Imperial Germany Revisited

Imperial Germany Revisited

Continuing Debates and New Perspectives

Edited by
Sven Oliver Müller and Cornelius Torp

Berghahn Books
New York • Oxford

First published in 2011 by

Berghahn Books
www.berghahnbooks.com

©2011, 2013 Sven Oliver Müller and Cornelius Torp
First paperback edition published in 2013

All rights reserved. Except for the quotation of short passages
for the purposes of criticism and review, no part of this book
may be reproduced in any form or by any means, electronic or
mechanical, including photocopying, recording, or any information
storage and retrieval system now known or to be invented,
without written permission of the publisher.

Library of Congress Cataloging-in-Publication Data

Imperial Germany revisited : continuing debates and new perspectives / edited by Sven Oliver Müller and Cornelius Torp.
   p. cm.
   Includes bibliographical references and index.
   ISBN 978-0-85745-252-8 (hbk.)--ISBN 978-0-85745-900-8 (pbk.)
   1. Germany--History--1871-1918. 2. Germany--History--1871-1918--Historiography. 3. Imperialism--History. 4. Politics and culture--Germany--History. 5. Social change--Germany--History. 6. Violence--Germany--Colonies--History. 7. Germany--Colonies--History. 8. Germany--Foreign relations--1871-1918. I. Müller, Sven Oliver, 1968- II. Torp, Cornelius.
   DD220.I65 2011
   943.08'4--dc23

2011018394

British Library Cataloguing in Publication Data

A catalogue record for this book is available from the British Library

Printed in the United States on acid-free paper.

ISBN: 978-0-85745-900-8 (paperback)   eISBN: 978-0-85745-921-3 (retail ebook)

Contents

List of Figures		ix
Acknowledgements		xi
Introduction *Cornelius Torp and Sven Oliver Müller*		1

PART I   THE PLACE OF IMPERIAL GERMANY IN GERMAN HISTORY

Chapter 1	When the *Sonderweg* Debate Left Us *Helmut Walser Smith*	21
Chapter 2	The Impossible Vanishing Point: Societal Differentiation in Imperial Germany *Benjamin Ziemann*	37
Chapter 3	Was the German Empire a Sovereign State? *Dieter Grimm*	51
Chapter 4	Theories of Nationalism and the Critical Approach to German History *John Breuilly*	67

PART II   POLITICS, CULTURE, AND SOCIETY

Chapter 5	The Authoritarian State and the Political Mass Market *James Retallack*	83
Chapter 6	Using Violence to Govern: The German Empire and the French Third Republic *Heinz-Gerhard Haupt*	97

Chapter 7	Women's Suffrage and Antifeminism as a Litmus Test of Modernizing Societies: A Western European Comparison *Ute Planert*	107
Chapter 8	Germany in the Age of Culture Wars *Olaf Blaschke*	125
Chapter 9	Their Favorite Enemy: German Social Historians and the Prussian Nobility *Stephan Malinowski*	141
Chapter 10	A Difficult Relationship: Social History and the Bourgeoisie *Manfred Hettling*	157
Chapter 11	Cultural Nationalism and Beyond: Musical Performances in Imperial Germany *Sven Oliver Müller*	173

PART III WAR AND VIOLENCE

Chapter 12	1914–1945: A Second Thirty Years War? Advantages and Disadvantages of an Interpretive Category *Jörg Echternkamp*	189
Chapter 13	The Enduring Charm of the Great War: Some Reflections on Methodological Issues *Roger Chickering*	201
Chapter 14	The First World War and Military Culture: Continuity and Change in Germany and Italy *MacGregor Knox*	213
Chapter 15	A German Way of War? Narratives of German Militarism and Maritime Warfare in World War I *Dirk Bönker*	227
Chapter 16	German War Crimes 1914 and 1941: The Question of Continuity *Alan Kramer*	239

PART IV THE GERMAN EMPIRE IN THE WORLD

| Chapter 17 | From the Periphery to the Center: On the Significance of Colonialism for the German Empire
Birthe Kundrus | 253 |
| Chapter 18 | The Kaiserreich as a Society of Migration
Thomas Mergel | 267 |

Chapter 19	Wilhelmine Nationalism in Global Contexts: Mobility, Race, and Global Consciousness *Sebastian Conrad*	281
Chapter 20	Imperial Germany under Globalization *Cornelius Torp*	297
Chapter 21	German Industry and American Big Business, 1900–1914 *Volker Berghahn*	313
Select Bibliography		325
Notes on Contributors		337
Subject Index		341
Index of People		345

List of Figures

8.1	Evangelischer Bund: Members 1887–1999 Volksverein für das katholische Deutschland: Members 1891–1933	127
8.2	Light entertainment literature with an anti-Catholic tendency, 1860–1917	128
8.3	Percentage of parishioners taking communion in the Lutheran Church in Bavaria to the right of the Rhine, 1830–1975	135
8.4	Men and women in the religious orders in the Bishopric of Trier, 1846–2006	136
8.5	Visitors to the Holy Tunic pilgrimage in Trier, 1844–1996	137
8.6	Number of religious wayside shrines (Flurdenkmäler) in the district of Vilsbiburg	137

Acknowledgements

An academic book is always the result of a long-lasting process at the end of which one has built up a considerable debt of gratitude. In this case, the origins go back to a conference we organized on the occasion of Hans-Ulrich Wehler's 75th birthday at the Wissenschaftszentrum in Berlin.

The conference was generously funded by the Fritz Thyssen Foundation. Jürgen Kocka, then director of the Wissenschaftszentrum was a perfect host and contributed substantially to making the event a success. All financial and institutional help would have been in vain, however, without the initiative and the intellectually stimulating contributions of all the speakers and discussants who breathed new life into the German Empire.

The current book is based on the edited volume *Das Deutsche Kaiserreich in der Kontroverse* which was the direct result of the conference and published two years after the event with the German publisher Vandenhoeck & Ruprecht. This volume, however, comprises only a selection of the original articles. Moreover, many contributions have been substantially revised. The introduction and eleven chapters (2, 3, 6, 8, 9, 10, 11, 12, 17, 18, 20) have been translated by Jeffrey Verhey who did a great job not only in bridging the language gap but also in patiently discussing all controversial cases with a group of demanding authors and editors. Again, here we would like to thank the Thyssen Foundation for financially supporting the translation. Berghahn Books and above all, Marion Berghahn herself from the very beginning showed intensive interest in the project and made publishing with them an enduring pleasure. We are grateful also to Iris Törmer who was an invaluable help in proof-reading and in setting up the index.

It is a happy coincidence that this book finally is being released in September 2011, the very same month in which Hans-Ulrich Wehler turns 80 years old. That his interpretation of the German Empire still forms a point of reference and a bone of contention for historical research shows how much we all as scholars of the Kaiserreich are indebted to his work.

Sven Oliver Müller
Cornelius Torp

Introduction

Cornelius Torp and Sven Oliver Müller

I

What sort of structure was the German state of 1871? What sort of powers and phenomena dominated it? What sort of potential for development did it possess? What inheritance did it leave behind? How did it shape the future course of German history? These questions have been at the heart of numerous historical controversies, in the course of which our understanding of Imperial Germany has fundamentally changed. Modern historical research on the German Empire was shaped by two important developments.[1] The first was the Fischer controversy at the beginning of the 1960s, which put the question of the continuity of an aggressive German foreign policy from the First to the Second World War onto the agenda, thus providing one of the key impulses for research into the period before 1918.[2] The second was a complex upheaval at almost exactly the same time in the historiography of modern Germany in which a particular interpretation of German history before World War I played a central role. The advocates of this interpretation immediately referred to it as a "paradigm change," a concept then in fashion.[3] Indeed, surprisingly quickly, a group of young historians were able to establish across a broad front a new interpretation of modern German history, which broke in many respects with old traditions.

In their methodology, the representatives of the so-called "historical social science" (*Historische Sozialwissenschaft*) turned with verve against the interpretation which had dominated mainstream historiography up till then, which saw the dominant, most important historical actions and actors in politics and the state. These historians concentrated instead on the forces underlying economic and social structures and processes. They preferred social science theories to the hermeneutical methodology of historicism, and made Karl Marx and especially

Max Weber their theoretical figureheads. The new work brought forth a new historical "master narrative," assembling lines of thought that already existed but which had not yet been put together in this condensed form. This narrative turned upside down the previous notion of a German *Sonderweg*, widespread in Imperial Germany, according to which Germany was superior to western societies. From the new perspective, analyzing Germany using the scale of an ideal development postulated by sociological modernization theory and in comparison to western societies which served as a reference, Germany possessed grave structural deficits in modernization, the origins of which lay deep in the nineteenth century. It was these deficits which in the final analysis paved the way for National Socialism.

The new, critical interpretations of German history were by no means fully successful; quite possibly their advocates remained a minority within the historical profession. However, these new interpretations were able to an extraordinary degree to force competing conservative interpretations into a defensive position and to promote an interdisciplinary research program which even their enemies were forced to participate in—if only to engage them in critical debate. Furthermore, the "historical social science" and the "*Sonderweg* historiography" had an impact far beyond the narrow boundaries of the discipline. Reflecting the political-didactic impetus of the protagonists, with this interpretation the German historical profession won back an authority in public political discourse it had previously lost. At the same time, the *Sonderweg* interpretation embedded itself deep into the dominant "official" picture of history in the Federal Republic of Germany.

The success enjoyed, at least for a while, by this interpretation can only partly be explained by the fact that it set forth a promising research agenda with considerable potential for innovation, that it created a bridge to related subjects in the social sciences, whose reputation at this time was growing immensely, and that its pioneers in the course of the expansion of the university system were quickly able to become professors and thus to provide the new "paradigm" with institutional security. More importantly, this paradigm supplied a new answer to the pressing question concerning the rise of National Socialism, an answer which many found convincing and which—in contrast to the interpretation which had dominated up till then, which had concentrated solely on the years leading up to the failure of the Weimar Republic—explained the historical faults of German history by looking at a longer, broader picture, reaching deep into the nineteenth century. At the same time, the *Sonderweg* interpretation made it possible to argue that 1945 was the end of a pathological path toward modernization, and that the political culture of the Federal Republic of Germany had broken with the disastrous German past. Thus, the historical interpretation completely turned the "*Sonderweg* model" on its head—a model which up till then had completely dominated historical interpretations, by acknowledging the total military and moral defeat in World War II; this reflected the upheaval experienced by German society. It also had a sort of therapeutic effect because it promised, fully in harmony with the modernization euphoria and the surge of reforms in the 1960s and 1970s, that Germany was advancing toward a better future, down the path of western modernity.[4]

From the very beginning the German Empire was something like the favorite child of the historians interested in the *Sonderweg*. Most of them did not themselves conduct research on the history of National Socialism or even the Weimar Republic. Rather, they believed that they could find in the years before the traces of all those strains and burdens which pulled Germany after 1933 into the abyss. The question which all representatives of the *Sonderweg* thesis asked first and foremost is why National Socialism, with its devastating effects, came to power in Germany and only in Germany. Because of this question, politics was always seen as the most important realm. Even if they grappled with the economic development or the class structure of the German Empire, theirs was a very political economic and social history which, to put it pointedly, served to assist the explanation of a political phenomenon.

The new interpretation of the second German Empire was expressed most cogently in Hans-Ulrich Wehler's influential synthesis from 1973.[5] The German Empire fell apart, one could read here, because of its basic dilemma: the "inability ... to adapt the structure of the state and society to the conditions of a modern, industrial state."[6] Against the background of the synchronicity of the different "partial modernizations" postulated by modernization theory, Germany's path into modernity, characterized by the "simultaneity of the non-simultaneous (*Gleichzeitigkeit des Ungleichzeitigen*)," appeared to be an abnormal aberration with fatal consequences. According to this interpretation, the list of debts and deficits is long and weighed down not only the history of the German Empire, but German history beyond that: the forestalled parliamentarization and the democratization which was stuck in a rut; the weakness of political liberalism, which corresponded to a deficit of bourgeois values; the outmoded supremacy of pre-industrial norms and ideals and, finally, the anachronistic predominance of the old power elite, who defended tooth and nail their traditional dominant position and whose strategies to achieve this purpose were as successful as they were far-reaching.

This dark picture of the German Empire as a backward-looking entity, ruled by sinister powers, has often been criticized and relativized, first, by a heterogeneous group of German historians. Thomas Nipperdey complained that by privileging only one of the possible lines of continuity, namely that which centered on 1933, the period before 1914 was degraded to a mere prehistory of National Socialism, that interpreting and explaining phenomena solely from the perspective of how these phenomena stabilized power underestimated and did not pay proper attention to either the accomplishments or the dynamic development of the German Empire.[7] Nipperdey, and especially historians such as Andreas Hillgruber and Klaus Hildebrand, also criticized Wehler's insistence on the "primacy of domestic politics," a thesis which Wehler and others developed on the basis of work done by the historian Eckart Kehr, who died in 1933. According to this thesis, the foreign policy of the German Empire resulted from the status quo policies of the Prussian-German ruling establishment, which was plagued by the nightmare of a social revolution, and which attempted to divert internal tensions by concentrating on foreign problems.[8] Wehler's critics insisted on the autonomy of foreign policy and saw the international system as central, as a factor which explains a great deal.[9] However, it could be argued that by interpreting Germany's foreign policy between 1871 and 1914 as being derived from its particular location in Central Europe critics did not truly distance themselves from the idea of a German *Sonderweg*. Instead of an explanation of the *Sonderweg* based on social structures and internal politics, they put forth an explanation of the German *Sonderweg* based on its geographical position.

Quite a different sort of criticism has come since the end of the 1970s from a group of English historians. Richard Evans, David Blackbourn and Geoff Eley have argued against the importance which representatives of the "historical social science" and those who support the idea of a *Sonderweg* have assigned to the elites of the German Empire and to the thesis of social control exercised from above. They argued that it was not "manipulation from above" which was the defining characteristic of Wilhelminian Germany but rather self-organization "from below."[10] They also criticized the claim that there were pathological characteristics among the German ruling and social structure before 1914, the thesis that there was a German *Sonderweg* extending far back into the past which flowed into National Socialism, as well as the assumption of a positive, "normal path" in the West.[11]

This critique became more powerful as the empirical work on the history of the bourgeoisie, which had been initiated in the 1980s and 1990s above all by prominent representatives of the *Sonderweg* interpretation, concluded that, although one could perhaps speak of a special orientation toward the state, one could not speak in general of a weakness of the bourgeoisie or of a "deficit of bourgeois values" in nineteenth and twentieth century Germany.[12] Perhaps the most significant revision was to the "feudalization thesis." According to this thesis, which had already been put forward by contemporary liberals, the bourgeoisie in the German Empire of its own free will embraced and submitted to the norms and the lifestyle of the aristocratic elites, demonstrating a specific German willingness to be subservient. Upon closer investigation it turned out that the bourgeois adoption of noble norms and styles of life, leading to a symbiosis of parts of the upper bourgeoisie and of the nobility, took place throughout Europe. Indeed, it appears that the "ennoblement" of the bourgeoisie took place later in Germany and was less developed than, for example, in England or France.[13]

In the meantime the smoke from the historiographical battles of the past few decades has cleared. Has the master narrative of the German *Sonderweg* also moved on, or does it continue to shape our historical understanding of Imperial Germany? Paradoxically, it seems both are true. Proponents of the *Sonderweg* thesis still hold to it and continue to use it as the foundation of their new historical syntheses of the German Empire during these years. However, one should not be deceived by this. We have witnessed a defensive movement in which the phalanx of historians in favor of the *Sonderweg* thesis, once so proud, have been reduced to individual combatants. Furthermore, we have seen that the prestige of the *Sonderweg* thesis has been declining, that its proponents are staging a well-ordered retreat to the narrow realm of state power.[14] What speaks in favor of the continuing influence of the *Sonderweg* interpretation, even if only indirectly, is that even those who have openly come out as its opponents have found it very difficult to escape its narrative logic. This is true, for example, for Thomas Nipperdey's history of the German Empire, large sections of which can be read as a counter-proposal to the *Sonderweg* narrative and which as a result remains deeply indebted to this narrative.[15] Perhaps even more important is the fact that the thesis of the German *Sonderweg* and the questions which this interpretation raises continue to structure the historical research on the German Empire. What we understand or do not understand especially well about Germany during these decades—where the specialized research has pointed out conspicuous blind spots—this is to a large degree the legacy of a master narrative and the controversies it provoked which is already over forty years old and which has turned a bit grey at the edges.

II

It cannot be overlooked, however, that our present view of Imperial Germany has moved away in many important regards from the questions, debates and lines of division associated with the *Sonderweg* paradigm. On the one hand, a fundamentally different interpretation of modernity has become increasingly important. On the other hand—directly related to this, although not completely submerged in it— new questions and methodologies have become increasingly important to the historians of modern Germany.

To turn to the first point: the concept of modernization which informs the *Sonderweg* theorizing—which sees modernization as a coherent and largely positive, Western process of development, characterized by industrialization, by the building of political classes, by urbanization, by the expansion of political participation, by the building of nation-states and by secularization—has lost a great deal of its attraction. Only at the beginning, in the debates of the 1980s, were historians especially interested in what modernization destroyed in regard to the traditional ways of life, turning a history of progress into a history of loss.[16] In a second step, the ambivalence of modernity, as well as the manifold forms which it could assume, moved to the forefront. It found its expression, for example, in the concept of "multiple modernities," developed by Shmuel N. Eisenstadt, which was directed against the assumption of a common, homogenous modernity.[17]

Especially influential was a reading of modernity which emphasized its negative, anti-emancipatory characteristics. Is it an exaggeration to see in this modernization paradigm, with its dark tones, already the shadowy outline of a new, alternative master narrative of modern German history? No longer are the social-economic processes of the "modernization" of the nineteenth century at the center of interest, but rather the nature of the "modernity" of the twentieth century, with the discourses which characterize it. Among the key elements of modernism according to this understanding are, on the one hand, a deep pessimism, a feeling of fundamental insecurity and of being threatened, the consciousness of a permanent crisis, brought forth by the decline of traditional values and structures and the emergence of a new, chaotic way of life, with new problems. This, however, is linked at the same time—this is one of the paradoxes of modernity—to extreme optimism, to a belief in the feasibility of things, that is, to the belief that it is possible to create order in societies which have gotten out of control. One can accomplish this with various sorts of models of social rationalization: city planning, health policy, education, the welfare state, etc. Modern social sciences have an important role to play here. First, they identify, define, classify and systematize the new threats and problems. Second, they "discover" the "solutions" to these and supply new technologies for their "control." This is especially true of the so-called "human sciences" such as eugenics and the biology of races, which, since the early twentieth century, have grown enormously, and which, through their biopolitics based on their reading of Darwin, shaped in important ways the contemporary perception of the crisis. They also supplied the means to overcome social problems which they had identified as pathological.[18]

Michel Foucault and Zygmunt Baumann were the leading theoretical figures of this dark concept of modernity; but it is based as well on a new reading of Max Weber, concentrating on his pessimistic, dark conceptions.[19] The first one to apply this perspective fruitfully to German history was Detlev J.K. Peukert, two decades ago.[20] The difference between his image of modernity (as well as the image of many who came after him) and that of the *Sonderweg* historians could not be greater. According to Peukert, the "project of modernity" is not characterized by the individual being freed from traditional bonds through liberalization and social reform, rather, it is characterized by the pathologizing of difference, social discipline, and increasing institutional pressure. From this perspective, systematic exclusion, concentration camps and the Holocaust no longer seem to be atavisms, not even regrettable aberrations, which could eventually be overcome, but are rather modernity's genuine sign, its most basic product. National Socialism, with its crimes, is no longer seen as something that needs to be explained through the incomplete modernization of Germany and the anachronistic persistence of pre-modern relics in society and in the political system. Rather, the National Socialist genocide, with its racist logic of selection and its use of the most modern technologies of extermination, is seen as the most terrible expression of an extreme, radical modernity. Thus, the crimes and brutality of the German case are not unique but rather an example of an ever-present potential which is always and everywhere capable of making itself manifest.[21]

Closely tied to this different understanding of modernity is that in the last few years the vanishing point of German historiography has changed.[22] To be sure, National Socialism is still the pivotal point of the historiography of the nineteenth and twentieth centuries; however, one is increasingly less interested in explaining its rise and its establishment, in short, in explaining how things led up to January 1933. The key period now appears to be 1939–1941, the starting point of the National Socialist policy of genocide, with the beginning of World War II and the military campaign against the Soviet Union. From this perspective, quite different questions and themes in regard to the history of the German Empire have moved into the focus of historical interest. Historians have looked more intensely than ever at the First World War with its experience of violence and its mental dispositions. Furthermore, historians have placed the discourse of those bio-political experts in eugenics and demography, in criminology and in social reform in the decades before 1933 at the centre of their interest, arguing that they contributed to the National Socialist policy of exclusion and extermination—to what degree is still a matter of controversy—by preparing the soil for it ideologically.[23]

For the historiography on Germany from 1870 to 1918 this means a shift in the research interests. This shift expresses itself in a moderate and a radical version. According to the moderate version, the German Empire remains important, even given the new understanding of modernity. However, this is not true for the period when the German national state came into being, or, indeed, of the whole Bismarck era, which, from the perspective of bio-politics and a disciplinary society, appears to belong to quite a different epoch. Instead, the period since the 1890s appears to be the key historic period, even if one conceives of modernity in the alternative way sketched above. It marks in many ways "a departure into modernity." One thinks here of the enormous increase in the importance of the natural and social sciences and the opinion of experts, of the beginnings of the welfare state, but also, if one looks beyond the limits of the bio-political "paradigm" and takes into consideration the manifold dimensions of modernity, of the emergence of modern mass culture and the Belle Époque of globalization.

More drastically, one could describe the present trend in the historiography as a "goodbye to the nineteenth century" (Paul Nolte). Whereas the nineteenth century with its successful or unsuccessful "double revolution" (Eric Hobsbawm) in economics and politics is the key period of the "*Sonderweg* history," historians are now focusing more and more on the twentieth century—with World War I as the turning point. For Germany this tendency to explain the twentieth century from developments within itself means that increasingly the National Socialist policy of genocide and its direct pre-history has moved to the forefront of the historian's interest. One can see in this, on the one hand, the expression of a necessary and unavoidable historicization of the twentieth century. On the other hand, we must continue to ask critically whether by forgoing long-term explanations there has not been a regrettable loss of historical depth of focus.

If today our understanding of the German Empire is in many regards quite different from that three decades ago, this is—as suggested above—not only because our understanding of modernity today is much more multi-faceted and problematic than before, but is in part as well because the historiography in this period, in a series of methodological "turns" and changes in perspectives reinvented itself a number of times. To name just some of the keywords here, without making any claim to completeness: the cultural turn, gender history and trans-national history. The increasing importance of cultural history with its claim to write not only the history of a certain sector but to be a general historical approach has moved people's modes of perceptions and thoughts, the form in which they make sense of the world around them, their practices and their shared norms and values to the center of historical research. At the same time, cultural history has attempted to keep step with the "holistic turn" in epistemology, by emphasizing the degree to which previously reified social entities are constructed and by studying the interaction between the "subjects" and the "objects" of history.[24] Gender history has shown the degree to which the attributions "feminine" and "masculine" are historical categories, which vary over time, and has turned the attention of historians to the symbolic and practical significance of gender-specific patterns.[25] Trans-national history questions the national historical perspective, with its self-evident assumption that the nation-state is the framework of historical analysis; this assumption has had an unbroken line of tradition in German historiography from the historicism of the late nineteenth century up through the "historical social science" and its critics. Trans-national history has concentrated on the transfers and constellations which transcend borders, on the effect of the colonies on the colonizing societies, and on the integration of the German Empire in the process of globalization.[26]

These innovations, in part intertwined with each other, in part taking place after each other, have had two sorts of influences on the panorama of the German Empire we have today. On the one hand, they have contributed to moving our perceptions away from the idea that the German Empire was a historical epoch *sui generis*. The de-politicization of the historiography of the German Empire in comparison to the "*Sonderweg* history" or, rather, its changing political connotations, the prominence of numerous new themes, all of which have had their own "time"—all this has meant that classical political caesurae, classical political boundaries are increasingly seen as less important and time periods which transcend them are becoming more important. On the other hand, there has been an enormous pluralization of the approaches, methods and themes in the historiography of the German Empire. This pluralization shows clearly that the narrative of a modernity characterized by discipline and compulsion has, till now, not been able to take the place of a paradigm which dominates broad sections of the research, such as was the case for social history and the "*Sonderweg*" thesis in the 1970s. All in all, this suggests that what is occurring here is less a "paradigm change" than the end of the "master narratives."[27]

This development can be criticized for a growing lack of consensus concerning the relevant research questions and research topics as well as the decreasing ability of the different branches of historical research to communicate with each other. One can also ask, as has Volker Berghahn, if historians have not lost sight of the "big" questions such as those concerning the origins of World War I, as a result of their enthusiasm for deconstruction, local agency and contingencies, in short, if we are not in danger of having "lost sight of the forest because we are so firmly focused on the trees."[28]

However, on the other hand, it can scarcely be denied that the new perspectives on the period before 1918 have achieved a great deal. The German Empire today appears much more complex and rich in nuances; it is less the authoritarian power state and is viewed less from a Prussian perspective than was the case only a couple of decades ago. The increase in the number of approaches and in the objects of study has led to the competition of multiple narratives, so that neither "never-ending shades" of grey determine the image of the German Empire, as Nipperdey claimed, nor that black-white dichotomy which he accused his opponents of in general and Wehler in particular.[29] Rather, our image is a mixture of bright colours, which—if that is at all possible—describe the historical reality better than was previously the case.

III

The present state of the historical research into the German empire, open, pluralistic and innovative in its methodology, is reflected in this volume. At the same time, this collection of essays demonstrates the degree to which the contemporary research builds on previous work and the degree to which we are still today affected by traditional questions. The variety of topics collected here is considerable: from social history to military history, from cultural history to economic history. Furthermore, the historians employ quite different methodologies in how they approach their topics. All of these approaches share an awareness of the historiographical tradition in which they stand, just as they are open and transparent in regard to the most important interests which inform their own work and their historical conditionality. That their own perspectives and interpretations themselves reflect the context in which they were written and that this itself needs to be historicized—these historians consider this self-evident.

This collection of essays brings together the work of experts, both young and old, on the history of Germany from 1870 to 1918 and links established questions with new approaches. Even where it seems that the "classical" questions and themes are at the center of interest, this collection of essays often opens up a new perspective on them—looking at cultural transfers, for example, from the standpoint of a broader understanding of the political opens up new and surprising perspectives on the history of the German Empire.

We concede that the collection presented here only partly reflects the present state of the historical research on the German Empire. In part this is because the historical debates of the last few years shed light on certain topics, leaving other topics—despite there having been much good research—in the shade. All the same, some will regret a number of empty spaces: for example, the history of the working class or foreign policy. There are also a number of topics in economic, intellectual and gender history which have not been treated here. To a large degree these gaps, as well as the topics that were chosen, can only be explained as the editors' decision, which is to a certain degree always subjective and arbitrary.

We have concentrated on four research perspectives, which have played a special role in the last few years: first, the place of the German Empire in German history; second, the relationship between society, politics and culture; third, the history of military violence and militarism with a concentration on World War I, and, last but not least, the trans-national integration of Germany against the background of the "first globalization."

1. The Place of Imperial Germany in German History

In the past three decades it has become increasingly less clear what sort of state the German Empire actually was—culturally, politically and socially. The picture of an economically well-developed, but politically and socially backward Germany, a picture we had believed to be well founded, has become increasingly confused. At the same time, and this is closely related, the historical site of the German Empire and the significance assigned to it in the course of German history, has undergone many important changes. Those authors who analyze this complex set of problems refer repeatedly to two aspects which are of crucial importance for the changing interpretation of German history between 1870 and 1918.

First, they emphasize the relevance of the definitions, concepts and categories developed by contemporaries and the following generations for our understanding of the German history of these years, or, indeed, for our understanding of history at all. This can be shown in an exemplary fashion with the concept of sovereignty and the competing constructions of the "nation."[30] Of crucial importance for our interpretation of the German Empire remains—as sketched out in detail above—the definition of the concepts modernization and modernity. The essays collected here not only reflect the shift in the focus of the historiography of the German Empire toward a paradigm of modernity with negative accents, and discuss the problems arising from that shift,[31] they suggest as well an alternative understanding of modernity, one which puts the German Empire into a quite different light. One author, for example, defines modernization, following the approach of sociological systems theory, as the increasing social differentiation of functional sub-systems with a corresponding method of reproducing self-observation.[32]

Second, the contributions make clear the importance of historiographical traditions. Only by understanding the decline of the Whig interpretation of history among British historians can one understand why British historians have made such an important contribution to the debate on the German Empire since the late 1970s.[33] The importance of the historiographical traditions is shown further by the fact that for most historians the *Sonderweg* narrative remains a central reference point. Even those who have distanced themselves from the narrative include it as a set piece. As a result, historical revisionism means—and this is true as well for the "critical" historiography of Germany during the 1960s and 1970s—never completely replacing one point of view with another, as is suggested by "paradigm change," but rather the sometimes quicker, sometimes slower, sometimes ephemeral, sometimes fundamental modification of traditional historiographical traditions.[34]

2. Politics, Culture, and Society

Historians no longer focus so strongly on social structures, conceptualized and understood as objective facts existing independent of the individual actors, but are rather turning increasingly to actors, behavior patterns and social practices. It is clearer than ever that societies have to be conceptualized as communicative communities, politics as a context of social actions, and culture as a framework of interpretations of meaning which shape our perceptions of reality. In this section new perspectives on classical areas of tension and conflict—such as the public sphere and media culture, the nobility and the bourgeoisie, or violence and order—have enhanced and expanded historical research: social history has been enriched by cultural historical interpretations, class as a category has been revised by investigating new social groups, the understanding of power relationships and institutions has been supplemented by the analysis of patterns of practices and receptions. What is important now is to bring politics, society, and culture as a pluralistic cross section back into the center of the history of the German Empire.

The German Empire in this volume is no longer just the product of the manner of its construction, but is rather seen as an epoch of constant political and social change. With their analysis of political developments, debates, and problems, the authors of this volume bring before our eyes a state which, even given all the incrustations, cannot be seen as a stiff and sclerotic power structure. Although one can have wonderful arguments about whether or not it still makes sense to describe this state as authoritarian, it is important to place the concept of the authoritarian state within the framework of the processes of the fundamental politicization and the social and political upheavals taking place at the same time. The political scandals of the era, which were transmitted into the public sphere through mass communication, mass media and mass politics, could not be put down with the means customarily used for political repression. An international comparison shows the ambivalence in regard to political violence. In Germany during these years, violent political conflicts were, for example, less common than in the Third French Republic; when they took place, however, the government responded with much more force than was the case in France.[35]

The authors here have questioned many of the judgements of the older historiography. Our understanding of the everyday living conditions of the Prussian nobility or of the new forms of communication and conflict among the bourgeoisie has been revised, and approaches and ideas with which we were well acquainted have been questioned and analyzed, opening up new perspectives for future research.[36] Something similar can be said for the work which describes the religious history of the German Empire not as a process of secularization, but as part of a neo-confessional age, lasting from 1830 till 1960.[37] From the perspective of gender history and in a Western European comparison, it is clear that the mere existence of a strong anti-feminist movement such as existed in Germany and in Britain cannot be considered evidence of a society's backwardness, but rather of its ability to undergo reforms, indeed, that there was a high chance that the reforms toward much more gender equality would be successful.[38]

A further focus of the present research into the history of the German Empire is the history of the cultural reception of political and social phenomenon. Here, researchers are less interested in institutions than in practices, and the degree to which cultural processes are interwoven with political and social developments becomes quite clear. The most important conflicts in German society turned out to be shaped essentially through the meanings given to them. Cultural preferences, for example, in the changing patterns of the reception of music, were linked inseparably with national demands, which for a long time were only a topic in classical political history.[39]

3. War and Violence

In the last few years, research into the history of the First World War, its preconditions and its consequences, has formed an important starting point for the new interpretation of the German Empire. Historians have been most interested in the changes in the history of experience and in the history of mentalities caused by the "total war."[40]

The focus here has been on militarism and the practice of military violence in Germany from 1870 to 1918, especially in World War I, and its power to shape the future course of German history. Lines of continuity between the First and the Second World War are suggested, for example, by the unlimited submarine warfare of the years 1915 to 1918. In this interpretation, the German approach to naval warfare in World War I appears not as the expression of a specific German militarism, but rather marks a significant break with the military ideas and practices of the pre-war years. Submarine warfare was part of a brutalization of war, a tendency which could be observed in the other nations fighting the war as well. In contrast, there is quite a different result if we look at the military culture of the German army, paying special attention to the characteristics of a specific German culture of organization. Here the lines of continuity extend far beyond the end of the Wilhelminian Empire in 1918. A direct comparison of the German War Crimes in the north of France and Belgium during 1914–15 and the war of extermination in Eastern Europe after 1941 shows similarities and lines of continuity, as well as, however, radically qualitative differences.[41]

That the search for lines of continuity was not just a privilege of the research into the *Sonderweg* comes out clearly in the contributions in this volume. Here, other lines of continuity, closely connected with the problems of war and violence, are at the center of attention. The concept of the "Second Thirty Years War" between 1914 and 1945, which is widespread among historians and which has been critically discussed here, extends the historical legacy of the German Empire well into the twentieth century.[42] Just as in the 1970s, the explosiveness of the historical judgement of the German Empire lies less in its own history than in the history of the events that happened after it.

4. The German Empire in the World

Macro processes, described with the terms globalization, Europeanization and international migration, have become increasingly important in the last few years. This has had significant consequences for our understanding of the German Empire. Changes in the everyday experiences of historians caused by these macro processes have inspired historians increasingly to question whether or not the nation-state should be the referential framework for the history of the German Empire. Furthermore, historians have increasingly paid attention to phenomena and relationships which transcend the boundaries of the nation-state. At present, historians consider analyzing trans-national contacts and processes of exchange to be one of their most important tasks. At the same time they are increasingly investigating patterns of reciprocal perception and how these have changed over time. Thus, studying the interaction of American and German business elites before World War I as well as the American perception of the German industrial world has shed new light on the German economic system.[43]

Important impulses for the present upswing in trans-national history have come from postcolonial studies, which thematized the social and cultural consequences of colonial rule and which have played a central role especially in Anglo-American research. The "postcolonial" perspective directs our attention to the colonial discourse, with its binary oppositions and the principles inscribed in this discourse concerning the construction of the "other." This perspective revises the perception of colonial relationships as a one-sided influencing of those being colonized by the colonizers and emphasizes the reciprocity of the colonial exchange and the hybridity of the identities which come about through it. What was the impact of the colonial experiences on justice and politics, on the society and culture of Germany? To what degree did new forms of demarcation, new images of fascinating foreignness and ethnic inequality distributed through the mass media shape the political culture of the German Empire? Given the short-lived and not very successful history of the German colonial experience, the question is also asked whether an approach which assumes that in the German case the colonial experiences had an influence analogous to that of the colonial experiences for great imperial powers such as England or France, with their long imperial tradition, is in danger of vastly overestimating the significance of colonialism for Germany.[44]

Globalization, which was highly developed in the years before World War I, appears to have been very important. This can be shown paradigmatically by looking at trans-national mass migration, which was closely linked with the internal migration and which thoroughly shook up traditional ways of life and values. Its consequences for the discourse on citizenship law and on nationalism allows us to see that the establishment of the nation-state as a territorial regime did not simply precede processes of global integration but can only be adequately understood in its complex interplay with them.[45] On the other hand, the development of a global market for capital, for factors of production, and for goods had a lasting and profound effect on Germany, for Germany was highly integrated into these markets. Because globalization had a quite different impact on the incomes of various social groups, it produced a profound shift in social and internal political power relationships and increasingly limited the German government's autonomous room to maneuver in its trade policy.[46]

Fifty years ago, the Fischer controversy gave the impetus for in-depth historical research into the history of Germany from 1870 to 1918. Since then our understanding of the history of this era has changed many times and in many important ways. At present there is no single dominant historical perspective on the German Empire; rather, there are a number of narratives from completely different perspectives, which at times compete with each other and at times live peacefully with each other, side by side. The fact, however, that the history of the German Empire is still able to supply new material for new historical controversies and debates shows its continuing relevance. The future of historical work on the German Empire appears today to be more open than ever before. All that is certain is that in the future two factors will continue to determine the narratives which historians compose of the German Empire: the weight of the historiographical tradition on which they build, and the changes in their own research interests that they bring to the German Empire and which allow us to continue to discover new aspects of its history.

Notes

1. For views of the German Empire before 1960 see E. Frie, *Das Deutsche Kaiserreich* (Darmstadt, 2004), 2–10; M. Jefferies, *Contesting the German Empire, 1871–1918* (Malden, MA, 2008), 7–18. The authors would like to thank Dirk Bönker for his critical remarks and productive suggestions.
2. The bone of contention was F. Fischer, *Griff nach der Weltmacht. Die Kriegszielpolitik des kaiserlichen Deutschland 1914/18* (Düsseldorf, 1961); edited version in English as *Germany's Aims in the First World War* (London, 1967).
3. Cf. T.S. Kuhn, *The Structure of Scientific Revolutions* (1962), 2nd ed., (Chicago, 1970). Kuhn developed the concept to explain developments in the natural sciences. Since its publication, the degree to which this concept can be applied to the humanities and the social sciences has been a topic of heated debate.
4. See D. Langewiesche, "Der 'deutsche Sonderweg.' Defizitgeschichte als geschichtspolitische Zukunftskonstruktion nach dem Ersten und Zweiten Weltkrieg," in *Kriegsniederlagen. Erfahrungen und Erinnerungen*, eds. Horst Carl et al. (Berlin, 2004), 57–65; id., "Über das Umschreiben der Geschichte. Zur Rolle der Sozialgeschichte," in *Wege der Gesellschaftsgeschichte*, eds. J. Osterhammel et al. (Göttingen, 2006), 67–80; T. Welskopp, "Identität *ex negativo*. Der 'deutsche Sonderweg' als Metaerzählung in der bundesdeutschen Geschichtswissenschaft der siebziger und achtziger Jahre," in *Die historische Meistererzählung. Deutungslinien der deutschen*

Nationalgeschichte nach 1945, eds. K.H. Jarausch and M. Sabrow (Göttingen, 2002), 109–39; J.J. Sheehan, "Paradigm Lost? The 'Sonderweg' Revisited," in *Transnationale Geschichte. Themen, Tendenzen und Theorien*, eds. G. Budde et al. (Göttingen, 2006), 150–60.
5. H.-U. Wehler, *Das Deutsche Kaiserreich 1871–1918* (1973), 6th ed., (Göttingen, 1988); engl. *The German Empire 1871–1918* (Leamington Spa, 1985).
6. Wehler, *Kaiserreich*, 18.
7. See T. Nipperdey, "Wehlers 'Kaiserreich.' Eine kritische Auseinandersetzung," *Geschichte und Gesellschaft* 1 (1975), 539–60.
8. See E. Kehr, *Der Primat der Innenpolitik*, ed. H.-U. Wehler (Berlin, 1965); H.-U. Wehler, *Bismarck und der Imperialismus* (1969), 2nd ed., (Frankfurt, 1985).
9. See only A. Hillgruber, "Politische Geschichte in moderner Sicht," *Historische Zeitschrift* 216 (1973), 529–52; K. Hildebrand, "Geschichte oder 'Gesellschaftsgeschichte'? Die Notwendigkeit einer Politischen Geschichtsschreibung von den internationalen Beziehungen," *Historische Zeitschrift* 223 (1976), 328–57; id., *Deutsche Außenpolitik 1871–1918* (München, 1989).
10. See R.J. Evans. ed., *Society and Politics in Wilhelmine Germany* (London, 1978); G. Eley, *Reshaping the German Right. Radical Nationalism and Political Change after Bismarck* (1980), 2nd ed., (Ann Arbor, 1991); D. Blackbourn, *Class, Religion, and Local Politics in Wilhelmine Germany. The Center Party in Württemberg before 1914* (Wiesbaden, 1980). Cf. also W. Mock, "'Manipulation von oben' oder Selbstorganisation an der Basis? Einige neuere Ansätze in der englischen Historiographie zur Geschichte des Deutschen Kaiserreichs," *Historische Zeitschrift* 232 (1981), 358–75.
11. See D. Blackbourn and G. Eley, *Mythen deutscher Geschichtsschreibung. Die gescheiterte bürgerliche Revolution von 1848* (Frankfurt, 1980); republished in English in expanded form as *The Pecularities of German History* (Oxford, 1984). For a retrospective view cf. the email interview with Blackbourn and Eley in *German History* 22 (2004), 229–45.
12. The literature on the German bourgeoisie is now enormous. An introduction to this literature can be found in the summary of the work of the Collaborative Research Centre in Bielefeld (*Sonderforschungsbereich*) on the modern bourgeoisie in P. Lundgreen, ed., *Sozial- und Kulturgeschichte des Bürgertums* (Göttingen, 2000).
13. See, e.g., H. Berghoff and R. Möller, "Unternehmer in Deutschland und England 1870–1914. Aspekte eines kollektiv-biographischen Vergleichs," *Historische Zeitschrift* 255 (1993), 353–86; H. Berghoff, "Aristokratisierung des Bürgertums? Zur Sozialgeschichte der Nobilitierung von Unternehmern in Preußen und Großbritannien 1870–1918," *Vierteljahrschrift für Sozial- und Wirtschaftsgeschichte* 81 (1994), 178–209; D.L. Augustine, *Patricians and Parvenus. Wealth and High Society in Wilhelmine Germany* (Oxford, 1994).
14. See H.-U. Wehler, *Deutsche Gesellschaftsgeschichte*, vol. 3 (Munich, 1995), 1250–95.
15. See T. Nipperdey, *Deutsche Geschichte 1866–1918*, 2 vols. (Munich, 1990/1992). Cf. also P. Nolte, "Darstellungsweisen deutscher Geschichte. Erzählstrukturen und 'master narratives' bei Nipperdey und Wehler," in *Die Nation schreiben. Geschichtswissenschaft im internationalen Vergleich*, C. Conrad and S. Conrad (Göttingen, 2002), 236–68; Welskopp, "Identität," 128f.
16. See e.g., Alf Lütdke, ed., *Alltagsgeschichte. Zur Rekonstruktion historischer Erfahrungen und Lebensweisen* (Göttingen, 1989).
17. See only S.N. Eisenstadt, ed., *Multiple Modernities* (New Brunswick, NJ, 2002); id., *Comparative Civilizations and Multiple Modernities* (Leiden, 2003).
18. See only E.R. Dickinson, "Biopolitics, Fascism, Democracy: Some Reflections on Our Discourse about 'Modernity,'" *Central European History* 37 (2004), 1–48; P. Nolte, "Abschied vom 19. Jahrhundert oder Auf der Suche nach einer anderen Moderne," in: *Wege der Gesellschaftsgeschichte*, 103–32; L. Raphael, "Radikales Ordnungsdenken und die Organisation totalitärer Herrschaft: Weltanschauungseliten und Humanwissenschaftler im NS-Regime," *Geschichte und Gesellschaft* 27 (2001), 5–40.
19. See, e.g., M. Foucault, *Discipline and Punish. The Birth of the Prison* (1975) (London, 1977); Z. Bauman, *Modernity and the Holocaust* (Cambridge, 1989); D.J.K. Peukert, *Max Webers Diagnose der Moderne* (Göttingen, 1989).
20. See in particular ibid., S. 102–21.

21. For the preceding paragraph see the contribution to this volume by Helmut Walser Smith.
22. For the concept of the "vanishing point" see H.W. Smith, "The Vanishing Point of German History. An Essay on Perspective," *History and Memory* 17 (2005), 269–95.
23. See only D.J.K. Peukert, *Grenzen der Sozialdisziplinierung. Aufstieg und Krise der deutschen Jugendfürsorge, 1878–1932* (Cologne, 1986); P. Weindling, *Health, Race, and German Politics between National Unification and Nazism, 1870–1945* (Cambridge, 1989); G. Eley, "Introduction 1: Is There a History of the Kaiserreich?," in *Society, Culture, and the State in Germany, 1870–1930*, ed. G. Eley (Ann Arbor, 1996), 1–42, here: 24–31; S. Stöckel, *Säuglingsfürsorge zwischen sozialer Hygiene und Eugenik* (Berlin, 1996); M. Kappeler, *Der schreckliche Traum vom vollkommenen Menschen: Rassenhygiene und Eugenik in der sozialen Arbeit* (Marburg, 2000); P. Becker, *Verderbnis und Entartung. Eine Geschichte der Kriminologie des 19. Jahrhunderts als Diskurs und Praxis* (Göttingen, 2002). For an overview of the recent literature see Dickinson, "Biopolitics."
24. See only U. Daniel, *Kompendium Kulturgeschichte. Theorie, Praxis, Schlüsselwörter* (2001), 5th ed., (Frankfurt, 2006); M. Bevir, "Meta-Methodology: Clearing the Underbrush," in *The Oxford Handbook for Political Methodology*, ed. J.M. Box-Steffensmeier et al. (Oxford, 2008), 48–70.
25. See only U. Frevert, *"Mann und Weib, und Weib und Mann." Geschlechter-Differenzen in der Moderne* (München, 1995); K. Canning, *Gender History in Practice. Historical Perspectives on Bodies, Class and Citizenship* (Ithaca, 2006); K. Hagemann and J. Quataert, eds., *Gendering Modern German History. Rewriting Historiography* (New York, 2007).
26. See, e.g., S. Conrad and J. Osterhammel, eds., *Das Kaiserreich transnational. Deutschland in der Welt 1871–1914* (Göttingen, 2004); Budde et al., eds., *Transnationale Geschichte*.
27. See also K. Ledford, "Comparing Comparisons. Disciplines and the Sonderweg," *Central European History* 36 (2003): 367–74; J. Retallack, ed., *Imperial Germany 1871–1918* (Oxford, 2008); G. Eley and J. Retallack, eds., *Wilhelmism and Its Legacies. German Modernities, Imperialism, and the Meanings of Reform, 1890–1930* (New York, 2003); Jefferies, *Contesting*.
28. V.R. Berghahn, "The German Empire, 1871–1914: Reflections on the Direction of Recent Research," *Central European History* 35 (2002): 75–81, here 77; cf. also M.L. Anderson, "Reply to Volker Berghahn," *Central European History* 35 (2002), 83–90.
29. Nipperdey, *Deutsche Geschichte 1866–1918*, vol. 2, 905.
30. See the contributions to this volume by Dieter Grimm and John Breuilly.
31. See the chapter by Helmut Walser Smith.
32. See the contribution by Benjamin Ziemann.
33. See Richard J. Evans, *Cosmopolitan Islanders. British Historians and the European Continent* (Cambridge, 2009).
34. Cf. also M. Bevir, "On Tradition," *Humanitas* 13 (2000), 28–53.
35. See the contributions by James Retallack and Heinz-Gerhard Haupt. Cf. also K.H. Jarausch and M. Geyer, *Shattered Past. Reconstructing German Histories* (Princeton, 2003); M. Kohlrausch, *Der Monarch im Skandal. Die Logik der Massenmedien und die Transformation der wilhelminischen Monarchie* (Berlin, 2005); F. Bösch, *Öffentliche Geheimnisse. Skandale, Politik und Medien in Deutschland und Großbritannien 1880–1914* (Munich, 2009).
36. See the contributions by Stephan Malinowski and Manfred Hettling.
37. See the chapter by Olaf Blaschke; as well as id., ed., *Konfessionen im Konflikt. Deutschland zwichen 1800 und 1970: ein zweites konfessionelles Zeitalter* (Göttingen, 2002).
38. See the chapter by Ute Planert; id., *Antifeminismus im Kaiserreich. Diskurs, soziale Formation und politische Mentalität* (Göttingen, 1998).
39. See the contribution by Sven Oliver Müller; M.P. Steinberg, *Listening to Reason. Culture, Subjectivity, and Nineteenth-Century Music* (Princeton, NJ, 2004); H.E. Bödeker, ed., *Le concert et son public. Mutations de la vie musicale en Europe de 1780 à 1914 (France, Allemagne, Angleterre)* (Paris, 2002).
40. For a concise overview of World War I research, see the contribution by Roger Chickering.
41. See the contributions by Dirk Bönker, MacGregor Knox, Roger Chickering and Alan Kramer. Cf. also I.V. Hull, *Absolute Destruction. Military Culture and the Practices of War in Imperial Germany* (Ithaca, 2006); A. Kramer, *Dynamic of Destruction. Culture and Mass Killing in the First World*

War (Oxford, 2007); S.O. Müller, *Deutsche Soldaten und ihre Feinde. Nationalismus an Front und Heimatfront im Zweiten Weltkrieg* (Frankfurt, 2007).
42. See the contribution by Jörg Echternkamp. Cf. H.-U. Wehler, *Deutsche Gesellschaftsgeschichte*, vol. 3, 1250–95; id., *Deutsche Gesellschaftsgeschichte*, vol. 4 (Munich, 2003), 985–94.
43. See the contribution by Volker Berghahn.
44. See the chapter by Birthe Kundrus; id., *Moderne Imperialisten. Das Kaiserreich im Spiegel seiner Kolonien* (Cologne, 2003).
45. See the contributions to this volume by Sebastian Conrad and Thomas Mergel. Cf. also S. Conrad, *Globalisierung und Nation im Deutschen Kaiserreich* (Munich, 2006); D. Gosewinkel, *Einbürgern und Ausschließen. Die Nationalisierung der Staatsangehörigkeit vom Deutschen Bund bis zur Bundesrepublik Deutschland*, 2nd ed., (Göttingen, 2003); E. Nathahns, *The Politics of Citizenship in Germany. Ethnicity, Utility and Nationalism* (Oxford, 2004).
46. See the contribution by Cornelius Torp; id., *Die Herausforderung der Globalisierung. Wirtschaft und Politik in Deutschland 1860–1914* (Göttingen, 2005).

Part I
———————

THE PLACE OF IMPERIAL GERMANY IN GERMAN HISTORY

Chapter 1

When the *Sonderweg* Debate Left Us

Helmut Walser Smith

German history has traversed a long complicated terrain, with the Reformation, the convulsions of the religious wars, the precarious hold of the Enlightenment, the shock of Napoleonic invasion, the failed Revolution of 1848, and the impact of Bismarck as important markers of a tortuous past that ended, insofar as history can end, in collapse. The Third Reich was not predetermined by this history, but nor can it be thought to be without it. Otherwise, the Nazi period would seem like an unfortunate accident, divorced from any connection to a longer view of German history and culture.

To most readers, the above may seem sensible enough, but the weight of orthodoxy among professional historians, especially in the Anglo-American branch of the guild, is of a different opinion. There the prevailing view tends to saw the twentieth century off from the nineteenth, making its central catastrophes into a product not of a long-term history as such, but of an apocalyptic twentieth century. Niall Ferguson's *War of the Worlds*, published in 2006, is only the most recent, and upfront, work to take this position. Ferguson insists that the bloodletting of the twentieth century cannot be traced to the extreme ideologies of the nineteenth, or the dynamics of national states, or the collapse of an international system locked in colonial competition, but instead to a combination of factors—ethnic disintegration, economic volatility, and the collapse of empires—that occurred in the last hundred years.[1] The real context of what Friedrich Meinecke called "the German Catastrophe" is, in this reading, not Germany at all.[2] As a phenomenon of historiography, this is something new. Previous generations of German historians, starting from Friedrich Meinecke and Gerhard Ritter, and including Hans Rosenberg and Hajo Holborn, possessed an acute sense of the chronological depth of German and European history. But this sense has left us. Why?

There are prosaic answers. The nineteenth century is farther away than it was for Meinecke and Ritter, both of whom were born in the nineteenth century, but also for Rosenberg and Holborn, born in the first decade of the twentieth. Moreover, for many historians 1989 ended the short, violent twentieth century, "the age of extremes," and forced us to take a stand on when it began.[3] As "the age of extremes" was palpably marked by global warfare, genocide, and competition among ideologically driven Empires, World War I became the fundamental break. The pressures of that war engendered the collapse of the Russian Empire, and allowed the seizure of power, first by Lenin, then by Stalin. The War also thrust most of Europe east of the Rhine into revolution, tore East Central Europe into a series of nation-states, gave cover for the Armenian genocide, and brought the United States into world politics and military struggle on a grand scale. Then too there was the senseless slaughter for "an old bitch gone in the teeth/a botched civilization," as Ezra Pound put it.[4]

For the twentieth century, World War I makes as much sense as a marker of its inception as does the French Revolution for the nineteenth. But as any such marker, it also obscures our view, and so we may well ask what the new marker means for our understanding of the century that preceded the "age of extremes." This seems all the more urgent in German history, where a powerful historiography once connected the nineteenth to the twentieth century. This was a historiography represented on both sides of the Atlantic. Fritz Stern begins the first body chapter of his recently published memoirs with the arresting sentence, "There have been five Germanys I have known since my birth in 1926, but it is the Germany I don't know, the Germany of the years before World War I, that I think I understand best."[5] It was the Germany of his professional life, driven by an abiding sense that nineteenth-century Germany offered the keys to understanding the twentieth-century catastrophe. He was not alone, even if other American scholars marked the dividing lines differently. For Peter Gay, the place of Enlightenment remained central, even as he insisted that the Kaiserreich was to contemporaries "anything but a chamber of potential horrors." For Gay, the enlightened spirit of liberal alertness and unrelenting but constructive criticism, which defined Weimar's community of reason (the outsiders of Wilhelminian Germany as insiders in the 1920s), was not finally forced into death, or exile, until 1933.[6] More ponderously, Hajo Holborn placed the decisive interpretive stress on the end of German idealism, circa 1840, when German intellectuals failed to address the social question, making it impossible for German idealism to "elevate itself to the level of a national culture" and "solve the practical and intellectual problems of all classes."[7] Like Stern and Gay (and George Mosse and Hans Kohn), Holborn shared a sense that in the nineteenth century the track switched, to use Max Weber's famous metaphor, even if the final destination of catastrophe was not clear until 1933.[8] A parallel tradition emphasized not the intellectual but the social dimension of nineteenth-century origins. Hans Rosenberg, to take only the most famous and influential example, argued that the agrarian constitution of East Elbia, even if formed much earlier, nevertheless proved especially deleterious in the context of nineteenth-century industrialization, creating the structural malformations that led, ultimately, to catastrophe.[9] Alexander Gerschenkron and Barrington Moore, historical sociologists for whom it was axiomatic that nineteenth-century structures shaped twentieth-century outcomes, followed similar lines of reasoning.[10]

This sense of the powerful shaping force of the nineteenth century is now passing, and it is passing in Germany too. This passing has recently been the subject of a wide-ranging historical reflection by Paul Nolte, entitled "Abschied vom 19. Jahrhundert: Auf der Suche nach einer anderen Moderne."[11] Suffice here that in the Federal Republic a powerful historiographical tradition analytically tied the deep structures of the nineteenth century to the catastrophes of the twentieth. This tradition included Werner Conze, who saw the Vormärz as the harbinger of a new industrial civilization; Friedrich Meinecke, who discerned a decisive break when German nationalism lost its idealist component; and Fritz Fischer, who traced strong continuities from the Wilhelminian to the Nazi period. It also included Gerhard Ritter, who saw the democratic moment of the French Revolution as the decisive break into a dark modernity—a view that, with different politics and different channels of influence, still resonates, especially in Israel and France.[12] In Germany, the tradition of seeing the nineteenth century as profoundly structuring for the twentieth century anchored the monumental synthetic works of Heinrich August Winkler and Hans-Ulrich Wehler.[13] Their interpretations of the *longue durée* of German history, however different in matters of detail, turned on nineteenth-century developments, the nation-state and industrial breakthrough, and a missed revolution in civil society. This was, of course, the central thesis of the German *Sonderweg*, which had appeared in many guises, from the self-critical reflections of Ernst Troeltsch, to the sweeping, chronologically deep, European-wide interpretation of Eugen Rosenstock-Huessy, to the profound if idiosyncratic essays of Hellmuth Plessner.[14] But nowhere did it appear with such concentrated vigor as in the work of a group of historians, including Winkler and Wehler, but also Jürgen Kocka and Volker Berghahn, who emphasized Germany's special path to modernity.

In what follows, I will argue that criticism of the *Sonderweg* thesis, while enabling historiographical innovation, also weakened our sense of the continuities of German history. This occurred because (a) no tenable continuity thesis was put in its place, and (b) the continuity thesis eventually offered—not to 1933 but to Auschwitz—ill accounted for fundamental aspects of the Third Reich's catastrophic violence. In its place, we—especially in the Anglo-American branch of the community of German historians—have come to accept an anti-*Sonderweg* consensus bereft of a sense for the deep continuities of German history. Put differently, when the *Sonderweg* left us, it left us without a convincing way to connect twentieth-century German history to the long nineteenth century. The result is a foreshortened sense, not of German history as such, but of a German history that serves to explain twentieth-century horrors.

I

The *Sonderweg*—that thread in German history that connected the centuries—came under attack not after 1989, but in the early 1980s, and in order to understand the current historiographical moment—characterized, I believe, by a sharp disjuncture between the nineteenth and twentieth centuries—it is necessary to return to that *Sonderweg* debate. In its crystallized form as a contest of two remarkable books, Hans-Ulrich Wehler's *Das deutsche Kaiserreich*, and David Blackbourn and Geoff Eley's *The Peculiarities of German History*, the debate left a set of interpretive signposts.[15] These signposts can now be queried, not with a view to deciding the issue—was Germany on a special path or not?—but rather with an aim of understanding when, and for what reasons, the *Sonderweg* debate left us.

As is well known, in *The German Kaiserreich*, Hans-Ulrich Wehler posited the political predominance of the nobility over the middle classes in a period of rapid industrial change, and this political predominance, cemented in constitutions and in political culture alike, undermined attempts at achieving democracy. It also generated a propensity to domestic and international violence that led, via a blind flight forward, into the chaos and bloodshed of World War I. The special path consisted of Germany's relative political backwardness, especially vis-à-vis the United Kingdom, and this expressed itself most profoundly in a failed bourgeois revolution, a feudalized bourgeoisie, and the political predominance of an aristocratic caste that controlled key institutions of government, including the army and bureaucracy. Not Germany's modernity, then, but its lack of it determined subsequent disasters. Blackbourn and Eley, conversely, emphasized the modernity of the Kaiserreich, the relative strength of the bourgeoisie, and the importance of the 1890s as a political *caesura* in which populist politics flourished. They also stressed the formation of political movements resistant to elite manipulation, and the crystallization of political ideologies that challenged rather than stabilized the status quo. If Wehler pointed to the sclerosis of feudal structures, Blackbourn and Eley underscored the disruptive impact of modern capitalism. The modernizers, not the feudal elite, were thus the main carriers of continuity. Nevertheless, both sides emphasized continuity between the Second and Third Empires, and by extension between the nineteenth and twentieth centuries. For Wehler these continuities rested with a feudal elite geographically centered east of the Elbe; for Blackbourn and Eley, carriers of continuity were located in the south, west and center of Germany rather than in the east, and were more important to civil society rather than to the state as such.

At the time, these positions polarized the discipline. Now, more than twenty-five years later, with smoke dissipated, similarities across battle lines appear with greater clarity. In the early 1980s, both sides shared an aversion to stand-alone intellectual or political history, and neither side emphasized diplomatic or military history or the crucial impact of the violence of war. The debate, in fact, largely turned on the form of domestic politics, whether manipulation from above or grass routes mobilization from below. The nation-state remained the frame, with the problem of how nations and societies permeate each other largely unaddressed.[16] Similarly, colonialism was important for reasons of domestic politics but was not particularly important as either experience or as the practice of domination. Most decisively, the Holocaust was not a reference point. In the final analysis, the *Sonderweg* debate was about 1933, not 1941, about politics, not mass murder. Clarify the failure of liberal democracy, and one has already gone far to explaining the onset of genocide, both sides tacitly concurred.

The great contribution of *deutsche Kaiserreich* was to anchor an analysis of state power in a structural analysis of economy and society, and to demonstrate profound continuities across the significant ruptures of war, revolution, and the temporary stabilization of bourgeois Europe. It also answered the question, central to the generation of Holborn and Rosenberg, of why Germany veered from the West in terms of its passage to modernity, and it accomplished this with a wide sociological frame. *Peculiarities*, by contrast, diminished the importance of this veering, and convincingly showed that the model depended on an idealized understanding of British developments. But Blackbourn and Eley did more than bring down a carefully wrought edifice. In *Peculiarities*, they also erected a new framework, centered on a "new style" of politics and the modern elements of the Imperial society, and this, in turn, opened a space that allowed historians to connect the Kaiserreich to the Third Reich in innovative ways. Civil society, once manipulated from above, suddenly seemed to matter on its own terms. As a result, the rest of Germany, and not just Prussia, came into sharper focus, while religion, local identities, associational life, and the law all assumed a new urgency. To be sure, these topics had been the subject of intensive research before, but the new research could now claim centrality.

This was heady stuff, and it inspired a great deal of new research, some of which, especially the researches of James Retallack, has concluded that the original debate centered on false dichotomies and that Blackbourn and Eley initially underestimated the importance of battles won by conservatives and overestimated the ability of populists in the 1890s to mobilize the masses.[17] Nevertheless, young scholars in the late 1980s benefited immensely from the possibilities that Blackbourn and Eley's challenge opened, in the same way that previous scholars had used Wehler's *das Kaiserreich* as a structuring device and a soundboard.

Yet the commitment in *Peculiarities* to German continuities was more ambivalent than the initially liberating emphasis on the modernity of politics in the 1890s implied. This is partly because this commitment also came paired with an explicit abnegation of longer-term German continuities. On this point Eley was especially clear, insisting that the argument in *Peculiarities* "redirects primary attention away from the deeper historical continuities and towards the immediate fascism-producing conjunctures."[18] Specifically, this entailed, according to Eley, placing the "stress [on] the more immediate circumstances under which the Nazis rose to power—namely, the succeeding conjuctures of the First World War, the post-war crisis of 1917–1923, and the world economic crisis after 1929." In his recently published work, *A Crooked Line: From Cultural History to the History of Society*, Eley returned to this issue, contending that the problem of the *Sonderweg* rested in its "anti-Marxist thrust," especially evident in its emphasis on the persistence of feudal and pre-industrial structures in explanations of Nazism. "By these means," he writes, "capitalism was being let off the hook."[19] Blackbourn's subsequently published reflections have hedged the question of continuity with more circumspection, but also with more equivocation. "Implicitly, our questioning of the rigid continuity from Bismarckian Germany to 1933 led us to underline the importance of the First World War as a *caesura*," Blackbourn explained in an interview with the journal *German History* in 2004. He then added that "one of the most interesting issues today is how we can reconcile the undoubted importance of continuities through the period 1890–1930, the era of 'classic modernity.'"[20]

Explicit articulations only tell part of the story, however. The structure of the argument in *Peculiarities* also shifted considerable weight away from the late 1870s, the second foundation of the Empire, and to the 1890s, which then became, to use Paul Nolte's term, "the key element of a larger interpretation of history."[21] But how did the 1890s actually structure subsequent history, insofar as that history had something to say about 1933? Eley, more than Blackbourn, has attempted to answer the question explicitly. In fact, he has given two answers, one indebted to a modified Marxist analysis, the other to Detlev Peukert. The first answer was focused on 1933 as such, the second on the brutality of the Third Reich. The answers are instructive—not just for understanding the state of the debate after the *Sonderweg* left us, but also for taking measure of our subsequent assumptions concerning the continuities of German history.

II

Eley's first answer, articulated in "What Produces Fascism," pointed not to the bodily experience of war, but to capitalist collapse as a result of war and revolution. This collapse occurred first in the crisis of 1917 to 1923, then in the Depression of 1929. These are Eley's "immediate conjunctures": they turned, in his analysis, not on an iron relation between structure and superstructure, economy and ideology, but on a "crisis of representation" and "a crisis of hegemony."[22] The first referred to the inability of "economically dominant classes and their major economic fractions" to pursue their interests in a democratic frame, the second to the collapse of democratic legitimacy. The dominant classes, which in Eley's analysis were not pre-feudal elites but capitalists, then sought radical solutions to the twin crisis of representation and hegemony. More than any other class, the bourgeoisie mobilized the wide field of civil society, and in this way came to exercise a kind of hegemony based on anti-Socialism, intensified after the Russian Revolution, and the frustrations of defeated nationalism. Class remained the driving force of this analysis, as it had been for Gramsci, and power is located not with the state but in civil society.[23] The 1890s remained an interpretive hinge, as this was the decade in which civil society became relatively autonomous from the state, which for Gramsci had been a precondition of hegemony in the sense he intended the term.

Eley's first answer, offered as a provisional program for future reflection, never achieved scholarly assent because it proved impossible to show that that "economically dominant classes and their major economic fractions" organized the rise of Hitler or his seizure of power.[24] Big business lent scant material support to the National Socialists during the Weimar Republic and the presidential cabinets. Even in 1932, financial subsidies proved extremely modest and, from the standpoint of the NSDAP, remained insignificant compared to contributions garnered from grass roots organizing and small and medium-sized businesses.[25] Not capitalists but the people financed the rise of Hitler. Hedging their bets, German capitalists spread their money among non-socialist parties.[26] Nor is it evident that influential business leaders played a significant role in the *Machtergreifung*. Instead, military and agrarian elites, especially those close to Hindenburg, were decisive for the internal maneuvering that brought Hitler to power.[27] Finally, any analysis of continuity that placed an emphasis on social class and modern carriers of continuity had to confront the results of Jürgen Falter's investigations of the basis of Nazi electoral success. These results show that not social class but previous politics and religion proved the most powerful indicators of support for the NSDAP; and that the Nazis received significantly higher levels of support than previously assumed from industrial workers, and significantly less from white-collar employees. The Nazis were also over-represented among educated elites and rural Protestant voters, especially in northern Germany.[28] In the end, neither the success of the NSDAP, nor its appeal, nor Hitler's Machtergreifung could be closely related to capitalist crisis, except in the generic and self-evident sense that the Great Depression constituted the broad background against which events unfolded, and that anti-Socialism and anti-Communism glued Hitler's supporters together.

The causal explanation that linked the alternative narrative of *Peculiarities* forward to the rise of fascism failed, therefore, to convince, and was not pursued, as far as I am aware, in a sustained manner throughout the nineties. Yet the new focus on the critical importance of the 1890s as a caesura of modern German history became significant in a different context. It was the initial decade of "classical modernity"—a term that Detlev Peukert borrowed from art history to denote a period of increased complexity and significant transformations in scientific research, social reform, city planning, consumer behavior, popular politics, the arts, and much else.[29] Within this rubric, a flood of illuminating research provided historians with a fuller sense of the social and intellectual experimentation that arched across three decades, giving us an infinitely richer picture of the Wilhelminian period and the Weimar Republic.[30] Moreover, historians framed that picture within a theoretically versatile conception of modernity, and this, in turn, has imparted to the specialized research wider appeal. Historians now draw lines of continuities from Wilhelminian Germany through the Weimar Republic, sometimes to the Third Reich, but as often to the Federal Republic of Germany.[31] Comparisons with other Western countries are not simply negative, and indeed the contradictions of Weimar have taken on the sheen of the universal.

Yet in its initial formulation, the argument for classical modernity posited close connections between cultural and political crisis. In *Die Weimarer Reublik*, for example, Detlev Peukert narrated the end of the Weimar Republic as "an attempt to combine technocratic efficiency with authoritarian methods of social control in order to resolve the tensions that had been created by modernization and heightened by the chronic crises of the 1920s."[32] Peukert took up insights of Michel Foucault, as well as of Jürgen Habermas and Norbert Elias. He emphasized the centrality of concentrated attempts at management, control, and social discipline in a society shot through with contradiction. And he placed instrumental reason and the spirit of science at the center of the Weimar Experience. Moreover, his insights remain remarkably suggestive, especially for the middle year of the Weimar Republic.

Yet what impresses at the end of Weimar is not control but loss of it, and especially the loss of initiative to the principled ideological parties of left and right, whose solutions were systemic and brutal. Little interested in neatly sewn technocratic solutions stitched together in committees, the NSDAP and the KPD both took to the street, rendering politics exciting, volatile, emotional, and violent.[33] Peukert convincingly argued that by 1930 the Republic proved unable to shoulder the modern welfare provisions on which it had based part of its legitimacy. In this way, a modernist experiment gone awry fueled further discontent. Yet this insight tells us about July 1930, when the Reichstag dissolved over the inability of capital and labor to compromise on social insurance, not September of the same year, when the NSDAP achieved its first significant electoral victory. Moreover, even after September 1930, a fascist outcome was hardly predetermined. But instead of following politics at the center, and asking about the possibility of an authoritarian course (which, however loathsome given the democratic promise of Weimar, would surely have been preferable to a genocidal regime), Peukert shifted the emphasis to political culture, which he then folded into a crisis of cultural modernity. The explanation emphasized broad political style rather than concrete political programs, modernist apocalyptic visions rather than older ideologies.[34] Nationalism and anti-Semitism are, for example, largely absent in his explanation. It is about the lapse into barbarity, not the seizure of power as such. If anything, Peukert's work, and the thesis of classical modernity more generally, elided the vortex of the vanishing point of 1933.[35]

With few exceptions, subsequent research has worked with a shifted vanishing point, and, in this context, Eley's second argument, which placed the 1890s as marking the onset of an ambivalent but dark modernity, assumed fundamental importance. As Edward Ross Dickenson has argued, this thesis represents the "outlines of a new master narrative of modern German history," and that narrative has "a function in German historiography similar to that long virtually monopolized by the Sonderweg thesis."[36] This paradigm, which gives prominence to rationality, science, and the disciplining of the body in arguments for continuity, renders German history as "a particular variant of modernity," and Germany in the early twentieth century "not as a nation having trouble modernizing, but as a nation of troubling modernity."[37]

The paradigm rests on a variety of scholarly contributions, but its theoretical bearings are also indebted to Detlev Peukert, and in particular his seminal essay, "the Genesis of the Final Solution from the Spirit of Science," first published in 1988. In "Genesis," Peukert posited a "fatally racist dynamic" that turned on the practical dilemmas of progressive social reform and the theoretical positions staked out by the turn-of-the-century human sciences. Fatally new, according to Peukert, was the qualitative division of humanity according to worthy (*Werte*) and worthless (*Unwerte*) coupled with a view that "man" is not the measure, still less individual men and women, but the body of the nation or the race. Peukert advanced this argument in a lecture in 1987, in the aftermath of the *Historikerstreit*, and it begins by centering the discussion not on 1933, or on the character of fascism, but on Auschwitz. This is one reason why the text is so crucial: it marks an important moment in the shift of the vanishing point of German history from 1933 to 1941–42. Peukert then defines the central question as what "might explain the origins of the decision, unparalleled in human history, to use high technology to annihilate certain abstractly defined categories of victims."[38] The modernist thrust inheres in the emphasis Peukert puts on "high technology" (*Großtechnik*) but also on "abstractly defined categories of victims." The latter term situates the victims of the Holocaust in the context of an enlightenment project of naming and counting individuals in terms of citizenship, ethnicity, and sexuality. Where religion fits in this scheme is more difficult to discern, and one senses that Peukert felt the tension as well. He explicitly argued his case against "the traditional history of anti-Semitism and the persecution of the Jews, despite the fact that Jewish victims constituted by far the largest group on the charge-sheet of Nazi terror up to 1945."[39] Not that Peukert denied the influence of anti-Semitism; rather, he subsumed it under a broader category of a "fatally racist dynamism present within the human and social sciences."[40] Telling, in this context, were turns of phrase such as "anthropological racism—with its centerpiece, anti-Semitism."[41]

Where does the difficulty lie? Self-evidently, Peukert understood that anti-Semitism and ethnic antagonism have a longer history than turn-of-the-century formulations drawn from the humane sciences. The question, however, is whether his explanation can incorporate them in theoretical terms.[42] Here the answer is less clear, and in any case incorporating the longer histories would necessitate abandoning the chronological marker, the switching point, which Peukert places circa 1900. It is possible to argue, for example, that nationalism and anti-Semitism were not particularly virulent in Germany; that they were more deeply anchored in France, and more violent in Russia. The older ideologies constituted part of a general background but were not as causal with respect to genocide. But then, given the switching point of 1900, it remains important to show a connection between German modernity, as marked by the human sciences, and the Holocaust. The evidentiary road typically traveled runs through murderous biopolitics: racial hygiene, sterilization campaigns, euthanasia, T-4, Belzec, and the extermination camps of Operation Reinhardt, which drew its specialists disproportionately from the euthanasia campaign. In this way, the Holocaust can be, at the very least, "genealogically related" (Dickinson) to turn-of-the-century biopolitics—the racial hygiene of Alfred Ploetz, for example.

The sociology of such an explanation remains extraordinarily thin, however. The German Society for Racial Hygiene had but 425 members in 1913, and fewer in the Weimar Republic.[43] By contrast, the large nationalist associations counted their numbers in the hundreds of thousands, and increased in popularity in the Weimar Republic. The anti-Semitic "German Defense and Offense League" (Schutz-ud Trutzbund), for example, reached nearly two hundred thousand members when it was banned in 1922; in 1930, the Stahlhelm, originally an organization of former frontline soldiers, counted its membership at about half a million.[44] Nor did eugenics have a discernable effect on government legislation. The Reichstag did not approve a single eugenics measure, whether in the Kaiserreich or in the Weimar Republic—in contrast, for example, to a number of American states, like Indiana, which passed compulsory sterilization legislation in 1907, and California, which passed such legislation in 1909 and sterilized over sixty-five thousand people, a third of the US total.[45] In Germany, there was one academic chair for racial hygiene, established in Munich in 1923, and two institutes for the study of human heredity, the Kaiser Wilhelm Institiute of Anthropology, Human Heredity, and Genetics, founded in Berlin in 1927, and Ernst Rüdin's Psychiatric Institute in Munich. But aside from the sterilization of French Moroccan troops, the so-called "Rhineland bastards," these institutes likewise had little influence on policy. While a discourse of eugenics existed prior to 1933, and had gained momentum in the last years of the Weimar Republic, it remained institutionally marginal and without influence on the social legislation so central to Peukert's broader analysis.[46] In fact, it never achieved significant successes until Adolf Hitler came to power. It therefore remains a thin reed of continuity, unable to bear the analytical weight the biopolitics paradigm has assigned to it.

One also wonders about the place of "high technology" in the explanation of the antecedents of the Holocaust. Here the figure of Auschwitz as a vanishing point exerts a great deal of force. But brutal face-to-face killings by the Wehrmacht, the Ethnic German Defense forces, the Order Police, and the Einsatzgruppen preceded Auschwitz.[47] Before Auschwitz, there were also the base and brutal slaughters at Ponary (Vilnius) and Fort IX (Kovno), Maly Trostinets (Minsk) and Rumboli (Riga), Babi Yar (Kiev) and Drobitzki Valley (Kharkov), and countless unnamed killings at the edge of makeshift pits, ravines, and anti-tank ditches throughout Eastern Europe. There was the explicitly colonial tactic of concentrating victims in ghettos and allowing them to starve, a policy that hard-line "attritionists" advocated against the more economically "rational" occupational authorities, the "productionists," who hoped to use the Jewish ghettos to enhance Jewish economic potential in the service of the Reich.[48] Even the initial extermination camps, Chelmno and the camps of Operation Reinhard (Belzec, Sobibor, and Treblinca) killed Jews not with high technology but with carbon monoxide running off internal combustion engines, a nineteenth-century technology already put to mass use in the automobile at the beginning of the twentieth century. Comparative consideration, moreover, suggests that genocide hardly requires "high technology." In Rwanda, militant Hutu groups killed over half a million and perhaps as many as a million Tutsi between early April and mid July 1994. What does this tell us? That most Tutsi, as well as Jews killed in the Holocaust, were not victims of high technology but of archaic forms of murder and ordinary kinds of technology. "The Holocaust," according to Ulrich Herbert, was "in a pronounced way a process of human destruction of very traditional, indeed archaic forms with a correspondingly high number of direct perpetrators."[49] These archaic forms seem as important as the Holocaust's vaunted modernity; they also have a history, in particular with respect to Jews, but also with respect to ethnic antagonism.

Eley's second argument relies heavily on Peukert, and works backwards from the shifted vanishing point of the Third Reich's murderous policies. For Eley, "biological politics" are "a unifying principle of Nazi practice, linking anti-Semitism and the racialist offensive of the war years to a complex of policies before 1939, including population planning, public health, welfare policies directed at women, euthanasia, sterilization, and eugenics." Like Peukert, Eley sought to situate the murderous dynamic of the Third Reich in normal life and to shift emphasis away from the "exegetical focus on Hitler's and other Nazi leader's immediate ideas and their etymology." As with Peukert, the impetus is clear: the attempt to encompass theoretically the range of victims. But the result is a Holocaust without reference to anti-Semitism. Instead, the murder of Jews and other groups is placed in a broader context of a "racialized social-policy complex in ideas and innovations that go back to the Weimar Republic and even further, to the period before 1914." In this reading, the question of "why the Jews?" (who constituted the overwhelming majority of murdered non-combatants) is answered by reference to their status as one of a number of culturally constructed target groups. Medicine, social policy, eugenics, hygiene—these are the motors, and the murder of the European Jews is the effect. Moreover, the "diffusion of eugenicist and related ideologies of social engineering ... had permeated the thinking of social policy and health-care professionals long before the Nazis themselves had arrived." Put differently, they are causally prior to the radical nationalist and anti-Semitic ideologies that, in a different narration, might be construed as independent forces in an explanation of the Holocaust.

III

Where, then, are we left—when the *Sonderweg* left us? With an argument for continuity that seems to place more weight for the German catastrophe on the theories of Alfred Ploetz than on the policies of Otto von Bismarck? Or with a narrative that eschews strong claims for continuity that reach deep into the nineteenth century? Hans-Ulrich Wehler's *Gesellschaftsgeschichte* is remarkable for many reasons, but perhaps most of all because it confronts the question of continuity with insistence, and stresses the thick braids rather than the thin. Paramount is nationalism, a powerful ideology throughout the nineteenth century with a wide social basis (and as Geoff Eley taught us many years ago, a radical new style) by the beginning of the twentieth. Transformed by war and defeat, it became among the most destabilizing forces of the Weimar period, fueling the radical right, cultivating discontent, searing enmities. Wehler argues that it was at the core of the problem. Aligned with Hitler's charismatic rule and an increasingly murderous anti-Semitism, nationalism accounted for Nazism's remarkable ability to mobilize large numbers of people. There are other elements to Wehler's interpretation—the extended account of the social and economic history of Imperial Germany and the Weimar Republic, the shift to a primacy of politics in the Third Reich, the insistence that inequalities of class structured society, the emphasis on the baleful role played by elites in the military and the bureaucracy, and on the continuing hold of authoritarianism.

Is it possible, then, to reconsider German continuities, and to posit deeper historical connections between the twentieth-century catastrophe and the nineteenth-century history that preceded it? The answer depends in part on our definition of continuity. Alexander Gerschenkron put forward five possibilities: the constancy of direction, the periodicity of events, endogenous change, the length of causal regress, and the stability of the rate of change.[50] By constancy of direction, he meant continual change in the same direction, admitting of setbacks, possibly fluctuating in the rate of change, but nevertheless history pressing forward or sliding irreversibly backwards. The second possibility, the periodicity of events, involves the reiteration of the past. If different in outward appearance, historical events nevertheless represent a reenactment of earlier occurrences—the victory, again, of conservative over liberal interests, the persecution of the Jews, as always. The third, endogenous change, points to the possibility that historical development, or deformation, occurs as a result of recurring mechanisms that inhere within a given system: the political preponderance of agrarian elites in a dynamic industrial economy vitiating attempts at achieving democracy, for example. Continuity as endogenous change was central to Wehler's formulation of the *Sonderweg*, since the causal link was located in the system, and exogenous shocks, like the impact of war, only affected the rate of change, not the mechanism per se. Then there is the length of causal regress, Gerschenkron's fourth category. It posits that cogent historical argumentation requires that causes be traced backwards, not infinitely, but significantly. He draws his example from the Russian Revolution, whose immediate origins may be discerned in World War I or in the failure of the reforms of 1905, but whose deeper causes lie in the Russian ordeal of serfdom and absolutism, and must be traced back to the reign of Catherine II. Here the case is for the preponderance of significant factors, serfdom and absolutism, "powerful currents in the causal stream." The explanation does not rely on the supposition that such factors were not extant elsewhere, but that they possessed remarkable weight in Russian history. Finally, there is stability in the rate of change. Here the question concerns the significant "kink" in continuity, the metaphor taken from economic take-off in a backward economy, with the element of continuity measured from the significant shift in the series.

Continuity, Gerschenkron insisted, is a term of scholarship, not politics; all five models are ordering devices, programs for research. And they are crucial for shaping the historical field. The *Sonderweg*, for example, necessitated that historians show not only the force of a causal factor, like nationalism, but also its peculiar force in relation to other countries. It also explained change in almost exclusively endogenous terms. Yet whether in regards to Germany's authoritarian traditions, its strident nationalism, or its virulent anti-Semitism, a great deal of historical research has chipped away at our sense of German singularity. But not at the salience of the causal factors themselves. This seems to me a crucial distinction. It allows us to emphasize nationalism and ethnic antagonism (in the East, for example) as "powerful currents in the causal stream" (Gerschenkron) without claiming a unique status for German variations on European ideologies.[51] This enables a reconsideration of the force of older ideologies, which the modernity thesis had likewise relegated to theoretical holding stations—in part because of the need to emphasize the modernity of the Holocaust itself, in part because of an emphasis on the modern carriers of continuity. But when we see the Holocaust as a brutal mix of archaic violence and ordinary technology and its perpetrators as more ideologically motivated than the modernity paradigm allowed, the importance of nationalism, ethnic and religious enmity, and absolute destruction as a military ethos, come more sharply into view.[52] Beyond the *Sonderweg*, then, is a concept of continuity as the length of causal regress. It allows us to impart a deeper chronological sense to our explanations of the twentieth century, and it opens the possibility that in our explanation of German history, and the twentieth-century catastrophe it brought forth, we can situate the German past in a denser weave of international and transnational history.

Notes

1. N. Ferguson, *The War of the World: Twentieth-Century Conflict and the Descent of the West* (London, 2006), xii.
2. F. Meinecke, *Die deutsche Katastrophe. Betrachtungen und Erinnerungen* (Wiesbaden, 1946).
3. E. Hobsbawm, *The Age of Extremes. A History of the World, 1914–1991* (New York, 1994).
4. E. Pound, "Hugh Selwyn Mauberly," in *Selected Poems of Ezra Pound* (New York, 1957), 64.
5. F. Stern, *Five Germanies I have Known* (New York, 2006), 13.
6. P. Gay, *Freud, Jews and other Germans. Masters and Victims in Modernist Culture* (New York, 1978), 19; P. Gay, *Weimar Culture: The Outsider as Insider* (New York, 1968), 145.
7. Hajo Holborn, "German Idealism in Light of Social History," in id., *Germany and Europe: Historical Essays* (New York, 1971), 4. This essay was first published in German in the *Historische Zeitschrift* 174 (1952), 359–84. See also Hajo Holborn, *A History of Modern Germany*, vol. 2, 1648–1840

(New York, 1964), 513, 531, where the decisive markers come with Hegel, whose "philosophy rejects the whole tradition of natural law, which had constituted one of the strongest liberalizing forces in western civilization," and with the failure of the idealistic aspirations of 1848, "causing the widespread loss of idealistic faith." In this reading, the embrace of pure power divorced from ideals defined the next half century, and cast the die.

8. For an astute review of this literature, see V. Berghahn, "Deutschlandbilder 1945–1965. Angloamerikanische Historiker und moderne deutsche Gechichte," in *Deutsche Geschichtswissenschaft nach dem Zweien Weltkrieg (1945–1965)*, ed. Ernst Shulin (Munich, 1989), 239–72.

9. G.A. Ritter, "Die emigrierten Meinecke-Schüler in den Vereinigten Staaten. Leben und Geschichtsschreibung im Spannungsfeld zwischen Deutschland und der neuen Heimat; Hajo Holborn, Felix Gilbert, Dietrich Gerhard, Hans Rosenberg," in *Historische Zeitschrift* 284, 1 (2007), 59–102. See also the contributions in the special edition, dedicated to Hans Rosenberg, of the journal *Central European History* 24 (1991).

10. A. Gerschenkron, *Bread and Democracy in Germany* (Berkeley, 1943); B. Moore, *Social Origins of Dictatorship and Democracy* (Boston, 1966).

11. P. Nolte, "Abschied vom 19. Jahrhundert," in *Wege der Gesellschaftsgeschichte*, eds. Jürgen Osterhammel, Dieter Langewiesche and Paul Nolte (Göttingen, 2006), 103–32.

12. See J. Talmon, *The Origins of Totalitarian Democracy* (New York, 1952); F. Furet, *The Passing of an Illusion: The Idea of Communism in the Twentieth Century* (Chicago, 1999); and, extremely fruitful and suggestive, A. Finkielkraut, *In the Name of Humanity*, trans. J. Friedlander (New York, 2000).

13. Monumental but with significant public resonance. H.A. Winkler, *Der lange Weg nach Westen. Deutsche Geschichte vom Ende des Alten Reiches bis zum Untergang der Weimarer Republik*, 2 vols., (Munich, 2000); H.-U. Wehler, *Deutsche Gesellschaftsgeschichte*, vols. 1–5 (Munich, 1987–2008).

14. For Troeltsch, see his *Schriften zur Politik und Kulturphilosophie (1918–1923)*, ed. G. Hübinger in association with J. Mikuteit, *Ernst Troeltsch Kritische Gesamtausgabe im Auftrag der Heidelberger Akademie der Wissenschaften*, eds. F.W. Graf, V. Drehsen, G. Hübinger, and T. Rendtorff (Berlin, 2002). On Rosenstock-Huessey, *Die europäischen Revolutionen. Volkscharactere und Staatenbildung* (Jena, 1931); and for the importance of this book to later formulations of the *Sonderweg* thesis, especially Wehler's line of argumentation, see H.-U. Wehler, *Eine lebhafte Kampfsituaion. Ein Gespräch mit Manfred Hettling und Cornelius Torp* (Munich, 2006), 66. On Plessner, see C. Dietze, *Nachgeholtes Leben: Helmuth Plessner (1892–1985)* (Göttingen, 2006).

15. H.-U. Wehler, *Das deutsche Kaiserreich 1871–1918* (Göttingen, 1973); D. Blackbourn and G. Eley, *The Peculiarites of German History: Bourgeois Society and Politics in Nineteenth Century Germany* (Oxford, 1984).

16. For the difference between comparative history, the method shared by Wehler, Eley and Blackbourn at the time of the debate, and a transnational history that treats as central the problem of mutual influence ("Galton's problem"), see J. Osterhammel, *Geschichtswissenschaft jenseits des Nationalstaats. Studien zu Beziehungsgeschichte und Zivilisationsvergleich* (Göttingen, 2001), 39–43.

17. See especially, J. Retallack, *The German Right 1860–1920: Political Limits of the Authoritarian Imagination* (Toronto, 2006), 77–78; also R. Chickering, "Language and the Social Foundations of Radical Nationalism in the Wilhelmine Era," in *1870/71–1989/90. German Unification and the Change of Literary Discourse*, ed. Walter Pape (Berlin, 1993), 61–78.

18. Blackbourn and Eley, *Peculiarities*, 50. Eley writes, "this argument has major implications for our understanding of the period after 1914 and for the origins of German fascism in particular. In effect, it redirects primary attention away from the deeper historical continuities and towards the immediate fascism-producing conjunctures." He also argued that the critique of pre-industrial traditions implies that "the deep historical view of the origins of fascism is also cast into doubt." See *Peculiarities*, 154–55; see also G. Eley, "What Produces Fascism: Pre-Industrial Traditions or a Crisis of the Capitalist State?," in Eley, *From Unification to Nazism: Reinterpreting the German Past* (Boston, 1986), 272.

19. G. Eley, *A Crooked Line: From Cultural History to the History of Society* (Ann Arbor, 2005), 81.

20. D. Blackbourn in "Forum: An interview with David Blackbourn and Geoff Eley," *German History* 22, 2 (2004), 233.
21. Nolte, "Abschied," 106.
22. Eley, "What Produces Fascism," 273.
23. On the role of Gramsci in these formulations, see now G. Eley and K. Neild, *The Future of Class in History. What's Left of the Social* (Ann Arbor, 2007), 143–47. But see also T. Nipperdey, who in his review of *Peculiarities* wryly noted, "Ich muß gestehen, ich lese Eley ohne Gramsci, und Blackbourn ohne die Frankfurter Schule." Nipperdey, *Historische Zeitschrift* 249 (1989), 436.
24. Eley, "What Produces Fascism," 273.
25. H.A. Turner Jr., *German Big Business and the Rise of Hitler* (New York, 1985), 340–49.
26. Ibid.
27. So too, and more than previously than assumed, were the nobility. See S. Malinowski, *Vom König zum Führer. Sozialer Niedergang und politische Radikalisierung im deutschen Adel zwischen Kaiserreich und NS-Staat* (Berlin, 2003).
28. Jürgen Falter, *Hitlers Wähler* (Munich, 1991).
29. D.J.K. Peukert, *Die Weimarer Republik. Krisenjahre der klassichen Moderne* (Frankfurt am Main, 1987). For a judicious appraisal of Peukert's contribution, see D. Crew, "The Pathologies of Modernity: Detlev Peukert on Germany's Twentieth Century," *Social History* 17 (1992), 319–28.
30. In lieu of a mountain of literature, *Germany at the Fin de Siècle. Culture, Politics, and Ideas*, eds. S. Marchand and D. Lindenfeld (Baton Rouge, 2004); *Jahrhundertwende: Der Aufbruch in der Moderne, 1880–1930*, 2 vols. eds. A. Nitschke, G.A. Ritter, D.J.K. Peukert, and R. vom Bruch (Reinbeck bei Hamburg, 1990); and Peukert, *Die Weimarer Republik*.
31. This is also true of politics. Exemplary, in this regard, is T. Mergel, *Parlamentarische Kultur in der Weimarer Republik. Politische kommunikation, symbolische Politik und Öffentlichkeit im Reichstag* (Düsseldorf, 2002).
32. Peukert, *Die Weimarer Republik*, 265.
33. On the contrast, see Mergel, *Parlementarische Kultur*.
34. Compare H.-U. Wehler, *Deutsche Gesellschaftsgeschichte*, vol. 4 (Munich, 2003), 589, where the explanatory emphasis is also on crisis and political culture, but with a reaffirmation of the *Sonderweg*—many countries struggled with the contradictions of modernity and capitalism but only Germany succumbed to fascist dictatorship—and a sense of the deep grounding of the problem.
35. On the concept of vanishing point, see H.W. Smith, "The Vanishing Point of German History: An Essay on Perspective," *History and Memory* 17,1/2 (2005), 269–95.
36. E.R. Dickinson, "Biopolitics, Fascism, Democracy: Some Reflections on Our Discourse About 'Modernity,'" *Central European History* 37 1 (2004). 1. Tim Mason may have been the first to see this as a "new paradigm: Nazism as an expression of biological politics." See C.S. Maier, "Foreword," to *Reevaluating the Third Reich*, eds. T. Childers and J. Caplan (New York, 1993), xiv.
37. Ibid., 5.
38. D.J.K. Peukert, "Die Genesis der 'Endlösung' aus dem Geist der Wissenschaft," in Peukert, *Max Webers Diagnose der Moderne* (Göttingen, 1989), 104.
39. Ibid. There is, moreover, a strong sense in which Peukert assumed a thoroughly secularized, demystified German modernity.
40. Ibid.
41. Peukert, "Genesis," 103.
42. According to Charles Maier, "Foreword," to *Reevaluating the Third Reich*, xiv, the historian Marion Kaplan already raised the question, in 1998, of whether Peukert's interpretation "threatened to become a Holocaust without Jews."
43. For the membership figures, and the overwhelmingly academic and medical composition of its members, see P. Weindling, *Health, Race, and German Politics between National Unification and Nazism, 1870–1945* (Cambridge, 1989), 146–49.
44. Membership figures in Wehler, *Deutsche Gesellschaftsgeschichte*, vol. 4, 502, 391.
45. I. Dowbiggin, *A Merciful End. The Euthanasia Movement in Modern America* (New York, 2003).

46. Dickinson, "Biopolitics."
47. This rendering anonymous was hardly unique to Peukert. See the general critique in A. Lüdtke, "Der Bann der Wörter: 'Todesfabriken.' Vom Reden über den NS Völkermord—das auch ein Verschweigen ist," *WerkstaatGeschichte* 5 (1996), 13. For a critique of the general approach from the perspective of the new research on perpetrators, G. Paul, "Die Täter der Shoah im Spiegel der Forschung," in *Die Täter der Shoah. Fanatische Nationalsozialisten oder ganz normale Deutsche?* (Göttingen, 2002), 24–27, 41. See, further, M. Mann, *The Dark Side of Democracy. Explaining Ethnic Cleansing* (Cambridge, 2005), 242, where the criticism is directed at Z. Baumann, *Modernity and the Holocaust* (Ithaca, 1989).
48. C. R. Browning, *The Origins of the Final Solution. The Evaluation of Nazi Jewish Policy, September 1939–March 1942* (Lincoln, NE, 2004), 113.
49. See U. Herbert, "Vernichtungspolitik. Neue Antworten und Fragen zur Geschichte des Holocaust," in *Nationalsozialistische Vernichtungspolitik 1939–1945*, ed. Ulrich Herbert (Frankfurt am Main, 1998), 57. With still more validity, the same may be said of genocide more broadly. "For genocide," as Omer Bartov writes, "is, ultimately, also about the encounter between the killer and the killed, usually with a fair number of spectators standing by." Bartov, "Seeking the Roots of Modern Genocide: On the Macro- and Microhistory of Mass Murder," in *The Specter of Genocide: Mass Murder in Historical Perspective*, eds. R. Gellately and B. Kiernan (Cambridge, 2003), 96.
50. A. Gerschenkron, *Continuity in History and other Essays* (Cambridge, MA, 1968), 21.
51. Wehler's *Gesellschaftsgeschichte*, vol. 4 argues that nationalism aligned with Hitler's charismatic rule and an increasingly murderous anti-Semitism, accounted for Nazism's ability to mobilize large numbers of people. The German story suggests the convergence of factors, but whether the individual histories of nationalism, anti-Semitism, or the pull of charismatic authority are German or European is perhaps another matter.
52. Crucial recent texts for reconsidering this question are, among many others, I.V. Hull, *Absolute Destruction. Military Culture and the Practices of War in Imperial Germany* (Ithaca, 2005); Mann, *The Dark Side*.

Chapter 2

The Impossible Vanishing Point
Societal Differentiation in Imperial Germany

Benjamin Ziemann

In the third volume of his *History of German Society*, Hans-Ulrich Wehler painted a broad and powerful picture of the political reform blockages in Germany from 1870–1914 and of the authoritarian remodeling of the political system of Imperial Germany. The military's special constitutional position, the absence of a genuine parliamentarization although parliament increasingly had more duties, the formally non-political, in fact however conservative-authoritative "government through the civil service," and the "radicalization" of a new "Reich nationalism"— these are just a few examples of Germany's negative record in regard to political reform from 1870–1914.[1] It is possible to criticize Wehler's insistence on the thesis of a German *Sonderweg* on grounds of formal logic, because National Socialism can be considered only partially a *Sonderweg* if one accepts, following a point convincingly argued by key experts, that fascism was a generic, European phenomenon in the interwar period.[2] But even then, the importance of his argument on the political reform blockade cannot be denied. In spite of the many revisions historians have made in the last two decades to the older views of the socio-historical causes for the *Sonderweg*, the power of the enemies of reform remains a central aspect of the political history of Imperial Germany.[3]

It is questionable, however, if this blockade in the political system can be taken as the yardstick for an overall assessment of the history of German society during these years. Wehler assigns politics a central role in German society. According to his interpretation, politics, together with the classes which supported this politics, was "largely responsible" for the *Sonderweg*, for the inability of German society to deal successfully with the social crisis produced by modernization. One cannot find a more explicit way of formulating Wehler's advocated primacy of politics in society than this.[4] One can, however, point out, arguing against this verdict, that the history of society since 1800, and especially in the late nineteenth century, won considerable stimulus from the progress of social differentiation.

The key message of this chapter is that the accelerating process of social differentiation during the final decades of the nineteenth century makes it impossible to see society in Imperial Germany as a compact, container-like entity. Thus, the deformation of one part of society cannot fairly be attributed to society as a whole and cannot determine the historical judgement on an entire era. Functional differentiation itself, that is, the development of fields or sub-systems of society which are independent against each other, is an important criterion for the process of modernization. It encapsulates modernity because it unleashes functionally specialized social practices and fields and leads thus to an increase in the amount of complexity society can allow for. If functional differentiation advances to a topic that contemporaries reflect upon, and through this is itself labeled and described as an important signature of a society's modernity, then differentiation is simultaneously a marker of modernity. Or, in other words: functional differentiation is both a structural "reality" of modern society and a form to describe these realities within society, a self-description of society.[5]

In a conventional sense, functional differentiation can be understood as the dissolution of the old, polyfunctional social configurations which defined the social history of the early modern period. The early modern church with its special privileges within society and for the aristocracy, the nobility which was understood and which saw itself as the ruling estate (*Herrschaftsstand*), the guilds of the artisans and merchants—all these configurations which merged political, economic and cultural functions made way for an institutional arrangement in which these functions were differentiated into different institutions. This development can be described as an empowerment of the state, which monopolized both political power and the enforcement of law through the police. At the same time, however, the state lost power because it gave up some of the economic and cultural competences it had maintained throughout the early modern period.[6] Such an understanding of functional differentiation, in which complex wholes break down into different parts, is called "decomposition" in the tradition of sociological theory, employing the biological analogy of cell division.[7] As an alternative to this approach, we can employ an understanding of functional differentiation that sociologists tend to call the "emergence" of differentiation. Why emergence? Because according to this theory, differentiation is a process where new forms of accessing and looking at the social world emerged and differentiated themselves. Incidentally, they developed their own structures inside society. Or, in other words: functional sub-systems of society are not the result of a division of larger entities, but develop when a specific code of communication does emerge and can be stabilized. This emergence of functions followed as "world views were cultivated, turned into partial entities and finally rendered in terms of absolutes," producing self-referential social forms in the process.[8] Hence, this form of differentiation also implies an "interruption of interdependence," because developments in one field or sub-system of society no longer automatically or completely affect other fields.[9] In modern society, for example, religious developments do not necessarily affect science or the arts, whereas science and art without religious underpinnings were largely inconceivable during the medieval and early modern period.

Based on these reflections on different sociological theories of functional differentiation, I will now try to highlight the fact that various processes of emergent differentiation occurred in Imperial Germany. One example is the vast increase in the number of daily newspapers, moving Germany literally to the "age of the mass press." This development can best be described by examining the rapid, quantitative increase in circulation, and through the inner diversification of this market; there were no less than 4,200 daily papers in 1914. Concerning the political tendencies, it is noticeable that in their public significance and in their reception the liberal press from the houses Ullstein and Mosse pushed the conservative daily papers to the "second rank." In the political pecking order, however, according to Wehler, the liberal newspapers stayed in a position of "political powerlessness."[10] It is questionable whether such a verdict, focusing on the political impact of the liberal press, adequately and sufficiently apprehends the genuine socio-historical relevance of the daily press, especially if we look at this development from the viewpoint of a theory of social differentiation and see the emergence of new codes of communication as one key criteria for modernization.

From this perspective, it can be seen that the mass media emerged as a differentiated sub-system of society in Wilhelmine Germany. To be sure, the press as an institutional complex which compiles, selects, and spreads the news in its printed form has a history that goes back to the early modern era. In Germany it was, however, only in the last decades of the nineteenth century that the press developed its specific mode of selecting and circulating information which turned the daily press as a mass medium into a coherent self-referential social system. Only now did the daily press, like every other differentiated sub-system of society, become a duplicate of the social world while it elaborated upon it, but from a certain perspective. In this case the perspective was that of information—the distinction or code that informs the workings of the mass media is that the information in the news was already basically old, non-news at its very moment of distribution, having to make space for new news.[11] The specific temporality and sociability of a world that was constituted through mass media was not unique to, but definitely most clearly tangible in the urban world of the big city metropolis, which the daily press both reflected and simultaneously reconstructed in its own context.

Berlin, the city that at the end of Imperial Germany had the largest concentration of daily newspapers in Europe, can be understood as a metonymy for information in printed form, for the "word city" that developed and decayed once again every day. This "word city" not only complemented the "real" city that was made of bricks and mortar; it also superimposed itself increasingly over the latter and represented it. The fleeting nature and urgency of the visual staging of metropolitan life pulsated in its own differentiated temporal structure. This was the rhythm of the "extra" issues, which were printed and circulated several times a day—at midday, in the evening, and again at night. A crucial example of this trend was the *BZ am Mittag* that Ullstein published from 1904 on. This newspaper relied solely on telephone reports. These newspapers with their "extra" editions, in their search for the latest news and sensations, did not allow for a single, "authoritative" reading and reception of the news; and precisely this openness to a multiplicity of readings constituted the social modernity of the mass media as an emergent reality. The "word city" in the Berlin daily press thus developed a life of its own, so that that the press advanced to an important reference point for the experiences and descriptions of modernity in the eyes of the contemporary observer.[12] In the plenitude of its reports and other textual genres, the Berlin daily press confirmed one thing—the big city, in which multiple social processes occur simultaneously, is itself an important example and site of functional differentiation.

The emergent differentiation of a functional sub-system of society and its specific perspective on the social "world" is not only reflected, it is simultaneously advanced by its internal differentiation.[13] The duplication or in fact multiplication of perspectives and observer positions in modern society implies that every perspective will develop zones of contact with other perspectives. This becomes especially clear in the modern daily press of the Wilhelmine Empire, in which, among other things, the internal differentiation of the papers into sections and departments increased. It was the culture section, the pages devoted to the economy, local news and articles about sports that gained in available space and importance, not politics.[14] This new, spectacle-driven style of reporting in the Berlin newspapers focused on theatrical effects and episodes. It thus also indicated a disruption in interdependence with other sub-systems as the news coverage increasingly made it difficult to attribute newsworthy events to a clear-cut political interpretation. A good example for this trend is the famous "episode in Köpenick" (*Köpenickiade*) of the cobbler Wilhelm Voigt. In October 1906, Voigt took command of a platoon of soldiers wearing a captain's uniform he had assembled from various secondhand shops. With the help of "his" troops, he was able to seize control of the town hall in Köpenick, a suburb of Berlin, to detain the mayor and get access to four thousand marks from the public purse. In the critical historiography on Imperial Germany, this episode has been interpreted as evidence of a widespread social militarism and its authoritarian values. From the perspective of the contemporary metropolitan press, however, it was first and foremost one theatrical buffoonery among many others, one that provided a welcome occasion for laughter and ridicule. Only for this reason could the *Köpenickiade* even hope to receive some attention from the metropolitan public, whose attention span was limited.[15]

The development of a social field that was based on the circulation of the most "recent" information—as in the urban mass media—was only one example of the emergent functional differentiation in Imperial Germany. Another prominent example was sports. The gradual extension of leisure time made possible the emergence of a life beyond the world of work. This allowed in particular the new bourgeois middle class of salaried employees to exert themselves, searching for ways to systematically fill the new budget of free time. To be sure, as with the mass media, emergent differentiation was preceded by and could partly built on older traditions, in this case those of "gymnastic exercises" (*Leibesübungen*). These had been practiced, for example, in the gymnastics clubs of the German Gymnastics Association (*Deutsche Turnerschaft*), which had been an important part of the nationalist movement since the early nineteenth century. Against this backdrop, however, modern sport brought a defining new element. Modern sport was focused completely on "performance and competition" and this vastly accentuated the "measurement of performance and time" as the central perspective of organized sports.[16] Winning or losing, based on performance, is the code of sports as a self-referential sub-system of modern society. The members of the German Gymnastic Association could at first not find much value in this code of winning and losing. The gymnasts were still primarily interested in the disciplining of their bodies for the larger, national "body politic."

A similar reluctance to adopt the code of competitive sports was displayed by the Social-Democratic workers' sports movement, which was an important part of the socialist milieu and hence more interested in cultivating the tightly-knit forms of sociability which sustained this milieu. For this reason, working-class sports associations tended to "emphasize less competitive physical activities such as gymnastics, cycling, hiking and swimming." Only in the 1920s did working-class athletes decide to support team sports and thus also the principles of competition.[17] Even then critics remained. In 1919, Heinrich Ströbel, at this time a member of the Independent Social Democratic Party (USPD), published a utopian vision of "future society." In this future utopia, he reckoned, hiking would be the most popular or perhaps even only sport, replacing the current "passion for one-sided stupid muscle sports and the even more stupid rubberneck passion of the masses" who attended sports events only as spectators.[18] Ströbel apparently not only resented the performance criteria of modern sports. He also wanted to revert the concomitant drive towards a differentiation between (in the terminology of Talcott Parsons) "performance roles" (physicians, journalists, athletes) and "audience roles" (patients, newspaper readers, spectators), which is a side-effect of the emergence of differentiated sub-systems of society. The emergent differentiation of sport as a sub-system was, as these examples indicate, not yet fully completed by the end of Imperial Germany.

Football (soccer, for the American reader) can serve as a good example of the setbacks and advances that accompanied the emergent differentiation of sports based on the principle of competition. Imported in the 1880s from England, football became steadily more popular in Germany, especially among students and salaried employees. However, popular enthusiasm for the German football league, founded in 1903, remained limited until the league embraced a competition in which the winner was determined by its standing in the league table. This enabled comparisons between the teams and established a clear standard for the evaluation of performance. In a long-term perspective, the establishment of the German Football Association (*Deutscher Fussball Bund, DFB*) in 1900 marked an important caesura in the differentiation and concomitant stabilization of the code winning/losing. This marked the shift from a "sociable game" that was based on the sociability of the middle classes to a "game of society," tending to be more socially inclusive because it was oriented solely on the performance of the players. In line with this development, the sport developed its own criteria for what constituted a fluent, professional style of football, and the competition for victory was increasingly cultivated as an end in itself.[19] In the perspective of a history of society, this emergence of football as a competitive sport was far more important than the militarization of the game which can also be observed before 1914.

The emergence of the printed, daily mass media and of competitive sports as self-referential sub-systems of society are two important examples of the ways in which functional differentiation shaped the trajectory of modernization in Imperial Germany. The key point is that the typical form of modernization was not the decomposition of poly-functional and hierarchically structured institutions, but rather the emergence and stabilization of new, specific forms of addressing the social world with codes such as information/non-information or winning/losing. It can be added in passing that the emergence of a scientized health system and the subsequent medicalization of health problems, which occurred during the final decades of the nineteenth century, could also be analysed in such a perspective.[20] The development of the media society and of the meritocratic, achievement- and profit-oriented sports system were part of the political reality of Imperial Germany and were in many ways influenced by politics. At the same time it becomes apparent that both systems cultivated their own social reality, and that in the formation and structure of this social reality, the values and the rationality criteria of the monarchical authoritarian state played a subordinate role at best. Emergent differentiation shows itself here in the form of a new, self-referential programming of the system's perspectives, which had already been independent for quite some time in institutional terms, as newspaper companies and sports associations.

Seen in this perspective, differentiation also involves a reprogramming of the codes of sub-systems which did already exist. An intriguing example of this can be seen in the arts, with its heart set on beauty. Of the arts, especially painting is relevant here, because the respecification of the ways in which the arts refer to "reality" can be shown most vividly in painting. The arts had already broken off and defined themselves as a differentiated field of society in the early nineteenth century. This field displayed its independence in the institutionalization of appropriate social forms for the presentation, assessment, and selling of artworks and through the possibility of articulating artistic individuality through changing art movements. The development of an audience that discussed and appreciated works of art, or of "audience roles," complemented this process. The further advancement of differentiation then showed itself in the specific way in which the arts reformulated the functional problem they address, i.e., the transformation of sensual perception into societal communication.[21] Towards the end of the century, the painters of "Berlin impressionism," among them Max Liebermann, Lovis Corinth, and Max Slevogt, broke away and made themselves independent of the reception of French impressionism, which up till then had dominated the conventional currents of idealism and realism in painting.

Although one can notice a curious restraint in the range of subjects the Berlin Impressionists tended to choose (in which scenes from daily life, like children, gardens, and streets took the place of allegorical and mythological subjects), there is at the same time an intensification of feeling and a modification of the perception of color and form.[22] The impressionists of the Berlin secession no longer conceived of their paintings as a depiction of the world around them, but concentrated on perception itself, on the "process of subjective seeing" that was supposed to be expressed through the "intrinsic dynamics" of the colors in the paintings. The next important step was taken by the German "artistic revolution" of expressionism. In expressionism, the formative elements of paintings—color, the form of shapes— were seen as an "autonomous structure." The development of this new, autochthonous visual vocabulary was related to the radicalization of the problem of depicting reality through images in the age of photography. Expressionism responded, therefore, to the recognizable "questionability of the world" through the "setting of signs, of meaningful images [Sinn-Bildern] with their own logic."[23] The goal of this art form was, as the painter Franz Marc formulated it, to "create symbols for their time ... behind which the technical creator disappears."[24]

Expressionism thus distanced itself radically from an artistic strategy that relies on a mimesis of the objective "reality." Its experimental visual vocabulary is only one important example, though a very important one in the German context, in regard to the groundbreaking transformation of the transcendental categories of space and time in the decades before World War I. Some historians might be inclined to see the arts as a rather marginal or unimportant sub-system in the framework of modern society. But even they cannot fail to acknowledge the invalidation of traditional hierarchies, which was triggered by these new artistic strategies, as a socio-historical phenomenon *sui generis*. This development in the arts formulated the artistic world view (and through this also the possibility of a reference to reality) in a new, radical, subjectivist form.[25] It was therefore with good reason that Thomas Nipperdey coined the seemingly tautological formulation that art in the German Empire was "first and foremost art," expressing the new intensity of emergent differentiation it had arrived at.[26] In 1917, the sociologist Max Weber highlighted—in a similar fashion and clearly alluding to the artistic avant-garde in Imperial Germany—the differentiation of art vis-à-vis the Christian religion: "Art now constitutes itself as a cosmos of always consciously apprehended autonomous values [Eigenwerte]. Art has taken over the function, regardless of how it is interpreted, of inner-worldly redemption."[27]

We can see similar developments in other societal fields, for instance in the social sciences. One example is the famous value judgment controversy (*Werturteilsstreit*) that from 1905 on took place annually at the convention of the

Association for Social Politics (*Verein für Socialpolitik*). This debate came to a climax in a committee meeting of the association in 1913, in which reports on this subject matter by all of the well-known opponents were presented.[28] Max Weber, a key protagonist of this debate, was keen to stress the specific and autonomous nature of scientific communication about the "world," in accordance with his approach to define sociology as a *Wirklichkeitswissenschaft*, a science that should focus on the realities of social life. He formulated this approach not in spite of but rather because he wanted science to serve as a reflection of "one's own ultimate values." Weber saw, however, only too clearly that the universal validity of political value judgments was illusionary. Here he differed from Gustav Schmoller and his students, who tried to base the need to develop the welfare state on their own political values. Any such claim to present universal values based on scientific investigation was, Weber knew, bound to fail in the modern, pluralized and differentiated society of Imperial Germany.[29] This controversy again highlights the further differentiation of the ways in which communication could refer to social reality, in this case through the accentuation of the difference between an academic "relation to values" and politically charged "value judgments."

Max Weber is important for an understanding of the societal history of Imperial Germany not only as evidence for the fact that the difference between scientific methodology and morality was prominently discussed in the scholarly community. His work also lays bare the extent to which analytical observations of the process of functional differentiation were part and parcel of a discourse about modernity. Emergent functional differentiation was, as mentioned above, not only a structural "reality" in turn-of-the-century society. It was also a self-description of society, a form in which the structures of society could be described, not least as an alternative to other descriptions such as, for instance, "class society." Apart from Weber, a few other prominent examples can be mentioned here briefly. Ernst Troeltsch, for example, Weber's "expert friend" (*Fachmenschenfreund*) and the most prominent Protestant theologian in Germany in the years before World War I, developed the program of an "European cultural synthesis" precisely against a perceived background of cultural and normative pluralism, a pluralism which had developed through the differentiation of social spheres, each with their "own rationality."[30] The reformulation of Christian tradition in "Cultural Protestantism," a project initiated and represented by Troeltsch, tried to preserve "religious autonomy" at a time when modern science and modern art had made a belief obsolete which tried to integrate society on normative religious grounds and thus wanted to reverse the advance of functional differentiation.[31] Protestantism for Troeltsch was supposed to become a religion that proved itself compatible with a functionally differentiated modernity—in contrast to the hopes of conservative Lutherans who strived for a religiously colored "culture of unity."[32] After assessing the state of affairs, it seemed to him that this could only be achieved through more individualized forms of piety. Through a more individualized piety, Protestantism would manifest itself as a "religiosity that is in its essence related" to modernity because it gave room to the trend towards functional differentiation.[33]

Individualization is also the header for the theoretical observations developed by Georg Simmel in his book "On Social Differentiation," which was published in 1892 as a central element of his overall œuvre. Under the heading "intersection between social circles," he discussed what is nowadays analysed by sociologists with the concept of the "social role"; the fact that the individual cannot truly fully develop his or her personality anywhere in modern society because he or she is forced to switch constantly between a multitude of social contexts and act, for instance, both as a customer, citizen, father, and religious believer.[34] Simmel understood differentiation as a variable that develops in correlation with other factors, most crucially a money-based economy.[35] The individual had therefore to "perceive in himself a number of demands which cannot be accomplished," that arose more and more through the "growth of the social macrocosm." Or, in other words: the ongoing differentiation made it increasingly difficult to be, at the same time, an informed customer in the economy, an active citizen in politics, a caring father and a pious believer. Simmel interpreted the increase in the number of "problematic natures in modern times" as a consequence of the concomitant fragmentation of individuals.[36] It seems difficult at times to contextualize Simmel's sociological theory properly, and his concepts often seem to lack historical specificity. There can be no doubt, however, with regard to his theories on individualization and differentiation, that Simmel wrote as an observer of contemporary German society. This is underscored by Simmel's specific interest in urbanism, if we consider that differentiation processes were especially tangible in the rapid urbanization of Wilhelmine Germany.[37] The idea of a "labyrinth" as the key metaphor for the diversity of social contexts in modern society, a diversity which cannot any longer be controlled by any hierarchy or authority, was recognizably based on the manifold forms of social life in the big cities.[38] In terms of an intellectual history of sociological theory, it should also be noted that Simmel developed many of his most important ideas on functional differentiation in a critical discussion of Wilhelm Dilthey's ideas, including the very concept of an "intersection between social circles."[39] Dilthey can therefore certainly be included among the group of reputable and relevant intellectual observers of Imperial Germany who described modern society as increasingly shaped by functional differentiation.[40]

At the end of these brief reflections, which conclusions can be drawn about the nature of Imperial Germany as a historical epoch when we take processes of functional differentiation into account? It should be clear by now that it is insufficient to put an authoritarian political system center stage when we write the history of Imperial Germany. This argument is, to repeat the point, not meant to deny that the political system in Imperial Germany was in fact authoritarian, and that fundamental reform blockages could not be lifted until the revolution in November 1918 pushed them aside, together with the monarchical system. But any historical assessment of Imperial Germany that is primarily focused on the lack of reform in the political system just takes a particularly visible part of society as a representative for the whole. To take politics as a benchmark for an assessment of Imperial Germany more generally does not duly acknowledge the multiplicity of perspectives which are necessary to describe modern society. The same is, by the way, true for the attempt to describe Imperial Germany and the whole nineteenth century as a "second confessional age."[41] Such an argument is helpful if it serves to strengthen our understanding of the importance of religion and of confessional opposites for German history after the *Kulturkampf*. But as a term to describe a whole era, "second confessional age" is flawed because *no* historical account can properly describe turn-of-the-century society when it posits that one field of society is central or more relevant than others.[42]

It is impossible, in other words, to write the history of late-nineteenth-century Germany in a vanishing point perspective where the lines of all societal fields meet. Such a vanishing point is impossible to describe. One might think that such an argument could be described as "postmodern." But that would be wrong. Postmodernism as a form of observing modern society is best described by its key thesis, the end of metanarratives such as progress, democratization, etc. But if the farewell to metanarratives is to be taken seriously, it should include postmodernism itself, and then contradicts itself. With good reasons the sociologist Niklas Luhmann has thus formulated: "If it is true, it is false."[43] In accordance with Luhmann I would insist that the multiplicity of contexts and codes in society is a distinctively modern, and not a postmodern phenomenon.

For these reasons I would like to suggest that Imperial Germany is best understood as an age of "polycontexturality." The philosopher Gotthard Günther has used this term to describe a situation in which a multitude of observer positions exist, various angles of observation which cannot be subsumed under each other or be brought into a hierarchical order. In a polycontextural environment, every event falls into the reference of different perspectives or contextures.[44] According to Günther, a contexture is a social domain where a distinction is used and the "*tertium non datur*" applies. Sports, for example, was the domain where winning/losing was the key distinction, whereas other distinctions did not really matter, so "no third position was given." In the same way, the Wilhelmine daily press distinguished between (relevant) information and (obsolete, because already reported) non-information. Catholic and Protestants strove to explain plausibly and to inculcate the distinction immanent/transcendent, so important for religious communication, in a way that was appropriate for contemporary society. But while all these sub-systems cultivated their own contextural distinctions, they all could also observe events in other sub-systems, and it was not possible to establish any superior vantage point for all observations in society.

Imperial Germany can be described as an age of polycontexturality because new perspectives on the world of meaningful social communication emerged, amongst others, the media, sports, the arts, and the value-free sciences. This description of this era also seems appropriate in the context of the sociological discourses in Germany at the turn of the century, which attempted with singular intensity, in a comparative perspective, to observe and analyze, with seismographic accuracy, the polycontextural differentiation of modern society. And any historical analysis of a certain period should not only consider social structures, but also the self-descriptions of a society.[45] Or, in other words, and formulated in a personalized manner: a history of Imperial Germany in which Max Weber figures only as a political commentator, but not as an analytical observer of contemporary society, is at best a partial history of society.

We must admit, however, that our description of Imperial Germany as an age of polycontexturality has to be taken with a pinch of salt. This is due, firstly, to the well-established conventions which historians follow when they write general histories. In spite of decade-long efforts to underpin historical research with theoretical insights from sociology and other disciplines, there are still clear limits to the use of more complex concepts in historical narratives. No publisher would like to publish a book titled "Imperial Germany as an Age of Polycontexturality," not only because it would not sell, but also because general histories still tend to serve a moral purpose and are certainly not the genre where irony and *Verfremdung* (alienation) are used to generate insight.[46]

Second, open questions remain when we consider the delineation of the period between 1871 and 1918. One has to keep in mind that "Imperial Germany" as a headline term already privileges the political perspective. In comparison with the first half of the nineteenth century, it is justified to emphasize polycontexturality as the signature of German history in the late nineteenth and early twentieth century, more broadly understood. In the first half of the nineteenth century, differentiation took place primarily through decomposition, whereas after 1870 we can observe ever more emergent processes and a greater dynamic of differentiation. This assessment remains true even if we consider the fact that sub-systems such as law and religion had, of course, already differentiated themselves long before the end of the nineteenth century. It should also be repeated that Wilhelmine Germany was characterized by intensive theoretical reflections on the multitude of observer positions in society, more than any previous period. Our description of an "age of polycontexturality" is much more problematic when we consider the end of Imperial Germany, as there is a noticeable continuity to the Weimar Republic with its unbroken dynamic of differentiation, which also shaped the self-descriptions of 1920s German society.[47] Thirdly, as a cipher for Imperial Germany "polycontexturality" has its limitations, because the very term itself denies the idea that historians can find one defining term that encapsulates a whole historical era. Unlike what is suggested by the historicist principle of individuality, historians cannot describe what an epoch "actually" was. The reconstruction of functional differences cannot, in contrast, provide anything other than a "different" view on the subject.

It is important, and so the argument of this essay, that politics is no longer privileged as the central analytical perspective for a historiographical assessment of Imperial Germany. Instead of privileging one perspective or sub-system of society, functional differentiation and the concomitant disruption of interdependence between sub-systems have to be considered as signatures of modern society. Such an approach then also has to go beyond the distinction of politics, economics, and culture, which is widely used in many textbook accounts.

Indeed, the dynamic of differentiation in the late nineteenth century can no longer be adequately understood with these categories. An interpretation which highlights the political costs of authoritarian reform blockades emphatically strikes an important point, but fails to account for the society of Wilhelmine Germany as a whole, which can only be understood in its differentiation. A history of society which describes the modernization around 1900 cannot be written without an adequate understanding of the complexities of the processes of differentiation.[48] It is exactly such an interpretation that is able, in spite of political reform blockages, to stress the modernity of German society around the turn of the century. Only after these facts have been analyzed that the question of the interdependency between the different "powers" (*Potenzen*) or societal fields in the history of Germany 1870–1914 can be considered once again.[49] Our focus on the modern aspects of functional differentiation, to be sure, is not the same as the notion of a pluralized "civil society" based on citizenship and voluntary associations.[50] While functional sub-systems can be charged politically both in liberal and authoritarian terms, the overall result of functional differentiation was fragmentation rather than a coherent civil society.

For any historical interpretation of modernization processes it seems advisable to dismiss the normative point which posits a general positive interdependency between the development of modern industrial capitalism and the implementation of a democratic constitutional state. Our emphasis on the polycontexturality of Imperial Germany suggests a different reading. It was the clearly pronounced dynamics of functional differentiation which created increasing resonance for a longing for community in Wilhelmine society. According to this view, only a community was able to provide proximity, safety, and unity to the individuals. These hopes have to be situated in a functionally differentiated society, where individuals are rather "dividuals"—that is, they were included into very different functional contexts and were here only addressed with regard to different aspects of their person. They were thus not addressed as a whole person, but only as a divided person, a "dividual."[51] For these reasons, it is not by chance that the idea of a "people's community" found widespread approval not only in the authoritarian, anti-democratic circles of late Imperial Germany. Also Liberals, Social Democrats and Catholics, who surely supported a political reform and the introduction of full parliamentary government, were fascinated by a concept of community which promised to compensate or even eradicate the negative side-effects of functional differentiation and thus of a society many Germans after 1900 perceived as shattered and fragmented. It is hence not by chance that the very term *Volksgemeinschaft* (people's community) gained widespread currency during World War I, when both the war effort and the fragmentation of a differentiated society made the search for more tangible forms of belonging and togetherness paramount.[52] Also, seen in this perspective, the political history of the cultural rejection of modernity since 1890 cannot be appropriately interpreted without considering the polycontexturality of society in Imperial Germany.

Notes

1. H.-U. Wehler, *Deutsche Gesellschaftsgeschichte, vol. 3: 1848/49–1914* (Munich, 1995), 1288, 1291. I would like to thank Helmut W. Smith and the editors of this volume for their critical feedback on a first draft of this article. The Department of History at the University of Sheffield contributed towards the translation of this piece, a support that is gratefully acknowledged.
2. R.O. Paxton, *The Anatomy of Fascism* (London, 2005).
3. On historiography see T. Kühne, "Das Deutsche Kaiserreich 1871–1918 und seine politische Kultur: Demokratisierung, Segmentierung, Militarisierung," *Neue Politische Literatur (NPL)* 43 (1998), 206–63; M. Jefferies, *Contesting the German Empire, 1871–1918* (Oxford, 2008). On the European context see B. Ziemann and T. Mergel, "Introduction," in *European Political History 1870–1913*, ed. idem. (Aldershot, 2007) XI–XXVI.
4. Wehler, *Gesellschaftsgeschichte*, 1294f.
5. See N. Luhmann, *Observations on Modernity* (Stanford, 1998).
6. J. Breuilly, "Modernisation as Social Evolution: The German Case, c.1800–1880," *Transactions of the Royal Historical Society* 15 (2005), 121.
7. H. Tyrell, "Zur Diversität der Differenzierungstheorie. Soziologiehistorische Anmerkungen," *Soziale Systeme* 4 (1998), 125–27; U. Schimank/U. Volkmann, *Gesellschaftliche Differenzierung* (Bielefeld, 1999); A. Nassehi, "Die Theorie funktionaler Differenzierung im Horizont ihrer Kritik," *Zeitschrift für Soziologie* 33 (2004), 98–118. The key text for the theory of functional differentiation is N. Luhmann, *Die Gesellschaft der Gesellschaft* (Frankfurt, 1997), 595–865. See idem,*The Differentiation of Society* (New York, 1982).
8. Schimank/Volkmann, *Differenzierung*, 9.
9. Tyrell, "Diversität," 127.
10. Wehler, *Gesellschaftsgeschichte*, 1283, 1249.
11. N. Luhmann, *The Reality of the Mass Media* (Cambridge, 2007).
12. P. Fritzsche, *Reading Berlin 1900* (Cambridge, MA, 1996), 10, 16f., 48f., 75f., 236ff.
13. R. Stichweh, *Inklusion und Exklusion. Studien zur Gesellschaftstheorie* (Bielefeld, 2005), 165.
14. See T. Nipperdey, *Deutsche Geschichte 1866–1918, vol. 1: Arbeitswelt und Bürgergeist* (Munich, 1990), 803f.
15. Fritzsche, *Reading*, 160f.; see B. Ziemann, "Der 'Hauptmann von Köpenick' – Symbol für den Sozialmilitarismus im wilheminischen Deutschland?," in *Grenzüberschreitungen oder der Vermittler Bedrich Loewenstein*, eds. V. Precan et al. (Prague 1999), 252–64.
16. Nipperdey, *Arbeitswelt*, 174.
17. R.F. Wheeler, "Organized Sport and Organized Labour: The Workers' Sports Movement," *Journal of Contemporary History* 13 (1978), 196f.
18. Cited in R. Graf, "Die Politik der reinen Vernunft. Das Scheitern des linken Sozialdemokraten Heinrich Ströbel zwischen Utopie und Realpolitik," in *Vernunftrepublikanismus in der Weimarer Republik*, eds. A. Wirsching and J. Eder (Stuttgart, 2008), 138.
19. C. Eisenberg, "Fußball in Deutschland 1890–1914. Ein Gesellschaftsspiel für bürgerliche Mittelschichten," *Geschichte und Gesellschaft (GG)* 20 (1994), 203. For the semantic shift in the meaning of *Gesellschaft* from "sociability" to "society" see A. Kieserling, "Das Ende der guten Gesellschaft," *Soziale Systeme* 7 (2001), 177–91.
20. Nipperdey, *Arbeitswelt*, 150–66.
21. D. Schwanitz, "Systems Theory and the Difference between Communication and Consciousness: An Introduction to a Problem and Its Context," *Modern Language Notes* 111 (1996), 488–505.
22. A. Wesenberg, ed., *Berliner Impressionismus. Werke der Berliner Secession aus der Nationalgalerie* (Berlin, 2006).
23. Nipperdey, *Arbeitswelt*, 705f., 711, 714; G. Simmel, "Tendencies in German Life and Thought since 1870," *International Monthly* 5 (1902), 96.
24. Cited in W.J. Mommsen, "Die Herausforderung der bürgerlichen Kultur durch die Avantgarde. Zum Verhältnis von Kultur und Politik im Wilheminischen Deutschland," *GG* 20 (1994), 439.

25. For a broader perspective, see S. Kern, *The Culture of Time and Space 1880–1918* (Cambridge, MA, 2003), 180–210.
26. T. Nipperdey, *Deutsche Geschichte 1866–1918*, vol. 2: *Machtstaat vor der Demokratie* (Munich, 1992), 894.
27. M. Weber, *Gesammelte Aufsätze zur Religionssoziologie*, vol. 1 (Tübingen, 1988), 555.
28. Cf. H. Nau, ed., *Die Äußerungen zur Werturteilsdiskussion im Ausschuß des Vereins für Sozialpolitik (1913)* (Marburg, 1996).
29. F. Tenbruck, *Das Werk Max Webers. Gesammelte Aufsätze zu Max Weber* (Tübingen, 1999), 257.
30. F.-W. Graf/H. Ruddies, "Religiöser Historismus: Ernst Troeltsch 1865–1923," in *Profile des neuzeitlichen Protestantismus*, vol. 2/2, ed. F.-W. Graf (Gütersloh, 1993), 315–17.
31. E. Troeltsch, "Die Selbständigkeit der Religion," *Zeitschrift für Theologie und Kirche* 5 (1896), 361–436; 6 (1896), 71–110, 167–218; see F.-W. Graf, "Protestantische Theologie in der Gesellschaft des Kaiserreichs," in *Profile des neuzeitlichen Protestantismus*, vol. 2/1, ed. idem. (Gütersloh, 1992), 16–22.
32. Graf, *Theologie*, 17.
33. V. Drehsen, "Die 'Normativität' neuzeitlicher Frömmigkeitsgeschichte. Zur aktuellen Bedeutung der klassischen Religionssoziologie Ernst Troeltschs," in *Protestantismus und Neuzeit*, eds. H. Renz and F.-W. Graf (Gütersloh, 1984), 276.
34. G. Simmel, "Über sociale Differenzierung" (1892), in: idem, *Gesamtausgabe*, vol. 2 (Frankfurt, 1989), 109–295.
35. Tyrell, "Diversität," 134f. From the rich literature on Simmel, compare only D. Frisby, *Fragments of Modernity. Theories of Modernity in the Work of Simmel, Kracauer and Benjamin* (Cambridge, MA, 1986), 81ff.
36. Simmel, "Differenzierung," 286.
37. G. Simmel, "Die Grossstädte und das Geistesleben," *Jahrbuch der Gehe-Stiftung zu Dresden* 9 (1903), 185–206; idem, "Tendencies."
38. Frisby, *Fragments*, 85f.
39. K.C. Köhnke, *Der junge Simmel in Theoriebeziehungen und sozialen Bewegungen*, (Frankfurt, 1996), 321–34, 380–97.
40. A. Hahn, "Die Systemtheorie Wilhelm Diltheys," *Berliner Journal für Soziologie* 9 (1999), 5–24.
41. O. Blaschke, "Das 19. Jahrhundert: Ein Zweites Konfessionelles Zeitalter?," *GG* 26 (2000), 38–75.
42. As a critique, see B. Ziemann, "Säkularisierung, Konfessionalisierung, Organisationsbildung. Aspekte der Sozialgeschichte der Religion im langen 19. Jahrhundert," *Archiv für Sozialgeschichte* 47 (2007), 497–501.
43. Luhmann, *Gesellschaft*, 1144.
44. G. Günther, "Life as Poly-Contexturality," in idem, *Beiträge zur Grundlegung einer operationsfähigen Dialektik*, vol. 2 (Hamburg, 1979), 283–306; U. Schimank, *Theorien gesellschaftlicher Differenzierung* (Opladen, 1996), 185ff.
45. See P. Nolte, *Die Ordnung der deutschen Gesellschaft. Selbstentwurf und Selbstbeschreibung im 20. Jahrhundert* (Munich, 2000). For a critique, see B. Ziemann, "Die Soziologie der Gesellschaft. Selbstverständnis, Traditionen und Wirkungen einer Disziplin," *NPL* 50 (2005), 56–61.
46. H.U. Gumbrecht, *In 1926: Living on the Edge of Time* (Cambridge, MA, 1998), 411–36.
47. Gumbrecht, *In 1926*, 253ff.
48. J. Osterhammel, "Gesellschaftsgeschichte und Historische Soziologie," in *Wege der Gesellschaftsgeschichte*, eds. idem, D. Langewiesche and P. Nolte (Göttingen, 2006), 100.
49. See the reflections in Nipperdey, *Machtstaat*, 894–903.
50. As a good overview on historiographical debates, see S.-L. Hoffmann, *Civil Society* (Houndmills, 2006).
51. A. Nassehi, *Differenzierungsfolgen. Beiträge zur Soziologie der Moderne* (Opladen, 1999), 117.
52. G. Mai, "'Verteidigungskrieg' und 'Volksgemeinschaft.' Staatliche Selbstbehauptung, nationale Solidarität und soziale Befreiung in Deutschland in der Zeit des Ersten Weltkrieges," in *Der Erste Weltkrieg. Wirkung – Wahrnehmung – Analyse*, ed. W. Michalka (Munich, 1994), 583–602. See also M. Föllmer, "The Problem of National Solidarity in Interwar Germany," *German History* 23 (2005), 202–31.

Chapter 3

Was the German Empire a Sovereign State?

Dieter Grimm

The Significance of Sovereignty

This essay treats a topic which is not at the heart of the historical research into the German Empire. Hans-Ulrich Wehler, for example, answers the question: "What was this new Empire, founded by way of a treaty on 1 January 1871?" by saying that its "principle of construction" was the establishment of a central state, to which the mediatized member states had transferred certain sovereign rights.[1] According to Wehler the "formal sovereignty" lay with the Bundesrat, which, however, was not the power center. Symbolically, the Kaiser was increasingly considered the "actual sovereign of the Reich," whereas the "key institutional position"—perhaps the "material" sovereignty?—was, in Wehler's eyes, held by the Chancellor. Wehler had a low opinion of the constitution. He describes it as the "statute of an association," as a "façade" behind which the old absolutist regime was able to survive. All in all, Wehler concedes the German Empire merely the character of an "autocratic, half absolutist pseudo-constitutionalism." Yet, he does not doubt that the Empire was a state, and its sovereignty is at any rate implicitly affirmed by naming its official holder.

Contemporary scholars of constitutional law saw this quite differently. For them, everything centered on the question of sovereignty, or, to be more exact, on the question of where the sovereignty was located in the federal state. In the first few years of the German Empire, no other topic stirred so many authors. There were few discussions conducted with a similar thoroughness. This cannot be unimportant for those who study the history of these years. The importance attached at the time to the question of sovereignty suggests that what is involved here is more than just juridical concepts. Rather, this was first and foremost a political problem, one which could be discussed in terms of sovereignty. There had been no comparable discussion concerning the predecessor of the German Empire, the German Confederation. There is therefore much to be said for the thesis that behind the question of sovereignty there were unresolved tensions in regard to the founding and the construction of Germany in 1871. The reason for the conspicuous interest in the question of sovereignty should therefore emerge when one asks what changed as a result of the transition from the German Confederation to the German Empire.

The German Confederation defined itself, according to Article 1 of the Viennese Final Act from 1820, as "a union under international law." Its members were, according to Article 1 of the Federal Act of 1815, "the sovereign princes and the free cities in Germany." Accordingly, the Confederation was composed of states, but was itself not a state, not even a federal state (Bundesstaat), but rather a confederation of states (Staatenbund). The distinction between these two forms was, according to a widely accepted notion, just the place of sovereignty. In a confederation of states, sovereignty was located in the individual member states; in a federal state, sovereignty was located in the central state. No one doubted that the German Confederation belonged to the first category. One can describe the German Confederation as an institution to defend the sovereignty of the princes in an era when large sections of the population longed for a nation state and for democracy. Article 57 of the Viennese Final Act set a clear boundary for the expansion of constitutionalism: because of the sovereignty of the princes, the public power had to be concentrated in the hands of the monarchs; constitutions could only bind them in the exercise of certain powers to the consent of the estates.

If one examines more closely the purpose and the construction of the Confederation, it becomes clear that the question concerning sovereignty was not at all as easily resolved as is suggested by the conceptual distinction between the federal state and the confederation of states. The purpose of the Confederation was not only to preserve Germany's external but also its internal security, as well as to secure the independence and the inviolability of the individual German states. By internal security was meant not only the peace between the member states, but also the existing order in them. This purpose could not be achieved through a mere alliance of sovereign states. If in one of the member states the internal peace was directly endangered "through insubordination of the subjects against the authorities," or if it was to be feared that "rebellious or revolutionary movements might spread" or an upheaval might develop, then, according to Article 26 of the Viennese Final Act, the Confederation had the right to intervene if asked to by the government of the state affected—in an emergency, even "without being asked." To accomplish this, however, the Confederation had to rely upon other member states, as it did not have its own executive.

The German Confederation possessed furthermore a permanent body, the Federal Assembly (Bundesversammlung), in which the princes of the member states were represented by ambassadors, who were bound by the instructions they received from their capitals. The Federal Assembly had the right to pass laws which were binding on the member states, but were applicable only after having been published in their law gazettes. The legislative powers were not listed in a catalog of competencies, but were rather, according to Article 3 of the Viennese Final Act, dependent on and limited by the purposes of the Confederation; the competencies thus were not rigid, but dynamic. Understood as a self-restraint of the member states, this would not have raised any problems concerning sovereignty, if the decisions of the Confederation could only be taken unanimously. No state could then have been forced against its will to obey the Confederation. But this was not the case. To be sure, all important questions required an unanimous decision. For less important questions, however, a majority was sufficient. It was thus possible for a member state to be required to carry out an order which it had not agreed to.

The larger South German states were able to prevent federal jurisdiction, which had been foreseen, by referring to their sovereignty. In return the members were, however, required by federal law to set up a court system with three instances. In case of a denial of justice, the person affected could turn to the Confederation, which was required to come up with a remedy. The subjects were also conceded a number of further quasi basic rights. The Confederation had at its disposal, as instruments to carry out its purposes in case of a conflict, both the federal intervention, which served to support a member state against rebellious movements, and the federal execution, which was directed against insubordinate governments and which was carried out by member states upon order from the Confederation. The "outer skin"[2] of the states in the German Confederation was thus not as impermeable as would have been the case in a purely international alliance. Some authors perceived the Confederation therefore as having an irregular or a mixed nature.[3]

However, as the center of particularism and of the reactionary movement, the German Confederation was unable to satisfy the hopes for national unity which had grown so powerfully after the Wars of Liberation. Merely a reform of the Confederation, a topic which was repeatedly discussed, would have failed to have achieved the goal. National unity meant a nation-state, although not necessarily a uniform state. Even the majority in the National Assembly in the Paulskirche in 1848 had not desired to create a uniform German state. Such a uniform state was much less likely after the attempt to found a German nation-state as the result of a revolutionary act against the monarchs had failed in 1849 and it appeared that a new attempt could only be successful in coalition with the princes. Under these conditions, the nation-state could only come into being as the creation of sovereign states. Hence, the foundation of a German Empire required a transformation from a confederation of states to a federal state and thus a shift in sovereignty. Without sovereignty there could be no state. No contemporary legal scholar doubted this.

This describes well the dilemma surrounding the formation of the new Germany. On the one hand, a national government without sovereignty was inconceivable. On the other hand, it would be bound to fail if the states which came together to create Germany, above all the South German states, were forced to give up their sovereignty. It is this dilemma that explains the central importance of the sovereignty question in the process of founding the new Germany. Everything depended on the solution of this question. Which solution could be considered compatible with one's sovereignty, which had to be eliminated because of sovereignty, depended on what one meant by "sovereignty." In other words it was a question of the meaning of sovereignty. The meaning of notions is outside the realm of political decision-making; however, at times it determines political actions, because it delimitates the political options. As a result political (and legal) disagreements are often debated in the form of a discussion of the key concepts. Conceptual questions are then the political questions of their time, and if, in retrospect, they appear to be only a "pseudo-problem,"[4] this is itself an ahistorical statement.

The Concept of Sovereignty in the Years Before the Unification of Germany in 1870

No definition of sovereignty has ever been universally accepted. Since 1576, however, all participants in the discourse on sovereignty have referred back to Jean Bodin. The concept of sovereignty, as developed by Bodin with the intention of overcoming the confessional civil war in France in the sixteenth century, was, however, not tailored for the federal state. Instead, Bodin laid the foundation for a centralized state. According to Bodin, sovereignty could be defined as the highest and comprehensive authority to rule. The sovereign neither derived his right to rule from anyone above him, nor did he have to share his rule with anyone beside him. In other words, it was not merely the possession of some public powers which constituted sovereignty, but rather the consolidation of all public powers into an all-encompassing public power in the singular. Sovereignty was not an umbrella term for a number of public powers, but rather a single term describing the right to rule. According to Bodin, sovereignty was indivisible. It therefore required a single responsible bearer, which Bodin could only imagine in the form of human beings. As things stood in France in the sixteenth century, this could only be the King. Yet in theory, Bodin did not commit himself to one individual person.

Bodin's teaching in regard to sovereignty quickly became extraordinarily popular, as one can see from the numerous editions of his *Six Livres de la Republique* and the numerous translations.[5] This is true for Germany as well, where the legal framework of the Holy Roman Empire, which was of a quite different kind, had to be described henceforth in terms of sovereignty, although a consolidation of the different sovereign powers into a unified public authority in one hand, had not taken place. If one were to apply Bodin's criteria for sovereignty, no German ruler could have been considered sovereign. The Holy Roman Empire lacked all the attributes of a state, whereas the larger territories within the Empire, where the process of state-building had been advancing, were prevented by the existence of the Empire in the full deployment of their sovereignty. Samuel von Pufendorf arrived at his famous conclusion that the Reich is an *"irregulare aliquod corpus et monstro simile"* from the idea of indivisible sovereignty.[6]

The majority of the publicists in the Holy Roman Empire did not agree with Pufendorf and claimed instead that there was sovereignty in the Holy Roman Empire as well. Of course, these attempts could only succeed if one was willing to sacrifice one of Bodin's key concepts, indivisibility. In order to be able to use the sovereignty concept, the majority of the authors insisted on a distinction between the commonwealth, which was supposed to possess complete sovereignty (*majestas realis*), and the Kaiser, who was limited in the exercise of sovereignty (*majestas personalis*). As Michael Stolleis has shown, this understanding became the dominant teaching among contemporary legal scholars, who aimed to uphold the rights of the estates.[7] Hence, a ruler whose rights were limited by the estates could still be called sovereign. Thus there was already a distinction between possessing and exercising sovereignty, similar to what would become necessary in the constitutional state. Within the constitutional state there is no sovereignty, there are only legally granted and limited powers, whereas sovereignty is exhausted in the act of constitution making.

After the Holy Roman Empire was dissolved in 1806, the individual territories became fully sovereign. However, attaining sovereignty coincided broadly with the transition to constitutionalism. Although the constitutions of the German states remained well behind the standards set in the American and French Revolutions, these constitutions hardly left monarchical sovereignty untouched. Granting basic rights placed concrete limits on the power of the monarch, and laws could only be proclaimed with the approval of the people's elected representatives. The paths taken by the United States and France which enabled both states to hold on to the idea of indivisible sovereignty by ascribing sovereignty to the people or to the nation were not available to Germany; here the unity of the public authority could only be maintained if one located sovereignty in the state. This was first done by Eduard Albrecht in 1837 in his famous review of Maurenbrecher's treatise on public law.[8]

With this, however, nothing had been achieved in regard to the location of sovereignty in nation-states composed by individual states joining together. Examples of this were quite rare at the time. Only with the creation of the United States of America in 1787 and of the Swiss Confederation in 1848 had independent states united in a federal state. Even after this, sovereignty remained an issue. In the United States, the southern states, theoretically equipped by John Calhoun,[9] insisted on their indivisible sovereignty, and only in the Civil War was this issue finally decided. In Switzerland the contradiction between national sovereignty, which could only be conceived of as a sovereignty of the people, and the sovereignty of the cantons could only be bridged with the formula in Article 3 of the Constitution of 1848, which stated that the cantons were sovereign, "insofar as their sovereignty is not limited by the federal constitution." This formula established the recognition of double sovereignty, even if some were able to see in this "only deception or swindle, only insanity or a lie."[10]

In Germany the question remained unimportant, as long as the German Confederation existed. Because the Confederation was not considered a state, the sovereignty of the member states remained untouched. But every attempt to follow the example of the USA or Switzerland inevitably raised the question of sovereignty. In the Revolution of 1848 this question was quickly decided in favor of a German nation-state, which had to be created. From the very beginning, the National Assembly saw its task, just like the Convention in Philadelphia, not in reforming the confederation, but in passing a national constitution, and they had for this, in contrast to the American Convention, a mandate from the people. The legitimation for their work was thus, as in the USA, the sovereignty of the people, the "people" being defined here not as the sum of the peoples in the individual states, but rather the German people as a whole. Heinrich von Gagern left no doubt about this in his opening remarks: "We want to create a constitution for Germany, for all of Germany. The authority to do this lies in the sovereignty of the nation."[11]

With the failure of the revolution and of the Prussian plans to unify Germany immediately after the revolution, the Confederation reappeared and with it the recognition of the sovereignty of the princes of the individual states. Of course, the people's hopes for a German national state did not die out. However, the failure of the attempt to bring about national unity from below had convinced many people that success could only be achieved if the people worked with the princes, not against them. Whoever pursued the idea of national unity had to prove the compatibility of a federal state and monarchical sovereignty. It was this very task that the Göttingen historian, Georg Waitz, attempted in his *Das Wesen des Bundesstaates* (The Nature of the Federal State), published in 1853.[12] In this text Waitz discussed the thesis that the Revolution of 1848 was doomed to failure because it was impossible to form a federal state out of monarchies; the defining characteristic of the monarchy being the monarchical sovereignty, which, in turn, could not be sustained in a federal state for the federal state would claim sovereignty.

If this was true, then the nation-state in Germany could only come about after the transformation of the individual states into republics or after their assimilation into a uniform state. Neither of these was likely in the foreseeable future. Waitz, himself a former representative at the Paulskirche and a member of its constitutional committee, responded "that the nature of the federal state in and of itself does not contradict the concept of the monarchy." The monarchy, in the full meaning of the word, means that the monarch is in possession of an independent authority, not merely a transferred authority, be it derived from a higher person or from the people. However, the concept of the monarchy does not require "the concentration of all of the state's powers and activities in one hand." Waitz had no doubt that within a federal state both the central state and the member states were states. Yet, as the state could not be conceptualized without sovereignty, one could only conclude that both the central state and the member states were sovereign.

Waitz believed that he could find evidence in favor of the possibility of a double sovereignty in one and the same territory in the USA, where, according to Tocqueville, the transition from a confederation of states to a federal state was made easier by the recognition of a double sovereignty. In fact, Tocqueville did speak of *"deux gouvernements entre lesquels la souveraineté allait se partager."*[13] If, however, the central state was able to achieve sovereignty without the member states losing their sovereignty, then the state's existence was no longer at stake; rather, what needed to be decided was only the functional allocation of powers between the central state and the member states. Waitz did not hesitate therefore to give up the indivisibility of sovereignty. Sovereignty was still defined as the highest power. However, it would suffice if each of the states belonging to a federal state was the highest power "in its sphere" and was thus able to exercise its share of powers independent of other states.

Waitz's idea of "not only but also" aimed to replace the "either or" idea which had existed for so long, that is, the stark opposition of a non-sovereign confederation of states and a federal state which was solely sovereign. This was convenient for the German bourgeoisie: the nation-state no longer had a price which could not be paid. The princes could keep that to which they were especially attached. Accordingly, Waitz's teaching found wide support. From the 1850s on, his argument was accepted by most scholars, such as Heinrich von Treitschke, who in his paper on the "Federal State and the Centralized State (Bundesstaat und Einheitsstaat)" from 1864, affiliated himself with Waitz's position and credited Waitz with having expanded on Hamilton's groundbreaking ideas concerning the federal state "systematically and with the deep seriousness of German scholarship ... The old battle between the different schools concerning the concepts confederation of states and federal state has been concluded through this masterly paper by Waitz."[14] This, of course, would turn out to be a mistake, as Treitschke himself would soon have to admit. The real battle was still to come.

The German Discussion on Sovereignty in the Empire

After Prussia's victory over Austria in 1866, the German Confederation was dissolved and the process of the small German unification began, at first with the North German states. Bismarck aimed nevertheless to make use of the "traditional" in the new constitution, "for something they are accustomed to and which is a matter of course is easier for governments to submit to than every new combination."[15] For this reason he rejected Duncker's rough draft for the constitution of the North German Confederation as being "too centralistic and too close to a federal state for the future accession of the South Germans."[16] Regarding the form, the constitution should resemble a confederation, in substance it should establish a federal state. In Bismarck's comments on the final Prussian draft, he stated that the theoretical question of whether or not the new structure was to be a confederation of states or a federal state was to be left unanswered.[17] As, according to the traditional understanding, the difference between the two was to be found in who possessed sovereignty, this meant that the question of sovereignty had to be left unanswered.

Treitschke was thus only half wrong when he wrote in 1867 that the constitution of the North German Union would not "represent a quick resting stop, but would rather most likely be the foundation for our political development for a generation."[18] Admittedly, already in 1871 the North German constitution was succeeded by the German constitution. Yet, as the North German constitution had already been written with an eye to the "accession of the South Germans," it could serve as the basis for the German constitution. Concerning sovereignty, there was no difference between the two. The preamble stated that the princes had concluded "an eternal union" which would have the name "German Empire." Nothing was said as to the site and the holder of sovereignty. Politically speaking, this vagueness was a precondition for the adoption of the German constitution. Legal scholars, however, could not leave the question unanswered if they wanted to understand systematically the legal nature of the German state, and if they wanted to the draw legal conclusions from this understanding. Therefore the question which had been left open on the political level, became the central question on the juridical level.

It certainly played a role in their treatment of this issue that with the founding of the German Empire in 1871 a new generation of constitutional law scholars came forth, who at the time were about thirty years old and who were replacing a generation whose formative experiences had been before 1848. If these had, either from a conservative or a liberal perspective, quarrelled with the existing constitutional conditions or their handling and as a result had not always sharply differentiated between their theoretical concepts of state and constitution on the one hand and the existing constitutional law on the other, the new generation made its peace with the fact that Germany had been founded from above and concentrated instead fully on the construction and interpretation of the new constitutional law. This constellation was fertile ground for a new methodological approach, juridical positivism, which aimed to purify the discourse on constitutional law of all non-legal embellishments and to analyse the legal norms in a logical, conceptual way such as had already been customary for a long time in the field of civil law.

The first systematic discussion of Germany's legal nature as a federal entity appeared in only the first year after the Empire was founded. The author was the 25-year-old Max Seydel. His first publication, *The Notion of the Federal State* (Der Bundesstaatsbegriff), came like a thunderbolt.[19] In contrast to previous approaches, Seydel sought to understand the peculiarity of the federal state not from the concept of sovereignty, but rather from the concept of the state. He considered the state to be the highest form of human association. There was no entity above the state; alongside the state there was no entity which was equal. The state was for the human beings who were its subjects the perfect and total entity: "One cannot conceive of a state existing next to a state for the same area because two perfect and total entities are a contradiction." This entity could only be ruled by a single highest will. "Two highest wills cancel each other out." The will appeared in the form of state power. State power is the highest power and does not accept or allow any other power above it or alongside it. Since Bodin, the expression "sovereign" has been used to describe this characteristic of state power.

From this position, Seydel approached the concept of the federal state, through a discussion of Waitz's teachings concerning double sovereignty. In this context he also discussed Calhoun extensively.[20] Like Calhoun, Seydel considered the idea of shared or divided sovereignty a logical impossibility. According to Seydel, the distinction between the unlimited content and the limited extent of sovereignty, which had been made by Waitz, is untenable, for "it is the nature of sovereignty that it is not limited in any way." Seydel concluded from this that in the federal state it was not possible for the central state and the member states to be sovereign at the same time. He went even further. As the state was defined by the possession of sovereignty, the central state and the member states could not be states at the same time. If this was true, then a federal state could not possibly exist at all. This was indeed Seydel's conclusion: "All state entities which are generally labelled federal states have to be either unitary states or confederations of states." There was nothing between a union of states and a centralized state.

Consequently, Seydel could no longer avoid the question which entity in the new Germany deserved the name state, whether it was the federal state or the member states. He sought the answer, once again following Calhoun, in the origin of federal states. They come into being by way of treaties concluded by existing centralized states. A treaty and not a law is their legal foundation. The quality of the new entity as state depends, under these conditions, upon whether the states who have entered into the treaty wanted to give up their sovereignty and transferred it to the newly formed polity. As it was not possible for there to be a non-sovereign state, the question was, more precisely, whether or not they had given up the quality of a state at the moment they entered the treaty. Seydel could not perceive such a will in the formation of the new Germany. Accordingly, the new German state founded in 1871 had not acquired sovereignty, and nor had it become a state. Compared with the German Confederation, the new Germany had merely changed the extent of its competencies, but not its legal nature. Germany remained a confederation of states, with a new name.

Seydel's paper became the starting point for an extraordinarily rich discussion on the concept of the federal state, which in this form has never been repeated. This discussion can only be broadly sketched here.[21] Waitz's dualistic theory, developed in order to show the possibility of national unity under post-revolutionary conditions, did not outlive the establishment of the nation-state. On this point, Seydel won across the board. "Sovereignty is a property whose nature is absolute, that is to say, it is incapable of being increased or diminished ... There is no half, no shared, no reduced, no dependent, no relative sovereignty; rather, there is only sovereignty or no sovereignty," wrote Paul Laband in his influential treatise.[22] Merely some authors of the older generation refused to give up the idea of the divisibility of sovereignty, among them the founder of the new methodological school in public law, Carl Friedrich Gerber.[23] Among the younger generation only

Rümelin was an exception, "without noticing the absurdity of a divided sovereignty," in Laband's critical words.[24]

Treitschke, too, distanced himself in 1874 from Waitz.[25] He admitted that ten years earlier he had not dared to challenge this theory but had shared in accepting "the general mistake." Now he could see more clearly, as he said. It was impossible for there to be several sovereignties existing alongside each other within a state. "The highest power is just that— the highest." Even the reference to the two contemporary federal states, the United States of America and Switzerland, and the theory of the two sovereignties which had been developed there, was, upon closer examination, not credible in light of the newest work on the topic. In the United States and in Switzerland there, too, could only be one sovereignty. Those who wrote the German constitution had learned from the weaknesses of these constitutions and destroyed the "sovereignty scam" of the German princes. Only Prussia had not given up its sovereignty in Treitschke's eyes, because it was able, with its seventeen votes in the Federal Council, to prevent any amendment to the constitution that it did not like. This could only be reconciled with the concept of the indivisibility of sovereignty if one identified Prussia with the Reich and saw it as a centralized state cloaked as a federal state. As a matter of fact, that is exactly what Treitschke's interpretation did.

Seydel was, however, unable to prevail with his position that the federal state is logically impossible, that there could only be centralized states or confederations of states. On this point, only one person agreed with him, namely Philipp Zorn.[26] However, Zorn drew exactly the opposite conclusion from Seydel's premises, namely that the new Germany was a centralized state. The member states were not states; they were only called this. Laband criticized this position quite harshly, culminating in the comment that Zorn uses his construction of the federal state in the only way possible: in the rest of his remarks he ignores it completely and therefore he himself takes all the significance out of his claim.[27] The sharp contrast between the confederation of states and the federal state was thus once again revived and with it the contrast between a treaty (in terms of international law) and constitutional law. The North German Confederation and the German Empire were created, to be sure, by treaties. With the founding of the German Empire, however, the contractual relationship had ceased and had been turned into a constitutional relationship.[28]

Seydel came to his understanding of the impossibility of the federal state because he saw an identity between state and sovereignty. Under the conditions of indivisible sovereignty, it was actually impossible for there to be a state composed of existing states. If the defenders of the idea of the possibility of the federal state did not want to become entangled in contradictions concerning the indivisibility of sovereignty, they had to contest the indissoluble bond of state and sovereignty. Laband took this step, pointing out that the theory of sovereignty had been developed in work on centralized states, in which indeed it could appear as if the state and sovereignty were interdependent. The formation of amalgamated states demanded, however, that the theory be refined.[29] This was worked out by Georg

Jellinek.[30] Jellinek claimed that equating state power and sovereignty was the fundamental mistake of the previous work on sovereignty. One should see sovereignty not as the essence of the state's authority, but rather as a quality whose absence did not affect the existence of the authority of the state.

This position came to be widely accepted. There was, to be sure, no longer any double sovereignty; there were, however, sovereign and non-sovereign states. Seydel protested, arguing that one could call a non-sovereign state "a state only in the same way that one could call a eunuch a man,"[31] but without success. Those who believed that sovereignty was indivisible, that there was a distinction between a sovereign and a non-sovereign state, now, of course, had to describe those characteristics which differentiated a sovereign from a non-sovereign state. The state was, according to Laband, that entity which exercised its own sovereign authority, not authority devolved to it or which it had been given, as was the case with provinces, districts, or communities. Merely being in possession of public powers, however, did not constitute sovereignty. The defining features of sovereignty required the state to always be the highest power. The sovereign state is characterized by the "negative characteristic" that there is no power above it which can legally order it to do something.[32]

Jellinek disagreed with this purely negative definition of sovereignty. He had originally, following up his assumption that the formation of a state could not be described purely in juridical terms, taken the position that a federal state created by existing states was in fact a completely new entity. The founding states disappeared and were newly created by the new state. These states then had the federal state to thank for their powers; they did not have any authority on their own.[33] Later, as a result of criticism, he moved away from this position; he continued, however, to emphasize that the highest power is not to be confused with unlimited powers.[34] The sovereign state's powers were only boundless in regard to limitations imposed on it externally, because otherwise there would be a higher power, whereas self-limitations did not contradict sovereignty, because there could be no state without laws. A state without laws would degenerate into anarchy. A state could not, however, wish for its own negation. A state could always disentangle itself from obligations imposed on it by laws. It did not, however, stand above the law in such a way that it could do away with all legal commitments.

Accordingly, Jellinek defined sovereignty as "the characteristic of a state's authority, by which the state has the exclusive capability of legal self-determination and self-limitation."[35] For the federal state this meant that the characteristic division of powers between the central state and the member states did not affect sovereignty inasmuch as these limitations were self-imposed. What is decisive in regard to the question of sovereignty is not the extent of the state's power, but rather only who determines the division of powers. In the federal state the sovereign is the one who is able to determine for himself his own powers and who thus at the same time determines what powers the other side is to have. What is decisive in regard to sovereignty is therefore the authority to decide on competencies (Kompetenz–Kompetenz).[36] This understanding now became a general conviction. That the Empire was sovereign, not the member states, was without a doubt. Amending the German constitution took place not through a treaty of the member states, but rather through a federal law. In the end, Seydel remained alone with his position. The German Empire was a sovereign state.

The Return of the Discourse on Sovereignty

Historians have paid little attention to the discussion on sovereignty in their portrayals of the history of the German Empire. This may have to do with two characteristics of the discussion: the forum in which it took place and the fact that after some initial confusion the lines of division were soon clear. The depth and the lucidity of the discussion on sovereignty resulted from the fact that here the old German opposition between particularism and unitarism once again came forth and that there was no clear answer to this question in the German constitution. As a result, legal doctrines became the preferred site of the conflict. Because of the preliminary methodological decision by constitutional legal scholars for juridical positivism, the clarification of the positions largely took place in a discussion about the definitions of the key notions and of the conclusions which were logically to be drawn from these. This ensured that the discussion had a remarkable lucidity. It meant, however, as well that the discussion was only to a limited degree able to serve as a basis for broader discourses.

Relatively quickly, the results were clear. Germany was a sovereign state—this was what almost everyone wanted. The federal states were not sovereign; however, they could nevertheless continue to exist as states—this is what most scholars thought. In political and historical categories, there was only the question of whether the present form of the German state was final or just a stage on the path to a more or less decentralized central state. Juridically the question came to the forefront of how those results which had slowly but surely been reached could be formulated in terms of constitutional law, so that they followed logically, without any contradictions, from the constitution. A consensus in this dispute was, to be sure, never reached. However, as Stolleis has shown, concentrating on the later treatment of the topic, especially among the representatives of the next generation of constitutional law scholars such as Heinrich Triepel who was born in 1866,[37] the discussion gradually exhausted itself. "All in all it appears that a certain disinclination to dispute concepts was spreading, combined with a pragmatic acceptance of the concrete development of the constitution, including the historic and political implications."[38]

Things remained like this in the following epochs, helped along by the fact that a scholarly jurisprudence which concentrated so strongly on concepts was questioned in the Weimar Republic; after World War II this methodology was completely rejected. The Weimar constitution had further reduced the importance of the federalist principle, so that only the question of whether Germany was still a federal state or had already become a decentralized central state was important. In contrast, as Richard Thoma wrote, "the questions which were politically and theoretically so important in the years after the founding of the new Germany and the constitution of 1871, whether this Germany is to be understood as a confederation of states or as a federal state, and if it were to be understood as a federal state, how was one to define in juridical concepts the structure of this complicated and contradictory entity, belong to the past." In a footnote Thoma added that because one had concentrated too much on formal concepts, one had neglected to develop a theory with respect to the subject matter of the federal state. However, he admitted that we are indebted to this theoretical discussion for "a permanent treasure trove of concepts and insights into the nature and the legal structure of unions of states."[39]

This did not mean that there were not any controversies around the idea of federalism in the Weimar Republic and the Federal Republic of Germany. However, these debates took place at the next lower level, concerning the allocation of powers between the central state and the member states and the forms of their cooperation. That only the central state was sovereign was in the Weimar Republic no longer in dispute, and in the Federal Republic was hardly even worth mentioning. In contrast, the question concerning the institutional arrangement remained on the agenda even after the Weimar constitution and the Basic Law of the Federal Republic. In the Weimar Republic the relationship between the central government and the member states became one of the most important constitutional questions, without, however, the solutions being considered leading to a constitutional amendment. In the Federal Republic, in contrast, no section of the constitution has been modified more often than that having to do with the structure of the federal state, including two major reforms, the first in 1969 and the second most recently in 2006 and 2009.

Things have, however, changed in the meantime insofar as we are once again in the midst of a fundamental discussion about sovereignty. Only now the discussion is not about the relationship between the central state and the member states, but rather about the relationship between the nation-states and the European Union. There can be no doubt that no member state of the EU is sovereign in the sense that the German Empire or the Weimar Republic was sovereign. On the other hand, the EU has also not achieved indivisible sovereignty. Whether or not this sort of sovereignty exists at all—and if so, where and how—is one of the most important topics of our time.[40] In this discussion, all of the controversies in the Empire are reappearing: the divisibility or the indivisibility of sovereignty, whether or not sovereignty is a uniform concept or an umbrella term, the degree of statehood of the member states and the EU, the difference between a treaty and a constitution, and the power to distribute the competencies as the most important distinguishing criterion. However, this discussion is taking place without the awareness that one is on a field which has already been well cultivated. Reflecting back on the "treasure" earlier legal scholars supplied seems today more useful than ever.

Notes

1. H.-U. Wehler, *Das Deutsche Kaiserreich 1871–1918*, 5th ed. (Göttingen, 1983), 60; the further citation here and on the next three pages. See also id., *Deutsche Gesellschaftsgeschichte*, vol. 3 (Munich, 1995), 301ff., 355ff., 849ff.
2. For this term see M. Stolleis, "Die Idee des souveränen Staates," *Der Staat* Suppl. 11 (1996) (*Entstehen und Wandel verfassungsrechtlichen Denkens*), 67.
3. Cf. W. von Humboldt, "Über die Behandlung der Angelegenheiten des Deutschen Bundes durch Preußen" (1816), in *Werke in fünf Bänden*, eds. A. Flitner and K. Giel, 3rd ed., vol. 4 (Darmstadt, 1982), 375.
4. U. Scheuner, "Struktur und Aufgabe des Bundesstaats in der Gegenwart," in *Staatstheorie und Staatsrecht* (Berlin, 1978), 416.
5. H. Denzer, ed., *Jean Bodin* (Munich, 1973), 494ff. (the first Latin edition in Germany 1591, the first German translation 1592).
6. S. von Pufendorf, *Dissertatio de Republica irregulari*, Heidelberg, 1608.
7. See M. Stolleis, *Geschichte des öffentlichen Rechts in Deutschland*, vol. 1 (Munich, 1988), 174ff.
8. *Göttingische gelehrte Anzeigen* 1837, 1489.
9. See J. Calhoun, *Works*, vol. 1 (New York, 1863), 109ff.; vol. 2, 271ff., 382ff.
10. See A. Kölz, *Neuere Schweizerische Verfassungsgeschichte* (Bern, 1992), 543ff., the quotation of Troxler on 387.
11. F. Wigard, *Stenographischer Bericht über die Verhandlungen der deutschen constituirenden Nationalversammlung zu Frankfurt am Main, Frankfurt 1848*, vol. 1, 17.
12. *Allgemeine Monatsschrift für Wissenschaft und Literatur* 1853, 494, also in id., *Grundzüge der Politik* (Kiel, 1862), 153, discussing Joseph Maria Radowitz' publication under the same title, *Gesammelte Schriften*, vol. 2 (Berlin, 1852).
13. See A. de Tocqueville, *De la Démocratie en Amérique*, vol. 1 (Paris, 1835). Quotation: ed. Paris 1951, vol. 1, 168.
14. H. von Treitschke, *Aufsätze, Reden und Briefe*, vol. 3 (Meersburg, 1929), 38.
15. O. von Bismarck, "Unmaßgebliche Ansichten über Bundesverfassung" (19 November 1866), in *Die gesammelten Werke*, Berlin, 1924–1935, vol. 6, no. 616.
16. Dictation from 30 October 1866, ibid., no. 615. For the draft see H. Triepel, "Zur Vorgeschichte der norddeutschen Bundesverfassung," in *Festschrift Otto Gierke zum siebzigsten Geburtstag* (Berlin, 1911), 631.
17. Bismarck, *Gesammelte Werke*, vol. 10, 314.
18. H. von Treitschke, "Die Verfassung des Norddeutschen Bundes," in *Aufsätze*, 364.
19. M. Seydel, "Der Bundesstaatsbegriff," *Zeitschrift für die gesamte Staatswissenschaft* 28 (1872), 185–256.
20. Ibid., 208–24.
21. A survey of the literature during the Empire is offered by A. Haenel, *Deutsches Staatsrecht*, vol. 1 (Leipzig, 1892), 200ff.; H. Rehm, *Allgemeine Staatslehre* (Freiburg, 1899), 86–146; P. Laband, *Das Staatsrecht des Deutschen Reiches*, vol. 1 (Tübingen, 1876, 1888, 1895), quoted from the 4th ed. from 1901, 51ff.; G. Meyer and G. Anschütz, *Lehrbuch des deutschen Staatsrechts*, 7th ed. (Leipzig, 1914), 11ff., 41ff., 121ff., 193ff., 224ff.; for a contemporary doctrinal history see S. Brie, *Der Bundesstaat* (Leipzig, 1874). For the time after see J.L. Kunz, *Die Staatenverbindungen. Handbuch des Völkerrechts*, vol. 2/4 (Stuttgart, 1929), 21ff., 61ff., 595ff.; M. Dreyer, *Föderalismus als ordnungspolitisches und normatives Prinzip. Das förderative Denken der Deutschen im 19. Jahrhundert* (Frankfurt, 1987); M. Stolleis, *Geschichte des öffentlichen Rechts*, vol. 2 (Munich, 1992), 365.
22. Laband, *Staatsrecht*, 68.
23. *Grundzüge eines Systems des deutschen Staatsrechts*, 3rd ed. (Leipzig, 1880), 247.
24. Laband, *Staatsrecht*, 60, fn. 1; E. Rümelin, "Das Beaufsichtigungsrecht des Deutschen Reiches," *Zeitschrift für die gesamte Staatswissenschaft* 39 (1883), 200.
25. H. von Treitschke, "Bund und Reich," in *Aufsätze*, vol. 4, 212.

26. P.K. Zorn, *Das Staatsrecht des Deutschen Reiches*, vol. 1 (Berlin, 1880), 46ff., 84f.; id., "Neue Beiträge zur Lehre vom Bundesstaat," *Hirth's Annalen* 1884: 425.
27. Laband, *Staatsrecht*, 71ff.
28. Laband, *Staatsrecht*, 84f.; further A. Haenel, *Studien zum Deutschen Staatsrecht*, vol. 1 (Leipzig, 1873), 31ff., 68ff., who, however, attributed sovereignty and statehood neither to the central state nor the member states but to the Empire as "the totality" of both (ibid., 63f.).
29. Laband, *Staatsrecht*, 60ff., 67.
30. G. Jellinek, *Allgemeine Staatslehre* (Berlin, 1900, 1905, 1914), quoted here from the 7th reprint of the 3rd ed. (Darmstadt, 1960), 461ff., 474ff., 737ff.
31. M. Seydel, *Kommentar zur Verfassungsurkunde für das Deutsche Reich*, 2nd ed. (Freiburg, 1897), 8; cf. also id., "Die neuesten Gestaltungen des Bundesstaatsbegriffes," *Hirth's Annalen* 1876, 641. Also in id., *Staatsrechtliche und politische Abhandlungen* (Freiburg, 1893), 101.
32. Laband, *Staatsrecht*, 68.
33. Jellinek, *Die Lehre von den Staatenverbindungen* (Tübingen, 1887), 295.
34. Jellinek, *Staatslehre*, 475ff. The criticism was mainly expressed by H. Rosin, "Souveränität, Staat, Gemeinde, Selbstverwaltung," *Hirth's Annalen* 1883, 265; S. Brie, "Die Lehre von den Staatenverbindungen," *Grünhuts Zeitschrift* 11 (1888), 85.
35. Jellinek, *Staatslehre*, 481.
36. Ibid., 495f.
37. See H. Triepel, *Unitarismus und Föderalismus im Deutschen Reich* (Tübingen, 1907).
38. Stolleis, *Geschichte des öffentlichen Rechts*, vol. 2, 367.
39. R. Thoma, "Das Reich als Bundesstaat," in *Handbuch des Deutschen Staatsrechts*, eds. G. Anschütz and R. Thoma, vol. 1 (Tübingen, 1930), 171 with fn. 6.
40. From the rich literature cf. only N. Walker, ed., *Sovereignty in Transition* (Oxford, 2003).

Chapter 4

Theories of Nationalism and the Critical Approach to German History

John Breuilly

Detaching Nationalism from National History

Nationalism began to be treated as a subject in its own right in the interwar period, though still as an aspect of nation.[1] It remained contained within the national framework that characterized historical writing.[2] This blocked the formation of an autonomous concept of nationalism.

Kedourie broke this link in his seminal 1960 study, as the opening sentence makes clear: "Nationalism is a doctrine invented in Europe at the beginning of the 19th century."[3] However, for two decades his book had little influence, as it treated nationalism as a radical doctrine, largely consigned to the past. Only from the early 1980s did theoretical work separate the study of mainstream nationalism from that of nations, and then very differently from the perspective of Kedourie.[4]

Two key arguments were advanced. Nationalism was modern (so had to be placed within some larger concept of modernity) and it shaped politics and culture so as to become a "natural" way of seeing the world. As Gellner put it in his seminal 1983 book *Nations and Nationalism*: nationalism invented nations.[5] These notions of nationalism as modern and constructive of nations have recently influenced German historical studies.[6]

However, there is a pervasive ambivalence in much of this work. One approach presents nations as products of modernization, one effect of which is nationalism. The other makes nationalism prior to nation-formation, even if appealing to real distinctions of language, religion, and other "markers." Nationalism becomes a contingent matter of elite agency. Writers like Gellner combine the two approaches, seeing the second form of nationalism as a reaction to the first form. That might carry conviction if one could identify two distinct classes of nationalism: "nation-based" nationalism of old nations and "invented nations" nationalism of new nations. However, most cases fail to fit (including Germany), and the idea becomes hopeless when historians shuffle between the two positions (because they lack clear concepts) in narrative accounts of particular cases.

This essay will argue for a modern, constructivist position which treats "nation" as a term deployed in nationalism, not an independent entity underpinning nationalism, and aim to show that it is impossible to combine this position with the methods of critical German *Gesellschaftsgeschichte*, focusing on particular problems in interpreting the German Second Empire.

First, it will be argued that a satisfactory treatment of nationalism must detach it from any prior concept of the nation; this is what it means to take up a modernist, constructivist theory of nationalism. Second, it will be suggested that such a treatment of nationalism is incompatible with approaches to German history which assume the "nation" as the underlying basis on which nationalism develops. Third, it will be contended that this criticism applies to critical German *Gesellschaftsgeschichte*. Finally, it will sketch ways in which the modernist, constructivist theory might be applied to interpreting German nationalism.

In looking at critical German *Gesellschaftsgeschichte* and the concept of the national the key terms are "German," "national," "*Gesellschaftsgeschichte*" (social history) and "critical." In the following sections these various terms and how they are used are considered.

German History and the Concept of the National

Any concept of German history presumes a concept of the nation. Before 1871 this cannot be the nation-state and we cannot identify a national economy or society. Meinecke proposed two concepts. First, that of the *Kulturnation*[7] referred to elite culture associated with Goethe and Schiller. However, a different cultural concept outlined by Herder centered on popular, vernacular culture. In neither case does the concept refer to nation as group but only to values propounded in different elite circles. We can best inquire into how these values came into being by bracketing out any underlying "national culture."

Meinecke's second concept of *Staatsnation* makes no sense of pre-1871 Germany.[8] It could only mean something else, such as we find in work on federalism in German history, seen as sustaining a political culture and system.[9]

However, the *Reich*, *Rheinbund* and *Deutsche Bund* cannot be equated with the coercive institution we call the state. Furthermore, before the mid-nineteenth century there were no widespread nationalist oppositional movements. We are left with the "doctrines" of nationalism which Kedourie highlighted. Again, nation becomes a term within a nationalist frame of reference.

There remains teleology. We know Germany will become a national state, economy and society, and that nationalism plays its part. So we can use such concepts to understand the process by which places and peoples became German.

The argument is weak. Modernist approaches stress transformation and emergent properties. Projecting back the national undercuts that approach, driving one into constraining the later history within a prior national context which itself is understood in terms of that later history.

The modernist view requires one either to demonstrate that nationalism as doctrines, movements and identities was operating and significant earlier than the mid-nineteenth century (empirically untenable) or abandon national frameworks. The latter move is intellectually difficult, going against the grain of national historiography.

Such arguments might seem less relevant after 1871 because a new term can be introduced: nation-state. However, there is a danger of conflating the actions of the nation-state with forms of nationalism. In the German case, the argument that nation-state formation induced "nation-building" is persuasive but tells us nothing about competing forms of nationalism, how national sentiments combined with other sentiments, the forms of "German" nationalism beyond the Second Empire, and how transnational forces shaped German nationalism.

Let us take two issues which exemplify these problems.

Nationalism and Nation-state Formation

There were intense anticipations of a Prussian-led German unification.[10] However, this was not an "expression" of long- or even short-run "national" developments. It links to certain bourgeois associational and political movements and their appropriation of ideas associated with state formation in Britain and France (constitutionalism, free trade, democracy). Their ideas and movements could find no place for popular nationalism or a strategy of alliance with Prussia. Only a rapid combination of unforeseeable events in the early 1860s (Austrian defeat by France and its financial and military repercussions; the adoption to military use of new technologies of mass production, transportation, communication and organization, the rise to power in Prussia of a gambler) enabled such ideas and movements to find "expression" in the wars of unification (a teleological term).[11] This was by hindsight converted into national fate, legitimizing the new state and coordinating new and old elites. The constructivist account of nationalism also recognizes there were other forms of nationalism which were no more obviously absurd or doomed to failure than the form which prevailed.

Nation-building

The same argument can be applied to "nation-building." Official nationalism—an uneasy blend of state worship and invoking of a cultural nation—was an obstacle to popularizing national identity and integrating popular political forces. That came about as the inadvertent consequence of many processes (establishment of imperial agencies, importance of Reichstag majorities, rapid urbanization and industrialization). The diverse political movements which opposed the official nationalism of the state and expounded alternative values (socialism, Catholicism) which official nationalism condemned, became locked in a nation-state framework. It was the insinuation of the nation as a "natural" category arising from these complex processes which were expressions of nation-building, not overt nationalism. This process can be observed taking place in comparable ways in other countries.[12]

Thus the forms of nationalism in the Second Empire are not primarily to be understood as expressions of a longer-run German history but as contemporary responses to an inadvertent process of cultural, political, and economic coordination around a state now deemed to be a nation-state.

Social History and the Concept of the National

The assumption of a national history prior to nationalism furnishes one with an object for social history. The concept of the nation is inclusive, transcending class, occupation, status group, region: a "whole society." Non-nationals within are strangers or minorities; those beyond are foreigners or exiles. Society, nation, and subjects of the (nation)-state are equated.

Yet the only concepts of the German nation which can be credibly deployed much before nation-state formation are those to do with (elite) culture and (elite) politics. These did not embrace most of the groups and aspects of life which are the concern of social history. To write German social history before the formation of a German nation-state is to take two concepts (nation as state/political system; nation as culture/society) without adequate objects and to combine them in a doubly inadequate manner.

Of course critical historians do not work so naïvely. Wehler differentiates society by means of the concepts of economy, domination, and culture, understood as ideal types, not real objects. However, the three concepts are treated as levels within a unitary field: although different forms of power (coercive, economic, cultural) which connect large numbers of people do not necessarily, or even normally, map on to the same territory or people.[13] By making these three concepts relate to the same "German society," which then exhibits particular features of "social inequality," Wehler makes an untenable assumption about a "German nation." Even if we disaggregated the different levels, this simply transfers the problem of the national from "society" to the specific concepts of culture, economy, and domination. Yet it is clear that regional-cum-political differences make assumptions of national culture or economy or domination untenable before 1871.

Once more the nature of the argument apparently changes following nation-state formation. One could argue that this "power container" creates a national society, or fields of interaction at the levels of culture, economy, and domination which can be characterized as national. However, this runs into further problems.

For many people for some time after 1871, living in a nation-state did not make much difference. Most state taxation and expenditure, on matters which affected large numbers of people like education or poor relief, remained at state level. Admittedly at elite level coordination of affairs through Berlin contributed to a stronger sense of national identity. It was again inadvertent processes such as urban and industrial growth, and a reduction in emigration coupled with an increase in internal migration which mattered more. Arguably what produced a shared sense of national identity—to the extent we can show that happening— was not shared cultural values, social practices or political ideals but the increasing importance of national institutions as places where conflicts over precisely these matters were handled. The nation was not what nationalists imagined it to be but, if the term has any other meaning, the common habits and routine actions that such institutionalized conflict shaped. Conversely, nationalism as an overt idea or movement inveighed against precisely those habits and actions. Rather than seeing nationalism as an expression of "society" we should see it as reactions against the way broad social strata were being coordinated in the increasingly national state.

Critical History and the Concept of the National

German critical history is associated with the idea of *Sonderweg*. This is framed in terms of comparisons with other "Western" national histories. However, if it is invalid to write of nations as societies before nation-state formation, and if these— insofar as they exist as categories of action—are the product of state activity after nation-state formation, then this approach is invalid. After the formation of a nation-state the *Sonderweg* idea operates principally at the level of political development. However, it would be better to deploy specific concepts about state power and oppositional forms of nationalism than to make sweeping "national" comparisons.

The notion of peculiarity makes sense not in terms of a "whole" national history but in relation to particular issues the historian wishes to highlight. Thus if one wants to highlight the role of violent revolution as a means to nation-state formation, it would be France that one might single out as peculiar; if apparent continuity of the process whereby a state becomes national, then Britain; if the role of military force in forcing a number of states into a common state legitimized by nationalism, then Italy and Germany.[14]

It is not an accident that these "peculiarities" refer to processes of state formation. *Sonderweg* has been about political culture and state forms rather than demography, economy, social inequality, or culture in a general sense. Indeed, Wehler and other critical historians have conceded ground where once they claimed German peculiarities in these areas, for example giving up the ideas about the "feudalization of the bourgeoisie" and "organized capitalism." Narrower political concepts have been introduced to interpret the peculiarities of the Second Empire, such as Bismarck as charismatic leader and the post-Bismarckian political order as "polycracy." These concepts are themselves highly problematic, but my point here is that the focus is not on German society but on political styles and state institutions.

Yet these concepts are used comparatively less to demonstrate distinctively German forms of legitimate authority than to account for a distinct and fateful course of foreign and military policy. The forms of nationalism which shaped such policies might be better understood not as rooted in some peculiar German system but as responses to international problems such as the inability of Britain to maintain its global hegemony in the face of the modernization of other states, including Germany. Yet military and foreign policy are excluded from German social history.

Where to Go From Here?

From this consideration of how the modern, constructivist theory of nationalism is incompatible with key assumptions of critical German social history, some conclusions can be drawn.

First, one must abandon the concept of the *prior national*. The concept is empirically untenable before nation-state formation and must be modified to account for the specifically state-institutional aspects of change after nation-state formation.

Second, one must abandon the idea that significant differences in modern history can be grasped as differences between nations. The study of nationalism must begin with nationalism, bracketing out nation and treating it as a term within nationalist discourse, although the term acquires an independent force when it becomes a practical category for competing political actors in nation-state institutions. This raises problems about defining and operating the concept of nationalism and treating it as an aspect of modernity.

So far as operating the concept of nationalism is concerned, a distinction is proposed between nationalism as ideas, as sentiments, and as politics. The whole subject is confused by seeing nationalism only as one of these aspects, or one aspect determining the others, or jumping from one aspect to another.[15]

Those who focus on ideas make the discourse and ideology of nationalism the principal creator of nations. This is the line taken by Kedourie and, in very different style, by postmodernists who see the nation as a discursive construct and nationalism as a "discursive formation."[16] I would be very reluctant to adopt these approaches for a number of reasons.

How do we measure the "creative" impact of different discourses and ideologies independently of their own content and claims? If we seek the national beyond discourse we imply that the nation, at a certain point, emancipates itself from the nationalism which created it. If we do not do that, we have no way of stepping beyond discourse and can only measure significance internally—e.g., by looking at how many people articulate one discourse rather than another. But even that does not tell us much about relative influence and relationships between different kinds of discourse.

There is also the problem of ignoring the conditions under which nationalism originated, embedded itself, and eventually naturalised the language of political legitimacy and identity. Nationalism in the Kedourian modernist or postmodernist approach becomes an incredibly creative force, making the nation which it claims to express. I use the word "incredibly" here in its original, literal meaning, i.e., not believable.

Similar objections can be made about the impact of nationalism as sentiments or as politics. Nationalist movements are clearly only one, often quite minor, element in the formation of nation-states. After nation-state formation, nationalist politics may disappear as a distinctive form, the nation-state being seen as the given framework within which all politics organizes, meaning that either all or no political actors are "nationalist." Alternatively it may take on competing forms which cannot be understood in terms of the nation-state itself.

Nationalist sentiments—that is a sense of national identity which is not necessarily framed in terms of doctrines or which underpins distinct political programmes and movements—are difficult to trace but the consensus is that prior to nation-state formation (except for nationalist discrimination practiced against minorities within an imperial state) these were rarely significant for large numbers of people.

Having made the differentiations, one must describe the origins, embedding and extension of these different levels of nationalism in particular cases, and how the levels interact. These will vary enormously from case to case. The plausible notions of moving from ideas to politics to sentiments, from intellectuals to elite politics to mass politics,[17] is more about a "logic" of description than an actual historical sequence. If we insist on describing nationalism in the first instance as a doctrine, then it must begin life as an "idea." However, historians of colonial resistance have written of nationalist movements before nationalist ideas, in the sense of movements which aim to throw off foreign rule and are socially and geographically extensive within the colonial territory. In some cases a long established set of national institutions within which large-scale social interactions take place, but in which there is no intellectual articulation of nationalist ideas or political need for an explicit politics seeking to construct or defend a nation-state, can give rise to a widespread sentiment of national identity without any corresponding doctrine or politics. That is arguably the case for eighteenth- and nineteenth-century Britain.[18]

Having provided such accounts of nationalism differentiated in this way, but maintaining a scepticism about the centrality of nationalism at all these levels for actually "making" nations, one needs to turn to the modern conditions which underlie nationalism. One must begin with some non-teleological concept of modernization which does not see modernity as the successful or failed project of nationalists. I have outlined elsewhere a concept of modernization as process not project which, specifically for the German lands, focuses on the transformation from a corporate to a functionally specialized societal division of labor. I argue that nationalism, understood primarily as a political idea, with sentiment and movement focused on achieving, maintaining and consolidating the independent nation, takes up particular functions in relation to the types of power—coercive, economic, ideological—which are associated with this modernization process.[19]

Within this framework, when one turns to the origins of nationalism, in the German case it is right and conventional to stress doctrines and elite discourse and how these became constituent of elite networks.[20] National ideas embedded themselves into elite culture, as in the pervasive influence of historicism in a range of academic subjects such as philology, art history, economics, and history.[21] Nevertheless, in roughly the first third of the nineteenth century, nationalism remained unimportant at the levels of popular sentiments and politics.[22] This has implications for how we study nationalist ideas and elite discourse. It is important to avoid a teleological selection which only picks up on particular nationalist ideas (e.g., in the propaganda and mobilizing appeals of 1813–14) because these ideas are seen to be of subsequent importance in nationalist sentiments and politics, while ignoring other variants of nationalist ideas and non-nationalist ideas which may have been as, if not more, important at the levels of sentiments and politics.[23] What is more, one should stress the transnational formation of a liberal and romantic discourse of nationality in which imitation of the most "successful" cases figures more prominently than distinctively national patterns.[24]

Embedding means nationalism as idea becomes linked to movements and institutions. Not all of these had political objectives. Key elements (a) were located outside Germany (exile movements, diaspora groups) and (b) had closer links to non-national elements than to other German nationalist elements. This transnational dimension again suggests that the nation is a term within nationalist ideas, sentiments, and politics, and not a condition for the development of nationalism. This can be reinforced by two other points. The distribution of nationalist ideas, sentiments, and politics is uneven through the "nation" geographically as well as socially, and "nationalism" is entangled with other ideas, sentiments, and politics which sometimes marginalize and sometimes make more central the nationalist element. Furthermore, a key aspect in the embedding of nationalist ideas, sentiments and politics is the constraining role of state institutions which cut across earlier conceptions of the national, for example in the way in which Austrian Germany was marginalized in the national discourse of the Second Empire.[25]

Here it is illuminating to point to national differences which become clearer in this embedding phase. Take the cases of Germany and Italy. There is a similar romantic-democratic discourse being constructed in the first third of the century, a discourse which not only transcends the political boundaries of a "fragmented nation" but is embodied in elite networks of nationalists. However, there are also major differences. There are national political and elite cultural institutions in the German lands to which nationalism can orient itself which are absent in the Italian case. Thus the *Deutsche Bund*, even if it worked to repress nationalist challenges, did so at a national level. There was a university and high school system in Germany which attracted students across political boundaries, developed similar curricula, and in which national historicist understandings were central. As a consequence, nationalism was able to articulate itself within as much as against established institutions in the German lands. By contrast, exile figures and radical-oppositional tendencies in early Italian nationalism were more prominent. This contrast reached its climax in the 1848–49 revolutions where national-level politics was simply not institutionalized in the Italian lands in the way it was in Germany with the German National Assembly. All this conditioned the forms and significance of different kinds of elite nationalist ideas and sentiments. But even in the German lands by mid-century, nationalist ideas remained politically marginal to state power and distanced from popular sentiments. What came to make it more central were shifts in the nature of power which rendered nationalism increasingly relevant and attractive. Here we must move beyond the elite networks in which nationalist ideas, sentiments and politics were most clearly embodied to the broader, emergent forms of modern power.

Modernization undermined local and "thick" forms of power embodied in privileged landownership, city patriciates, urban guilds, and personal monarchies. One can see it, for example, in the commercialization of agriculture and craft manufacture which increasingly produced for non-local markets and in turn made supra-local purchases. This is not to be equated with industrialization in the form of new machine technology and large plant, which only began to impact on the economy in the 1840s and became much more significant after mid-century.[26] Nor is it to be understood in terms of a national economy because these increasingly commercial and supra-local networks were European, even global in character, and brought different regions of "Germany" into more intense contacts with non-German regions than with one another. We should not therefore see nationalism as some expression of the national at economic level, any more than at political or cultural level. Instead one can interpret the appeal of nationalism in two ways.

First, in relation to more developed economies in Western Europe, Germans involved in these transnational connections lacked the powerful backing of an extensive territorial state. The attraction of the early *Zollverein* lay in its capacity to integrate Prussia's western provinces with her core central and eastern territories and to boost the state revenue of smaller states, but also to give these smaller states a capacity to bargain with existing national states such as Britain and France.[27] The point was not to cut oneself off from that international economy but to participate in it more effectively.

Second, the national idea could help people understand and coordinate the "society of strangers" which modernity was forming.[28] This was articulated most effectively in the dominant liberal idiom, an idiom in which an abstract "society" (conceptualized as a collection of individuals), economy (market), and polity (constitutional and parliamentary state) were culturally unified through the notion of German nationality.[29]

With the rapid industrial growth of the late-1850s and 1860s, as well as with the marginalization of radical-democratic versions of nationalism through the failure of mid-century revolution and subsequent repression, this liberal articulation of nationalism became increasingly dense and institutionalized. The *Zollverein* turned into a powerful national institution, constraining the power of individual states. The web of associations and media extended beyond governmental control, even if censorship and restriction was practiced. Above all, a political-cultural vision of Germany came to dominate liberal discourse.[30] What is more, that discourse was extended downwards socially, even if concentrated in the towns, among the middling sorts of people, and in Protestant rather than Catholic regions. And again, one can compare this with markedly different developments in Italy where there was no equivalent to the *Zollverein* or the national gymnastic and choral societies. This inhibited the formation of a strong nationalist ideology capable of bridging the gap between the revolutionary-romantic discourse of exiles and the manipulative statism of Piedmont.

Nationalism as liberal-modernist discourse articulated closely with new forms of economic and ideological power associated with the growth of a commercial and industrial economy and increasingly popular media and associational life. Nevertheless, until the mid-1860s the principal function of nationalism was to coordinate elites from modern sectors of culture and economy and help orient them politically. It did not have much significance for popular mobilization or state legitimation. Counter-revolution marginalized popular politics for some time. So far as the state legitimation was concerned, as late as 1865 the Austrian and Prussian governments defied "national" opinion in their refusal to frame the war against Denmark in national terms or create a new German state under the Augustenbergs. Only after 1866 and the expulsion of Austria from Germany would the Prussian state seek to use German national-historical discourse to legitimate itself. Yet the very fact that the Prussian state did this is linked to the compelling need to involve modern forms of ideological and economic power in the legitimation of the state, a state which in its constitutional, bureaucratic, and military aspects was itself rapidly modernizing coercive power and promoting the abstract reasoning appropriate to a "society of strangers."

What we know least about is nationalism as popular sentiment. We can point to top-down processes—especially following the formation of the Second Empire—such as the construction of mass welfare institutions, military conscription, and the routinization and extension of electoral competition for seats in a national parliament with increasing influence. It seems plausible to assume that the larger these "national" achievements figured in the everyday lives of ordinary people, the more embedded would become some sense of national identity. Yet we know little about how the formation of mass institutions within the nation-state actually did or did not promote the appropriation of national identity at a popular level. Social history or "history from below" has tended overwhelmingly to concern itself with issues of class, region, or confession; while the history of nationalism has tended to be written from top-down and in terms of ideas and symbols which are with difficulty, if at all, connected to the concepts and perspectives of social history.[31]

Given this lack of knowledge, in addition to calling for more research we need to avoid certain hazards. We should not assume that national sentiment is something that percolates from above downwards. However, equally we should not see the popularization of national sentiment as an upward appropriation of the national. Both conceptions smack of a manipulative relationship. One can easily see why elites would wish, under conditions of mass politics in the nation-state, to induce a popular consent to their own views of national identity and interest. But precisely because one can see that, one can also see why such a project is unlikely to succeed. The rise of the Centre Party and the Socialist Party as the most successful mass parties of the Second Empire is a clear indication of the degree of failure.

In the bottom-upwards approach the manipulation is more persuasive in terms of rational analysis. If class interest is taken to be dominant, then for a subordinate class to express its interest in national forms makes more sense than for it to accept another class definition of that interest. However, the question then is why use the "cloak" of national discourse at all. The answer is to see the deployment of national language not in terms of serving some sectional interest, or as motivational, but as providing cognitive orientation under modern conditions. There is a nation-state developing various institutions which permit popular participation and an increasingly abstract society of strangers. (Class and confession are as much "imagined communities" as is the nation.) Nation provides a way of conceptualizing the field within which political conflict takes place and envisaging what, beyond political institutions, holds together these competing groups. The price that is paid for accepting this concept of nation is that one cannot just invent it *ab nihilo*; rather it is constrained to commence with the existing forms in which it has been constructed by nationalism. In the German case, the notions of power, progress, and modernity are central to those existing forms. This presents different challenges to different subordinate groups. The history of "popular nationalism," still largely unwritten, should focus on these different kinds of interactions between existing elite discourses of the national and popular, originally non-national, discourses. In this process nationalism becomes multi-layered and conflictual. Yet rather than undermining the power of nationalist discourse this increases it, although at a price. The very framing of political conflict in terms of conflicting conceptions of the national "naturalizes" the national, making it appear as something which underlies these competing conceptions. However, this argument needs empirical underpinning and an analysis of just what the significance of naturalized or routinized or "banal" forms of nationalism are in relation to politicized, "hot" forms of nationalism.[32]

Notes

1. C. Hayes, *The Historical Evolution of Nationalism* (New York, 1931); H. Kohn, *The Idea of Nationalism: a study in its origins and background* (New York, 2005): Transaction. This was originally published in 1944. See also P. Lawrence, *Nationalism: History and Theory* (London, 2004), chap. 2–4.
2. S. Berger, M. Donovan, and K. Passmore, eds., *Writing National Histories: Western Europe since 1800* (London, 1999).
3. E. Kedourie, *Nationalism* (London, 1960), 1.
4. For surveys U. Ozkirimli, *Theories of Nationalism* (London, 2010); A.D. Smith, *Nationalism and Modernism* (London, 1998).
5. E. Gellner, *Nations and Nationalism*, 2nd ed. (Oxford, 2006).
6. J. Echternkamp and S-O. Müller, eds., *Die Politik der Nation: Deutscher Nationalismus in Krieg und Krisen 1760–1960* (Munich, 2002); H-U. Wehler, *Nationalismus. Geschichte – Formen – Folgen* (Munich, 2000).
7. F. Meinecke, *Cosmopolitanism and the Nation State* (New Jersey, 1970). Originally published in German in 1911. G. Schmidt, "Friedrich Meineckes Kulturnation. Zum historischen Kontext nationaler Ideen in Weimar-Jena um 1800," *Historische Zeitschrift* 284 (2007), 597–621.
8. Although one could in theory apply it to an existing state such as Prussia or Saxony.
9. D. Langewiesche and G. Schmidt, eds., *Föderative Nation. Deutschlandkonzepte von der Reformation bis zum Ersten Weltkrieg* (Munich, 2000).
10. J. Breuilly and R. Speirs, eds., *Germany's Two Unifications: Anticipations, Experiences, Responses* (Basingstoke, 2005).
11. J. Breuilly, *Austria, Prussia and Germany and the Making of Germany, 1806–1871* (London, 2011), chap. 8.
12. E. Weber, *Peasants into Frenchmen* (London, 1976). For Weber's arguments generalized to other countries, including Germany, see M. Cabo and F. Molina, "The long and winding road of nationalization: Eugen Weber's *Peasants into Frenchmen* in Modern European History (1976–2006)," *European History Quarterly* 39/2 (2009), 264–86.
13. M. Mann, *The Sources of Social Power. Vol 1: A History of Power from the Beginning to AD1760* (Cambridge, 1986), chap. 1. Mann's later treatment in Volume 2 of the nation-state as "power-contain" does imply that the different levels of power are integrated to some extent over all, and only, the people living in the territory of the nation-state.
14. I argue this point at length in "Conclusion: National Peculiarities," in J. Breuilly. *Labour and Liberalism in 19th Century Europe: Essays in Comparative History* (Manchester, 1992), 273–95.
15. J. Breuilly, "Culture, Doctrine, Politics: Three Ways of Constructing Nationalism," in *Nationalism in Europe. Past and Present*, ed. J. Beramendi et al. (Santiago de Compostela, 1994), 127–34.
16. C. Calhoun, *Nations Matter: Culture, History, and the Cosmopolitan Dream* (London, 2007).
17. M. Hroch, "From National Movement to the Fully-Formed Nation: The Nation-building Process in Europe," in *Mapping the Nation*, ed. G. Balakrishnan (London, 1996), 78–97.
18. P. Mandler, *The English National Character: The History of an Idea from Edmund Burke to Tony Blair* (New Haven, 2006).
19. J. Breuilly, "Modernisation as Social Evolution: The German Case, c.1800–1880," *Transactions of the Royal Historical Society, Sixth Series* 15 (2005), 117–47; J. Breuilly, *Nationalism, Power and Modernity in Nineteenth-Century Germany* (London, 2007).
20. B. Giesen, *Intellectuals and the Nation: Collective Identity in a German Axial Age* (Cambridge, 1998); D. Düding, *Organisierter gesellschaftlicher Nationalismus in Deutschland (1808–1847). Bedeutung und Funktion der Turner- und Sängervereine für die deutsche Nationalbewegung* (Munich, 1984).
21. W. Hardtwig, *Nationalismus und Bürgerkultur* (Göttingen, 1994).
22. U. Planert, *Der Mythos vom Befreiungskrieg. Frankreichs Kriege und der deutsche Süden. Alltag – Wahrnehmung – Deutung, 1792–1841* (Paderborn, 2007).

23. A good example is the treatment of Fichte's *Reden an die deutsche Nation* which I consider from this perspective in J. Breuilly, "The Response to Napoleon and German Nationalism" in *The Bee and the Eagle: Napoleonic France and the End of the Holy Roman Empire, 1806*, eds. A. Forrest and P. Wilson (Basingstoke, 2009), 256–83.
24. A good recent study of this transnational dimension is L. Riall, *Garibaldi: Invention of a Hero* (New Haven, 2007). For an transnational approach to the early formation of national(ist) ideas see J. Leerssen, "Nationalism and the Cultivation of Culture," *Nations and Nationalism* 12 (2006), 559–78.
25. J. Vermeiren, *Brothers in Arms: The Dual Alliance in World War One and German National Identity* (PhD, University College London, 2009).
26. F. Lenger, *Industrielle Revolution und Nationalstaatsgründung (1849–1870er Jahre)* (Stuttgart, 2003).
27. J.R. Davis, *Britain and the German Zollverein, 1848–1866* (Basingstoke, 1997).
28. B. Anderson, *Imagined Communities: Reflections on the Origins and Spread of Nationalism*, 2nd ed. (London, 1991).
29. Calhoun, *Nations Matter*, argues that the construction of the individual and the nation follow parallel and linked paths.
30. R. Parr, "Identity in Difference: Collective Symbols and the Interplay of Discourses in the Two German Unifications," in Speirs and Breuilly, *Germany's Two Unifications* (2005), 76–100.
31. S. Weichlein, *Nation und Region. Integrationsprozesse im Bismarck-Reich* (Düsseldorf, 2004).
32. The contrast of banal with hot nationalism is taken from M. Billig, *Banal Nationalism* (London, 1995).

Part II

POLITICS, CULTURE, AND SOCIETY

Chapter 5

The Authoritarian State and the Political Mass Market

James Retallack

In this chapter I consider how research on my principal themes has evolved since the 1980s.[1] In the process I will identify some open questions for future research. Some initial observations are required to place my twin subjects in the context of three discussions found elsewhere in this volume, dealing with World War I, culture, and transnationalism. They also begin the task of explaining why the two bodies of scholarly writing on the authoritarian state and on the political mass market have relied so heavily on each other in the past—and should continue to do so.[2]

I. Don't Fence Me In

Did World War I decide the fate of the German authoritarian state or deflect the evolution of mass politics? Yes and no. Many elements of the thesis about Germany's *Sonderweg* (special path) to modernity hinge on what happened at the beginning and end of the war. Whether the German Revolution of 1918–19 represented a likely or even plausible outcome to the processes of democratization and constitutional reform is a question that has been tackled less often in recent years than we might suppose. Nevertheless, the prospects of democracy in the transition from empire to republic have drawn the attention of such scholars as Stanley Suval, Brett Fairbairn, and Margaret Lavinia Anderson. They have argued that an undemocratic political culture inherited from the pre-war era was *not* one of the burdens afflicting the Weimar Republic.[3] Instead they have stressed the importance of "affirming voting," legal guarantees underpinning the secret ballot, and the concept of electoral "fairness." Germans learned about "democracy in the undemocratic state"—this is Fairbairn's provocative term—by practicing it *avant la lettre*.

What of the war's beginning and middle? With reference to the "polarized" and "stalemated" condition of Imperial Germany's political parties, Volker Berghahn has argued that the most important question of Kaiserreich historiography remains "Why did Germany go to war in 1914?"[4] I disagree not with the question but with the priority assigned to it. There are more interesting questions about Germany's political modernization that cannot be cast in the harsh spotlight of July 1914. We are immeasurably better informed than we were just twenty years ago about the authoritarian state's loss of legitimacy in the middle years of the war—as seen, for example, from the trenches and from the cities, towns, and villages of southern Germany.[5] When we speak of burdens that exhausted the resources and undermined the legitimacy of the authoritarian state, it is there that we are finding new clues about why the dysfunctional German state of 1914–18 was essentially the same state that Bismarck had put in the saddle in 1871. Should we, then, give that state credit for flexibility, generosity, and commitment to serving the interests of a pluralistic society in either the war years or the decades that preceded them?

Historians of German political culture, second, are by definition interested in culture. This interest has grown more intense with each passing decade since the 1970s. Symptomatic here is the evolution of approaches to confessional conflict, class conflict, gender relations, and the antagonism among political camps (*Lager*). We can appreciate how far we have traveled when we contrast, say, Ronald Ross's study of Bismarck's *Kulturkampf*, which was already more skeptical of the power of the authoritarian state than anything written in the 1970s, with more recent books written by David Blackbourn, Michael Gross, and Róisín Healy.[6] Each of these authors considered confessional conflict from the vantage point of perceptions, meanings, and experiences. They each questioned the operation of gender norms as well.

Third, transnational history focuses attention on relationships, constellations, and "flows" rather than on events. Transnational history helps us move beyond a fixation on the German nation-state as the self-evident, paradigmatic unit of analysis. But these strengths are no less constitutive of political culture research in which the authoritarian state and political modernization figure centrally. Two examples are provided by Thomas Kühne's study of electoral culture in Prussia and Thomas Mergel's study of parliamentary culture in the Weimar Republic.[7] Despite contemporary complaints about the hateful Americanization of German electioneering, the old adage "All politics is local" reminds us that the "play of scales" can be helpful in assessing just where and when and how the "mass" in mass politics operated. Margaret Anderson showed us what mass politics looked like at the local level; but she also reassessed German political culture in European and global contexts. Contemporaries judged the norms and practices of their political culture not just as seen from the village church steeple but in light of cultural transfers across national borders.

Border-crossers enjoy other advantages. Consider the colonizing efforts of Germany's political parties to win new territory in the political mass market. One can emphasize manipulation from above, self-mobilization from below, or—better still—the sparks that flew between them when different ways of "fishing for popularity" collided.[8] One might also consider the willingness of traditional notables to recruit female auxiliaries before 1918. My point is that crossing borders helps to reveal how asymmetrical relations of power and alterities emerged as smaller political cultures became enmeshed in larger ones. As they did in transnational settings, they might alleviate marginality and misery but also cause loss and humiliation. "Playing with scales" also helps us discover how winners and losers transgressed or transcended established political boundaries, for example when they left small-town politics and "arrived" in Dresden, Munich, or Berlin. As Michael Geyer has written, "even the most parochial and inward-turned worlds are imbricated in other worlds of action and imagination that range beyond parish and nation."[9] Yet that imbrication was not quite as "natural" as we sometimes think. To say that politics at a given time and place was "parochial" still seems to imply that what happened in local and regional settings was necessarily more small-minded than what took place on a larger stage.[10] This implication echoes an early, untenable variant of modernization theory. It also reflects the disdain we tend to feel for the authoritarian state, the politics of notables, and the "anachronistic" élites who defended them. We look right through them or hope they will hurry off the stage because they are too arrogant to belong there any longer. Yet if we avoid historical hubris and redirect our gaze, we can profit from Geyer's advice about how to study border-crossers: "you notice them only when the transnational 'pie' is no longer in the sky, but manifestly in your face."

II. The Authoritarian State

Konrad Jarausch and Michael Geyer claimed in their book *Shattered Past* that to speak of the "authoritarian" Empire is to invoke an "empty cliché."[11] Because their book appeared in English, it is unclear whether they would have used the German term *autoritär* or *obrigkeitsstaatlich*. But that distinction is hardly the central issue, because in neither case are we invoking an empty cliché. Let me suggest five reasons why it may still be helpful—even if only heuristically—to describe Imperial Germany as an authoritarian state.

One way to determine whether a concept has become a cliché is to examine its linguistic usage and to parse its changing inflections over time. Authority (*Obrigkeit*) and the authoritarian state (*Obrigkeitsstaat*) do not appear in the *Geschichtliche Grundbegriffe*.[12] But this should not distract us from its use as a polemical term before, during, and after World War I. Otto von Gierke and his pupil Hugo Preuß lent the authoritarian state currency when they asserted its opposition to a people's state or one where the rule of law prevailed. By 1915 Preuß's use of the term had become even more barbed. It conjured up a host of hateful associations, each of which identified realms in which the state helped preserve "anomalous" spheres of power—the police and the military, for example—and made them immune from the constitutional and political influence of a bourgeois society.[13] From Max Weber's perspective in 1917, the authoritarian state was bankrupt: it had failed to produce the charismatic leaders and talented parliamentarians who might have educated Germans politically.[14] Then came Gustav Radbruch's famous comment (1930) that governmental non-partisanship was the "life-giving lie" (*Lebenslüge*) of the authoritarian state.[15] Arguably the concept of the authoritarian state is with us still—as a polemical super-weapon and as part of historiographical memory. Before 1918, socialists and left liberals used the term as a catch-all for everything they disliked about Imperial Germany. Have liberal historians avoided this pitfall?

Second, we should acknowledge (but not accept) that the concept of the authoritarian state has frequently been deployed in ways that make it functionally equivalent to other terms that serve as a polemical lightning-rod. A symptom of this usage is historians' uncertainty about whether the term "Prussia-Germany" is to be understood as Greater Prussia or Lesser Germany. Hartwin Spenkuch has argued convincingly that Prussian particularities have often been ignored by critics of the *Sonderweg* idea.[16] When historians use terms like *Junkerstaat*, *Militärstaat*, *Machtstaat*, and *Beamtenstaat*, they may be striving for both precision and nuance. Often they deliver neither. Such ersatz terms allow historians to avoid thorny questions about how the authoritarian state actually functioned—or failed to function.

A third strategy is to break down the false polarity between society-centered and state-centered analyses. An exaggerated distinction between state and society veils interesting questions about how a modern society can accommodate an authoritarian state, and vice versa. Of course to speak of "the state" in the singular is to start on the wrong foot. Different authorities existed in Prussia, Bavaria, Saxony, Württemberg, Baden, and the other federal states. Yet only recently have historians of modern Germany begun in earnest to follow the example of Abigail Green, whose book *Fatherlands* was pioneering.[17] Green demonstrated for the pre-1870 period that the middle-sized German states used schoolbooks, press policies, and various symbols of nationhood to enhance the authority of German princes and their administrations. Green's findings chart a different path from the one pioneered by Celia Applegate, whose work illustrated that attachment to one's homeland (*Heimat*) was perfectly compatible with a modern sense of nationalism. Still, more work is required before we will understand how a "nation of provincials," understood sociologically, evolved in tandem with authoritarian states at the sub-national level when they faced new challenges.[18]

Fourth, it is worth asking whether state and society "tolerated" one another only to the extent that each sought to instrumentalize the other to guarantee its own hegemony. David Blackbourn has remarked that the German state was never particularly successful at wringing "wide-eyed obedience" from politically emancipated citizens. Yet where did the "mystique of the state" begin and where did it end? Was the authoritarian state the "provider" or the "scourge" of bourgeois hegemony? Or did it function mainly as a "sternly benevolent umpire" among competing social, economic, and political interests?[19] And what other forms of authority filled this role when the deficiency of the central German state was plain to see? Mark Hewitson, Christoph Schönberger, and Thomas Kühne, building on earlier work by Dieter Langewiesche and others, have helped clarify why the "silent parliamentarization" thesis is a dead letter: they have correctly distinguished between the political, institutional processes of parliamentarization on the one hand, and the social, emotional significance of democratization on the other.[20] This distinction helps explain why suffrage reform movements generated far more resonance—in speeches, printed propaganda, street demonstrations, and riots— than, say, efforts to reform or abolish the upper chambers in Prussia and other federal states.[21] This distinction also suggests why parliamentarization and democratization are best understood as learning processes: they both required practice and habituation. Unfortunately the *longue durée* still often gets lost from view.[22] I am tempted to agree with the British political scientist Peter Stirk, who has posed the question: When did the authoritarian state die? Not yet! some might say. Or it died in November 1918. "A more interesting possibility," Stirk suggests, "is that it was in a sense dead even before then. It was a façade of strength lacking true substance. The 'life-giving lie' gave life to a walking corpse."[23]

Fifth and lastly, the authoritarian state is invoked less frequently than we might imagine in descriptions of Imperial Germany's constitutional structure. In his *Gesellschaftsgeschichte*, Hans-Ulrich Wehler conceded that the couplet "constitutional monarchy" is not sufficiently precise to get at the real nature of the German Empire.[24] He preferred to explore the contours of charismatic rule. Thomas Nipperdey took a different tack to describe his *Machtstaat vor der Demokratie*. The authoritarian state was conspicuously absent: "The Empire of 1871 was many things rolled into one: federal state, constitutional state, imperial state, Prussian hegemonic state, a powerful and a military state, above all it was a national state."[25] Winfried Becker hitched up the same wagons and sent them off on the *Sonderweg* at the outset of his brochure of 2000 entitled *Das Bismarck-Reich – ein Obrigkeitsstaat?* Yet in his conclusion Becker conceded that his principal question can only be answered if we continue to explore what Karl Mannheim in the 1930s referred to as the fundamental politicization of German society.[26] In suggesting that a new socio-political dynamic in Imperial Germany conditioned the principle and *Praxis* of authority, Becker put it this way:

> The politicization of wide circles of the population, which already began in the Bismarckian era, was by no means only the reflex of authoritarian state action that deliberately awakened and conflated the interests of the dominated in order to guarantee its own hold on power. Rather, precisely the many conflicts at the regional and national levels led members of various classes of the population toward political life via increased participation. The disputes leading up to elections created and reflected a growing multiplicity of highly diverse motivations, which included not only burgeoning class, confessional, and milieu loyalties, which tended to stiffen

quickly, but also everyday problems as well as questions about political culture and about the common welfare viewed either as a particularist or a nationalist matter.[27]

Coming at the same problem from a different direction, Thomas Kühne has asked whether the "authoritarian essence"[28] of Imperial Germany was fundamentally transformed by the processes of democratization. Did the beginnings of political pluralization overcome the socio-cultural fragmentation of the party system? In each instance, Kühne answered no.[29] It is no simple matter to reconcile Becker's and Kühne's conclusions; but what is centrally important here, and will remain so for future scholars, is that the idea of the authoritarian state is not a cliché. On the contrary, further study will underscore just how unpredictably representatives of the German authoritarian state reacted to social, economic, and political transformations they could not control.

III. The Political Mass Market

What elements of a political system or a political culture have the strongest "transmissive function" between state and society? Elections play such a role, as has long been recognized.[30] But so do electoral cultures, regional political cultures, and the public sphere, including the press, associational life, and civil liberties. In studying each of these areas, scholars writing in the past fifteen years have made tremendous strides. They have linked political and cultural ways of invoking authority. They have demonstrated the reciprocal relationship between parliamentarization and democratization, whereby the latter actually inhibited progress of the former. And they have helped us learn to balance (though not necessarily to reconcile) the views of statesmen, political leaders, ordinary voters, and other citizens who entertained one of two very different visions of Germany's future. On the one hand we find those who viewed Imperial Germany as dysfunctional, hamstrung by irreconcilable religious, ideological, ethnic, and other conflicts, teetering on the brink of revolution or collapse. On the other hand we find those who viewed Imperial Germany as amazingly liberal and likely to become more so every day: its pluralistic, modern face was Germany's most recognizable feature.

Historians' attempts to "emphasize the positive" in the German Empire have achieved mixed results. Some have elicited groans of impatience or howls of protest. Such studies include the volume that purported to find *Another Germany*, Chris Lorenz's attempt to move us "beyond good and evil" empires, and Marcus Kreuzer's categorization of Kaiserreich historians into optimists, pessimists, and skeptics.[31] Done well, a refusal to see only Imperial Germany's dark side has its merits. For example, Edward Ross Dickinson, Kevin Repp, and Andrew Lees have demonstrated the breadth and cohesion of a reformist movement in Wilhelmine Germany, principally in Germany's municipal arenas though not only there.[32] Two handbooks on Germany's reform and *völkisch* movements have also demonstrated the priority Germans placed on "overcoming" perceived deficiencies in their country's cultural and political heritage.[33]

Unfortunately, the existence of a modern, pluralist, steadfastly reformist Empire is often asserted but not demonstrated by scholars whose research agendas have become narrow and self-referential and who rely on theories that spiral inward on themselves.[34] How many valences of modernity do we really need? Such arguments are particularly unconvincing when they present a caricature of Imperial Germany as sclerotic, backward-looking, and ruled by pre-modern élites. This caricature is then used to prop up two other unsupportable claims: that if Imperial Germany was "modern" it cannot also have been authoritarian, and that Bismarckian and Wilhelmine styles of politics were so fundamentally different that they are best studied separately.

Scholars thus hold divergent opinions about Hans Rosenberg's concept of a "political mass market." Does the term satisfactorily describe a polity that had been transformed by the introduction of universal manhood suffrage in 1867–71 but continued to evolve?[35] For critics of Rosenberg's thesis, the notion of a political mass market connotes a passivity among voters that is belied by the evidence. Some such historians say we cannot regard the German voter as a "consumer" of politics because he did not choose his party or candidate like a supermarket shopper chooses one brand over another.[36] (Stanley Suval's thesis about the "affirming" habits of Reichstag voters runs in the same groove.) Others claim that voters expressed their political preferences in groups and not, like a consumer, by individual choice.[37] But arguably these criticisms miss the mark, for reasons that will be outlined briefly in the balance of this chapter.

Why should we focus on voters as individual consumers when speaking of a political mass market? Why not consider the cut-throat competition among the purveyors of political wares—the parties? With the de facto deregulation of the electoral arena, the government gradually became unable to control either the medium or the message of politics. Both aspects were denigrated when contemporaries complained about the unseemly business of cattle-trading in the political market place. But one can argue that the chief commodity being bought and sold was influence. Influence was bartered on a new scale, in new venues, and with new middlemen wanting a piece of the action. Such middlemen included party functionaries, newspaper editors, and municipal counselors, to list only a few categories. But each of these in turn tended to focus their attention on parliamentary candidates who, if they were elected, could serve the interests of local constituents and wire-pullers.[38] Thus, when a voter entered a polling booth, he could legitimately ask: if I cast my vote for this candidate over that one, what is it going to cost me, and how might I profit by doing so? Thinking in these terms helps us understand why historians like Anderson, Fairbairn, and Suval are correct to stress the agency of voters who were once considered "voting fodder" by local notables and historians alike. But it is just as important to recognize that each voter's cost-benefit analysis had its own short-, medium-, and long-term ramifications.

Collectively these voters determined whether a candidate was given the opportunity to represent them in the next legislative period of a municipal, state, or national parliament. However, the daily business of political agitation, recruitment, and organization usually had implications that stretched far into the future. Even the most future-oriented politicians, among whom we can count the Social Democratic leader August Bebel, sometimes had to be reminded not to let their energy sag. Consider the words Friedrich Engels directed to Bebel in May 1883. Bebel had recently expressed some satisfaction that he was now sitting as a member of the Saxon Landtag, not in Berlin's Reichstag. (In 1881 Bebel had lost the Reichstag constituency of Dresden-Altstadt to the "parties of order.") Forced to live away from his family in the village of Borsdorf because the Minor State of Siege had been imposed on Leipzig and its environs by the Saxon government in June 1881, Bebel was trying to recover his health and recharge his political batteries. Yet Engels urged him to invest in the future, roll up his sleeves, and get back to work:

> My dear Bebel! That you would rather *not* sit in the Reichstag I can well believe. But you see what your absence has made possible. ... Certainly agitational and parliamentary work become very boring in the long run. It is the same as with advertising, launching promotions, and traveling around on business: success comes only slowly and, for many, not at all. But there's no alternative, and once you're in it, the thing must be carried through to the end or else all the previous effort is lost.[39]

Were the Social Democratic Party and the Catholic Centre Party the Walmarts and Best Buys of Imperial Germany? At the very least, these parties' activities in the first years of the German Empire helped to create a marketplace of ideas, niches of opportunity, where none had existed before. Who can doubt that they sought to mobilize a particular kind of acquisitiveness—the hunger to be heard—among the little men of society? Had not the defenders of throne and altar, the leaders of veterans' associations, and other agents of the authoritarian state been market-testing their own brand of subliminal advertising for years before Bismarck fell from power? Insofar as they learned the art of successful political mobilization, they could calculate their profit and market share easily, by counting the number of votes and Reichstag seats they won. Consensus-building and coercion, too, went hand in hand, as they do in any good marketing strategy or public relations campaign. Anti-democratic parties learned their trade even while rival parties learned theirs by pitching the ideals of liberty and democracy. New political practices were tested and retested under constantly changing marketplace conditions, but it was the collision of these strategies that transformed political styles and gave rise to new ones. For all these reasons, to look for the agents of change in only one camp is to narrow our conception of mass politics in unnecessary and unhelpful ways.

Rosenberg's term also helps focus attention on the modern methods and unprecedented competitiveness of national politics in Imperial Germany. Under the new suffrage introduced for elections to the North German Confederation in 1867 and then for the German Reich in 1871, no one could accurately predict which strategies would work in competitive environments still largely shaped by local, personal relationships. William Sheridan Allen, in his pioneering study of Nazism's rise in the town of Nordheim, stressed the self-correcting, "capitalist" principle that forced rank-and-file Nazis to learn (on the job) what moved voters and what alienated them.[40] Who can say that the same principle did not operate in the political culture of Bismarckian Germany? The liberal Gustav Freytag certainly thought it did. Even in the midst of the first Reichstag election campaign in the winter of 1866/67, Freytag was exhausted by the demands of his voter-clientele. "Fie, Bismarck, that was no master stroke," Freytag wrote, referring to the principle of one man, one vote. "Worst of all ... no one knows whether he'll be elected or not."[41]

It is not difficult, lastly, to discover why the advent of "mass politics" has so often been ascribed to the 1890s. It is plausible to portray this decade as a turning point. According to this line of argument, the mobilization of previously passive social constituencies was accompanied by the appearance of new economic interest groups and nationalist pressure groups, perhaps even by the development of new technologies (for instance, slide-shows and naval displays) to "spread the word." Moreover, Carl Schorske's term "politics in a new key" *was* meant to describe post-1890 innovations.[42] Rosenberg himself endorsed Friedrich Naumann's withering critique of agrarian self-interest as exemplified by the Agrarian League after its founding in 1893.[43] An "agitating aristocracy" and "authoritarian types with democratic gloves" were cited by Rosenberg, and then subsequently by Wehler and others, as evidence that pre-modern élites learned to play the modern game of politics with unheard-of skill and cunning. Offering an "outward accommodation with democratization," those élites accepted the need to participate in a political competition with its inevitable "leveling" tendencies.[44]

It is ironic that many historians who have stressed the "modern," dynamic nature of German politics after 1890 have themselves provided arguments that highlight the historically more significant period of political innovation and mobilization between 1867 and 1881. For example, David Blackbourn convincingly demonstrated the newness of political institutions set in place by Bismarck at the founding of the Empire. These included the constitutional, administrative, parliamentary, and electoral institutions that remained largely unchanged over the next half-century. Geoff Eley has drawn attention to the relatively early date—not later than the mid-1870s—by which time both bourgeois and (national) liberal Germans exerted not only economic, social, and cultural dominance but irrepressible political influence as well. Margaret Anderson and Helmut Walser Smith, among others, have illustrated that although openness and dynamism characterized the 1870s due to conflicts pitting the authoritarian state against the Catholic Church and Social Democracy, those battle lines had already hardened by the early 1880s into political polarities that remained largely static until the end of the Empire.[45]

According to one view of Germany's political modernization, the decade of the 1890s witnessed the "reconstitution of the political nation," "a major moment of flux," a "vital moment of transition," a time of political "fission," a "populist moment," a "major enlargement of the public sphere," a "reordering of the public domain," and "a fundamental change in the scale and intensity of public life."[46] But a growing number of historians, including Alastair Thompson and Axel Grießmer, have shown that it is misleading to single out the 1890s so categorically.[47] To be sure, we are hampered by a paucity of good studies of domestic politics in the 1870s and 1880s, especially ones that take the performative aspects of Germany's electoral and parliamentary cultures seriously. Hans-Peter Goldberg's study of "Bismarck and his opponents" is a notable exception. Yet when we consider the decades in which truly innovative strategies were not just formulated but actually implemented by the political parties, economic lobby groups, and nationalist associations, the 1890s recede as a decade of fundamental change.

Exaggerating only slightly, one could say that mass politics arrived in Germany as a Christmas market when, to Freytag's dismay, that first Reichstag election campaign heated up in December 1866. There was no turning back. The participation rate for Reichstag elections rose from 1867 through to 1887, when it reached 77.5 percent: that figure was not exceeded until 1907. The Catholic and Social Democratic milieus were mobilized in the 1870s and 1880s respectively. Antisemites, whether in the Conservative Party or outside it, were conspicuously unoriginal in their take on the "Jewish question" in the 1890s. SPD membership climbed steeply after 1903. And the nationalist camp, if it existed at all, was consolidated only once the agrarian movement, mass imperialist agitation, and popular anti-socialism were fully functional, that is, after 1900. Women, too, found opportunities in the new century to become active in voluntary associations, suffrage movements and, eventually, the political parties themselves. When Eve Rosenhaft proposed an expanded definition of "mass" politics almost twenty years ago, she feared that scholars had no choice but to accept the conscious, regretful exclusion of women from historical accounts that chart the formal structures and practices of politics.[48] Happily, other scholars have shown that Rosenhaft was too pessimistic. The proliferation of works on the political activities of right-wing women alone, spanning the divide of 1918/19, suggests the vibrancy of this field.[49]

All new? New and improved? These make good marketing slogans. But they do a poor job of describing Germany's political culture in 1900.

IV. Conclusion

Obrigkeitsstaat is still regularly used by historians as a shorthand description of Imperial Germany *tout court*, even though the term itself is so obviously state-oriented. The closest approximation to an "authoritarian society" one finds in the literature is reference to a society of subjects or a spirit of servility. But the general trend of recent research has been in the opposite direction. It depicts a bourgeois society where subjects have been replaced by citizens; where civil liberties, individual rights, and the rule of law are protected; where professional, entrepreneurial, and intellectual merit are rewarded in ways typical of modern societies; and where Germans enjoyed many opportunities not only to "reform" and adapt their society to new circumstances but to "transform" it fundamentally—as the authoritarian state and its institutions could not be transformed.

As these remarks have tried to suggest, there is no longer any need to ask students of Imperial Germany to choose between such stark alternatives. Recent works with titles like "political styles in the Kaiserreich," "elections and election campaigns," and "parties in transition," represent promising avenues of research.[50] No single decade, no single party, and no single political "idiom" can be privileged in the way they once were. As more research is carried out along these lines, scholars will probe more deeply into the cross-cutting pressures that contributed to both the "unchaining" (*Entfesselung*) and the "taming" (*Zähmung*) of the political mass market. In doing so they will reveal new facets of authoritarianism as well.

Notes

1. For research funding I am grateful to the Gerda Henkel Foundation and the Connaught Program at the University of Toronto. As a Henkel Research Fellow I benefited particularly from the support of my host in Berlin, Jürgen Kocka. Although I have added references to this chapter—as few as necessary—I have tried to retain the informal, inquiring tone of my original oral presentation.
2. Short surveys with a historiographical component include E. Frie, *Das Deutsche Kaiserreich* (Darmstadt, 2004); M. Jefferies, *Contesting the German Empire, 1871–1918* (Oxford, 2007); and H.-P. Ullmann, *Politik im Deutschen Kaiserreich 1871–1918* (Munich, 1999).
3. Cf. S. Suval, *Electoral Politics in Wilhelmine Germany* (Chapel Hill, 1985); B. Fairbairn, *Democracy in the Undemocratic State: The Reichstag Elections of 1897 and 1903* (Toronto, 1987); M.L. Anderson, *Practicing Democracy: Elections and Political Culture in Imperial Germany* (Princeton, 2000).
4. V. Berghahn, "The German Empire, 1871–1914: Reflections on the Direction of Recent Research," *Central European History* 35 (2002), 75–82.
5. See inter alia B. Ziemann, *War Experiences in Rural Germany, 1914–1923* (orig. German ed. 1997) (Oxford, 2007); R. Chickering, *The Great War and Urban Life in Germany: Freiburg, 1914–1918* (Cambridge, 2007).
6. R.J. Ross, *The Failure of Bismarck's Kulturkampf: Catholicism and State Power in Imperial Germany, 1871–1887* (Washington, DC, 1998); D. Blackbourn, *Marpingen: Apparitions of the Virgin Mary in Bismarckian Germany* (Oxford, 1993); M. Gross, *The War against Catholicism: Liberalism and the Anti-Catholic Imagination in Nineteenth-Century Germany* (Ann Arbor, 2004); R. Healy, *The Jesuit Specter in Imperial Germany* (Boston, 2003).
7. T. Kühne, *Dreiklassenwahlrecht und Wahlkultur in Preussen 1867–1914. Landtagswahlen zwischen korporativer Tradition und politischem Massenmarkt* (Düsseldorf, 1994); T. Mergel, *Parlamentarische Kultur in der Weimarer Republik. Politische Kommunikation, symbolische Politik und Öffentlichkeit im Reichstag* (Düsseldorf, 2002).
8. See J. Retallack, *The German Right, 1860–1920: Political Limits of the Authoritarian Imagination* (Toronto, 2006), esp. Chap. 2.

9. M. Geyer, "Forum: Reviewsymposium, 'Transnationale Geschichte': The New Consensus," H-Soz-u-Kult, 27 September 2006, <http://hsozkult.geschichte.hu-berlin.de/rezensionen/id=812&type=revsymp>.
10. See D. Blackbourn and J. Retallack, eds., *Localism, Landscape, and the Ambiguities of Place: German-Speaking Central Europe, 1860–1930* (Toronto, 2007).
11. K.H. Jarausch and M. Geyer, *Shattered Past: Reconstructing German Histories* (Princeton, 2003),19.
12. O. Brunner et al., eds., *Geschichtliche Grundbegriffe. Historisches Lexikon zur politisch-sozialen Sprache in Deutschland*, 8 vols. (Stuttgart, 1972–1997); cf. H. Rabe, "Autorität," 1:382–406; H. Günther et al., "Herrschaft," 3:1–102; H. Boldt et al., "Staat," 6:1–154.
13. H. Preuß, *Staat, Recht und Freiheit* (Tübingen, 1926), pts. I and III and pp. 365–68; Preuß, *Das deutsche Volk und die Politik* [1915] (Jena, 1919), esp. 170–99. Cf. J. Hatschek, *Das Parlamentsrecht des Deutschen Reiches* (Berlin, 1915); D. Lehnert, *Verfassungsdemokratie als Bürgergenossenschaft. Politisches Denken, Öffentliches Recht und Geschichtsdeutungen bei Hugo Preuß* (Baden-Baden, 1998), esp. Chap. 8.
14. M. Weber, "Parlament und Regierung im neugeordneten Deutschland. Zur politischen Kritik des Beamtentums und Parteiwesens" [1917], in Weber, *Gesamtausgabe*, vol. 15, *Zur Politik im Weltkrieg. Schriften und Reden 1914–1918*, ed. W. J. Mommsen (Tübingen, 1984), 432–596. See also Klaus von Beyme, *Die parlamentarische Demokratie. Entstehung und Funktionsweise 1789–1999*, 3rd ed. (Opladen, 1999).
15. G. Radbruch, "Die politischen Parteien im System des deutschen Verfassungsrechts," in *Handbuch des deutschen Staatsrechts*, eds. G. Anschütz and R. Thoma, (Tübingen, 1930), 1:289.
16. H. Spenkuch, "Vergleichsweise besonders? Politisches System und Strukturen Preußens als Kern des 'deutschen Sonderwegs,'" *Geschichte und Gesellschaft* 29 (2003), 262–93. Cf. C. Clark, *Iron Kingdom: The Rise and Downfall of Prussia, 1600–1947* (Cambridge, 2006).
17. A. Green, *Fatherlands: State-Building and Nationhood in Nineteenth-Century Germany* (Cambridge, 2001).
18. See, for example, S. Weichlein, "Saxons into Germans: The Progress of the National Idea in Saxony After 1866," in *Saxony in German History: Culture, Society, and Politics, 1830–1933*, ed. James Retallack (Ann Arbor, 2000), 166–79; Weichlein, *Region und Nation. Integrationsprozesse im Bismarckreich* (Düsseldorf, 2004); C. Applegate, *A Nation of Provincials: The German Idea of Heimat* (Berkeley, 1990).
19. D. Blackbourn, *Populists and Patricians. Essays in Modern German History* (London, 1987), 18f.
20. C. Schönberger, "Die überholte Parlamentarisierung. Einflußgewinn und fehlende Herrschaftsfähigkeit des Reichstags im sich demokratisierenden Kaiserreich," *Historische Zeitschrift* 272 (2001), 623–66; M. Hewitson, "The Wilhelmine Regime and the Problem of Reform. German Debates about Modern Nation-States," in *Wilhelminism and Its Legacies: German Modernities, Imperialism, and the Meanings of Reform*, eds. G. Eley and J. Retallack (New York, 2003), 73–90; T. Kühne, "Demokratisierung und Parlamentarisierung: Neue Forschungen zur politischen Entwicklungsfähigkeit Deutschlands vor dem Ersten Weltkrieg," *Geschichte und Gesellschaft* 31 (2005), 293–316. Cf. M. Rauh, *Die Parlamentarisierung des Deutschen Reiches* (Düsseldorf, 1977); D. Langewiesche, "Das Deutsche Kaiserreich: Bemerkungen zur Diskussion über Parlamentarisierung und Demokratisierung Deutschlands," *Archiv für Sozialgeschichte* 19 (1979), 628–42.
21. Cf. S. Lässig, "Wahlrechtsreformen in den deutschen Einzelstaaten. Indikatoren für Modernisierungstendenzen und Reformfähigkeit im Kaiserreich?" in *Modernisierung und Region im wilhelminischen Deutschland. Wahlen, Wahlrecht und Politische Kultur*, 2nd ed., eds. idem., K.H. Pohl, and J. Retallack (Bielefeld, 1998), 127–69.
22. Anderson, *Practicing Democracy*. Cf. reviews by G.A. Ritter, "Die Reichstagswahlen und die Wurzeln der deutschen Demokratie im Kaiserreich," *Historische Zeitschrift* 275 (2002), 385–403; Kühne, "Demokratisierung."
23. P. Stirk, "The Obrigkeitsstaat: When was it Born and When did it Die?," unpublished paper delivered at the Annual Meeting of the Political Science Association, April 2004; cf. Stirk, *Twentieth-Century German Political Thought* (Edinburgh, 2006), Chaps. 2–3.

24. H.-U. Wehler, *Deutsche Gesellschaftsgeschichte*, vol. 3, *Von der "Deutschen Doppelrevolution" bis zum Beginn des Ersten Weltkrieges 1849–1914* (Munich, 1995), 361f.
25. T. Nipperdey, *Deutsche Geschichte 1866–1918*, vol. 2, *Machtstaat vor der Demokratie* (Munich, 1992), 80.
26. K. Mannheim, *Man and Society in an Age of Reconstruction* (New York, 1967), 44.
27. W. Becker, *Das Bismarck-Reich – ein Obrigkeitsstaat? Die Entwicklung des Parlamentarismus und der Parteien 1871–1890* (Friedrichsruh, 2000), 34. Becker takes issue with the idea (in Ullmann, *Politik*, 31–3) that political mobilization began around 1900 and worked principally through the ideologies of nationalism and antisemitism.
28. Kühne's term was *obrigkeitsstaatliche Verfaßtheit*.
29. T. Kühne, "Die Jahrhundertwende, die 'lange' Bismarckzeit und die Demokratisierung der politischen Kultur," in *Otto von Bismarck und Wilhelm II. Repräsentanten eines Epochenwechsels?*, ed. L. Gall (Paderborn, 2000), 85–118.
30. This is a central theme in my forthcoming monograph, *Red Saxony: Election Battles and the Specter of Democracy in Germany, 1860–1918*.
31. J.R. Dukes and J. Remak, eds., *Another Germany: A Reconsideration of the Imperial Era* (Boulder, CO, 1988); C. Lorenz, "Beyond Good and Evil? The German Empire of 1871 and Modern German Historiography," *Journal of Contemporary History* 30 (1995): 729–65; M. Kreuzer, "Parliamentarization and the Question of German Exceptionalism, 1867–1918," *Central European History* 36 (2003), 327–57 (cf. the mild rebukes from Jonathan Sperber and Kenneth Ledford, ibid. 359–74).
32. E.R. Dickinson, "The bourgeoisie and reform," in *Imperial Germany 1871–1918. The Short Oxford History of Germany*, ed. J. Retallack (Oxford, 2008), 151–73; K. Repp, *Reformers, Critics, and the Paths of German Modernity: Anti-politics and the Search for Alternatives, 1890–1914* (Cambridge, MA, 2000); A. Lees, *Cities, Sin, and Social Reform in Imperial Germany* (Ann Arbor, 2002).
33. D. Kerbs and J. Reulecke, *Handbuch der Deutschen Reformbewegungen 1880–1933* (Wuppertal, 1998); U. Puschner, W. Schmitz, and J.H. Ulbricht, eds., *Handbuch zur "Völkischen Bewegung" 1871–1918* (Munich, 1996).
34. See for example the unfortunate trans-Atlantic polemic over G. Eley, ed., *Society, Culture, and the State in Germany, 1870–1930* (Ann Arbor, 1996); H.-U. Wehler, "A Guide to Future Research on the Kaiserreich?" *Central European History* 29 (1996), 541–72; Eley, "Theory and the Kaiserreich. Problems With Culture: German History After the Linguistic Turn," *Central European History* 31 (1998): 197–227.
35. H. Rosenberg, *Große Depression und Bismarckzeit. Wirtschaftsablauf, Gesellschaft und Politik in Mitteleuropa* (Berlin, 1967), Chap. 4.
36. See inter alia Blackbourn, *Populists and Patricians*, 222.
37. E.g., Anderson, *Practicing Democracy*; cf. Suval, *Electoral Politics*; Fairbairn, *Democracy*; K. Rohe, *Wahlen und Wählertraditionen in Deutschland. Kulturelle Grundlagen deutscher Parteien und Parteiensysteme im 19. und 20. Jahrhundert* (Frankfurt a.M., 1992).
38. See T. Kühne, "From Electoral Campaigning to the Politics of Togetherness: Localism and Democracy," in Blackbourn and Retallack, eds., *Localism*, 101–23.
39. Friedrich Engels to August Bebel, 10 [–11] May 1883, in A. Bebel, *Aus meinem Leben*, 3rd ed. (Berlin-GDR, 1961), 822–23.
40. W.S. Allen, *The Nazi Seizure of Power: The Experience of a Single German Town, 1922–1945*, 2nd rev. ed. (New York, 1984). Cf. R. Chickering, "Political Mobilization and Associational Life: Some Thoughts on the National Socialist German Workers' Club (e.V.)," in *Elections, Mass Politics, and Social Change in Modern Germany*, eds. L.E. Jones and J. Retallack (Cambridge, 1992), 307–28.
41. Gustav Freytag to Duke Ernst von Coburg, 21/30 Jan. 1867, in *Gustav Freytag und Herzog Ernst von Coburg im Briefwechsel 1853 bis 1893*, ed. E. Tempeltey (Leipzig, 1904), 212–17.
42. Albeit with reference to Karl Lueger and Christian Socialism in Austria; C. Schorske, "Politics in a New Key: An Austrian Trio," *Journal of Modern History* 39 (1967), 343–86.

43. F. Naumann, *Demokratie und Kaisertum* (Berlin, 1900), 92f.; H. Rosenberg, "Die Pseudodemokratisierung der Rittergutsbesitzerklasse" [1958], in Rosenberg, *Probleme der deutschen Sozialgeschichte* (Frankfurt a.M., 1969), 11f.
44. See inter alia Wehler, *Gesellschaftsgeschichte*, 3:825.
45. D. Blackbourn, "New Legislatures: Germany, 1871–1914," *Historical Research* 65 (1992), 201–14; G. Eley, "Society and Politics in Bismarckian Germany," *German History* 15 (1997), 101–32, esp. 111, 121, 128; M.L. Anderson, "Voter, Junker, *Landrat*, Priest: The Old Authorities and the New Franchise in Imperial Germany," *American Historical Review* 98 (1993), 1448–74; H.W. Smith, *German Nationalism and Religious Conflict* (Princeton, 1995), esp. 113.
46. G. Eley, "Anti-Semitism, Agrarian Mobilization, and the Conservative Party: Radicalism and Containment in the Founding of the Agrarian League, 1890–93," in *Between Reform, Reaction, and Resistance: Studies in the History of German Conservatism from 1789 to 1945*, eds L.E. Jones and J. Retallack (Providence, RI, and Oxford, 1993), 194; Eley, "Notable Politics, the Crisis of German Liberalism, and the Electoral Transition of the 1890s," in *In Search of a Liberal Germany*, eds. K.H. Jarausch and L.E. Jones (New York, 1990), 192, 210–11; Eley, *Reshaping the German Right: Radical Nationalism and Political Change after Bismarck* (New Haven, 1980), 184–205.
47. A.P. Thompson, *Left Liberals, the State, and Popular Politics in Wilhelmine Germany* (Oxford, 2000), 21; A. Grießmer, *Massenverbände und Massenparteien im wilhelminischen Reich. Zum Wandel der Wahlkultur 1903–1912* (Düsseldorf, 2000), 49f.; H.-P. Goldberg, *Bismarck und seine Gegner. Die politische Rhetorik im kaiserlichen Reichstag* (Düsseldorf, 1998). Cf. H.W. Smith's contribution to "Forum. The Long Nineteenth Century," *German History* 26 (2008), 79f.
48. E. Rosenhaft, "Women, Gender, and the Limits of Political History in the Age of 'Mass' Politics," in Jones and Retallack, eds., *Elections*, 149–73.
49. See inter alia A. Süchting-Hänger, *Das "Gewissen der Nation." Nationales Engagement und politisches Handeln konservativer Frauenorganisationen 1900 bis 1937* (Düsseldorf, 2002); E. Schöck-Quinteros and C. Streubel, eds., *"Ihrem Volk verantwortlich." Frauen der politischen Rechten (1890–1933)* (Bremen, 2007); K. Heinsohn, *Konservative Parteien in Deutschland 1912 bis 1933. Demokratisierung und Partizipation in geschlechterhistorischer Perspektive* (Düsseldorf, 2009).
50. D. Langewiesche, *Politikstile im Kaiserreich. Zum Wandel von Politik und Öffentlichkeit im Zeitalter des "politischen Massenmarktes"* (Friedrichsruh, 2002); G.A. Ritter, ed., *Wahlen und Wahlkämpfe in Deutschland. Von den Anfängen im 19. Jahrhundert bis zur Bundesrepublik* (Düsseldorf, 1997); D. Dowe et al., eds., *Parteien im Wandel. Vom Kaiserreich zur Weimarer Republik* (Munich, 1999). The following reference to "taming" alludes to Peter Steinbach, *Die Zähmung des politischen Massenmarktes. Wahlen und Wahlkämpfe im Bismarckreich*, 3 vols. (Passau, 1990).

Chapter 6

Using Violence to Govern
The German Empire and the French Third Republic

Heinz-Gerhard Haupt

There is little in the historical literature on either the German Empire or the Third Republic on the structure of the violence within these countries. The parliament, developments in individual states and the structures of civil society are seen as significant, within the framework of a liberal interpretation of Germany from 1870–1918 and the development of its political culture, but not the structure of violence. Even in the cultural and political histories of the French Republic, the army and the police are not among the central actors. One of the reasons for the relative unimportance that both historiographies attentions assign to internal violence may be that "governance" in both societies took place under structurally similar conditions. In both countries, the process of state-building had largely been completed before these states were founded. In both France and Germany, the state had established a monopoly of legitimate physical violence; in both societies the development of police forces was well underway and the use or application of violence was illegal and was punished—inasmuch as this use of violence did not take place by order of or through state institutions.[1] Emphasizing the structural similarities, however, leads us away from the analytically interesting question, which is whether or not the monarchical form of government differed significantly from the republican in its relationship to political violence, and how both of these responded to various different manifestations of violence. For in both countries it was not only labor disputes that were violently fought; some of the conflicts associated with the separation of church and state were also accompanied by violence.[2] And both societies had to come to terms with terrorist attacks.

Some basic considerations concerning the fundamental nature of the political systems suggest that the republican society should have dealt with these challenges differently from monarchical Germany. Political participation was one of the founding principles of the republic—a political participation which went beyond simply protecting individual rights, but which emphasized that people had to use these rights. From this perspective, being educated to participate in political life was one of the central elements of republicanism, and anything which led to a violent exclusion from the political space was in conflict with these efforts. At the same time, however, as Pierre Rosanvallon has repeatedly emphasized, universal male suffrage, introduced in 1848, was, for Republicans, less an instrument with which to argue out conflicts of interests and more a symbol which represented political and social unity.[3] Placed in the discrepancy between cohesion and unity on the one hand, and social participation on the other, republican governments could either defend national unity against violent powers which threatened to divide society or choose to perceive the acts of violence as part of a legitimate political expression. In the June 1848 uprising, the government defended the republic against a social movement which had questioned the republic; with the amnesty in 1880 for those who had participated in the Paris Commune it appeared that the government was going to have understanding and sympathy for past acts of violence and not rigorously prosecute them.[4] In regard to both the idea of participation and of education as well as the perception of the political space and its attitude to past acts of violence, the policies of the authorities—to employ a concept of Hans-Ulrich Wehler—were different in the Third Republic from those in Germany. In Germany, the strategies traditional elites employed to rule set the tone, and social militarism predominated.[5]

Did the republic and the monarchy have a different understanding of political violence? To answer this question we need to look at the government's response to violent acts both in the Third Republic in France and in Germany. The answer is to be sought not only in the state response to violent acts, but also in the discursive strategies which established or negated the legitimacy of certain forms of violence. Accordingly, the following problems are at the center of this study:

1. How did the state authorities in France and in Germany respond to violent forms of conflict between workers and employers? How and when did the police, the gendarmerie and the army intervene? Were there differences between the two societies in regard to the frequency of actions, the threshold at which the state took action and the intent of the state actions? And if this was the case, how are we to explain them?
2. In both societies, the state's monopoly on violence was threatened by terrorist acts. Were these terrorist acts intended to be provocations with a propagandistic intent—as is suggested by the new research into terrorism—or are they instead better interpreted as declarations of war on the respective states? What methods and instruments did the state employ in both countries to fight these attacks, and what were the consequences of these actions for the structure and borders of the political space?

These questions address problems whose importance has been underlined by recent research into violence. This research has concentrated less on determining the motives and the causes of the violence and more on the forms of violence and the ways society dealt with it. This research locates acts of violence in the relationship between actors, victims, the audience, and society. The methodology of comparison, in this case comparing France and Germany, not only brings out national characteristics, it also helps us to better understand, analytically, the role of violence in the self-understanding of these two societies and these two states, who had two quite different forms of government. Special attention will be paid to the problem of whether or not the state's apparatus of violence was similarly developed in both societies, if and to what degree violence functioned as a means of reaching a settlement—in the sense of "bargaining by riot" (Eric J. Hobsbawm)— and whether or not already at the end of the nineteenth century the beginning of a development could be seen which has continued up to the present day, according to which in France violent forms of political arguments are more widespread in social conflicts and are also more widely accepted by the political actors. Furthermore, we will pay attention as well in a transnational perspective to the similarities which existed between the states fighting terrorism, so that the reactions of the individual nation-states can be better integrated into a broader context.[6]

The labor conflicts were especially numerous; they led repeatedly to violent conflicts between police forces and the strikers as well as between the police and corporate leaders. As the strikers were always suspected not only of pursuing their specific interests, but also of trying to change society as a whole—this was expected or feared from the working class as the revolutionary subject—the strikes were a neuralgic point in the system both in Germany and in France. Here was an important site for testing the waters, in terms of both weighing one's interests and achieving one's goals. What was involved here was to determine the degree of risk to public peace and order as well as to determine the necessity of using the military. Thus, the German government stated in an internal memo on 7 July 1904 that the military was to be employed "when one can assess, on the basis of past experience, that at the beginning of the strikes the composed demeanor of the working-class population will reach such a stage of ferment that it is to be feared that violent activities could take place to a much larger degree and that it is no longer likely that the civilian police will be able to rein in the passions."[7]

The terrorist attacks in both countries moved other forms of the use of violence to the forefront of the public's attention. In these other forms the violence was not usually undertaken by interest organizations, but rather by individuals, who the authorities then linked to existing or fictive associations. Terrorist violence made public appearances by the rulers potentially unsafe, as well as sites such as cafés or public squares. In this way the violence provoked a reaction from the state, which was responsible for peace and security. Whether or not the state's actions remained within the framework of the existing legal and constitutional order or whether or not they were exceptional will have to be examined by looking at individual cases.

If one accepts the results of the research done into the comparative history of strikes between 1899 and 1914, then the number of labor conflicts and of working days lost in them was much higher in Germany than in the Third Republic. According to Friedhelm Boll, Germany lost 4.6 million working days during these years, whereas France lost only 3.5 million. On average, 2.058 strikes per year took place in Germany, while there were only 976 in France. However, the number of participants per strike was on average higher in France, with 215 per strike, than it was on the other side of the Rhine, with 109. The length of the conflicts was on average higher in Germany at 21 days, whereas in France it was only 15 days. Germany's higher degree of industrialization and much more developed heavy industry are the reasons for these quite different numbers.[8]

Although the labor disputes in Germany were more numerous, lasted longer and had more of an economic impact than in France, they were also accompanied by less violence. According to the statistics (which are without a doubt in need of improvement) put together by Charles und Richard Tilly on violent protests in which at least twenty people participated and in which either people or material goods were damaged, there were 500 violent protests in France and only 214 in Germany.[9] Different social conditions are reflected in these numbers. On the one hand, one could perceive here confirmation of the thesis that the degree of violence in labor conflicts depends on the degree to which labor relations have been inscribed into law and to which there are corporatist structures of negotiation. The higher degree of peaceful and consensual resolution of labor conflicts in Germany before 1914 could point to a level of development of the welfare state and of the legal order that was more advanced than in France.[10] It can, however, also be the expression of a power relationship between capital and the working class which enabled employers in Germany to employ the lock-out to a much larger degree.[11] On the other hand, this difference can also be interpreted as the expression of the stronger acculturation of German workers in manners and behaviors which frowned on violence or even an expression of the German worker's faith in government, were there not the physical attacks against strike-breakers and the manifold forms of violence which Thomas Lindenberger has documented in his study of street politics in Berlin before 1914; Lindenberger's study speaks against this thesis.[12] Michelle Perrot has emphasized, for the period between 1867 and 1890 in France, how much the acceptance of the constraints of industrial labor itself, but also the experiences of the strikes, contributed to the fact that violent actions in labor conflicts remained relatively rare. According to her, violent labor actions occurred most often at the end of long labor conflicts and above all in the textile industry, in mining, and among diggers and excavators. Just like Lindenberger, Michelle Perrot emphasizes that violence among the workers themselves was much more common than conflicts with police forces, and that symbolic and verbal expressions of violence played an important role in their protest culture.[13]

Finally, one can see in these different national developments the soothing influence of German Social Democracy and the Free Trade Unions, who distanced themselves already during the Socialist Law from popular violence and who condemned violent actions. Thus, *Vorwärts* wrote on 15 April 1892 in regard to the terrorist attack by Ravachol: "given the disgust which the only revolutionary class, the proletariat, feels for such crimes and criminals, no one should ever think that the working class sympathizes with types like Ravachol and that it will follow men like him as their leaders. In contrast, the working class has a lively interest in shaking off this group, for it gives them a bad name." In France, socialists distanced themselves from violence as a means of politics as well. Yet the socialist organizations themselves were divided on this issue so that they would never have been able, before 1900, to have agreed on a single position. Above all, the socialists were not able to move the revolutionary syndicalists, who had set themselves the goal of a general strike, to reject violence, clearly and without reservations.[14] On this question the positions within the French working-class movement were more varied and widespread than in the German working-class movement.

Alongside the breadth of violence, there were also differences in regard to the manner of fighting violence. As violent acts in France produced more victims than in Germany—39 protesters and five policemen died in France, 19 protesters and two policemen died in Germany—a look at the state's monopoly on violence is necessary. This monopoly was more pronounced in France than it was in Prussia, which here shall stand, *pars pro toto*, for Germany. In 1907 there were 26.000 French policemen, whereas there were only 5.597 in Prussia, although the number of local policemen in both societies increased significantly toward the end of the nineteenth century; as a rule, however, the number was higher in the French cities than in the Prussian.[15]

If one wanted to interpret the use of the military in labor conflicts as a consequence of the lack of police forces, then one could surmise that Germany probably used the military more often than did the Third Republic. This, however, was not the case. Rather, in her study Anja Johannsen comes to the conclusion that the civilian authorities in France used the military much more often and for a longer period than was the case in Prussia. Although there were exceptions, Prussian authorities generally hesitated to call in the troops. Behind these different approaches were different experiences and strategies of ruling. In the French case, it is clear that the French authorities were afraid that local unrest could get quickly out of control—the memory of the Parisian Commune was very strong—and accordingly, such unrest had to be restrained quite early on through repressive measures. The authorities' actions were characterized by the logic of prevention. The presence of the military was supposed to have an educating and soothing effect. In contrast, the Prussian authorities only called in the military as a last resort. When called in, however, the Prussian military was rarely inactive. Whether or not these different strategies led to different forms of violence needs to be investigated concretely.[16] It is likely that the massive military presence in the Third Republic not only had a soothing effect, but that it also provoked violent reactions. The historical research into protests has repeatedly pointed out this dialectic of repression.[17]

The Third Republic as well as the German Empire experienced at different times similar waves of terrorist attacks. After the two attacks on Emperor

Wilhelm I, which the government used to pass the Anti-Socialist Law, the next few years saw many acts of terrorist violence—above all in 1882 with the murder of the shoe manufacturer, Merstallinger. The violence continued in the following years with, for example, a failed bomb attack at the dedication of the Niederwald memorial. The terrorist violence reached its peak with the murder of the Frankfurt policeman Rumpf, who was known as the "Anarchist eater."[18] In France, the years between 1892 and 1894 saw many terrorist attacks. These were associated not only with the name Ravachol, who attempted to murder judges, but also with Henry, who threw a bomb into the Café Terminus at the Gare St. Lazare. On 24 June 1894 Caserio murdered the French President Sidi Carnot in Lyon. All in all, nine people were murdered in France in eleven dynamite bombings.[19] The wave of terror in France was larger than it was in Germany.

In spite of these differences, there were a number of similarities in regard to the terrorist attacks. In both countries, the individual terror, carried out and legitimated by anarchists, remained limited to a certain historical period. In both countries, disappointed socialists, who did not agree with the legalistic course of the socialist party or parties, no longer counted on a collective uprising, but rather believed in the symbolic value of individual acts of terror. The murder of Tsar Alexander II served here as a positive example. Both in Germany as well as in France, those socialists with a terrorist orientation remained an extremely small minority in the working-class movement and quickly lost their political influence after the terrorist attacks.[20]

Both governments counted not only on national measures to fight terrorism; they also attempted to organize international measures. In the German Interior Ministry, extensive dossiers were set up on "The State of the Anarchist Movement Abroad and the Efforts to Combat It," which not only tracked the legal developments in France and Spain, but also in the United States, Argentina, and Mexico. Terrorism was seen not as a national but rather as an international phenomenon.[21] Thus, the *Hamburger Nachrichten* wrote on 12 December 1892: "given that anarchism has international branches, one has to consider the international struggle against anarchism as the most important precondition of any genuine success." The international cooperation of the police was to be accompanied by a tightening of internal security. The German ambassador in Paris, Graf Münster, commented with satisfaction on the harsher laws in France: "the energetic efforts of the government have made a good impression. This is seen as a good beginning, one worthy of being imitated in the fight against anarchism" (12 December 1893).[22] It was therefore not an accident that Germany and France belonged to the hardliners in the international anti-anarchist conference in 1898, demanding extradition, the sharing of information, and standardized mug shots.[23]

In spite of the international cooperation and transnational surveillance, the responses to terrorist attacks differed in each country. This can be seen both in the legal and in the public discussions. In Germany, fighting terrorism took place within the framework of an Anti-Socialist Law, a Special Law against the "efforts constituting a public danger of Social Democracy"; the Special Law was renewed a number of times. This strategy allowed the authorities to link the goals and methods of Social Democracy with those of the anarchist terrorists and to justify the continuing prosecution of the Social Democrats. This Special Law was itself based on provisions in the criminal law code: either on §130 of the penal code, which provided for fines and terms of imprisonment for those who "incite the different classes in our population to violence against each other in a way which endangers the public peace and order," or on §86, which set the framework for the prosecution of an action in preparation of a traitorous enterprise.[24] In 1881, the German Supreme Court, established in 1879, based its decision in the trial proceedings against Dave and comrades on these last paragraphs. Although the court carefully examined whether individuals had actually belonged to the group of "traitors," and found some individuals not guilty, the court found Dave and his comrades guilty. Working on the basis of the ideas of Johann Most, the court perceived an act of high treason already in the fact that Most had formed a group: "the formation of groups is, according to the evidence of the history of revolutions, a suitable means to prepare for violent modifications of the constitution and has been chosen for this purpose by Most and is accepted by the majority of the members."[25] Not so much the concrete goals of the group or the actions of the members of the group were at the center of the court's attention; rather, the court focused on the revolutionary purpose, which was seen in the group's very existence.

In France, the authorities and the courts attempted to bring the terrorists to justice within the framework of the existing criminal law. When, however, in the so-called "trial of the thirty," the court had to decide about both anarchist activists as well as the allegation that the accused were members of a criminal association, the evidence was so patchy that twenty-seven of the thirty accused were found innocent. Only in 1893, in the final terrorist phase, were three laws, which critical journalists called *"lois scélérates,"* pushed through parliament, disregarding parliamentary procedure. These three laws forbade newspapers to incite to violence or to legitimate or justify violent acts. Criminal associations were to be punished, not just criminal acts. Associations were considered criminal if they put forth anarchistic propaganda.[26] The boundaries between criminal acts and criminal ideas became blurred. In contrast to the prosecution of terrorists on the basis of existing Special Laws—as in Germany—this intensification of criminal legislation took place after the anarchist's actions. In both societies state strategy made not only the criminal prosecution of potential terrorist activists possible, but also initiated preventive actions.

Both in Germany and in France, the public responded to the terrorist attacks. In Germany the public tended to blur the distinction between Social Democracy and terrorism, whereas in France the socialists actively participated in a broad criticism of terrorist activities. In the most recent discussions on violence, influenced by the "cultural studies" in Great Britain, historians and social scientists have introduced the concept of "moral panics" for this reaction. Stanley Cohen sees "moral panics" as a phenomenon which took place during business cycles, in which events, people, or groups were presented and discredited by the media as a danger to society.[27] It is indeed possible—as Kenneth Thompson has emphasized—to differentiate in moral panics between the danger to society and the danger to individuals. The discrimination of a person or of a group is often tied up with the media's representation of a threat to the public: "There should be a high level of 'concern' over the behaviour of a certain group or category of people and that there is an increased level of hostility toward the group or category regarded as a threat."[28]

The media's representation of dangers and enemies can be influenced by certain groups, by "influential claim-makers, each with a set of interests or a political agenda."[29] This approach allows us to investigate public discourses in regard to central patterns of presentation and to name the actors who were responsible for these public images. The historical research on both countries has not yet advanced far enough to allow us to reach fully reliable conclusions. It appears, however, that in Germany the terrorists were instrumentalized for a "moral panic" against alleged social revolutionaries, whereas in France the press stirred up a hysterical fear of future violent acts.[30] Further research should look carefully at the initiators of moral panics, on the message and its staging within the political public sphere, and on how the messages of the respective threats were received.

In light of the foregoing, it cannot be claimed that the republic and the monarchy differed greatly in their use of violence. Protecting peace and order, as well as defending the state's monopoly on violence, were central components of the respective policies of both forms of government. Beneath this level of general consensus, however, there were clearly differences between the republican form of government and the monarchical, which were especially important in regard to how citizens could shape their own lives and take political action. Using the military against strikers had in the Third Republic an educational, preventive purpose, whereas in Germany it had more of a repressive character. In the pursuit of terrorists, the French justice system remained within the framework of the existing criminal law and did—at least for a certain time—not fall back on the Exceptional Laws of an authoritarian state. In France, in the public discussion concerning the terrorist acts, it was the violence and less the condemnation of the political position that was more at the center of the discussion; the expressions of fear in the press concentrated more on worries about injuries to individual citizens than on dangers to general state and social values. Beyond this, the questions asked above will help us determine the similarities and differences between the principles underlying the construction of political space in Germany and in the Third Republic in France.

For the German Empire, which is the focus of this collection of essays, the results of our comparison speak against too liberal an interpretation of the German development. The state's monopoly of violence was not only continually expanded; this monopoly, when used, was used with force. The threats, both real and imagined, repeatedly provided the state with the opportunity to limit civil rights in regard to personal liberty and the right to participate in politics, and supplied fuel for the repression carried out against Social Democracy.

Notes

1. W. Knöbl, *Polizei und Herrschaft im Modernisierungsprozeß. Staatsbildung und innere Sicherheit in Preußen, England und Amerika 1700–1914* (Frankfurt, 1998).
2. M. Borutta, "Pflanzstätten des Aberglaubens, der Dummheit und des Verbrechens: Moabiter Klostersturm und deutscher Kulturkampf," *Comparativ* 12 (2002), 63–80; J.-P. Chantin and D. Moulinet, eds., *La séparation de 1905. Les hommes et les lieux* (Paris, 2005); C. Clark and W. Kaiser, eds., *Culture Wars. Secular-Catholic Conflict in Nineteenth-Century Europe* (Cambridge, 2003).
3. P. Rosanvallon, *La démocratie inachevée: histoire de la souveraineté du peuple en France* (Paris, 2002).
4. C. Latta, ed., *La commune de 1871: l'évènemnet, les hommes et la mémoire* (St. Etienne, 2004); P. Starr, *Commemorating Trauma: The Paris Commune and Its Cultural Aftermath* (New York, 2006).
5. Cf. H.-U. Wehler, *Das Deutsche Kaiserreich.1871–1918* (Göttingen, 1973); idem., *Deutsche Gesellschaftsgeschichte*, Vol. 3 (Munich, 1995).
6. Cf. H.-G. Haupt, "Comparative History – a Contested Method," *Historisk Tidskrift* 4 (2007), 697–716; B. Anderson, *Under Three Flags. Anarchism and the Anti-Colonial Imagination* (London, 2005).
7. A. Funk, *Polizei und Rechtsstaat. Die Entwicklung des staatlichen Gewaltmonopols in Preußen 1848–1914* (Frankfurt, 1986), quote 310.
8. F. Boll, *Arbeitskämpfe und Gewerkschaften in Deutschland, England und Frankreich. Ihre Entwicklung vom 19. zum 20. Jahrhundert* (Bonn, 1992), 101.
9. C. Tilly, *The Rebellious Century* (Cambridge, 1975), 62, 212.
10. Cf. G.A. Ritter, *Der Sozialstaat. Entstehung und Entwicklung im internationalen Vergleich* (Munich, 1991).
11. Cf. Boll, *Arbeitskämpfe*, 109.
12. T. Lindenberger, *Straßenpolitik. Zur Sozialgeschichte der öffentlichen Ordnung in Berlin 1900–1914* (Bonn, 1995).
13. M. Perrot, *Jeunesse de la grève. 1871–1890* (Paris, 1984), 568.
14. J. Juillard, *Fernand Pelloutier et les origines du syndicalisme d'action directe* (Paris, 1971); G. Heuré, *Gustave Hervé, itinéraire d'un provocateur* (Paris, 1997).
15. Cf. A. Johansen, "Policing and Repression: Military Involvement in the Policing of French and German Industrial Areas, 1889–1914," *European History Quarterly* 34 (2004), 69–98; idem., "A Process of Civilisation? Legitimisation of Violent Policing in Prussia and French Police Manuals and Instructions 1880–1914," *European Review of History* 14 (2007), 49–71.
16. Cf. A. Johansen, *Soldiers as Police. The French and Prussian Armies and the Policing of Popular Protest, 1889–1914* (Aldershot, 2005); R. Jessen, *Polizei im Industrierevier. Modernisierung und Herrschaftspraxis im westfälischen Ruhrgebiet 1848–1914* (Göttingen, 1991).
17. C. Tilly, *The Politics of Collective Violence* (Cambridge, 2003).
18. R. Jessen, "Daggers, Rifles and Dynamite: Anarchist Terrorism in Nineteenth Century Europe," *Terrorism and Political Violence* 16 (2004), 116–53; U. Linse, "Propaganda by the Deed and Direct Action, two Concepts of Anarchist Violence," in *Social Protest, Violence and Terror in Nineteenth Century Europe*, eds. W.J. Mommsen and G. Hirschfeld (London, 1982), 201–29.
19. J. Maitron, *Le mouvement anarchiste en France*, 2 vol. (Paris, 1975), vol. 1, 75–85, 151–250; idem., *Ravachol et les anarchistes* (Paris, 1992).
20. M. Fleming, "Propaganda by the Deed. Terrorism and Anarchist Theory in late Nineteenth-Century Europe," *Terrorism. An International Journal* 4 (1980), 1–23. Cf. the interesting approach by A. Sedlmaier, "The Consuming Visions in Late Nineteenth and Early Twentieth Century

Anarchists: Actualizing Political Violence Transnationally," *European Review of History* 14 (2007), 283–300.
21. Berlin. Bundesarchiv. Reichsministerium des Inneren R 13581 / 7 – Stand des Anarchismus im Auslande (1886–1909).
22. Berlin. Bundesarchiv. R 13581 Graf von Münster to Caprivi, 12 December 1893.
23. R.B. Jensen, "The International Anti-Anarchist Conference of 1898 and the Origins of Interpol," *Journal of Contemporary History* 16 (1981), 323–47.
24. Cf. D. Blasius, *Geschichte der politischen Kriminalität in Deutschland, 1880–1980. Eine Studie zu Justiz- und Staatsverbrechen* (Frankfurt, 1983); J. Wagner, *Politischer Terrorismus und Strafrecht im Deutschen Kaiserreich von 1871* (Hamburg, 1981).
25. Cf. Blasius, *Geschichte*, 341.
26. Cf. Maitron, *Mouvement*, 252.
27. S. Cohen, *Folk Devils and Moral Panics* (London, 1972), 9.
28. K. Thompson, *Moral Panics* (London, 2001), 9.
29. Thompson, *Moral Panics*, 15.
30. Cf. Maitron, *Mouvement*, 257; F. Chauvand, *De Pierre Rivière à Landru. La violence apprivoisée au XIXe siècle* (Paris, 1991); A. Owzar, *Reden ist Silber, Schweigen ist Gold. Konfliktmanagement im Alltag des wilhelminischen Obrigkeitsstaates* (Konstanz, 2006).

Chapter 7

Women's Suffrage and Antifeminism as a Litmus Test of Modernizing Societies
A Western European Comparison

Ute Planert

How "modern" was the German Empire in comparison to other European countries? How willing was it to undertake necessary reforms? The answer to these questions has changed considerably during the last few years. While some authors still include the German Empire as part of Europe's "conservative east,"[1] from the perspective of comparative social history the German *Sonderweg* has merged into the variety of European paths of development.[2] Although Hans-Ulrich Wehler still holds with verve to his stimulating formula of the German *Sonderweg*, he has acknowledged considerable modernizing successes during the German Empire. Nevertheless, the doyen of German social history attests the state a considerable series of deficiencies, including society's inability to "loosen the traditional definitions of gender roles."[3]

On this point, August Bebel would have strongly disagreed. No other movement, stated the author of the bestseller *Die Frau und der Sozialismus* (The Woman and Socialism) in 1909, "has achieved such positive results in such a short time."[4] The leader of the National Liberal Party, Ernst Bassermann, was also convinced that in the years before World War I the women's movement had become a "powerful actor in public life."[5]

Since these appraisals differ considerably from older conceptions of Imperial Germany's fossilized political landscape, this chapter will compare the response to women's claims for suffrage in Great Britain, France and the German Empire. My criteria for measuring a society's willingness to undertake political reforms are not just the degree of organization of the respective women's movements, but also their significance within society, as well as the importance and influence of their opponents. My thesis is that anti-feminist movements should not be understood as evidence of a tendency to reject political modernization. Instead, the generation of defensive strategies indicates a society in motion. With regard to the level of female participation in politics, it appears that Germany was no more backward than its Western European neighbors. However, whereas anti-feminist currents in other countries were often accompanied by nationalistic chauvinism, only in Germany did anti-Semitism and antifeminism enter into a symbiotic relationship.

1. Antifeminism and Social Change

Throughout the Western world, debate on the legal and political position of women intensified after the turn of the twentieth century, not only in Germany but also in Great Britain, France, and many other countries. During the second half of the nineteenth century, women's movements focused on improving opportunities in education and in the professions. When slowly but surely the question of political participation moved to the forefront, the calls for political participation were met with both support and resistance. In Great Britain, an antisuffrage league was founded, inspiring the formation of a broader antifeminist organization in Germany a few years later.[6] In France, political discussions and decisions were apparently influenced by antifeminist sentiments without leading to formal organization. This comparative study aims to understand the reason for, and the significance of, western societies' developments for these divergent reactions to a common challenge.[7]

The starting point here is the recognition that the structure and strength of antifeminist movements can serve as a reliable indicator of social change. In many European countries, women obtained the ballot during periods of warfare and political upheaval. Hence older works have tended to understand enfranchisement as a gift of revolution or a reward for women's war assistance. Yet this approach neglects the centuries-old struggle for equal rights and opportunities as well as the dynamics of social change besides revolutionary upheavals and disruptions. On the other hand, the comparison between France, Great Britain, and Germany shows that the sheer size of women's organizations does not supply us with sufficient information concerning their influence and strength. Antifeminist movements, however, can serve as a litmus test and measuring tool, and allow us to develop appropriate categories with which to judge societies' willingness to undertake reform.[8] From their social and political composition, we can infer not only the strength of resistance and hence women's movements' chances for success, but also the political mentalities of the respective states. By comparing Imperial Germany's development with that of other nations, the question of the Kaiserreich's ability to reform itself can be re-examined, without, however, losing sight of the specific character of the German path. All in all, the comparative perspective demonstrates that the existence of antifeminist movements is not indicative of a society's backwardness. Instead, it represents an indicator of social change.

The International Debate on Women's Suffrage

In order to understand the foundations of antisuffrage and antifeminist efforts in their respective national contexts, this essay will first give a short survey of the debate on women's political rights conducted in all Western societies, before taking a closer look at the gradual and partial realization of these demands in Great Britain, Germany, and France. Before World War I, no society granted full female suffrage. However, considerable advances had been made in all three societies through the admittance of women to a number of boards of welfare institutions, urban committees, and public bodies.

Nevertheless, neither the independence of the United States nor the Age of Revolution in Europe had brought considerable advances in granting political and legal equality. Instead, the question of civic rights receded, not only in the respective societies as a whole, but also on the agenda of women's organizations. Given the enormous economic and social upheavals of the early nineteenth century, priority was given to improving women's educational and professional opportunities, as well as to fighting female poverty. When women's organizations were institutionalized on a great scale in most European countries between the 1860s and the 1880s, they primarily worked to improve women's position in both family and civil law. However, when male suffrage was being extended toward the end of the nineteenth century, the experience of political powerlessness led to a renewed awareness of the significance of women's suffrage. Since the women's movements had formed ever stronger transnational networks through conferences and personal and organizational contacts, the examples of other states played an increasingly important role in national discussions. After 1900 the debate on female suffrage was, in all Western societies, once again firmly on the political agenda.[9]

Great Britain acted as Europe's front-runner. In the course of the nineteenth century, suffrage, which had always been bound to property qualifications, was extended to an ever larger group of male citizens. The intense battles and debates over male suffrage provided the stage for female voting rights activists and their male supporters, who repeatedly raised the question of female suffrage in endless debates. English women's organizations had pushed for the right to vote as early as the mid-1860s. From 1869 female taxpayers in England and Wales could participate in communal elections—a right explicitly denied to them in the Reform Act of 1832. Three years later, however, this right was restricted to unmarried women. Between 1870 and 1894 women were admitted to the boards of school administrations and the poor relief boards, as well as to district and church councils, and from 1907 they were even allowed to vote for city and district councillors.[10] For many supporters of female suffrage, it was clear that the political participation of women at the local level represented a down payment on the general right of women to vote in the state as a whole.

In the 1880s women became involved in party politics, both with Whigs and Tories. The British House of Commons repeatedly addressed numerous motions proposing female suffrage, each slightly different. By the outbreak of World War I, more than thirty such bills were under discussion in parliament. On five separate occasions a majority for such a bill was secured, only for the legislation to be blocked by rules of procedure. It took the emergence of the Labour Party to impose decisive advances, since the new political actor broke up the back and forth between the Whigs and the Tories which had characterized British politics for centuries. To be sure, the Labour Party's leadership only slowly brought itself to support female suffrage, but now the women's associations had a further potential ally alongside the hitherto ambivalent Liberals.

When the Liberal government again raised the question of universal male suffrage in 1912, Labour decided to vote in favor of these plans on the condition that women were also included. As a result, the suffragettes annulled their disappointing alliance with the Liberals and opened negotiations with the Conservatives, proposing to reject universal male suffrage in favor of extending limited suffrage to upper-class women. As a result, at the beginning of World War I, the governing Liberal Party was under pressure from two sides. Finally, the all-party coalition which guided Great Britain through the war agreed upon a compromise and in 1918 passed a law granting universal male suffrage. Women were only partially enfranchised; they had to be over 30 years old, married to an enfranchised man, head of their household or an academic. The rest of Britain's female population, including many former munitionettes, had to wait until 1928 to receive the vote.[11]

Whereas in Great Britain the gradual expansion of male suffrage kept the question of political participation permanently on the agenda—and in so doing helped move along the debate on the emancipation of women—the prompt adoption of universal male suffrage following the founding of the German Empire meant that such a debate rarely came up in Germany. The efforts of the bourgeois women's movement to solve the "bread question" were well received, but hopes that women might participate in the "dawn of a new age"[12] and make advances in both education and the professions were in vain. In fact, in 1900 the newly adopted Civil Code discriminated more strongly against women's civil and marriage rights than had been the case in many of the older legal codes. Furthermore, women had been debarred from political activity in Prussia since the failed revolution of 1848–49, a prohibition that was only revoked as a by-product of a law governing associations passed in 1908.[13]

The 1908 law set the starting point for the feminization of Germany's party politics and irrevocably changed the political landscape. Previously, only the Social Democrats had attempted to organize their female supporters. Indeed, the social democratic leadership, more progressive than their own party base, had been calling for women's suffrage since 1891. However, after 1908 the other parties were forced to adapt to the new political realities. They quickly began, one after the other, to accept female members. By 1913 not only the left-wing and the Liberal parties, but also the Centre Party and the German Conservative Party, had their own women's organizations. These women's organizations pressed to have their voice heard, aiming at first to integrate women into church and district politics—as a gradual development. During World War I, women did increasingly participate in municipal institutions; indeed, in some states they already had the right to participate in decision-making. Even in Prussia, women were given the right to vote in welfare and school commissions before the war had ended.[14]

The Kaiser's Easter Proclamation in 1917 gave a broad impetus to a debate on parliamentarization. The so-called "women's question" profited from these discussions, although it was not explicitly mentioned. Even the German Fatherland Party, on the far right, now sought support from women. For the first time, the large Bund Deutscher Frauenvereine (Federation of German Women's Associations) moved away from its tactical reserve vis-à-vis women's suffrage, that had—apart from opposition in some of its branch associations—for the main part been motivated by political considerations. The cooperation with bourgeois and Social Democratic women in the Nationalen Frauendienst (National Women's Service) during the war had made it easier for moderate feminists to cooperate politically, something that they had previously viewed with scepticism, at least at the federal level. In 1918 the Bund Deutscher Frauenvereine, with its half a million members, and the Social Democratic women's organizations unanimously demanded civic rights for women in an attempt to gain influence in the restructuring process of German politics beyond class and party borders after the war. To be sure, just as with the introduction of the universal male suffrage, the crucial steps were not taken slowly. Instead, success was achieved through a political cataclysm. The dynamics of the developments after 1908 and the rapid acceptance of universal female suffrage in all the parliamentarian camps of the early Weimar Republic suggest, however, that the decisive factors—a general trend toward parliamentarization, pressure from women's associations across party lines and the parties' own interests—were in place and that sooner or later, even without a revolution, perhaps through the path of local government, the women's movement would have been successful.[15]

In France too, at the beginning of the twentieth century, the women's movement made advances. The celebrations commemorating the hundredth anniversary of the Code Napoléon politicized French women, making them more aware of how they were discriminated against in civil law. In the following years, women's position in family law was gradually improved. Single mothers, for example, were granted the right to be the guardians of their children, and married women were allowed to dispose of their own income. By 1908 women had achieved the right to vote for positions in chambers of commerce, professional associations and commercial courts. At the level of the departments, school commissions also started to elect female members.[16]

In the National Assembly around a third of the approximately six hundred members joined the Groupe parlementaire de défense de droits de la femme (Parliamentary Group for the Defense of Women's Rights), an informal association that aimed to advance women's legal position. As early as 1906 a law was proposed to introduce female suffrage for communal elections, but it was never passed. The factions of the bourgeois women's movement, previously divided, unanimously agreed in 1908 to support female suffrage. A year later, an extensive report in parliament opted in favor of political equality. Since the legal situation was left unchanged, half a million French women placed a symbolic ballot in the boxes during the 1914 parliament elections.

As on the other side of the Channel, French women's movements used contemporary debates on male voting rights for their own purposes. However, it soon became clear that even pro-feminist members of parliament were not ready to endanger the complicated and difficult reform of the intensely discussed proportional representation suffrage system by linking it to female suffrage. The question of political equality was postponed and was only taken up again after the war, even though French Justice Minister Viviani had in 1917 given women hope that the right to participate in communal elections would soon be introduced. In 1919 a majority of the members of parliament voted in favor of universal female suffrage, citing what women had done during the war and referring to the example of other states. Yet, the resolution had neither the support of France's postwar governments nor of the mighty Senate. After being delayed for a long time, the Senate ultimately rejected the proposal.[17]

All in all, up till World War I, the situation in the Western European states did not differ significantly in terms of female suffrage. Everywhere women's rights associations were united behind the issue of voting rights—even if they may have differed in details—and everywhere they linked their demands to ongoing debates. In all countries there was progress below the threshold of national representation. At the local or regional level, more and more women were able to participate in public bodies. And everywhere women's growing influence on party politics as well as the parties' own self-interest proved to be a decisive motor of change.

2. The Opponents' Arguments

Accordingly, the arguments put forward by the opponents of women's emancipation differed little in the three countries. From London to Paris to Berlin, opponents argued that, as assumedly could be seen from their physique, nature has made men and women for different tasks. Transgressing natural boundaries would lead to degeneration and chaos. A woman's holy destiny was to be a mother. If women were to become politicized, the home and the family, and ultimately the state, would be destroyed. Their emotionality made them incapable of making rational political decisions, while physically they were unable to perform demanding activities. Furthermore, a state governed by women, held the opponents of gender equality, would be incapable of surviving in the natural competition between the nations, not to mention that it would be unable to make a claim to world power and to rule colonies.[18]

This mixture of a Christian ideology of motherhood, pseudo-scientific biology and imperialistic masculinity was found throughout Europe. The prevalence of this argument is evidence of the ubiquity and the power of the medical-scientific discourse. It shows furthermore the continuing importance of Christian traditions and demonstrates the strong imperialistic bias of the three prewar societies under investigation. Yet, the monolithic lack of differentiation makes it difficult to situate the ubiquitous antifeminist discourse in any one place. A pure discourse analysis does not bring us much further, for it conceals significant differences in the political and social spheres of the respective countries. Instead, a closer look at the composition of the antifeminist opposition could be used as a key to judge the assertiveness of antifeminist concepts and thus, in reverse, the ability of the respective societies to adapt to new challenges.

3. Antifeminism in Western Europe

There were opponents of women's emancipation in all political camps. Antifeminism was not just a specific characteristic of conservatives or the political right. It could be found among Liberal and Social Democratic groups as well as in the trade unions, although with quite different characteristics and frequency.[19] In Europe, however, only in Great Britain and in Germany did the opponents of the women's movement feel that it was necessary to found their own organizations to defend their interests. In both cases it was the fear of women's suffrage which mobilized opponents. In the Third Republic there was no such association—a clear hint that in France granting women the right to vote was not on the political agenda in the years before World War I.

3.1 Great Britain

Great Britain's Antisuffrage League was at the forefront of antifeminist movements in Europe. Extending communal voting rights to women in 1869 and the echo throughout the world to John Stewart Mill's passionate plea against the "subjection of women" brought the British opponents of women's suffrage out in full force. The opponents' arena was, alongside newspaper columns and petitions, above all the House of Commons. In 1875, a cross-party "Committee for Maintaining the Integrity of the Franchise" was formed. On top of that, two thousand signatures collected in 1889 provided evidence that popular opposition to female suffrage could easily be mobilized through the conservative Primrose League. Despite this, antifeminist activities declined and the cross-party committee was dissolved after a couple of years, as the influence of the British women's organizations receded and feminist motions introduced in the House of Commons declined significantly by the end of the nineteenth century.

Things started to pick up again after the turn of the century. In 1906, when the Liberal Party came to power and the workers' movement had developed its own parliamentary representation in the Labour Party, many opponents of emancipation feared the worst. Indeed, many more Liberal members of parliament did come out in favor of women's suffrage, whereas the party leadership adhered to an antisuffragette position. In the meantime, the Labour Party flirted with the militant wing of the women's movement. Unlike the majority of the constitutionalists, the suffragettes did not want to accept a voting law which merely extended the class barriers of male suffrage to women. Acts of civil disobedience reinforced their demand for equal suffrage.

Against this background, many opponents of women's suffrage started once again to write articles in the larger English newspapers, and they submitted a petition against the extension of the franchise to women with forty thousand signatures to the House of Commons. In order to give more substance to the campaign, the Women's National Anti-Suffrage League was formed in 1908. By the end of the year, the all-female association was joined by a Men's Committee whose members came largely from the milieu of the parliamentarian opponents of female suffrage. When the two branches united, the antifeminists had over twenty-two thousand members and by 1914 they had extended the number of supporters to forty-two thousand. They were organized into about 290 branches. These were concentrated mainly in the southwest of England, but there were also branches in Scotland, Wales and Northern Ireland. The league sought publicity through articles in *The Times* and public demonstrations, and they were able to collect over three hundred thousand signatures against the introduction of women's suffrage in parliament.[20]

Some 85 percent of the members of the antisuffrage association were women. Influential ladies of the London society belonged to the League, alongside social reformers such as Violet Markham and authors such as Mrs Humphry Ward, who would later become a war reporter. All of them used their well-attended salons to exert political influence. Even the wife of the Liberal Prime Minister, Asquith, joined the association. She was, "if that is at all possible, an even more bitter opponent of female suffrage than he was himself."[21] As is shown by the case of Gertrude Bell, a famous explorer who played an important role in the reorganization of the Near East in her role as a liaison officer of the British Secret Service after World War I, neither professional independence nor an unusual biography meant that one could not oppose women's suffrage.

The association's agenda was, however, not determined by the female members, who, although they were in the majority, spent most of their efforts canvassing for new followers. Instead, the agenda was set by a small, very elite group of male members who sought donations and political support in their exclusive circles. Donations came from the nobility and from the City, and also, in a similar manner to the United States, from the brewing industry, which feared the influence of the women-dominated temperance organizations.

Politically, the activities of the association were shaped by two former colonial politicians, Lord Cromer and Lord Curzon. They established contacts with members of parliament and used their extensive networks in order to raise money for the antifeminist league. Up till 1916, Cromer had been Consul-General in Egypt. Curzon was Viceroy and Governor-General in India until 1905 and was afterwards installed as chancellor of the University of Oxford. Curzon was a Tory

MP, while Cromer belonged to the Unionist Party, which had split from the Liberal Party over the question of Irish Home Rule and merged with the Conservative Party in 1912. The two leading men were paradigmatic not only in regard to their party allegiances but also in regard to their occupation. Many of those in Great Britain opposed to women's rights were imperialists, working in the colonial administration. There were also numerous military men and noble names, a disproportionate percentage of peers and their wives, and on top of that an illustrious network of former Oxford graduates, who met repeatedly in the exclusive, men-only London clubs. Taken as a whole, the opponents were a collection of elderly "rich and titled people,"[22] whose political ideas were stuck in the Victorian Age.

British antifeminism was fed essentially by the opposition of the closely knit and interrelated British upper class, who in their majority thought in traditional categories and fought against any extension of voting rights beyond the higher ranks of society. Announcements to recruit members of the lower classes were most likely rhetorical, given the level of membership fees. Although activists did not shy away from introducing motions in parliament, from distributing questionnaires, and from writing occasional articles for the press, the emphasis of political work was less on winning the public than on exerting personal influence behind the scenes. The British Anti-Suffrage League was largely an organization of honorables, who had not yet adapted to the conditions of modern mass communication. Consequently, it disappeared from the political stage during World War I.[23]

3.2 Germany

As in Britain, those with doctoral and noble titles were also disproportionately represented among the ranks of the German antifeminists. Yet the backbone of their organization was not in high society, but rather in the predominantly middle-class networks of the nationalist opposition.

The German antifeminist association was composed above all of members of the national and the *völkisch* movements. The associates who joined ranged from the Pan German League to the Deutschbund (German League), from the Gobineau-Gesellschaft (Gobineau Society) to the Reichshammerbund (Reich Hammer League), the Gesellschaft für Rassenhygiene (German Society for Racial Hygiene) and the Verband gegen die Überhebung des Judentums (Society against the Presumption of Jewry) on to the deutschvölkischen Schutz- und Trutzbund (German Nationalist Protection and Defiance Federation). Conservative, National Liberal and *völkisch* members of parliament also took part. On top of this, the antifeminist association received support from orthodox Lutherans and from a series of professional associations whose members believed they were suffering from the new female competition. These included teacher and student organizations as well as associations of clerks, paralegals and salesmen, railway officials, post office employees and veterans hoping for positions in public service that were slowly but surely being infiltrated by female clerks.

The most important functionaries of the so-called Bund zur Bekämpfung der Frauenemanzipation (Alliance for the Combat of Women's Emancipation) were civil servants, largely from the ministries, along with professors, teachers, and ministers—in short the upper, public sector bourgeoisie. These members were overwhelmingly male and many of them saw themselves as the guardians of German culture. The broad mass of the antifeminists, however, wore more petit-bourgeois clothing. The Verband der Militäranwärter (Alliance of the Military Aspirants) and the Deutschnationale Handlungsgehilfenverband (German National Clerks Association), with its one hundred and forty thousand members, joined the antifeminist league as a group. Unlike Great Britain, in Germany women were clearly underrepresented among the antifeminist members although about a quarter of the functionaries were women, often with a background in welfare or clerical organizations.

In contrast to their English model, the German antifeminist league was unable to count any governors or Prime Ministers among its members. The German league had to make do without the networks of influence centered on the clubs of Westminster or the salons of the London nobility. With only a few exceptions, there were also no prominent deputies from the established parties. However, unlike the British honorable organizations, the German antifeminists were better adapted to the conditions of modern mass society. There were numerous journalists and teachers among their followers. In the Berlin business office, a paid functionary was responsible for the public relations work, ensuring that in the years before World War I the dispute with the women's movements was conducted professionally, working closely with modern mass media.[24]

The close contacts with the male professional organizations and with the radical right could be clearly seen in the program and in the strategies of the German antifeminists. Unlike their British sister organization, the German league was no single-issue organization. Whereas in Great Britain feminists and antifeminists alike focused on the voting question in the prewar years, the German discussions had a broader range. Women's associations were far from unitarily claiming the ballot. Instead, the large Bund Deutscher Frauenvereine (Federation of German Women's Associations) was composed of a variety of clubs whose interests ranged from gender equality to charity work. Hence, antifeminists fought not only against female suffrage, but against everything which threatened traditional gender relations. This ranged from women studying at university or earning a living outside of the household, to increased participation in the church and in the community all the way to the demand for sexual self-determination.

Whereas the antifeminists in the official journal of the association used a relatively moderate tone in articles on the "un-German" feminism, the same authors issued a clarion call in *völkisch* newspapers and magazines for all "pure race Germans" to combat the "degenerate" women's movement. They accused feminists of belonging "to a race for which internationalism and the breakdown in national cohesion arising from this means that they will be able to extend and strengthen the bonds of their own racial solidarity over all countries."[25] In contrast to Great

Britain, anti-Semitism and antifeminism went hand in hand in the Deutscher Bund zur Bekämpfung der Frauenemanzipation (Alliance for the Combat of Women's Emancipation).[26] The British opponents of voting rights may have believed in the self-evident superiority of the white race—this at least is suggested by their proximity to the colonial administration. They were not, however, anti-Semites.

Much to the displeasure of the enemies of emancipation, towards the end of World War I, many *völkisch* organizations gradually began to open up their associations to women from their own milieu.[27] The intransigent position of the antifeminist league was therefore not uncontested, even in their own political camp.[28] The German Fatherland Party, the annexationists in the war from the far, nationalist right, had accepted women as members since it was founded in 1917. After the November Revolution gave women the right to vote, parties such as the DNVP (German National Folk Party), a party with a broad base on the right, hurried to adapt to the new conditions. Even the antifeminist league had to change sides. In December 1918 it announced: "All of the thoughts and worries which we put forward earlier against giving women the right to vote, no longer pertain."[29]

Since German antifeminists had not, unlike their English model, intimately connected their faith to the suffrage question, they were able to survive into the postwar era. Reorganized as Bund für deutsche Volkserneuerung (Association for the German People Instauration) they intended to make the public aware of the dangers of gender equality and attempted to block the reforms of the Weimar government that, for instance, admitted women to the legal professions. However, after the November Revolution, for many radical nationalist and *völkisch* opponents of emancipation it was no longer enough simply to pursue gender politics. They decided to fight the whole so-called Weimar System. Very soon, therefore, German antifeminism moved into the *völkisch* camp of the Weimar Republic. It was the Deutschvölkische Schutz- und Trutzbund (German Nationalist Protection and Defiance Federation) which first took on, both in terms of content and membership, the legacy of the Anti-Feminist League. Many of the opponents of emancipation, after a couple of intermediate stages, finally found their new political home in the NSDAP.[30]

3.3 France

Whereas German antifeminism came from the right and British antifeminism from above, French opposition to the emancipation of women came from the middle of society. French antifeminism was fed by many sources: a strong Catholic tradition, in which the man was seen as the master of the house, who the woman had to obey; a republican tradition that viewed women not so much as citizens than as the mothers of future generations; the patriarchal nature of the Code Napoléon, that shaped the private legal relationships and treated women not as individuals but rather as a part of the family; and finally the artistic and intellectual avant-garde of the Fin de Siècle, whose members passionately promoted, perhaps with more success than elsewhere, their belief that the two sexes were incompatible.

On top of this, the segmented French trade union and working-class movement considered women less as companions than as wage-depressing competition.[31] "La classe ouvrière," wrote Madeleine in July 1912, resigned, "sera la dernière à venir au féminisme ... Esclave du patron, il [l'ouvrier] veut être le maître de sa femme."[32] (The working class will be last to become feminist ... Being the slave of his boss, the worker wants to be the boss of his wife.)

After the traumatic defeat by Germany in 1870–71, the misogynist currents were accompanied by a propagandistic pronatalism found in all sections of society. Since the 1880s, numerous voices had harshly criticized the decline in the birthrate—a demographic trend that started in France earlier than elsewhere—as evidence of national decadence. Supporters argued that France would be outbred by the German enemy and proclaimed that increasing the birthrate was a precondition for military revenge. Firms and insurance companies offered rewards for babies, numerous pronatalist organizations were founded, and in the years before World War I even progressive and liberal newspapers joined the chorus of the *"repopulisateurs."* In this atmosphere of fear of degeneration and pronatal propaganda, women's calls for emancipation could all too easily be defamed as the selfish pursuit of particular interests at the cost of the *"grande nation."*[33] This accusation drew its power from a political and mental tradition that had always denied women the right to their own individuality, and instead considered them as part of the nation or family. Examining the political culture of the Anglo-Saxon countries with their different orientation, Pierre Rosanvallon emphasized: "Le véritable obstacle au suffrage des femmes en France réside ainsi dans la difficulté qu'il y a à considérer la femme comme un individu."[34] (In France the veritable obstacle to women's right to vote thus lies in the difficulty in considering the woman as an individual.)

Alongside this figuration of political mentality, what turned out to be disadvantageous for women's suffrage was the self-interest and self-understanding of the political parties, especially those of the Republican middle. Whenever France's political institutions dealt with the question of women's suffrage between 1906 and 1922, whenever there were votes, it was always the left-leaning Parti républicain radical et radical-socialiste (Radical Republican and Radical Socialist Party), and thus the dominant force of the Third Republic, which blocked women's suffrage. Although numerous socialists spoke up for the cause and supporters were even found among the Conservatives, politicians with a republican and anticlerical orientation revealed a deep mistrust towards the female half of the population. This reserve was, on the one hand, the expression of a republican tradition which understood the state and politics to be exclusively male. On the other hand, ever since Michelet had accused women of treason vis-à-vis the French Revolution, they were considered supporters of clericalism, who would collaborate with antirevolutionary forces and an antirepublican priesthood. The Parti républicain radical et radical-socialiste was founded with the explicit goal of defending the republic against Catholicism. They had pushed through the separation of church and state, outlawed numerous religious orders and secularized the education system. In an era of conflict between the church and the state, the party never tired of painting the "black danger" of female suffrage. As the radical republicans played an important role in shaping the history of the Third Republic, political equality had no real chance, although the pressure of the French women's movement in the last years before the war was no less strong than in neighboring countries. In the light of this political constellation, the establishment of an antifeminist organization obviously seemed unnecessary.[35]

This did not change after the war, even though the French parliament in May 1919, influenced by the events in Great Britain and Germany, for the first time in its history put women's suffrage on the agenda. After a heated debate, the proposal was passed with an unexpectedly clear majority, 329 against 95. However, a closer look reveals that a majority of supporters had merely voted in favor so as to ensure that their main goal—suffrage for families—was not blocked. The case was taken to the Senate for approval, yet here the party of the radical republicans, who were still opposed to women suffrage, held a clear majority. As pro-vote representatives—mainly from the northeast of France and the Paris basin—were clearly overruled, the issue was buried in committees for a further three years. When finally in 1922 it was debated again, former prominent supporters such as René Viviani and Aristide Briand were conspicuously reserved. After the euphoric mood of the immediate postwar period, many politicians had returned to their previous political agendas and things continued as before. The memory of the "*union sacrée*" (Holy Union) had faded, other questions had moved to the forefront, and the weight attached to the women's issue was no longer large enough to move the political elite to a noticeable engagement.[36]

The following decades showed a mixed picture. On the one hand ever more women were working, participating in public discourse, and engaging in strikes and political demonstrations. For a short period there were even three female Ministers of State in the cabinet of the socialist Léon Blum. On the other hand, mothers with many children were rewarded with medals and it was illegal to inform people about contraceptives. The radical republicans continued to block women's suffrage, while the democratic left was divided on whether or not to privilege a family-based vote over women's individual rights. The increasing polarization of the political camps in the interwar period also was mirrored in the disunity of women's organizations that were no longer able to cooperate broadly, as they had in the years directly before the war. Finally, the increasing urgency of events abroad, the outbreak of the Spanish Civil War, and the endangering of the international order by Fascist Germany, all pushed women's suffrage from the political agenda.[37]

The Link between Antifeminism and Anti-Semitism was Peculiarly German

In conclusion, it seems clear that wherever women's movements were able to achieve significant success and where the introduction of women's suffrage appeared not to be too far off, the opponents to emancipation were also organized. Hence, the mere existence of an antifeminist movement is not evidence of the backwardness of a society, but rather indicative of significant underlying social change. In other words, the absence of antifeminist organizations is not proof of the political liberality of a society, but rather just the opposite—it is evidence that the emancipatory demands had little chance of being realized. On the eve of World War I, the German Empire underwent a significant modernization process with regard to gender relations and the so-called "women's question." Wilhelmine society was much closer to female suffrage than the Third Republic, although it still could not match Great Britain's long tradition of improving gender equality.

Whereas British antifeminism had a clear class bias and focused on female suffrage, its counterparts in France and Germany encompassed a much broader spectrum of concerns. These concerns ranged from political, religious, and economic questions to fears of degeneration. All were underpinned by a deeply rooted misogyny. Unlike in Britain, continental antifeminism tended to be a middle-class phenomenon. British and German liberalism was divided over the "women's question" and organized antifeminists tended to belong to the conservative or right-wing elements. It was only in France that political liberalism was almost unanimously opposed to women's emancipation.

British antisuffragism was, therefore, class-based, while French antifeminism was shaped by liberal fears of recatholicization. The comparison of the three states does, however, reveal an element specific to Germany, one that did not play a role in Britain and only a marginal one in France. This was the prominence of the *völkisch*-radical nationalistic milieu, in which both antifeminism and anti-Semitism were intertwined.

British antifeminism was, as a result of the people participating in the movement, no less imperialistic in its orientation than the German. Here, too, some of its arguments had clear racist contours. Nevertheless, one does not find in its publications anti-Semitism or the accusation that the women's movement was part of a Jewish international conspiracy.

Such accusations were, however, made on the Continent and in this respect there are some German-French parallels. On both sides of the Rhine, those on the political right regarded women's suffrage as a foreign eccentricity, inappropriate for the natives. Like the *völkisch* activists in Germany, the right-wing Action française (French Action) considered feminism to be a Jewish invention, maintaining that their goal was the destruction of the state and the French family, in order to take power itself.[38]

However, the coupling and interweaving of antifeminism and anti-Semitism remained limited in France to the milieu of the Action française. In France, antifeminists of all political camps could count on the scepticism of the political parties vis-à-vis women's suffrage and on the intransigence of the Senate. Therefore, the French political right did not act as a melting pot for all opponents of women's emancipation. At the same time, the royalism of the Action française and its condemnation by the Pope prevented it from becoming a mass party.[39] The power to shape society through an anti-Semitic code with anti-feminist implications remained therefore, just like the breadth and the virulence of the proto-fascist movement, a German phenomenon.

Notes

1. E.g., M. Görtemaker, *Geschichte Europas, 1850–1918* (Stuttgart, 2002).
2. Cf. J. Kocka, *Das lange 19. Jahrhundert. Arbeit, Nation und bürgerliche Gesellschaft*, 10th ed. (Stuttgart, 2001), 141.
3. Cf. H.-U. Wehler, *Deutsche Gesellschaftsgeschichte*, vol. 3, *Von der Deutschen Doppelrevolution bis zum Beginn des Ersten Weltkrieges, 1849–1914* (Munich, 1995), 1289.
4. Cf. A. Bebel, *Die Frau und der Sozialismus*, 50th ed., Preface (Stuttgart, 1910), XXXI (first published 1879).
5. Cf. *Verhandlungen des Reichstags*, XIII. Legislaturperiode, 1. Session, vol. 283: Stenographische Berichte, Berlin 1912, 16. Sitzung vom 29.2.1912, 339.
6. Whereas antisuffragism focuses on denying women the right to vote, the broader term antifeminism refers to opposing female participation in the public sphere in a more general sense. Yet this differentiation is heuristic; in practice, these segments are often part of an intertwined broad range of attitudes.
7. In accordance with the guidelines laid down for publication, the number of bibliographical references given in this version of my article had to be reduced to a minimum. For more detailed references, see the original (German) version: U. Planert, "Wie reformfähig war das Kaiserreich? Ein westeuropäischer Vergleich aus geschlechtergeschichtlicher Perspektive," in *Das Deutsche Kaiserreich in der Kontroverse – Probleme und Perspektiven*, eds. S.O. Müller and C. Torp (Göttingen, 2009), 165–84.
8. Cf. T.L. Mottl, "The Analysis of Countermovements," *Social Problems* 27 (1980), 620–35; U. Planert, "Antifeminismus im Kaiserreich: Indikator einer Gesellschaft in Bewegung," *Archiv für Sozialgeschichte* 38 (1998), 93–118.
9. Cf. G. Bock, *Frauen in der europäischen Geschichte. Vom Mittelalter bis zur Gegenwart* (Munich, 2000); K. Offen, *European Feminisms 1700–1950. A Political History* (Stanford, CA, 2000); J. Rendall, *The Origins of Modern Feminism: Women in Britain, France and the United States, 1780–1860* (Basingstoke, 1985); B. Bader-Zaar, *Das Frauenwahlrecht: Vergleichende Aspekte seiner Geschichte in Großbritannien, den Vereinigten Staaten von Amerika, Österreich, Deutschland und Belgien, 1860–1920* (Vienna, 2008); S. Paletschek and B. Pietrow-Ennker, eds., *Women's Emancipation Movements in the 19th Century: A European Perspective* (Stanford, CA, 2004); A. Schaser, *Frauenbewegung in Deutschland, 1848–1933* (Darmstadt, 2006); C. Bolt, *The Women's Movement in the United States and Britain from the 1790s to the 1920s* (New York, 1993); L.J. Rupp, *Worlds of Women: The Making of an International Women's Movement* (Princeton, 1997).
10. Cf. P. Hollis, "Women in Council: Separate Spheres, Public Space," in *Equal or Different: Women's Politics 1800–1914*, ed. J. Rendall (Oxford, 1987), 192–213.
11. Cf. E. Crawford, *The Women's Suffrage Movement: A Reference Guide, 1866–1928* (London, 1999); C. Rover, *Women's Suffrage and Party Politics in Britain, 1866–1914* (London, 1967); S.S. Holton, *Feminism and Democracy: Women's Suffrage and Reform Politics in Britain, 1900–1918* (Cambridge, 1986); A.V. John and C. Eustance, eds., *The Men's Share? Masculinities, Male Support, and Women's Suffrage in Britain, 1890–1920* (London, 1997); S.A. VanWingerden, *The Women's Suffrage Movement in Britain, 1866–1928* (Basingstoke, 1999); B. Caine, *English Feminism, 1780–1980* (Oxford, 1997).
12. Cf. A. Schmidt, 1870, "Zur Erkenntnis der Zeit," *Neue Bahnen* 5 (20), 153–55; quotation on 153.
13. U. Gerhard, ed., *Frauen in der Geschichte des Rechts: Von der Frühen Neuzeit bis zur Gegenwart* (Munich, 1997).

14. With special respect to political parties' attitudes towards female claims for emancipation, cf. Schaser, *Frauenbewegung*; A. Schaser, *Helene Lange und Gertrud Bäumer: Eine politische Lebensgemeinschaft* (Cologne, 2000), 128–43; U. Planert, ed., *Nation, Politik und Geschlecht. Frauenbewegungen und Nationalismus in der Moderne* (Frankfurt, 2000); J. Sneeringer, *Winning Women's Votes: Propaganda and Politics in Weimar Germany* (Chapel Hill, 2002).
15. Cf. U. Planert, *Antifeminismus im Kaiserreich. Diskurs, soziale Formation und politische Mentalität* (Göttingen, 1998), 224–40; U. Rosenbusch, *Der Weg zum Frauenwahlrecht in Deutschland* (Baden-Baden, 1998).
16. Cf. M. Albistur and D. Armogathe, *Histoire du féminisme français*, 2 vols. (Paris, 1977); C.G. Moses, *French Feminism in the Nineteenth Century* (Albany, 1984); L. Klejman and F. Rochefort, *L'égalité en marche: le féminisme sous la Troisième Républíque* (Paris, 1989); J.W. Scott, *Only Paradoxes to Offer. French Feminists and the Rights of Men* (Cambridge, MA, 1996).
17. C. Bard, *Les Filles de Marianne. Histoire des Féminismes, 1914–1940* (Paris, 1995); P. Smith, *Feminism and the Third Republic: Women's Political and Civil Rights in France, 1918–1945* (Oxford, 1996); S.C. Hause and A.R. Kenney, *Women's Suffrage and Social Politics in the French Third Republic* (Princeton, 1984).
18. Cf. Planert, *Antifeminismus*; B. Harrison, *Separate Spheres. The Opposition to Women's Suffrage in Britain* (London, 1978), 55–90; A. Maugue, *L'identité masculine en crise au tournant du siècle, 1871–1914* (Paris, 1987); C. Bard, ed., *Un siècle d'antiféminisme* (Paris, 1999); A. Howard and S.R.A. Tarrant, eds., *Antifeminism in America. A Collection of Readings from the Literature of the Opponents to U.S. Feminism, 1848 to the Present*, 3 vols. (New York, 1997); C.D. Kinnard, *Antifeminism in American Thought: An Annotated Bibliography* (Boston, MA, 1986).
19. Cf. R. Symonds, *Inside the Citadel. Men and the Emancipation of Women, 1850–1920* (Basingstoke, 1999); J.S. Chafetz and A.G. Dworkin, "Action and Reaction: an Integrated, Comparative Perspective on Feminist and Antifeminist Movements," in *Cross-National Research in Sociology*, ed. M.L. Kohn (Newbury Park, 1989), 329–50.
20. Cf. Harrison, *Seperate Spheres* and M. Pugh, *The March of the Women. A Revisionist Analysis of the Campaign for Women's Suffrage, 1866–1914* (Oxford, 2000).
21. Mrs Humphry Ward to Frederic Harrison, 27 Dec. 1912, quoted after Harrison, *Seperate Spheres*, 132.
22. Such was the comment of an eyewitness about an "anti"-meeting at the noble Royal Albert Hall in London 1912, cf. Harrison, *Seperate Spheres*, 137.
23. Cf. Harrison, *Separate Spheres*, 91–107, 126–46 and Pugh, *March of the Women*, 162; furthermore cf. R. Owen, *Lord Cromer. Victorian Imperialist, Edwardian Proconsul* (Oxford, 2004).
24. Cf. Planert, *Antifeminismus*.
25. Cf. E. zu Reventlow, "Die Frauenbewegung – Nationale Zersetzung," *Alldeutsche Blätter* 19 (39) (25 Sept. 1909), 333–35.
26. Cf. U. Planert, "Reaktionäre Modernisten? Zum Verhältnis von Antisemitismus und Antifeminismus in der völkischen Bewegung," *Jahrbuch für Antisemitismusforschung* 11 (2002), 31–51.
27. Cf. K. Heinsohn, "Germany," in *Women, Gender and Fascism in Europe, 1919–45*, ed. K. Passmore (Manchester, 2003), 33–56.
28. Planert, *Antifeminismus*, 124–25.
29. Cf. M. Diers, "Das Stimmrecht der Frauen," *Deutsche Tageszeitung*, Nr. 632 (12 Dec. 1918).
30. Cf. Planert, *Antifeminismus*, 251–58.
31. Cf. Maugue, *Identité*; C. Bard, 1999, "Les antiféminismes de la première vague," in *Siècle*, Bard, 41–68.
32. La Suffragiste, no. 30 (July 1912), quoted after R. Huard, *Le suffrage universel en France, 1848–1946* (Paris, 1991), 197–98; C. Sowerwine, *Sisters or Citizens? Women and Socialism in France since 1876* (Cambridge, MA, 1982).
33. Cf. K. Offen, "Depopulation, Nationalism, and Feminism in Fin-de-Siecle France," *American Historical Review* 89 (1984), 648–76; C. Dienel, *Kinderzahl und Staatsräson. Empfängnisverhütung und Bevölkerungspolitik in Deutschland und Frankreich bis 1918* (Münster, 1995).

34. P. Rosanvallon, *Le sacre du citoyen. Histoire du suffrage universel en France*, Paris, 1992, 396.
35. Cf. F. Rochefort, 2004, "The French Feminist Movement and Republicanism, 1868–1914," in *Women's Emancipation Movements*, Paletschek and Pietrow-Ennker, 77–101; Huard, *Suffrage universel*, 198–99.
36. Cf. the differentiated analysis of electoral behavior provided by Hause/Kennedy, *Women's Suffrage*, 221–47. With special respect to familial suffrage, cf. J.-Y. Le Naour and C. Valenti, *La famille doit voter: le suffrage familial contre le vote individuel* (Paris, 2005).
37. Concerning the question of women's rights during the (inter)war period, cf. the articles by Bard/Thébaud, Bard, Reynolds und Thalmann in Bard, *Siècle*. With respect to the enforcement of women's suffrage, cf. H. Diamond, *Women and the Second World War in France, 1939–1848: Choices and Constraints* (Harlow, 1999).
38. Cf. M. Borély, *L'Appel aux Françaises. Le Féminisme politique* (Paris, 1919).
39. With regard to the Action française cf. E. Weber, *Action française: Royalism and Reaction in 20th Century France* (Stanford, CA, 1962); Y. Guchet, *Georges Valois: l'action française, le faisceau, la république syndicale* (Paris, 2001); E. Nolte, *Der Faschismus in seiner Epoche. Action française, Italienischer Faschismus, Nationalsozialismus*, 5th ed. (Munich, 2000).

Chapter 8

Germany in the Age of Culture Wars

Olaf Blaschke

The "Age of Culture Wars"—to stress this point first—was coined neither by the author of this chapter nor by the editors of this volume, who were kind enough to ask him to write about this topic. Rather, it was coined by Albert Ehrhard. The historian of the Catholic Church wrote over one hundred years ago: "Throughout Europe conflicts have come up between governments and the Catholic Church which may one day give our age the label of the 'Age of Culture Wars'" (*Zeitalter der Kulturkämpfe*).[1]

The forty-year-old Erhard had to wait a long time for this labelling to happen. Rather, the events of the twentieth century, the "century of war," pushed aside the deeper understanding of the religious dynamics of that era. In 1902, when Ehrhard was writing, he was referring to all of Europe, not just Germany. It took eight decades to rescue the "culture wars" from their position on the sidelines. Now it has become increasingly common to refer to the second half of the nineteenth century as the "Age of the European Culture Wars"[2] or as "an era of culture wars"[3] with a phase of "hot culture wars" raging from 1860 till 1880.[4]

A controversy has not yet developed over the question of whether the second half of the nineteenth century was truly an "Age of Culture Wars." Perhaps the last couple of decades of the nineteenth century can be called this. Let us look at this more closely. Even if, at first glance, much speaks against the idea that the *Kulturkampf*, such as we know it, covers only the period after 1870, one can argue that contemporaries such as Ehrhard, decades after the "actual" *Kulturkampf* in Prussia and in Germany between 1871 and 1887, were still employing this and other similar expressions. They were of the opinion that the conflicts were not fully over, and perceived through the lens of this topic a basic unity of the era. Such interpretations were found not only in Germany, but also in Belgium, Switzerland, Austria, and other countries. When Ehrhard wrote his book, *Der*

Katholizismus und das 20. Jahrhundert, the conflict in France concerning the separation of the church and state, hotly discussed since 1879, was coming to a head; the complete separation finally came in 1905.[5]

In Germany the tensions around 1900 no longer manifested themselves so much at the level of the state fighting against the church—although there was still the Anti-Jesuit Law and the Pulpit Law and still no Catholic Chancellor (with the exception of the anti-clerical Chlodwig Hohenlohe-Schillingsfürst). Rather, the *Kulturkampf* conflicts had moved to a different level, an everyday level, between liberals and ultramontanists, anticlericals and clericals, reformers and traditionalists, Protestants and Catholics.

Especially in associations and societies, a new confessionalism was blossoming. Although the three major confessions—Lutheranism, Calvinism and Roman Catholicism—shared the same religion (Christianity), they started to emphasize their differences. The term "confessionalism" made its way into dictionaries in the twentieth century, meaning that the adherents of a confession praised their profile while putting down the beliefs of others. The participants in the confessionalization were not satisfied with just consolidating their own identity in order to design a positive distinction. They rather were interested in spreading confessional heterostereotypes, indeed, in formulating intrigues and schemes against their confessional opponents. Protestants considered Catholics dull and superstitious. In 1886 the evangelical theologian Willibald Beyschlag founded the anti-ultramontanist "Evangelische Bund" (Evangelical League) because he was upset that, officially, the *Kulturkampf* had ended. He did not want the common enemy to disappear, since Roman Catholicism was important for a divided Protestantism and was used for its negative integration. When Ehrhard wrote of the "Age of Culture Wars," the Evangelische Bund had one hundred and forty-two thousand members; in 1914 it had half a million members. At the same time, the "Volksverein für das katholische Deutschland" (The People's Association for Catholic Germany), which was founded later, had two hundred thousand members and in 1914 even had over eight hundred thousand members. Everyone who has worked on the history of Germany from 1870–1918 knows that these are impressive numbers. The Volksverein, an organization of German Catholics that was opposing social-democracy and standing for the defense of Christian order in society, which was a bit more moderate in its polemics than the Evangelische Bund, went bankrupt after World War I and was dissolved in 1933. The Evangelische Bund however still exists, with approximately ten thousand members. Yet it does just the opposite of what it did earlier. Now it is working for ecumenism instead of deepening the division between the confessions, as it did a hundred years ago.[6]

Given the energy which both sides, Catholics and Protestants, invested in opposing not only each other but also the reformed and the orthodox within each group, and given the importance of religion, of the church and the confessions, not to forget the socialists, the atheists, the anticlerical, laicists, monists, free-thinkers, the Pan Germans, the "Los von Rom" movement in Austria and many others, a strong argument can be made in favor of the concept of the Age of

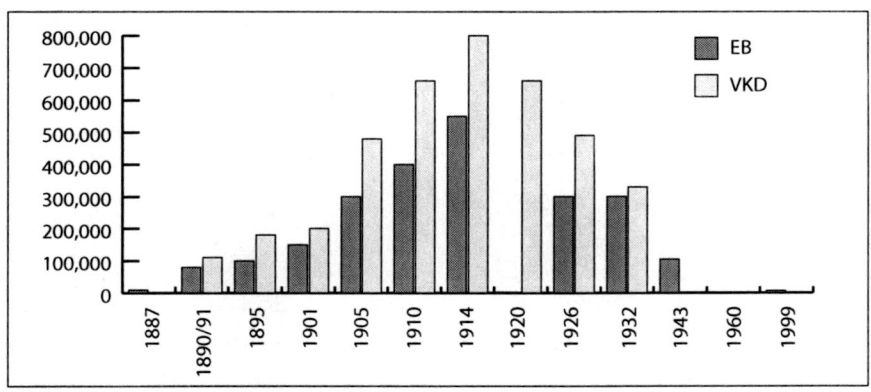

Figure 8.1 *Evangelischer Bund (EB): Members 1887–1999; Volksverein für das katholische Deutschland (VKD): Members 1891–1933. Figure by Olaf Blaschke.*

Culture Wars. The lines dividing orthodoxy and reform also existed within the Christian population itself, within Protestantism and Catholicism. Indeed, questions like supporting a small Germany (without Austria—the solution of 1866) and how loyal one should be towards the pope often divided Catholic families in two.

The period of these conflicts was not limited, however, to that suggested by Ehrhard, that is, from the *Kulturkampf* in Baden in the 1860s up to the turn of the century. Rather, one can go back even further, for example, to the conflicts in Switzerland after its defeat in the *Sonderbund* war in 1847, or, if one wants to remain purely within the German context, to the Cologne turmoils (*Kölner Wirren*) in 1837, which is treated in the literature as the "first *Kulturkampf*."[7] One can also look forward to the National Socialist dictatorship. In the historical literature, one often finds, mistakenly, the concept "battle of the churches" (*Kirchenkampf*) to describe the difficulties of the National Socialist period. Many contemporaries spoke instead of a "second *Kulturkampf*,"[8] comparing the measures against religion and the repressions of the Hitler regime with Bismarck's *Kulturkampf*. This turned out to be just another fatal misinterpretation of the real dimensions of what happened.

Looking for a superordinate term to cover the phenomena between the mid-nineteenth and mid-twentieth centuries, one could feel encouraged to speak of an Age of Culture Wars. The fact that this term allows us to compare historical developments internationally and across regions speaks in favor of such a term. The "culture wars" between Catholic and anticlerical powers were a "pan-European phenomena," extending over almost all of Europe, from Upper Silesia to Cantabria, from Oldenburg in northern Germany to the Campo Fiori in Rome.[9] There are three reasons, however, why one might not wish to agree with an "Age of Culture Wars" and not extend the terminology beyond these borders.

Chronological Limits of the Age of Culture Wars

First, this terminology would be restricted to a limited time span. The concept "*Kulturkampf*," coined by Rudolf Virchow in 1873, specifies in German historiography the period from 1871 to 1886. It should not be expanded arbitrarily to other decades, but should rather continue to refer to the period of concerted measures by the state, the administration, the police, and the press against the religious orders and organizations of the Catholic Church.

For the Weimar Republic—the Catholic Centre Party participated in almost all the governments of the period—it is difficult to perceive any conflict which came close to the *Kulturkampf*. In the second German Republic, after 1949, led by the former Member of Parliament for the Centre Party, Konrad Adenauer, there was no *Kulturkampf*. However, the Adenauer era can be considered, as for example Thomas Gauly does, as a phase of massive "confessionalism and clericalism." Certainly there are clear lines of social and cultural continuity with the German Empire; these are, however, described better with the concept of confessionalism than with the concept of the *Kulturkampf*.[10]

Without a doubt the confessionalism reached a peak during the *Kulturkampf*, although the two developments did not coincide completely. The *Kulturkampf* was fed by more than just purely confessional motives. At the same time it had political, social, and gender dimensions. Furthermore, the confessionalism also found other forms of expression than just the *Kulturkampf* legislation which began in 1871. The *Kulturkampf* itself had more dimensions than laws and countermeasures. The image of the *Kulturkampf* was strongly influenced by caricatures which depicted a masculine Bismarck and dubious clergymen and Jesuits, as well as by numerous polemical publications.

As a matter of fact, the number of novels ridiculing Catholic institutions and organizations and representatives reached a peak in the early 1870s. Each year

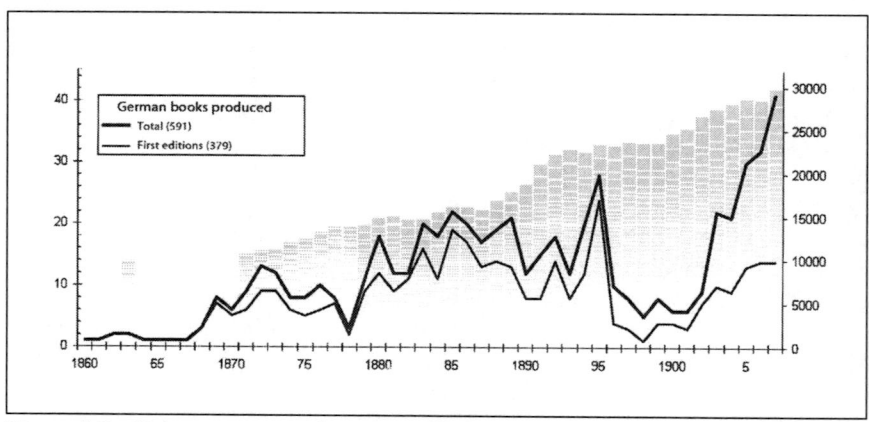

Figure 8.2 Light entertainment literature with an anti-Catholic tendency, 1860–1917. Figure and calculations by Olaf Blaschke, data from Keiter, *Brunnenvergiftung*, 1908, p. 209–23.

there were about a dozen new such products on the market. This increase, however, had clearly begun before the new German state was born and thus 1870 is not a caesura. In 1908, Bernhard Stein published an annotated bibliography of over four hundred novels and light pieces of entertainment, using criteria which we would consider overly sensitive today. This bibliography includes Wilhelm Busch's *Heiliger Antonius* (1870) and his *Pater Filuzius* (1873), Felix Dahn's *Kampf um Rom* (1876) and his *Die Schlimmen Nonnen von Poitiers* (1886), as well as less famous works (by unknown authors) such as *Im Netze der Jesuiten* (1896) and *Leben und Lieben der Kapuziner* (1908). The output reached a low in 1878, the year of the turnaround in the *Kulturkampf*, the death of Pius IX and the introduction of the antisocialist laws. However, already by the middle of the 1880s, in comparison to the years of the *Kulturkampf*, there were twice as many writings on the market which could be identified as antichurch. The anti-Catholic literature reached a new height after the turn of the century, whereby the reprints and new editions of classical pieces easily exceeded the first editions. These statistics on the amount of light fiction unfriendly to Catholics, which are certainly incomplete, are an indication of the popularity of confessional resentments and of the intensity of the confessionalism. In this light the actual *Kulturkampf* appears to have been a short episode. Yet the polemics did not come to an end. The German people are "not united today," summed up Stein in 1908. "The basic opposition of the anti-Catholic denominations to the church has been brought into a sharper focus than was earlier the case. In literature there is a sneaky, fanatical *Kulturkampf* being fought against the church." Stein still used the term *Kulturkampf* at the beginning of the twentieth century, such as Ehrhard did. This rhetoric was thus part of a religious polemic. For the purpose of historical analysis the term is contaminated.[11]

Therefore the formula of an Age of Culture Wars should remain reserved for periods for which it was originally intended, at the very least because the concept is already pretty well set. However, one should not lose sight of the long prehistory and the long repercussions of the *Kulturkampf*. The prehistory reaches back to 1789 and the subsequent separation of church and state (civil constitution of the clergy, 1790). The aftereffects in *les deux Frances* can be followed well into the twentieth century; in Germany it extends well up to the "battle between the churches" under Hitler and further on into the neo-confessionalism in the politics of the Federal Republic of Germany as well as in the mixed marriage problematic of the 1960s. How can we employ the concept *Kulturkampf* to help us understand the formation of Belgium as a national state in 1830? Catholic Belgium separated from the Protestant Netherlands because of religious reasons, thus confessionalism covers the phenomenon much better than culture war. There was a culture war in Belgium, however. The first battle over the schools from 1879–1884 was waged as an "ideological civil war," and this fits exactly in the scheme of the Age of Culture Wars; the second battle over the schools from 1954–1958, however, falls outside of this framework, although scenes which were similar to those of the *Kulturkampf* were played out here and the masses were mobilized: two hundred thousand people demonstrated in Brussels in 1955 against promoting state schools at the cost of Catholic schools; a petition to the King had two million signatures.[12]

The anticlericalism after the middle of the nineteenth century and the increasing compartmentalization of society into confessional clubs as well as the confessional divisions in social life and in one's professional life can hardly be interpreted as miniature forms of the *Kulturkampf* before the actual *Kulturkampf*. Rather, the increasing confessionalism since the 1830s is to be made responsible for this. How is one to understand all of this within the framework of the *Kulturkampf* terminology? In the 1950s the rhetoric of the "Christian Occident" was very popular. With its massive anti-Bolshevist line of attack, it paid tribute to interconfessionalism, which obviously was not there, otherwise there would had been no need to demand it. Here again Culture War does not cover the phenomenon. The demand for interconfessionalism and the vision of a united Christianity rather indicated the existence of confessionalism. The Age of Culture Wars had long passed, but confessional resentments continued to live on in Europe. They are one of the reasons why in 1951 Anglican England and High Church Lutheran Sweden shied away from joining the European Community. All of the six foreign ministers who in Paris in April 1951 signed the treaty creating the European Community for Coal and Steel were members of a Christian Democratic Party. All six member states were governed by Christian Democratic Parties, either single-handedly or as members of a coalition. France, Belgium, and Italy were Catholic anyway; on top of this there was Catholic Austria, whereas Spain and Portugal were ruled by dictators friendly to the church. All of Western Europe, the so-called "Christian Occident," appeared to be Catholic—which made Scandinavian and British politicians feel uncomfortable. Sweden's Prime Minister Tage Erlander stated that these were the reasons for his reticence vis-à-vis Europe. And the Labour politician Kenneth Younger, Minister of State in the British Foreign Office and advisor to Foreign Minister Ernst Bevin, noted in his diary in May 1950 that while he generally favored European economic integration the new proposals might "on the other hand ... be just a step in the consolidation of the Catholic 'black international' which I have always thought to be a big driving force behind the Council of Europe." In short, confessional dislikes and antipathies inhibited prominent politicians, even half a century after the "Age of Culture Wars."[13]

In debates on the social and cultural history of Germany, historians have rightly questioned the political signposts 1871 and 1918 and demanded that historians move beyond them. The German Empire stood in the middle of the "Age of Culture Wars." World War I is, in spite of the *Burgfrieden* and the existential crisis, not a clear historical break. Rather this era was itself only the highpoint of a prolonged era in which the church and secular forces, clerical and anticlerical, Catholic and anti-Catholic camps, and—in Germany, the Netherlands, and Switzerland—Catholics and Protestants struggled against each other. Therefore, the time frame has to be extended.

The Representational Scope of the Age of Culture Wars

Second, it is obvious that the concept of the *Kulturkampf* not only has limitations in terms of chronology, but also in terms of its ability to describe the facts. The concept, as presently employed, remains strongly limited to the conflict between the official church and the state. Other phenomena are often ignored: the polemics in the press, so-called "disgust thresholds" between members of different denominations in everyday life, religion as *one* dimension of inequality, religion as *one* factor which influenced political, economic, and social decisions. On top of this, the concept of the *Kulturkampf* is limited exclusively to the conflict and quarrel between Catholics and the Catholic Church on the one side, and the state and anti-clerical powers on the other, concerning the place of religion in a modern political culture. Protestants do not appear here either as prosecutors or as those being persecuted. However, many Protestants were, because of their religious background, very much interested in an effective anti-Catholicism, not only to help them construct their own identity, but also as something that defined their political activity. "Most Protestants are biased against the church because of their religious prejudices," complained the Catholic journalist Heinrich Keiter in 1896, while insisting that "there is nowhere among Catholics any hatred of Protestants, at most regret and, perhaps, some reservations." In contrast, "the hatred of the Catholic Church is the fertilizer which keeps the tree of Protestantism alive."[14]

Given the atmosphere in which such a semantic prevailed, how should we interpret the inspection report of a priest in a small town who even in the middle of the *Kulturkampf* emphasized that "it was always peaceful among both denominations." Historians who believe such formulas to be an adequate description of reality conclude that "there is not the least sign of an antagonism between the denominations," at least not in the small town of Steinbach in Oberamt Esslingen (near Stuttgart).[15] However, those who read such formulations against the grain must ask the question why it was necessary at all in Württemberg to report that there was always peace between the two denominations. Is the person not referring rather to a latent potential for conflict, which fortunately has not manifested itself? In 1874 it was necessary to mention whether or not there was peace among the denominations. But would such a formula have been necessary in 1974?

Even in a cosmopolitan city such as Hamburg, whose population was largely alienated from the church, there were distinct, never completely impervious boundaries of segregation between social classes, ethnicities, genders, and confessions, for example, in conversations in bars, in breaks at work, and in one's social and club life. After the rise of political Catholicism, the Liberal patricians in Hamburg treated Catholic citizens once again with reserve; the social circles of the bourgeoisie remained "homogenous in their composition in regard to their denomination"; those who had a different religion found no admittance to "good society."[16]

As a matter of fact, denominations set up invisible boundaries, and religion in the German Empire was a permanent cause for conflict. A variety of social strategies and creative mechanisms were set up to prevent open conflict as, for example, had taken place during the *Kulturkampf*. However, the etiquette "Age of Culture Wars" remains too narrow, because it is limited to the periods of actual struggle and because it does not encompass the larger framework of the religious stereotypes and ways of making distinctions. The concept of the *Kulturkampf*, no matter how broadly one defines the term, is unable to describe why and how nonreligious phenomenon such as Social Democracy or, later, National Socialism were infused with religious and anticlerical elements, moreover, with elements that were specific to certain denominations. Whether or not a wide definition of denomination would be able to declare socialism or liberalism or—in France— the heterogeneous camp of the anticlericalists, the free thinkers, the atheists and the anticlericalists as "competing denominations" remains open for discussion. At any rate, contemporaries such as Ferdinand Buisson spoke of 'La foi laïque' (1912), of anticlericalism as a statement of faith. The term "confession" itself became a fighting word in the nineteenth century; after 1933 the concept "deconfessionalization" (*Entkonfessionalisierung*) pretended to bridge the Christian gap between the denominations and to keep politics free of clerical influence. But, in fact, deconfessionalization was a totalitarian approach. It intended to delegitimate Christian churches as a whole.[17]

Historiographic Breadth of the Age of Culture Wars

Third, the Age of Culture Wars cannot compete with concepts which have long been accepted for the German Empire and for the long nineteenth century. Historians talk about the bourgeois period or the century of nationalism or the age of secularization. These established concepts are useful and should not be replaced. But in order to balance the view we need to find a counterweight. The historian Franz Schnabel wrote in 1936, "once again a confessional age [*konfessionelles Zeitalter*] came forward," referring to the fights between Catholics and Protestants in the early nineteenth century. He left it open at the time when this new confessional age came to an end. However, seventy years later, after the shift in values of the long 1960s, we are wiser than our colleagues were in 1936. The confessional age ended in the 1960s. Schnabel spoke at the same time of a "century of the bourgeoisie" and of the dominant secular "spirit."[18] These perspectives are not mutually exclusive. If one can speak of a "bourgeois era," albeit with many reservations—think of the rural population and the working class, of the fact that women did not have voting rights—then one can also speak of a confessional age, once again albeit with many reservations.

The notion of a second confessional age is in this respect a notion of relationships. It would be carrying coals to Newcastle if one emphasized that "the nineteenth century was neither an age of secularization or of confessionalization but rather both at the same time." Superfluous polemics against the "primacy of confessional patterns of interpretation in the nineteenth and twentieth century," a claim which no one has ever made, do not move our understanding forward, but only push it back.[19] The confessional age took place alongside the age of secularization and nationalism; we are not required to see denominations as the defining element of the epoch. Historians who repudiate the thesis of an age of neoconfessionalism because they find patterns of cooperation between Catholics and Protestants should also ask of the age of nationalism whether or not it can be shown that there were peaceful contacts between Germans and non-Germans in the border regions. It is helpful to apply the same standards when making historical judgements.

The idea of an age of secularization continues to dominate the historiography of these years. The Parisian historian of religion, René Rémond, recently distinguished between a first 'Age of Secularization' from 1789 till 1905, in which the state broke apart from the church, and a 'Second Age of Secularization,' the twentieth century, in which the population distanced itself from the church.[20] The culture wars are an expression of a secular age but also of a confessional age. However, whereas one can easily agree with the concept of the "Age of Culture Wars" for the German Empire, it seems that the formulation of a "new" or of a "second age of confessions" still creates enough discomfort among historians to provoke constructive counterarguments. One of them was suggested by Helmut W. Smith. In his view, a "more modest and truer formulation" would be to call the period "not a confessional age but an age of confessionalism," because evidently confessionalism played an important role but not enough to dominate other tendencies.[21] Some historians mobilize all the arguments which speak against such a label, without, however, trying to apply the same arguments to the idea of a secular, bourgeois or nationalistic age. These approaches need to be measured in the same way, need to be critically challenged and questioned with the same enthusiasm. Why this asymmetry, why this dogged and tenacious defense? The concepts "bourgeois" or "industrial century" or the "Age of Nationalism," the "Age of Secularization," etc., have simply had a clear head start. One has grown accustomed to them. Whereas Schnabel's "confessional age" has slumbered, undiscovered, for decades in the fourth volume of his German History on page 271, all of the other concepts have had a career as titles of chapters or even of books. There are innumerable books about the "bourgeois age." Recently the publisher Wallstein introduced a new series with the title, "Building Blocks for a European History of Religion in the Age of Secularization,"[22] as if one had to emphasize that religion still existed in the age of secularization, which seems a matter of fact.

It cannot be claimed that the Age of Secularization or the bourgeois century as concepts have not been criticized. Friedrich Wilhelm Graf has repeatedly questioned the argument that secularization was a necessary concomitant of the modernization process. And even Jürgen Kocka, in his standard work on the 'long nineteenth century,' in the chapter that treats the 'century of nationalism,' points out that there were competing identities. He even puts a question mark on his chapter entitled the "bourgeois century." The boundaries of the "bourgeois" were the nobility, the country, the people, and the churches.[23]

Is anything gained by the concept of a confessional age? Why all this argument? Has there not been in the last two decades a genuine boom in the historiography of the history of religion in Germany from 1870–1918? In spite of this "religious turn," the results have not been adequately integrated into the general historiography. Therefore Oliver Zimmer has recently demanded that, by looking at religious denominations and religious groups, those historians "doing research on nationalism should finally take up their blind spot: the question ... concerning the understanding of the processes of nationalisation in one's everyday environment." There were complex amalgamations and transformations of nationalism and religion. And what would nationalism have been without the Protestant parsonage? Nationalism cannot be understood without the confessional dimension, and confessional practice cannot be understood without nationalism.[24]

If nationalism and bourgeois identities were, so to speak, confessionally intertwined, if religious denominations were a dynamic factor in the German Empire, then why should this factor be ignored? Why should religion not receive, just like the other dynamic factors, its own label? Of course one has to show the limits of the confessionalism, just like one has to show the limits of nationalism. In the end, one has to consider whether this factor does indeed need to be discussed at the same level. Over the long term—and indeed well into the 1960s—it appears to be plausible to deal with confessionalism, at least more plausible than retaining the monopoly enjoyed by the concept of the (first and second) age of secularization.

No Linear Secularization: Re-Christianization and Confessionalism as a Parable

Many historians have rejected the thesis of an "epoch of linearly progressing secularization."[25] Still, one often comes across the idea that in the nineteenth century society became ever more secular—even if this process was not always linear, but happened in waves.

The data concerning people leaving the churches supports this observation. For the Protestant church one can use Lucian Hölscher's four volume atlas of data—regardless of where one opens it up, the results are always the same. There is especially good data, that is, full data, concerning the percentages of those who took communion in Bavaria (Figure 8.3). If in 1830 about 80 percent of the Bavarian parishioners (excluding Palatine) still participated in communion, a hundred years later it was only 57 percent.[26]

The downward trend is obvious; yet it was not a linear trend, as it was interrupted by small waves of Christianity as in World War I. Catholics, in contrast, remained diligent churchgoers and continued to participate in communion. Therefore, until the beginning of the twentieth century the Catholics did not believe it necessary to collect statistics. The actual rate of decline only increased in the 1960s, at times from 50 to 20 percent. It is important here that

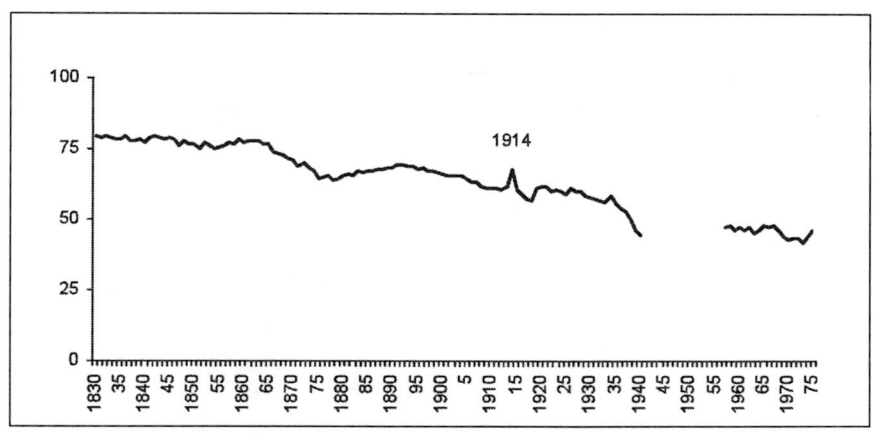

Figure 8.3 *Percentage of parishoners taking communion in the Lutheran Church in Bavaria to the right of the Rhine, 1830–1975. Figure by Olaf Blaschke.*

the tendency to break away from the church is not equated with de-Christianization or with secularization. There were other developments which contradict distinctly the picture of an inexorably declining line and suggest instead that we should interpret the new confessional era as a curve which increased in the early nineteenth century, or to be more precise, as the sum of various curves we can measure (membership in clubs, the amount and level of propaganda activity, the growth rates in the number of members in the religious orders, in the participation in rites which were evidence of piety, etc.). The high point of these curves often lay in the period 1870–1918 or even later; after that they started to decline and the decline increased in most cases in the 1960s.

The graph (Figure 8.1) concerning the Evangelische Bund and the *Volksverein* showed that their membership had reached its zenith at the end of the German Empire. The numbers we have, however, do not cover the whole period. There are three other examples that let us show this parabolic curve, which can also be observed in other indicators. For example, we could look at anti-Semitism—one could measure statistically the ups and downs of stereotypes—or book production: religious books, astoundingly, became the most popular types of books in the middle of the nineteenth century, against all of the assumptions of secularization. Before the nineteenth century, the popularity of religious books had greatly declined.[27]

The first example shows quite plainly the so-called "springtime for the religious orders." Since the middle of the nineteenth century, many new members joined especially the female religious orders. After the Prussian-German *Kulturkampf*, the number joining in the diocese of Trier, for example, reached new heights. A decline in the number of new members only came during the Adenauer era, and only in the 1960s did the numbers begin to decline seriously. Since 1848, liberalism had been increasingly worried about this upswing. It found one of its most important sources of strength in its anti-Catholicism, so much so that one of the historians of this topic, Michael B. Gross, recently spoke of the "century of anti-Catholicism."[28]

The parabolic curve becomes especially clear when we calculate the number of visitors in the last six pilgrimages to the Holy Robe in Trier, which is, alongside the shroud in Turin, one of the most important Catholic relics. We see (Figure 8.4) the total number of visitors as well as the daily average. Far more people participated in the spectacular pilgrimage in 1844—an estimated seven hundred thousand pilgrims—than in the famous national democratic Hambach festival (four days in 1832, with thirty thousand participants). Yet it is the Hambach festival which is found in every history book. In the pilgrimage the Catholic Church not only demonstrated the strength of its organization and the solidarity of its membership; the activity also made, as a "*demonstratio catholica*," an "essential contribution to the renewed confessionalization of the population."[29]

In the next pilgrimage, in 1891, the number of participants once again increased enormously; the record number of visitors was achieved in July 1933. After this, the attractiveness of this sort of event declined. To be sure, each pilgrimage had a slightly different content because of the different historical contexts, and the number of visitors depended upon the transport possibilities at the time. The decline in the number of visitors in 1959 is therefore that much more conspicuous. Even the length this pilgrimage was open—a record 64 days— did not help. Parallel to the total numbers of visitors from 1810 till 1933, the average number of daily visitors also increased, from over ten thousand to about forty-three thousand, and then fell after World War II. The form of both curves is that of a parabola, and the curve covers the space from approximately the beginning up till the end of the second confessional era.

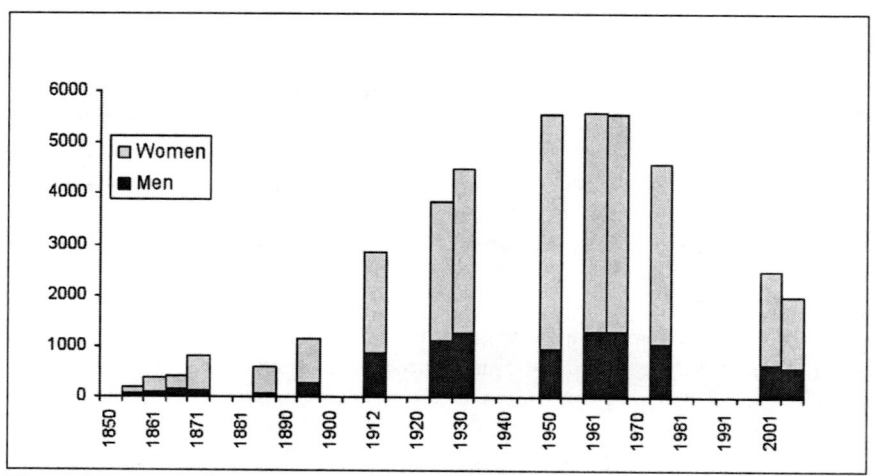

Figure 8.4 *Men and women in the religious orders in the Bishopric of Trier, 1846–2006. Figure by Olaf Blaschke.*

Germany in the Age of Culture Wars 137

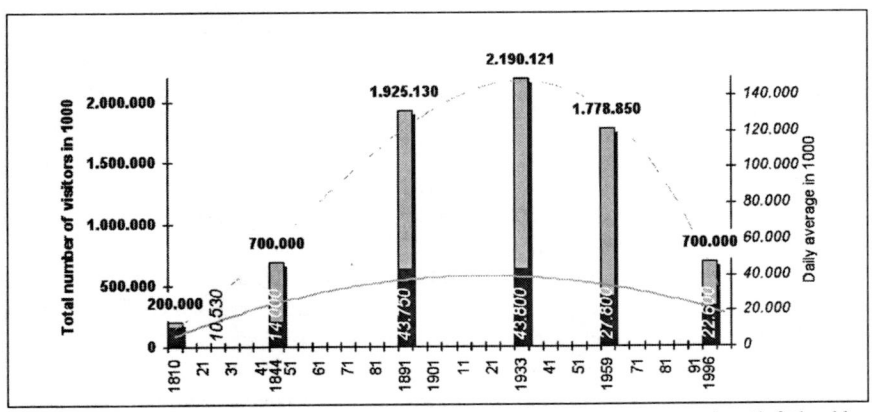

Figure 8.5 Visitors to the Holy Tunic pilgrimage in Trier, 1844–1996. Figure by Olaf Blaschke.

There was a similar development concerning wayside shrines (*Flurdenkmäler*), those crosses or statues of Maria put up where paths and roads meet, especially in Bavaria. Many people imagine they were put up in the eighteenth century and have been there ever since, slowly decaying. The opposite is true; the stock grew up through the early twentieth century and only began to decline in the 1950s, as is shown by looking at the example of the district of Vilsbiburg in Bavaria.[30]

Such characteristics suggest that one should not think of the religious developments of the last 150 years as a downward line, as often appears to be the case, at least unconsciously. Rather, much seems to suggest that the re-Christianization,

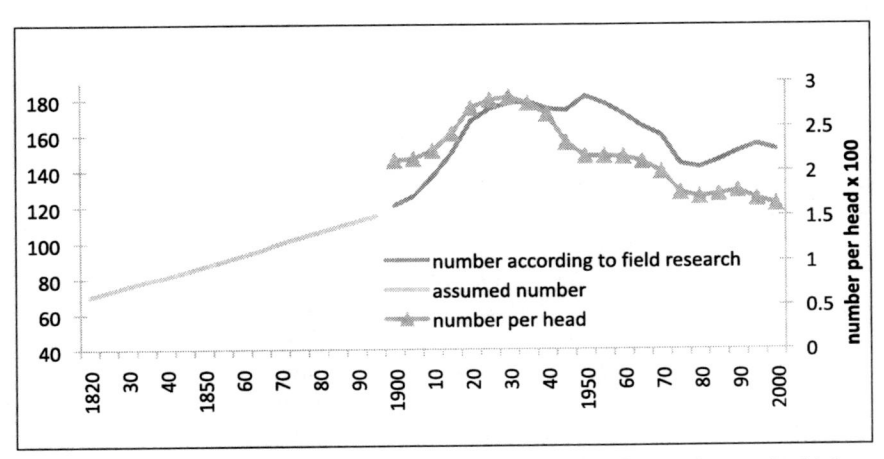

Figure 8.6 Number of religious wayside shrines (Flurdenkmäler) in the district of Vilsbiburg. Figure by Olaf Blaschke, data from Florian Obermayer, Durch Annufung der heiligsten Dreifaltigkeit. Religiöse Flurdenkmäler im Gemeindegebiet Vilsbiburg 1900–1999, Vilsbiburg 2000.

the consolidation of the churches, the confessionalism, as well as the corresponding counter-reaction, even the persistence of religious patterns of interpretation can be accommodated under the broad umbrella of a confessional age between 1830 and 1970. In this regard, what we see here is much more a parabolic curve than a declining line.

Individually, the curves reach different peaks, depending on the different manifestations of the different religious and political needs and conditions of the time. The religious orders, which had been blossoming and expanding since 1848, were unable to reach the zenith of their popularity under the restraints and limitations of the *Kulturkampf*; the societies and associations were able to grow only alongside the general growth of the societies and associations as a whole. However, no wave and no cusp lies outside of the second confessional age. If there were religious phenomena in which confessions set themselves apart or believers engaged in their religious community, then they were rarely before 1830 or after 1960. The general decline of religious and denominational attitudes and practices has speeded up since the 1960s on all levels—in the churches themselves, in the media, in the world of symbols, in associations and clubs, in politics, in how people spend their free time. Today, no one has a need to emphasize that in his high school Catholics and Protestants live peacefully together. As a result the beginning point and above all the landing point of the parabolic curve lie in the same decades, regardless of different internal cycles.

The German Empire, Ehrhard's Age of Culture Wars, takes the place in this narrative of only one stepping stone—admittedly a very important one. The continuities are evident. There is, however, no German *Sonderweg*. The Dutch with their "pillarization" wanted to differentiate even more strongly than the Germans. Functional differentiation was so to speak wantonly and wilfully undermined by segmentary differentiation. In the 1960s, the "de-pillarization" finally won.

The Age of Culture Wars and of religiosity belongs to the past. The *Kulturkampf* was a catalyst of the religiosity and assisted in stabilizing the Catholic milieu. The *Kulturkampf* deepened the fissures in German society and in the German party system. The history of Germany from 1870–1918 was strongly influenced not only by the *Kulturkampf* and its consequences—well into World War I, Germany was characterized by a lingering confessionalism. This confessionalism was found among Protestant elites and the Catholic minority, which during the Wilhelminian period worked hard to be seen as an integral part of the nation. In the neoconfessional age, in the middle of which lay the German Empire, secularization, science and liberalism were the driving forces behind industrialization, secular ideologies, and nationalism, as well as behind the tendency to become bourgeois. However, the churches, religion, and confessionalism were just as important, perhaps even more important than before. The term confessionalism mobilizes the memory of conflicts which were at times quite bitter. The cultural struggles which took place at the time, the political, social, and gender struggles, cannot be reduced to a confessional dispute. Quite often these lines of conflict ran straight down the middle of the confessions themselves. On the other hand, the category "confessionalism" receives too little prominence in the formula, the "Age of Culture Wars." The confessionalism was built up long before the actual culture wars and continued to have an effect decades later. The suggestion to incorporate and integrate the German Empire into a second confessional age attempts to make us more aware of the multidimensional and enduring effects of religion in politics, society, and culture.

Notes

1. A. Ehrhard, *Der Katholizismus und das zwanzigste Jahrhundert im Lichte der kirchlichen Entwicklung der Neuzeit*, 12th ed. (Stuttgart, 1902), 287.
2. M. Borutta, *Liberalismus als Antikatholizismus. Deutschland und Italien im Zeitalter der europäischen Kulturkämpfe* (Göttingen, 2008).
3. W. Kaiser, "'Clericalism – that is our enemy!' European Anticlericalism and the Culture Wars," in W. Kaiser and C. Clark, eds., *Culture Wars. Secular–Catholic Conflict in Nineteenth-Century Europe* (Cambridge, 2003), 50.
4. C. Clark and W. Kaiser, "The European Culture Wars," in Clark and Kaiser, *Culture Wars*, 1–10, 6, 8. Clark and Kaiser translate the German term "Kulturkampf" as "struggle of cultures"; "culture wars" in contrast is used as a deliberate mistranslation of "Kulturkampf," because the expression would contain the essence of the German term while at the same time being more encompassing.
5. To France cf. D. Mollenhauer, "Symbolkämpfe um die Nation. Katholiken und Laizisten in Frankreich (1871–1914)," in *Nation und Religion in Europa. Mehrkonfessionelle Gesellschaften im 19. und 20. Jahrhundert*, eds. H.-G. Haupt and D. Langewiesche (Frankfurt, 2004), 202–30.
6. Data: A. Müller-Dreier, *Konfession und Politik, Gesellschaft und Kultur des Kaiserreichs. Der Evangelische Bund 1886–1914* (Gütersloh, 1998), 80; data for 1926, 1932, 1943, 1999 W. Fleischmann-Bisten, "Evangelischer Bund," in *Die Religion in Geschichte und Gegenwart. Handwörterbuch für Theologie und Religionswissenschaft (RGG)*, vol. 2 (1999), 1728–31. Volksverein: G. Klein, *Der Volksverein für das katholische Deutschland 1890–1933. Geschichte, Bedeutung, Untergang* (Paderborn, 1996), 420–27.
7. H.-U. Wehler, *Deutsche Gesellschaftsgeschichte*, vol. 2 (Munich, 1987), 473.
8. Cf. O. Blaschke, "Kulturkampf," in *RGG*, vol. 4 (2001), 1838–1843.
9. The pan-European dimension and comparability is a central argument for Clark and Kaiser, *European Culture Wars*, 1–3, for the internationally transferable term "culture wars." About the battles in the "levitical city" Santander (Kantabrien) as well as in Rome, where a provocative statue of Giordano Bruno was uncovered in 1889, cf. the contributions of J. de la Cueva, "The Assault on the City of Levites: Spain," in Clark and Kaiser, *Culture Wars*, 181–201; M. Papenheim, "Roma o morte: Culture Wars in Italy," in Clark and Kaiser, *Culture Wars*, 202–26.
10. Cf. T.M. Gauly, *Katholiken. Machtanspruch und Machtverlust* (Bonn, 1991), 127–200.
11. B. Stein (Bearb.), *Heinrich Keiter, Konfessionelle Brunnenvergiftung*, 2nd ed. (Essen, 1908), 12.
12. Cf. E. Witte, "The Battle for Monasteries, Cemeteries and Schools: Belgium," in Clark and Kaiser, *Culture Wars*, 102–27, quote, 118.
13. Cf. T. Judt, *Postwar* (London, 2005), 158.
14. H. Keiter, *Konfessionelle Brunnenvergiftung. Die wahre Schmach des 19. Jahrhunderts* (Regensburg, 1896), 2f.
15. H. Pahl, *Die Kirche im Dorf. Religiöse Wissenskulturen im gesellschaftlichen Wandel des 19. Jahrhunderts* (Berlin, 2006), 242. The weak "Kulturkampf" in Württemberg does not allow any generalization about "the" rural community. A most solid work is: T. Dietrich, *Konfession im Dorf. Westeuropäische Erfahrungen im 19. Jahrhundert* (Cologne, 2004).

16. A. Owzar, *"Reden ist Silber, Schweigen ist Gold."* Konfliktmanagement im Alltag des wilhelminischen Obrigkeitsstaates (Konstanz, 2006), 193.
17. Mollenhauer, *Symbolkämpfe*, 205. Concerning the history of the terms denomination ("Konfession") and "Konfessionalismus" indispensable: L. Hölscher, "Konfessionspolitik in Deutschland zwischen Glaubensstreit und Koexistenz," in *Baupläne der sichtbaren Kirche. Sprachliche Konzepte religiöser Vergemeinschaftung in Europa*, ed. L. Hölscher (Göttingen, 2007), 11–53.
18. F. Schnabel (1937), *Deutsche Geschichte im neunzehnten Jahrhundert*, vol. 4 (Munich, 1987), 271; O. Blaschke, "Das 19. Jahrhundert: Ein Zweites Konfessionelles Zeitalter?," *Geschichte und Gesellschaft* 26 (2000) 38–75; O. Blaschke, ed., *Konfessionen im Konflikt. Deutschland zwischen 1800 und 1970: ein zweites konfessionelles Zeitalter* (Göttingen, 2002). For a brief English account of the second confessional age cf. Blaschke, *Offenders or Victims? German Jews and the Causes of Modern Catholic Antisemitism* (Nebraska, 2009), 41–51.
19. C. Kretschmann and H. Pahl, "Ein 'Zweites Konfessionelles Zeitalter?' Vom Nutzen und Nachteil einer neuen Epochensignatur," *Historische Zeitschrift* 276 (2003), 369–92, 386, however, only repeats the argument of the coexistence and competition of secularization and sanctification, cf. O. Blaschke, "Der 'Dämon des Konfessionalismus.' Einführende Überlegungen," in Blaschke, *Konfessionen*, 13–69, 28f.
20. R. Rémond, *Religion und Gesellschaft in Europa. Von 1789 bis zur Gegenwart* (Munich, 2000), 18, 209–13.
21. H.W. Smith, "Review of Blaschke, Konfessionen," in German Historical Institute London, *Bulletin* 25 (2003), 101–6.
22. M. Geyer, "Einleitung: Religion und Nation – Eine unbewältigte Geschichte. Einführende Betrachtungen," in *Religion und Nation. Nation und Religion. Beiträge zu einer unbewältigten Geschichte*, eds. M. Geyer and H. Lehmann (Göttingen, 2004), 11–32, 20.
23. F.W. Graf, *Die Wiederkehr der Götter. Religion in der modernen Kultur* (Bonn, 2004); J. Kocka, *Das lange 19. Jahrhundert. Arbeit, Nation und bürgerliche Gesellschaft*, 10th ed., vol. 13 (Stuttgart, 2002), 82. The other two main chapters are: "Das Jahrhundert der Industrialisierung" and "Das Jahrhundert der Bevölkerungsexplosion und der Wanderungen."
24. O. Zimmer, "Nation und Religion. Von der Imagination des Nationalen zur Verarbeitung von Nationalisierungsprozessen," *Historische Zeitschrift* 283 (2006), 617–56, 618.
25. Kocka, *Das lange 19. Jahrhundert*, 123.
26. L. Hölscher, *Datenatlas zur religiösen Geographie im protestantischen Deutschland von der Mitte des 19. Jahrhunderts bis zum Zweiten Weltkrieg*, 4 vols. (Berlin, 2001), vol. 3, 135; http:/www.fowid.de/fileadmin/datenarchiv/Kirchliches_Leben_Landeskirche_Bayern_1957-2003.pdf (Erstelldatum 6.11.2005; zuletzt gesehen: 13.1.2008).
27. Cf. more detailed O. Blaschke, "Das zweite konfessionelle Zeitalter als Parabel zwischen 1800 und 1970," zeitenblicke, (http://www.zeitenblicke.de/2006/1/Blaschke/index_html/fedradocument_view).
28. Data for Figure 8.4: B. Schneider and M. Persch, eds., *Geschichte des Bistums Trier*, vol. 4, *Auf dem Weg in die Moderne 1802–1880* (Trier, 2000), 242f.; B. Schneider and M. Persch, eds., vol. 5, *Beharrung und Erneuerung 1881–1981* (Trier, 2004), 218; M.B. Gross, *The War against Catholicism. Liberalism and the Anti-Catholic Imagination in Nineteenth-Century Germany* (Ann Arbor, 2004), 1.
29. B. Schneider, "Die Hl.-Rock-Wallfahrten von 1810 und 1844," in Schneider and Persch, vol. 4 (2000), 567–80, 577. M. Persch, "Die Hl.-Rock-Wallfahrten 1891, 1933 und 1959," in Schneider and Persch, vol. 5 (2000), 720–30. Data for 1996: www.trier.de/stadt/hr.htm.
30. F. Obermayer, *Durch Anrufung der heiligsten Dreifaltigkeit. Religiöse Flurdenkmäler im Gemeindegebiet Vilsbiburg 1900–1999* (Vilsbiburg, 2000).

Chapter 9

Their Favorite Enemy
German Social Historians and the Prussian Nobility

Stephan Malinowski

In German social history, the nobility has for a long time had about the same position that "backward peoples" had in the work of American modernization theorists.[1] Since the 1950s, Berber, Bantu, Southeast Asian rice farmers and the Prussian nobility were perceived to have shared a modernization deficit, diagnosed by social scientists inspired by modernization theory. This analogy is not completely ridiculous for a number of reasons. For one, already in 1830 German liberals made fun of the nobility as an "exotic Indian tribe,"[2] and between the French Revolution and the founding of Germany in 1870–71 the nobility worked hard to reinvent itself not only as a nonmodern but also as an antimodern institution.[3]

Just like the "backward people" depicted in the modernization texts of the 1950s and 1960s,[4] the nobility resembled (at least in the rough drawings sketched by early German social historians, following earlier critics of the nobility such as Lujo Brentano, Gustav Schmoller, Hugo Preuß and Max Weber[5]) a group which clung to backward traditions, traditions which no longer had any meaning, which were in opposition to the industrial and democratic dynamic, in other words, to progress. These "backward people" were a problem for society as a whole, with fatal consequences. The search for the "drivers and spoilers of change," a search inspired by modernization theory, which still today informs development aid projects,[6] played a prominent role in the search for the causes of the "mistaken paths" of German history.

In the 1950s and 1960s, in Germany or as an exchange student or professor abroad, many German academics were fascinated with modernization theories. As a result of these theories it was possible to undertake a large, broad, interdisciplinary analysis of societies, to interpret modernity as an "uncompleted project." This interpretation was consciously founded on a teleology. German social scientists did not share the optimism, sense of mission, overestimation of their capabilities, or the proximity to power and the misuse of that power by the American "mandarins of the future."[7] Yet the euphoria which was described by Talcott Parson's student, Clifford Geertz, of being able to participate in the "social science equivalent of the Newtonian system,"[8] was not fully foreign to the founders of the German school of social history.[9] There were further similarities as well in the emphatic affirmation of "Western values" and the empathy and support for the "long path to the West."

Even if the interpretations were nuanced and the German authors were well aware of the dark sides of modernity,[10] social historical discourse continued to be characterized by the use of normative concepts, by an adherence to a positive understanding of modernity and by a sharp criticism of modernity's enemies, especially among past mandarins.[11] Concepts from modernization theory made possible the development of theories and judgements of broad scope. Quite early, prominent critics accused these social scientists of following the principle, when analyzing structures, of if the theory does not fit the facts, too bad for the facts.[12] The mandarins of the future and the mandarins of the past shared the pragmatic belief that you have to break an egg to make an omelette.[13] It is not my purpose here to discuss how many of these basic assumptions turned out to be true. Rather it should be emphasized that for a long time the nobility was more a by-product of historical research than a carefully examined object of study. Social historians, who concentrated on change, on the dynamics of modernization, and on the forestalled modernization, had little sympathy, for obvious reasons, for the nobility. For reasons which are more difficult to understand, however, historians also did not pay much attention to the nobility—in spite of the enormous importance assigned to the "old elites." Among the important social groups, the Prussian nobility has remained the favorite enemy of social historians; they wrote a great deal about the nobility but did little empirical research on the nobility.[14] In Germany only the boom of research into the bourgeoisie, which led to a new discussion of the older motif of the feudalization of the German bourgeoisie, finally made the nobility acceptable as a social historical subject.[15]

Among the historians living in exile who brought back to the postwar generations of the Federal Republic some of the traditions destroyed after 1933, Hans Rosenberg was without a doubt the most important mediator of these analytical interpretations of the Prussian nobility.[16] Just like Max Weber before him, Rosenberg was writing about a group who belonged at the heart of his political enemies and about whom he continued to express reservations even after July 1944.[17] In New York during World War II, Rosenberg came up with a project for a large study of the Prussian landowning nobility, encompassing approximately seven hundred years.[18] When this project was conceptualized, the important question was still: what were the conditions which had brought about National Socialism. In spite of considerable efforts, far from the sources, the book was never finished. Instead, the most important work on the book market and the market for interpretations—less so among historians than among the general public—was the informative and apologetic account by Walter Görlitz. Görlitz's work was written as a narrative, at the end of which "the terrible barbarians from the Asian steppe" raged among Prussia's "best names," like in a painting by Brueghel.[19] Rosenberg, however, was able to extract from the uncompleted book a number of essays, which are still impressive today, and which have strongly influenced our interpretation of the nobility. Rosenberg himself described very precisely the early breakup of the Prussian nobility into powerful estate owners as well as a "reserve army of noble Déclassés."[20] However, just like later historians, he did not pay much attention to this last group when analyzing the behavior and position of the "old elite."

If one may use the limited space of an essay as an excuse for rough simplifications, then arguably seven basic topics concerning the Junkers were formulated by authors from Max Weber to Hans Rosenberg to the social historians of the Federal Republic.[21] These will be sketched first and then discussed critically.[22]

First, historians have stressed the alleged "consolidation" of noble and bourgeois estate owners into a homogenous "class of noble landowners" (*Rittergutsbesitzerklasse*)—the concept "Junker" can be applied equally to noble and bourgeois estate owners, suggesting more homogeneity than was actually the case.[23] Second, the inability of this class to adapt resulted in an "economic death struggle." Third, this death struggle could only be postponed by state protectionism, which itself guaranteed the Junkers a degree of power incongruous with their level of economic success. Fourth, the social scientists perceived a modernization deficit, a successful blockade of tendencies to modernize, in other words a successful defense against revolution, liberal reforms and meritocratic principles of promotion and advancement. Fifth, historians perceived the successful manipulation of the rural population through the use of "pseudo-democratic" techniques. Sixth, historians saw a bourgeoisie which attempted to imitate the noble way of life, in their self portrayal and in their political attitudes—this reproach had been formulated already in 1870–1918. Under the title "feudalization thesis," it has had a limited career in academic discourse. Seventh, historians saw an effective, long-term, noble-bourgeois "coalition of elites," which outlasted the clear political caesuras, with ominous lines of continuity extending from 1871 till 1945.

Large landowners were and have remained the benchmark for understanding the German nobility. The large landowners were the strongest faction in the nobility, economically and politically, and the most important site of (re-) production of the noble cultural model and self-understanding. It is without a doubt reasonable to study this group to try to answer the question of how the German nobility was able, successfully, in the midst of a highly dynamic industrial society, to hold on to power. However, historians examined and studied the outer parameters, things which could be counted; and, among the large landowners, where the lines of division ran directly through individual families, they only counted the eldest sons, never those sons who came after or the daughters. The obsession with the size of the estate, the harvest numbers, the manipulation of laws, and the analysis of the ranks and the positions displays a tendency "to discount what cannot be counted," as David Blackbourn has written.[24] What is ignored in a view of history fixated on the Junker's power is the quite colorful variety within the noble living environment, which will provide fascinating topics for cultural historians for decades to come. What is also absent in this sort of analysis is how strongly the nobility were already breaking down during the Kaiserreich into heterogeneous groups, groups which were often socially, culturally, and politically in opposition to one another. It has also been widely overlooked is that the nobility was often more "being driven" than it was a driving force. Finally, from this perspective one loses sight of the fact that the most important tendencies in the nobility were not the rigidity, the stubbornness, the refusal to modernize, but rather the break-up, the building of factions, the improvization, and the tendency to become more radical, more ideological. This is even more the case if 1933 is what needs to be explained.

The results of the new research into the nobility contradict the assumptions of the three models, assumptions which for decades, beginning with Weber and Rosenberg, determined our understanding of the relationship between the nobility and the bourgeoisie. On the basis of the empirical evidence, one can speak neither of a feudalization of the bourgeoisie, nor of the "bourgeoisification" of the nobility, nor of a fusioning of the two groups.[25]

It would seem more appropriate to distinguish between two contradictory basic tendencies within the nobility. Without a doubt rich and important groups from the nobility and the bourgeoisie became closer. Sponsored by Wilhelm II, who acted as the "man in the middle" between these two groups (Nicolaus Sombart), there developed at the Berlin court, in the wealthy residential districts of Berlin as well as in private salons, associations, and clubs an independent culture, which cannot be labelled either bourgeois or noble. However, and this is the central point, never more than a small minority of the nobility participated. This process was accompanied by the decline of an ever larger section of the nobility into the middle class and the development of a noble proletariat, which was supported with meagre donations of potatoes, clothes and fuel, without, however, having given up its claim to leadership in society. This group, which grew quickly during the Kaiserreich, was unable to retain its association with the power, wealth, education, and sociability of the noble-bourgeois power elite.

In the ideology of the lower nobility, banks and commerce were deemed something that "Judified" the offspring; the low nobility often regarded the high nobility a "guard to protect the Jews" (*Judenschutztruppe*) and the Kaiser, who mingled with the noble and bourgeois millionaires at the "Kieler Woche" or on trips on the North Sea, was considered a businessman, a Byzantine, a traitor or even worse: a liberal. In the words of Friedrich Naumann, he was "the dictator of industry," yes, a very despicably modern Kaiser.[26] Democracy and liberalism were not something the nobility believed in—this is once again not a German, but rather a European pattern. What was problematic and incompatible with all the tendencies toward democratization was less the figure of the large rich landowner than the groups, which in Prussia were unusually numerous, which combined increasingly meagre means with exorbitant demands. The chance to solve the problem by reforming the nobility itself was missed in the first third of the nineteenth century. Various diverse models to reform the nobility were formulated both by the nobility and by those outside the nobility; all failed. All of these projects to reform the nobility included efforts to establish fixed minimum wealth standards in order to be noble.[27] The attempt, which began in the Kaiserreich, to build up out of the lower classes in the Prussian nobility a cult of meagre means, shaped by a militarist, antimaterialist perspective, in other words, to transform the real hardship of numerous Prussian noble families into an imaginary virtue, can also be viewed as a defensive movement both against the projects to reform the nobility and against the real coalition between the rich and the powerful minorities within the nobility and the bourgeoisie. These real coalitions were sprouting up in the Kaiserreich as if in a greenhouse.

Little attention has been paid by historians, who have oriented their research to the line suggested by Weber and Rosenberg, to the development of strong factions within the nobility, the accelerated widening of the gap between the rich minority, which remained part of the elite, and the part which was sinking in the direction of the middle class or even proletariat. It is, however, just this gap, which worsened in the Kaiserreich under the dynamics of accelerated social change, which brought forth processes which were specific to the nobility, which radicalized the nobility, and which determined the relationship of various noble groups to various non-noble groups.

Concerning Weber's and Rosenberg's statements on the Junkers—their "economic death struggle," their refusal to participate in capitalism, to become capitalists or even businessmen[28]—this describes at best only a part of the noble realities and should furthermore not be read as an analytical but rather as a political statement. In the countryside the differences between noble and bourgeois landowners remained strongly accentuated and detectable up through the Third Reich. The empirical studies of the last few years, and there have been not many of them, suggest that one should emphasize the differences between the various groups which have been pooled together as the class of owners of so-called noble estates (*Rittergut*) or as Junkers. The capitalist logic of maximizing profits remained foreign to significant portions of the nobility. Instead, they tried to hold on to their possessions, which was logical enough within the framework of their economic position, and something they pursued with considerable success.

Max Weber's distortions, and their adoption in historical interpretations of the nobility inspired by modernization theory, are less astounding if one interprets them not as part of an academic discourse, but rather of a political discourse. Weber's statements concerning the nobility were part of his political writings, writings by a "class conscious bourgeois," as he described himself in 1892 during his study into agricultural laborers.[29] His assessment of the Junkers was enriched, if not with Jacobin, then at the very least with Girondist elements, and he formulated a normative criticism of the nobility on the basis of the liberal spirit of capitalism and its promise of modernization. In the final analysis, Weber was formulating here tactical and strategic positions for the liberal, capitalist cause. This is true as well for those analyses which can compete with Weber's analysis of the Junker in terms of their sharp, incisive quality, as, for example, Hugo Preuß's work published in 1897.[30] The knives which were sharpened here were for everyday political battles; even when these knives were later used in the historiography they were unable to shake off completely their genuine intention, to teach the nobility about their actual task. The link to the teleological tendencies of American modernization theory only further increased this tendency.

The feudalization thesis is based, either explicitly or implicitly, on the idea that the German bourgeoisie did not behave as it should have. This thesis has been contradicted by recent research into the bourgeoisie and the nobility. Irrespective of whether one employs so-called soft or hard historical criteria such as the choice of wife, career choice, education, or promotion into the noble ranks, it is as hard to see a fusion of the bourgeoisie and the nobility as it is to see a general bourgeois accommodation into the nobility. Paul von Schwabach or the von Siemens brothers did not become any more noble through their titles and their acquisition of villas than did, for example, Friedrich von Schiller or Johann Wolfgang von Goethe. At second glance, the air-conditioned nightmare of the Krupps' accommodation in the Villa Hügel has as little to do with noble standards as the style of life which was developed in the newly formed, largely bourgeois, wealthy districts of Berlin such as Grunewald, Wannsee, Lichterfelde, and Nikolassee.[31]

It appears that what is unusual and special about the German development is not fusion, feudalization, and a coalition of the elite but the weak synthesis among the elites.[32] From the perspective of the nobility, the synthesis of the elites remained weak during the Kaiserreich, and alliances of those who were losing their social status, among all classes, remained strong. In a Western European comparison, what is most striking is that the convergence between the leading groups of the nobility and the bourgeoisie took such a long time and required so much effort. There had been "coalitions of the elites" in many places much earlier and with greater intensity than in Germany. In Italy, where many noble families had long been a part of the urban setting, it had always been necessary to newly invent, almost artificially, the boundaries between the nobility and the bourgeoisie. In France, such coalitions happened as a result of the fact that the power and the prestige of the nobility had been broken quite early, in the revolutions between 1789 and 1871 and in the forced compromises in the elite society of the Third Republic. In England, a different understanding of the concept of the nobility, strict settlement, and the restrictive policy of granting noble titles produced an incomparably greater degree of freedom but also the obligation for sons who were not first born to consider careers in bourgeois occupations in the city, in trade and empire.[33] Around 1900 the Prussian lower nobility considered these occupations appropriate only for "Jews and their comrades."

For the three countries under consideration, one can see an "amphibious lifestyle" between the country estate and the city palace. It was above all the Prussian nobility which at the end of the nineteenth century retired from this practice or, indeed, never got into this practice. Whereas selected sections of London and Paris continued to be economically and culturally noble sites, the German capital, Berlin, had become in 1900 the hated city of parvenus, a New Jerusalem where only a few rich Prussian families had a city palace. The actual retreat from the cities and the development of a hatred of big cities, with its anti-Semitism, closed off the path to a synthesis of the elites. Furthermore, it remains confusing that noble social activity in Caritas, and in clubs and associations and the noble's hyperactivity in the public realm, which Hans Rosenberg has analyzed as a "pseudo-democratization," can be interpreted differently—many of the activities presented here correspond quite precisely with those activities which for a number of years have been discussed positively with the framework of "civil society."[34]

Max Weber modernized and made even more pointed the old bourgeois criticism of the nobility's idleness, of their "fat ways of living," stating that they, in their "degeneration," had become useless, even harmful to the state.[35] Concerning the nobility's refusal to agree to accept the meritocratic rules of the modern, achievement-oriented society, one cannot say that either Weber or Rosenberg or those who came after them are necessarily incorrect; however, there are two things that need to be pointed out. First, looked at from the perspective of an international comparison, the nobility limited itself to a remarkable degree to a few occupations: mainly agriculture, government service, and the military. Second, they had considerable success in these areas. A crude estimate suggests that the percentage of German nobles who before 1914 pursued a career in the bourgeois occupations of industry, trade, or science could scarcely have been more than 5 percent. The suggestion that the nobility rejected modernity in part because of a lack of empathy—empathy defined here, in the words of Daniel Lerner as a flexible adaption to novel situations[36]—is captured in this percentage. However, if one examines the social nucleus of the old nobility in the three occupations in which it concentrated its efforts, then the performance record, even if meritocratic criteria are applied, does not look that bad.

First of all in agriculture: the thesis of an "economic death struggle," asserted by Max Weber and taken up by Hans Rosenberg and his students as a motif, has been strongly questioned in the empirical studies of the last ten years. At the very least this is not true of the upper strata, the large landowners, the group which historical researchers have always had in mind when referring to the "Junkers." The upper third of the rich, landowning families, that is to say, the social-economic backbone of the old nobility, was able to consolidate its possessions to an amazing degree.[37] This is especially true if one takes into account the noble forests; they were run by their wealthy owners in a modern fashion, successfully competing against the bourgeoisie and the state.[38] The "death struggle" which liberalism claimed to have perceived, the long-awaited death of the Junkers, did not come about because the diagnosis was mistaken. Although the National Socialist state did not in fact do anything to the large landowners, this was not because the anti-noble aspects were absent in Darre's vision of a new nobility based on blood and the land (*Blut und Boden*), but because the competence and aptitude of the large farms were considered irreplaceable in the midst of the total war.

In 1913, about 35 percent of all officers were noble. In the General Staff, in the highest ranks and in the elite troops, the guards, the percentage of noble officers was between 50 and 90 percent, which, given that the nobility made up only about 0.2 percent of the population, was indeed considerable.[39] Of course, the fact that the nobility protected itself by recruiting from its own ranks played a big role here. However, this degree of recruiting from one's own ranks was probably less than among modern German managers; according to a 2007 study by Michael Hartmann, 80 percent of the managers of the top three hundred German firms have been recruited from families in management.[40]

In both cases there is little that logically speaks against this sort of selection. It is possible that the sons of the managers of leading German companies make especially good managers. It is also possible that the sons of noble cavalry officers can become especially good cavalry officers. One's background and heritage and one's professional abilities can be complementary. Looked at from a professional standpoint, traditional noble military abilities and military professionalism are thoroughly compatible, even in the era of industrial warfare.[41] That the nobility still made up an amazing 21 percent of the officer corps of the Weimar army and that the Nazi leadership did not want to do without the functionally quite significant contribution of the nobility in the development of the army, in the planning and carrying out of an aggressive war, may have had less to do with "feudal relics" than with the modern professional abilities of the nobility in these disciplines.

The "accomplishments" in the third area—in government service and diplomacy—do not need to be described in detail here.[42] Instead, there is a fourth area in the noble record, one which is difficult for historians to examine. This could be called the "charismatic mission" of the nobility. This can only be described using the tools of cultural history and is therefore of such importance because here one can examine those positive attributes which many contemporaries assigned to the nobility both before and after 1918. In both the right's and the left's search for authenticity beyond the boundaries of bourgeois norms, standards and work disciplines, many referred again and again to the nobility. The motif of the nobility is found in aesthetic-elitist revolts and insurrections such as are found in Stefan George and Rudolf Borchardt up through the despair and despondency of Robert Musil's "Ulrich" concerning the "brilliant racehorse," up through the reformist youth movements. The *völkisch* movement's relationship to the nobility remained as ambivalent as the *völkisch* movement itself. However, the nobility remained a conspicuous reference point for the formulation of anti-bourgeois, anti-industrial and anti-urbane ideas.[43] With the material deterioration of ever larger sections of the nobility toward the middle classes and the varied efforts to integrate the *völkisch* movement with the nobility, attempts which inevitably came from the middle class, both developments meant that the two groups inevitably moved closer to each other, with serious consequences. The nobility supplied a broad public with eccentrics and colorful characters, with individualists, and it cultivated in its military parades a symbolic discourse which was read even by many in the working class with open or secret enthusiasm. And the nobility brought forth a Kaiser who was a master at representing himself in the world of glitter and dreams.[44]

Ernst Jünger, who in *Das abenteuerliche Herz* described the bourgeois dream as the "most boring dream" humanity had ever had,[45] hit the powerful attraction of the nobility on the nose with this formulation. The question, what sort of developments would have been possible in regard to the nobility and bourgeois dreams of the nobility without World War I or with a different result to World War I, cannot be answered, like all such contra-factual questions. To ask this question, however, is useful, in order to realize how little it appeared at the time that the decline of the nobility was inevitable.

Concerning political modernization, the peculiarity of the German situation lay less in the conservative and un-modern positions than in the turning away from conservatism and in the thoroughly modern diffusion into the new right,[46] which already in the Kaiserreich affected a considerable portion of the lower nobility. Conservative and reactionary positions among the nobility would have been neither remarkable nor fatal. Italian *marchesi*, French *vicomtes* and English dukes have rarely possessed much Social Democratic willingness for reform. The image, for example in Hans Rosenberg, of an English nobility open to the industrial working class is not corroborated by empirical studies.[47] The peculiarity of the situation in Germany from the Kaiserreich up till January 1933 was less the conservative rigidity than the dynamic convergence of a phalanx of right-wing radical organizations, which were essentially bourgeois. Here, too, concerning the noble contribution to the right-wing extremist movements before and after 1918, the European comparison shows that the German peculiarity was not in the unusual strength of the (landowning) nobility, but rather its weakness in defending conservative positions against right-wing extremist positions, and its inability to prevent a considerable part of the younger generation from joining the dynamic organizations of the new, radical right, even though this new, radical right broke all of the old rules. In as much as the—still very vague—state of the historical research allows us to make international comparisons, it appears the ability of the nobility to defend itself against right-wing extremist deployment before and after 1918, to differentiate itself clearly through conservative counter models, was larger in other states.[48] There is much to be said for the thesis that right-wing extremist and fascist movements were most able to put through their ideas where they came across an especially divided, that is to say, weak, "old elite."[49]

The phalanx of the "new right" was neither created nor led by the nobility. Rather the Pan German League was, in the words of Roger Chickering, a child of German liberalism; at its heart were members of the German academic bourgeoisie and it was supported by a rather dispersed group of nobles.[50] The development of a modern "Führer" discourse, which caused lasting damage to the traditional concept of the monarch, was not a noble invention. It took place in the league and in other, similar organizations, and was largely completed by 1908.[51] Journalistic front men such as Maximilian Harden and Heinrich Claß were as bourgeois in their contributions as was, for example, Friedrich Naumann. Martin Kohlrausch has recently shown, quite convincingly, how large the pressure from the public and the free press became. He also showed how strongly the bourgeoisie demanded that the monarch change, that he become a modern leadership figure.[52] The remarkable sentence, "we demand a leader for whom we would willingly go through fire," was stated in 1913 not in a Potsdam barracks, but in a university (by Friedrich Meinecke).[53] What is important here was the alliance between the lower nobility and middle class groups. These groups were aware of their distance from the monarch, the court and the higher nobility, and they poured their resentment into an aggressive, anti-Semitic ideology of the Führer. This discourse grew steadily up through 1918, and after that, of course, exploded. The pressure exerted on the nobility from a heterogeneous milieu, the majority of which was middle class, through an extremely aggressive criticism of the nobility, was thus considerable.[54]

Finally, and this point was and remains central to our understanding of the landed nobility, we need to question their ability to manipulate the rural population. If the nobility accomplished this, then it was through the Agricultural League, the apparatus of which was in the hands of bourgeois professionals, who understood mass organization and mass agitation.[55] Furthermore, the most recent empirical studies on the changes in the power relationships in the countryside to the east of the Elbe emphasize that the rural population had considerable scope of action vis-à-vis the noble landowners. The famous description of the putting down of the revolution of 1918 provided in 1936 by Elard von Oldenburg-Januschau, a noble landowner to the east of the Elbe, a man who loved to tell stories and who was a close friend of Hindenburg, was part of the noble efforts to construct their self-image. This account is, of course, not absent in Hans Rosenberg's footnotes, just as it is not absent in the footnotes of all those authors who have written about the Prussian nobility since then. However, the scene in which the noble landowner forces his servant to the ground and restores social peace with the sentence "I'm going to beat your brains out" (*Ich hau Dich in die Fress' bis Du Kopp stehst*),[56] did not reflect the realities of the Kaiserreich. The noble's ability to manipulate was limited, as has most recently been shown by Patrick Wagner in his work on the rural power relationships in the nineteenth century,[57] and by Rainer Pomp in a recent regional study for the period after 1918. Pomp has shown that the farmers were able to exert considerable pressure on the landed nobility. Pomp's study of the pressure group's policies in Brandenburg furthermore suggests that in the final stages of this development it was not necessary to lead the farmers to the National Socialist movement.[58] Rather, if one examines the causality carefully—where there was one—it appears that it was most often the other way around. The picture described above, where the nobility was more often being driven than being the driving force, is true here as well.

In late Marxism and early Bielefeldism the idea of a "coalition of the elites" was one of the central explanations of January 1933. The question concerning the lines of continuity between 1871 and 1945, which is what Fritz Fischer was referring to with this catchy formula,[59] will remain an important question. However, the formula does not adequately reflect the historical reality concerning the social structure and the power position of the nobility. There is little empirical support—at least in the history of the nobility—for a coalition between the nobility and the bourgeoisie, which guaranteed the continuity of conservative power structures from 1870 to 1945.

There is no denying the fatal and destructive role played by the Prussian nobility in the course of the nineteenth and twentieth centuries. If we take a closer look at the empirical evidence concerning the negative role played by the nobility between 1870 and the end of World War II, assumptions found in many historical works, from Max Weber to Hans Rosenberg up through the works of the social historians in the Federal Republic of Germany, concerning this negative role will not change; indeed, the negative image may become even stronger. There is much to be said for revising aspects of the explanation of this role, taking away some parts, adding other parts to the picture. A closer examination of the nobility brings forth less the image of overly powerful and lazy "Junkers"; rather, the nobility was breaking apart socially, and only a minority were able to grow into an elite constellation of noble-bourgeois. The central concepts are not conservatism, inertia, or a rigid rejection of modernity, but rather a dynamic radicalization; not the materialistic goal of maximizing profits by a homogenous "class of noble landowners," but rather the antimaterialist production of images by sons and daughters who had little chance of success; not a class of capitalists and a synthesis of the elites, but rather fragmentation, social decline, and a *völkisch*, middle-class ideology.

It is certain that the heterogeneity among the nobility was incomparably larger, and the internal dynamics among individual groups of nobles was incomparably more complicated, than has been suggested by the recent historiography on the nobility and the manhunt for the Junkers. However, the present historiography, too, has difficulties coming up with meaningful concepts with which one can analyze the history of the nobility in the twentieth century. There has been no convincing synthesis between, on the one hand, the hastily developed construct of groups of nobles and of "noble qualities" which did not exist in reality, and, on the other hand, the proposal to place "the" "Prussian" "nobility" in quotation marks, alongside all of the analytical concepts, and thus to eliminate the essence of the nobility.[60] It is likely that a possible solution will employ the methods of cultural history. In 1943, in a proposal to American research institutions for the book he never completed on the Prussian nobility, Hans Rosenberg announced that he planned to use a "cultural approach to history" as his method.[61] Rosenberg describes here, using empirical data such as the reconstruction of the living conditions, social realities, and collective experiences, the tool with which one can reconstruct the mixture of real accomplishments—the holding on to power of a few functional elites—and the social decline and radicalization. The ideal analytical unit in the history of the nobility, as the works of Eckert Conze have shown for Germany, would be the family—in the noble sense of the word, that is, the group bearing the name.[62] The changes which took place so quickly in that group, long assumed to be inert, would become clearer if those subgroups within the nobility which have largely been ignored—women, and the sons subsequent to the first-born—were more closely examined and studied. Whether or not when looking at these groups we will see genuine possibilities[63] or whether or not we would establish that there was indeed a gradual sinking into bourgeois patterns of behavior, remains an open question. At any rate, when looking at the noble scope for action, the research into the nobility, which up till now has been mostly the history of the male nobles, must also rigorously examine the position of all these groups to the political questions—there is still, for example, no explanation of the high percentage of noble women, well above average, in the NSDAP.[64]

The majority of the lower Prussian nobility, thrown by the defeat in the war and the revolution into a world for which they were unprepared, could not have been feudalized by anyone and were unable to forge any elite coalitions. Their power, however, did suffice to move noble families so that in 1933 they would move into the study of the notorious manor house in Neudeck.[65] This history needs to be told from "below," from the perspective of the nobles, not from the perspective of the heights which the nobility themselves so gladly claimed, and which social historians have believed they occupied for far too long.

Notes

1. Here and in the following I am referring to the versions of modernization theory which were developed in the USA beginning in the 1950s. On the politics of those involved in modernization theory, see the excellent study by N. Gilman, *Mandarins of the Future. Modernization Theory in Cold War America* (Baltimore, 2003).
2. So Heinrich Laube in 1833, quoted in H.-U. Wehler, *Deutsche Gesellschaftsgeschichte*, Vol. 3 (Munich, 1995), 805.
3. S. Malinowski, *Vom König zum Führer. Sozialer Niedergang und politische Radikalisierung im deutschen Adel zwischen Kaiserreich und NS-Staat* (Berlin, 2003), 144–97, 299–320.
4. On the discussion of backwardness and modernity in the context of late colonialism and development aid, see F. Cooper, *Colonialism in Question. Theory, Knowledge, History* (Berkeley, 2005), 113–52; G. Rist, *The History of Development. From Western Origin to Global Faith* (London, 2002), 69–108.
5. Weber's criticism of the nobility is well summarized in C. Torp, *Max Weber und die preußischen Junker* (Tübingen, 1998).
6. M. Radseck, "Leitfaden zur Erstellung einer Politökonomischen Kurzanalyse," Internes Papier aus dem Bundesministerium für Wirtschaftliche Zusammenarbeit und Entwicklung, Oktober 2006.
7. Following Gilman's title, *Mandarins*.
8. Gilman, *Mandarins*, 77.

9. See the biographical sections in R. Hohls and K.H. Jarausch, eds., *Versäumte Fragen. Deutsche Historiker im Schatten des Nationalsozialismus* (Munich, 2000), and H.-U. Wehler, *Eine lebhafte Kampfsituation. Ein Gespräch mit Manfred Hettling und Cornelius Torp* (Munich, 2006).
10. T. Mergel, "Geht es weiterhin voran? Die Modernisierungstheorie auf dem Weg zu einer Theorie der Moderne," in *Geschichte zwischen Kultur und Gesellschaft. Beiträge zur Theoriedebatte*, eds. T. Mergel and T. Welskopp (Munich, 1997), 39–70.
11. Here only one prominent example: H.-U. Wehler, *Die Herausforderung der Kulturgeschichte* (Munich, 1998), above all the section on Michel Foucault, who is dissected here as a "rigorous ascetic."
12. T. Nipperdey, "Wehlers 'Kaiserreich.' Eine kritische Auseinandersetzung," *Geschichte und Gesellschaft* 1 (1975), 539–60.
13. See the balanced discussion of modernization theory, which is ultimately a resolute defense of modernization theory in H.-U. Wehler, *Modernisierungstheorie und Geschichte* (Göttingen, 1975), 58–63.
14. The most important study of the nobility to come out of the Bielefeld school, which inspired much of the most recent work on the nobility, treats neither the Kaiserreich nor "the Junkers." H. Reif, *Westfälischer Adel 1770–1860. Vom Herrschaftsstand zur regionalen Elite* (Göttingen, 1979).
15. J. Kocka, "Das europäische Muster und der deutsche Fall," in *Bürgertum im 19. Jahrhundert. Deutschland im europäischen Vergleich*, vol. 1, ed. J. Kocka (Göttingen, 1995), 9–75.
16. *Friedrich Meinecke. Akademischer Lehrer und emigrierte Schüler. Briefe und Aufzeichnungen 1910–1977*, ed. G.A. Ritter (Munich, 2006), 69–81.
17. Letter from Hans Rosenberg to his wife, 24.7.1944, in *ibid.*, 348.
18. There is a proposed outline of the Junker book in *ibid.*, 357.
19. W. Görlitz, *Die Junker. Adel und Bauer im deutschen Osten* (Limburg, 1956) (reprint, 1981), 404–31, quotation on p. 405.
20. H. Rosenberg, "Die Pseudodemokratisierung der Rittergutsbesitzerklasse," in *Machteliten und Wirtschaftskonjunkturen. Studien zur neueren deutschen Sozial- und Wirtschaftsgeschichte*, ed. H. Rosenberg (Göttingen, 1978), 83–101.
21. On the concept of the Junker, see H. Reif, "Die Junker," in *Deutsche Erinnerungsorte*, vol. 1, eds. E. François and H. Schulze (Munich, 2001), 520–36.
22. Cf. the literature review in H. Reif, *Adel im 19. und 20. Jahrhundert* (Munich, 1999).
23. This is the formulation employed by Rosenberg in his most influential essay on the history of the nobility, first published in 1958: "Pseudodemokratisierung."
24. D. Blackbourn, "A Thoroughly Modern Masterpiece. Wehler's Deutsche Gesellschaftsgeschichte. Vol. 3, 1849–1914," *Neue Politische Literatur* 41 (1996), 189–92, quotation on p. 191.
25. Malinowski, *König*, 121–44 (with a discussion of the most recent literature).
26. Ibid.,170–97; M. Kohlrausch, *Der Monarch im Skandal. Die Logik der Massenmedien und die Transformation der wilhelminischen Monarchie* (Berlin, 2005), 417 (Naumann).
27. H. Reif, "Adelserneuerung und Adelsreform in Deutschland 1815–1874," in *Adel und Bürgertum in Deutschland 1770–1848*, ed. Elisabeth Fehrenbach (Munich, 1994), 203–30.
28. M. Weber, "Der Nationalstaat und die Volkswirtschaftspolitik. Akademische Antrittsrede," in *Max Weber Gesamtausgabe*, vol. I/4, ed. W.J. Mommsen (Tübingen, 1993), 543–74, quotation on p. 567.
29. Torp, *Weber*, 62–79, quotation on p. 75.
30. H. Preuß, *Die Junkerfrage* (Berlin, 1897).
31. D.L. Augustine, *Patricians and Parvenus. Wealth and High Society In Wilhelmine Germany* (Oxford, 1994).
32. See the literature review in Reif, *Adel*.
33. T. Kroll, "Dynastische Adelspolitik und gesellschaftlicher Wandel im Italien des Risorgimento. Der toskanische Adel in der bürokratischen Monarchie," in *Adel und Moderne. Deutschland im europäischen Vergleich im 19. und 20. Jahrhundert*, eds. E. Conze and M. Wienfort (Cologne, 2004), 19–39; D. Cannadine, *Lords and Landlords. The Aristocracy and the Towns 1774–1967* (Leicester,

1980); C.I. Brelot, *La noblesse réinventée. Nobles de Franche-Comté de 1814 à 1870*, 2 vols. (Paris, 1992).
34. S. Malinowski, "Wie zivil war der deutsche Adel? Anmerkungen zum Verhältnis von Adel und Zivilgesellschaft zwischen 1871 und 1933," in *Zivilgesellschaft als Geschichte. Studien zum 19. und 20. Jahrhundert*, eds. R. Jessen et al. (Wiesbaden, 2004).
35. Quoted in Torp, *Weber*, 24, 52.
36. D. Lerner, *The Passing of Traditional Society* (Glencloe, IL, 1958).
37. Two of the richest empirical studies on this are: R. Schiller, *Vom Rittergut zum Großgrundbesitz. Ökonomische und soziale Transformationsprozesse der ländlichen Eliten in Brandenburg im 19. Jahrhundert* (Berlin, 2003); I. Buchsteiner, *Großgrundbesitz in Pommern 1871–1914. Ökonomische, soziale und politische Transformation der Großgrundbesitzer* (Berlin, 1992).
38. W.G. Theilemann, *Adel im grünen Rock. Adliges Jägertum, Großprivatwaldbesitz und die preußische Forstbeamtenschaft 1866–1914* (Berlin, 2004).
39. D. Bald, *Der deutsche Offizier. Sozial- und Bildungsgeschichte des deutschen Offizierskorps im 20. Jahrhundert* (Munich, 1982).
40. M. Hartmann, *Der Mythos von den Leistungseliten. Spitzenkarrieren und soziale Herkunft in Wirtschaft, Politik, Justiz und Wissenschaft* (Frankfurt, 2002).
41. The most thorough analysis of this can be found in M. Funck, *Feudales Kriegertum und militärische Professionalität. Der Adel im preußisch-deutschen Offizierkorps 1860–1935* (Berlin, 2010).
42. Among recent works, the best is: H. Spenkuch, *Das Preußische Herrenhaus. Adel und Bürgertum in der Ersten Kammer des Landtags; 1854–1918* (Düsseldorf, 1998).
43. A. Gerstner, *Rassenadel und Sozialaristokratie. Adelsvorstellungen in der völkischen Bewegung (1890–1914)* (Berlin, 2003); U. Puschner, *Die völkische Bewegung im wilhelminischen Kaiserreich. Sprache – Rasse – Religion* (Darmstadt, 2001).
44. N. Sombart, *Wilhelm II. Sündenbock und Herr der Mitte* (Berlin, 1996); Kohlrausch, *Monarch*.
45. E. Jünger, *Das Abenteuerliche Herz (1929)* (Stuttgart, 1987), 131.
46. S. Breuer, *Ordnungen der Ungleichheit. Die deutsche Rechte im Widerstreit ihrer Ideen 1871–1945* (Darmstadt, 2001).
47. Rosenberg, "Pseudodemokratisierung," 95.
48. For a comparative perspective on the French nobility of the Third Republic, see S. Malinowski, "A Counter-Revolution *d'outre-tombe*: Notes on the French Aristocracy and the Extreme Right during the Third Republic and the Vichy Regime," in *European Aristocracies and the Radical Right 1918–1939*, ed. K. Urbach (Oxford, 2007), 15–34, as well as the essays collected here on, amongst others, England, Spain, Italy, Belgium, and Holland.
49. S. Payne, *Geschichte des Faschismus. Aufstieg und Fall einer europäischen Bewegung* (Munich, 2001).
50. R. Chickering, *We Men Who Feel Most German. A Cultural Study of the Pan-German League 1886–1914* (Boston, 1984), 303.
51. See, on this phenomenon, from three different perspectives: I. Hull, *The Entourage of Kaiser Wilhelm II 1888–1918* (New York, 1982); M. Funck, "Vom Höfling zum soldatischen Mann? Entwürfe und Umwandlungen adliger Männlichkeit vom Kaiserreich zum Nationalsozialismus," in *Adel und Moderne. Deutschland im europäischen Vergleich im 19. und 20. Jahrhundert*, eds. E. Conze and M. Wienfort (Cologne, 2004); and Kohlrausch, *Monarch*, 156–300.
52. Kohlrausch, *Monarch*, 139–46, 461–69.
53. F. Meinecke, "Deutsche Jahrhundertfeier und Kaiserfeier. Freiburger Universitätsrede vom 14.6.1913," *Logos* 4 (1913), 161–75.
54. Malinowski, *König*, 145–97.
55. Still unsurpassed: H.J. Puhle, *Agrarische Interessenpolitik und preußischer Konservatismus im Wilhelminischen Reich (1893–1914). Ein Beitrag zur Analyse des Nationalismus in Deutschland am Beispiel des Bundes der Landwirte und der Deutsch-Konservativen Partei* (Hannover, 1966).
56. E.v. Oldenburg-Januschau, *Erinnerungen* (Berlin, 1936), 208f.
57. P. Wagner, *Bauern, Junker und Beamte. Der Wandel lokaler Herrschaft und Partizipation im Ostelbien des 19. Jahrhunderts* (Göttingen, 2005).

58. R. Pomp, *Bauern und Großgrundbesitzer auf ihrem Marsch ins Dritte Reich. Der Brandenburgische Landbund 1919–1933* (Berlin, 2000).
59. F. Fischer, *Bündnis der Eliten. Zur Kontinuität der Machtstrukturen in Deutschland 1871–1945* (Düsseldorf, 1979), 11–15, 63–75.
60. Recently C. Tacke stated in her critical review of recent works on the nobility, in which she discusses, amongst other topics, the weaknesses and the limits of the "nobility" as a concept: "it is important to avoid the hasty application of the conceptual language to the political history." "Adel" und "Adeligkeit" in der modernen Gesellschaft, *Neue Politische Literatur* 1 (2007), 91–123.
61. Hans Rosenberg's outline of his proposed research for a book on the "Junkers," submitted to an American foundation, is reprinted in *Friedrich Meinecke*, 345–48, quotation on p. 347.
62. E. Conze, *Von deutschem Adel. Die Grafen von Bernstorff im zwanzigsten Jahrhundert* (Stuttgart, 2000).
63. This was recently suggested by M. Wienfort in "Adlige Handlungsspielräume und neue Adelstypen in der 'Klassischen Moderne' (1880–1930)," *Geschichte und Gesellschaft* 33 (2007), 416–38.
64. Malinowski, *König*, 577f.
65. Most recently: W. Pyta, *Herrschaft zwischen Hohenzollern und Hitler* (Munich, 2007).

Chapter 10

A Difficult Relationship
Social History and the Bourgeoisie

Manfred Hettling

German social history and working-class history were so closely linked like partners in a long marriage. Beginning with the studies of the "Vereins für Socialpolitik" in the late nineteenth century, research into the working class was at the center of social historical studies; historians were especially interested in the material conditions of the lower classes during industrialization. In the Federal Republic of Germany, this interest in living conditions was especially strong in the 1960s and 1970s. Part of the motivation for this interest came from the way East German historians investigated the history of the working-class movement, concentrating on the movement's political forms of organization. In the west as in the east, the interest in the history of the working class was given an impetus by the desire to be working on the history of the underdogs and the underprivileged. In terms of its methodology, for a long time social history in Germany was considered innovative. An example of this was the turn to working-class culture, which took place quite early.[1] Thus, the working class was the only social group which was the subject of a large research project, which brought together some of the best known social historians in the Federal Republic of Germany. The completion of this impressive project, which was to be a number of volumes, has been postponed for a number of reasons. One of these is that in the last two decades German social historians have moved to other topics, especially the bourgeoisie. In this essay I will attempt, first, to offer a balance of the work done on the German bourgeoisie and to sketch out the significance of this body of historical work for the interpretation of the German Empire. In so doing I will make clear how the investigation of the bourgeoisie and bourgeois culture has challenged the theoretical and methodological arsenal developed by social historians. In the second part I will sketch the perspectives for future work on the history of the German bourgeoisie—where are the new interesting directions, what are the most interesting questions?

I

Since the 1980s the bourgeoisie, a glimmering, appealing object, has been studied intensely by social historians.[2] At the beginning the project was limited in size. The "Working Group on Modern Social History," which brought together some of the most influential West German historians, had discovered the academic bourgeoisie (*Bildungsbürgertum*) as a historical topic, and quickly invested more time and energy in this topic than it had planned. At the beginning, one had still hoped to be able to define and describe the bourgeoisie as a social formation of the nineteenth century as, for example, one could describe the urban bourgeoisie of the early modern period or the bourgeois third estate of the eighteenth century.[3] However, after numerous meetings of the working group, after four anthologies and after culture had been discovered as an interesting field of investigation by social historians, Jürgen Kocka opened the final meeting of the group with the resigned question, whether the academic bourgeoisie was not a construction of the historian's imagination rather than a social formation.[4] The object one had fallen in love with had turned out to be extremely enigmatic.

In spite of this scepticism, the bourgeoisie continued to remain an attractive topic. According to the program of the Collaborative Research Centre in Bielefeld (*Sonderforschungsbereich*), which has existed since 1986, investigating this concept should provide the answer to three very important sets of questions. First, was the nineteenth century a "bourgeois century" and the society of the nineteenth century a bourgeois society? Second, was the German *Sonderweg* tied up with the weak development of bourgeois characteristics? And third, how can historians participate in a meaningful discussion of modernity?[5]

The central questions listed above are all indebted to the critical attitude, the spirit of criticism of the 1970s. As a result of this critical attitude, "society" became the most important category for the historical social sciences. Ironically, however, the "critical reappraisal" of the German past by a "critical social science" did not lead to extensive empirical studies of bourgeois society. Because historians assumed there was a deficit of bourgeois characteristics, they believed that there was little to be gained from costly and difficult empirical work. Indeed, it was the gradual vanishing of the critical judgement of the past which appears to have made it possible for there to be open-ended empirical studies.

There have been two major areas of interest among West German historians since the 1980s. First, at the Collaborative Research Centre in Bielefeld the question of how one was actually to define the unity of the bourgeoisie as a social formation has become ever more important. To the degree that historical studies on the bourgeoisie have become more empirical, to that degree have historians more and more turned away from the category of class and, instead, have begun to see culture as a bracket, as attributes which define one's identity.[6] Second, in the working group, "city and bourgeoisie," initiated by Lothar Gall, which met at the same time, the interest has centered on the analysis of the slow transformation of the premodern urban bourgeoisie up through the German Empire.[7] In spite of differences, very quickly a consensus was reached. In a number of comparative studies, based on intensive research, historians concluded that the lack of bourgeois values, long postulated as a German deficit, was a myth.[8] The bourgeoisie was quite able to shape experiences as well as social and cultural perceptions in the cities. It became ever clearer that the German Empire could not be adequately described either as a society of meek subjects or as a Wilhelminian court society.

One of the most important, if indeed not the most important finding of the research, was to have discovered and to have investigated the internal variety, the quantitative weight, and the political and social power of the bourgeoisie. The bourgeoisie, defined here as an ensemble of class positions determined by wealth and education, proved to be both numerically and in terms of its social standing much more successful than the old *Sonderweg* interpretations had postulated. Many researchers employed in their studies a broad concept of class. Although in the "Frankfurt school" around Lothar Gall there was a special emphasis on law— to be more exact, on urban law, which privileged a small group of residents in Germany—there has been a wide consensus among the various researchers concerning the importance of material interests and forms of social and political interaction. In many cases it has only recently become possible, on the basis of work done during this period, to describe more exactly the social reality of the bourgeois world of the nineteenth century.

The research done by social historians into the bourgeoisie has broadened our understanding of the concept of class. At present, historians largely agree that class has to be understood as "social class" and not in the traditional Marxist sense as the ownership of the means of production. Recently, Charles Tilly listed five quite different characteristics of the modern concept of social class. First, there are the hierarchical arrangements in realms such as esteem and reputation, health, and power; second, the power of control over markets; third, self-consciousness and culture; fourth, the relationship to the means of production; and fifth, a description of numerous and heterogeneous dimensions of inequality, which was in terms of its classification units a simplification, and which would have been better described in another manner. In Germany, Marxist historians have concentrated on the fourth dimension, with varying degrees of success. Hartmut Zwahr's attempt to investigate the bourgeoisie and the proletariat as complementary figures, closely intertwined and developed during the course of the industrialization, has proved to be the most profitable; Zwahr has also made an important distinction between the bourgeoisie and the *Bürgertum*.[9] In contrast, West German historians, unlike the East German, defined the bourgeoisie as an ensemble of classes defined by what one owned and where one worked. They were especially interested in the "academic bourgeoisie," especially those who were self-employed. (In Tilly's terms, based on Max Weber, this is his second criteria.) Hierarchical differences in the various spheres of life (Tilly's first criteria) are at the forefront of the social science analysis and their description of contemporary societies. There are almost no historical studies on this; as a rule, the problem is the sources. In the last couple of decades the most innovative work has been in studies which investigated classes primarily by analyzing their common forms of consciousness and cultural forms of expression. This has, however, led to an increased awareness of the differences within the bourgeoisie, raising the question: what is actually meant by the concept and the phenomena "bourgeoisie." This discussion is still continuing.

On the basis of this recent work we see that those studies which employ a modern concept of class have made visible a broad variety of material and intellectual interests. Thus, our understanding of the "economic bourgeoisie" becomes more differentiated. The concept of the bourgeoisie is no longer reduced to industrial entrepreneurs. Rather, the part of the bourgeoisie involved in trade was far more important in the nineteenth century, not only quantitatively. Empirical studies have shown the broad, varied possibilities of earning money among the bourgeoisie. The large industrial entrepreneurs of the late nineteenth century, the Krupps, Siemens, Rathenau, and so on, typical of the large industrial firms and their new technical possibilities, were for a long time considered exemplary of an imputed "feudalization of the bourgeoisie." Yet they were a group that appeared late on the stage and were a small minority. The social influence of the bourgeois lifestyle came largely from the influence of the economic lower-middle and middle class. They had an income and possessions which were well above the average of the population. However, they were not exactly synonymous with wealth and they did not become wealthy.

If there was one social-economic characteristic that individual occupations in the bourgeoisie shared, it was "independence," understood as a composition of social, cultural, political, and economic dimensions, not as property. Economic wealth was combined with social respect, with political participation (for many decades, the right to vote depended upon a degree of economic independence) and with cultural representation.[10] A broader definition of class lets us see that in the concept of economic independence one can find an anchor, a common foundation between the economic bourgeoisie and the academic bourgeois subgroups. Independence could be based on one's possessions—but it could also be based on a particular profession. It has often been overlooked that although classic representatives of the academic bourgeoisie such as doctors or lawyers possessed academic patents, they were at the same time self-employed and forced to comply with the laws of the market. For the historical analysis of the bourgeoisie it has therefore been fruitful to employ a broader definition of class, one which does not reduce interests merely to their material dimension.

The discovery of the bourgeoisie by historians had thus a number of quite different sources. For one, through empirical studies many wanted to rebut Geoff Eley, David Blackbourn and others, who had questioned the thesis, long postulated, of a deficit of bourgeois characteristics.[11] Moreover, the development of new theoretical issues forced historians to pay more attention to new aspects of bourgeois society. The transformation of cultural theory meant that historians had to concentrate on subjective perspectives, on systems of symbols, on interpretations and meanings. Accordingly, we can investigate the bourgeoisie today in a much more differentiated, complex, and interesting manner than was the case with the analytical tools we used to study the working class. It is not the lack of, but rather the excess of subjective statements by bourgeois men and women which scared away historians. And, even more important, not only characters in novels like *Werther* discovered the newly conceptualized subjectivity; rather, bourgeois contemporaries developed their own subjective and independent cosmos. Since Humboldt an empathetic understanding of such worlds has been the program of historicism.[12] The historicist methodology has been neglected because of developments in the methodology of social history since the 1960s; there has been a fundamental break in the methodology of writing history, making it "independent of historicism" (Wolfgang J. Mommsen). A world which had faded away from the everyday experiences of the modern historian now became attractive as a research field, and this interest was intensified under the banner of cultural history. This was the charm of the new research field; the historian's relationship with the bourgeoisie began with the discovery of the world of inner and outer subjectivity.

Topics which only a few years earlier were of peripheral interest, such as duels, court theatre, the education of children, troubles in love, clothes and fashion, were now being studied intensively and, even more importantly, were the topic of programmatic discussions.[13] The charm of the new was that it opened up undiscovered areas which social historians had been unable to describe well with traditional categories such as interests or social positions. There is now a broad consensus that the bourgeoisie cannot adequately be described in terms of class. However, it still remains an open question as to how the bourgeoisie is to be defined in cultural terms. This may be the result of the fact that the historical perspective on the culture of the bourgeoisie, on bourgeois values and attitudes, in spite of all the modifications, has tended to remain indebted to objective criteria. If social formations cannot be defined by their interests, then one wanted "to take as the benchmark those social situations and figures in which the bourgeois cultural practice presented itself as a concrete social context for their actions." One hoped that through this analysis one would be able to decipher quickly that hidden power which "held the bourgeoisie together."[14] However, this hope turned out to be misguided. In most cases the turn to culture has privileged small scale, at best micro-historical studies. Historians found out quite quickly that the culture of the bourgeoisie is at least as manifold and contradictory as the class attributes. And, given an undisputed differentiation of bourgeois cultural practice and social formations, historians were unable to give a satisfactory answer to the question of the political consequences of the deficit of bourgeois values, which had long been imputed.

German society in the age of industrialization and urbanization was transformed very quickly from an agrarian to an industrial society, with a rapid urbanization. The large social groups in the German Empire were thus in the midst of a rapid development. Since contemporaries were unable to describe or analyze adequately these groups in valid empirical studies, the terms employed to describe them are more often presentations of ideological interpretations than anything else. Contemporary scholars such as Sombart had already responded to this challenge by increasingly investigating the intellectual and ideological content of these concepts.[15] They distinguished between various large groups within the category of "social classes," according to their place in the economic system. Even allowing for all the methodological scepticism which one needs to have in regard to Sombart, his concept is similar to Max Weber's socialization concept, which is theoretically much more stringent and methodologically realizable, or to Josef Schumpeter's conception of social class. For similar reasons, historians have worked with great success, repeatedly, with concepts such as milieu, camp, even the "middle." These concepts became especially fruitful if through them the mechanisms of the linkage between the diverse social groups were investigated. It is indispensable therefore, even if one is concentrating on the culture of the bourgeoisie, to ask about those mechanisms which worked to integrate, to hold together the partial formations of a bourgeoisie which was becoming more diverse, more differentiated.

One of the conclusions of recent research is that there is not a clear identity between "class" and "culture." The popularity of the concept "social class" reflects the theoretical challenges. Numerous previous studies have made visible many new aspects; however, there are few new ideas being offered, at least which are conceptionally convincing, which would help synthesize these perspectives.

II

In the last few years, German social historians have often employed the concept of socialization (*Vergesellschaftung*) introduced by Rainer M. Lepsius.[16] However, there has been no empirical work, such as was suggested by Max Weber. It is thus not surprising that the most convincing attempts to define theoretically the relationship between culture and the bourgeoisie have not come from historians. Friedrich Tenbruck and Karl Eibl have developed functional definitions of bourgeois culture which avoid the danger of social-historical reductionism.[17] According to them, forms of socialization develop in the tension between economic interests and ideas of political order (Lepsius); in other words, "cultural socialization" can be understood as an interpretation of the reality beyond social borders. According to Tenbruck and Eibl, bourgeois culture describes a specific way of interpreting reality. This method of understanding reality is constituted through the self-reflection on this reality and not through the social interests themselves. Eibl has remarked sarcastically—referring to Hans-Ulrich Wehler and Thomas Nipperdey—that whoever speaks of a deficit of bourgeois values aims to repair a deficit in academic concepts through the recourse to a norm and defines the theoretical deficit as the defect. Instead, according to Eibl, it makes more sense to look for "sets of identical problems" which were addressed with genuine attempts to find cultural answers.[18] Eibl describes three fundamental cultural problems. First, there was the problem of social disintegration, second, the challenge of individuality (the development of the concept of the self, including the ability to reflect on one's self as someone who plays various roles), and third, the discovery of contingency, the openness of the world.[19] One of the ironies of the research landscape is that in spite of the turn to culture and the opening up to cultural history, those theoretical concepts which enable one to analyze empirically the object of study through processes of cultural socialization have scarcely been used.[20]

Investigating such processes makes it possible, instead of searching for deficits in "bourgeois values," regardless of how one defines them, to understand bourgeois values as an answer to specific challenges, and then to investigate the interpretations and possibilities stimulated by this. This shifts the perspective from a deficit to a challenge, and opens up a perspective on what sort of different answers were developed to this challenge. A comparative historical perspective appears to me to be especially fruitful here, for it enables us to update our work. In order to explain how this might be possible, in the following pages I have formulated some hypotheses and wish to sketch, briefly, some recommendations. If one looks from this background at the debates on bourgeois values in the German Empire, then old questions can be asked in a new way, without having to repeat the old battles. It seems to me that six aspects are most likely to offer the most fruitful perspective for theoretically challenging work on those social formations which were fragmenting in the late nineteenth century and their further development in the twentieth century. Working on these problems should provide new answers to the old question of how Germany met the challenges of social modernity. Of course, I make no claim to completeness.

1. One of the most remarkable deficits in the social history of the modern bourgeoisie lies in the neglect of the family. In contrast to the early modern period, the influence of family ties and the structures of relationships between relatives in the formation of social classes in the nineteenth and twentieth century has only been cursorily investigated. Recent research has shown that in the eighteenth and nineteenth centuries the family had a special significance, indeed, that the formation of class structures was closely intertwined with a revalorization of the concept of the family. Family was a special pattern of relationships and functioned as a supportive and stabilizing framework. When the traditional estate-based society broke up, indeed, family increasingly became the environment, which enabled one to develop one's personality along new lines.[21] Around 1900, however, it appears that this emphasis on family relationships, which had been reflected marriages inside the family (e.g. between cousins) broke down—across Europe. It is likely that only because of this change in the meaning of family were

other forms of relationships—such as the developing social-moral milieus—able to become more important. What consequences this had for the modern bourgeoisie has yet to be investigated.

2. The cultural criticism (*Kulturkritik*) was a reformulation of bourgeois patterns of interpretation. If one defines bourgeois values as a pattern of culture, which around 1800 offered answers to the challenges of the breaking apart of a society which was divided up into estates and the ever developing modernity, then the cultural criticism at the turn of the century can be seen as a discussion within the bourgeoisie itself concerning the redesigning and reshaping of the patterns of bourgeois culture. The "cultural pessimism" of Lagarde, Langbehn and Moeller van den Bruck is as much a part of this discussion as is the cultural optimism of Ernst Haeckel, or the emphatic criticism of Friedrich Nietzsche, or the heroic skepticism of Max Weber.

Therefore we need to investigate the heterogenous bourgeois answers to the special problems of modernity since the late nineteenth century. Concepts, circles, and directions which were developed around 1900 brought about a profound change in the shape of bourgeois values which had developed around 1800. The "dissolving" of the bourgeoisie since the end of the nineteenth century, an interpretation of Hans Mommsen's which has had a good deal of influence in the historical profession, captures only one aspect of the bourgeois past. At the same time there were numerous laboratories where the bourgeoisie experimented with the challenges of modernity—from the right to the left, in large cities and in small towns, with an emphasis on aesthetics or on politics or on social reform.

It is therefore necessary to question those contemporary interpretations which did not overcome the social disintegration, but which, through reference to political and social arrangements and institutions of mediation sought, as it were, to make the consequences of social disintegration manageable. Furthermore, we need to ask about the changing conceptions and practices of individuality and the formation of the self in regard to what degree they thematize the ability of people to step outside of themselves, to perceive themselves as someone who plays a number of social roles—without sketching out solutions which promised to remove this role-playing and thus the tension of the autonomy of the world. Thus, the great debate around 1900 concerning capitalism and how it threatened to destroy the social order stimulated, on the one hand, a flight into new, harmonious social models such as the *Volksgemeinschaft*, and, on the other hand, considerations concerning the "limits of community" (Plessner). Both of these can be characterized as a bourgeois answer and both of these answers broke with traditional bourgeois values. Finally, one needs to ask to what degree the counter-world to the tangible reality can, to be sure, be represented and thematized, without however suggesting that this counter-world has been tamed or that we have surrendered to it. For all of these areas there is enough evidence, especially in regard to the critique of contemporary culture at the turn of the century, where there was an intensive discussion over bourgeois as well as non-bourgeois answers.[22] The intensity of this debate over culture in the decades after 1890 and its dynamic which transcends political caesura have been only partly analyzed. What is lacking, above all, is an intensive discussion of the rise of mass culture as both a threat and a possibility—the research on bourgeois values has scarcely looked at this topic.[23]

Furthermore, we also need in this discussion to move beyond the historical period usually discussed when we discuss the history of "bourgeois culture" as cultural socialization. The theoretical concepts developed by Tenbruck and Eibl apply above all to the period when bourgeois values were being developed, around 1800. Both authors reflect only in passing on the degree to which changes—Klaus Tenfelde's "transformation"[24]—have actually taken place in the last two centuries. The question therefore needs to be asked, does the theoretical understanding of bourgeois values which had as its reference point the beginning of the bourgeois world around 1800 still apply under the conditions of mass culture in the twentieth century? Or is there here a completely differently constituted "dissolving" of bourgeois values beyond politics? Here is a continuing weakness of our study of the bourgeois way of life. Even the modern debate on civil society has taken place—and still is taking place—separate from the historical discussion of bourgeois values.

3. In this context, one of the greatest challenges historians face is to analyze the bourgeois answers to the rise of mass culture. Mass culture became visible before 1914 and spread quickly after 1918 under the difficult conditions, in material and social-psychological terms, of a society which had lost the war. The analysis of the bourgeois response can only be profitable if bourgeois values and mass culture are not set up as simple opposites, for then one reduces bourgeois values to high culture and we are confronted once again with the old degeneration thesis. Instead, we need to analyze problems and constellations. It is clear that the transformation of bourgeois values in Germany in the early twentieth century cannot just be reduced to the effects of the decay of the political order and the destruction of material goods during the inflation, but that it is also tied up with the challenges of mass culture. We need more work here. For the changes in bourgeois values in and since the early twentieth century cannot be sufficiently understood merely as a reaction to external crises (defeat, revolution, inflation, world economic depression). On the one hand, the collapse of the political and social foundations—so to speak, the outer framework—was important. On the other hand, the collapse of classical "bourgeois ways of thinking and living" (Kondylis) due to mass democracy and mass culture was also important, and these developments took place in parallel. This concurrence has been scarcely investigated in terms of the history of ideas, especially in regard to its political explosiveness.[25] Even the many attempts to anchor "community" as a central political argument can be related back to this constellation.

4. Any discussion of the *Sonderweg* necessarily includes, besides the analysis of the political problem under investigation, a discussion of the relationship between

long-term and short-term explanations.[26] This is often forgotten. From our perspective today, one can certainly criticize the picture of German history moving unfailingly in the direction of 1933, such as was put forward by Wehler in his book in 1973. However, do those interpretations which emphasize the "numerous continuities" (Thomas Nipperdey) or the "numerous faces" (Dieter Langewiesche) really advance our understanding?[27] If one asks, as Weber might have, "what chain of circumstances led to the fact"[28] that in 1933 only in Germany did a totalitarian-fascist system come to power, and after 1939 during the war, increasingly developed, planned and carried out genocide—are those explanations which emphasize short-term factors sufficient? This problem comes up especially when one emphasizes the special importance of the state in German bourgeois values. That one's self-understanding as bourgeois in Germany did not include political participation (except in the realm of self-administration, which, however, was conceived of as unpolitical) can be shown quite well in a comparative perspective.[29] The question comes up here as well, how did short-term factors mix with these long-term structural patterns in the changed constellation after 1918?

Classical historical explanations differentiated between short-term and long-term factors. Now historians tend to emphasize short-term factors in their explanations of the end of Weimar and the rise of National Socialism, and pay less attention to long-term factors. In so doing, historians are privileging contemporary explanations—one thinks of the Revolution of 1918, the end of the monarchy, the inflation, and such like. To the degree that cultural history privileges subjective factors such as perception, this has certainly contributed to our moving away from looking at long-term structural patterns (forms of socialization, mental character, behavioural patterns, and so on).

Today the "continuity history,"[30] as Nipperdey once sarcastically called it, has lost a good deal of its public and political impact. Pleas for the openness of history, for accepting the ambivalence of historical reality, are becoming increasingly common. Yet it seems that one of the goals of the old as well as the new research into the history of Germany from 1870 to 1918 is still all too seldom achieved. The key "question of attribution" remains "not a question of laws but of concrete causal relationships; it is not a question of the subsumption of the event under some general rubric as a representative case but of its imputation as a consequence of some constellation."[31]

To formulate the question in Weberian terms means to ask about the specific constellation, about the "interlinkage of factors and circumstances." To ask this question is still appropriate if the question is about the explanation, about a phenomenon. A "history of continuity" as well as every "history of pluralities" fails to develop this potential; none ask questions regarding historical events about the "structure of what made things possible," nor do they sound out the mutual interlacing of "inevitable developments" and "room to manoeuvre."[32]

Finally, one more point which so far does not seem to have been brought up in the discussion on the *Sonderweg*. The strength of the older literature on the *Sonderweg* was that it asked about continuities, about long-term developments and conditions in order to apply the answers to its narratives of German history. This was certainly compatible with historicism, so long as historicism was not reduced to a mere narrative of events. However, linking the question concerning long-term conditions with a turning away from this tradition, rooted in the experiences of a new generation, led to a radicalization of this interpretation. If the *Sonderweg* theory is so closely tied to a collective experience which was specific to a certain generation, then to what experiences are those tied who criticize the theory?

The new interpretations of those who were born later—are they also tied up with a change in their life's experiences? One can perceive here at any rate less of a methodological development than was the case with social history. Social history was justified, even if it was an exaggeration, to claim in the 1970s that it represented a paradigm change. Influenced by Koselleck, one could argue that the experience of the break represented by National Socialism led to a privileging of structures, to examining their long-term formation and their long-lasting durability—in the shape of the old *Sonderweg* thesis. To turn this around, it appears that the experience of social and democratic stability has animated those born after 1945 to concentrate increasingly on short-term explanations. Making these generational experiences more explicit could possibly be one way of moving the debate out of the rut it has fallen into.

5. There remains in the current discussion, which emphasizes the social and cultural creative power of bourgeois groups in the German Empire, an amazing gap in regard to an old event that needs to be explained, namely the collapse of Weimar political democracy. In this discussion the bourgeois culture of the German Empire, generally described in positive terms, is analyzed separately from the collapse of the Weimar Republic. By emphasizing the short-term factors to explain 1933—World War I, the Revolution of 1918, the Great Depression—one is turning one's back on longer perspectives. In so doing, one endeavors, once again, to use the political events as an *explanans*, or even the subjective interpretations of the actors. This is a result of the fact that one is asking much less than one did earlier about the political power and persuasiveness of groups and ideas. This may also be the result of the specific bias of cultural history not to privilege questions of political power. Thus, the discussion concerning the "democratization" of political life in the German Empire has produced impressive results in regard to changes in voting culture and the deep popularity and acceptance of certain election procedures and election standards among broad sections of the population of the German Empire.[33] To what degree, however, a possible parliamentarization could have been a result of this democratization—this needs to be addressed much more skeptically. In this context, one has scarcely discussed the significance of the cultural fragmentation of the bourgeoisie for the bourgeoisie's political orientation.[34] The discussion which has recently broken out concerning the German Empire's potential for reform, to democratize, has in the final analysis ignored the debate concerning bourgeois culture. Whereas the old deficit thesis set forth its argument with the assumption of a (as we have come to

realize) mistaken conception of the social weakness of the bourgeoisie, the new narrative of the bourgeois creative power in the German Empire hardly pays any attention at all to the political dimension. This is reflected in the fact that the discussion concerning the degree to which the political order of the time could be reformed[35] is still being argued within the framework of traditional political history. To be sure, historians have investigated in great detail the political culture of elections; however, the attempt to create a link between bourgeois culture and the politics of the citizens has not been successful.

With this, historians repeat a division such as was already found in the perception and political practice of the German Empire. Max Weber's father, for example, who was a salaried city councillor first in Erfurt and then from 1869 in Berlin, cultivated in Berlin a salon where political issues were discussed. There was a great discrepancy between the work of the salaried city councillor—civil engineering, especially road construction—and the discussions which took place in the salon. There people discussed intensely and passionately the political themes of the day, especially Bismarck's policies and actions. However, the bourgeoisie remained largely excluded from having any influence on these large questions of the day, in spite of all their accomplishments, their scope of action and creative power in regard to canalization, energy supply and city planning.[36]

6. It seems to be necessary to go beyond the traditional borders of the epochs, which are still set in terms of political and state history—and thus to go beyond 1918. There is certainly a great deal of profit in crossing temporal borders not only in regard to understanding bourgeois values, but also in opening up perspectives for further work on the German Empire. When Jürgen Kocka for example emphasizes that one has to keep in mind the special constellation surrounding the origin of the German Empire, this is at least as true for its end; in both cases constellations emerged for which there was nothing comparable in Europe. This could perhaps prove to be more profitable than simply overcoming the territorial borders under the auspices of trans-nationality. Only with works which span the arc from the 1890s till 1933 and beyond can we investigate long-term developments. The old Marxist interpretations of the bourgeois origins of National Socialism are quite unconvincing; just as insufficient are the conventional interpretations of the political disintegration of the bourgeoisie as a precondition for 1933. A research perspective which asks about the changes in the structures of bourgeois social formations, patterns of behavior, objectives and political models could be more profitable—in regard to both the bourgeoisie and the nobility. The increasing importance, even dominance, of concepts of community in quite different realms, while keeping their orientation to the state, was accompanied by the loss of the traditional state order, by material war losses, by inflation, and by a world economic crisis, and was linked to a fundamental intellectual insecurity. In this lay the significance of the radicalization, which in all likelihood characterizes better the changes in the political and cultural structures of the 1920s and 1930s, and thus the transformation of bourgeois values, than does disintegration. In the

processes of radicalization there were also possibilities for new coalitions between noble and bourgeois actors and positions; at the same time the customary definitions of what was noble or bourgeois became blurred. From this perspective, the decades between the turn of the century and 1933 can be understood as a period of transformation, in which new answers were formulated concerning what it meant to be bourgeois—culturally, socially, and politically.

It is certainly worth analyzing the conditions of this radicalization and the changing form of bourgeois values associated with this. If this analysis were to be successful, then the relationship between social history and the bourgeoisie would not be just a temporary exertion, but would remain fruitful for a long time.

Notes

1. G.A. Ritter, "Workers' Culture in Imperial Germany: Problems and Points of Departure for Research," *Journal of Contemporary History* 13 (1978), 165–89.
2. One should not forget here older studies which, however, remained isolated efforts: H. Henning, *Das westdeutsche Bürgertum in der Epoche der Hochindustrialisierung 1860–1914. Soziales Verhalten und soziale Strukturen*, vol. 1: *Das Bildungsbürgertum in den preußischen Westprovinzen* (Wiesbaden, 1972); or F. Zunkel, *Der Rheinisch-Westfälische Unternehmer 1834–1879* (Cologne, 1962); P.E. Schramm, *Neun Generationen. Dreihundert Jahre deutscher "Kulturgeschichte" im Lichte der Schicksale einer Hamburger Bürgerfamilie (1648–1948)*, 2 vols. (Göttingen, 1964).
3. W. Conze and J. Kocka, "Einleitung," in *Bildungsbürgertum im 19. Jahrhundert*, vol. 1, eds. idem (Stuttgart, 1985), 9–26, here 9.
4. J. Kocka, "Einleitung," in *Bildungsbürgertum im 19. Jahrhundert*, vol. 4, ed. idem (Stuttgart, 1989), 9–20.
5. Idem, "Bürger und Bürgerlichkeit als Probleme der deutschen Geschichte vom späten 18. zum frühen 20. Jahrhundert," *Bürger und Bürgerlichkeit im 19. Jahrhundert*, ed. idem (Göttingen, 1987), 21–63.
6. J. Kocka, "Bürgertum und bürgerliche Gesellschaft im 19. Jahrhundert. Europäische Entwicklungen und deutsche Eigenarten," in *Bürgertum im 19. Jahrhundert*, 3 vols., ed. idem (Munich, 1989), vol. 1, 11–76. In fact, most authors still just study subgroups or fall back on the indefinite plural of "bourgeoisie" (Bürgertümer). M.R. Lepsius, "Zur Soziologie des Bürgertums und der Bürgerlichkeit," in *Bürger und Bürgerlichkeit*, ed. J. Kocka, 79–100, calls on scholars to investigate the socialization process. His appeal has been often quoted, but seldom put into practice.
7. L. Gall, ed., *Stadt und Bürgertum im Übergang von der traditionalen zur modernen Gesellschaft* (Munich, 1993).
8. P. Lundgreen, "Fragestellungen und Forschungsgeschichte des Sonderforschungsbereichs zur Geschichte des Bürgertums," in *Sozial- und Kulturgeschichte des Bürgertums*, ed. idem (Göttingen, 2000), 13–39; one of the few dissenting voices: J. Kocka, "Bürgertum und Sonderweg," ibid., 93–110; M. Hettling, *Politische Bürgerlichkeit* (Göttingen, 1999), with an emphasis on the difference between the urban and the national stage.
9. H. Zwahr, *Proletariat und Bourgeoisie in Deutschland. Studien zur Klassendialektik* (Cologne, 1980); methodically still stimulating: idem, *Zur Konstituierung des Proletariats als Klasse* (Berlin, 1978).
10. Hettling, *Politische Bürgerlichkeit*.
11. D. Blackbourn and G. Eley, *The Peculiarities of German History. Bourgeois Society and Politics in Nineteenth-Century Germany* (Oxford, 1984).

12. "I examine my own being, and find there a world" (Ich kehr ein mich selbst zurück, und finde eine Welt), in Johann Wolfgang von Goethe, *Die Leiden des jungen Werther*, vol. 6 (Munich, 1981), 13 (letter from 22 May).
13. U. Frevert, *Ehrenmänner. Das Duell in der bürgerlichen Gesellschaft* (Munich, 1991); U. Daniel, *Hoftheater. Zur Geschichte des Theaters und der Höfe im 18. und 19. Jahrhundert* (Stuttgart, 1995); G.-F. Budde, *Auf dem Weg ins Bürgerleben. Kindheit und Erziehung in deutschen und englischen Bürgerfamilien 1840–1914* (Göttingen, 1994); A.-C. Trepp, *Sanfte Männlichkeit und selbständige Weiblichkeit. Frauen und Männer im Hamburger Bürgertum zwischen 1770 und 1840* (Göttingen, 1996); S. Brändli, *"Der herrlich biedere Mann." Vom Siegeszug des bürgerlichen Herrenanzuges im 19. Jahrhundert* (Zürich, 1998).
14. W. Kaschuba, "Deutsche Bürgerlichkeit nach 1800. Kultur als symbolische Praxis," in *Bürgertum im 19. Jahrhundert*, vol. 3, ed. J. Kocka, 9–44, here 10; J. Kocka, "Bürgertum und bürgerliche Gesellschaft," ibid., vol. 1, 11–76, here 27.
15. W. Sombart, *Die deutsche Volkswirtschaft im 19. Jahrhundert* (Berlin, 1903); J.A. Schumpeter, "Die sozialen Klassen im ethnisch homogenen Milieu," *Archiv für Sozialwissenschaft und Sozialpolitik* 57 (1927), 1–67.
16. Lepsius, *Soziologie des Bürgertums*.
17. F.H. Tenbruck, "Bürgerliche Kultur," in idem, *Die kulturellen Grundlagen der Gesellschaft* (Opladen, 1989), 251–72; K. Eibl, Die *Entstehung der Poesie* (Frankfurt, 1995).
18. Ibid., 197.
19. Ibid., 46.
20. Pioneering work: G. Hübinger, *Kulturprotestantismus und Politik. Zum Verhältnis von Liberalismus und Protestantismus im wilhelminischen Deutschland* (Tübingen, 1994); see also M. Hettling, "Bürgerliche Kultur – Bürgerlichkeit als kulturelles System," in *Sozial- und Kulturgeschichte des Bürgertums*, ed. P. Lundgreen (Göttingen, 2000), 319–39; idem and S.-L. Hoffmann, eds., *Der bürgerliche Wertehimmel* (Göttingen, 2000).
21. D. Sabean and S. Teuscher, "Kinship in Europe. A new approach to long term development," in *Kinship in Europe. Approaches to long term development (1300–1900)*, eds. idem (New York, 2007), 1–32.
22. For example: I. Buruma and A. Margalit, *Okzidentalismus. Der Westen in den Augen seiner Feinde* (Munich, 2004), 151, argue that the enemies of the West used in fact Western arguments and that "more than every other European nation Germany was the battlefield and the origin of these ideas."
23. A. Schulz, *Lebenswelt und Kultur des Bürgertums im 19. und 20. Jahrhundert* (Munich, 2005), presents a good overview of the "classical" bourgeois world but does not thematize the impact of mass culture.
24. K. Tenfelde, "Stadt und Bürgertum im 20. Jahrhundert," in *Wege zur Geschichte des Bürgertums*, eds. H.-U. Wehler and K. Tenfelde (Göttingen, 1994), 317–53, here 320.
25. P. Kondylis, *Der Niedergang der bürgerlichen Denk- und Lebensform. Die liberale Moderne und die massendemokratische Postmoderne* (Weinheim, 1991).
26. Kocka, *Sonderweg*, 96.
27. Wehler, *Kaiserreich*, 12; T. Nipperdey, "1933 und die Kontinuität der deutschen Geschichte," in idem. *Nachdenken über die deutsche Geschichte* (Munich, 1990), 225–48, here 245; D. Langewiesche, ed., *Das deutsche Kaiserreich 1867/71 bis 1918. Bilanz einer Epoche* (Freiburg, 1984), 13f.
28. M. Weber, *Gesammelte Aufsätze zur Religionssoziologie*, 9th ed., vol. 1 (Tübingen, 1988), 1.
29. Hettling, *Politische Bürgerlichkeit*; R. Koselleck, "Drei bürgerliche Welten? Zur vergleichenden Semantik der bürgerlichen Gesellschaft in Deutschland, England und Frankreich," in *Bürger in der Gesellschaft der Neuzeit*, ed. H.-J. Puhle (Göttingen, 1991), 14–58.
30. Nipperdey, "1933," 240.
31. M. Weber, *The Methodology of Social Sciences*, transl. and ed. E.A. Shils and H.A. Finch (New York, 1949), S. 78f.

32. R. Koselleck, "Erfahrungswandel und Methodenwechsel. Eine historisch-anthropologische Skizze," in *Historische Methode*, eds. C. Meier and J. Rüsen (Munich, 1988), 13–61, here 51.
33. M.L. Anderson, *Practicing Democracy. Elections and Political Culture in Imperial Germany* (Princeton, 2000).
34. H. Mommsen, "Die Auflösung des Bürgertums seit dem späten 19. Jahrhundert," in Kocka, *Bürger und Bürgerlichkeit*, 288–315.
35. T. Kühne, "Demokratisierung und Parlamentarisierung: Neue Forschungen zur politischen Entwicklungsfähigkeit Deutschlands vor dem Ersten Weltkrieg," *Geschichte und Gesellschaft* 31 (2005), 293–316.
36. J. Radkau, *Max Weber. Die Leidenschaft des Denkens* (Munich, 2005), 107.

Chapter 11

Cultural Nationalism and Beyond

Musical Performances in Imperial Germany

Sven Oliver Müller

Successful politics requires successful exaggeration. If one wants to conquer the political realm, there is no such thing as too much exaggeration. Both the ruler and his subjects are anxious to define the desired situation through their own public portrayal. Those who want to structure the interaction in the political arena must do so within the framework of the existing conditions in society, in order to define their interests in their own words. This can be seen not only when one examines election campaigns but also when one examines the musical culture of the German Empire. Here the manifestations of power and sovereignty were based on a sensual dramaturgy—that is to say, on the audibility and visibility of political processes.

Opera and concert performances enabled and enforced a political representation. The social possibilities of the musical life gave a political dimension to an allegedly nonpolitical form of entertainment. Operas and concerts can be understood as part of an implicit or explicit governing strategy of the ruling elite, as an institution as well as a performance.[1] The rulers were determined to create and legitimize their power and their status through their representations in the musical venues of the European metropolises. Cultural rituals, regularly repeated, produced the political structure of the state, ordering the nation to their ideal. The performances in opera houses and concert halls stimulated public communication. The ornamented auditorium, especially the richly decorated boxes, staircases and foyers, illustrated the transition from everyday life to the world of the rich and powerful. Particularly the cultural rituals in the auditorium and the social division between different classes and social ranks contributed towards creating and cementing political models of society.

In the rapidly changing late nineteenth century there was a large demand for the political staging of power and the powerful. Especially the German Empire, faced with growing foreign-policy pressures and intensifying social inequalities after the unification of the German Empire, needed to find a way of addressing these challenges by developing a stronger national community. The cultural representation of the German nation increased the nation's political status, both at home and abroad. This music scene offered numerous opportunities for nationalist politicians. Operas and concert halls could be used as the setting for media events, for it was exactly these places, these sites of power which the ruling elite frequented; here they displayed political, social, and cultural competence. A gala held in the opera placed leadership figures such as Otto von Bismarck and Kaiser Wilhelm II in the center of an imaginable, tangible national community.[2] One can even speak of an age of theatricality, or, to put it more precisely, of an increasingly theatrical political landscape.

In regard to the public music performances in Berlin, this meant that their political reach was a function of their ability to be perceived within a context capable of dramatization. Evenings in the court opera house or the philharmonic were, admittedly, a strictly controlled event for the powerful, but they required that the powerful participate and that the powerful be observed by the public. Furthermore, in the audience the Berlin aristocracy and upper classes were united in the shared consumption of classical music. Repeatedly the cream of society strove to be admitted, indeed, desired the most prestigious seats in order to play a part in the cultural ceremonies of state. Evidently, participating in a political gala not only cemented the role of the German Emperor, it also enabled the elite audience to move up in the public's estimation. A steadily growing public sphere was a part of this cultural symbiosis because the expansion and differentiation of the media environment allowed many more people to partake in the festivities. Newspaper articles, bulletins from the court, graphics and pictures allowed the subjects in the empire to participate in a sensual, personal manner in the national music festivities. People read bulletins on the event, viewed pictures in the press, or played and sang popular pieces at home. Music performances in opera houses and in concert halls therefore presupposed a form of participation which by no means relied on equal participation. They did, however, presuppose the willingness to experience the news as a "German" event. Through the presence of the public every observer potentially became an equal part of the national musical festivities. Even in the German Empire the representatives of the state were not able to get by without society's participation. The state's staging of musical performances and the reception by an elite audience, personally present, and a wider audience, present through the media, makes clear how German nationalism was created through cultural communication.[3]

In order to emphasize the process-like and actor-focused dimension of the phenomenon, this article discusses not nationalist music, but rather the nationalization of the musical culture, and the focus is on the political attribution of public events. This definition is fundamentally different from the assumption of a "natural" division of the spheres of art and politics. Musical performances in public spaces should be seen far more as a potential political attribution: to love German music is to love the German nation. Concentrating on the public space of the opera and concert halls helps us understand that the ceremonial practices which already existed in those places could be freely acquired for nationalistic purposes. The splendor of these houses and of the embellished elite—in other words the "pomp and circumstance" of the rulers—established a symmetrical relationship between the audience and the stage. Our first and foremost interest in this essay is the behavior of the audience in a performance; the musical piece is only secondary. We need to understand better how the audience up to the turn of the century perceived the auditorium as an extension of the opera's stage in political ceremonies and themselves as social artists. The symmetries and asymmetries between the observer and the observed need to be shown, since the audience largely regulated the nationalization of the musical life. It was the audience, after all, which transformed musical pieces into German legends and cultural ceremonies into nationalist goals. Accordingly, this essay will first discuss the public dimensions of musical performances, the attempts by the audience and the press to unite the lovers of music with German history by referring to the German nation. Next, the essay will turn to the scope of this cultural nationalism; more precisely, it will discuss the belief in German cultural superiority over France and the analogous ascent of the musical nationalization and the musical Europeanization in the late nineteenth century. It is no surprise, therefore, that it was especially the lovers of music themselves who simultaneously celebrated the cultural unity and the cultural hostility between the nations in the auditorium.

The history of German cultural nationalism began long before the unification of Germany. The synthesis of culture and power so widely desired was proclaimed already in 1856 by the Berlin critic, Ludwig Rellstab, according to whom "the masters of the German musical art ... have turned into the leaders in the world."[4] The success hoped for in achieving German political unity, hoped for by many before, during, and after the era of German Empire, rested on the shared belief in the supremacy of the uniform musical culture. The proclamation by those responsible in Germany after 1871 of a common music for the individual German states had an impact on the community of the German Empire. If one does not shy away from possible exaggeration, then the audience in the different German cities did not simply visit public music performances—they were the performance itself. Or more exactly: the public became a nationalist public through the act of collectively consuming music.

Music performances in Germany developed into a paradigm of nationalism. The praising or criticizing of opera performances in foreign languages in Germany arose out of the political worldview of the "nationalist" music aficionados in Berlin. German musical culture seemed to offer the promise that in music one could overcome all conceivable social divisions within Germany. The demonstrated reverence for the German musical tradition by the bourgeoisie and the nobility provided additional legitimacy to the German national community after 1871. By commenting on and criticizing the music of other nations, one paid tribute to a perceived superiority of the German cultural tradition.[5] The "Signals for the Musical World" explained in 1908 in regard to the "national aspect in the music," which supposedly only in Germany was so clearly defined, so unshakeable:

> In a musical center such as Berlin musical differences must be more discernable than in other places. Since the beginning of time foreign countries have been sending virtuosos and composers of relevance, but they remain isolated appearances and only in the rarest cases did they leave behind strong traces of the essence of their art. ... If we admit—which nobody doubts—to a difference between the cultures, then, solely through logical deduction, music must be a national matter.[6]

The cultural communication stimulated the political communication within the empire's capital, Berlin. The Prussian theater director, Friedrich Wilhelm Redern, wrote in his memoirs in 1883: "back then Berlin had no politics, no press, the theater alone had to fill the void for the general public."[7] Regardless of whether one was celebrating the emperor or a state visit for foreign guests—ultimately the political, social, and economic elite of the empire celebrated themselves in their role as German representatives. The reverence for the monarchs formed the representational focal point. Of course the magnificent staging of nationalism in the opera, the singing of hymns and the solemn recitation prologues also moved the visitors emotionally. In a review of the celebration of the birthday gala for Wilhelm II at the Royal Opera House in Berlin in 1892, one author wrote: "Already before the last verse, the harp in the orchestra started to play the national anthem in quiet chords ... Mightily the melody of 'Heil Dir im Siegerkranz' sounded through the house and the entire audience stood and turned towards the box of the Emperor. The Emperor had risen from his chair and remained standing, solemnly, until the last tone faded away."[8] The political rituals in the auditorium helped secure and even increase the importance of the German monarchy in national terms, both in regard to constitutional law as well as in regard to the organization of the personnel of the German monarchy. Of course, there was no German musical "*Sonderweg.*" In almost all existing and developing nation states, patriotic hymns such as the Marseillaise and Rule Britannia as well as the *Wacht am Rhein* dominated the musical life of the nineteenth century.

Did the aristocratic elites confine themselves to the realm of musical ceremonies, disconnected from the political challenges of their time? This finding is deceptive, because it is precisely by focusing on national musical ceremonies that one can observe how the aristocracy adjusted flexibly to the political culture of the nineteenth century. Those close to the court responded to these new political impulses by restaging and newly staging their luxury, their wealth, in spectacular surroundings, that is to say, they continued to insist on exclusivity and uniqueness for their part of the "stage" during a celebration. Against a background of growing legitimization problems, increasingly the presence of monarchs at official state acts as well as their private amusements became a topic of public interest. It seems certain that every opera gala in the nineteenth century became more nationalist by becoming more public.[9] The perfect performance of the society at court stimulated and created a perfect national unity. Through their public presence and their political forms of distinction, the top of the aristocracy was able to keep their social rank, to assert their position even in the face of complicated challenges. Thus, the masters of visibility cultivated aristocratic traditions which were supposed to vouch for century-old traditions and enable them to meet the new challenges in the German Empire.

One can observe a communicative diversification of politics in selected music performances: the ruler and his subjects interact closely in and in front of the opera houses in a reciprocal performance, a mélange of sounds and pictures, rituals and ceremonies. The success of these performances lay, first, in their portrayal of competence in regard to state power, but also in the sensuous presence of the imparted messages. As a result, the emperor and his aristocrats became simultaneously the performers and the audience for the opera performance—they became, in other words, their own audience. But even when the political success this achieved generated new political success, as a rule this form of endowing authority created a setting of constraint. The beauty of the political staging made the monarchs and their audience captives of their own nationalist music festival. Both combined in themselves a network of subjugation and supervision, within which they themselves became vulnerable if they acted uncomely or if they breached the expected etiquette of representative communication. When, for example, the British king Edward VII arrived in Berlin in February 1909, the combination of the court packing his schedule too densely and his personal aversion to his "dear nephew" Wilhelm II ended in—"the most brilliant failure in history."[10] The gala performance in the court opera, required but not much appreciated by the King, was the last straw. Exhausted after a demanding day, Edward VII dozed off during the historic pantomime *Sardanapal*, until he was suddenly awoken by the special effects of the pompous final scene (when Sardanapal is burned at the stake) and inquired pleadingly after the status of the fire-fighting operations on the stage. Luckily, the German Empress managed to calm him down.

Integrating music into the practice of nationalism became one of the most distinctive cultural rituals of consensus within the German Empire. Of course, the social boundaries, the limits of cultural nationalism as a politically unifying force cannot be overlooked. The aristocracy and middle classes came together at nationalist musical festivities, but workers and peasants, Social Democrats and Catholics, did not. The allocation of seats and the formal dress code already illustrated the point that to be a music aficionado one had to follow the social, cultural, and economic rules of the elites. Admission was only for those who were appropriate for a formal, nationalist gala. Most German citizens had neither the means nor the knowledge of protocol to enter the court opera; rather, they were interested in observing the attending ruler. They sought their own musical pleasures at the vaudeville and on the fairgrounds.

It was not solely formal and habitual criteria which determined whether or not music could be appropriated as a means of national and social power. If one accepts the position of the academic musical press, the journalists, and wide parts of the bourgeois public, then the "correct" assessment of German music made all people equal. Those who did not have sufficient command of cultural rules were excluded by the elites.[11] Accordingly, all lovers of music were equally German, but the educated just a little more so. This understanding of music served not only as a legitimation for musical performances, it also accentuated their characteristic as an attribute of social distinction, as something that divided society. The most important Social Democratic newspaper remarked on this harshly on the eve of World War I. According to *Vorwärts* in 1912, the high regard for and the attendance at what was allegedly the most important public institution for entertainment, the opera, only further solidified the hated political relations of inequality within the Empire. High culture music in Germany, according to *Vorwärts*, made the bourgeoisie as well as the proletariat subordinate, for it made them dependent. The "royal Prussian enterprise" is:

> "not unsubstantially subsidized at the expense of the taxpayers ... the costly royal opera is an institution to amuse the court and those who are noble by birth or who have been ennobled because of their wealth. The people do not participate ... The German opera is in principle simply not ready for or prepared for snobs ... Who wants to demand that the Prussian three class state should accommodate those of lesser means?"[12]

One of the most important difficulties of the musical life was defining authoritatively the social reach of cultural nationalism in the German Empire. Neither the working class nor the rural population had the slightest chance of experiencing the national community though music by attending important concert and opera performances. The social and economic inequalities limited the cultural equality. Nonetheless the elitist musical practices did not completely exclude the wider population. On one hand, the Social Democrats in particular went to great lengths in their newspapers and their festivities to spread popular music pieces by well-known composers and to make it possible to attend inexpensive concerts.[13] On the other hand, the communication about these events in the media, the presence of musical rituals within the press, brought together, in conversations and in shared leisure-time experiences, Germans of different social standings, denominations, backgrounds, and genders. Maybe workers scorned the aristocracy within the opera, but they managed to talk about it to one another, and often decided to chant a hymn or participate in music during a political demonstration.

The cultural nationalists in Berlin needed their partners and opponents in Europe, in particular in Paris, London, and Vienna. The depiction of the German nation revealed to all of Europe to what extent politics was not a clearly definable category, but could rather be the object of projection for collective attributions.

Cultural nationalism's public face created the belief in one's own political power—and this enabled boundaries to be drawn vis-à-vis the friends and enemies of one's personal music taste. With the help of "national music," considered eminently important, two borders—that between the European cultures and that within one's own culture—could be drawn, which generally could be removed only with difficulty. Examining the audience's participation within the framework of a musical performance in the opera house or concert hall revealed that the "nation" did not necessarily exist, but was rather formed as an imagined, practicing community. For exactly this reason, music aficionados in Germany, France, and Great Britain revered not an abstract, ascertainable state, but rather savored in these moments the independent involvement in their own "nation."

What speaks against the idea that the musical nationalization of musical culture was consensual is the evidence of a massive nationalistic differentiation in and between almost all European societies in the nineteenth century. One can observe a gradual development toward thinking in nationalistic categories in the approach to music as an art form; these categories reveal little about the music itself, but quite a bit, however, about the ascent of nationalism. Especially in the genre of opera one can detect a downright wave of nationalization.[14] The goal of these national myths performed to music on the opera stages of Europe was ultimately to transform the past into a form of legitimacy. "National" music developed as an expression of the politically motivated necessity to use music to generate meaning. The best of one's own cultural tradition was understood by the bourgeois elites to be specifically "national." For this the music had to be either reinterpreted or newly created. This invention of national traditions was triggered by no means from a cultural void, but rather expressed first and foremost a creative reassessment and a new ordering of the existing body of knowledge and existing social practices. Against this backdrop of an increasing politicization and secularization, and of the breaking down of traditional lifestyles and securities, art music seemed to convey a special form of orientation. Some middle-class intellectuals understood music, especially the opera, as a medium for nationalist emancipation.

The audience composed of opera aficionados in the German Empire understood the myth of the Germanic not only as a timeless parable, but also as part of Germany's history.[15] Themes from prehistory and ancient history had the added advantage that the storyline could be freely formed dramaturgically but tightly woven politically. The opera houses in Berlin, Dresden, and Leipzig in the first two decades after the founding of the German Empire performed numerous operas about the Germanic, with such picturesque titles as "Folkhunger," "Heinrich der Löwe," "Thusnelda und der Triumphzug des Germanicus," and "Armin." The actors on stage were dressed the way the public imagined their Germanic ancestors: heavily armed and clothed in coarse fabrics, fur, and helmets. The critics praised not only the art of illusion, but also—and primarily—the attentive "envisioning of time, place, and nationality."[16]

This nationalization of music, however, transcended borders in the nineteenth century. By mid-century at the latest, all European musical metropolises saw calls by music critics for a nationalist orientation in art music, for national music schools and for national operas. Carl Maria von Weber and Ludwig van Beethoven in Germany, and somewhat later Bedřich Smetana in Bohemia and Edward Elgar in Great Britain, were known to their contemporaries not only as great artists but also as the embodiment of their nation. The funeral march from the Eroica symphony promised insight into the depth of the German "soul of the people," Elgar's collection of folk songs promised to reveal a British national treasure. The perception of the people was crucial. Art music did not become a nationalist affair through various musical renditions of the "colloquial" (songs, dances, marches), but through the "faith" of its recipients.[17]

Not only in German-speaking Europe can one notice a gradual trend toward assessing art music in nationalist categories; this trend says little about the music itself and much about the rise of nationalism. Historic subjects and local flavor came together in dramatic musical works which not only told a historic story but which also dealt with history. The irony was that in practically all European nations an allegedly specifically "national" music was created. For example, Weber's "Freischütz," for many of his contemporaries the German subject par excellence, borrowed elements of form from French opera. Of course this was in no way detrimental to the euphoric "national" reception by German-speaking audiences.[18] It was indeed the universality of the art forms opera and symphony which enabled their nationalistic acquisition.

What was true for the public reception of Weber was of course also true for the positive political reassessment of Johann Sebastian Bach, Ludwig van Beethoven and Richard Wagner in the German Empire. A comparison of the reception of Bach in Germany, France, and Italy shows that the journalistic emphasis on the "German" in Bach was without a doubt an obstacle to the reception of his work outside of Germany. With the help of a nationalist invention, the provincial Saxon cantor Johann Sebastian Bach became a German hero inside and outside the boundaries of the German state. The same is true for Ludwig van Beethoven, who lived in Vienna, but who was born and raised in the Rhineland, and who was furthermore of Flemish descent. In the era of modern nationalism the origin of a composer, which in the eighteenth century was still largely irrelevant, became a measure of his musical-national "authenticity."[19] In 1887 an article about "Richard Wagner's national relevance" appeared in the magazine Der Kunstwart. The German master advanced in the article to a "genius," to the embodiment of the German and his music to a "singular outlet of the Germanic soul."[20] The reverence for Wagner broke down all traditional categories of the musical life, and it was exactly this that outraged the critics. Around 1900 his musical dramas attained a preeminent share in Berlin and other major opera houses in Germany.

This reveals clearly that the music aficionados in the German Empire mercilessly pursued cultural nationalism with reference to the myth of the German genius. Richard Wagner unfailingly linked the standing of his own work with that of the political standing of Ludwig van Beethoven. In 1870—the year of the Franco-German War and the hundredth anniversary of Beethoven's birth—Wagner used his cultural nationalism in an excursion against his French enemies. He declared Beethoven to be a hero of musical freedom, who in the empire of sound put an end to the world sovereignty of the traditional enemy and who has "broken the domination of the foreigners forever." Through Beethoven German music had succeeded in asserting itself as a "bold, powerful fighter against French domination."[21]

In the second half of the nineteenth century a musical canon began to be developed in the European musical repertoire. Only those pieces considered "great" and "classic" achieved a canonical status in the performance programs. Compositions by Beethoven, Verdi, and Wagner acquired a lasting market value in Germany, France, and Great Britain through the number of their performances and ticket sales; works by Cherubini and Spohr never approached these numbers. The international cultural alignment was a result of the acquisition of relatively few symphonies, concerts, and operas which the music aficionados integrated into their repertoire. The differences between the selected composers therefore accounted for little, their similarities for a lot more. Those pieces one was already well acquainted with and whose significance one progressively learned more about were especially large successes.

The development of a repertoire in Europe accessible to everyone musically and socially, however, is not discernable. Rather, the canon excluded socially. In the struggle to have a work achieve a certain rank in the musical culture, the competitors regularly fought with economic and social means. Canonically organized concert programs stabilized the rulers because this elitist selection distinguished primarily between members of a knowledgeable and paying audience and the others. Canons excluded aesthetically, that is to say, they conserved musical culture by both excluding unacceptable styles and works as well as by including the "great" creations by musical masters. Canons excluded in terms of both domestic and foreign policy. The rise of cultural nationalism altered the behavior of audiences in Europe because these believed, more strongly than ever, that they had to protect themselves against allegedly foreign musical styles and works. Middle class and aristocratic elites in the German Empire paid fastidious attention to regulating the admittance of foreign cultures—be it the Social Democrats or the French.

The concert performance of the French composer Camille Saint-Saëns in 1886 in Berlin lent itself splendidly to this cultural nationalism. For many members of Berlin society in the audience at the philharmonic concert, Saint-Saëns personified an unwanted Frenchman. Days earlier the press had published accounts of his views on art, especially his commentary on Wagner's operas. Directly before his visit to Germany, in the magazine *La France* he had taken a stance against a performance of *Lohengrin* in Paris. In so doing, the composer distinguished himself publicly as a business-oriented manager. Some patriotic Berlin music aficionados were unwilling to overlook this and accused him of having a position hostile to Wagner (and therefore hostile towards Germany): "And so it came to a demonstration against Mr. Saint-Saëns yesterday. ... Mr. Saint-Saëns had already sat down at the piano ... when at his arrival the prevalent silence was broken by the clumsy attempt of a few audience members to welcome him with applause ... This applause we met with impetuous hissing, whistling, loud howling and yells of 'Lohengrin.'" Saint-Saëns chose to accept his defeat with grace. He maintained his composure against the vocal opposition and tried to play what he could.[22] The German nationalists reacted much more mercilessly. Perceiving a difference between French and German music, they demanded a contest for the German opera *Lohengrin* in Paris—which was viewed as "superior"—with the hope that the French, who were becoming more intelligent through music, would be forced to acknowledge this superiority. After the German cultural nation lost World War I, the public self-staging of the music aficionados went too far for the son of the master, Siegfried Wagner, and in 1925 he posted the following notice in Bayreuth: "The audience is kindly asked to refrain from singing after the end of the Meistersinger. We're dedicated to the arts!"[23]

The impact of these quarrels points out the important relationship between nationalization and Europeanization, between reception and cultural transfer. It was exactly the universality of the musical genres—the operas, symphonies, dances and songs—that enabled their nationalistic acquisition. Regardless of how emphatically music newspaper critics from Berlin to Paris discussed the musical styles allegedly typical for each country, the late nineteenth century was actually characterized by musical styles throughout Europe becoming increasingly similar. In a word, the increasing similarity of the repertoire and of the aesthetic preferences meant that a supposedly specific national phenomenon could also increasingly be read as a commonly shared European convention. The "national" music styles were products of a successful transfer of culture.[24] The practices of nationalistic differentiation and European adjustment were not only parallel developments, both spatially and temporally, they also reinforced each other, required one another. Asking about the causes of this dichotomy directs the focus towards the reciprocal relationship of these two phenomena. On closer inspection, the supposedly tense relationship between differentiation and alignment can be seen as the result of complex communicative processes. It is important that the relationship between societies and cultures is written along the allegedly separate axes of transfer and communication on the one hand and power struggles and antagonism on the other.[25]

The results of our investigation appear almost trivial: musical culture and political conflict do not mark alternatives in German history. As the evaluation of music as an art form in Europe shows, there is a simultaneous interaction of nationalism and a successful transfer of culture. Enforcing "national" music meant exchange, communication, and imitation as well as resistance and exclusion. Successful cultural transfers did not take place outside the framework of the charged nationalist frictions, but were rather part of their development. Most German nationalists rebelled against those hegemonic cultures from which they took the norms which energized their own movement. Musical contacts, therefore, strengthened not only mutual learning and tolerance but also alienation and differentiation. Often the music aficionados in Germany and in France hated each other, not despite, but rather because they came in contact with the works of the other nation's composers. The optimistic pedagogical belief that getting to know one another better, that communication and transfer are equally important for engendering cultural harmony and understanding between European societies has been rebuked by the history of the nationalistic reception of music.[26]

The cultural nationalism in the musical culture of the German Empire executed exactly the plot that it created, exactly the world which it showed: a community of Germans communicating through music. Musical performances constituted the political reality—a reality which developed through the perception and behavior of the audience. For this reason, participating in musical performances or viewing these not only reflected existing political values and identities, but also generated them. The audience created a nationalist regime through its own behavior. Following the concept of the performance, participating in a musical performance can be defined as an exercise which established the nationalistic order by creating it. Physical, linguistic, and habitual expressions of the audience altered the nation; the particular practices brought forward exactly this desired order. To interpret the musical representation on the stage as merely superficial, or even as the imaginary disguising of political facts, misses the point. It could be argued that what mattered politically was not that which was, but that which the people believed to be, what they staged as the nationalist reality. Display therefore implies construction, the musical performance of an ideal state, the creation of a victorious nation.

The cultural nationalism in the German Empire as well as in the rest of Europe illustrates the degree to which politics is not an easily definable category, but instead can be an object of projection for collective attribution. Through mutual understanding actors decide what is political and what becomes political. Contingent on the actors and their communication, even apparently nonpolitical performances transform themselves into political spaces. This phenomenon not only puts the given "natural" spheres of art and politics into perspective, but focusing on the (potential) political dimension of music as an art form requires that we see performances both as collectively desired political facts as well as controversial incidents. That is to say, cultural nationalisms can play a role in forming European norms and practices, one which is not to be underestimated. Europe therefore should not be understood as a framework, but rather as a category which formed during the nineteenth century, in part because of "cultural nationalization." Essential aspects of this process were a specific appreciation of music as an art form, the development of a communal repertoire and of a uniform listening behavior, the development of networks, and assessing music through nationalist categories in all of Europe.

Music performances in the German Empire were different from other art forms.[27] It was the performances and reviews themselves which transformed the allegedly passive observers—or rather listeners—into negotiating actors. To put it pointedly: the act of listening to music itself not only reflected, it also generated a nationalist reality. From a historical perspective, the musical importance is produced not through the reproduction of a score but through the public reception of a performance, through the political realization of the music as an art form. Without following the radical constructivism of Ola Stockfeld completely, who claimed that "the listener, and only the listener, is the composer of the music,"[28] it is evident that describing how a music piece was rated means understanding that this was never a purely aesthetic phenomenon. To conceptualize music through the eyes of a historian therefore means to understand that the significance of musical performances in opera houses and concert halls depended less on their artistic rank then on their political reach. From this, however, we certainly cannot conclude that the music itself did not matter. Actually, it is only the reception of the music by the audience which created a fusion between musical productions and historical societies. Only this interaction between musical and political praxis explains the behavior of the audience and the development of a nationalist meaning for music.[29]

Notes

1. Cf. R. Bereson, *The Operatic State. Cultural Policy and the Opera House* (London, 2002); U. Daniel, *Hoftheater. Zur Geschichte des Theaters und der Höfe im 18. und 19. Jahrhundert* (Stuttgart, 1995); J.F. Fulcher, *The Nation's Image. French Grand Opera as Politics and Politicized Art* (Cambridge, 1987); S.O. Müller, "Analysing musical culture in nineteenth-century Europe: towards a musical turn?," *European Review of History* 17 (2010), 835–859.
2. Cf. J.C.G. Röhl, *Kaiser, Hof und Staat. Wilhelm II. und die deutsche Politik* (Munich, 1988); J. Plunkett, *Queen Victoria. First Media Monarch* (Oxford, 2003); J. Paulmann, *Pomp und Politik. Monarchenbegegnungen in Europa zwischen Ancien Régime und Erstem Weltkrieg* (Paderborn, 2000); A. Biefang, M. Epkenhans and K. Tenfelde, eds., *Das politische Zeremoniell im Deutschen Kaiserreich 1871–1918* (Düsseldorf, 2008).
3. Cf. C. Applegate, *Bach in Berlin, Nation and Culture in Mendelssohn's Revival of the St. Matthew Passion* (Ithaca, NY, 2005); C. Applegate and P. Porter, eds., *Music and German National Identity* (Chicago, 2002); H. Danuser and H. Münkler, eds., *Deutsche Meister – böse Geister? Nationale Selbstfindung in der Musik* (Laaber, 2000); J. Samson, "Nations and Nationalism," in *The Cambridge History of Nineteenth-Century Music*, ed. J. Samson (Cambridge, 2002), 568–600; B. Anderson, *Die Erfindung der Nation. Zur Karriere eines folgenreichen Konzepts* (Frankfurt, 1993).
4. Cf. J. Rehm, *Zur Musikrezeption im vormärzlichen Berlin. Die Präsentation bürgerlichen Selbstverständnisses und biedermeierlicher Kunstanschauung in den Musikkritiken Ludwig Rellstabs* (Hildesheim, 1983), quote 154.
5. Cf. Applegate, *Bach*, 234–63; C. Dahlhaus, *Die Musik des 19. Jahrhunderts* (Wiesbaden, 1980), 29–34.
6. *Signale für die musikalische Welt* 66 (1908), 1501–3.
7. F.W. Redern, *Unter drei Königen. Lebenserinnerungen eines preußischen Oberstkämmerers und Generalintendanten*, ed. S. Giesbrecht (Cologne, 2003), quote, 120. Cf. J. Andres, A. Geisthövel and M. Schwengelbeck, eds., *Die Sinnlichkeit der Macht. Herrschaft und Repräsentation seit der Frühen Neuzeit* (Frankfurt, 2006).
8. *Neue Zeitschrift für Musik* 88 (1892), 559. Cf. T. Blanning, *The Triumph of Music. Composers, Musicians and their Audiences, 1700 to the Present* (London, 2008), 231–85.
9. Cf. Daniel, *Hoftheater*, 120–25; M. Kohlrausch, *Der Monarch im Skandal. Die Logik der Massenmedien und die Transformation der wilhelminischen Monarchie* (Berlin, 2005), 31–51.

10. Cf. L. Reinermann, *Der Kaiser in England. Wilhelm II. und sein Bild in der britischen Öffentlichkeit* (Paderborn, 2001).
11. Cf. S.O. Müller and J. Toelle, eds., *Bühnen der Politik. Die Oper in europäischen Gesellschaften im 19. und 20. Jahrhundert* (Vienna, 2002); S.O. Müller, "Distinktion, Demonstration und Disziplinierung: Veränderungen im Publikumsverhalten in Londoner und Berliner Opernhäusern im 19. Jahrhundert," *International Review for the Aesthetics and Sociology of Music* 37/2 (2006), 167–87.
12. *Vorwärts*, 20 November 1912.
13. The *Vorwärts*, 26 July 1914, tried to convince workers in Berlin to attend a performance of a symphony by Antonin Dvorak.
14. D. Beller-McKenna, "How deutsch a Requiem? Absolute Music, Universality, and the Reception of Brahms's Ein deutsches Requiem, op. 45," *19th Century Music* 22 (1998), 3–19.
15. Cf. R. Kipper, *Der Germanenmythos im Deutschen Kaiserreich. Formen und Funktionen historischer Selbstthematisierung* (Göttingen, 2002).
16. *Dresdner Journal*, 16 October 1877.
17. Cf. E.E. Bauer, *Wie Beethoven auf den Sockel kam. Die Entstehung eines musikalischen Mythos* (Stuttgart, 1992); S.C. Meyer, *Carl Maria von Weber and the Search for a German Opera* (Bloomington, 2003); M. Hughes, *The English Musical renaissance and the Press 1850–1914: Watchmen of Music* (Aldershot, 2002).
18. C. Dahlhaus, "Webers Freischütz und die Idee der deutschen Oper," *Österreichische Musikzeitschrift* 38 (1983), 381–88.
19. Cf. H.-J. Hinrichsen, "Johann Sebastian Bach zwischen Deutschland und Frankreich. Konstruktion und Zurückweisung einer nationalen Identifikationsfigur," *Journal of Modern European History* 5 (2007), 119–38.
20. *Der Kunstwart* 1 (1887), 121–25.
21. *Leipziger Illustrierte Zeitung*, 17 December 1870. Cf. D.C. Large and W. Weber, eds., *Wagnerism in European Culture and Politics* (Ithaca, 1984).
22. *Neue Preußische Zeitung*, 24 January 1886. Cf. *Vossische Zeitung* (AA), 23 January 1886; *Neue Zeitschrift für Musik* 82 (1886), 79.
23. Cf. W. Gebhardt and A. Zingerle, *Pilgerfahrt ins Ich. Die Bayreuther Richard-Wagner-Festspiele und ihr Publikum. Eine kultursoziologische Studie* (Konstanz, 1998), 60–63.
24. Cf. J.C.E. Gienow-Hecht, *Sound Diplomacy. Music and Emotions in Transatlantic Relations, 1850–1920* (Chicago, 2009); "Demarcation and Exchange, 'National' Music in 19th Century Europe," *Journal of Modern European History* 5 (2007), eds. S.O. Müller and L. Raphael.
25. Cf. N.Z. Davis, "What is Universal about History?," in *Transnationale Geschichte. Themen, Tendenzen und Theorien*, eds. G. Budde et al. (Göttingen, 2006), 15–20.
26. Cf. S.O. Müller, "A musical clash of civilisations? Musical transfers and rivalries around 1900," in *Wilhelmine Germany and Edwardian Britain – Essays on Cultural Affinity*, eds. D. Geppert and R. Gerwarth (Oxford, 2008), 305–29.
27. T.W. Adorno, "Bürgerliche Oper," in idem, *Musikalische Schriften I–III* (Frankfurt, 2003), 24–39. Cf. J. Früchtl, "Der Schein der Wahrheit. Adorno, die Oper und das Bürgertum," in *Ästhetik der Inszenierung. Dimensionen eines künstlerischen, kulturellen und gesellschaftlichen Phänomens*, ed. idem (Frankfurt, 2003), 164–82.
28. R. Finnegan, "Music, Experience, and the Anthropology of Emotion," in *The Cultural Study of Music. A Critical Introduction*, eds. M. Clayton, T. Hervert and R. Middelton (London, 2003), 181–92, quote, 184.
29. Cf. S. Bennett, *Theatre Audiences. A Theory of Production and Reception* (London, 1990); C. Small, *Musicking. The Meanings of Performing and Listening* (Middleton, 1998); H.-J. Hinrichsen, "Musikwissenschaft: Musik – Interpretation – Wissenschaft," *Archiv für Musikwissenschaft* 57 (2000), 78–101.

Part III

WAR AND VIOLENCE

Chapter 12

1914–1945: A Second Thirty Years War?
Advantages and Disadvantages of an Interpretive Category

Jörg Echternkamp

The idea that there are clear lines of continuity from the First to the Second World War is hardly new. Already toward the end of the 1970s, the American diplomat and historian George F. Kennan interpreted the First World War as "the great seminal catastrophe of this century," perceiving a break in the course of world history from 1914–18 to 1939–45, the influence of which extended even into the Cold War.[1] The end of the Cold War in 1989–90 made one think once again about the beginning of this period, increasing the interest in the First World War seen from this perspective. The dates 1914 and 1990 set the boundaries for the "short twentieth century."[2]

In the last few years this interpretation—especially the idea that both world wars were part of one large conflict and that the period between the wars represents less a break than a link—has received a good deal of support not only from professional historians but also from the broad public. Repeatedly, above all in the context of the ninetieth anniversary of the beginning of the First World War in 2004, one has come across the succinct and catchy formula of the "second Thirty Years War"[3] to describe the first half of the twentieth century.[4]

In the context of this essay this analogy is to be analyzed as a heuristic model for the discipline of military history for the First and Second World Wars. One can also call these years the "Age of the World Wars," or in French in the singular: "*l'ère de la guerre.*" As a historiographical category, this concept aims to help us analyze a complex conglomeration of cause and effect as well as experiences. However, the mere existence of, or the catchiness of, this concept says little about its plausibility. We must address the central question of any periodization: is what is gained by such a break worth the price of paying less attention to other continuities and other breaks?

In this chapter I shall, first, explain and then question this concept. I will conclude by investigating its heuristic value. I am not interested here in "playing through" the scenario in order to test it—such "playing through" already accepts the scenario in principle. Instead I will ask, at a somewhat greater distance, what are the advantages and disadvantages of the concept, what is its relationship to other heuristic models, as well as considering the possible implications for the narrative logic of the military history of the late nineteenth and early twentieth century.

I

What is true of a classification such as the "short twentieth century" is also true for the subclassification, "Age of the World Wars." Such a subclassification, which divides the past into epochs, allows historians as well as contemporaries to situate themselves quickly.[5] To the degree that the world wars have become history, and fewer and fewer people who experienced them are still living, to that degree is it easier to examine the wars in their relationship to one another. Whereas professional historians are always discovering new and interesting details, in the collective memory it is largely the overall picture which is becoming more important. If one furthermore considers that the need for orientation through history takes place within the context of the present and the future, because it depends on contemporary experiences and expectations, then the fact that war has returned to Europe has certainly played a role in the contemporary discussion—there is now an increased public awareness of the history of (one's own) warfare. From this perspective one could see more clearly than before both wars as world wars, as total wars. The contrast to the present-day asymmetric warfare made it easier to situate these wars historically, to see their contours.[6] Accordingly, many of the public debates about recent German history have centered on the two wars. The list of the occasions and topics extends from the so-called "Wehrmacht exhibition" of the Hamburg Institute for Social Research and the compensation of forced laborers up to the recent discussion concerning the end of the war in 1945. In this recent discussion there has been a tendency to see Germans as victims in the Second World War, rather than to put the victims of the Germans at the center, and to do so as if one was breaking a taboo. Therefore, approximately ninety years after its outbreak, the First World War was rediscovered in Germany, and the concept of the "seminal catastrophe" experienced a renaissance. In 2004 numerous academic conferences, numerous publications,[7] television productions and exhibitions, for example in the German Historical Museum, reminded us of the war.[8]

The image of a second Thirty Years War is part of the contemporary rhetoric, expressing expectations (the worries about a future global conflict) and experiences (understanding the meaning of the Second World War). Thus Charles de Gaulle stated in 1941, in a radio talk in London exile as the Head of Free France, that the war against Germany had begun in 1914 and did not end with the Treaty of

Versailles: "En réalité, le monde fait la guerre de trente ans, pour ou contre la domination universelle du germanisme."[9] (In reality, the world is making the Thirty Years War, for or against the universal domination of Germanism.)

II

If we look more closely, what patterns of interpretation are hidden behind the analogy, the "Second Thirty Years War?" How is the relationship between the two wars established? What are the parameters of a possible network of relationships? It is comparatively easy and plausible to argue *ex negativo* that for approximately thirty years we lacked a stable peace. Who could possibly disagree? However, when one talks of a second Thirty Years War, a certain causal relationship is implied. The First World War, in the words of Hans-Ulrich Wehler, predetermined "to a large degree" the Second World War. It is this context which constitutes the internal unity of the concept, the "Second Thirty Year War." 1914–18 is the "prelude," the "model" for 1939–45.[10]

The value of this interpretive category lies in its ability to shed light upon central dimensions of these processes, in order to do justice to their complexity. As a rule, one chooses a comparative approach, most often implicitly, sometimes explicitly.[11] Unfortunately, historians engaged in the comparative history of the world wars are at a disadvantage because of the inequality in regard to the research. Whereas the First World War has been investigated since the 1980s using many new methods and concepts, the Second World War has remained for years, in spite of the early interest in the history of everyday life, in the shadow of earlier wars. Since the 1990s this has gradually changed. Today, research on the Second World War goes well beyond reconstructing events, ideas and military campaigns. Researchers investigate the "war society" and the social and cultural conditions of the war as well as, to turn this around, the impact of the war on everyday life.[12]

In order to establish how the events of both wars are related to one another, methodologically and theoretically, and to establish the structural relationship, we can employ another heuristic model, "The Age of Total War" (Eric Hobsbawm)[13]— "total war" is understood here as an ideal type.[14] According to this, not only both world wars, which are already widely accepted as "total wars," but all violent conflicts since the American Civil War need to be examined in regard to certain criteria concerning their totality. Even if there has been no agreement concerning the definition, one can name at least four central criteria: (1) total mobilization, that is, the maximum use of the human and material resources of a state through compulsion and propaganda so that the civilian population is fully included and involved in the war effort; (2) total war aims as the result of an imagined, existential threat from outside, which extends from physical subjugation all the way to total destruction; (3) a disregard for humanitarian law and the law on armed conflict, using the methods of total war to achieve the war aims, using the technological possibilities which are offered by new weapons, including against the civilian population; and finally (4) total control by the state, which intervenes in all social and economic regions. Bruno Thoß has proposed for diachronic comparison the following levels: (a) the extension of military violence, its means and methods, under the conditions of an industrialized warfare, (b) the extension of the geographical space of the war, and (c) the elimination of the borders limiting warfare.[15] The list can be (with Hirschfeld) extended to include a fourth level: (d) the ideological and propagandistic preparation of the world wars, the "intellectual mobilization."[16]

It is not by chance that one talks here of the dissolution of borders, of widening, and broadening. Slight differences as a rule are seen as resulting from the process of radicalization. This radicalization gives the developmental model of total war its dynamic continuity. Against this background, the First and the Second World Wars are discussed as parts of the same picture, each displaying a respective level of radicalization.

This approach is far more appropriate than the attempt to merge the First and the Second World Wars into a European, a World Civil War, as was done by National Socialist ideologues in order to legitimate their war of extermination.[17] In the postwar version of this interpretation, the unity of the epoch was seen in the putative continuity of a basic ideological constellation—the battle between the European bourgeoisie and Bolshevism. These ideologues turned the "National Socialist War"[18] into an act of "putative self-defence by the German bourgeoisie," which in 1939, as the representative of the European bourgeoisie so to speak, preempted the Bolshevik's putative war of extermination. It should be noted that the World War began before the October revolution in 1917, indeed, that without the war the Bolsheviks most likely would never have come to power, that the war was also fought in the West, and that the right in the Weimar Republic attacked liberalism (always meant pejoratively) at least as strongly as it attacked Bolshevism.[19] At best, the concept of the World Civil War refers to two real aspects of modern war: the extension of war to society as a whole and the radicalization of war into a "war of values." This explains perhaps why the concept has not yet been forgotten.[20]

In the comparative work on the history of the world wars, above all French historians have suggested that research be conducted into "the culture of war."[21] The interest here is in the experiences and the interpretation of the meaning of the war, the "war of ideas," and the social context of the interpretations of the meaning of the war in the memoirs. The culture of war is about death, mourning, and trauma, about being wounded and about disability as well as about the attractiveness of nationalism in the face of the experience of increasing social inequality—the burdens of war were not equally distributed.[22]

The study of these topics has received new impulses from the analysis of violence, for violence, of course, is at the center of armed conflict. The material foundations and the social practice of the use of military violence remained up till the 1990s a *terra incognita*.[23] Now, the study of the practice of violence in the Age of the World War asks whether or not there were early effects of habituation which allow one to see the extraordinary violence of the Germanization policies in the East, the "ethnic cleansing," as something with which people were in principle well acquainted, which they had already practiced. This was, for example, shown in a study on the Sondereinheit Dirlewanger (Dirlewanger Brigade), which was composed of men with a criminal record. Of special interest here was Oskar Dirlewanger, born in 1895, who spent more than half of his adult life at war: as a soldier in the First World War, as a Freikorps (Free Corps) leader, as a member of the Legion Condor, and finally as a member of the Waffen-SS. As a member of the SS his troop hunted down alleged partisans behind the front, at first in Poland and later in the Soviet Union. In these actions, and especially in the response to the Warsaw uprising, he displayed unusual brutality.[24] The practice, experience and cultural shaping of military violence is at the center of one of the most recent synthesis of the years 1914 to 1945, which here—misleadingly, and because of the global dimension much too narrowly—are characterized as a "European Civil War."[25]

III

To return to the question asked at the beginning: what are the heuristic advantages and disadvantages of the formula, a "Second Thirty Years War?" Instead of putting together a detailed list, adding up the strengths and weaknesses of the current research, for which it is at any rate much too early, my aim here is to put forward some ideas in regard to methodology and historiography. Whoever investigates the "Age of the World Wars" crosses over widely accepted caesura and often the boundaries of disciplines.[26] As a rule, this is refreshing, because it opens up new perspectives. However, this in itself is not a sufficient argument in favor of a comprehensive categorization of the period from 1914 to 1945 as an "epoch."

More is offered by the suggested interpretation if one asks about the genesis, development, and significance of the Second World War, without, of course, falling into the trap of a teleological reduction. Looking at military violence over a timeframe of thirty years makes it very difficult to understand an event like the Second World War as, in the literal sense of the word, extraordinary, and in so doing to cut the Second World War out of the course of (German) history. This is, of course, a volatile perspective in terms of the politics of memory. Whoever sees the links with the prewar period and with the First World War is no longer able to see the second as an exceptional event, as an "accident."

Furthermore, there are longer lines of continuity, which go back before 1914 and extend beyond 1945. The history of imperialism, of militarism, of social Darwinism, is characterized by continuity. To speak of an Age of the World Wars makes it therefore easier from a historiographical perspective to sketch the broad lines with which to interpret (German) history in the nineteenth and twentieth centuries—and to recognize possible projections into the "Cold War." Viewed like this, it is, for example, not a mistake to see the interwar period as a sort of cease-fire, during which German imperialism rearmed. This is what de Gaulle suggested in 1941, and it is worth noting that Fritz Fischer in the 1960s saw Germany as having the major responsibility for both world wars.[27]

However, the advantages of extending our perspective into the early twentieth century also points to one of the weaknesses in the periodization, as can be seen by looking first at the cornerstones 1914 and 1945, then at the narrative logic of this interpretive category. The starting point must be the break in 1914, the experience of the break in 1914. Yet the explanatory model of radicalization used in the recent scholarship on the war and interwar years also applies to the first prewar period (without, of course, interpreting the outbreak of the war as the necessary result of Europe's militarism and nationalism). Armament races and imperial rivalries destabilized the peace (this does not mean, however, that war was inevitable). Although people were frightened by the probable extent of a war—this fear made many assume that a large suicidal conflict was improbable—the industrial mass war of 1914 was not a surprise; there had been warnings, and there had not been any lack of martial rhetoric. Looked at from the colonial perspective, it is clear that there were regularly wars of extermination and expulsion in the colonial empires before 1914, which aimed to destroy systematically foreign societies and cultures. This radical type of warfare had thus been often tested and practiced *before* the Age of the World Wars. Accordingly, Aribert Reimann has spoken of a "colonization" of warfare after 1914, which corresponded to a "discursive colonization of the stereotypes of the enemy."[28] Something similar is true as well for the increasingly scientific rhetoric of perceptions and interpretations. In the final analysis, the power of nationalism and of anti-Semitism is based on their alleged scientific character.[29] This murderous rationality is characteristic of the First as well as of the Second World War; however, it has its origins in the late nineteenth century, just like central elements of the "military culture."[30]

On the other hand, many of the developments for which the First World War is generally considered the spark did not continue, or continued only in part, after the war ended. "Brutalization," for example, was by no means as widespread a phenomenon as has long been assumed. Broad social developments cannot be explained by individual biographies.[31] Rather, the First World War can also be interpreted as a pressure cooker, as an "event which transformed ... the cultural potential for violence from the colonial empires to the European battlefields."[32] In this case, the First World War belongs to the continuity of the "long nineteenth century" and not to the "short twentieth century," not to the "Second Thirty Years War."[33]

There is a second problem in regard to the end of the era. The interpretive category "Second Thirty Years War" necessarily includes the interwar period. The concept of the "interwar years" came from the Second World War; for contemporaries, in contrast, it was at first simply a postwar period, in spite of a revisionist rhetoric which predicted future world wars. If one takes the idea seriously that the period after the war was a postwar period, the advantage is that one can present in more detail central patterns of socialization influenced by the war. One of the strengths of the concept of the "Thirty Years War" is that it attempts to include the 1920s and the 1930s from the perspective of the history of the influence of the First World War.

However, is this not true for the years after 1945 as well? Should not this phase, which in the German case was for a long time reduced to a prehistory of the founding of the two postwar German states, likewise be interpreted and understood in close connection to the war? To be sure, the end of the war marks a clear break, especially in German history. The defeat and the condemnation of the war of extermination in the East, with its racist legitimation (which German propaganda attempted to make more palatable as the continuation of the First World War), the collapse of the National Socialist dictatorship, and finally, the formation of a new bi-polar world order which was speeded up by the end of the war: all this speaks in favor of the concept of a historical break. However, new research has shown how much can be gained by going beyond the political and military caesura of 1945 and investigating the continuities in the first ten to fifteen years after the end of the war in regard to, for example, the elites and popular mentalities as well as the social and cultural consequences of the war.[34] A new perspective would include, among other things, seeing this second postwar period in relation to the first and investigating the significance(s) of the first postwar period for the history of the second. 1918–19 and its consequences played an important role in, amongst other things, the apologetic discourse of the late 1940s and 1950s.[35] Still today "revisionists" feel an affinity for the formula of a second Thirty Years War because it allows them to project the responsibility for 1939–45 back to the key transition of the "shameful peace treaty (*Schandfrieden*) of Versailles" and the policies of the victorious powers in 1918–19.[36] (Another question is whether the influence of the First World War extends so far that—as is suggested by the talk of the "short twentieth century"—in 1989 a period ended which began in 1914.)

Thus, at the end of this essay there is a paradox of the periodization. The formula, the Age of Total Wars, becomes that much more imprecise to the degree to which its shortcomings are to be overcome by expanding the period before 1914 and after 1945. Is not the research into the history of the world war in danger of relinquishing the advantages that were hoped for, that is, opening up new fields of research by drawing a new epochal boundary around the Age of the World Wars? Is there not a danger that academic historians will be satisfied with a historiography of the two world wars which takes little note of each other: those viewing the First World War do so with a strong interest in the history of Germany from 1870–1918, whereas the others are so occupied with further deep investigations in the field of the Second World War that only from a great distance do they see the long nineteenth century? This dual system of research into the world wars can only be understood in a positive sense if the research is done with a systematic division of labor. However, historians doing research on the world wars who take seriously the concept of the Age of the World War, in which the concept is not watered down to a military history of militarism from the German Empire up to the "remilitarization" of the Federal Republic of Germany and the GDR, are well advised to approach methodologically the specifics of the Age of Total Wars through systematic, longitudinal analysis and diachronic comparisons within an international context.

There appears to be a consensus concerning the totality of these wars—concerning the extensive and far-reaching dissolution of the boundaries limiting violence, ultimately leading to the radical nullification of the distinction between the combatant and the civilian population. Given this consensus, is it not necessary to pay special attention to this problem in all its ramifications? It is propitious that at the very latest since the 1990s military historians have had at their disposal a well-stocked arsenal of questions and methods which aim ultimately to study the interaction of war, military, and civil society.[37] Here lies the social relevance of military historical studies. The idea that military historians were dealing with a subject matter *sui generis*, which, accordingly, no one could understand who, lacking a military training, was unable to understand the arcane realms of military strategy and their jargon—this idea would be the equivalent of a methodological step backwards, a retreat into a protective niche. It would furthermore be counterproductive if what was involved here was to integrate a history of military operations into military history so that military history profited from the results of this study in its various subsections—be it the political, the technical, or the social or cultural historical dimensions of military history. In terms of military history, the military strategy and the conduct of war has to be historicized, has to be placed in a larger historical context. Uniform longitudinal analysis and selected diachronic comparisons are an effective way of operationalizing the second Thirty Years War as a heuristic category. That these need to be designed so that they are transnational and not reduced to part of the history of individual nations, who could question this when the unit of study itself can only be described from a European perspective?[38]

A further disadvantage of this interpretive category can be found, finally, in the manner in which the history of war is narrated. The reservations which are called for in dealing with the concept of the "total war" apply here as well, although to a lesser degree. If the Second World War is seen as the temporary culmination of the development to total war, this has consequences for the narrative logic. For if earlier wars are measured by their structural proximity to the Second World War, then modern military history will all too quickly employ a "master narrative" in which 1939–45 is the perspective for everything, that is to say, the culmination of a development which began at the end of the eighteenth century with the people's war of the revolutionary periods. Roger Chickering, Stig Förster, and Bernd Greiner have attempted to mitigate this problem for the first half of the twentieth century by suggesting a "nominalistic" reading, according to which a "total war" can only be considered that which contemporaries already called a total war. This accordingly limits the framework chronologically and also shortens the length of the teleology.[39]

In this context it is worth noting that recent historical work has also shown the limitations of the idea that the Second World War was a total war. There were, for example, different geographical core areas, completely different degrees of economic mobilization and social control. Indeed, in many regards the Second World War was a little less total than its predecessor. Life on the German "home front," for example, was for a long time much less affected by the war than was the case in the First World War. Traditional gender roles limited the degree to which women could be used for military purposes in Germany as well as in Great Britain.

In all these structural relationships, in all the processes of development, acceleration, and radicalization, one needs to remember the relative contingence of historical processes. Even *post festum* one cannot perceive any inevitability, not to mention any rule suggesting that 1918 had to produce 1939. It is not the case that the peace treaty of Versailles or the war of ideas or becoming habituated to violence had to lead, as if on a one-way street, to the Armageddon of a war of extermination. Not only internally were different developments conceivable, but in terms of foreign policy as well; the National Socialist war could probably have been prevented by a timely signal from the Western powers. Looking back, Germany's entrance into the League of Nations in 1926 would have had quite a different significance as the final point of the postwar period.

The problem of finality is rather a methodological one. The historian's problems in regard to the content, in contrast, centers around the question of whether the quantitative and qualitative differences in regard to the level of destruction and annihilation in both wars is not so large that it is not possible "to think them together"—even if this is not to be mistaken with saying that they were equivalent. There were around sixty million dead in the Second World War, a far higher number of wounded, crippled, and orphaned, and the devastation of whole continents; just this list suggests that there is a break in the history of war. The most important question, however, remains, as it always has: did the war not obtain a new quality from the fact that—as has been convincingly shown by the most recent research—it was closely intertwined with the genocide?

By December 1941 at the very latest, when the war widened into a genuine World War, the decision was taken for the "final solution of the Jewish question," which would cost six million Jews their lives. Whether or not the "Fall Weiß" and the execution of the Polish elites after the surprise attack on Poland was the "prelude to a war of extermination" is a matter of debate and can certainly be questioned.[40] What is certain is that the "Operation Barbarossa" was planned from the very beginning as a war of extermination, leading to a far-reaching depopulation of the European part of the Soviet Union and to the enslavement of those who survived. If the National Socialists had been able to carry out their policy of Germanization in Eastern Europe, far more Soviet citizens would have been expelled or murdered. In contrast, the mass murder of the Armenians in 1915–16 was not initially part of the war planning. Only the NS-regime put genocide explicitly on its agenda. This clearly went far beyond the basic approaches of a radical Anti-Semitism in the First World War.[41]

To be sure, one could, looking at the concept of the "total war," point out other instances of radicalization: for example, the radicalization of the war aims up to the point that a peace treaty, such as was still possible at Versailles, was no longer possible, only unconditional surrender. Or one could refer to the radicalization of the conduct of the war, especially the strategic air war, directed against civilians, which went far beyond either the atrocities of the Germans or the partisan warfare in occupied Belgium and northern France in August 1914.[42] Or one could discuss the phantasmagoria, the conceptualizations of a German military state in "Oberost" through General Ludendorff[43] or the hunger blockade conducted by the British. Included here as well must be the radicalization of the mobilization for the war through the use of women, old men and youths in the "final battle" (*Endkampf*).

However, *the* break which most clearly contradicts the coherence of the category, "Thirty Years War," is the crime against civilization, the Shoah. To be sure, there are also continuities in this regard which go back into the nineteenth century, for example, the *völkisch*-racist anti-Semitism, which had its roots in the nineteenth century and which was radicalized after 1916. Genocide, however, so argues, for example, Gerhard Schreiber, "explodes the framework in which civilized people normally demarcate their war aims, and it is this which makes it absolutely impossible to see the Second World War as a legacy of the Great War."[44] It is on exactly this point that there are very different opinions when one is discussing whether or not to accept or reject the concept of the "Second Thirty Years War."[45]

IV

One does not have to go as far as Stig Förster, who has criticized the concept of a second Thirty Years War especially in regard to the break with civilization: "this is more a caricature than an adequate description of the historical reality."[46] The heuristic model, the "Second Thirty Years War," is certainly worth testing further. This must, however, be done with great care—especially in education. Where the "Second Thirty Years War" is not reduced to just a succinct and catchy formula, a merely formal classification scheme, but is rather used for a systematic analysis of an epoch, the model has advantages and disadvantages, depending on whether or not one is involved in research on the First or on the Second World War, on the first postwar period or on the second postwar period. In short, from the perspective of the "Second Thirty Years War," the "Great War," which was in the final analysis a world political catastrophe in large part because it led to another, is in danger of being reduced as an object of historical interest to a prelude to something else. Further problems are that by looking at the postwar period as an interwar period one easily loses sight of alternative developments; the second postwar period remains under-investigated in comparison to the first. Finally, if the period being investigated is expanded too much, if the object of study becomes too large, this reduces the marginal utility of the model. Therefore the following is true for the historiography of what the British call the "German Wars:" the proof of the pudding is in the eating.

Notes

1. G.F. Kennan, *The Decline of Bismarck's European Order. Franco-Russian Relations, 1875–1890* (Princeton, 1979), 3. I would like to thank Jeffrey Verhey for his meticulous translation.
2. E. Hobsbawm, *Age of Extremes. The Short Twentieth Century, 1914–1991* (London, 1994).
3. H.-U. Wehler, "Vom Beginn des Ersten Weltkriegs bis zur Gründung der beiden deutschen Staaten, 1914–1949," in *Deutsche Gesellschaftsgeschichte* (Munich, 2003), vol. 4, XIX.
4. Cf. the comprehensive bibliography by S. Audouin-Rouzeau et al. "Les sociétés, la guerre et la paix. Europe, Russie puis URSS, Etats-Unis, Japon 1911–1946," Bibliographie, in *Historiens et Géographes* Nr. 388 (2003), 137–212 (online: http://www.ihtp.cnrs.fr/spip.php?article114&lang=fr).
5. K. Tenfelde, "1914 bis 1990: Die Einheit der Epoche," in *Was ist Gesellschaftsgeschichte? Positionen, Themen, Analysen*, eds. M. Hettling et al. (Munich, 1991), 71–80.
6. Cf. however as early examples R. Aron, *The Century of Total War* (Garden City, NY, 1954); H. Arendt, *Elemente und Ursprünge totaler Herrschaft* (Frankfurt, 1954).
7. Cf. for example G. Hirschfeld et al., eds., *Enzyklopädie Erster Weltkrieg* (Paderborn, 2003); S. Burgdorff and K. Wiegrefe, eds., *Die Urkatastrophe des 20. Jahrhunderts* (Stuttgart, 2004).
8. Der Weltkrieg 1914–1918. Ereignis und Wirkung, Deutsches Historisches Museum, 13 May–15 Aug 2004.
9. C. de Gaulle, *Discours et messages*, 18 septembre 1941, radio de Londres, T 1, Pendant la guerre (Paris, 1970), 102–3.
10. Wehler, *Der zweite Dreißigjährige Krieg*, in Spiegel special 2004/1, 138–143.
11. S. Audoin-Rouzeau et al., eds., *La Violence de guerre 1914–1945. Approches comparées des deux conflits mondiaux* (Brussels, 2002); B. Thoß and H.-E. Volkmann, eds., *Erster Weltkrieg – Zweiter Weltkrieg: ein Vergleich. Krieg, Kriegserlebnis, Kriegserfahrung in Deutschland* (Paderborn, 2002).
12. J. Echternkamp, ed., *German Wartime Society 1939–1945: Politicization, Disintegration, and the Struggle for Survival* (Oxford, 2008); Ibid., ed. *German Wartime Society 1939–1945: Exploitation, Interpretations, Exclusion* (Oxford, forthcoming).
13. Hobsbawm, *Age of Extremes*.
14. Cf. the series of conferences started in 1992: S. Förster and J. Nagler, eds., *On the Road to Total War. The American Civil War and the German Wars of Unification, 1861–1871* (Cambridge, 1997); M.F. Boemeke, ed., *Anticipating Total War. The German and American Experiences, 1871–1914* (Cambridge, 1999).
15. B. Thoß, "Die Zeit der Weltkriege – Epochen als Erfahrungseinheit?," in idem. / Volkmann, ed., *Erster Weltkrieg – Zweiter Weltkrieg*, 7–42.
16. G. Hirschfeld, "Erster Weltkrieg – Zweiter Weltkrieg: Kriegserfahrungen in Deutschland. Neuere Ansätze und Überlegungen zu einem diachronen Vergleich," in *Zeitgeschichte online*, 2004. Thema: Fronterlebnis und Nachkriegsordnung. Wirkung und Wahrnehmung des Ersten Weltkriegs, May 2004.
17. E. Nolte, *Der europäische Bürgerkrieg, Nationalsozialismus und Bolschewismus (1987)* (Munich, 2000).
18. N. Frei and H. Kling, eds., *Der nationalsozialistische Krieg* (Frankfurt, 1990).
19. U. Herbert, "Der Zweite Weltkrieg in der europäischen Geschichte," in B. Martin, ed., *Der Zweite Weltkrieg und seine Folgen. Ereignisse – Auswirkungen – Reflexionen* (Freiburg, 2006), 315–331, 315.
20. This is what is assumed by Geyer, *Urkatastrophe*, 29.
21. Cf. the syntheses by J.-J. Becker et al., eds., *Guerre et cultures 1914–1918* (Paris, 1994); S. Audoin-Rouzeau and A. Becker, *14–18. Understanding the Great War* (New York, 2003).
22. S. Delaporte, *Gueules cassées: les blessés de la France pendant la Grande Guerre* (Paris, 2001); cf. S.O. Müller, *Deutsche Soldaten und ihre Feinde. Nationalismus an Front und Heimatfront im Zweiten Weltkrieg* (Frankfurt, 2007).

23. Cf. J. Keegan, *A History of Warfare* (London, 1994); S. Audoin-Rouzeau, "Au cœur de la violence de guerre: la violence du champ de bataille durant les deux conflits mondiaux," in *La Violence de guerre*, eds. idem et al., 73–97.
24. C. Ingrao, *Les chasseurs noirs. La brigade Dirlewanger* (Paris, 2006).
25. Enzo Traverso, *À feu et à sang: de la guerre civile européenne 1914–1945* (Paris, 2007).
26. Cf. the series "Zeitalter der Weltkriege" edited by the German Research Institute for Military History (MGFA) (Paderborn, 2006) et seqq.
27. Cf. S. Förster, "Eine Katastrophe von dreißig Jahren," *Der Bund*, 5/6/2005, 2.
28. See A. Reimann, "Der Erste Weltkrieg – Urkatastrophe oder Katalysator?," *Aus Politik und Zeitgeschichte B* 29–30 (2004), 30–38.
29. C. Geulen, *Wahlverwandte. Rassendiskurs und Nationalismus im späten 19. Jahrhundert* (Hamburg, 2004).
30. Cf. the article by MacGregor Knox in this volume.
31. D. Schumann and A. Wirsching, eds., *Violence and Society after the First World War* (Munich, 2003). For the critique cf. B. Davis, "Experience, Identity, and Memory: The Legacy of World War I," *Journal of Modern History* 75 (2003), 111–31.
32. Reimann, *Der Erste Weltkrieg*, 33.
33. Cf. V. Ullrich, *Die nervöse Großmacht. Aufstieg und Untergang des deutschen Kaiserreichs* (Frankfurt, 1997). D. Bönker, in contrast, underlines the rupture of former warfare using the example of the unlimited U-boat warfare; cf. his article in this volume.
34. For research on the continuity of elites cf. N. Frei, ed., *Hitlers Eliten nach 1945* (Munich, 2003); for the postwar perspective cf. J. Echternkamp, *Nach dem Krieg. Alltagsnot, Neuorientierung und die Last der Vergangenheit 1945–1949* (Zurich, 2003).
35. J. Echternkamp, "Zwischen Selbstverteidigung und Friedenskampf. Zur Wirkungsgeschichte des Ersten Weltkriegs 1945–1960," in *Erster Weltkrieg – Zweiter Weltkrieg*, eds. Thoß and Volkmann (2002), 641–68.
36. Cf. only G. Schulze-Rhonhof, 2006, *Der zweite Dreißigjährige Krieg [Hörbuch]*; ders., *1939 – Der Krieg, der viele Väter hatte. Der lange Anlauf zum Zweiten Weltkrieg* (München, 2007).
37. T. Kühne and B. Ziemann, eds., *Was ist Militärgeschichte?* (Paderborn, 2000); G. Krumeich, "Militärgeschichte für eine zivile Gesellschaft," in *Geschichtswissenschaften. Eine Einführung*, ed. C. Cornelißen (Frankfurt, 2000), 178–93.
38. Cf. J. Echternkamp and Stefan Martens, eds., *Experience and Memory. The Second World War in Europe* (Oxford, 2010).
39. R. Chickering et al., "Are We There Yet? World War II and the Theory of Total War," in *A World at Total War*, eds. idem et al. (Cambridge, 2005), 1–31, 13.
40. This is the thesis by J. Böhler, *Auftakt zum Vernichtungskrieg. Die Wehrmacht in Polen 1939* (Frankfurt, 2006).
41. Cf. S. Bruendel, *Volksgemeinschaft ohne Volksstaat. Die "Ideen von 1914" und die Neuordnung Deutschlands im Ersten Weltkrieg* (Berlin, 2003). This cesura is also stressed by Alan Kramer, cf. his article in this volume.
42. J. Horne and A. Kramer, *Deutsche Kriegsgreuel 1914. Die umstrittene Wahrheit* (Hamburg, 2004); A. Kramer, *Dynamic of Destruction. Culture and Mass Killing in the First World War* (Oxford, 2007); cf. his article in this volume.
43. V.G. Liulevicius, *Kriegsland im Osten. Eroberung, Kolonisierung und Militärherrschaft im Ersten Weltkrieg* (Hamburg, 2002).
44. G. Schreiber, *Der Zweite Weltkrieg* (Göttingen, 2004), 7–8.
45. Cf. Wehler, *Der zweite Dreißigjährige Krieg*, 143.
46. Cf. S. Förster, 2005, "Eine Katastrophe von dreißig Jahren," in *Der Bund*, Verlag, 2.

Chapter 13

The Enduring Charm of the Great War
Some Reflections on Methodological Issues

Roger Chickering

Several years ago, American audiences were riveted to their televisions by Ken Burns' epic history of "The War."[1] Burns did not have to identify the war in question, for in the United States the Second World War (which is what everyone in Burns' audience understood "the war" to mean) figures as the pivot in America's twentieth century, the "good war" fought by the "greatest generation"—an event that rivals the American Revolution and the American Civil War as this country's defining historical moment.[2] The First World War, by contrast, occupies a much more modest, peripheral place in the American national memory. One finds no World War I memorial on the Washington Mall. In the United States the First World War figures as a first, reluctant, tentative American introduction to the turbulent and obsolescent politics of the old Europe, the overture to the great coming-of-age that Burns documented anew and with great effect on American public television.

On the other side of the Atlantic, the First World War occupies a much more central place in the narratives of Europe's twentieth century. The fact that the effects of this war were by a wide margin more profound, far-reaching, and traumatic than in North America is the most obvious reason. Although it speaks to issues broader than its comparative marginality in the United States, a case can be made that European interest also reflects the fact that the First World War poses more exciting, troubling, and broadly interesting methodological problems than the Second. In any event, interest in the First World War not only remains broad, but is clearly growing.

A lot of evidence supports this conclusion. The point was recently institutionalized in the establishment of an International Society for First World War Studies. The roots of this organization lie in Europe, but in 2007 its conference convened in Washington, DC, where dozens of young North American scholars presented their findings. Another piece of evidence is the recent explosion of scholarly literature on the First World War.[3] One can now even find books in libraries and on the internet that deal exclusively with the historiography of the First World War—books about the history of the history of the Great War. The most thorough and significant of these volumes, Jay Winter's and Antoine Prost's *The Great War in History*, offers some rough statistical calculations about the proliferation of literature on the First World War. The authors note, for example, that the number of volumes that were catalogued in the British Library under the rubric of "The World War, 1914 to 1918" quadrupled between 1980 and 2001.[4]

Whatever the value or meaning of these numbers, the fascination of the First World War, which began in fact to rivet the attention of historians almost from the moment it broke out, has not only persisted but also intensified. This fact itself represents a significant historiographical problem. How should one explain the enduring popularity of the Great War, particularly in this day and age? And what are the implications and methodological challenges of its popularity?

Four considerations are central to answering these questions. In the first place, anniversaries are important. A case in point was the gathering of a group of distinguished historians (together with President Carter) in Atlanta in October 2004 to observe ("celebrate" is surely not the right word) the ninetieth anniversary of the Great War's outbreak.[5] The special volume that was published by the German magazine *Spiegel* on the same occasion, the enormous German *Encyclopedia of the First World War*, and its no less enormous French counterpart were likewise commemorations of this anniversary.[6] We can anticipate with certainty that the volume of literature will swell as we near the year 2014, if only on the strength of the conference volumes and companion-volumes to the TV series that will mark the centennial. Plans are already underway in the German Studies Association to meet in 2014 in Kansas City, at the new National World War I Museum; and we can anticipate that a spate of publications will emerge from this meeting as well.

Another date offers a more durable explanation than the approaching centenary in 2014 for the war's popularity. This date is 1989. Insofar as they brought the "short twentieth century" to a close and established it as a coherent historical unit, the events of 1989 drew the attention of historians immediately to the violent onset of this historical era in 1914 and to the beginning of what George Kennan had already, in 1979, labeled the "seminal catastrophe of the twentieth century."[7] In keeping with the political triumphalism that pervaded Western commentaries in the 1990s—the belief that the "short" twentieth century had ended in freedom's triumph over totalitarianism—the epoch-making character of the First World War stood out for its catastrophic consequences.[8] These consequences now unambiguously included the Bolshevik Revolution and its hideous offspring, the Soviet Union. The resulting change in perspective on the First World War was evident in the work of Hans-Ulrich Wehler, who is arguably the most important German historian of the twentieth century's second half. When, in 1973, Wehler first addressed the broader significance of the First World War, he put his analysis at the end of his little volume on the German Empire, as if to affirm that the importance of this conflict lay primarily in its role as outcome and conclusion of developments that had gone before it.[9] In 2003, by contrast, the First World War stood at the beginning of the fourth volume of Wehler's massive *Gesellschaftsgeschichte*. Here the author characterized the war as the "great transformer," the epochal event that constituted a "dividing line between the long nineteenth and the fundamentally different twentieth century."[10]

Characterizing the war as catastrophe and tragedy speaks as well to the enduring moral ambivalences—or better, the ironies—that have attached to this seemingly endless "war to end war" and enhanced interest in it. Attempts have generally failed to portray the First World War in the same light as the Second World War—as a contest of moral absolutes. Outside the Soviet Bloc, few historians were willing after 1961 to follow Fritz Fischer's arguments to their conclusion that Germany's hegemonic designs during the First World War rivaled those of Nazi Germany during the Second World War.[11] A number of British historians—one thinks primarily of Brian Bond—have admittedly argued this case, noting that the vast majority of British soldiers remained persuaded (by implication correctly) that they were fighting naked German aggression during the First World War, no less than they (or their sons) were during the Second.[12] Still, few historians have quarreled with the proposition that general disillusionment, a broad questioning of the stark moral oppositions that had guided wartime mobilization on both sides, set in Britain and elsewhere shortly after the conclusion of the First World War, as this conflict metamorphosized into memory—in other words into history.[13]

This disillusionment with the First World War has in a sense never disappeared. It reflects the proposition, which Kennan's famous phrase captured, that the world in the twentieth century would have been a much better place had the war not taken place. Recent controversies about a "second Thirty Years War," in which the Second World War figures as the conclusion to the First, have revolved about this proposition.[14] "World War II," as the economic historians Stephen Broadberry and Mark Harrison have recently written, "was just World War I with more countries, more soldiers, more time, more money, more guns, more death, and more destruction."[15]

Disillusionment over the aftermath doubtless explains why a whiff of irony continues to hover over the Great War—a lingering sense of "in vain" spawned by the vast discrepancy between hopes and consequences, between expectations and the frightful results of this conflict. In fact, if one follows Paul Fussell, in the English language at least, irony represents the quintessential trope of this war, the only adequate literary form for framing what can be portrayed as the systematic and pointless squandering of life, wealth, and well-being.[16] Recent historical studies have only confirmed the impression that irony lurked everywhere in this vast conflict. Analyses of soldiers' letters have emphasized how the ironic proximity of boredom and sudden, gruesome death was a defining feature of life on the front lines.[17] Meanwhile, on the "home front" (this expression, a product of the war's first months, is itself ironic), the irony lay in the growing daily tedium of an extraordinary situation. In Germany, where it corresponded to the very normality or *Alltäglichkeit* of war, the irony took the dismal form of acute material shortages, which seeped into every phase of life, accompanied by omnipresent anxiety about the fate of friends and loved ones who daily confronted mortal danger at the front.[18]

Vast dimensions offer a third reason for the enduring interest in the First World War. In this dreadful war, combat—the failure to break the operational stalemate—continues to exert a powerful fascination on military historians; so does the experience of the front-line soldiers who were the objects of this catastrophic failure.[19] Powerful accounts of this front-line dimension continue to appear.[20] But life on the home front has also represented a fascinating object of study, on which the interest of several generations of social historians has been fixed since the 1960s. Thanks in part to their work, we now recognize that the great secular processes of social and economic development—industrialization, urbanization, capital concentration, class formation, class tension, demographic change, social mobility, and criminality—were by no means suspended. Instead they continued—transformed, warped, or intensified in the crucible of war. The development of these secular processes has been the subject of impressive scholarship from the moment, in the immediate aftermath of the war, in which the Carnegie Endowment launched its great series of studies on the war's impact on belligerent societies. Some of these volumes remain indispensable today.[21] The most impressive testimony to the renewed vitality of this genre is the two volumes of Jay Winter and Jean-Louis Robert's *Capital Cities at War*, for they have given the war's social history a powerful comparative dimension.[22] They have also documented how much the purview of interest has broadened to other social institutions and cultural dimensions of life in war, be they sexuality, confession, schools, sociability, or voluntary associations.

A final entry in the list of reasons for the ongoing interest in the war has to do both with the social history of the war and the date 1989. The First World War has functioned as a crucible for historical methodology as well. The "turn" toward cultural history began long before the fall of the Berlin Wall. As the work of Fussell, Eric Leed, John Keegan, and others attests, historians had begun in the 1970s, if not earlier, to exploit letters from the front and other autobiographical sources to analyze the "subjectively experienced history" of the front-line soldier.[23] The implications of this work increasingly informed the agenda of historians of the war during the 1990s. The emphasis now fell on the "meaning" of the war, or, as Gerhard Hirschfeld has recently put it, "the question of what the war meant to those human beings who experienced it."[24] This question has pointed toward a dimension of the war that was more direct, basic, or somehow more genuine than the broad material processes that had occupied the social historians. Cultural history thus appeared to present a fundamental challenge to social history. And this challenge was all the more troubling once the collapse of the Soviet Empire—and with it, rightfully or not, the appeal of Marxist historiography—put social history further on the defensive.

As it relates particularly to the history of the First World War, one can see both the impact and the implications of this challenge from cultural history in the book by Jay Winter and Antoine Prost, which can be read as a manifesto of sorts. In their survey of the historiography of the Great War, the authors write of a progressive development through a series of phases or tendencies. In the first phase, which set in immediately with the end of the war and continued into the 1960s, the interest of historians was riveted to the military, diplomatic, and political history of the war. A second phase followed until the end of the 1980s. This one featured a stronger emphasis on the social history of the war, and it was often guided by materialist assumptions and a variety of Marxist or neo-Marxist approaches. In the last stage, whose commencement the authors find well symbolized in the foundation in 1992 of the *Historiale de la Grande Guerre* in Peronne in northern France, historians have turned increasingly to the "culture of war" broadly understood.[25] By this term Winter and Prost write of a realm of identity, emotions, memory, and "*mentalités*," collective ideas and representations of war. The two historians invoke "a new kind of historical idealism," "a dematerialization of historical study, a turn towards ideas and representations as independent of material conditions." Are we not in fact dealing, they ask, with the "reversal of the materialist assumptions of the second generation, for which identities emerged out of social conditions?" They write of these developments as a kind of evolution or maturational process (although it is also possible to detect traces of an intellectual trajectory that the two authors themselves have followed). In the initial phase, they write, the historiography of the war lay in its infancy, while the behavior of individual actors—heroes and antiheroes—figured as the driving forces in the story. In its adolescence, the historiography of war grew to encompass the material conditions of war, as the actions of classes and other social groups took on greater analytical power. Now, however, as it enters its maturity, the historiography of war has recognized culture as the proper object of study. Culture, write Winter and Prost, has emerged as the "driving force of history."[26]

These two scholars have identified a basic reason for the growing interest in the First World War in the last two decades. There is no gainsaying the energy and excitement that the "cultural turn" has injected into the recent scholarship on the war (and more generally). At the same time, however, the historiographical trends that these authors have identified, and embraced, have raised big and important methodological problems. One of the welcome effects of their book—and surely it was by design—was to provoke discussion of just these issues.

The persistent interest in the Great War has been fueled in a way that reflects differences in national historiographical traditions. The book by Winter and Prost emphasizes developments in British and French historiography, where the turn to cultural history has been particularly marked, and productive. Their analysis of the situation in Germany is more tentative, in large part because social history has remained more entrenched in this land, and the cultural history of the war has, for better or worse, encountered more resistance. Scholars here, particularly those who have trained in Bielefeld or otherwise been linked to the so-called "Bielefeld school," have been reluctant to abandon the methods and questions of the "old" social history of the war. Jürgen Kocka's study of class society at war remains a monument to an approach to history whose practitioners tend, as David Blackbourn once quipped, to discount everything that they cannot count.[27] To scholars who view the war in this light, the kind of history that Prost and Winter are championing hardly represents a step forward. German scholars have noted with alarm that cultural history threatens to bring a historiographical regression, a retreat into the old, discredited methodologies of the nineteenth century. The new "primacy of mentalities" and emotions has, so runs the argument, encouraged a resurgence of historical (and philosophical) idealism and what was once known as historicism, including the hermeneutics of *Einfühlung* or empathetic intuition, which was prominently associated with the name of Ranke. To judge from the criticism that this hermeneutic tradition has drawn in Germany, it offers license to undisciplined subjectivity.[28] It lacks the careful quantitative controls that historians around Wehler and Kocka had worked out in the name of "historical social science" in the 1970s. Like consciousness, as Kocka charged in the mid-1980s, experiences can be false.[29]

This kind of skepticism bristles at the terms in which the new paradigm of cultural history is being laid out. The principal objects of this reconfiguration of the war's history, claim Prost and Winter, are to be "the victims, who do not act, but suffer." These are "ordinary people in their anonymous individuality ... people, as they live, love, endure pain, because they are trapped in an exceptional situation which they are unable to change and which at any moment threatens to crush them." What is more, in the new paradigm of cultural history, social groups, economic interests, and political institutions appear to be foreign or irrelevant. This history, Prost and Winter insist, "does not consider people in constituted groups, but as a collection of individuals," each of whom is legitimate. The challenge of this "humanist vision" is accordingly, they conclude, "to identify meanings, to reconfigure the symbolic universe of the time."[30]

One can only admire the work of Antoine Prost and Jay Winter, two scholars whose contributions to the scholarship on the Great War are simply unsurpassed. Still, aspects of their new paradigm raise troubling questions, as well as the fear that what they are advocating may result in the isolation of cultural history—that it may deepen the gulf between cultural history and the "other" histories of the war; and this would be a most unfortunate outcome. In any case, the provocation issued by these two historians begs for a response. So here it is.

Although the proposition may appear to be immodest, coming as it does from one of the principals, the foundation of the *Historiale* in Peronne was not the only reason why the year 1992 was important in the historiography of the First World War. In March of the same year, the first in a series of conferences took place in Washington, DC, on the history of total war. This conference was followed by five more, all of which explored aspects of total war from the era of the American Revolution to the Second World War.[31] One of these conferences, in 1997, was devoted to the First World War; and Jay Winter was one of the participants. The conferences failed in a sense, for they did not achieve the purpose that had inspired them in the first place, which was to frame a definition of "total war" that would find general assent among the participants. It is still not clear what total war was. Participants could agree on little more than the idea that the great industrial wars of the twentieth century could claim a certain "totality," insofar as distinctions between the military and civilian realms of warfare practically disappeared. Civilians became no less vital than soldiers to sustaining the war effort, and, as a consequence, they became no less vulnerable to military violence—be it in the form of strategic bombing from the air, starvation caused by naval blockade, or calculated genocide in a factory-like setting. More civilians than soldiers died during the Second World War. The monster wars of the last century thus directly and comprehensively affected every man, woman, and child in the participating states (and to a significant extent in many neutral states as well).

Although the point may strike some as banal, this proposition itself established what one might call a "causal nexus," insofar as the effects of war extended into every phase or dimension of life in the belligerent societies. War itself provided, in other words, the analytical center of its own comprehensive history. Total war left nothing, absolutely nothing untouched. This principle applied to the home front no less than the fighting front—to the conduct of military operations, the politics and diplomacy of war, the development of economies and societies, and the culture of war in all of its many, many manifestations. Even the subjective experiences of war could be anchored within this all-embracing analytical context.

This perspective raised a host of problems of its own, which were also well in evidence at the conferences on total war. At issue now was the definition of military history.[32] How might one write the history of such comprehensive wars, whose effects spared no one and no thing in the belligerent societies? How might one distinguish military history from the history of everything else? At least in the era of total war, in the great wars of the twentieth century, must not the history of war logically be total history—a kind of history that strives to capture every dimension of the vast experience that war had become?

These struck me as compelling questions, so I resolved to confront them practically. To the alarm of some of my colleagues, who charged me with trying to rob military history of its identity, I began to play with the idea of writing such a total history of total war, for I had persuaded myself that it might be possible. The effort would require combining cultural history not only with social history, but also with economic history, political history, and the history of operations. To anticipate the end of this story, I also had to make major compromises in the interests of practicality. These included limiting myself to one world war (the first), one country (Germany, because I knew it best), and one city, Freiburg im Breisgau, because it was the right size, offered a surviving documentary basis, and was a nice place to work.[33] This total history was to be of total war in a lovely place.

One of the attractive things about the project was that it compelled me to think a lot about my own philosophy of history, and about methodological assumptions with which I had been working for most of my professional life but had not articulated well, even to myself. I also found myself wondering about the bases on which I held these assumptions. In the end, I found myself forced to reason back to original principles that I had accepted on grounds that were not historical; these principles had grown instead, as I realized, out of considerations that are best characterized as moral and aesthetic.

The moral assumptions were of two orders. The first I found triggered in phrases like "precision bombing," "surgical strike," or anything else that suggested that the effects of warfare might be confined to an immediate theater of operations. The analogue, with which I was also uncomfortable, was the proposition that the history of war was properly confined to the history of operations. Perhaps naively, I had long wondered whether at least some of history's wars might have been prevented had their proponents foreseen the vast and pervasive effects of their decisions to resort to military means, had they appreciated that the furies of war are violent and volatile and that the consequences have tended historically to become as comprehensive as they have been unhappy.

A second order of moral conviction had to do with the analytical imperatives that these dynamics pose to historians. The responsible intellectual reaction to the last century's catastrophic wars is, I concluded, to seek to understand how and why they happened as they did, to exercise the analytical powers that historians possess to weave causal connections (as historians tend to understand them). I myself took this imperative to mean that I should try to trace the dynamics and scope of one of these wars on one of these societies—to study the ways in which the furies that were unleashed in August 1914 plagued everyone in ways that were impossible to imagine at the outset. Who could have anticipated the olfactory experience of war on the German urban home front, which was due to shortages of alcohol and soap, which were due in turn to shortages of vegetable oils and fats, which were due to the crisis in German agricultural production, which was due to the army's voracious demands for foodstuffs, animals, and farm labor? Establishing these connections would require wearing the hats of economic historian, social historian, political historian, cultural historian, and historian of operations, for the city in question was a principal staging area for the Alsatian sector of the western front, as well as a theater of allied strategic bombing operations out of eastern France.

The aesthetic considerations that guided my thinking were, by contrast, entirely practical. They had to do with the organization of such a study of a war's consequences. How does one arrange a total history of a total war? If the war left nothing untouched, nothing is irrelevant to the account. It thus became necessary to think about analytical priorities or the hierarchies of explanatory categories that would organize the account most efficiently and persuasively. What kinds of historical causes produced what kinds of historical effects? Historians ask explanatory questions—about why things happened as they did—but the challenge was to devise an elegant explanatory network, one that was at once comprehensive, coherent, and plausible. As if to adumbrate this problem, I speculated that it might be possible, had the sources existed, to write a postmodern history of this German city at war—as a random series of eighty-five thousand personal biographies of ordinary people. The end product would have chronicled how these inhabitants of the city lived, loved, and endured pain, and were trapped in an exceptional situation. The result would have been comprehensive; but it would not have been coherent, because it would not have linked the experiences of these people in any meaningful way. It is impossible to determine even whether it would have been a plausible account either, because no one would have wanted to read, much less publish it.

The challenges of composing the account in the most efficient and coherent way recommended a number of methodological premises, working hypotheses, or what one might call with Carlo Ginzburg "cognitive wagers."[34] The ultimate test of their validity struck me as a practical one. It would be the effectiveness of these premises in organizing the surviving sources and in organizing the account in a persuasive fashion.

These premises were fourfold. The first was to posit on practical grounds the fundamental materiality of the war. This premise challenged frontally the thinking of Antoine Prost and Jay Winter about a basic order of explanatory categories. I had to admit it: I was a historical materialist. I assumed that the war really happened, that it was not, as some advocates of the "linguistic turn" appeared for a while in the 1990s to argue, a phenomenon whose ultimate reality was cultural because it could be apprehended metaphorically, in language alone. Instead, I posited that the war had, as one might say nowadays, "pretextual materiality." The war was in the first instance about bodies—complex organisms—that were destroyed, maimed, or otherwise traumatized, undernourished, exhausted, and rendered more vulnerable both to the natural elements and to the noxious microorganisms that thrived in an environment made hospitable to them by mass killing and deprivation.

A second wager flowed directly from the first. This one had to do with the "textuality of the war." I wagered that the culture of war was constituted in attempts to fix the meaning of the war, and that these attempts in turn required textualizing it, locating it in a broader narrative framework of significance—as a story with a beginning and an end, be it a narrative of national fulfillment or survival, class conflict, religious renewal, racial regeneration, or something else. I also assumed, however, that the principal reference points of this textualization lay in the material impact of the war, in the effort to fix the meaning of death, troop movements, hunger, and the chemical processes that issued in foul smells. The culture of war was in this sense secondary or epiphenomenal; it was generated in constant, dialectical interaction with the war's massive and comprehensive impact on bodies.

In addition, I wagered that the experience of war was a social phenomenon. Those who lived through the war did not experience it as an amorphous collection of individuals, independent of political institutions or social affiliations. The culture of war consisted of efforts to endow the war with meaning, but these meanings were constructed, represented, and communicated within social groups. These processes were, moreover, constituted in language, in collective dialogues called discourses, among human beings who shared basic social characteristics or identities (many of which were rooted in common experiences of war itself). Almost all of the German participants, for instance, shared ties of ethnic identity. However, the vast majority of those who shared the experience of the war at the front were male. As officers or enlisted men, they shared social traits; as members of locally recruited military units they shared regional and confessional traits. The majority of those who shared the experience of the war on the home front were female or, if they were male, young or elderly; here at home they shared commonalities of gender, class, confession, regional identity, and age cohort. The experiences of war reflected and refracted the complex loyalties, identities, and counteridentities that were rooted in all these social affiliations

Finally, I wagered that all those who experienced the war were not merely passive objects. To regard them in this way obscures the basic ways in which the men, women, and children who lived through the war composed their own experiences of the ordeal. They all faced the challenge of making sense of the war's impact on people like themselves. They sought accordingly to situate their ordeal in historical time and social space, to locate the war's impact not only in a coherent narrative framework, but also in a system of social categories, like class, confession, and age-cohort. Insofar as they attempted to understand, interpret, comprehend, or otherwise to "construct" it, they all made their own war. And their "constructions" of the war in turn authorized a broad range of social and political practices—most, but by no means all of which ensured the continuation of the war, and the prolongation of its material burdens, however these had been textualized.

These assumptions defined the principal tasks of writing a history of the war. As some German scholars have been arguing, the main challenge was to undertake an "'empathetic' structural history" (*'verstehende' Strukturgeschichte*) of this titanic conflict.[35] The object was not only to understand the experiences of the war, as these were constituted in language and other symbols—in rituals and other collective practices—but also to situate these experiences, to answer the question of which experiences were shared by whom and why.

This approach can lay no claims to originality. It reflects instead methods and techniques that have begun to inform the most interesting new cultural histories of this war, a category that includes the Janet Watson book or Maureen Healey's history of wartime Vienna (both of which were, like my own work, published in Jay Winter's *Studies in the Social and Cultural History of Modern Warfare*), or the scholarship of the young German scholars in the "Working Group for the History of Mentalities in the First World War," which was anchored in Tübingen.[36] The signs are clear that young historians are now seeking, with some success, to synthesize the analysis of cultural practices in wartime with an analysis of their contexts, both at home and at the front.

The historiography of the First World War is thus vibrant. But one is tempted to think less of an evolution or maturation of methods than of a broadening, or the expansion of the understanding of what constitutes legitimate objects of study. The scholarship has not so much outgrown old approaches to the war as it has accommodated new ones. The picture of the First World War is becoming more comprehensive; and this is a welcome development, as Jay Winter and Antoine Prost will surely agree. The result suggests in any event the wisdom and rewards of employing a broad range of methodologies in seeking to understand everything that this terrible war let loose.

Notes

1. An earlier version of this essay is in M.S. Neiberg and J.D. Keene, eds., *Finding Common Ground: New Directions in First World War Studies* (Leiden, 2011), 3–180.
2. The iconic statement is in T. Brokaw, *The Greatest Generation* (New York, 2004). See K. Scholz, *The Greatest Story Ever Remembered. Erinnerung an den Zweiten Weltkrieg als sinnstiftendes Element in den USA* (Frankfurt a. M., 2008).
3. Just among the surveys, for instance: D. Stevenson, *Cataclysm: The First World War as Political Tragedy* (New York, 2004); E. Dorn Brose, *A History of the Great War: World War I and the International Crisis of the Twentieth Century* (New York, 2009); S. Neitzel, *Weltkrieg und Revolution 1914–1918/19* (Berlin, 2008); W.J. Mommsen, *Die Urkatastrophe Deutschlands: Der Erste Weltkrieg 1914–1918* (Stuttgart, 2002); V.R. Berghahn, *Der erste Weltkrieg* (Munich, 2008); A. Carrère, *La Première Guerre Mondiale: Anthologie* (Paris, 2006).
4. J. Winter and A. Prost, *The Great War in History: Debates and Controversies 1914 to the Present* (Cambridge, 2005), 17.
5. H. Afflerbach and D. Stevenson, eds., *An Improbable War? The Outbreak of World War I and European Political Culture before 1914* (New York, 2007).
6. S. Burgdorff and K. Wiegrefe, *Der Erste Weltkrieg. Die Urkatastrophe des 20. Jahrhunderts* (Munich, 2004); G. Hirschfeld, et al., eds., *Encyklopädie Erster Weltkrieg* (Paderborn, 2004); P. Cabanel, u.a., eds., *Encyclopédie de la Grande Guerre 1914–1918* (Paris, 2004). The German encyclopedia has now appeared in a second edition and will be published in English by Brill.
7. G.F. Kennan, *The Decline of Bismarck's European Order: Franco-Russian Relations, 1875–1890* (Princeton, 1979), 3.
8. E. Hobsbawm, *The Age of Extremes: A History of the World, 1914–1991* (New York, 1996).
9. H.-U. Wehler, *Das Deutsche Kaiserreich 1871–1918* (Göttingen, 1973), 192–226.
10. Wehler, *Deutsche Gesellschaftsgeschichte: 1914–1919* (Munich, 2003), 3, 57.
11. F. Klein, "Die Weltkriegsforschung der DDR," in Hirschfeld, *Enzyklopädie*, 316–19.
12. B. Bond, *The Unquiet Western Front: Britain's Role in Literature and History* (Cambridge, 2002).
13. See the fine study by Janet Watson, *Fighting Different Wars: Experience, Memory, and the First World War in Britain* (Cambridge, 2004).
14. Wehler, *Gesellschaftsgeschichte*, 985.
15. S. Broadberry and M. Harrison, *The Economics of World War I* (Cambridge, 2005), 34.
16. P. Fussell, *The Great War and Modern Memory* (New York, 1975).
17. See B. Ulrich and B. Ziemann, eds., *Frontalltag im Ersten Weltkrieg: Wahn und Wirklichkeit* (Frankfurt a. M., 1994).
18. B. Ziemann, *Front und Heimat: Ländliche Kriegserfahrungen im südlichen Bayern* (Essen, 1997).
19. The seminal account is John Keegan, *The Face of Battle: A Study of Agincourt, Waterloo and the Somme* (New York, 1977).
20. For example, L. V. Smith, *The Embattled Self: French Soldiers' Testimony of the Great War* (Ithaca, 2007); A. Watson, *Enduring the Great War: Combat, Morale, and Collapse in the German and British Armies, 1914–1918* (Cambridge, 2008).
21. For example, F. Aereboe: *Der Einfluss des Krieges auf die landwirtschaftliche Produktion in Deutschland* (Stuttgart, 1927); A. Skalweit, *Die deutsche Kriegsernährungswirtschaft* (Stuttgart, 1927); M. Liepmann, *Krieg und Kriminalität in Deutschland* (Stuttgart, 1930).

22. J. Winter and J.-L. Robert, *Capital Cities at War: Paris, London, Berlin, 1914–1919*, 2 vols. (Cambridge, 1999–2007).
23. E. Leed, *No Man's Land: Combat and Identity in World War I* (Cambridge, 1979); A. Cochet, "Les paysans sur le front en 1916," *Bulletin du Centre d'Histoire de la France contemporaine*, No. 3 (1982); 37–48; S. Audoin-Rouzeau, *Men at War: National Sentiment and Trench Journalism in France during the First World War* (Providence, 1992).
24. G. Hirschfeld, "Vorwort", "*Keiner fühlt sich hier mehr als Mensch …* " *Erlebnis und Wirkung des Ersten Weltkriegs* (Frankfurt a. M., 1996), 7.
25. See also L.V. Smith, S. Audoin-Rouzeau, and A. Becker, *France in the Great War* (Cambridge, 2003).
26. Prost and Winter, *Great War*, 26–30.
27. J. Kocka, *Klassengesellschaft im Krieg 1914–1918* (Göttingen, 1973).
28. See W. Hardtwig and H.-U. Wehler, eds., *Kulturgeschichte heute* (Göttingen, 1996).
29. J. Kocka, *Alltagsgeschichte der NS-Zeit. Neue Perspektiven oder Trivialisierung?* (Munich, 1984), 53–54.
30. Prost and Winter, *Great War*, 209–10.
31. S. Förster and J. Nagler, eds., *On the Road to Total War: The American Civil War and the German Wars of Unification* (New York, 1997); M. Boemeke, R. Chickering, and S. Foerster, eds., *Anticipating Total War: The German and American Experiences, 1871–1914* (Cambridge, 1999); R. Chickering and S. Foerster, eds., *Great War, Total War: Combat and Mobilization on the Western Front, 1914–1918* (Cambridge, 2000); R. Chickering, S. Foerster, and B. Greiner, eds., *A World at Total War: Global Conflict and the Politics of Destruction, 1939–1945* (Cambridge, 2005); R. Chickering and S. Foerster, eds., *War in an Age of Revolution: The Wars of American Independence and the French Revolution, 1775–1815* (Cambridge, 2010).
32. R. Chickering, "Militärgeschichte als Totalgeschichte im Zeitalter des totalen Krieges," in *Was ist Militärgeschichte?*, eds. T. Kühne and B. Zieman (Paderborn, 2000), 301–12.
33. R. Chickering, *The Great War and Urban Society in Germany: Freiburg. 1914–1918* (Cambridge, 2007). A German translation has now appeared, *Freiburg im Ersten Weltkrieg: Totaler Krieg und städtischer Alltag 1914–1918* (Paderborn, 2009).
34. C. Ginzburg, "Microhistory: Two or Three Things That I Know about It," *Cultural Inquiry* 20 (1976); 32.
35. Hirschfeld, *Encyklopädie*, 313.
36. M. Healy, *Vienna and the Fall of the Habsbrug Empire: Total War and Everyday Life in World War I* (Cambridge, 2004); A. Lipp, *Meinungslenkung im Krieg. Kriegserfahrungen deutscher Soldaten und ihre Deutung 1914–1918* (Göttingen, 2003); S.O. Müller, *Die Nation als Waffe und Vorstellung: Nationalismus in Deutschland und Großbritannien im Ersten Weltkrieg* (Göttingen, 2002); C. Geinitz, *Kriegsfurcht und Kampfbereitschaft: Das Augusterlebnis in Freiburg. Eine Studie zum Kriegsbeginn 1914* (Essen, 1998).

Chapter 14

The First World War and Military Culture
Continuity and Change in Germany and Italy

MacGregor Knox

The First World War, for all its horrors, was not in all respects the primordial catastrophe allegedly at the root of the far greater horrors of the quarter-century that followed. The two powers in the middle of the scale of 1914–18 destruction, Germany and Italy, passed through the cataclysm with their civil societies largely intact. Their institutions fared less well. But even in Germany, much of the political and institutional landscape remained eerily in place; this essay is above all a study in continuity.

The forty-year gap—as of 1914—between Italy and Germany in economic development and literacy might suggest that comparison of the two armies' responses to the Great War is problematic.[1] But the two societies and polities were similar enough in significant ways so that comparison may prove fruitful, both in highlighting the Kaiserreich's undeniable peculiarities and in understanding the eventual outcomes in both countries. Both suffered—in the minds of both intellectuals and soldiers—from ethnic-territorial incompleteness and from an "internal fragmentation" (*innere Zerrissenheit*) that only a great war and—if war failed—perhaps only "the mighty will of a dictator" could ostensibly heal.[2] At the core of both states, however battered by war or truncated by defeat, lay the most vital and durable institutions of all: their armies. And like other armies and institutions, the Regio Esercito Italiano (Italian Royal Army) and the Imperial German Army and its *Reichswehr* successor possessed unique organizational cultures that determined how they understood the surrounding world, defined their resulting missions, and framed the means for their accomplishment. In this connection, the extensive anthropological and sociological debates about the nature and causal role of culture offer useful analytical tools for understanding the unspoken and unexamined assumptions of groups and organizations—and thus for explaining otherwise bafflingly dysfunctional or seemingly irrational behavior.[3]

Cultures are notably persistent. Their unspoken assumptions and tacit codes normally derive, directly or indirectly, from historical experience. And they offer those who partake of them a "tool kit" or repertoire that inevitably frames, shapes, and constrains perceptions, decisions, and actions.[4] Armies in particular possess peculiarly pervasive and rigid organizational cultures.[5] That characteristic derives in part from their paradoxical mission: they deploy violence, which is inherently chaotic, to impose order. And conversely only order—the fiercely enforced decision-making hierarchy characteristic of modern western armies—can compel violence to remain a means to an end, and prevent its metastasis into an irrepressible and ever-expanding end in itself.[6] Armies resist change because they fear, above all else, loss of control over their troops, over events, and over their own destinies. They strive desperately to minimize the disruption of actual fighting to their hierarchies, structures, routines, images of war, and understanding of their place in the world.[7] The chaos and slaughter of the greatest war in history—until its 1939–45 sequel surpassed it in all respects—accordingly posed existential challenges.

The Imperial German Army of 1871 was far richer in tradition than the Regio Esercito Italiano that had emerged a decade earlier. The uniqueness of the Royal Prussian contingent at the army's core was already long-established, as was the wider national culture's implacable belief in the sovereign power of mind over matter, of "fighting spirit" (*Geist*) and willpower over mere material factors.[8] The war of 1870–71, the second existential struggle with a French empire and republic in living memory, consolidated and transformed Prussia's military-cultural heritage and created a unique mental world resting on four salient and mutually reinforcing characteristics:

1. First, the pinnacle of Prussia-Germany's social pyramid, the officer corps, was even more self-referential than most military castes. Direct subordination to the monarch and the charisma of victory largely insulated the officer corps even from lay criticism—much less the civilian control that Prussia-Germany's civilians were incapable of exercising not merely institutionally, but also because they too partook of the army's culture.
2. Second, the army's authentic virtues at the tactical level of warfare determined its responses to virtually every question it confronted. The Prussian system of mission tactics (*Auftragstaktik*) and cult of self-reliance and initiative demanded, along with the usual professional knowledge and technological expertise, rare personal qualities: a controlled amalgam of boldness, will to victory, and murderous implacability: "*Kühnheit—Siegeswille—Vernichtungswille.*"[9] The officers of the Prussian and federal armies, bound by a code of honor that mandated short-range pistol duels that killed up to a third of those engaged, were in any event predisposed by upbringing and training to view caution as cowardice. Their ideal was the tactical "whole-hearted decision" (*ganze Entschluss*), the cheerful decisive contempt for risk and frenetic aggressiveness demanded of junior infantry leaders,

but scaled up to embrace areas—operations, strategy, and life—in which such attitudes guaranteed eventual disaster. Wagering one's existence or that of the nation on the steadiness of the individual trigger-finger or on an entire society's throw of the "iron dice" of war was so self-evidently the preferred course of action that Prusso-German officers almost invariably derided as feeble even the few alternatives their blinkered vision did perceive.[10]

3. The third fundamental characteristic of Prusso-German military culture was a totalizing vision of war as a merciless limitless zero-sum struggle for national existence. That apocalyptic image derived both from 1806–15 and from the murderous post-Sedan "war between peoples" (rather than mere armies) of 1870–71, reinforced by misunderstood Darwinism. And total victory demanded—with a lasting fervor not matched even by France's devotees of *offensive à l'outrance*—the attack: "warfighting means attack."[11] That Bismarck had by preference sought decision by more subtle and controllable methods than battle: "Many roads led to my objective, and I was compelled to try them in sequence, one after the other—the most dangerous last"—completely escaped those who had executed his strategy with striking tactical élan.[12] Clausewitz's evident enthusiasm for war's "absolute perfection," as the total struggle practiced by the French revolutionaries and Napoleon, inspired the learned Prusso-German soldiers of later decades. Yet the later Clausewitz's analytical distinction between the "complete, untrammeled, absolute expression of violence" inherent in his Kantian "pure concept" of war, and the effects of chance, friction, politics, and perhaps even moral misgivings that constrained "real war," wholly eluded his successors. Under their stewardship, Clausewitz's ruling concept of battlefield "annihilation of the enemy armed forces as the first-born son of war" mutated into something infinitely more sinister.[13] Negotiation even with a beaten enemy was unacceptable because it would mean success had been less than total—an outcome that mortally threatened the army's institutional prestige, essence, and role in life. The German army thus came to prefer annihilation (*Vernichtung*) in a literal sense, if as yet only in the colonies; in the new century the general staff gloatingly celebrated, in its official history of Germany's 1904–6 war against native insurrection in Southwest Africa, the army's "ruthless energy" in seeking "the annihilation of the Herero *Volk*"—a proud public tribute to genocide that suggests the extremist dynamism of the army's belief system, and Germany's exceptionalism even in its colonial pursuits.[14]

4. Finally, these tendencies both nourished and fed upon a radical and incipiently totalitarian notion of "military necessity" that trampled on moral and legal restraints and ignored or scoffed at political considerations. The contempt expressed, in the general staff's pre-1918 manual on the usages of land warfare, for "humanitarian attitudes that frequently degenerate into sentimentality and pathetic emotion-mongering (*weichlicher Gefühlsschwärmerei*) ... in complete contradiction to the nature and ultimate purpose of war" was no momentary aberration, but rather the expression of a long-consolidated system of belief.[15]

The resultant of these forces was a cultural dynamic that consistently, long after Imperial Germany's resulting demise in 1914–18, inspired German decision-makers, both military and civilian, to regard entire enemy nations as unconditionally subject to "military necessity," to underestimate almost invariably the fighting spirit, willpower, and material strength of adversaries, to escalate implacably in the face of failure, and to select or accept the most extreme or high-risk course from any given set of options. "All or nothing" and "victory or ruin" were not slogans, but rather the central strand of the intellectual DNA of the Prusso-German military elite and—through youthful military service, reserve officer commissions, and osmosis—of the civilians as well.

The Regio Esercito Italiano was a wholly different beast. Its Piedmontese forebear had responded only fitfully to the stimulus of Napoleonic conquest and French annexation after 1796. In its single-handed wars against Austria in 1848–49 and 1866, its faction-ridden and uninspired higher officer corps proved as incapable of campaign planning as it was lacking in boldness and will to victory. Garibaldi's democratic freebooters excelled in battlefield initiative and military success, but after 1861 the Piedmontese generals jealously excluded all but a few from the new national army. Recurring defeats by Austria and the African disaster at Adua in 1896 ensured a measure of formal civilian control wholly absent in Prussia-Germany. But defeat also reinforced the army's cultural deficits by depriving it of the prestige required to recruit brains. As Giovanni Giolitti despairingly observed in 1915, Italian society had for decades sent to the army the "stupidest sons of the family," the "black sheep and half-wits."[16] The army's one area of relative success was domestic counter-guerrilla warfare: the scorched-earth campaigns after 1861 against southern and Sicilian "brigandage" that required commitment of up to half the army's line units. But battlefield creativity and the ability to learn from experience remained rare and deeply suspect. In the words of Lucio Ceva, a preeminent student of the Regio Esercito's career, Italian military memoirs give "the impression that initiative and the proclivity to observe and emulate [other armies] indeed existed, but as forces striving against the current and almost constituting breaches of discipline." The Regio Esercito's ideal was passive faithfulness unto death, not the "good judgment ... boldness and self-confidence" that Moltke the Elder's 1888 infantry regulations and its successors demanded even of the lowly rifleman.[17] And while the Italian army shared with its Prusso-German counterpart a faith in the sovereignty of mind over matter, it often applied that faith too literally to areas, such as tactics, in which the German army normally employed a measure of cold reason.

Europe's first industrial war taxed the ability of all participants to learn from experience. Yet the war's origins, course, and end testify to the persistence and intensification of the German military-cultural syndrome already described. With the single exception of Falkenhayn's improvised eastern offensives of 1915, every major German "strategic" decision, as well as lesser exploits such as technological escalation through poison gas, fit the inherited pattern. Schlieffen's plan scaled up that well-understood tactical formula, envelopment, by a factor of 200 to embrace an entire theatre—and staked Germany's future on a single blow. His successor Moltke the Younger, despite awareness of the risks, cheerfully assumed responsibility in July 1914: "He said yes! We will do it."[18] When the plan failed, Falkenhayn attacked murderously in Flanders, and reduced the army, in his own words, to a "broken tool."[19] His subsequent momentary lucidity and insistence on a negotiated peace with one of Germany's three antagonists soon passed; the chancellor, Theobald von Bethmann-Hollweg, whose frequent wartime appearances in uniform testify to his personal fidelity to "the King's coat," held grimly to Germany's extravagant war aims program. Further escalation in the face of failure at Verdun was the result. The supposedly rational Württemberger, Wilhelm Groener, summed up in June 1916 the high command's wisdom on that battle with the astonishing comment that "the army with the stronger resolve [Wille] will win in the end."[20]

Falkenhayn's successors, Ludendorff and Hindenburg, stunned by Britain's industrial firepower and alarmed by the stubbornness of its amateur soldiers on the Somme, appreciated by late 1916 that the allegedly indisputable "spiritual superiority of the German soldier" was not enough, especially in the face of enemy numerical superiority. "Superiority in munitions, cannon, and machine guns" and "continuous progress in tactics and technology" were now required to economize Germany's waning manpower, for the World War had now "in essence, even in its [purely] military aspects, become a war of attrition [Erschöpfungskrieg]." Yet as Ludendorff's immediately following remark demonstrated, German military culture could only accommodate such momentary strategic insights by forcing them into its inherited tactical framework: "the concept of annihilation [also] seeks to achieve its objective in *this* fashion." Any concession to reality was thus momentary and instrumental: "Offensive struggle seeking decision in movement and in great battles ... remains our ultimate military ideal, upon which Germany's future will be founded even in time to come."[21]

Yet alongside the stubborn persistence of inherited patterns, novelties nevertheless emerged in tactics, operations, and ideology. Ludendorff, the general staff, and the major commanders in the west showed far more tactical imagination, flexibility, and willingness to learn from adversity than their British, French, and Italian counterparts. Ludendorff nevertheless confessed, in an admirably self-critical moment, that "we have in many respects learned more slowly than our adversaries."[22] But the remedy lay at hand; throughout the autumn of 1916, as the British offensive ground onward on the Somme, a cooperative effort by the high command, key staff officers at the front such as Fritz von Lossberg, and the forward units devised—amid heavy losses and successive crises—the standard defensive techniques of modern armies for the rest of the century and beyond.

Machines, not riflemen, were the key: "The *skeleton of the defence* is the machine guns." Battle henceforth was not "around lines, but in battle zones" filled with inconspicuous strong points configured to "scatter enemy fire in both space and time." German troops would mass, if at all, only beyond enemy artillery range or observation, not under observed fire in the forward lines. An enemy penetrating the battle zone would meet "ever greater and more unnerving difficulties ... the deeper he advances." And once the attackers were pinned by enfilade fire from concealed machine guns and by carefully preregistered artillery fires, immediate counterattacks by "small reserve forces acting on their own initiative" would annihilate the intruders.[23]

Unprecedented intensities of fire, the collapse of communications, the preexisting tradition of mission tactics, and the flexibility of the higher officer corps thus combined to give even riflemen a degree of tactical freedom wholly without precedent. The high command disseminated the new wisdom effectively through a multiplicity of training programs for staff officers, commanders, and units. And by the end of 1917, as the British offensive at Ypres petered out in the mud, defence in depth had mutated into attack in depth: the new techniques, pioneered in 1915–17 by special assault units—*Stosstruppen*—and by the German artillery that made breakthrough and deep penetration possible first against the Russians and Italians in September–October 1917, and then against the British and French in spring 1918.[24]

At the operational level, as 1916 grimly ended, the general staff and the army group and field army commanders briefly overcame their visceral culturally overdetermined loathing of defensive warfare. Verdun, the Somme, and the massive British and French offensives in prospect for 1917 faced the overstretched German army with catastrophe. The German response was unprecedented: the evacuation of the Somme salient—110 kilometers from north to south and up to 45 kilometers deep—and withdrawal to a carefully prepared network of defenses-in-depth, the SIEGFRIED position. But Ludendorff and the Prusso-German officer corps managed to turn even defensive warfare into massive strategic escalation. They built the SIEGFRIED position—the greatest engineering project of the war—largely through forced labor by prisoners of war and by French and Belgian civilians. And the Wagnerian complement to SIEGFRIED was ALBERICH: the merciless removal of a French population of up to one hundred and fifty thousand souls, and the destruction by high explosives of all towns, villages, farms, churches, wells, springs, dams, bridges, roads, and railroad lines within the evacuated area, along with the flooding of all low-lying areas. The perfection of destruction by the self-reliance, initiative, joy in responsibility, and the "meticulous, obsessively detailed" work of Germany's combat engineers was a fitting complement to the apprenticeship of the officer corps as slave-masters. As Michael Geyer has ironically noted, "the road to the [1941] war of annihilation was paved with the good intentions of upright men."[25]

In the realm of ideology, a new and equally sinister innovation emerged. Total war for the German fatherland and the Kaiser's perceived feebleness corroded the bonds between officer corps and monarchy.[26] On the staffs, technological expertise and radical nationalism went hand in hand. Colonel Max Bauer of the high command, patron of the *Stosstruppen*, cool-headedly damned the persisting traditionalism of higher commanders and staff officers, for whom "everything 'technical' savored of inconsequence; only tactics counted!" Which, Bauer nevertheless insisted, were in reality "nothing more than the rational and appropriate application of technical means to both attack and defence." Yet Bauer was also the foremost and fiercest apostle of a Hindenburg-Ludendorff dictatorship, to be forcibly imposed upon the German people out of military necessity. His technological-tactical clear-sightedness anticipated the blinkered goal-rationality characteristic of German forces in their next great war.[27] A new kind of officer—the technocratic-fanatical-charismatic military *Führer*—was emerging from the broken shell of aristocratic-monarchical Prussia-Germany. Such figures inevitably intensified further the institutional extremism of their inherited military culture.

And in the end, within the framework of German military culture the application of technical means could be authentically rational and appropriate only in the attack. The ultimate purpose of SIEGFRIED and ALBERICH was to husband Germany's resources for the titanic spring 1918 decisive offensive struggle in the west that Ludendorff had projected from early 1917 onward.[28] Yet that inane effort lacked even an operational concept, much less a strategic one. Ludendorff famously insisted "I prohibit the word 'operation'; we [shall] hack a hole in them; the rest can be improvised [*das Weitere findet sich*]." In March the army valorously and expertly hacked that hole in its first great western offensive since Verdun. But as in 1916 "the rest" proved disappointing. And the supreme command's tactical monomania insulated it, then and later, from realization that merely defeating Britain and France in the field could no longer decide a war that Germany had willfully expanded—with Ludendorff's hearty approval—to include the United States. The result was almost nine hundred thousand casualties from the army's best units by the end of July 1918, and the end of any chance of halting, however briefly, the final Allied drive toward the Rhine.[29]

Yet defeat was unthinkable and therefore impossible. It would create a world in which, as a key member of the high command lamented in October 1918, German officers would no longer constitute the pinnacle of Germany's elite, but rather "eke out their existence impoverished and but little regarded."[30] A *Nibelungen-Endkampf*, one last escalation in the face of failure, was the army's response: a scorched-earth retreat that would apply the techniques developed in ALBERICH to the entire territory—potentially including parts of Germany itself—that the army was to relinquish in its final withdrawal. Correspondingly, a German *levée en masse* would ignite the *"furor teutonicus"* to fight a final objectless and merciless battle that Ludendorff himself happily accepted might end in national annihilation.[31] Ludendorff's successor, the putatively level-headed Groener, and associates such as the general staff operations chief, Joachim von Stülpnagel, later the most influential *Reichswehr* war-planner, projected a centerpiece for this pageant of national self-immolation: a death-ride by the Kaiser and a select party from the high command into the artillery and machine-gun fire of the advancing Allies.[32] But military and national suicide was premature by almost thirty years; defeat had so diminished the high command's prestige that politicians and Kaiser could at last opt for surrender in all but name.[33] Only the legend of a "stab in the back" by the home front—a notion implicit in the meaning that officer corps and German elites had given to the World War from its inception—could now serve to explain disaster and to eliminate any need to learn strategically from it.[34]

The Italian army's wartime trajectory likewise followed the templates of the past. The army's leaders saw war predominantly as a moral rather than a military-technical test. Failure could only be the consequence of cowardice. "[I]ndomitable faith [*fede incrollabile*] in success" was the principal prerequisite of that success, while "the demoralization of the enemy" conversely "determined" victory.[35] The Regio Esercito's Ludendorff, General Luigi Cadorna, lacked even Schlieffen's relative tactical and operational sophistication. Cadorna and his staff concluded in winter 1914–15 that "modern weapons" offered the offensive "more favorable conditions for success today than in the past"—a fact "only apparently contradicted by that which is occurring in the current armed conflict."[36] And until September–October 1918, the Italian army lacked a doctrine that explained what its higher formations—divisions, army corps, and armies—were supposed to *do* in combat.[37]

From summer 1915 Cadorna drove his infantry frontally onto the Austrian wire in successive waves with all the sadistic relish of an *ancien régime* drill sergeant.[38] When units inevitably collapsed he dismissed commanders indiscriminately for "absence of faith in the attack and consequent inability to instill that faith in subordinates."[39] Concurrently, the control mania at the heart of Italian military culture stifled initiative; Cadorna's tactical instructions openly denounced the *"excessive individualism"* that had allegedly been the *"principal cause of the setbacks that we have encountered in almost all our wars."* "[O]bedience—the irreplaceable foundation of military discipline" stamped out tactical freedom, even while Cadorna contrasted the alleged "intellectual superiority" of the Italians with the "heavy-handed and rigidly methodical conduct of the enemy."[40] As the high command's historical officer concluded bitterly in June 1917, in reality the Austro-Hungarians were "in [their] entire conception of war less rigid than are we ... who constantly celebrate Latin geniality."[41]

Cadorna thus closed off inquiry into the true causes of failure and invited further and greater failures. He and his army commanders indiscriminately dismissed senior officers at the least setback or sign of dissent, removing roughly nine hundred by late 1917. That system both expressed and accentuated the long-standing lack of mutual trust prevalent throughout the officer corps and the wider society. Reciprocal accusations of "absence of faith," cowardice, and incompetence, and a resulting "reticence and insincerity" divided junior officers from their superiors, and pitted line officers against the despised and hated staffs.[42] The periodic despairing protests, born of repeated bloody failures, by Italy's largely peasant infantry in turn inspired the *generalissimo* and his chief subordinates to hunt down and exterminate the slightest sign of disaffection: "Superior officers have the sacred authority [*sacro potere*] to immediately execute recalcitrants and cowards." The alleged "morbid sentimentalism" of the army's military courts also inspired Cadorna to order decimation without trial of offending units.[43] Between 1915 and 1918 Italy shot roughly 750 men after trial, and several hundred more on the simple order of an officer, compared to the 48 executed by Prussia-Germany in the course of the war. Cadorna's reward for military malpractice and for enforcing passive obedience through terror was the Caporetto catastrophe of October–November 1917. Exhaustion from the preceding offensives, insufficient depth of position along the Isonzo, a surprise *Stosstrupp*-style assault by German divisions sent to shore up Austria-Hungary, and the fragility of the Italian "front community" led to the disintegration of 2nd Italian Army. Germans and Austro-Hungarians took 294,000 prisoners of war and seized Venetia to the Piave River, just short of Venice itself. Cadorna characteristically—and delusionally—blamed disaster on cowardice, and on subversion by the socialist "internal enemy."

Yet the Regio Esercito learned a few things. It successfully mobilized and supplied—however chaotically—over five million men. It ran or coordinated the industries that grew rapidly to feed the war's limitless appetite for steel and high explosive. It ruled northeast Italy almost free of civilian control. By late 1916 its doctrine, if not its practice, included the notion that defenses—while still linear—should be sited in depth, and that the troops in the forward trenches should be thinned out in order to lower casualties; artillery fire and hasty counterattack would hold the line.[44] Italy's artillerymen and *Stosstruppen*—the *Arditi* created in summer 1917 following the Austro-Hungarian example—received grudging license to innovate. Even the line infantry, in the confused November–December 1917 fighting on the Mt. Grappa massif that halted the German-Austrian Caporetto offensive, benefited from communications failure and involuntary decentralization of command, and mounted a largely unplanned but effective defence-in-depth. Junior officers mobilized the myths of the *Risorgimento* to propagate hatred of the Teutonic invaders and instill a "discipline of conviction" that made soldiers into "*combattenti*"—a direct counterpart to Germany's *Kämpfer*—and partially replaced disciplinary terrorism: a significant if largely involuntary cultural change.[45] Yet even in 1918, the army's attack formations remained Cadorna's "close-packed assault waves" of riflemen rather than agile *Stosstruppen* armed with light machine guns and trench mortars.[46]

In both Italy and Germany the war persisted after November 1918 in ways not found elsewhere.[47] The passionate moralizing nationalist indignation that German defeat and post-1918 territorial loss engendered found its fitting counterpart in Italy's myth of the *vittoria mutilata* and concurrent hatred of the "internal enemy," the "evil brood of *caporettisti*" who had purportedly "stabbed the nation in the back."[48] Only force could thus reassemble societies and political systems shattered in the Great War. The Italian officer corps demobilized the army and surrendered its power to the civilians slowly and grudgingly. Its junior officers, whom battlefield experience—as in Germany—had freed from all respect for authority, flocked first to Gabriele D'Annunzio's Fiume sedition, then to Benito Mussolini's *Fasci di combattimento*. Their fanaticism, resourcefulness, and tactical flexibility and skill were the essential ingredient in the Fascist assault on the "internal enemy" that convulsed north Italy in 1920–22.

But the war's military-cultural novelties—ideology and a measure of unplanned tactical initiative—had little effect on the army itself. For the next two decades the hierarchy, with an implacable continuity of outlook, stolidly contemplated a war of aggression against Austria-Hungary's hated and despised successor, Yugoslavia. It swiftly dismantled the *Arditi*, removed from its units the infantry support weapons that had provided a measure of battlefield mobility, and recreated the prewar barracks army. The "generals of victory" trusted in men and mules, not machines, and revered numerical superiority, frontally applied, as the preeminent source of victory.[49] Such beliefs were strikingly mismatched to the ambitions of the Fascist regime that those same generals heartily welcomed in 1922.

The *Reichswehr*, distilled essence of the "old army," by contrast learned a great deal from the World War, and nothing from German defeat. War, as the "total war faction" in the camouflaged general staff conceived it from the mid-1920s onward, was a total social process to be prepared—in Groener's words of May 1919—"long beforehand with foresight and ruthless consistency," aiming at world domination, and remorselessly consuming the resources of the entire nation and of any subject peoples acquired along the way.[50] Germany could, must, and would do it again— under new more charismatic leadership, with more effective ideological indoctrination, with pitiless suppression of "defeatists," "shirkers," "cowards," and deserters, and with the ruthless exploitation of all available technological means. Only force—as Stülpnagel, now the foremost general staff young Turk, put it in a now-famous 1924 briefing on "the war of the future"—could "decide the question whether a hundred [sic] million Germans must become the slaves of forty million Frenchmen." And as Stülpnagel added in a later memorandum for the German foreign office, force would in all likelihood likewise decide Germany's final confrontation with Anglo-America.[51]

The army's tactical focus and all-or-nothing mentality did not change.[52] The *Reichswehr*'s 1921–24 distillation of the wisdom painfully acquired in 1914–18, "Leadership and Combat with Combined Arms," enjoined leaders "to shape an 'ordinary victory' into an annihilational decision [*vernichtende Entscheidung*]" without the slightest awareness that the vacuous pursuit of annihilational decisions at the tactical and operational levels had been instrumental to German defeat.[53] And in the realm of strategy, Stülpnagel proclaimed without the slightest indication that 1914–18 had taught common sense that "German *Geist* must defeat French materiel!" Yet his 1924 plan for apocalyptic guerrilla war against the French invaders, inspired by "national hatred raised to the furthest extreme" was merely a "struggle to gain time." A final Schlieffenesque "struggle for the annihilation of the enemy" would duly follow—even if the political preconditions, as Stülpnagel remarked in a personal letter from this same period, were as yet absent: "It is our misfortune to lack in Germany a man of remarkable qualities who can and will rule as a dictator. We would support such a man, but we neither wish to nor can play the role ourselves."[54]

The man whom the *Reichswehr* eventually found was one the army had itself trained both in war and in political indoctrination.[55] His movement, led by veterans turned onto the streets by Versailles, successfully applied mission tactics to politics, and embodied all the fanaticism of the front officers of the lost war. The coalition that formed between the German army and the National Socialist German Workers' Party in 1932–33 was the encounter of two organizations with a shared military culture and community of values.[56] And the Party's leader, as he launched Germany's second bid for world mastery in August 1939, could appeal to his commanders in the language of that culture, and in the name of those values: *"without risk-taking, no whole-hearted decision."* Nor could Hitler's momentous equation of the "annihilation of Poland" with the "elimination of its life-force," and his consequent exhortations—then and later—to banish "all thoughts of compassion" have aroused comment. For such sentiments, if not the full extreme to which Wehrmacht and National Socialist Party were about to take them, had long been at the center of German military culture.[57]

Notes

1. Socio-economic data, and the overall comparability of northern Italy to Germany: M. Knox, *To the Threshold of Power, 1922/33: Origins and Dynamics of the Fascist and National Socialist Dictatorships* (Cambridge, 2007), 59–70.
2. Quotations: H. Class (chief of the Pan-German League, 1908–39), pseud. D. Frymann, *Wenn ich der Kaiser wär* (Leipzig, 1914), 54.
3. See the fundamental work of I.V. Hull, *Absolute Destruction: Military Culture and the Practices of War in Imperial Germany* (Ithaca, NY, 2004), 93–98.
4. "Tool kit": A. Swidler, "Culture in Action: Symbols and Strategies," *American Sociological Review* 51, no. 2 (1986), 277.
5. Hull, *Destruction*, 97–103; also E. Kier, *Imagining War: French and British Military Doctrine between the Wars* (Princeton, NJ, 1995), 29–31.
6. See especially Hull, *Destruction*, 100.
7. A tendency strikingly illustrated by the well-known Vietnam-era remark—entirely credible in the author's experience—of an anonymous senior officer: "I'll be damned if I permit the United States Army, its institutions, its doctrine, and its traditions to be destroyed just to win this lousy war": G. Lewy, *America in Vietnam* (Oxford, 1978), 138.
8. The roots of this salient element of German ideological peculiarities, especially in evidence in 1914–18, lie deep indeed. A glance at G.W.F. Hegel, *Grundlinien der Philosophie des Rechts* (Berlin, 1821), §§340–42, §344, §347, §359 is nevertheless helpful; see also the surveys and cited literature in Knox, *Threshold*, 48–51, 54–56, 119–31, 138, and especially 169–74.
9. On the tradition and its implications, Hull, *Destruction*, 115–17, and Knox, *Common Destiny* (Cambridge, 2000), chap. 5.
10. See Knox, *Threshold*, 77, and note 34, 101, and note 81.
11. C. von der Goltz (1890), quoted in G. Gross, "Das Dogma der Beweglichkeit," in *Erster Weltkrieg Zweiter Weltkrieg*, eds. B. Thoss and H.-E. Volkmann (Paderborn, 2002), 146.
12. O. von Bismarck, *Die gesammelten Werke*, vol. 9 (Berlin, 1926), 50.
13. C. von Clausewitz, *On War*, eds. and trans. M. Howard and P. Paret (Princeton, NJ, 1976), 593, 87, 119, 99.
14. Grosser Generalstab, *Die Kämpfe der deutschen Truppen in Südwestafrika*, vol. 1 (Berlin, 1906), 207; also Hull, *Destruction*, part 1, and idem, "Military Culture and the Production of 'Final Solutions' in the Colonies: The Example of Wilhelminian Germany," in *The Specter of Genocide*, eds. R. Gellately and B. Kiernan (Cambridge, 2003), 141–62. The extensive recent German-language debate over the long-term consequences and international comparability of the destruction of the Herero has so far failed to address the implications of the army's public celebration of its "final solution" as a shining exemplar of German military tradition.
15. Grosser Generalstab, *Kriegsbrauch im Landkriege* (Berlin, 1902), 3.
16. O. Malagodi, *Conversazioni della guerra (1914–1919)*, vol. 1 (Milan, 1960), 58 and 199–200.
17. *Exerzier-Reglement der Infanterie* (Berlin, 1888), 93 (Part II, A, para. 16).
18. K. Riezler, *Tagebücher, Aufsätze, Dokumente*, ed. Karl Dietrich Erdmann (Göttingen, 1972), 275 (25 May 1915).
19. F. Fischer, *War of Illusions* (London, 1975), 545.

20. Groener diary, 29–30 June 1916, in W. Groener, *Lebenserinnerungen* (Göttingen, 1957), 550–51; also Hull's analysis of Falkenhayn's escalatory self-deception: *Destruction*, 220–25.
21. "Geistige Überlegenheit": Hindenburg (Ludendorff) to Bethmann Hollweg, 2 November 1916, in *Ursachen und Folgen*, eds. H. Michaelis and E. Schraepler, vol. 1 (Berlin, 1958), 15–16; remaining quotations from Hindenburg (Ludendorff) circular, "Kriegführung und Generalstab," 22 November 1916, in Reichsarchiv, *Der Weltkrieg*, vol. 12 (Berlin, 1939), 56–57 (my emphasis).
22. Reichsarchiv, *Der Weltkrieg*, vol. 12, 57.
23. "Allgemeines über Stellungsbau," and "Grundsätze für die Abwehrschlacht im Stellungskriege," in E. Ludendorff, *Urkunden des Obersten Heeresleitung über ihre Tätigkeit 1916/18* (Berlin, 1920), 594–95, 606–7, 613, 615; and T.T. Lupfer, *The Dynamics of Doctrine*, Leavenworth Papers 4 (1981), chap. 1.
24. "Der Angriff im Stellungskriege," in Ludendorff, *Urkunden*, 641ff.; Lupfer, *Dynamics of Doctrine*, chap. 2.
25. All from Geyer, "Rückzug und Zerstörung 1917," in *Die Deutschen an der Somme 1914–1918*, eds. G. Hirschfeld, G. Krumeich, and I. Renz (Essen, 2006), 163–79 (quotations: 174, 171).
26. Knox, *Threshold*, 192.
27. M. Bauer, *Der Grosse Krieg in Feld und Heimat* (Tübingen, 1921), 70; B. Thoss, "Nationale Rechte, Militärische Führung und Diktaturfrage in Deutschland 1913–1923," *Militärgeschichtliche Mitteilungen* 42 (1987), 44–47, 52, 57–58, 60.
28. F. von Lossberg, *Meine Tätigkeit im Weltkriege 1914–1918* (Berlin, 1939), 274–75.
29. Ludendorff quotation: Rupprecht, Kronprinz von Bayern, *Mein Kriegstagebuch* (Munich, 1929), vol. 2, 372; casualties: Reichsarchiv, *Der Weltkrieg*, vol. 14 (Berlin, 1942), app. 42.
30. A. von Thaer, *Generalstabsdienst an der Front und in der OHL* (Göttingen, 1958), 240 (9 October 1918).
31. E. von Eisenhart-Rothe, *Im Banne der Persönlichkeit* (Berlin, 1931), 122–23.
32. See especially Hull, "Military Culture, Wilhelm II, and the End of the Monarchy in World War I," in *The Kaiser*, eds. A. Mombauer and W. Deist (Cambridge, 2003), 235–58.
33. But see B. Wegner, "The Ideology of Self-Destruction: Hitler and the Choreography of Defeat," *German Historical Institute London Bulletin* 26, no. 2 (2004), 18–33.
34. Antecedents and inner logic: Knox, *Threshold*, 172–73, 198–99, and B. Barth, *Dolchstosslegenden und politische Desintegration* (Düsseldorf, 2003), chaps. 1–3.
35. Ministero della Guerra, *Le istruzioni tattiche del Capo di Stato Maggiore dell'Esercito degli anni 1914–1915–1916* (Rome, 1932), 20, 24, 79–80, 84, 143, 267, 299.
36. The army's fundamental 1915–17 doctrinal document, "Attacco frontale e ammaestramento tattico," 25 February 1915, in Ministero della Guerra, *Istruzioni tattiche*, 82–83.
37. E. Pino, "La regolamentazione tattica del Regio Esercito Italiano e la sua evoluzione nell'ultimo anno del conflitto," in *Al qua di là del Piave*, eds. G. Berti and P. Del Negro (Milan, 2001), 295–96.
38. For the doctrinal basis of these and later efforts, see Ministero della Guerra, *Istruzioni tattiche*, particularly 70–83, 143–45, 266–67.
39. Cadorna, quoted in L. Ceva, *Le forze armate* (Turin, 1981), 133.
40. Ministero della Guerra, *Istruzioni tattiche*, 93–94 (italics in original), 71, 267.
41. A. Gatti, *Caporetto*, ed. Alberto Monticone (Bologna, 1964), 140, 154–56.
42. See the merciless analysis of Italian military culture—in part drafted by generals—in Commissione d'Inchiesta, *Dall'Isonzo al Piave, 24 ottobre–9 Novembre 1917*, vol. 2 (Rome, 1919), especially 356.
43. M. Pluviano and I. Guerrini, *Le fucilazioni sommarie nella prima guerra mondiale* (Udine, 2004), XIII–XIV, 9–10, 33–34, 100, 269; see also *Dall'Isonzo al Piave*, vol. 2, 346–49, 357–59.
44. Pino, "Regolamentazione tattica," 289, 293–94; lack of depth and of operational reserves were however major causes of the Caporetto disaster.
45. See M. Mondini, *La politica delle armi* (Rome, 2006), 43; "combattenti": N. Papafava, *Appunti Militari 1919–1921* (Ferrara, 1921), 146.
46. Pino, "Regolamentazione tattica," 300–301.
47. See Knox, *Threshold*, chap. 4.

48. B. Mussolini, *Opera omnia*, vol. 11 (Florence, 1953), 402.
49. Knox, *Hitler's Italian Allies* (Cambridge, 2000), chap. 3.
50. Groener's famous situation briefing, 19–20 May 1919, in *Zwischen Revolution und Kapp-Putsch*, ed. H. Hürten (Düsseldorf, 1977), 121; for the "total war faction," M. Geyer, *Aufrüstung oder Sicherheit* (Wiesbaden, 1980), 76–97; and Knox, *Threshold*, 286–91.
51. Stülpnagel, in *Das Krisenjahr 1923*, ed. H. Hürten (Düsseldorf, 1980), 268, and in *Akten zur deutschen auswärtigen Politik*, Serie B, vol. 1/1 (Göttingen, 1966), 345 and 343.
52. See especially G. Vardi, "The Enigma of German Operational Theory: The Evolution of Military Thought in Germany, 1919–1938" (PhD diss., The London School of Economics and Political Science, 2009), chap. 2.
53. H.Dv. 487, *Führung und Gefecht der verbundenen Waffen*, Part 3 (Berlin, 1924), 31.
54. Stülpnagel, in C. Dirks and K.-H. Janssen, *Der Krieg der Generäle* (Munich, 2001), 208, 207, and in Hürten, *Krisenjahr 1923*, 268, 243 (emphasis and exclamation point in original).
55. A. Joachimsthaler, *Hitlers Weg begann in München 1913–1923* (Munich, 2000), 223–55, and E. Deuerlein, "Hitlers Eintritt in die Politik und die Reichswehr," *VfZ* 7 (1959), 177–227.
56. J. Förster, "Geistige Kriegführung in Deutschland 1919 bis 1945," in *Das Deutsche Reich und der Zweite Weltkrieg*, vol. 9/1 (Munich, 2004), especially 487.
57. "Ohne Risiko kein ganzer Entschluss": Hitler, 22 August 1939, in F. Halder, *Kriegstagebuch*, vol. 1 (Stuttgart, 1962), 24–26 (my emphasis); compare Halder's own bloodthirsty anticipation: "[W]e must and shall pounce on Poland and crush it to a pulp [*zermalmend herfallen*]": C. Hartmann and S. Slutsch, "Franz Halder und die deutschen Kriegsvorbereitungen im Frühjahr 1939," *VfZ* 45 (1997), 490.

Chapter 15

A German Way of War?
Narratives of German Militarism and Maritime Warfare in World War I

Dirk Bönker

I

The narrative of an authoritarian German militarism set against political modernity and civil society has long served as a master narrative for modern German military history. But by now, the validity of this narrative has been successfully called into question. The narrative fails to situate the German experience with militarism within common European and transatlantic war cultures and politics of militarization; it offers too simple and overdrawn a portrayal of societal and cultural militarization in Germany; it ignores the importance of technocratic reasoning and industrialized warfare in understanding the German military; and it pays too little attention to transformations and ruptures after 1900.[1]

If recent scholarship has brought the limits of the notion of an authoritarian German militarism into sharp relief, new work on German military culture and pursuit of war strikes a different chord. John Horne and Alan Kramer's study of German military atrocities in Belgium and France in 1914 and Isabel Hull's book on the Imperial German military's conduct of war and institutional extremism stress the peculiarities of German warfare and military culture and emphasize direct continuities from 1870 to 1945. Reviewing their work, historians such as Margaret Anderson and Kevin Cramer have explicitly reopened the question of German exceptionalism, even if conceptualized differently from the "critical" narratives of Imperial Germany and the *Sonderweg* that found their classic expression in Hans-Ulrich Wehler's book on the Second German Empire, published in 1973.[2]

These two provocative studies raise anew the question of German militarism from the perspective of military-professional warfare and they direct our attention to World War I as a key moment in the convoluted history of German *Vernichtungskrieg* as a way of waging war against civilian populations. This essay aims to offer some thoughts on the Imperial German military's pursuit of war by asking whether there was a distinct German way of war that reflects a special German militarist condition. It will focus on the German navy's conduct of unrestricted submarine warfare in World War I, which offers not only a novel way of understanding the German military's conduct of war and its role in the twentieth-century "de-bounding of warfare" (Michael Geyer), but also refers directly back to the issue of German militarism. Like the German invasions of 1914 and the subsequent atrocities (*Kriegsgreuel*) in northern France and Belgium, Germany's submarine campaigns provided key images for the narrative of German authoritarian militarism that emerged as part of a European and transatlantic identity politics of alleged national difference in the age of the World Wars. To explore unrestricted submarine warfare is to tread some of this narrative's formative terrain and reflect upon its strengths and limitations.

This essay will argue that the German navy waged a maritime war of extermination during World War I. The submarine campaigns against Britain involved the professional-military conduct of war against the entire enemy nation, including its civilian population, and aimed at the destruction of the very integrity of the enemy's society through mass starvation and death. But Germany's maritime *Vernichtungskrieg* was not the natural product of a distinctly German military tradition and way of war, radically different from those of other powers. First, this way of waging war was the product of wartime choice and contingency, representing an important break with prewar naval ideas and practices, which stressed military restraint and legal limitation. Second, conduct of a maritime war of extermination was not an exclusively German practice; rather, it was also part of the Allied conduct of war and became one of several ways in which professional militaries came to use military force against civilian populations in the two global wars of the twentieth century.[3] Subsequent scandalization of German submarine warfare as part of exceptionalist German militarism ignored this commonality and resulted directly from the ideological confrontations of the Great War, which helped to create dominant national images that came to suffuse academic narratives of national histories.

II

The German navy waged a maritime war of extermination against Britain during World War I. It did so in the form of an unrestricted submarine campaign against all shipping, whether enemy or neutral, military or civilian, armed or unarmed, within an officially declared war zone (*Kriegsgebiet*) surrounding the British Isles. Predicated on the indiscriminate sinking without warning of all ships sighted, this war was unleashed on 1 February 1917, after the official decision for it had been made on 9 January 1917. The U-boat campaigns of 1917–18 followed on the heels of several somewhat more restricted submarine campaigns that had served similar purposes but had followed the prewar protocol of commerce warfare, with its rules concerning the search and seizure of ships, cargoes, and contraband, in relation to neutral shipping.[4]

The purpose of the maritime war of extermination was to assure military victory over Britain and achieve the island nation's violent subjugation. German naval leaders conceived of unrestricted submarine warfare as a war of trade and commerce, aiming at the economic strangulation of Britain.[5] This method of warfare, which the German Admiralty Staff defined in 1915 as an "economic war of extermination" (*wirtschaftlicher Vernichtungskrieg*), was designed to hit Britain at its most vulnerable spot, its "life nerve" (to invoke an oft-used metaphor in this context)—namely, British dependence on the sea-borne import of foodstuffs and other raw materials.[6] Geared towards the complete starvation of Britain and the paralysis of the British war economy, the submarine campaign waged war on civilian populations and their subsistence in order to break the enemy's will and impose a victorious peace. The very cohesion of British society was to be destroyed, and the submarine campaign became a strike against "life" itself, against the *Erhaltung des Lebens*, as the Chief of the Admiralty Staff explained to the Chief of the General Staff in December 1916.[7] Accordingly, considerations of the timing and yields of harvests on the British Isles and their major overseas importers of foodstuffs, such as Argentina, cast a long shadow on any demands for unrestricted submarine warfare. The poor worldwide harvest of 1916 thus played a central role in the debate about launching unrestricted submarine warfare in 1917.

The unrestricted submarine campaign that the Imperial German navy waged took place outside the bounds of the prewar framework of maritime law, both official and customary, as embodied in the Declarations of Paris (1856) and London (1909). The same was true already for the earlier submarine campaigns of 1915 and 1916, as the sinking without warning of enemy merchantmen and passenger ships was at odds with prewar law of maritime seizure at sea, which prescribed procedures for stopping a ship and the subsequent search and condemnation of both ship and cargo on the open seas. Moreover, besides the issue of the indiscriminate sinking of any and all ships in an officially declared "war zone," the German submarine campaign violated a fundamental tenet of prewar maritime law by making foodstuffs its primary concern. Prewar law had allowed for the classification of foodstuffs as conditional contraband liable to seizure only when there was clear proof that the items were destined for consumption by enemy armed forces or members of the enemy's state administration.[8]

III

Germany's pursuit of a submarine-based maritime war of extermination was a matter of choice driven by military-professional calculations.[9] That is, the navy's leadership willfully decided to pursue this course of action; it was not the natural outcome of new conditions of war as defined by industrial machine warfare or new weapons technologies. Still less was it an inevitable and "justifiable" response to the military action of the opposing side or to the breakdown of maritime law as occasioned by the British blockade and its toleration by the United States as the most powerful neutral power. Underlying this decision was the basic premise that entire nations had become the subjects and objects of war.

Germany's naval elite chose a naval exterminist strategy as a way of securing military victory in a war that had spiraled out of professional-instrumental control by the fall of 1914 and had turned into a drawn-out, siege-like war of attrition that raised the possibility of defeat. The navy leadership saw an opportunity to defeat Germany's chief opponent, the British Empire, the alleged leader of the Allied coalition. According to the Germans, that empire had started the war in order to eliminate Germany as its political and economic rival. Moreover, it was now showing its true colors in its relentless conduct of a war of economic strangulation through an all-encompassing blockade of Germany beyond any legal or military limitation. The defeat of Britain would irrevocably decide the war in Germany's favor, or so the navy's representatives argued.[10]

The prospects of making the decisive contribution to Germany's victory in the ongoing conflict fitted in with the navy's other needs as well. Winning the war by maritime action promised to shore up the credentials of the navy and safeguard its future. A successful maritime war of extermination would have answered all critiques lodged by the army, the foreign policy establishment, and civilian governmental leaders against the navy and its pursuit of *Weltpolitik* and maritime force. Those who criticized the navy argued that its pursuit of global power and maritime force had been a major mistake, both provoking Britain into anti-German action and diverting resources and attention away from the army and Continental power.[11]

Moreover, unrestricted submarine warfare promised a way out of the major military impasse the navy confronted in and after the fall of 1914. The non-occurrence of a decisive defensive battle against the British Royal Navy spelled the ruin of prewar naval strategy. The German battle fleet proved incapable of taking decisive action against the British fleet and preventing the British blockade. It also lacked military alternatives. New ideas about the use of capital ships for oceanic warfare against British trade lanes in the Atlantic, which had been offered by some senior officers such as Admiral Franz von Hipper, lacked a military foundation at that time.[12]

The navy settled on submarines as its new "wonder weapons" to win the war singlehandedly and secure its own glorious future in a postwar Germany.[13] It was this vision that grounded the navy's relentless, if not fanatical, commitment to unrestricted submarine warfare, which manifested in vigorous political lobbying, vicious denunciations of skeptics, dismissive attitudes towards the specter of U.S. entry into the war, and a cavalier disregard for the limited number of available submarines or the impact of possible British countermeasures.[14] Senior officers were so committed to unrestricted submarine warfare that in the spring of 1915 Admiral Hugo von Pohl, the commander-in-chief of the High Seas Fleet, and Commander Hermann Bauer, the official leader of the fleet of submarines, conspired to secretly order submarines to engage in "unrestricted" warfare against any ship, enemy or neutral, although the current political and military leadership had officially decided to wage a more restricted campaign.[15]

The faith that victory would be achieved through relentless submarine warfare left little space for voices of military moderation within the service. Most German submarine commanders, for example, had followed prewar protocols of search and seizure against enemy ships in 1915 and 1916 with remarkable military success, regardless of orders to follow other rules. Yet the leaders of the U-boat arm and of the larger fleet ignored these practices. They insisted that only "relentless" submarine warfare, pursued with utmost force, would yield decisive results, regardless of the catastrophic consequences for Germany's diplomatic relationship with the United States.[16]

Similarly, the commitment without compromise to unrestricted submarine warfare shaped the navy's actions after the summer of 1917 when the initial promise of victory within five to eight months proved illusory, despite the fact that it had originally appeared to be firmly grounded in calculations about British dependence on maritime imports, available maritime merchant tonnage, and likely shipping losses. The navy simply insisted on a continuation of the campaign and military escalation through accelerated submarine production. The navy leadership refrained from rethinking the premises of its submarine campaign and refused to change course. Institutional extremism, to use Isabel Hull's term, was not just an attribute of the Imperial German army.[17]

IV

The desire to secure a victorious peace by maritime means shaped the navy's thinking about unrestricted submarine warfare until the bitter end. But the navy's pursuit of unrestricted submarine warfare was nonetheless not a foregone conclusion. It was not the natural outgrowth of a particular long-standing military tradition or the product of a distinct way of war. Instead, Germany's conduct of a submarine-based war of maritime extermination represented a break with prewar naval strategy and planning. In 1914, the Imperial German navy set out to fight a conventional war in the image of battle fleet warfare, a paradigm of maritime war that, when developed in the 1890s, had drawn explicitly on the example of land warfare.

Accordingly, prewar naval planners defined the military mission of submarines in terms of the contests between battle fleets—"the fight of fleets against fleets," as the famous Service Memorandum IX, authored by Alfred von Tirpitz, had phrased it in 1894—and thus not in terms of direct operations against the enemy's seaborne trade.[18] Submarines were viewed as a secondary weapon; their construction was not a priority. On the eve of World War I, Germany's submarine fleet was smaller than those of Britain, France, the United States, and even Russia.[19] The German navy remained so devoted to the primacy of battle fleet warfare that this doctrine anchored all discussions of future naval strategy and construction during the war itself.[20]

Before 1914, German naval planners conceived of a war of commerce within clearly defined military and legal confines. Prioritizing the combat between battle fleets, prewar German naval strategy did not foreground operations against trade, commerce, and civilian populations. Schemes for direct operations against enemy trade remained a secondary issue within the overall planning that focused on the "defensive battle" against the Royal Navy and the prevention of a British blockade of German coastlines. The limited cruiser-based commercial warfare against Britain that naval strategists had planned for was designed to cause some economic and financial dislocation, strike a blow to the enemy's war morale, and tie down substantial naval forces that otherwise could be deployed against the German battle fleet. Creation of "anxiety" among the British "trading community" and the larger population was the official goal. Planners explicitly denied that it could have any decisive impact upon the outcome of the war.[21]

Before 1914, the German navy also did not approach maritime law, which simply did not provide room for the pursuit of a maritime war of extermination, with the same dismissive attitudes as the army approached the laws of land warfare. The army categorically placed military necessity, as a matter of principle, above military law. By contrast, the navy's policy-makers prior to 1914 respected maritime law as setting firm limits on the use of force and the pursuit of military necessity in wartime; and they enshrined this respect in their official Prize Order. Maritime law could simply not be ignored, the navy's representatives argued, because naval warfare in general, and a maritime war of trade and economic pressure in particular, always involved the interests of neutral powers that could insist on the law's recognition by belligerent powers.[22]

The respect for maritime law was also on full display when, in the spring of 1914, the head of German Submarine Inspection outlined a plan for a future submarine campaign against British trade. His proposal, which was the first of its kind that can be found in German naval records, assumed that the campaign would be waged within the existing confines of legal limitation. Several months later, in August 1914, the German government and navy leadership confirmed their commitment to the current framework of maritime law on request of the U.S. administration. This declaration corresponded with the Operations Orders of 31 July 1914.[23]

Nevertheless, prewar German naval thinking also prepared some of the grounds for the wartime turn to exterminist warfare. The concept of waging a maritime war of extermination fed off prewar discussions about the new vulnerabilities of industrial nations in a global age.[24] According to these discussions, industrial nations were becoming vulnerable because of economic specialization within a flourishing world economy and an increasing dependency on imports of foodstuffs and raw materials. Considerations of industrial Germany's need to keep its maritime routes of trade and communication open in times of war had already emerged as a major issue in the early 1890s when German war planners envisioned a war on two fronts, against Russia and France, that could turn into a long war of attrition. Such considerations reached a new urgency during the diplomatic crisis of 1904–5, and then in response both to the open Anglo-German rift and to Germany's alleged "encirclement." The German discussion took place in the context of similar and interrelated public debates among military theorists and economic writers in Britain, the United States, and elsewhere. Naturally, German naval officers closely followed the British debate about Britain's ever-increasing economic dependency and the need for military protection of vital import routes in times of war.[25]

A dialectics of danger and opportunity molded prewar German naval discourse about the maritime vulnerability of industrial nations. On the one hand, there were the potentially catastrophic consequences of a comprehensive British blockade, which the German Empire would not be able to bear over a longer period of time. On the other hand, naval planners all agreed that the "Achilles' heel" of Britain was its dependence on seaborne imports. They predicted deadly consequences for the British population if it were cut off from continuous supplies of foodstuffs from abroad, and thus German planners identified one possible direction for a successful conduct of war against Britain.[26]

Another part of the genealogy of the maritime war of extermination was the German navy's prewar view of the British Empire.[27] The navy's image of that empire, as it coalesced at the turn of the twentieth century, helped to construe the sort of ruthless enemy against whom it became conceivable to wage an all-out war. Central to this image was the perception of the British Empire as a world power whose elites thought in terms of unmitigated economic antagonism and trade envy, continually strove to eliminate commercial rivals, such as the German Empire, by all necessary means, and responded only to an assertive politics of maritime threat and deterrence. The fear of a British military strike against the German Empire's ever-increasing battle fleet and its flourishing civilian "maritime interests" weighed heavily on the minds of German naval officers. Accordingly, they viewed the war as a product of Anglo-German trade rivalry and identified pernicious intentions towards Germany and its national industry as Britain's driving force.

V

Direct or indirect use of military force against civilian populations was not an exclusive German practice during World War I. German military elites turned towards a maritime war of extermination at a time when Britain was already waging this kind of war against Germany. The British conducted exterminist warfare through the comprehensive blockade of German coastlines, which cut Germany off from any incoming seaborne trade from the Atlantic. British naval strategists had planned for an unlimited war of economic strangulation against Germany since the spring of 1904. The blockade was intended to break the Germans' will to wage war and to destroy the cohesion of German society through starvation and disease. "Grass would sooner or later grow in the streets of Hamburg and widespread death and ruin would be inflicted," summarized Vice-Admiral Charles Ottley, the Secretary of the British Committee on Imperial Defence, in 1908.[28]

Before and during World War I, British naval planners perceived the blockade of Germany as an offensive military strategy that transgressed existing strictures of military law and international diplomacy. It was not the Germans but the British who explicitly set military necessity against and above maritime law when they prepared for war. In 1914 they went to war with the clear intent to violate the existing regime of maritime law and impose an illegal and exterminist blockade. In contrast to the situation in Germany, the British maritime war of extermination was neither the product of wartime improvisation nor a reckless adventure. While the British blockade attested to the "extremism" of the Royal Navy in its pursuit of military victory, it also rested on the willing support of British elites and publics. Unlike in Germany, the blockade was not a matter of extreme controversy that eventually entailed the surrender of civilian government officials to the demands of the military in times of a deep political and military crisis. Civilian control and politics did not guarantee military restraint and legal limitation.

The British practice of a maritime war of extermination differed from its German counterpart in another way. While the British blockade contributed to the death of more than seven hundred thousand civilians, its violent character was less visible.[29] An act of strictly "indirect" military violence against civilian populations, the blockade did not involve the indiscriminate sinking of ships on the high seas or the killing of civilian crews and passengers of torpedoed enemy and neutral ships. By contrast, Germany's unrestricted submarine warfare went beyond the more indirect use of military force against civilian populations. It offered the world the spectacle of direct, massive military action against civilian ships and civilians, which involved the killing of about thirty thousand seamen and passengers. Seemingly providing further proof for all the stories about "German militarism" and its *Kriegsgreuel* in the wake of German invasions of neutral Belgium and France, German submarine warfare was an easy target for condemnation and became a monumental public relations disaster.

The scandalization of German unrestricted submarine warfare as an unparalleled, "uncivilized" act of war and its linkage to the notion of a singular authoritarian German militarism was accomplished by an ideological politics. The indictment of the German submarine campaign, and the moralizing distinction between "good" British navalism and "bad" German militarism contained therein, involved the willful denial of more complicated realities of war, as they were defined by the loss of civility, military restraint, and legal limitation across the board, and the conduct of maritime wars of extermination on both sides.[30] The scandalization served ideological ends in a war that was framed as an existentialist war of entire cultures that set Germany against the "West" and contrasted Western democracy, civilization, and civil society to German statehood, militarism, and *Kultur*.[31]

One result of the wartime indictment of German militarism, to which the discourse on Germany's submarine warfare contributed in profound ways, was the marginalization of the sense of militarist commonality and convergence that had united many observers of the arms races, global politics, and militarization before and even during World War I. In prewar Germany, for example, such diverse thinkers as Otto Hintze and Rosa Luxemburg had identified the dynamics of militarization across Europe and North America in strikingly similar ways.[32] Woodrow Wilson, too, the U.S. president who issued a powerful public indictment of German submarine warfare and took the United States to war over it, had taken a similar view. Before and after the outbreak of World War I, Wilson offered a general understanding of militarism as a common European condition, while expressing a nagging fear that the United States itself was in the process of transforming into an authoritarian, militarized state in response. Nevertheless, Wilson ended up forcefully contributing to the exclusive identification of militarism with Germany, denouncing its "barbaric" method of warfare, and linking the latter to the alleged "autocratic rule" of Germany's "military masters." Wilson did so while accepting, against the opposition of the U.S. navy, the British conduct of a maritime war of extermination, and willfully glossing over its illegal and exterminist character.[33]

Historians of the German military and its conduct of war in the late nineteenth and early twentieth centuries are well advised to move beyond the ideological polarities that coalesced as transnational formations during World War I and that were then reinforced by World War II. Germany's policy of unrestricted submarine warfare was a product of the professional extremism of the Imperial German navy under the specific conditions of World War I and the political-military dualism of the German Empire; yet it was also one of many emerging ways of waging war against civilian populations for instrumental purposes—a common feature of professional-military warfare in the great power wars of the twentieth century. Military elites in Europe and the United States settled on these ways of war as they engaged in large-scale wars of nations, industry, and military machines in a new global age—an age, that is, in which global power and economic interconnection shaped the ends and means of war. It was Nazi Germany and its *Wehrmacht* that combined these ways of war with the pursuit of genocidal war in Europe.

Notes

1. T. Kühne and B. Ziemann, "Militärgeschichte in der Erweiterung: Konjunkturen, Interpretationen, Konzepte," in *Was ist Militärgeschichte?*, eds. T. Kühne and B. Ziemann (Paderborn, 2000), 9–46.
2. I.V. Hull, *Absolute Destruction: Military Culture and the Practices of War in Imperial Germany* (Ithaca, 2005); J. Horne and A. Kramer, *German Atrocities 1914: A History of Denial* (New Haven, 2001); M.L. Anderson, "A German Way of War?," *German History* 22 (2004), 254–58; K. Cramer, "A World Of Enemies: New Perspectives on German Military Culture and the Origins of the First World War," *Central European History* 39 (2006), 270–98.

3. M. Geyer, "Gewalt und Gewalterfahrung im 20. Jahrhundert. Der Erste Weltkrieg," in *Der Tod als Maschinist. Der industrialisierte Krieg 1914–1918*, R. Spilker and B. Ulrich, eds. (Bramsche, 1998), 241–57.
4. The brief U-boat-campaign of the fall of 1916 refrained even from the sinking without warning of unarmed enemy merchantmen. A summary of the various German submarine campaigns is in J. Schröder, *Die U-Boote des Kaisers: Die Geschichte des deutschen U-Boot-Krieges gegen Großbritannien im Ersten Weltkrieg* (Bonn, 2003).
5. *Die deutsche Seekriegsleitung im Ersten Weltkrieg*, ed. Gerhard Granier, 4 Volumes (Koblenz, 1999–2004).
6. Chief of Admiralty Staff to Wilhelm II, 7 December 1915; *Seekriegsleitung*, ed. Granier, Vol. 1, 339–42.
7. Chief of Admiralty Staff to Chief of the General Staff, 22 December 1916; *Seekriegsleitung*, ed. Granier, Vol. 3, 456–61.
8. G. Hankel, *Die Leipziger Prozesse. Deutsche Kriegsverbrechen und ihre strafrechtliche Verfolgung nach dem Ersten Weltkrieg* (Hamburg, 2003), 396–415.
9. For this paragraph I have leaned on some of the language in Michael Geyer, "War and Terror: Some Timely Observations on the German Way of Waging War," *AICG Humanities* 14 (2003), 47–69.
10. See Note 5.
11. For a summary of this critique see A. von Tirpitz, "Aufzeichnung von Oktober 1915," German Military Archive (henceforth referred to as BA-MA), N 253/100. On this entire issue see also M. Epkenhans, "Die kaiserliche Marine im Ersten Weltkrieg: Weltmacht oder Untergang," in *Der Erste Weltkrieg: Wirkung, Wahrnehmung, Analyse*, ed. W. Michalka (Munich, 1994), 319–40.
12. W. Rahn, "Strategische Probleme der deutschen Seekriegführung 1914–1918," in *Weltkrieg*, ed. Michalka, 341–65.
13. Compare Hull, *Destruction*, 222–24, 295–98.
14. H.H. Herwig, "Total Rhetoric, Limited War: Germany's U-Boat Campaigns 1917–1918," in *Great War and Total War: Combat and Mobilization on the Western Front, 1914–1918*, R. Chickering and S. Förster, eds. (Cambridge, 2000), 189–206; Raffael Scheck, "Der Kampf des Tirpitz-Kreises für den uneingeschränkten U-Boot-Krieg und einen politischen Kurswechsel im deutschen Kaiserreich 1916–1917," *Militärgeschichtliche Mitteilungen* 55:1 (1996), 69–92.
15. Hugo von Pohl, *Aus Aufzeichnungen und Briefen während der Kriegszeit* (Berlin, 1920), 108–9, 110–11; Schröder, *U-Boote*, 95–110.
16. For more see Lehmann, *U-Boote*, 146ff., 203ff., 219ff.
17. *Seekriegsleitung*, ed. Granier, Vols. 3 & 4. See also Lehmann, *U-Boote*, 386ff.; G.P. Groß, *Die Seekriegführung der kaiserlichen Marine im Jahre 1918* (Frankfurt, 1989).
18. Service Memorandum IX is printed in Eva Besteck, *Die trügerische "First Line of Defence." Zum deutsch-britischen Wettrüsten vor dem Ersten Weltkrieg* (Freiburg, 2006), 123–208 (Quote: 127).
19. Baldur Kaulisch, "Zur Klärung der Einsatzmöglichkeiten der U-Boote in der deutschen Marine am Vorabend des Ersten Weltkrieges," *Militärgeschichte* 24 (1985), 369–76; Richard Lakowski, *U-Boote: Zur Geschichte einer Waffengattung der Seestreitkräfte* (Berlin, 1985), 34–57; Lehmann, *U-Boote*, 28–34, 41–44.
20. Representative are the various memorandums on the future development of the navy from 1916 in BA-MA, RM 3/10; and the documents in A. von Trotha, *Volkstum und Staatsführung. Briefe und Aufzeichnungen aus den Jahren 1915–1920* (Berlin, 1928).
21. Chief of Admiralty Staff to Secretary of Imperial Naval Office, 27 March 1907, BA-MA, RM 5/998; Vice-Admiral von Krosigk, "Denkschrift über den Kreuzerkrieg im Kriege gegen England," 1911, BA-MA, RM 5/5925; A, "Handelskrieg: Fragen des Seekriegsrechtes," 4 December 1913, BA-MA, RM 5/1013 (quote).
22. On the army, see Hull, *Destruction*, esp. 122–26; Hankel, *Prozesse*, 240–47; M. Messerschmidt, "Völkerrecht und 'Kriegsnotwendigkeiten' in der deutschen militärischen Tradition seit den Einigungskriegen," *German Studies Review* 6 (1983), 237–70.

23. Marinearchiv, *Der Handelskrieg mit U-Booten*, 4 vols. (Berlin 1932–1941), Vol. 1, 153–55 (spring 1914 proposal); Hanke, *Prozesse*, 401 (U.S. request); *Seekriegsleitung*, ed. Granier, Vol. 1, 67–68 (Operations Order).
24. Rolf Hobson, *Imperialism at Sea: Naval Strategic Thought, the Ideology of Sea Power and the Tirpitz Plan, 1875–1914* (Boston, 2002).
25. E. von Halle, "Die englische Seemachtpolitik und die Versorgung Großbritanniens in Kriegszeiten," *Marine-Rundschau* 17 (1906), 911–27, and 19 (1908), 804–15.
26. Exemplary are Tirpitz to Chancellor von Bülow, 28 February and 20 April 1907, *Große Politik der Europäischen Kabinette, 1871–1914*, Johannes von Lepsius et al., eds., 40 volumes (Berlin 1922–1927), Vol. 23, 350–53, 359–67.
27. V.R. Berghahn, *Der Tirpitz-Plan. Genesis und Verfall einer innenpolitischen Krisenstrategie unter Wilhelm II* (Düsseldorf, 1971); I.N. Lambi, *The Navy and German Power Politics, 1862–1914* (Boston, 1984); M. Epkenhans, *Die wilhelminische Flottenrüstung 1908–1914: Weltmachtstreben, industrieller Fortschritt, soziale Integration* (Munich, 1991).
28. A. Offer, *The First World War: An Agrarian Interpretation* (Oxford, 1989) (Ottley quote: 232). See also A. Lambert, "Great Britain and Maritime Law from the Declaration of Paris to the Era of Total War," in *Navies in Northern Waters, 1721–2000*, R. Hobson and T. Kristiansen, eds. (London, 2004), 11–38.
29. The estimate of deaths is from D. Blackbourn, *The Long Nineteenth Century: A History of Germany, 1780–1918* (New York, 1998), 475. According to Gustavo Corni, about eight hundred thousand people died of undernourishment in wartime Germany. G. Corni, "Hunger," in *Enzyklopädie Erster Weltkrieg*, G. Hirschfeld et al., eds. (Paderborn, 2003), 566.
30. Fittingly, British maritime warfare included military action that directly targeted civilian shipping. But the use of contact mines in the North Seas and the submarine campaigns in the North and Baltic Seas and in the Mediterranean in 1914–15 yielded only limited results. P.G. Halpern, *A Naval History of World War I* (Annapolis, 1994).
31. M. Jeismann, "Propaganda," in *Enzyklopädie*, ed. Hirschfeld et al., 198–209; *Kultur und Krieg: Die Rolle der Intellektuellen, Künstler und Schriftsteller im Ersten Weltkrieg*, ed. W.J. Mommsen (Munich, 1996).
32. O. Hintze, "Staatsverfassung und Heeresverfassung," in O. Hintze, *Staat und Verfassung: Gesammelte Schriften* (Göttingen, 1962), 52–83; R. Luxemburg, *Gesammelte Werke*, Volume 1 (Berlin, 1982).
33. R.A. Kennedy, "Woodrow Wilson, World War I, and an American Conception of National Security," *Diplomatic History* 25 (2001), 1–31; J.W. Coogan, *The End of Neutrality: The United States, Britain and Maritime Rights 1899–1915* (Ithaca, 1981).

Chapter 16

German War Crimes 1914 and 1941
The Question of Continuity

Alan Kramer[1]

For professional historians it is no longer a matter of debate that the German army committed war crimes both in the First and the Second World War. Interest has shifted, in a revival of the old controversy about the *Sonderweg* (special path) of German history, to the question of possible continuities. Clearly, few would today claim that Nazi warfare represented a linear continuation of the warfare of Imperial Germany, merely embellished by racist ideology. But does that mean a radically new type of warfare emerged in 1939, revealed by the disposition to commit massive war crimes and genocide?

At first it is the differences in the magnitude and motivation of the crimes that are most striking. The total number of civilians killed during the three months of the invasion of France and Belgium in 1914 was about 6,500. In the best-known case, that of Louvain in Belgium, German troops killed 248 citizens; in the town of Dinant 674 were executed.[2] By contrast, in just two days in September 1941 more than 33,000 Jewish men, women, and children were killed in the ravine at Babi Yar near Kiev, Ukraine. In the first five weeks of "Operation Barbarossa," the German invasion of the Soviet Union, up to the end of July 1941, *Einsatzgruppen* (murder squads) liquidated 63,000 civilians, 90 percent of them Jews. Self-evidently this reflected a policy of racial extermination, although a plan for genocide had not yet been decided.[3]

Rather than reopen the debate on the dating of the decision to launch the genocide, the focus here is on concrete actions: in the period from late July to mid-December 1941 the *Einsatzgruppen* and police and army units put into practice the intention frequently voiced by the Nazi leadership to murder all Jews living within the German area of control. Initially, only male Jews were shot, but as from late July in Lithuania and Poland more and more women and children were killed.[4] In the southern part of the Soviet Union the transition to genocidal killing took place in the area of *Einsatzgruppe D* in September; the majority of the Jews of the Ukraine, by contrast, remained at liberty until early 1942.[5] In Serbia, too, initially only men were murdered: in October 1941 Wehrmacht units shot over two thousand men as 'hostages'; Jewish women and children were interned in concentration camps in Serbia and killed in March 1942, by gas.[6]

Racial motivation was not absent from the mass executions in 1914, but the main factor was the troops' widespread fear of *francs-tireurs*, or civilian irregular fighters. In addition, violent anti-Catholic prejudice analogous to racism caused German troops to accuse Catholic clergy of fomenting the fanatical armed resistance of the Belgian people. The destruction of Louvain and its famous medieval university library was partly motivated by anti-Catholicism because the university was regarded as the intellectual center of Belgian Catholicism, and hence of Belgian national identity. Numerous Belgian priests were arrested and beaten; at least forty-seven were killed.[7]

The violence against civilians in 1914 was not the result of a breakdown in discipline or the random brutality of individual officers. It occurred throughout the invasion zone, in 129 major incidents in which ten or more civilians were deliberately killed. Of the 300 regiments in the invasion in August 1914, 150 were responsible for such major incidents; many more were involved in other killings.[8]

The German and French or Belgian documentation agrees on one point: German troops thought they saw *francs-tireurs* fighting everywhere. Yet the *francs-tireurs* existed only as a chimera in the imagination of the Germans. Apart from some isolated cases of individual resistance the real source of unidentified shooting was the regular Belgian and French armies; even in 1914 rifles had a range of 1.8 kilometres, and in the hands of experienced soldiers they were accurate at 600 metres: a distance that made it impossible to identify the assailant. Sometimes there were 'friendly fire' incidents between inexperienced, nervous, and exhausted German soldiers. The soldiers selected their victims arbitrarily: they usually did not even try to identify armed men who might have been responsible for the firing, but simply executed all male inhabitants of a house or street from which shots had ostensibly been fired. Sometimes no distinctions were made, and women, children, and old people were also killed.

This draconian procedure rested on a concept of international law that deviated significantly from the international consensus. True, Germany had signed the Hague Law of Land Warfare of 1907 (Annex IV: "The Convention Respecting the Laws and Customs of War on Land"), which afforded protection to non-combatants, and even reproduced it in the Field Service Regulations carried by every officer. However, the army leadership openly stated that German doctrine differed: the war academy taught that article 2 of Hague, which allowed the civilian population to take up arms and resist invasion, "did not conform with the German view." *Francs-tireurs*, who were to be expected everywhere on enemy territory, were therefore criminals, "murderers," and "beasts" who had to be "eliminated" without further ado, hanged, or shot.[9] The culture of the army, its mental world in 1914, also predisposed it to draconian solutions: the institutional memory of the war of 1870–71, fed by countless officers' memoirs, biographies, and regimental histories, and military training inculcated the expectation that there would be a *levée en masse* and *franc-tireur* resistance. After all, there had been real *francs-tireurs* in the Franco-Prussian War.

Finally, specific orders issued by commanders were decisive. Generals von Einem and von Bülow (Second Army) issued orders at the start of the invasion "to burn down the villages and shoot everyone" because of the "treacherous firing by the Belgian population." The commander of XII Army Corps (Third Army) issued an order on 15 August 1914 stating that civilians who failed to turn in firearms, who were caught with weapons in their hands, or who tried to sabotage the German advance, were to be shot. Moreover, "Where the culprits cannot be found, ... hostages and also villages will be held liable with life and property for the damage."[10] By any standard these were criminal orders, and the execution of civilians was a war crime. During the war the Allies resolved to prosecute alleged war criminals, and after the war attempted to have 844 suspects extradited for war crimes trials.

Clearly, Nazi warfare against civilians in the Second World War, whether genocidal or in the context of antipartisan warfare, was on an entirely different scale. But when did the transition to genocidal killing take place, and why? Traditionally, the turning point has been seen as the year 1941, but some historians argue that the invasion of Poland in 1939 already marked the opening of genocidal war.[11] Germany's invasion of the Soviet Union in 1941 showed how the new warfare evolved out of the spirit of the old. The first draft decrees to prepare the invasion appeared to be almost identical to orders issued in 1914: the draft decree on "war jurisdiction" of 28 April 1941 by Lieutenant-General Eugen Müller, head of the armed forces legal department, stated that "Francs-tireurs are to be eliminated without mercy by the troops in combat or while escaping." In an order formulated together with chief of staff General Franz Halder on 13 May 1941, Müller proposed to have the troops shoot dead "potential francs-tireurs, saboteurs, or resisters in combat or while escaping." There were to be "collective measures of violence against villages."

In fact, violence against civilians in Eastern Europe often developed in the context of war against partisans, suppressing imagined and sometimes real uprisings. On 11 June 1941 Müller explained to general staff officers and court martial judges that "in the coming campaign military necessity on occasion will have to take precedence over the sense of justice. A return to the old customs of war will be required ... One of the two enemies must perish; supporters of the enemy ideology are not to be conserved, but liquidated."[12] The Wehrmacht commanders of 1941 denied the population the right to defend themselves; just as in 1914 that was a conscious breach of international law: "Paragraph 2 of the Hague Convention is out of the question."[13]

Almost all of this might have been said in the First World War, including the rhetoric of 'annihilation' which Ludendorff, effectively the head of the army,

1916–18, had used. What was new was the radical ideological component. In a speech on 30 March 1941 Hitler prepared the armed forces commanders for Operation Barbarossa. The fundamental idea was that the coming war would be a "struggle between two ideologies," that the "Jewish-Bolshevist system" had to be wiped out: "We must forget the concept of comradeship between soldiers. A communist is no comrade before or after battle. This is a war of annihilation."[14]

The Commissar Order of May 1941, which laid down that Soviet "political commissars," whether military or civilian, were to be executed upon capture, arose from Hitler's speech of 30 March. The army was a willing accomplice. Army commander-in-chief Field Marshal von Brauchitsch told top commanders on 27 March: "The troops have to realize that this struggle is being waged by one race against another, and proceed with the necessary harshness."[15]

Since the military leaders to a large extent shared Hitler's equating of Jews with bolshevism and since military propaganda relentlessly hammered in this enemy stereotype, there was little open protest in the army at this clearly illegal order. The Commissar Order and the Jurisdiction Decree brought about the unprecedented radicalization of the war of racial-ideological annihilation which distinguished the war of 1941 from that against Poland in 1939. The pattern of violence in the invasion of Poland showed more distinct parallels with France and Belgium in 1914 than with that of 1941. In the first eight weeks of the invasion and occupation of Poland, 16,336 civilians were killed, mostly on the pretext that they had resisted.[16] Most victims were men, not women and children, and the killing thus lacked one essential feature of genocide. Even the language echoed that of 1914: the victims were not "partisans," but *"francs-tireurs"* (*Franktireurs* or *Freischärler*).[17]

Naturally, given two changes of regime between 1914 and 1939, and in the apparent absence of connecting elements, it is problematic in methodological terms to claim continuity. However, just as the war of 1870–71 left a deep imprint in the cultural memory of the army, it is reasonable to assume that the "cultural memory" of the Great War only twenty-one years later in many ways conditioned military conduct. In addition, there was an explicit learning process. Hitler, most Nazi party leaders, and almost all senior Wehrmacht officers had fought in the Great War, and their constant use of stereotyped notions of that war is unmistakeable. Military training, independent of the influence of the Nazi regime, reflected the presumed lessons of the First World War. Military theory was dominated by the concept of "total war" in which not only the armed forces but also the entire civilian population would be involved. The essential characteristics were "total mobilization" of all human and material resources, "total control" by the state, "total war aims," and "total methods of war" that erased the distinction between the combatants and non-combatants. Obsolete relics such as moral scruples and international law were to be discarded.[18] As the semi-official (but not Nazi-inspired) "Handbook of Modern Military Science" stated in 1936, the target of the future "total ... people's war ... was not only the enemy combatant but the entire people ... Such a war knows no mercy towards the enemy people."[19]

Then there was the development of strategic doctrine to overcome the stasis of trench warfare by means of motorized warfare, autarky policy as an answer to a renewed Allied naval blockade, and the ruthless exploitation of the occupied countries in order to avoid a repeat of the 1918 trauma, in which the revolutionary civilian population allegedly stabbed the German army in the back. Such selective memory and distorted histories were a part of the "constructed experience" of the war. In relation to the East there was a bundle of fatal misperceptions: a stereotypical contempt of the quality of Russian military leadership that lasted until the end of the Second World War, and the *idée fixe* of the backwardness, cruelty, and cultural and racial inferiority of the peoples of Eastern Europe. Paradoxically, these ideas coexisted with a fear of the "Russian peril" and of the "Asiatic warfare of the Russians."[20]

The necessity of terror, too, was derived from the "experience" of the First World War. Hitler insisted on the need for draconian repression of the civilian population to combat partisan activity, referring to the measures of General Colmar von der Goltz, as Governor-General of Belgium in 1914, who supposedly "had all the villages burnt within a radius of several kilometres [of sabotaged railways], after having had all the mayors shot, the men imprisoned, and the women and children evacuated. There were three or four acts of violence in all, then nothing more happened."[21] Hitler made no mention of the mass executions of 1914: to do so would have cast doubt on the German "innocence" campaign against Versailles. Goltz himself mentioned only one incident of killing civilians who had, he claimed, shot at German troops near Ghent in October 1914; he was not responsible for the wave of executions in August–September.[22]

Yet when Germany invaded Poland in 1939, it was no conventional war. The new racial-ideological component meant that the Polish elite and the clergy were targeted, as were Jews as saboteurs and ringleaders of the *franc-tireur* resistance.[23] Reinhard Heydrich, head of the Reich Security Main Office, informed the army on 8 September 1939 that the intention was not arrests or deportations, but killings: "The nobility, the priests, and the Jews" were to be shot or hanged summarily.[24] Heydrich repeated this on 19 September and 14 October, speaking of the "liquidation of the Polish leadership."[25] Nazi warfare thus went far beyond the scale of violence of the imperial army in the First World War, both in discourse and in practice, in autumn 1939.

However, the violent excesses in the invasion of Poland cannot be ascribed solely to the fascist doctrine of war. As from the end of the First World War it was an article of faith in the German military that the existence of Poland was "intolerable," as the chief of the troop office, General Hans von Seeckt, put it in 1922.[26] It was not merely a question of border rectifications, such as the elimination of the Polish corridor: Poland, Seeckt said, had to "disappear." The destruction of Poland was always the goal for Germany's secret rearmament, even before 1933.[27] General Halder, too, despite his later opposition to Hitler, for which he was sacked in 1942 and arrested after 20 July 1944, tapped into the common creed of the military leadership when, in a speech before officers in spring 1939, he demanded that "Poland must be not only defeated as fast as possible, but liquidated."[28] In a hitherto unremarked continuity, the lethal anti-Catholic prejudice, too, recalled that of 1914.

It would be incorrect to conclude that Halder and the Wehrmacht shared the Nazis' aim of liquidating the Polish elites, and even carried it out, as the American historian Alexander Rossino has suggested.[29] Halder said, "For Germany the task is to liquidate the new eastern front as fast and as completely as possible, so that it does not take on unforeseen dimensions. In destroying this enemy we have to set a speed record."[30] His rhetoric of "annihilation" was no longer narrowly restricted, as that of Clausewitz had been, who rejected the killing of prisoners of war and the devastation of enemy territory. The concept of annihilation that emerged from the First World War had already been radicalized by Falkenhayn and Ludendorff. They accepted the mass killing of enemy soldiers and the mass killing of their own soldiers, the devastation of entire regions, the deliberate breaches of international law, the starving of civilian populations in occupied territories, deportations, forced labor, and torture. Since all this was implicit in the concept "war of annihilation" in 1939 and within the sphere of experience of professional officers, the moral threshold to genocide was accordingly low. Halder's expectation of a Polish "small war" behind the front thus prompted planning for the internment of all male Poles and Jews aged from 17 to 45 years. The participation of civilians and paramilitaries in the defense against the invasion confirmed the army's expectations and encouraged the Wehrmacht's direct participation in the executions of "suspicious elements"; it also made it easier to transfer security tasks to the *Einsatzgruppen*.[31] Nevertheless, a moral threshold still separated the Wehrmacht from the *Einsatzgruppen*. Halder was at first appalled by the "bestialities [*Schweinereien*] behind the front," but he attempted to ignore the nature of the new annihilation warfare.[32]

It was not Nazi racial propaganda, moreover, that was decisive in crossing the threshold to illegal violence, but two assumptions deeply rooted in German military culture since 1870: first, that (Polish) civilians and volunteer units would join in the defense of their homeland, and secondly, that this was illegal and was thus to be ruthlessly punished. The fighting between Polish militia units and ethnic German paramilitary units in the early days of the war in the mixed border areas, and the Polish units' guerilla tactics, were by contrast with Belgium in 1914 not imagined, but a reality in several places. This heightened the German soldiers' fear and rage, contributing to the significantly higher civilian death toll than in 1914.

In addition, Goebbels exploited the fact that the Polish army and civic guard killed a large number of ethnic Germans during the fighting in Bromberg to stoke the hatred of Poland, using exaggerated reports of the "Bromberg Bloody Sunday." (Recent Polish estimates range between 103 and 165 deaths, German estimates between 366 and 1,000.)[33] Holding attacks by Polish "irregulars" in Upper Silesia caused the commander of VIII Corps, General Ernst Busch, to order the ruthless suppression of the "free-shooter nuisance" on 2 September.[34] Many of the "irregulars" were not civilians, however, but members of the Polish army who had lost contact with their units in the retreat, and banded together to take up the fight on their own initiative. Yet the army obeyed Hitler's request to treat these soldiers as irregulars and carry out death penalties immediately after summary trials, without confirmation from court martial chiefs (usually a divisional commander).[35]

The *Einsatzgruppen* were also assisted in autumn 1939 by the *Volksdeutscher Selbstschutz* militias, recruited from members of the German minority in Poland or those who had fled from the Polish territories after 1918. Motivated partly by revenge, and partly by Nazi racial ideology and propaganda alleging that fifty-eight thousand had been killed (in fact up to six thousand ethnic Germans were killed in Poland),[36] the militiamen killed twenty thousand Poles and Polish Jews, often in arbitrary actions, characterized by extreme brutality and torture.[37] The racist mobilization of violence from below was a historically new aspect of this war. There was also widespread military violence against Jews, thought to be the ringleaders of subversion, but also because of many soldiers' anti-Semitism, drummed into them by years of Nazi propaganda.

Nevertheless between 1939 and 1941 there were important distinctions. In 1939 the army mainly assisted by arresting members of the Polish elites and male Jews, and handing them over to the *Einsatzgruppen* for executions. However, it was in fact the army that put an end to the lynch-type murders by the *Volksdeutscher Selbstschutz* in November 1939. Several commanders tried to keep the army clear of the anti-Jewish actions. While involvement in the executions of suspected resisters accorded with German military culture, commanders regarded the Jewish population as mostly peaceful, refused to participate in the cruel, pogrom-like killings, and even protested against them. In contrast to the army's conduct in Operation Barbarossa two years later, when it largely identified itself with the aim of destroying "Jewish Bolshevism," the army commanders feared in 1939 that the measures against the Jews might provoke resistance against the occupation and violence against the ethnic Germans.

The army's protests against the *Einsatzgruppen* atrocities culminated in the memorandum by General Johannes Blaskowitz, Commander-in-Chief East, of 27 November 1939. Blaskowitz stated that "the army refuses to be identified with the atrocities of the Security Police." This was not only moral outrage ("Every soldier feels sickened and disgusted by these crimes"), but also expressed the concern that spreading fear in the population would create "a military state of unrest" and "prevent the exploitation of the country for the benefit of the troops and war industry."[38]

Still, from these utterances of some high-ranking officers, important though they were, we should not deduce the views of the entire army. General Walther von Brauchitsch, army Commander-in-Chief, voiced no objections to the "executions in Poland" in his meeting with Hitler on 12 September. Evidently he was satisfied when Hitler stated that "If the Wehrmacht wants to have nothing to do with it, it will have to accept that the SS and Gestapo will go into action alongside it."[39] Brauchitsch shared Himmler's view that harsh measures against the Polish population were essential for the success of the *Lebensraum* policy, and he had critics of Nazi racial policy silenced. The army was weaned off its moral outrage in 1939–40 by deploying it at certain points as an accessory to prepare for its future role as active accomplice.[40]

Yet there was absolutely no automatism in the downward slide into barbarization, no linear continuity. When the German army invaded France and the Low Countries in spring 1940, the civilian populations, remembering the atrocities of 1914, feared the worst. They were amazed to find that the conduct of the German army was almost without exception correct, even "chivalrous." The explanation lay in a policy decision: because of the racial distinction the Nazis made between Western and Eastern Europe, and the desire to avoid giving grounds for atrocity propaganda, German units were under strict orders to behave impeccably.[41]

If we extend the perspective from war crimes to encompass warfare more broadly, we find an analogous pattern of continuities and radical change. First World War soldiers showed and recorded their strong feelings in the face of destruction and death; Second World War soldiers used a detached language, expressed no empathy with other people, and showed no emotions. Killing in the Second World War was frequently described with cold objectivity as a technical process.[42] That had a great deal to do with the socialization of male youth in the Third Reich, their premilitary training, and their receptivity for social-Darwinist and racist ideology as a framework to interpret their experience on the eastern front.[43]

Soldiers in the Second World War accordingly had a different perception of the enemy. In the First World War there was much talk in trench newspapers and soldiers' ego documents of German cultural superiority, and there was also a perceptible discourse of the racial inferiority of the Slavs.[44] The Russians were already regarded as barbarians, even before their invasion of East Prussia in 1914 provided the occasion for charges of atrocities. Of course, a racial-ideological war of annihilation was not on the agenda in the Great War. Nevertheless, some ominous signs were visible in popular culture: in a teenage fiction trilogy by Richard Skowronnek, *Sturmzeichen*, *Das große Feuer*, and *Die schwere Not*, which had sold a quarter of a million copies by 1916, and was reprinted in 1933–34, the Russians in the war were depicted as drunken and bestial. The author has a kidnapped East Prussian district administrator say: "There can be no peace with this dehumanized people ... One has to beat them to death, man for man."[45]

The experience of victory in the East and political violence after 1918 were further important connections. Through the experience of the occupation and the short-lived dream of the Eastern Imperium, the terms *Volk* and *Raum* were reconfigured and interpreted in a racial sense; *Ostforschung* (research on the East) provided pseudo-scientific legitimation; and the collective memory of the primitive chaos of the East was skilfully transformed by the Nazis into their vision of the racial utopia.[46]

The brutality of the Freikorps units in the Baltic in early 1919 was another important link. Motivated by promises of colonial settlement, racialism, and hatred of the Bolsheviks, they spread fear and terror. Anticipating the extreme violence of the invasion of Poland twenty years later, the "Baltic Landwehr" killed over three thousand people in May/June 1919 in Riga alone, and several hundred more in other towns.[47] The three hundred or more murders committed by members of extreme right-wing associations from 1919 to 1923 inside Germany are testimony to the increased readiness to resort to violence against political opponents. The memory of heroic deeds in the Great War and the Freikorps fighting was kept alive with a macabre cult of martyrdom and death through countless publications and commemorations of the fallen.[48]

The history of anti-Semitism also appears to show a continuity from the First to the Second World War. Steffen Bruendel locates the germ of the idea of elimination in the notion of the "exclusion of the Jews" circulating in the Fatherland Party in 1918–19.[49] However, it can hardly be denied that lethal anti-Semitic violence in the Weimar years was the absolute exception, not the rule. "Exclusion" meant just that: the Nazi aim of a "Jew-free" Germany, through deprivation of rights and forced emigration, not through the unthinkable murder of all European Jews.

Certainly, anti-Semitism emerged as a mass phenomenon in the war with a first peak represented by the "Jew census" in 1916; the period of the defeat and the Revolution in 1918–19 saw another, more dangerous, spike in anti-Semitism. Anti-Semitism was a constant under-current in political culture after 1918, and an openly violent anti-Semitic party came to power in 1933. However, it is not the continuities, but the discontinuities in the history of anti-Semitism which are more evident.[50] In the Great War and the Weimar Republic the German state tried to stop the spread of anti-Semitism; the perpetrators of anti-Semitic violence were enemies of the state. The Nazi regime, by contrast, made anti-Semitism into state doctrine. The army demonstrated its complicity with the Nazi regime by anticipating the anti-Jewish measures of the Nuremberg racial laws in 1935 in its own ranks; in the same year a War Ministry circular described Soviet party officials as "usually dirty Jews." By the time of the invasion of the Soviet Union the specter of "Jewish Bolshevism" was a fixed enemy stereotype in the Wehrmacht.[51]

Above all, Nazism's genocidal intention was new: it had not been a part of traditional anti-Semitism, and in fact it only became the aim of the regime in 1941. Two decisive turns were necessary to make it not only regime but also army policy. The first turn from situational war crimes, committed against the background of systematic racial propaganda, to complicity in the massive war crimes against Poles and Jews, took place in 1939. The entry-point was the *franc-tireur* phobia and the will to mete out collective punishments, based on ideas that can be traced back to 1914 and 1870. The second turn was to genocidal killing, which only took place in the course of Operation Barbarossa in autumn and winter 1941. Jochen Böhler's argument that the attack on the Soviet Union in 1941 was not a watershed in warfare cannot in my opinion be maintained in view of the intention to commit genocide.[52]

The fate of the prisoners of war shows the distinctions clearly. The great majority of the 694,000 Polish soldiers taken prisoner in 1939 were adequately nourished and subsequently released during the winter of 1939–40; only about 7,500 of them died in captivity, a rate that did not differ greatly from those in the First World War.[53] By contrast, the 3.35 million Soviet soldiers whom the Germans took prisoner in 1941 were treated appallingly; two million had died by 1 February 1942, from deliberate neglect resulting in hunger, cold, and disease, or killed by shooting or poison gas. The extent of this war crime far exceeded even the killing of half a million Jews in the same period.[54]

In sum, the war of 1941 was *sui generis*. Nazi warfare, characterized by the readiness to commit massive war crimes and genocide, differed fundamentally from the war of 1914, but it was unthinkable without the reconfigured memory of the First World War, defeat, postwar right-wing violence, and the war of 1939.

Notes

1. I should like to thank Sven Oliver Müller, Cornelius Torp, and Michael Wildt for their comments and suggestions.
2. J. Horne and A. Kramer, *German Atrocities 1914. A History of Denial* (London, 2001); on the context of the cultural history of violence see A. Kramer, *Dynamic of Destruction. Culture and Mass Killing in the First World War* (Oxford, 2007).
3. W. Wette, "Babij Yar 1941. Das Verwischen der Spuren," in *Kriegsverbrechen im 20. Jahrhundert*, eds. W. Wette and G.R. Ueberschär (Darmstadt, 2001), 152–64.
4. C. Browning, *The Origins of the Final Solution. The Evolution of Nazi Jewish Policy, September 1939–March 1942* (London, 2004), 260–61.
5. J. Matthäus, "Operation Barbarossa and the Onset of the Holocaust," ibid., 282–94.
6. W. Manoschek, "'Gehst mit Juden erschießen?' Die Vernichtung der Juden in Serbien," in *Vernichtungskrieg. Verbrechen der Wehrmacht 1941–1944*, eds. H. Heer and K. Naumann (Hamburg, 1995), 39–56.
7. Horne and Kramer, *German Atrocities 1914*, 104–7, 276.
8. Ibid., 74–78.
9. Ibid., 145–52.
10. Ibid., 18, 162.
11. J. Böhler, *Auftakt zum Vernichtungskrieg. Die Wehrmacht in Polen 1939* (Frankfurt, 2006).
12. Quoted in Horne and Kramer, *German Atrocities 1914*, 406f.
13. Ausführungsbestimmungen des AOK 6/Abt. I c v. 16. Juni 1941, quoted in F. Römer, "'Im alten Deutschland wäre solcher Befehl nicht möglich gewesen.' Rezeption, Adaption und Umsetzung des Kriegsgerichtsbarkeitserlasses im Ostheer 1941/42," *Vierteljahrshefte für Zeitgeschichte* 56 (2008), 53–99, here 57.
14. Cited from the Halder diaries in J. Förster, "Operation Barbarossa as a War of Conquest and Annihilation," in *Germany and the Second World War*, vol. 4: *The Attack on the Soviet Union*, Oxford, 1998, ed. Militärgeschichtliches Forschungsamt (Stuttgart, 1996), 481–521, here 497.
15. Förster, "Operation Barbarossa," 485.
16. Browning, *Origins of the Final Solution*, 29.
17. Michael Wildt was the first to point out the semantic concordance with 1914: *Generation des Unbedingten. Das Führungskorps des Reichssicherheitshauptamtes* (Hamburg, 2002), 436f.
18. J. Hürter, *Hitlers Heerführer: Die deutschen Oberbefehlshaber im Krieg gegen die Sowjetunion 1941/42* (Munich, 2007), 113; S. Förster, "Introduction," in *Great War, Total War. Combat and Mobilization on the Western Front, 1914–1918*, eds. R. Chickering and S. Förster (Washington, DC, 2000), 7f.
19. Quoted in Hürter, *Hitlers Heerführer*, 114f.

20. R. Bergien, "Die Ostfront des Ersten Weltkries und das Kontinuitätsproblem," in *Die vergessene Front. Der Osten 1914/15. Ereignis, Wirkung, Nachwirkung*, ed. G.P. Groß (Paderborn, 2006), 396; J. Hürter, "Kriegserfahrung als Schlüsselerlebnis? Der Erste Weltkrieg in der Biographie von Wehrmachtsgeneralen," in *Erster Weltkrieg, Zweiter Weltkrieg. Ein Vergleich. Krieg, Kriegserlebnis, Kriegserfahrung in Deutschland*, eds. B. Thoß und H.-E. Volkmann (Paderborn, 2002), 759–71, here 766–69; Hürter, *Hitlers Heerführer*, 81f.
21. *Hitler's Table Talk 1941–44. His Private Conversations*, introduced by H.R. Trevor-Roper (1951; English translation, London, 1953), 29 (14–15 September 1941).
22. Horne and Kramer, *German Atrocities 1914*, 407.
23. On the question of anti-Semitic violence in autumn 1939 and the long-term plans of the RSHA, see Wildt, *Generation des Unbedingten*, 455–73.
24. H. Krausnick and H.C. Deutsch, eds., *Helmuth Groscurth. Tagebücher eines Abwehroffiziers 1938–1940. Mit weiteren Dokumenten zur Militäropposition gegen Hitler* (Stuttgart, 1970), diary 8 September 1939, 201.
25. Wildt, *Generation des Unbedingten*, 452f. On 19 September: H.-A. Jacobsen, ed., *Generaloberst [Franz] Halder. Kriegstagebuch. Tägliche Aufzeichnungen des Chefs des Generalstabes des Heeres 1939–1942*, vol. 1: *Vom Polenfeldzug bis zum Ende der Westoffensive (14.8.1939–30.6.1940)* (Stuttgart, 1962), 79.
26. F. von Rabenau, ed., *Seeckt. Aus seinem Leben 1918–1936* (Leipzig, 1941), 316.
27. A.B. Rossino, *Hitler Strikes Poland. Blitzkrieg, Ideology, and Atrocity* (Lawrence, KS, 2003), 8; Hürter, *Hitlers Heerführer*, 157.
28. C. Hartmann and S. Slutsch, "Franz Halder und die Kriegsvorbereitungen im Frühjahr 1939. Eine Ansprache des Generalstabschefs des Heeres. Dokumentation," *Vierteljahrshefte für Zeitgeschichte* 45 (1997), 467–95, here 489.
29. This is the impression given by Rossino, who in quoting passages from Halder's speech of spring 1939 distorts his meaning by omissions, and places it in the context of a truncated description of the mass murder of members of the Polish elites and the Jewish population. See Rossino, *Hitler Strikes Poland*, 1–7.
30. Hartmann and Slutsch, "Halder," 483f.
31. Rossino, *Hitler Strikes Poland*, 26, 58.
32. Halder, *Kriegstagebuch*, vol. 1, 68.
33. Wildt, *Generation des Unbedingten*, 430f.
34. Rossino, *Hitler Strikes Poland*, 74ff.
35. H. Krausnick and H.-H. Wilhelm, *Die Truppe des Weltanschauungskrieges: Die Einsatzgruppen der Sicherheitspolizei und des SD, 1938–1942* (Stuttgart, 1981), 49.
36. Browning, *Origins of the Final Solution*, 31.
37. C. Jansen and A. Weckbecker, *Der "Volksdeutsche Selbstschutz" in Polen 1939/40* (Munich, 1992), 154ff.; Wildt, *Generation des Unbedingten*, 440.
38. Commander-in-Chief East to Army Commander-in-Chief, in Krausnick and Deutsch, *Groscurth*, 426f.
39. Memorandum Lt.-Col. von Lahousen on meeting in Hitler's train, ibid., 358.
40. Browning, *Origins of the Final Solution*, 80f.
41. Horne and Kramer, *German Atrocities 1914*, 402–5.
42. P. Knoch, "Gewalt wird zur Routine. Zwei Weltkriege in der Erfahrung einfacher Soldaten," in *Der Krieg des kleinen Mannes. Eine Militärgeschichte von unten*, ed. W. Wette (Munich, 1992), 313–23, here 313f.
43. Cf. W. Wette, "Ideology, Propaganda, and Internal Politics as Preconditions of the War Policy of the Third Reich," in *Germany and the Second World War*, vol. 1: *The Build-up of German Aggression*, eds. W. Deist et al. (Oxford, 1990), 9–155, here esp. 104–10 and 147–55.
44. P. Hoeres, "Die Slawen. Perzeptionen des Kriegsgegners bei den Mittelmächten. Selbst- und Feindbild," in *Die vergessene Front. Der Osten 1914/15. Ereignis, Wirkung, Nachwirkung*, ed. G.P. Groß (Paderborn, 2006), 179–200, here 192ff. However, Hoeres denies the racial element in the perception of the Slavs and finds that "the perception of the east and of the Slavs of 1914–18 can

hardly be compared with that of the Barbarossa campaign" (p. 200). H.-E. Volkmann by contrast writes of the negative racial clichés in propaganda and journalism which "accumulated as a racist sediment in the memory of the German soldier." Volkmann, "Der Ostkrieg 1914/15 als Erlebnis- und Erfahrungswelt des deutschen Militärs," ibid., 263–93, here 281.

45. Quoted in M. Vogt, "'Illusionen als Tugend und kühle Beurteilung als Laster.' Deutschlands 'gute Gesellschaft' im Ersten Weltkrieg," in *Der Erste Weltkrieg. Wirkung, Wahrnehmung, Analyse*, ed. Michalka (Weyarn, 2000), 622–48, here 645.
46. On this see V.G. Liulevicius, *War Land on the Eastern Front. Culture, National Identity and German Occupation in World War I* (Cambridge, 2000); M. Burleigh, *Germany Turns Eastwards. A Study of Ostforschung in the Third Reich* (Cambridge, 1988). In general on the continuities and discontinuities of political concepts such as "nation" and "*Volksgemeinschaft*" between the First and Second World Wars see S.O. Müller, *Deutsche Soldaten und ihre Feinde. Nationalismus an Front und Heimatfront im Zweiten Weltkrieg* (Frankfurt, 2007), 29–84.
47. B. Barth, *Dolchstoßlegenden und politische Desintegration. Das Trauma der deutschen Niederlage im Ersten Weltkrieg 1914–1933* (Düsseldorf, 2003), 258–66.
48. Ibid., 544–47.
49. S. Bruendel, *Volksgemeinschaft oder Volksstaat. Die "Ideen von 1914" und die Neuordnung Deutschlands im Ersten Weltkrieg* (Berlin, 2003), 305.
50. I. Kershaw, "Antisemitismus und die NS-Bewegung vor 1933," in *Vorurteil und Rassenhaß. Antisemitismus in den faschistischen Bewegungen Europas*, eds. H. Graml et al. (Berlin, 2001), 29–48, here 29. P. Hoeres has found that the German army in the East was characterized rather by philosemitism, but noted that "the German military partly also displayed antisemitic attitudes." Hoeres, "Slawen," 192. Volkmann ('Der Ostkrieg 1914/15, 279ff.) points out that encounters between German soldiers or the military administration and East European Jews were often positive.
51. Matthäus, "Operation Barbarossa," 248.
52. Böhler, *Auftakt zum Vernichtungskrieg*, 247.
53. Rossino, *Hitler Strikes Poland*, 179; R. Overmans, "Die Kriegsgefangenenproblematik des Deutschen Reiches 1939 bis 1945," in *Germany and the Second World War*, vol. 9/2: *Die deutsche Kriegsgesellschaft 1939 bis 1945*, part 2: *Ausbeutung, Deutungen, Ausgrenzungen*, ed. J. Echternkamp (Munich, 2005), 729–875, here 745–55.
54. L. Herbst, *Das nationalsozialistische Deutschland, 1933–1945. Entfesselung der Gewalt: Rassismus und Krieg* (Frankfurt, 1996), 376.

Part IV

THE GERMAN EMPIRE IN THE WORLD

Chapter 17

From the Periphery to the Center
On the Significance of Colonialism for the German Empire

Birthe Kundrus

For a long time, the German colonial experience had a shadowy academic existence. German colonialism came on the scene too late, was too superficial and lasted too short a time to have left behind any deep tracks.[1] And, in truth, the period of German colonial rule lasted only a little more than thirty years—from 1884 till 1918. As a consequence of its defeat in World War I, Germany was required by Article 119 of the Versailles Treaty to give up its overseas "possessions to the allied and associated Great Powers." The first German Chancellor, Otto von Bismarck, had opposed the wishes expressed by sections of the bourgeoisie toward colonies and had instead placed his hopes on private initiatives, in order to keep the state as far as possible out of the colonial engagement. Only beginning in the 1880s, under Wilhelm II, did the turnaround to a more active *Weltpolitik* take place. The "protected territories" occupied by Germany were generally areas no other power was interested in. In Africa this was German South-West Africa (Namibia today) and German East Africa (today parts of Tanzania, Burundi and Ruanda, Cameroon and Togo). In the Pacific this was German Samoa and German New Guinea, the Marshall Islands and some islands in what is today Micronesia, as well as Kiautschou in China. The attractiveness of a colonial empire, measured against the British or French possessions, was the subject of hefty debates—some contemporaries made fun of the sandboxes that one had acquired in Africa, others referred to the fantastic prospects of these territories and of others which were still to be acquired. Yet only a very few Germans actually moved to the transatlantic territories. In 1912, only about eighteen thousand Germans were living in the German colonies.[2]

If one looks only at the dry facts, then one could agree with the judgement above concerning the insignificance of the German colonies and of German colonialism. However, as so often, taking a second look from a different perspective shows that the colonial period was neither irrelevant to German society nor to the societies of the overseas colonies. This at least is the conclusion of a number of recent studies into Germany's colonial past.

This chapter will describe the development of this historiography and the increasing relevance of German colonialism. My thesis is that a way of looking at the history of colonialism that is limited to the phase of formal German colonial rule, or which only looks at the German colonies, fails to take into consideration essential dimensions and dynamics of German colonial—or even imperial— efforts. These efforts were always directed in the nineteenth and twentieth centuries to the already acquired colonies as well to territories that Germany did not possess. We need to look not only at the territories overseas, in Africa, Oceania, and in the Far East, but also to the Near East, to South America, and to the European continent. The overwhelming absence of formal colonial or imperial rule and the territorial movement to find territories, especially moving between the overseas territories and Middle and Eastern Europe, describes the two points where reflecting on German colonial history is presently most interesting. What is the significance for German history of this special constellation of a late entry and an early departure, even if it was not so desired, from the lengthy imperial expansion? What tensions resulted from the short but intensive history, both of events and of intentions? And do the various attempts by Germany to reach out into the world have a common origin—or not?

The dates 1884, 1918, and 1945 are important for the answers to these and other questions. However, the degree to which these dates are really breaks in German history has repeatedly been questioned. For example, there is a debate concerning the relationship between the colonial expansion and that of the National Socialists. Can both be subsumed under the larger category of "imperialism," or are we dealing here with quite different phenomena?[3] On top of this, the actual period of formal German colonial rule between 1884 and 1918 has become more the center of attention. Especially interesting here is the question of whether, and to what degree, the German manner of ruling differed from that of other imperial powers. Recently, the discussion concerning the importance of colonialism for the history of Germany from 1870–1918 has gathered momentum. What results have been brought forth by this research, what are the characteristics of this research, what still needs to be done, where are the weaknesses—this will be investigated in the following.

A New History of Colonialism?

At present we are witnessing a considerable upswing in the journalistic and academic interest in Germany's past engagement overseas. Especially the interdisciplinary exchange between historians, cultural studies, and literature studies has been profitable.[4] The cause for the present upswing in the work on colonialism lies in the transformation, even the new constitution, of research fields such as colonial and postcolonial studies, and the impulse for this has come largely from the United States. Furthermore, the integration of transnational and global perspectives into national histories has required Germany to look more closely at its colonial past. Our understanding of colonialism and of its importance has received a fresh impetus because of these works. The older studies were limited to investigating policies which were oriented to acquiring and exploiting overseas territories. In other words, they were interested in an event which took place exclusively "there," and they interpreted this event essentially on the basis of its power-political and economic aspects. This classical approach, the approach of the sociology of politics and government, to the history of colonialism cannot and should not be replaced nor ignored in the new work—this point has recently been made by Jürgen Osterhammel and Sebastian Conrad.[5]

Today, however, colonialism is also understood as part of European history; both histories are interwoven. This interaction not only had an impact on the colonies themselves, albeit different and often contradictory from country to country—but also in the metropole.[6] In a certain sense the metropolitan significance of colonialism is the question asked already in the influential social imperialism thesis of Hans-Ulrich Wehler. The present research into the history of colonialism goes beyond this more instrumental way of comprehending the topic by assigning to the object of study a significance *sui generis*, although sometimes this significance is exaggerated. Colonialism's ability to shape society was true, first of all, in regard to the fact that high imperialism was an event with a timeless and global significance. It created political and economic power relationships, or rather, structural inequalities, which broke down in places, but which in general appear to have held up quite well over the period of decolonization and the foundation of new states. Second of all, new approaches show how important non-European cultures were for the self-understanding of Western European civilization, Western European culture.[7] It is also characteristic of the new approaches that they attempt to understand colonialism as a global, European, and national phenomena—all at the same time. In Germany between 1870 and 1918 there was, albeit very limited, immigration of (former) colonial subjects from, amongst others, Africa.[8] Traces of colonialism could be found on top of this in such different realms as literature,[9] film,[10] social science,[11] medicine,[12] advertising,[13] urban geography,[14] legislation,[15] infrastructure planning,[16] small retail trade with so-called "colonial shops,"[17] scandals,[18] the conduct of war and military strategy,[19] and leisure activities, for example, parlour games.[20] Furthermore, colonialism was a part of the political-administrative planning for the future, even a part of the demands for more political participation by parties and associations of almost every shape and form.[21] In short, colonialism was part of the broad spectrum of thoughts and experiences of German society. In the German discussions on colonialism, which took place largely among the academic bourgeoisie (*Bildungsbürgertum*), collective as well as individual projections, hopes, and fears were reflected—and with this German sensitivities. As a result, the comparatively new experience of formal colonial rule contributed to the increasing popularity of models of social order based on hierarchy and race around 1900.[22] This profiling of difference as something essential took place at a time when liberal, democratic, and socialist demands for more individual freedom, more equality, and more political participation, be it in the women's movement or in Social Democracy, were becoming ever louder.

The change in perspective not only to the real, historical experiences of colonialism, but also to the discursive practices, the debate in the culture sections of the newspapers, the fantasies and the plans, produces an image of Germany between 1871 and 1914 with which we are in many ways unacquainted. On the one hand, a more vital understanding of identity developed—with corresponding effects on how one displayed power in political realms or on the excited application of violence in the colonies.[23] On the other hand, one can see a remarkable and explosive curiosity in foreigners and in the foreign.[24] Already long before 1884, German businessmen, missionaries, travelers, scholars and academics, as well as engineers and technicians, had travelled extensively in the non-European world, and there was an active group lobbying for colonialism,[25] to be found around 1900 in all political camps, including the Social Democrats—this is true of the opponents of colonialism as well. The interest in colonies became explosive because here was a site of competing models of society, of competing models of solutions to German problems—always at the cost of those being colonized. The fascination with colonies, which was different for every region and their populations, was not limited exclusively to one's own colonies, and it was not only always about political and military rule. One thinks here of Orientalism, with the plans for colonies in the Orient, the trips to the Orient of Kaiser Wilhelm II, and the Baghdad railway.[26] In the nineteenth century, one thinks of how China and Egypt experienced similar periods when they were objects of projections, just like the classical versions of Rome and Greece.

Alongside this there was a large interest in Middle and Eastern Europe as a former site of German settlements; the *völkisch* right especially called for the annexation of these territories. If and to what degree, however, these quite different cravings for expansion, for "moral"[27] and military conquests, were related to one another, or were in competition with one another—these questions have received little attention. Were, for example, the *völkisch* dreams of a "German East" around 1900 a response to the frustrating results of the German efforts to get more colonies? To what degree can we agree with Philipp Ther that the imperial dimension of the Kaiserreich is to be found not only in the overseas possessions, but also in the rule over the Polish population in the Prussian Eastern provinces?[28] Did "Poland" assume more and more the role of a "compensatory colony"[29]—or was it not the actual colony of the German Empire, an imperial nation-state which came onto the world's political stage too late? It appears to be a quite fruitful line of investigation to bring together all of these various threads. In this regard, the considerations of David Blackbourn are very suggestive.[30] He regards the charge of Eastern Europe as the specific German colonial history. Already in the Wilhelminian period, it had become clear that for Germany the actual counterpart to India or Algeria was not Cameroon but rather Middle Europe. Blackbourn comes to the conclusion that it was not the end of formal colonial rule in 1919 but rather the end of the German settlements in Eastern and Middle Europe in 1945 which marks the real break in German colonial policy. It remains an open question, if, and if yes to what degree, colonialism and the German "aspirations" in Eastern Europe influenced each other. Furthermore, it is worth asking if one should differentiate in terms of a typology of government between overseas colonialism, imperialism and National Socialism. Besides, continuity is in question, a most difficult theoretical and methodological problem.[31] There is very little agreement as to what constitutes continuity. Since there are rarely clear, linear relationships and chains of causality, especially over longer periods and distances, one solution to the dilemma of continuity might be to examine the productive adaptation of ideas, structures, images, knowledge, experience, and practices. Further research might thus consider how British or American (rather than German) imperialism was adapted to Nazi plans and practices, and assess what conceptual modifications emerged in the course of such transfers. In what way did empires—be they Roman, American, or British—function as a kind of sounding board for Nazi attitudes and practices?[32]

For Gerhard Ritter, at any rate, National Socialism and colonialism were quite different forms of expansions. In a suggestive passage from 1958 on the end of colonialism, Ritter stated, astonished, that all German efforts to win colonies overseas had failed, and that, in contrast to 1919, this failure now had to be seen positively. Given the worldwide decolonization, this failure meant that Germany's image abroad was less burdened than that of the former imperialists. Ritter's point was that losing the colonial competition had helped Germany to shake off the negative image of the country which had been formed during the Nazism and World War II—indeed, that one was able to turn the international allocation of sympathy upside down. This was at best a very indirect bridge to the National Socialist epoch. In Ritter's words, the end of the period of:

> European colonialism [has] created a completely different situation in the world, so that today we no longer perceive the loss of our colonial empire in the First World War as a heavy loss. Just the opposite: the fact that we have not been a colonial power for a long time has saved us from that enormous level of resentment, yes, even of hatred, which our Western European neighbors presently suffer. The loss of colonies has allowed our Federal Republic to be the only large, European industrial country whose business agents are greeted everywhere warmly, without political mistrust. What a strange and fully unexpected twist at the beginning of a completely new and novel epoch of world history![33]

A Specific German Form of Colonialism?

Colonialism was and is an integral part of Western societies. What was specific to German colonialism, what made it different in comparison to the other European colonialisms? At first glance, it seems that what was true for Germany was true for European imperialism.[34] Prestige was very important in German colonialism, fluctuating between self-assertion and feeling threatened by the foreign. "The white German woman" as the savior of culture as, in general, the sexual metaphor of conquest, were important tropes. There was a highly developed clannishness in the German colonies, and local factors were of great importance in the social and political practice of ruling; in other words, instructions from Berlin had a relatively minor influence on the practice of colonial rule in the colonies. As in France, Great Britain or the United States, power and sovereignty was demonstrated and documented by displaying the conquered "other" and by observing the "other's" way of life with a mixture of idealization and distance. In German colonies, too, there was a creed of inequality, of physical segregation in terms of space, of paternalism, and of condescension vis-à-vis the native cultures as well as systematic exploitation and forced labor. And in German colonialism, too, one finds the repudiation of these claims, the structural instability of colonial rule, a structure of power which provided a show of force on the outside, but which on the inside was always unstable and which tended to disintegrate. This conglomeration of wild desires, a claim to absolute power and the unlimited, licentious living out of these desires led to regular conflicts with the indigenous population, which often ended in the application of extreme violence.

However, there were also other ways to respond. Often, although not always, the interpretation of Africa, Asia, or Oceania, or respectively, the interpretation of their natives was mistaken. Occasionally there were also clear-sighted observations concerning the mutual insecurities, the misunderstandings, and the stage directions. Brutality, domination, and exploitation were the basic structure of every kind of imperialism. Nevertheless, new research on colonial systems stresses that colonizers and colonized need to be interpreted not just in terms of perpetrators and victims, and that the concrete lives of the "natives" need to be understood not only in terms of force and compulsion. To do so reduces the complex realities of imperial experiences, the diverse strategies of agency by the colonized, and succumbs to the fantasies of omnipotence created by the colonizers.[35] Also the colonized learned to play on the imperial instrument and produced themselves their own form of knowledge concerning the "foreign."[36] Within the manifold varieties of interaction between the Europeans who were on site, between the local administration and the administration in the cities back in Europe, between the natives and the Europeans as well as among the natives themselves, there was resistance to the Europeans as well as strategies of arrangement and cooperation. Furthermore, colonial rule remained at first limited to a sparse network, usually along the coast, with few stations inland. Those historical atlases, in which thousands of square kilometres are marked with the colors of the respective colonial power, lead one astray and are evidence more of desire than of reality. The colonialists were only gradually able to win control of the territorial space and in many areas not at all—for example, they were unable to accomplish this in the Caprivi-Streifen or in Ovamboland in German South-

West Africa. The will to control the population came even more slowly.[37] Here, it is believed there is a further area that needs more research, namely comparative studies or studies of the transfer of ideas, not only between Germany and the other European colonial powers, but also between the individual German colonies. It appears as if things were different in the protectorates in Africa and in the South Seas;[38] the colonial state was not even close to being able to portray a semblance of order. Of course, in this regard German colonialism had much in common with other forms of European colonialism. Furthermore, many German conceptions of how to conduct its colonial empire, be it the "distribution" of women or the control of immigration, was oriented on models put forth by other imperial powers, especially by the British.

Perhaps Germany differed from the other colonial powers only in the enthusiasm with which it attempted, as an imperial latecomer, to catch up with France and Great Britain. This sporadic overacting gave rise to an oversized bureaucracy and a constant improvization, which did not end even when Bernhard Dernburg was appointed the new State Secretary in 1907. In this respect, some things in the German protectorates may have developed more quickly, more compressed, with greater tension; they were seldom more relaxed or more reserved. A vivid example of these extremes can be found in the discourse on intermarriages or so-called "mixed marriages" between white German men and indigenous women in the colonies. Many colonial powers asked themselves around 1900 whether or not they should or could politically prevent these couples and their offspring. In 1903, in Southern Rhodesia a law was passed which made sexual relations between European women and black men illegal, but not, however, between European men and African women. Beginning in 1902–03, in the Cape Province, Natal and in Oranjeland, unmarried sexual relations between black men and white women were outlawed, as part of the struggle against prostitution; in Transvaal beginning in 1897 they even outlawed sexual relations between married black men and white women. In 1909 Great Britain finally deviated from its previous course of not having the state get involved in private affairs—at least in regard to its colonial civil servants—and prohibited them from marrying natives.

In Germany the intervention of the authorities went even further. In German South-West Africa, German East Africa, and in Samoa, the leading civil servants in the colonial administration decided to interfere not only in the private lives of German women and of a group of men (such as civil servants) but forbade all white men in the three colonies from marrying indigenous partners. On the one hand, the problem was solved by all powers in a relatively similar manner: rules of social exclusion and discrimination. On the other hand, German colonial administration chose even stricter controls in the question of mixed marriages than did the other imperial powers. In the German parliament, in contrast, things were different. In May 1912 parliament asked the Federal Council to introduce a draft law which would legalize all marriages between "whites and natives" in all German colonies. In other words, race was not to be an obstacle to marriage.

These two German decisions, conflictive as they were, are remarkable in the European colonial context. A vote for equality before the law stood diametrically opposed to a vote for inequality. Thus intensification of ambivalence could be an answer to the question asked above concerning the specific qualities of German colonialism. Although there were generally similar patterns of behavior and structures during the period of actual colonial rule, German colonial rule was characterized by a tendency to take more radical positions—and in all likelihood this was not restricted to the field of colonial policy.

A second answer to the question concerning the distinctiveness and peculiarity of the German colonialism could be made directly: it was above all the overwhelming absence of German colonial rule which characterized German colonialism. This finding presents a challenge for researchers in the coming years. Were there repercussions from the special constellation of a long period of colonialism without colonies and a short imperial phase for the course of German history and, if so, what were they?[39] Was it the "backwardness" which generated the mercantile, scientific political energies, which increased the virulence of the colonial discourse?[40] Did the shock effects triggered by the "expropriation" in 1919 outweigh this sudden turnaround from power to powerlessness?[41] Did the German colonialism without colonies contribute to the German hubris because Germany did not have the experience that their power was limited in everyday colonial life?[42] What effect did the absence of this phase of decolonization, the absence of a meaningful discussion with the colonized nations, the almost non-existent migration into German cities have upon German policies and societies? Did it strengthen German "provincialism?" (Erich Kästner criticized, ironically, Bertolt Brecht's Song Surabaya-Johnny in 1930: "You speak of colonies, / Johnny, sunny Johnny,/ and you only know Berlin.")[43] Or did one come to terms with it; did not sections of the German elite feel, like Kästner, "relieved?" Thomas Mann responded in 1927 to a questionnaire sent to two hundred important personages in regard to the question of whether Germany needed colonies: "the idea of freedom and of self-determination has awakened everywhere, and will nowhere retire. I believe that events have taught us to perceive our freedom from the colonial baggage as an advantage."[44] It is especially regrettable that the contemporary critique of colonialism has still not received much attention.[45] And finally, what effects did the colonial amnesia, the creation of the myth that Germany had never actively pursued colonies, have after 1945 in the relationship of both German states to the "Third World?"[46]

Academic Ardor?

Even though the epoch of colonial rule was short, colonial topics and mentalities continue to have a lasting effect. Explicit positive references to the colonial period were a persistent feature of post-1945 German society, as evidenced, for example, in the names given to army bases. Some implicit patterns in popular culture or in perceptions of "foreigners" and "the foreign" are also relics of the colonial experience. But it is important to note that these were often drawn not from a specific German but rather from a European reservoir. During the years 1870–1918 as well as during the Weimar Republic, Germany's cultural avant-garde generally refrained from any form of involvement in its own national colonialism: it was "Surabaya Johnny" rather than "Kiaochow Johnny." If German cultural elites were engaged with colonial issues, then their inspiration came mainly from French and British literature—or even Dutch colonialism.[47]

Alongside the need to contextualize German colonialism within the larger framework of European colonialism, a further issue warrants closer consideration: how influential was the firsthand and secondhand experience with colonies? Especially many American scholars have emphasized the importance of colonialism for German history.[48] There is a tendency here to label nearly every form of illegitimate rule, every informal perception of the exotic "colonial" and to say the Germans have a rich—or perhaps one should say, a catastrophic—colonial legacy. This is a problematic overextension, as it underestimates the different contexts in which colonial effects were just one factor among others. More telling would be an analysis of the interplay of all these factors to determine in what constellations colonial topics were activated, by which actors, and for what purposes. For example, during the Weimar Republic blacks were seen in new roles that transcended colonial stereotypes. As jazz become more popular in Germany in the second half of the 1920s, not only Afro-Americans but also Afro-Germans performed as jazz musicians and as dancers. Although they still served as a surface onto which the political right could project Social Darwinist scenarios of degeneration, the coordinates of those visions changed, with blacks now also decried by the right—or lauded by others—as embodiments of the dynamics of modernity.

Sometimes categories are being stretched to breaking point also by the entry of the post-structuralist turn in colonial studies. As Frederick Cooper recently admonished, "looking for a 'textual colonization' or a 'metaphoric constellation' distinct from the institutions through which colonial power is exercised risks making colonialism appear everywhere—and hence nowhere."[49] His message is a call for a more nuanced and constructive approach, a call for greater conceptual clarity. A similar confusion can be found in sections of German pedagogy. These teachers see their challenge no longer in producing a "multi-cultural" society of immigrants, but rather a post-colonial society of immigrants.[50] This narrowing of the processes of globalization to a problem resulting from colonialism represents a reduction of complexity. It fails to acknowledge the distinctiveness of German immigration with its own traditions, especially in comparison to Great Britain and France, and thus misses the peculiarities of the German colonial past. In all likelihood, this oversubscription is a response to the neglect over many decades of colonial themes.[51] Despite German colonialism having been for a long time only considered a footnote of German history, now it is supposed to have initiated a thorough transformation or even to have functioned as a laboratory for the National Socialist expansionist and racial policies.

It is to be feared that through such blurring of contours the concept "colonialism" will lose its ability to clarify and explain. This tendency will lead to conceiving of the colonial topos as an absolute, in other words, to taking the colonial experience out of its context. We will lose sight too quickly of the boundaries of colonial experiences or the boundaries of the normalization of racism. Sonja Levsen provides a good example of what is meant here in her study of the students in Cambridge and Tübingen between 1900 and 1929.[52] Students in Cambridge came to define their identities through British imperial power. Accordingly, although in 1909 there were only a hundred students from the Commonwealth, an "Indian Problem" developed, that is, an increasing exclusion of Indian students. In contrast, imperial pride and prejudice were not important for German students. Colonies played no role in the formation of their identities; there were no "colored" students and they let out their racist resentments vis-à-vis their Jewish fellow students. Clearly, German colonialism played only a subordinate role in the formation of a racist consciousness, at least among these elites. For the development of a colonial habitus among the social elite, the colonialism would never have sufficed. The colonies played an important role, to be sure, in the discussion concerning new civil rights, as Dieter Gosewinkel was able to show. Decisive, however, was the exclusion vis-à-vis Poles and Jews.[53] It would be desirable if the research into the history of colonialism would increasingly pay more attention to the multi-causality of developments which were speeding up and which were compressed, especially after 1900.

We need finally once again to question and investigate how long-lasting the racist patterns of interpretations, stereotypes, and references actually were. We still do not have a systematic understanding of the abiding stability and the historical transformations of the idea of foreignness and of the power constellations and racist ideas which underlay this idea. How, for example, did the rules concerning what one could say publicly and privately about "race" change between 1871 and 1990?[54] Germans have made much acquaintance in the course of the twentieth century with "foreigners," in part through National Socialism.[55] How this worked in practice has not really been much investigated. That the colonial discourse or the colonial paradigm played a significant role here can be doubted. Yet more research is needed.

Sounding out the colonial or imperial dimension in German history is a vital and crucial task. We need to ask about the mechanisms of perception or non-perception of colonialism in Germany and to investigate how deeply it influenced political thought, political and social practices, and the cultural identity of the Germans, from the elites to the middle class to the lower classes. When writing German imperial history from this point it will be a challenge to bring together the two strands which are so in opposition to each other—the history of the colonized and the history of the colonizers—and to disband the constant role of the non-Europeans as extras on the colonial scenery.

Notes

1. Most recently H.-U. Wehler, "Transnationale Geschichte – der neue Königsweg historischer Forschung?" in *Transnationale Geschichte: Themen, Tendenzen und Theorien*, eds. G. Budde et al. (Göttingen, 2006), 161–74.
2. S. Conrad, *Deutsche Kolonialgeschichte* (Munich, 2008); H. Gründer, *Geschichte der deutschen Kolonien* (Paderborn: 2000); B. Kundrus (regional ed.), "Section: Germany," in P. Poddar, R. S. Patke, and L. Jensen (main eds.), *A Historical Companion to Postcolonial Literatures – Continental Europe and its Empires* (Edinburgh, 2008), 198–259; D. van Laak, *Über alles in der Welt: Deutscher Imperialismus im 19. und 20. Jahrhundert* (Munich, 2005); W. Speitkamp, *Deutsche Kolonialgeschichte* (Stuttgart, 2005).
3. J. Zimmerer, "The Birth of the 'Ostland' out of the Spirit of Colonialism: A Postcolonial Perspective on Nazi Policy of Conquest and Extermination," *Patterns of Prejudice* 2 (39), (2005), 197–219; B. Kundrus, "Continuities, parallels, receptions: Reflections on the 'colonization' of National Socialism," *Journal of Namibian Studies* 4(1), (2008), 25–46.
4. A. Honold and O. Simons, eds., *Kolonialismus als Kultur: Literatur, Medien, Wissenschaft in der deutschen Gründerzeit des Fremden* (Tübingen, 2002); A. Honold and K.R. Scherpe, eds., *Mit Deutschland um die Welt: Eine Kulturgeschichte des Fremden in der Kolonialzeit* (Stuttgart, 2004); B. Kundrus, ed., *Phantasiereiche: Zur Kulturgeschichte des deutschen Kolonialismus* (Frankfurt, 2003).
5. S. Conrad and J. Osterhammel. "Einleitung," in *Das Kaiserreich transnational: Deutschland in der Welt 1871–1914*, eds. Conrad and Osterhammel (Göttingen, 2004), 16.
6. H. Uerlings, "Kolonialer Diskurs, Globalisierung und postkoloniale Analyse," in *(Post-)Kolonialismus und deutsche Literatur. Impulse der angloamerikanischen Literatur- und Kulturtheorie*, ed. A. Dunker (Bielefeld, 2005), 17–44, here 17.
7. S. Friedrichsmeyer et al., eds., *The Imperialist Imagination: German Colonialism and Its Legacy* (Ann Arbor, 1998).
8. P. Mazon and R. Steingrover, eds., *Not So Plain as Black and White: Afro-German Culture and History, 1890–2000* (Rochester, 2005).
9. S. Zantop, *Colonial Fantasies: Conquest, Family, and Nation in Precolonial Germany, 1770–1870* (Durham, NC, 1997).
10. J. Schöning, ed., *Triviale Tropen: Exotische Reise- und Abenteuerfilme aus Deutschland 1919–1933* (Munich, 1997).
11. P. Grosse, *Kolonialismus, Eugenik und bürgerliche Gesellschaft in Deutschland 1850–1918* (Frankfurt, 2000); H.G. Penny and M. Bunzl, eds., *Worldly Provincialism: German Anthropology in the Age of Empire* (Ann Arbor, 2003); A. Zimmerman, *Anthropology and Antihumanism in Imperial Germany* (Chicago, 2001).
12. W.U. Eckart, *Medizin und Kolonialimperialismus: Deutschland 1884–1945* (Paderborn, 1997).
13. D. Ciarlo, *Advertising Empire: Race and Visual Culture in Imperial Germany* (Harvard, 2011).
14. U. van der Heyden and J. Zeller, eds., *Kolonialmetropole Berlin: Eine Spurensuche* (Berlin, 2002).
15. H.-J. Fischer, *Die deutschen Kolonien. Die koloniale Rechtsordnung und ihre Entwicklung nach dem Ersten Weltkrieg* (Berlin, 2001).
16. D. van Laak, *Imperiale Infrastruktur: Deutsche Planungen für eine Erschließung Afrikas 1880 bis 1960* (Paderborn, 2004).
17. See the essays in A. Epple and D. Wierling, eds., "Globale Waren," *Werkstattgeschichte* 45 (16), (2007).
18. F. Bösch, "Are we a cruel nation? Colonial Practices, Perceptions and Scandals," in D. Geppert and R. Gerwarth, eds., *Wilhelmine Germany and Edwardian Britain: Essays on Cultural Affinity* (Oxford, 2008), 115–42.
19. I. Hull, *Absolute Destruction: Military Culture and the Practices of War in Imperial Germany* (Ithaca, 2004).
20. N. Badenberg, "Spiel um Kamerun: Kolonialismus in Brett- und Gesellschaftsspielen," in Honold and Scherpe, *Mit Deutschland um die Welt* (2004), 86–94.

21. L. Wildenthal, *German Women for Empire, 1884–1945* (Durham, 2001).
22. C. Geulen, "The Common Grounds of Conflict: Racial Visions of World Order 1880–1940," in *Competing Visions of World Order: Global Moments and Movements 1880s–1930s*, eds. S. Conrad and D. Sachsenmaier (New York, 2007), 29–68.
23. M. Perraudin and J. Zimmerer, eds., *German Colonialism and National Identity* (London, 2009).
24. Conrad and Osterhammel. *Kaiserreich transnational*, 19.
25. M. Fitzpatrick, *Liberal Imperialism in Germany: Expansionism and Nationalism, 1848–1884* (New York, 2008).
26. M. Fuhrmann, *Der Traum vom deutschen Orient: Zwei deutsche Kolonien im Osmanischen Reich 1851–1918* (Frankfurt, 2006).
27. E.-W. Pöppinghaus, *Moralische Eroberungen? Kultur und Politik in den deutsch-spanischen Beziehungen der Jahre 1919 bis 1933* (Frankfurt, 1999).
28. P. Ther. "Imperial Instead of National History: Positioning Modern German History on the Map of European Empires," in *Imperial Rule*, eds. A. Miller and A. Rieber (Budapest, 2004), 47–68.
29. S. Conrad, *Globalisierung und Nation im Deutschen Kaiserreich* (Munich, 2006), 29. See also R.L. Nelson, ed., *Germans, Poland, and Colonial Expansion to the East: 1850 Through the Present* (Houndmills, 2009).
30. D. Blackbourn, "Das Kaiserreich transnational. Eine Skizze," in *Kaiserreich transnational*, eds. Conrad and Osterhammel (2004), 302–24, here 322. See also Blackbourn, *The Conquest of Nature: Water, Landscape and the Making of Modern Germany* (London, 2006), chapter 5.
31. Kundrus, Continuities; H.W. Smith, *The Continuities of German History. Nation, Religion, and Race across the Long Nineteenth Century* (Cambridge, 2008), and the reviews on http://www.sehepunkte.de/2009/01/forum/mehrfachbesprechung-brhelmut-walser-smith-the-continuities-of-german-history-61, especially the critique by Dieter Langewiesche: *Wie Helmut Walser Smith Kontinuitätslinien in der deutschen Geschichte erzeugt und was dabei verloren geht.*
32. M. Mazower, *Hitler's Empire. Nazi Rule in Occupied Europe* (London, 2008).
33. G. Ritter, *Lebendige Vergangenheit. Beiträge zur historisch-politischen Selbstbesinnung* (Munich, 1958), 152.
34. H.L. Wesseling, *The European Colonial Empires, 1815–1919* (Harlow, 2004).
35. J. Osterhammel, *Die Verwandlung der Welt: Eine Geschichte des 19. Jahrhunderts* (Munich, 2009), 662–72.
36. A. Eckert, *Herrschen und Verwalten. Afrikanische Bürokratien, staatliche Ordnung und Politik in Tanzania, 1920–1970* (Munich, 2007).
37. M. Pesek, *Koloniale Herrschaft in Deutsch-Ostafrika. Expeditionen, Militär und Verwaltung seit 1880* (Frankfurt, 2005).
38. G. Steinmetz, *The Devil's Handwriting: Precoloniality and the German Colonial State in Qingdao, Samoa, and Southwest Africa* (Chicago, 2007).
39. P. Grosse, "What does German Colonialism have to do with National Socialism. A Conceptual Framework," in *Germany's Colonial Pasts*, eds. E. Ames et al. (Lincoln, 2005), 115–34.
40. Dunker, "Einleitung," in Dunker, *(Post-)Kolonialismus*, S. 14.
41. W. Struck, "'Ein renegatisches Machtabenteuer unter den Negern.' Der phantasierte Kolonialismus der literarischen Moderne in Deutschland," in Dunker, *(Post-)Kolonialismus* (2005), 179–202, here 195–96.
42. F. Cooper, *Colonialism in Question. Theory, Knowledge, History* (Berkeley, 2005), 183.
43. E. Kästner, "Surabaya-Johnny II. Frei nach Kipling und Brecht," in Kästner, *Wir sind so frei. Chansons, Kabarett, Kleine Prosa*, ed. by H. Kurzke (Munich, 1998), 334–35.
44. Th. Mann, in *Europäische Gespräche. Hamburger Monatshefte für Auswärtige Politik* 5 (1927), 626.
45. M.-T. Schwarz, *"Je weniger Afrika, desto besser." Die deutsche Kolonialkritik am Ende des 19. Jahrhunderts. Eine Untersuchung zur kolonialen Haltung von Linksliberalismus und Sozialdemokratie* (Frankfurt, 1999). See by contrast the eight volume series edited by P.J. Cain, *The Empire and its Critics, 1899–1939. The Classics of Imperialism* (London, 1998). Just published: Benedikt Stuchtey, *Die Europäische Expansion und ihre Feinde. Kolonialismuskritik vom 18. bis in das 20. Jahrhundert* (München, 2010).

46. See the essays in A. Kruke, "Dekolonisation: Prozesse und Verflechtungen" (1945–1990), *Archiv für Sozialgeschichte* 48, (2008).
47. Struck, *Machtabenteuer*, 179–80.
48. U.G. Poiger, "Imperialism as Paradigm for Modern German History," in *Conflict, Catastrophe and Continuity: Essays on Modern German History*, eds. F. Biess, M. Roseman, and H. Schissler (New York, 2007), 177–99. Astutely argued is P. Gilroy, *After Empire: Melancholia or Convivial Culture* (Oxford, 2004).
49. Cooper, *Colonialism*, 47.
50. Kolonialismus bis heute? *Politisches Lernen* (2006), 1–2 (24).
51. The question has also been raised as to whether the British Empire, even at the height of its power, was as constitutive for British culture and the lives of most British citizens as has often been asserted. B. Porter, *The Absent-Minded Imperialists. Empire, Society, and Culture in Britain* (Oxford, 2004).
52. S. Levsen, *Elite, Männlichkeit und Krieg. Tübinger und Cambridger Studenten 1900–1929* (Göttingen, 2006), 150–71.
53. D. Gosewinkel, *Einbürgern und Ausschließen. Die Nationalisierung der Staatsangehörigkeit vom Deutschen Bund bis zur Bundesrepublik Deutschland* (Göttingen, 2001).
54. H. Fehrenbach, *Race after Hitler. Black Occupation Children in Postwar Germany and America* (Princeton, 2005).
55. K.K. Patel, Analysen und Alternativen – Der Nationalsozialismus in transnationaler Perspektive, *Blätter für deutsche und internationale Politik* 9 (49), (2004), 1123–34.

Chapter 18

The Kaiserreich as a Society of Migration

Thomas Mergel

Historians have only gradually become aware of the degree of mobility in nineteenth century society. This holds especially true with respect to imperial Germany—its society is perceived as being notoriously static among traditional social historians. Yet millions of Germans emigrated out of Germany, and hundreds of thousands of non-Germans, perhaps even more, either temporarily or permanently immigrated during this period. Internal migration, which mobilized a large section of the German population, took place on an even greater scale, yet remained largely unnoticed for a long time. Indeed, there was considerable movement within the authoritarian fabric of the Kaiserreich.

There was scant mention of these processes in works such as Hans-Ulrich Wehler's *The German Empire* (1973); the reason for this, however, is not to be found in a supposed ignorance on behalf of the author, but in the fact that not much research had been conducted in this area up to that point. It was not until the second half of the 1970s that a school of sociohistorical migration research arose which footed on systematic deliberations—sociological or demographical—that had been formulated in the seventies.[1] Migrational history, as a discipline, has witnessed a veritable boom since the 1980s. Out of the approximately 3,900 titles that the Berlin State Library lists under the keyword "migration," 2,900 appeared after 1980, a third of which were published in the twenty-first century. In Germany, migrational history is primarily associated with the Osnabruck-based historian Klaus Bade.[2] Bade had stressed colonial emigration in a study of German colonial policy from 1975; his professorial dissertation from 1979 examined the transnational and internal migration in northeastern Germany up until 1914.[3] He was the first to follow in the footsteps of American and English studies, systematically investigating the structures of migration as a substantial corollary of industrial society. It would not be far-fetched to assume that this amounted to a historicization of a contemporary phenomenon, namely the immigration into the European and North American welfare states and the breaking-up of national societies after the Second World War. The boom in migrational history is a response to the contemporaneous political discussion concerning the degree to which the rich societies of the West are immigrant societies, and to what extent migration is to be understood as a permanent phenomenon instead of a temporary one. Klaus Bade had always stressed that migration was not merely a current phenomenon; history is always also the history of migration. These movements, however, do not follow a continual pattern. The nineteenth century brought with it a tremendous intensification, and imperial Germany in particular was characterized by extensive movement, far stronger than in the decades that followed. Migrational history can reveal a great deal about the internal structures of the Kaiserreich, both as a sociohistorical phenomenon as well as an object for the study of authority.

It is therefore no surprise that the third volume of Wehler's *Deutsche Gesellschaftsgeschichte* (1995) dealt with this issue extensively.[4] Wehler emphasizes the extent of change and the impositions and demands on those affected. He describes how different migratory streams were intertwined with each other— emigration to the United States, for example, simply cannot be adequately conceived of without factoring in the enormous internal migratory movements that took place inside Germany. One of the key findings is that in many ways, the extent of migration did not differ from "American" conditions. This chapter will investigate the effect these processes of mobilization have on our understanding of the Kaiserreich. What are the implications with regard to social conflicts and the political order, and what is their meaning in terms of historical experience? These issues will be discussed by looking at the three most important migratory processes: transnational emigration, internal migration, and immigration.

I. Emigration

Unlike temporary labor migration, which regularly transcended national boundaries and often had long regional traditions,[5] permanent emigration in Germany only began to develop in the early nineteenth century. The number of emigrants increased dramatically as a result of the great agrarian crisis of 1816–17. The 1840s saw the beginning of a European-wide boom that led to tens of millions of Europeans emigrating overseas up until the beginning of the First World War.[6] Approximately 8.5 million Europeans emigrated to the United States alone. Germany played no small part in this: 1.1 million Germans emigrated between 1846 and 1857. Roughly one million left in a second wave (1864–73), peaking at 1.8 million between 1880 and 1893. All in all, approximately 2.85 million people emigrated overseas during the period of the Kaiserreich. These waves of emigration were part of the first surge of globalization, which resulted in an enormous increase in worldwide economic integration in the last third of the nineteenth century.[7]

Although quite large in absolute terms, the numbers of German emigrants do not appear to be particularly prominent when compared to those of other European nations, especially when these numbers are seen relative to their populations as a whole. Whilst the average number of Germans emigrating annually was anywhere between 0.1 and 0.3 percent of the entire population, emigration rates were two to three times as high in England and Austria-Hungary shortly before the First World War. In each year of the mid-1880s, Ireland saw almost 1.5 percent of its population emigrating; Italy experienced even higher emigration rates before the First World War. These rates were up to ten times as high as those in Germany.

Alongside these movements, however, there existed a long tradition of temporary labor migration—often neglected—that saw Germans working in neighboring countries. Roughly one hundred and twenty thousand Germans worked in France at the onset of the First World War, a quarter of which worked in Paris.[8] They worked in construction, as service staff, or as streetcleaners. In Switzerland, there was a steep increase in the percentage of Germans from the 1880s onwards. Approximately two hundred and twenty thousand Germans were employed there in 1910, working in construction, crafts, and tourism. There existed long-standing regional traditions such as the migration of Lippian brickworkers to Holland every year. This migration had been taking place since the seventeenth century, and despite its cessation in the nineteenth century, it gave rise to a migratory tradition that saw about a quarter of all male adults from Lippe employed as migrant laborers on the eve of the First World War, most of whom worked in the brick trade.[9] Germans also made up one-third of the French Foreign Legion. Incidentally, roughly half of all foreign legionnaires were men from Alsace-Lorraine who did not want to absolve their military service in Germany.[10]

An important characteristic of all these migrations was that they were predominantly migrations of males. This was one of the significant differences compared to the early modern transatlantic settlement migrations: most of the emigrants were jobseekers, who, unlike families, were very flexible when it came to accommodating themselves to local labor markets. This mobility also required information, which became available not only through a dense letter-writing culture, but also through very detailed newspaper reports and personal transnational networks. Migrants were thus not travelling into the unknown; people in Hamburg or London knew exactly how much could be earned in various professions in New York. Around 1900, many a job seeker nonchalantly calculated how much a trip across the Atlantic would earn him, quite possibly turning his attention elsewhere in a year or two. Hence there existed a transatlantic labor market which, incidentally, caused approximately one-third of German emigrants to America to return before the First World War, and some of them did this several times over.[11] One must keep this mobility in mind when considering the influence of migratory experience upon the Kaiserreich. After all, these emigrants did not simply vanish from the purview of their relatives, as they communicated with them quite intensely through letters or in conversations upon their return. Migration was a normal experience for the Germans, and many of them participated in this experience.

Most recent findings—which can only briefly be summarized here—have either relativized older conceptions or expelled these into the realm of myths. This applies to two areas in particular:

1. The classic uprooting thesis has proven itself to be false. Contrary to being the "uprooted" in Oscar Handlin's sense, migrants were jobseekers with a high degree of mobility. Most of them were chain migrants who were well informed—often through solicitors or agencies, but also through personal relationships—and knew what they were getting themselves into. Of the German emigrants to the United States, 95 percent traveled either to relatives or acquaintances! These ever-improving personal relationships led to a rapid decrease in the importance of emigration agencies in the 1880s, whose role was essentially reduced to selling tickets on behalf of shipping companies.[12] Quite often, an emigrant would spur others on to do the same thing. It was therefore no coincidence that the majority of emigrants from Cottbus went to southern Australia; a pioneer migrant had dared to undertake the adventure, sending back positive news. An agency specializing in Australia directed the stream that followed in this direction. Two-thirds of emigrants to America from the district of Arnswalde (East Elbia) went to Wisconsin for similar reasons.[13] Even in the provinces people were thus quite well aware of what it looked like beyond the horizon.

2. Contrary to the popular thesis concerning American society, the destination was not transformed into a "melting pot" as a result of these migratory structures. Rather, newly arriving emigrants often sought out what was customary to them. They settled in ethnically or nationally familiar milieus, as Kathleen Conzen has convincingly demonstrated in her pioneering study on Milwaukee.[14] In Ohio, a destination for many emigrants from Germany's northwest, Low German (*Plattdeutsch*) was the everyday language up until the First World War, and the inhabitants of New Bremen and Minster made fun of the dialects spoken in their respective neighboring towns.[15] The Germans, who predominantly came from the provinces, often only became aware of their national affiliation after arriving at their destination: only here did immigrants from Helmstedt and Biberach notice that they had things in common. Labor migrants thus did not automatically become integrated members of society wherever they moved, yet they shed themselves of their parochial background and increasingly perceived themselves and each other as Germans. The decisive element in all this was language, which signalized an affiliation that could also transcend national boundaries. In Brazil, the Swiss and Germans thus perceived each other as Germans—in the sense of German-speaking Europeans—and came to develop a shared sense of community vis-à-vis the indigenous population.[16] Accordingly, the rate of endogamy was very high: between 80 to 90 percent of Germans married other Germans.

II. Internal Migration

Internal migration in Germany increased tremendously within the context of industrialization and urbanization. Wolfgang Köllmann has described it as being the "greatest mass movement in German history," and rightly so.[17] Agricultural workers, small farmers, and rural manual laborers moved to the industrial regions in droves, not simply because the wages were higher, but also because they were paid in cash and there was far less social control. Statistics on urbanization reveal the true extent of mobility, albeit at second glance.[18] Between 1880 and 1890 the population of Chemnitz, an industrial city in Saxony and a pulsating center of machine-building, grew by 44,000, increasing by a half (it had 100,000 inhabitants in 1883). However, these numbers describe merely the surface of the massive movements into the cities and out of them. Whilst 260,000 people moved to Chemnitz, 227,000 left it during the same period. The total volume of migration was roughly eleven times as high as the net population and almost fifteen times higher than pure net migration. This implies a quasi-nomadic level of mobility among contemporaries. In search of work, they would move to a city and often move away again after a short period. They lacked the time and security necessary to build up a household, and the fact that rental agreements in cities such as Frankfurt (Main) were often limited to one month is suggestive of the degree of fluctuation among the population.

This applied to most industrial cities. Berlin counts among the most notable examples; its total population grew by 950,000 between 1880 and 1910, effectively doubling in size, whereas the total volume of migration exceeded 11.3 million. The largest industrial cities thus acted as huge sluices for an enormously mobile mass of people—predominantly from lower social strata—passing through at great speed. As many as 40 percent of Berlin's population changed residence in 1895. In Bochum, only 36.5 percent of inhabitants were long-time residents in 1907: 40 percent were migrants from nearby, and almost one-quarter came from far away.[19] Despite a reduction in the speed of these developments at the beginning of the twentieth century, West German industrial cities still registered annual net accession rates of 15–17 percent in the years before the First World War.[20] In terms of speed and structural transformations, the growth of these cities is on a par with that of the widely discussed American cities during this time. The process of urbanization in Germany—which, compared to other large European countries, began much later—gathered a unique momentum by the end of the century. The speed of migration only began to slow down during the First World War, eventually grinding to a halt in the 1930s. Only the second or third generation of these lower-class migrants would become sedentary.

With these migrants, too, it became apparent that they did not fit the familiar image of the immigrant or emigrant without reservations. For one, these people were usually migrants who were merely passing through, either as industrial migrants looking for work (with a high degree of fluctuation) or as migrants on a stopover in the big cities before going abroad. It should not be assumed that the majority followed a strategic plan. Looking for work, they either wandered to the nearest large city or were put on a train to a remote industrial center by an agent. If they were unsuccessful—as indeed many were—they would turn to the next destination, which either meant moving on to the next city or venturing the trip to America, but it could also mean returning home. Such a decision often depended on how strong the ties were to their home, the availability of information about the country of destination, and the established contacts there.

What is often overlooked, however, is that there were also many seasonal migrants traveling between the countryside and cities. Hundreds of thousands lived this way: they resided in cottages in the countryside, where they cultivated a small patch of land. In springtime they came to the city, looking for work and living the life of a so-called bed lodger, who, instead of renting a room, merely rented a bed which often had to be shared with others. The countryside, with its structures of solidarity, and where there was possibly a wife who cultivated the garden, served as an appealing niche of retreat, not only because it was cheaper to live there during winter, but also in case of failure in one's endeavors. This form of internal migration was not linear but circular. James Jackson Jr. has argued that this movement increased in both directions.[21] Focusing on unidirectional migration into the city alone therefore obscures the view for migration out of the city, which was also of a temporary nature. Therefore mobilization—and not urbanization—can be identified as *the* central movement: between one-quarter and one-third of the urban population only lived in the city temporarily.

Internal migration came to exceed transnational emigration in its scope over time. As Germany transformed into an industrial power, many considered staying in the country and heading for the industrial areas to be more lucrative than traveling abroad to the United States. The overall distances covered during internal migration increased accordingly, as people no longer simply moved to the nearest big city but instead headed for the industrial areas in Saxony or the Ruhr, with clear intentions. As a result of this gigantic mobilization, by 1907 half of all Germans no longer lived in their place of birth, and one-third lived outside their state or province. Between sixteen and seventeen million Germans crossed borders this way, and 20–40 percent of the urban population came from the countryside; internal migration can thus also be understood as a big machine that industrialized the rural population.[22] The implications are equally difficult to envision: a significant part of the urban population was composed of newcomers. They lived the life they knew from the countryside, which could mean that they kept pigs in their apartments, or that they transferred rural forms of leisure or rural cultures of violence into an urban setting.[23]

Prussian Poles and Masurians made up the largest group of this sort in Germany. They had been recruited to the Ruhr area as industrial workers because the regional labor reservoir no longer sufficed.[24] The Poles were not the only immigrants in the Ruhr. Coal miners from England and Ireland settled in Herne and Gelsenkirchen in the wake of investments in coal mines there by English and Irish companies around 1850. The names given to these coal mines—Shamrock

(Herne) and Hibernia (Gelsenkirchen)—are far from incidental. There was even an English school in Herne.[25] The dimensions of Polish labor migration to the West, however, outdid all other movements across Europe. Their numbers had already increased from forty thousand in 1880 to three hundred and thirty thousand by 1900. Approximately half a million Poles and Masurians lived in the Ruhr area shortly before the First World War, which amounted to one-tenth of the population and one-fifth of the industrial workforce. They also largely came from the countryside, and although they were Prussian citizens, they spoke Polish, and the Poles (unlike the Masurians) were Catholic.

The Ruhr has been called "Germany's America."[26] Indeed, the structural similarities between Germany and the United States in terms of processes of migration and thus also processes of urbanization are striking. In both cases, an agrarian population was integrated into an industrial, urban society. In neither case are we dealing with uprooted people; these were migrant colonies with a high degree of social coherence that reconverged according to ethnic and regional criteria, provided its members had not already previously been channeled into the coal mines through local networks. Another commonality is that, despite the alleged emergence of a new "Ruhr people" (*Ruhrvolk*) consisting of the various ethnic groups—something postulated by theoreticians of the Ruhr such as Wilhelm Brepohl—the Ruhr area did not become a "melting pot."[27] The Poles largely kept to themselves, and the fact that they developed parallel, separate Catholic associations of their own is testimony to this: there were Polish rosary brotherhoods, Polish gentlemen's clubs, Polish prayer groups, and a Polish workers' union.[28] The sociocultural distances corresponded to the political distrust on behalf of the Prussian state, which kept migrants under surveillance, despite the fact that they too were Prussian citizens. It also prohibited the hiring of Polish clerics and the use of the Polish language, because it feared a strengthening of the Polish national movement. This in turn led to secondary nationalization among the diaspora, a phenomenon that can similarly be observed among Irish immigrants in the United States: Poles only came to experience the meaning of being Polish as a result of segregation and discrimination. The weakness of the "melting pot" also became apparent after the First World War: a significant number of Ruhr Poles either returned to Poland or headed to the industrial areas in the north of France. At the end of the Weimar Republic, the Polish colony in the Ruhr had shrunk to one-third of its original size.

III. Immigration

This internal migration was a consequence of a large-scale restructuring of workplace geography in Germany, away from an agrarian economy with centers of craft and cottage industries, and toward industrial centers and growing cities with centralizing functions. It was accompanied by various waves of emigration, which, combined with internal migration, acted as a valve for the oversupply of labor which still existed in Germany. By the mid-1890s, however, the pendulum had swung in the other direction: the demand for labor began to permanently outweigh the supply. Germany, which had become the third largest industrialized nation worldwide, was being transformed from a country of emigration into a country of immigration. Moreover, it became the second largest importer of labor in the world (behind the United States) up until the First World War.

Although it never reached the sheer mass-character of emigration and internal migration, immigration was also a movement of enormous dimensions. According to official Reich statistics from 1907, 3.6 percent of Germany's workforce was born abroad—this figure was only again surpassed in 1963![29] In addition to this, however, one must also consider the number of unknown cases. According to an official estimate from 1914 there were about 1.2 million foreign workers in Germany at that time, and this figure probably underestimates the scope of seasonal work in the countryside and the number of temporary migrants. One could therefore proceed on the assumption that approximately 5 percent of the workforce comprised people from abroad. These numbers would only be reached again in the second half of the 1960s.

Two-thirds of the immigrants were employed in industry, and a large proportion of foreign workers came from neighboring countries: German-speaking Austrians composed one-quarter of all foreign workers in industry and were often sought out for technical jobs that required certain qualifications. Another quarter came from northern Italy, where a stable tradition of chain migration had developed in Friuli and Venetia. There were roughly two hundred and twenty thousand of them before the First World War, predominantly employed in mining and construction. Italians were a familiar fixture on large construction sites across Europe.[30] Like other groups of migrants, they were generally temporary labor migrants who remained in their place of employment for several months or years and would often travel back to their native land (especially during winter), where the inflow of German wages became a decisive component of the local economy. René del Fabbro has demonstrated how the regional economic structures in Friuli underwent fundamental changes under the influence of migration: pauperized mountain towns, from which the young men had once departed in droves, eventually became so wealthy that they began lending money to those towns which previously had been much wealthier (they had since fallen behind in economic terms because they had no need for emigration). New, spruce houses were built, and under the influence of the migrants, a previously unknown consumer culture emerged, with an upscale, "finer" form of alcohol consumption, and women who smoked and wore Bavarian garbs which their husbands had brought back for them.[31]

They too were highly mobile people who did not simply remain glued to their destination. Luigi Brodevini's path led him to Bielefeld in 1899 before the Venetian construction worker moved to Annen near Dortmund in 1900–1901 and traveled to South Africa in 1902. One year later, he returned to Europe—to Köflach in Styria, where brown coal was being mined—and eventually landed in Haltern, in the northern part of the Ruhr area in 1904.[32] All the same, these people were anything but worldly global players; they were shaped by the province in their country of origin, and this remained so. Only slowly did they, and the Italians in particular, lose their provincial gaze, their *campanilismo*. Migration often took the form of a group activity: a few men would leave their town together, arrive at a destination together and eventually depart again as a group. It seems likely that a confined mental horizon and the experience of isolation at the destination complemented each other. These labor migrants did not integrate themselves into the receiving societies. They lived in barracks and remained amongst themselves. Their main goal was to earn as much money as possible in the shortest amount of time. This is why Italians did not have a good reputation amongst German workers: they were considered to be strike-breakers and workers who would work for any wage. As they came from the agrarian provinces, they hardly thought in terms of class affiliation, and unionizing them was nigh impossible. Moreover, due to the fact that almost half of them were illiterate, it was easy for the proud German Social Democrat to develop a sense of superiority towards his foreign colleagues. International solidarity was a luxury one had to be able to afford, and this also applied to the working class.

One-third of foreign workers were employed in agriculture, which can be seen as an indirect result of internal migration or, more precisely, the exodus of the indigenous agricultural workforce into the industrial centers. Foreigners were predominantly hired for seasonal work in the agrarian border regions. In 1871, there were approximately twenty to thirty thousand Scandinavians—especially Danes and Swedes—working as farm hands or in construction in Schleswig-Holstein. They acted as compensation for the agricultural workers from Schleswig-Holstein who moved to the industrial centers.[33] But the employment of foreign agricultural workers was most pronounced in East Elbia: since the foundation of the empire, the necessity for people (*Leutenot*) had become an existential threat to the estate system here.[34] The Prussian Poles now no longer flocked to East Elbia for agricultural work, as they increasingly traveled farther to work in West German industry, which they found to be much more lucrative. At the same time, however, there existed a reservoir of laborers in Russian and Austrian Poland which the landowners had begun to use since the early 1880s, not least because the wages there were significantly lower. Yet this interest in hiring foreign workers in large numbers stood in direct conflict with the political ruling interests in Berlin, where they feared nothing more than a Polonization of East Elbia. In order to prevent this, they even briefly considered importing coolies from China, as their assimilation was considered to be less likely. A compromise between the economic interests of the landowners and the political interests of the Prussian government was reached in the form of an infamous contract system. Amounting to little more than a slave-like system of exploitation where it was possible to get rid of people promptly when they were no longer needed (during winter), it was meant to make the exploitation of labor possible, but without the risk of people eventually settling. The essence of the system was the recruitment of workers from the Russian and Austrian parts of Poland for a specific job. Workers could not freely choose their jobs, and there were no provisions for termination on their behalf. Furthermore, they were forced to leave Germany again in the late fall.

The contract system also distorted the foreign population statistics significantly, as these were compiled annually on 1 December, by which time most Polish agricultural workers had already left the country. In actual fact, the number of foreign workers in agriculture far exceeded the three hundred thousand figure mentioned in the official statistics. The Prussian Central Office of Agricultural Workers recorded about four hundred thousand migrant workers up until 1914, yet one has to assume a significant number of unknown cases, which would increase the total number by at least 20 percent. In all probability, approximately half a million Polish migrant workers were employed in the Prussian estate system.

This dark figure sprung from a market advantage on the part of the Polish workers. The worker shortages were so severe that that many landowners were compelled to disregard the strict regulations regarding the hiring and dismissal of their workers. A worker who left his employer of his own volition was supposed to be reported to the police, prohibited from taking up another job, and promptly deported. Some landowners, however, would turn a blind eye in case of severe farm labor shortages. Nonetheless, conditions were oppressive: wages were miserable (although they were about 50 percent higher than in the Russian parts of Poland), families were torn apart, and pregnancy was grounds for dismissal.

The animosities that Poles and other migrants were confronted with emanated from an ever-increasing tendency of Germanization which the German Reich succumbed to. It was not only directed from above, but also promoted by various associations, as well as through propaganda in the media. An increasingly pronounced *völkisch* conception of Germanness developed in the last third of the nineteenth century. It provided a breeding ground for the racist radicalization which came to determine ideas of Germanness, not only before but especially after the First World War, and was further aggravated by the inclusion of the Jews who had come to the German Reich from Eastern Europe after 1880. Twenty thousand "Eastern Jews" were registered in Germany in 1890, with their numbers rising to seventy thousand in 1910. Most of them came from the Russian and Austrian parts of Poland.[35] These Jews also experienced rejection by German Jews because they were considered to be primitive and superstitious.

Last but not least, transit migration is not to be forgotten alongside these great immigratory movements. Millions of people entered Germany during the Kaiserreich with the sole purpose of leaving again via the sea ports, usually heading overseas. About three million came from Austria-Hungary and 2.3 million came from Russia—most of them illegally because emigration required an expensive permit.[36] In many cases, they too were Jews fleeing from increasing persecution, especially in Russia. In Germany, they were collected in special registry stations and promptly sent on their way. The Berlin-Ruhleben train station was the largest collection point of its sort. Although transit migrants were prohibited from entering the German capital, the stereotypical "Eastern Jew" seeped deep into the collective consciousness of Kaiserreich nationalism.

IV. The Kaiserreich Through the Lens of Migrational History

Considering these findings in a preliminary summary, the scope of migratory movements in the Kaiserreich becomes clear: almost three million emigrants, over eleven million internal migrants, far more than a million foreign workers and more than five million transit migrants. So what exactly are the implications of these findings with regard to the Kaiserreich?

Considering the political system of the bureaucratic authoritarian state, the Kaiserreich has for a long time enjoyed the reputation of being rather static. Considering what happened in terms of migration, however, one is left with the impression of a society that was extremely mobile. This society was acquainted with an enormous number of people in its midst who were on the move—both close and far—and it was also acquainted with a similarily impressive number of people coming from elsewhere. These broad experiences with migration, however, were not spread evenly throughout Germany. Large construction sites and factories, ships and ports, as well as the large estates in Eastern Elbia were among the centers of such migratory experiences. So, places of work were the primary place where such experiences were made. New social and religious cleavages opened up. Catholics moved in droves to areas that had previously been dominated by Protestants, and Polish Jews became a familiar sight on East Elbian estates with their anti-Semitic landowners and day laborers. We still know far too little about how local societies were transformed as a result of these experiences.

Class solidarity similarly eroded; immigration generally led to a process of substratification, which placed foreign workers below the Germans in terms of employment, salary, and social status. We know a good deal about the treatment of and the attitude towards migrants in the working-class movement, where foreign colleagues were more likely to be perceived as strikebreakers rather than comrades.[37] One could advance the thesis that Social Democracy's compensatory nationalism schooled itself through this everyday experience. Migrational experience and tolerance were anything but congruent.

Experience with migration was less common in small cities and villages, in areas shaped by agriculture that were dominated by medium-scale farmers. Whereas up to 10 percent of the population in the Ruhr were composed of foreigners, rural areas might have been completely unaware of it all. This also meant that there were considerable experiential disparities on a regional level when it came to encounters with strangers. The consequences of these processes of migration for the political order and the structure of political participation were equally important. One could justifiably interpret the mass emigration to the United States as "exit" instead of "voice" in Hirschman's sense: the emigrants fled from a miserable situation, not only in economic but also political terms. Although it remains speculative, the question must be posed nonetheless: what would have happened if all these emigrants had decided to stay, demanding work and political participation? It is quite conceivable that Karl Marx's vision of a revolutionary wave through the proletarian masses would have suddenly become highly relevant.

Migrations had an even greater effect on participation within German political society. The Reich Citizenship Law of 1913—which established the *jus sanguinis* principle—aimed at the homogenization of the nation-state, yet had to be applied to a heterogeneous population.[38] Both on a communal and national level, the electoral law rewarded residency: it was a general precondition that one had to be registered in one's place of residence for over one year in order to vote. Migrants— including a considerable number of internal migrants—were thus excluded from any form of political participation. Beyond this, they rarely appeared on the local political scene. Although the trade unions, the local Social Democratic chapter, or the Catholic Kolping Club were among the first institutions to which a migrant would turn, he would soon leave again, which means that it is difficult to find traces of migration in the everyday work of these institutions. The question of what this enormous degree of mobility meant for local political cultures has not been posed strenuously enough. On the one hand, we know that almost all of the workers who were responsible for transforming Social Democracy into a significant political force and life-world had firsthand experience of migration and were shaped by this experience. What, however, did it mean for the construction of local working-class culture when the local barkeeper at the inn on the corner was almost the only one who guaranteed continuity in the neighborhood? It is quite possible that these fluctuations strengthened the position of local functionaries who would still be there tomorrow. Unlike the working world, the world of political discourse largely remained untouched by the experience of, and with, migrants.

A further consequence, regarded as completely self-evident for the period after 1945, is often underestimated with regard to the Kaiserreich: the transfer of goods, lifestyles, and values. As a result of labor migrants working in construction in southern Germany, conventional forms of securing one's existence dwindled in importance. In 1900, the total sum of money labor migrants sent back home to Friuli was five times as high in value as Friuli's entire grain harvest. However, money was not the only thing being transferred: words, fashion, and customs were also included in these movements. Germany's first ice-cream parlor was opened in Munich in 1879, and Düsseldorf and Würzburg were soon to follow.[39] The extent of this transfer of goods—and the transfer of lifestyles which accompanied it—becomes apparent when one considers the fact that Germany was the largest European importer of Italian foodstuffs on the eve of the First World War. Much of this was sure to be consumed by the migrant workers themselves, but this much is clear: it did not take a wave of tourism after the Second World War to acquaint Germans with pasta and Italian ice-cream. Conversely, similar transfers can be identified with regard to German culture in Brazil and in the United States.

Finally, there is the matter of how national consciousness and affiliations were affected. If emigrants from Braunschweig and Nuremberg discovered only after arriving in the Ohio valley how much they had in common as Germans, then this amounted to a virtualization of the nation. The nation became something that could only truly be experienced in a foreign environment, away from home.

Conversely, this effect could be observed in cases where colleagues at the construction site did not belong to one's own nation, although one had perhaps known them for a long time. Everyday experiences of migration meant a new density of these experiences. Ethnic and national differences were constantly negotiated and balanced with other experiences such as class affiliation. This experiential dimension of migration in everyday life also forces us to be careful when it comes to judging these experiences as being overly positive. When conceiving of the Kaiserreich as a society of migration, we must keep in mind that we are dealing with a society that became acquainted with a completely new presence of otherness, in which large sections reacted rather defensively and with *völkisch* aggression. Radical nationalism, which finally spilled over into a great European war, took shape in the midst of this society, which had been confronted with domestic and foreign migrants to such a high degree.

Notes

1. H.-J. Hoffmann-Nowotny, *Migration. Ein Beitrag zu einer soziologischen Erklärung* (Stuttgart, 1970). H. Esser, *Aspekte der Wanderungssoziologie. Assimilation und Integration von Wanderern, ethnischen Gruppen und Minderheiten – eine handlungstheoretische Analyse* (Darmstadt, 1980).
2. K.J. Bade, *Europa in Bewegung Migration vom späten 18. Jahrhundert bis zur Gegenwart* (Munich, 1998); K.J. Bade, P.C. Emmer, L. Lucassen, J. Oltmer, eds., *Enzyklopädie Migration in Europa. Vom 17. Jahrhundert bis zur Gegenwart* (Paderborn, 2007).
3. K.J. Bade, *Friedrich Fabri und der Imperialismus in der Bismarckzeit. Revolution – Depression – Expansion* (Freiburg, 1975). Bade's postdoctoral thesis, completed in 1979, was first published online in 2005: K.J. Bade, 2005, *Land oder Arbeit? Transnationale und interne Migration im deutschen Nordosten vor dem Ersten Weltkrieg.* http://www.imis.uni-osnabrueck.de/BadeHabil.pdf (29.07.2009).
4. H.-U. Wehler, *Deutsche Gesellschaftsgeschichte. 1849–1914*, 5 vols. (Munich, 1995), vol. 3, 543–45 (on emigration), 545f. (immigration), 22f., 503–10 (internal migration).
5. For example the trek to Holland by Lippian brickworkers: P. Lourens and J. Lucassen, *Arbeitswanderung und berufliche Spezialisierung. Die lippischen Ziegler im 18. und 19. Jahrhundert* (Osnabrück, 1999).
6. For an overview: K.J. Bade, "German Transatlantic Emigration in the Nineteenth and Twentieth Centuries," in *European Expansion and Migration. Essays on the Intercontinental Migration from Africa, Asia, and Europe*, eds. P.C. Emmer and M. Mörner (New York, 1992), 121–55. Figures, unless stated otherwise, taken from I. Ferenczi and W.F. Willcox, 1929–31 (reprinted 1969), *International Migrations*, 2 vols. (1929), New York: National Bureau of Economic Research.
7. T.J. Hatton and J.G. Williamson, *The Age of Mass Migration. Causes and Economic Impact* (Oxford, 1998).
8. M. König, ed., *Deutsche Handwerker, Arbeiter und Dienstmädchen in Paris. Eine vergessene Migration im 19. Jahrhundert* (Munich, 2003).
9. Lourens and Lucassen, *Arbeitswanderung*, 44.
10. E. Michels, *Deutsche in der Fremdenlegion 1870–1965. Mythen und Realitäten* (Paderborn, 1999), 45.
11. J.D. Gould, "European Inter-Continental Emigration. The Road Home: Return Migration from the USA," *Journal of European Economic History* 9 (1) (1980), 41–112. At this time, the remigration rate in Britain amounted to up to 60 percent.
12. A. Bretting and H. Bickelmann, *Auswanderungsagenturen und Auswanderungsvereine im 19. und 20. Jahrhundert* (Stuttgart, 1991), 85.

13. U. Reich, *Aus Cottbus und Arnswalde in die Neue Welt. Amerika-Auswanderung aus Ostelbien im 19. Jahrhundert* (Osnabrück, 1997), 122ff., 222.
14. K. Conzen, *Immigrant Milwaukee 1836–1860. Accommodation and Community in a Frontier City* (Cambridge, 1976).
15. A. Aengenvoort, *Migration – Siedlungsbildung – Akkulturation. Die Auswanderung Nordwestdeutscher nach Ohio, 1830–1914* (Stuttgart, 1999), 268f.
16. R.W. Wagner, *Deutsche als Ersatz für Sklaven. Arbeitsmigranten aus Deutschland in der brasilianischen Provinz Sao Paulo 1847–1914* (Frankfurt, 1995), 125ff. In 1872, Germans made up 13 percent of the population, making them the second largest minority in the province. During his research there in the mid-1980s, Wagner met a 90-year-old woman who still spoke Low German: Wagner, *Deutsche als Ersatz*, 159.
17. W. Köllmann, *Bevölkerung in der Industriellen Revolution* (Göttingen, 1974), 37.
18. D. Langewiesche, "Wanderungsbewegungen in der Hochindustrialisierungsperiode," *Vierteljahrsschrift für Sozial- und Wirtschaftsgeschichte* 64 (1) (1977), 1–40.
19. G.A. Ritter and K. Tenfelde, *Arbeiter im Deutschen Kaiserreich, 1871–1914* (Bonn, 1992), 190.
20. J.H. Jackson jr., *Migration and Urbanization in the Ruhr Valley, 1821–1914* (Atlantic Highlands, NJ, 1997), 306.
21. Jackson jr., *Migration*, 254ff.
22. W. Köllmann, "Industrialisierung, Binnenwanderung und 'Soziale Frage': Zur Entstehungsgeschichte der deutschen Industriegroßstadt im 19. Jahrhundert," *Vierteljahrschrift für Sozial- und Wirtschaftsgeschichte* 46, (1959), 45–70; W. Köllmann, 1973, "Der Prozeß der Verstädterung in Deutschland in der Hochindustrialisierungsphase," in *Gesellschaft in der Industriellen Revolution*, eds. R. Braun and W. Fischer (Cologne, 1973), 243–58.
23. Regarding hygiene and the keeping of animals: R.J. Evans, *Tod in Hamburg. Stadt, Gesellschaft und Politik in den Cholera-Jahren 1830–1910* (Reinbek, 1990), 155–58.
24. On the following: C. Kleßmann, *Polnische Bergarbeiter im Ruhrgebiet 1870–1945. Soziale Integration und nationale Subkultur einer Minderheit in der deutschen Industriegesellschaft* (Göttingen, 1978).
25. S. Peters-Schildgen, *"Schmelztiegel" Ruhrgebiet. Die Geschichte der Zuwanderung am Beispiel Hernes bis 1945* (Essen, 1997), 16ff.
26. Wehler, *Gesellschaftsgeschichte* vol. 3, 505f.
27. W. Brepohl, *Der Aufbau des Ruhrvolkes im Zuge der Ost-West-Wanderung* (Recklinghausen, 1948).
28. J. Mooser, 1991, "Das katholische Vereinswesen in der Diözese Paderborn um 1900. Vereinstypen, Organisationsumfang und innere Verfassung," *Westfälische Zeitschrift* 141, 447–61.
29. U. Herbert, *Geschichte der Ausländerpolitik in Deutschland* (Munich, 2001), Tab. 19, 198f.
30. A. Wennemann, *Arbeit im Norden. Italiener im Rheinland und Westfalen des späten 19. und frühen 20. Jahrhunderts* (Osnabrück, 1997).
31. R. del Fabbro, *Transalpini. Italienische Arbeitswanderung nach Süddeutschland im Kaiserreich 1870–1918* (Osnabrück, 1996).
32. Del Fabbro, *Transalpini*, 44.
33. C.H. Riegler, *Emigration und Arbeitswanderung aus Schweden nach Norddeutschland 1868–1914* (Neumünster, 1985), 58.
34. Herbert, *Ausländerbeschäftigung*, 15–81.
35. J. Wertheimer, *Unwelcome Strangers. East European Jews in Imperial Germany* (New York, 1987).
36. M. Just, *Ost- und südosteuropäische Amerikawanderung 1881–1914. Transitprobleme in Deutschland und Aufnahme in den Vereinigten Staaten* (Wiesbaden, 1988), 36.
37. Cf. J. Kulczycji, "Nationalism over Class Solidarity: The German Trade Unions and Polish Coal Miners in the Ruhr to 1902," *Canadian Review of Studies in Nationalism* 14 (1987), 261–76.
38. D. Gosewinkel, *Einbürgern und Ausschließen. Die Nationalisierung der Staatsangehörigkeit vom Deutschen Bund bis zur Bundesrepublik Deutschland* (Göttingen, 2001), 278–327.
39. P. Bernhard, "Italia nel piatto. Per una storia della cucina e gastronomia italiana in Germania nel XX secolo" in *Italiani in Germania tra Ottocento e Novecento. Spostamenti, rapporti, immagini, influenze*, eds. G. Comi and C. Dipper (Bologna, 2006), 263–87.

Chapter 19

Wilhelmine Nationalism in Global Contexts
*Mobility, Race, and Global Consciousness**

Sebastian Conrad

Between 1880 and 1914, the integration of the international economy, the political and imperial expansion of the West, and the increase in cultural exchanges across national borders contributed to a complex set of cross-border engagements that historians have begun to call globalization. This did not go unnoticed by contemporaries who closely witnessed this process with enthusiasm, or apprehension. Not much unlike today, the question of how to grasp the relationship between the nation and the process of transborder exchange received much attention. The most common interpretation was one that perceived globalization—or internationalization, in contemporary parlance—as a natural stage of development in human history. After nations had consolidated into organized nation-states, conventional opinion had it, they would gradually relate to each other, internationalize, and engage in world trade and world politics. "The family forms a tribe, and several tribes form a state and the nation," as the Social Democrat August Bebel typically phrased it, "and finally the close interaction of nations will result in internationality. That is the historical process."[1] First the nation, and then entanglements—these were the generally accepted stages of global development.

This interpretation—what I call the paradigm of consecutiveness—has largely been reproduced by much of recent scholarship. When analyzing the "mechanics" of internationalism in the late nineteenth century, historians stress the *a posteriori* character of cross-border interaction. Only fully fledged nation-states—and civil society groups within these nations—seemed in a position to engage in negotiations and exchange across borders. "Nationalism was," writes Leila Rupp using the example of women's movements, "a precondition of internationalism, or at least a necessary condition."[2]

It is interesting to note that in the historiography of German nationalism the issue of internationalism has only begun to be raised in recent years. It is probably no exaggeration to say that historians of Germany have clung to the internalist paradigm more stubbornly than elsewhere.[3]

The main concern, instead, was with the radicaliszation of German nationalism since the final decades of the nineteenth century.[4] This transformation revealed itself, the standard interpretation went, on two levels. First, in the Wilhelmian period nationalism was popularized and began to reach far beyond the educated elites as its original constituency.[5] Second, the structures and ideological contents of nationalism changed as well. Social hygienic as well as eugenic practices and technologies were employed to foster the alleged "purity" of the nation, both without and within. The reconfiguration of the nation under the influence of racial practices and biological theories like anti-Semitism was the central characteristic of this radicalization of *fin de siècle* nationalism.[6]

The emergence of mass-nationalism and its concomitant radicalization was primarily explained internally: German history as a peculiar path, a *Sonderweg*.[7] What was frequently eclipsed was the larger—European and non-European—context within which the German Empire was situated. Historians, in other words, largely took German nationalism out of the world at precisely the moment when the notion of "the world" assumed center stage in German politics and the public sphere. The logic here was one that resembles the stages-theory pronounced by August Bebel: the mass base and racial radicalization of nationalism was seen as the cause and precondition of later imperialism and "world politics." Colonial acquisitions, free-trade imperialism, and racialized wars were seen as the result of Wilhelmian hubris—while not in turn affecting the nature of German identities. German nationalism changed from within, the received wisdom had it, before aggressively reaching out.

Recent cultural histories of nationalism have done much to modify this perspective. Scholars like Michael Jeismann and Dieter Langewiesche have demonstrated that the dynamics of nationalism cannot be fully understood without reference to other societies. Most prominent in this regard is France, the "fatherland of the enemies," and later the "internal enemies," the Jews and the Poles.[8] In addition, much recent scholarship has illuminated the extent to which Germany was implicated in processes of colonial and global integration before World War I. On the one hand, the colonial past has received wide attention, frequently informed by postcolonial studies and an interest in the effects of the colonial encounter in the metropole.[9] On the other hand, scholars have begun to inquire into the mechanisms of international and global integration and have reconstructed Germany's role as one of the major players in the process of globalization before 1914.[10] In what follows, this growing literature will be built on to argue that in order to understand the dynamics of Wilhelmine nationalism we need to take into account the global context that reached deep into the German Kaiserreich.

Among the many dimensions of the increasing entanglement of the world, it was the process of mobility and migration that particularly affected the global discourse on what it meant to be a nation. The mobility of large numbers of people was one of the defining characteristics of globalization in the late nineteenth century. Recent scholarship has shown that between 1840 and the 1930s, more than a hundred and fifty million people left their countries of origin for elsewhere, often times to settle permanently.[11] However, these global movements were accompanied by the erection of global walls. The movement and circulation of people, in other words, proved to be a rather paradoxical process: a truly transnational phenomenon that at the same time reinforced national borders and mechanisms of exclusion.

In the case of Germany, too, migration was one of the forms through which large segments of the population experienced the global entanglement first hand. The third wave of transatlantic migration between 1880 and 1893 led close to two million people overseas, mainly to the United States.[12] It was accompanied by intense public debate in which the alleged "loss of national energies" was pitted against the advantages of migration as a "safety valve" that ridded the Empire of "revolutionary elements." When outbound movements subsided, immigration figures began to soar, mainly from Russia and Austrian Galicia, but also from Italy and the Netherlands. Germany effectively turned into a country importing cheap labor on scales only second to the United States.[13] In addition, migrants from Eastern Europe continued to travel through Germany on their way across the Atlantic. Their temporary sojourn had repercussions in Germany, on different levels: in West of Berlin, the train station in Ruhleben was built in 1890 for the sole purpose of channelling incoming laborers to the outbound sea ports; meanwhile on the national level, it was the high proportion of Jewish migrants that particularly aroused public suspicion in a climate increasingly dominated by anti-Semitism.

As Klaus Bade and others have convincingly argued, cross-border migration since the 1880s increasingly emerged as a central site where questions of belonging, citizenship, and nation were negotiated.[14] This is not to imply, to be sure, that the concept of the nation originated in the years of intensified global exchange since the 1880s. German nationalism, as elsewhere, was shaped by a longer tradition that reached back at least to the Napoleonic wars. Romanticism, the 1848 revolution, and the unification movement further contributed to the dynamics of nationalism that was by no means a new phenomenon in the late nineteenth century.[15] Rather, it was in many respects the product of a complex set of social conditions and political discourses *within* German society. These seemingly internal trajectories, however—and that became increasingly clear after the 1880s—need to be situated in a global context fundamentally shaped by cross-border entanglement.

Diasporic Germanness and Rejuvenation

The re-territorialization of the world in the context of mobility and migration took different forms. An important strand of discussion was the emergence of diaspora nationalism and its appropriation by the *völkisch* factions within Germany. There, the debates about mobility, for the most part, were dominated by a concern with outward migration. Over the course of the nineteenth century, successive waves of emigration had propelled more than four million Germans overseas, mainly to the United States. For many decades the discussion centered on the benefits and costs that the German states incurred through this outward movement. This changed at the end of the century when migration was seen almost like a natural phenomenon accompanying industrialization and modernization. Now the focus of debate shifted to issues of geography. Among the explicit goals of the colonial movement, for example, was the redirection of population flows to the colonies—so that Germans would remain Germans, albeit overseas, and not deteriorate into what was called "fertilizer of the peoples" (*Völkerdünger*) in contemporary parlance, a comment on the allegedly too rapid assimilation of Germans in the United States.

As Bradley Naranch has suggested, the shift in the meanings associated with outward mobility can be observed in a terminological adaptation. While German migrants overseas had for a long time been referred to as *Auswanderer* (emigrants), this began to change in the last third of the nineteenth century. Supplementing the centrifugal overtones of emigration, the term *Auslandsdeutsche* (diaspora Germans) became hegemonic in the Kaiserreich as its use was extended from German diasporas in Central Europe to overseas migration. The term was an expression of the social and cultural fears that were aroused by increasing mobility. In light of the fact that notions of belonging in the German states were deeply influenced by the concept of being rooted in a territory, emigration was associated with the danger of losing one's national identity. The modified terminology stressed the timelessness and stability of belonging to a nation defined by culture and language. The perceived gap between *Heimat* and overseas settlements was here translated into the conviction that a national identity that presupposed a cultural (and soon *völkisch*) essence could not be cast away.[16]

The result was, mainly on the nationalist fringe and among those that reported on the diaspora Germans in a booming print culture, a discourse of Germanness (*Deutschtum*) and a call for a politics of Germanification in places of German settlement. The fear of rapid assimilation in the North American "melting pot," where German migration was primarily headed, eventually led to attempts to redirect the flow of German emigrants elsewhere, in particular to Africa, but also to South America, the Levant, and Australia. Here, the reasoning went, Germans did not dissolve into the majority population, but were able to retain and even foster their German national characteristics. The ideology of diaspora Germanness was shaped by these different contexts, but the general thrust of the rhetoric exhibited many similarities.

In the focus of public attention were the settlement projects in the newly acquired African colonies where migration was supported by state subsidies. German South-West Africa, in particular, was envisioned to turn into a settler colony, and the first governor Theodor Leutwein initiated a series of measures to establish large planter and settler communities there.[17] In the end, however, the politics of colonial settlement proved unsuccessful. Before 1914, there were never more than twenty thousand Germans living in all the overseas possessions combined. The largest diaspora community outside the United States instead emerged in southern Brazil. The more than two hundred thousand *Auswanderer* were lured by the prospects of allegedly uninhabited land and bountiful nature, and by proactive immigration measures on the part of the Brazilian government that aimed at reinforcing the European elements in a politics of *embranquecimento*.[18]

Brazil was present in Germany through the activities of the Brazil lobby— people like Friedrich Fabri, the large shipping companies, and also the Protestant Church—but also through letters, migration handbooks and countless travelogues that reported from this new promised land. In these texts, the German settlements were typically represented as a "fountain of youth" that was immune to the kind of degeneration often associated with modern civilization. "If you want to know and appreciate the power and energy of the German nation," as one travelogue claimed, "then you have to follow the Germans to the far end of the world, into the swamps and jungles of South America."[19] The German colonies in Brazil not only seemed to remain "German" longer than other diaspora communities, but in fact they appeared as manifestations of the true Germany. Struggling with and overcoming nature, in particular, enabled the German colonist to discover a potential and virtues that purportedly "he had not known in Germany for a long time."[20] German Brazil was different: "Here," it was held, "the German is not in danger of degenerating."[21]

The German colonies in Brazil were thus appropriated, more by the radical nationalists than by the emigrants themselves, as laboratories of a specific vision of German society, informed by the nostalgia of preindustrial countrysides, of large families and patriarchal gender-relations, of the limited impact of the state and its bureaucracy, and of the levelling of social differences. It is important to note, however, that these utopias were not confined to Brazil. Rather, they were geared towards an audience in Germany, mainly to the educated and bourgeois classes. More importantly, the project of rejuvenation itself was not only directed at the diaspora community, but rather targeted German society as a whole. The return to some kind of German essence, the "rejuvenation of the race"[22] was not only a project for subtropical Brazil, but primarily a model laid out for the German Kaiserreich: "The old fatherland, too, can learn from these German colonies overseas."[23]

Indeed, there were numerous connections between the German colonists overseas and other agents of social renovation, in particular agrarianists and the life reform movements that shared the critique of industrial society, division of labor, and mass politics. The parallels between these two projects were striking, in particular in the rhetoric of the bourgeois press that appropriated the diaspora Germans, many of them of non-bourgeois backgrounds and hardly conversant with the ideals of the social renovation movements.[24] But there were not only similarities in scope and world vision, but also direct interactions with the Brazilian colonies that were often referred to as privileged sites for the realization of the goals of the life reform movement. The founder of the vegetarian garden colony "Eden" for example, Bruno Wilhelmi, had lived in Brazil for two years and had been inspired by the "life reform settler colonies there."[25] In many texts, "Brazil" assumed a metonymic presence and implicitly evoked the promises of authenticity, simplicity, and national reawakening. "I cannot stop thinking about Brazil," confessed the young writer Herman Hesse in 1895. "The longing for a healthy and sane existence, for a simple culture, for true and authentic life, for Brazil, does not cease within me."[26]

"The diaspora Germans," in the eyes of the governor of German East Africa, Eduard von Liebert, "are our most important colony."[27] This quote illustrates how close colonial territories and settlement colonies had become in nationalist discourse. But the reformist claims went further. The German settlements were represented as a veritable laboratory of the nation. Brazil, as a shorthand for the *Auslandsdeutschtum*, was referred to as a place where Germanness—and eventually the Kaiserreich itself—could be transformed. The diaspora communities thus served a function similar to that which Frederic Jackson Turner envisioned for the American frontier: immigrants, Turner famously held, would get rid of their "European" traits—hierarchical thinking, social stratification, decadence—and turn them into free and equal people. Brazil, likewise, appeared as a utopian space where *Gesellschaft* was still *Gemeinschaft*: Here all "class differences disappear," as Robert Gernhard reported in his travelogue, "and most social problems solve themselves."[28] For German nationalists and members of the life reform movement, too, the diaspora communities, in Brazil and elsewhere, served as the location for the transformation of the German nation under conditions of global mobility.

Racialization of Nationalism

Since the mid-1890s, the trajectories of mobility experienced a fundamental transformation. While the settler lobby was still occupied with agitating for an emigration law that was finally passed in 1897, the real currents of mobility had begun to go in the opposite direction. Partly as a consequence of emigration, but also in response to the increasing demand for labor in the industrialized centers, immigration figures soared. More than half a million people from the Polish-speaking provinces settled in the emergent conglomerations in the Rhine and Ruhr region (so-called *Ruhrpolen*). In addition, an estimated 5.1 million people from Eastern Europe travelled through Germany between 1880 and 1914 alone, many of them on their way across the Atlantic. Finally, migration to the cities created a demand for agricultural workers that was increasingly met through immigration. Seasonal workers in the Prussian countryside, many of them from the Polish territories in Russia and Austria, numbered more than 360.000 before World War I.[29]

These inward movements, then, were of considerable size. Their significance was enhanced, moreover, by the fact that many observers treated them not as local phenomena confined to the Eastern provinces; rather, they were connected in public debates to the expansion of capitalist flows, to large-scale mobility, and to the emergence of global labor markets. This contextualization opened up a space, in contemporary debates, to link immigration to an issue that increasingly dominated discourses of belonging and practices of exclusion on a global scale, namely race.

The relevance of racial concepts as part of the dynamic of German nationalism since the 1890s is well established. What is striking, however, is the extent to which the scholarly literature treats the gradual racialization of nationalist discourse as part of a history internal to Germany, or at least internal to Europe. The standard narrative is almost exclusively concerned with the rise of anti-Semitism. What is almost entirely absent from these accounts, however, is the larger global context in which these European debates unfolded. While the world around 1900 was permeated by discourses and practices of racism under conditions of high imperialism and colonialism, the genealogy of German racism continues to be located safely within the boundaries of Europe.

In recent years, there have been attempts to look closer at the colonial dimension of German racism. A number of studies have demonstrated how the colonial "rule of difference" (Partha Chatterjee) came to be organized along the concept of "race." The degree to which politics of ethnic segregation occupied center stage after the Herero war has led Jürgen Zimmerer to speak of a "racial state" in German South-West Africa. In Kiautschou (Jiaozhou) in China, the colonial government radically organized urban structures, social relations, and legal provisions according to the principle of ethnic segregation.[30] The most ambitious, and most controversial, attempt to link the racial politics in the colonies to the metropole analytically has focused on the question of continuities between the Herero war in 1904 and the genocidal practices of the Nazi period. The "extermination order" (*Vernichtungsbefehl*) of General von Trotha is then seen as a direct precursor of fantasies, and practices, of elimination that eventually culminated in the Holocaust.[31] These works promise to denationalize the discourse of race and to reinsert it into the colonial context within which it was developed and practiced.

One of the crucial areas where issues of race were directly implicated in notions of nationality was the debate about "racial mixing" and miscegenation in the colonies, in particular in South-West Africa with the largest German settler community. The growing population of mixed race origin was increasingly an issue of concern for colonialist and nationalist circles, in particular in the German homeland. On the one hand, the critique was aroused by the fact that legally, the offspring of the mostly unofficial "mixed marriages" between German men and indigenous women (there were no reverse cases) were entitled to German citizenship. On the other hand, miscegenation was seen to undermine the cultural essence of Germanness abroad and thus threatened to cut off the colonies from the *Heimat*.[32]

The colonial government reacted with a legal ban on interracial marriages promulgated in 1905 with the explicit aim of protecting the "purity" of the German nation. This measure bespeaks a fear of non-identifiability and a lack of clearly marked boundaries that are typical, as Ann Stoler has argued, for colonial frontiers.[33] It was followed by similar prohibitions in East Africa and in Samoa, even if in the Pacific the rationale was more ambiguous as Governor Solf aimed at protection not only of Germanness, but also of what he thought of as pristine and pure island identities. The prohibitive measures were complemented by a large-scale campaign to bring German women to South-West Africa. Some of them were trained specifically in colonial women's schools in order to inculcate the virtues of *Deutschtum*, femininity, and domesticity. Eventually, over two thousand women settled in the colony, intended by the mostly male colonial activists as bearers of German culture to a predominantly male colony in danger of going native.[34]

These interventions were accompanied, in the metropole, by broad popular debates that spilled over into the proceedings of the Reichstag. "Once the issue of racial difference was raised," as Lora Wildenthal has concluded, "it was not easily laid to rest." It proved increasingly difficult, in the years to come, to insist on racial segregation at the colonial periphery without allowing for a transfer of this principle to the German Kaiserreich.[35] The contexts of formal and informal imperialism as well as global migration were instrumental in overdetermining notions of belonging by supplementing a "colonial" dimension to concepts of the nation. Politics of ethnic segregation and racial difference, so characteristic of the colonial experience, thus began to be superimposed upon social practices of inclusion and marginalization in Europe as well.

This can be further illustrated using the example of Polish migration into Germany and the accompanying discourse of racial difference that emerged in the final decades of the nineteenth century. To be sure, "Race" in the Prussian East did not hold the same connotations as in the overseas colonies; the most notable difference was the access of most Poles to German citizenship. But an argument can be made that the Polish-speaking population in Germany was increasingly defined through a language of race, as was the case in Gustav Freytag's novels, in the ubiquitous rhetoric of the cultural mission, in the politics of a "Germanization of the soil" and the denaturalization of property with the aim of settling German colonists. An interesting offshoot of this gradual racialization was the tendency to treat Jews and Poles, for example in cases of immigration and naturalization, as part of the same group. In the eyes of the bureaucracy, this seemed legitimate as both groups frequently overlapped. What it also shows, however, is the complex process in which the radicalization of anti-Semitism and the racialization of anti-Polish sentiments informed each other.[36]

This was particularly evident in the debates about the so-called "Eastern Jews" (*Ostjuden*) that preoccupied the public in Wilhelmine Germany. The immigration and subsequent settlement of almost eighty thousand Jews from Russia unleashed an arsenal of xenophobic, apocalyptic scenarios of an imminent "flood from the East," exacerbated by the alleged backwardness if not outright "barbarity" of the Jews.[37] These fears, not infrequently supported by German Jews, were nourished not only by social resentment, but also by their connection to the much larger flow of over five million transitory migrants (*Durchwanderer*), mostly Poles and Jews, who passed through Germany on their way across the Atlantic. The association of *Ostjuden* with political radicalism, with poverty, with the trafficking of women in the 'White slave trade,' with a lack of hygiene, and with the spread of diseases as in the case of the cholera epidemics in the early 1890s, further contributed to a mechanism in which anti-Semitic stereotypes were connected to the fear of the "East" and "Asian" influences, just as the threat of "Polonization" was associated with anti-Semitic notions. This mechanism was not confined to the level of rhetoric, as the case of forced expulsion of forty thousand Poles and Jews without Prussian citizenship in 1885 demonstrated.[38] The 1890s, as Massimo Ferrari Zumbini has concluded, were characterized by a fusion of anti-Slavism and anti-Semitism in Imperial Germany.[39]

It is this gradual racialization of Polish migration that rendered conceivable an otherwise entirely unlikely proposal made by a certain Adolf Hentze in 1907 to Bernhard Dernburg, Secretary of State of the Colonial Office. Hentze suggested employing sixteen thousand Herero and Nama who lived as prisoners of war in South-West African camps since the Herero war in 1904, as agricultural workers in the Prussian East. There they were supposed to learn the necessary "civilized customs, the language and the cultivation of the land" and over the course of time be "educated to work." From the perspective of the government in Windhoek this project may have appeared as part of the civilizing mission and the overall "improvement" of colonial subjects while at the same time contributing to the security of the colony. But Hentze's initiative had broader implications, in particular since moving the Herero to Prussia was meant to replace Polish seasonal workers. This plan was only thinkable in the context of a radicalization of difference along the Polish border. Only now could Africans stand in for, and indeed serve as substitutes for, Polish workers.[40]

Borders and Border Control

It is important to recognize that changes in the notion of Germanness triggered by mobility and diaspora did not remain confined to the level of rhetoric and ideology. In fact, they had palpable effects as they translated into legal provisions as well as into measures to reinforce the boundaries of the nation. They were most palpable where new immigration regulations changed the very materiality of the border. This is an issue that as been entirely ignored by studies of German nationalism. It would be fascinating to study further the way new provisions of control and surveillance fundamentally changed the physical shape of the landscape. This is most obvious in the case of the control stations where immigrants from Russia and Austria were subjected to scrutiny before entering the country as seasonal workers. Thirty-nine of these stations were erected along the Eastern Prussian border by the Central Office of Agricultural Workers (*Feldarbeiterzentralstelle*). Here, the incoming laborers needed to prove that they had a valid contract with a German employer. A medical doctor attached to each control station ensured that hygienic measures were taken so that "the threat of a spread of epidemic diseases would not rise to unmeasurable heights."[41] The border stations were nodal points at which checks on mobility were connected to notions of cultural superiority and hygienic nationalism. The Prussian Ministry of Agriculture in 1913 internally discussed plans of disinfecting every single non-German seasonal worker when he/she entered the country.[42]

The border was a site where difference was marked, enforced, and also constructed. It is important to note, in this context, that the German practices were not the result of the radicalization of German nationalism alone, but rather coincided with the nationalization of mobility on a global scale. In many countries, authorities reacted to the apparent borderless movements with renewed technologies of exclusion, of identification, and of citizenship in order to channel, control, and counter the steady human flow in and out of the country. The most prominent example was the Chinese Exclusion Act in 1882 that "transformed the United States into a gatekeeping nation."[43] In Australia, the so-called "Chinese Crisis" in 1888 initiated a series of exclusionary measures to prop up the politics of "White Australia." In Europe, too, we can observe a growing concern for border control and the managing of transnational mobility in many societies, such as the Alien Act, triggered by a massive influx of Jewish migrants and introduced in Great Britain in 1905.

These exclusionary measures were clearly sparked by mobility and the menace of vanishing borders in an age of globalization, and cannot be solely attributed to what could be called an internal "closing of the national mind." They were the result, partly, of close international monitoring and observation. Max Weber, for example, looked to Australia where "the immigration of Chinese is banned," only to warn that "the Poles are even more dangerous due to the possibility of mixing and of bringing down German culture."[44] Calls for an exclusion of Poles, in other words, were not only connected to long-standing anti-Semitic traditions, but at the same time embedded in a consciousness of synchronous interconnectedness on a global scale. The Prussian government complied with a very specific form of exclusionary regulation that was unparalleled in other countries: the urgently needed agricultural laborers from Polish Russia and Austrian Galicia were annually forced to leave the country temporarily (during the so-called *Karenzzeit*) in order to inhibit permanent settlement and an unsettling of the unstable ethnic and national balance in Eastern Prussia.[45]

While border controls and techniques of identification were designed to check the alleged borderlessness and fluidity of the globalizing world, citizenship emerged as the most important factor in establishing fixity and stability. Here, too, one can observe an adaptation of practices and regulations in accordance with the changing scales and trajectories of mobility. In fact, the revisions of German citizenship law in 1913 can be read as a direct response to the changes in German notions of belonging under conditions of global migration. These revisions are reminiscent of the shift from *Auswanderer* to *Auslandsdeutsche* referred to above. While the law of 1870 had foreseen that citizenship ended ten years after leaving the country, this stipulation was revoked in 1913: from now on, citizenship could not expire and was even transferred to descendants. This provision was a reaction to the changing conditions of mobility. During the nineteenth century, the vast majority of emigrants had moved to the United States, presumably for good, and this was considered to be a loss to the national substance. The acquisition of colonies since 1884 was motivated, to a large extent, by the intention to provide emigrants with opportunities without severing their ties to the German nation. In the face of political support for the colonial project, it seemed mandatory to enable Germans to settle in the colonies without risking their legal status. The modification of the durability of citizenship thus was a direct outcome of the debates about global mobility. This was no mere legal cosmetic, rendered insignificant by the dissolution of the colonial empire just shortly thereafter; rather, it concerned central dimensions of belonging and participation. It is instructive to note that the effects of this legal adaptation survived the end of empire. When in the 1990s large groups of descendants of former emigrants (*Aussiedler*) "returned," as it came to be called, from the Soviet Union, they still benefited from this redefinition of Germanness under colonial/global conditions.[46]

Nationalism and Global Consciousness

The impact of trans-border mobility on the trajectories of German nationalism was palpable on different levels. Diasporic nationalism, the racialization of national belonging, and the reinforcement of material and legal borders were among the most striking effects of transnational interactions on the sense of nation in the Kaiserreich. Different social milieus were affected by these developments in very different ways. The educated classes were particularly quick to respond to global challenges. While the *Bildungsbürgertum* was a minority, its influence in shaping the appropriation of the world went well beyond the confines of its constituency. The commitment to secure access to world markets enlisted the support of industrialists and entrepreneurs for expansionist schemes, while the churches were invested around the world through the missionary project. They helped to transmit the desire for tangible and spiritual acquisitions in exotic regions to social classes that might otherwise not have found it in their interest to support them. Presumably least affected by intensifying global exchange were petty bourgeoisie and the lowest social strata. The working class, however, increasingly felt the dependency upon global demand structures, and the trade unions experienced highly emotional debates about the internationalization of the labor market. It is important to take these different actors and interests into account; engagement with the world was always of a contested nature.

On the whole, however, there can be little doubt that the increasing global entanglement left its traces on the way the German nation was conceived. Mobility—as the focus of this paper—was only one dimension of this globalizing process; other aspects affected the dynamics of nationalism as well. Among them, most famously, was the notion of world politics (*Weltpolitik*) that tied national interests to places like the Taku Forts, Venezuela, and Agadir. The integration of the world market went hand in hand with a renationalization of the economy along neo-mercantilist lines. Increasingly social actors connected their sense of community and belonging to larger contexts. In the Wilhelmine period, the rhetoric of the "world" became almost ubiquitous. German nationalism at the turn of the century was informed by what can be called a form of global consciousness.[47]

As a result, central tropes of the nation emerged that articulated nationalist discourse with the geopolitical context. Among them was the quest for a larger lebensraum for the German folk, a term coined by geographer Friedrich Ratzel but influential far into the twentieth century.[48] The notion of lebensraum, like many others, fed into one of the founding binaries that continued to structure German nationalism for some time to come: namely, the figure of German "culture" as a third way beyond Western "civilization" and "barbarism" in the East. The popularity of this trope surged in the early years of the twentieth century and culminated in the war years, but has retained a powerful grip on the German imagination since.[49] It has conventionally been traced back to the romantic period and to longstanding traditions represented by a class of mandarins detached from politics.[50] From the perspective of a history of globalization, however, the trope can equally be understood as the effect of a peculiar reading of the world political status of the Kaiserreich: Germany as latecomer when compared to France and Great Britain, both in terms of nation-building and as a global player; and Germany as superior compared to Europe's East, and to the colonial world, that appeared backward economically and was not yet organized into nation-state units.

Also, the notion of "German work" (*Deutsche Arbeit*) can be read as a concept that articulated Germany's particular location in the globalization process with nationalist discourse. It served as an ideological template that enabled the translation of the culture-vs.-civilization paradigm into practice. To be sure, the idea of national work has had repercussions in other countries as well, as the French debate on *travail national* illustrates. But the conviction that German work was different and unique was widespread in Imperial Germany. This trope was the expression of a quest for uniqueness and an attempt to come to terms with the peculiarities of a nation that—unlike France and Britain—could not be defined through Empire; a nation whose power did not rest, like Britain's, on maritime hegemony, capital investment, and trade; a nation that had no internal frontier at her disposal, as did the United States, as a resource of seemingly perennial rejuvenation; a nation, finally, that unlike the Poles and many colonial societies did not define their characteristics vis-à-vis an imperial oppressor. In the global context of the turn of the century, the notion of "German work" can be understood as a typical latecomer discourse, a form of protest against the underprivileged role Germany appeared to play in the international arena.[51]

At the same time, the concept was an expression of the pride in Germany's achievements and ambitions. "German work" was at the heart of the Kaiserreich's attempt to assert the place it deserved, both within Europe and beyond. The concept clearly had an expansionist ring, as is clear from its frequent use to describe colonial settlement, conquest, and occupation. The most important developmental project in the African colonies, as in other European possessions as well, was the "education of the negro to work." "German work" was a foundational term suggesting that Germany's position in the world was the product of her own efforts and achievements. Not unlike the naval arming, the rhetoric of "German work" can be read as the expression of an ambivalent mix of pride and minority complex, and it is indicative of the mechanisms through which global contexts translated into the grammar of nationalism. The afterlife of the trope—the "soldiers of work" in National Socialism, "German *Wertarbeit*" as the basis for the economic miracle of the 1950s, and the East German version of a "state of work" (*Staat der Arbeit*)— attests to the mark it has left on notions of Germanness.

Conclusion

The Wilhelmian Kaiserreich was deeply implicated in global conjunctures, and the specific dynamics of German nationalism were shaped and transformed in the course of transnational entanglements. This is not to deny the importance of complex national traditions, as social actors in late-nineteenth-century Germany frequently referred to continuities of the nationalist imagination. But these traditions were instrumentalized in the context of current problematics and concerns, and the way historical legacies were appropriated was increasingly shaped by the constraints of global integration. The connection of national themes with larger issues allowed social actors to connect their particular interests with global contexts. These contexts, to be sure, did not create nationalism, but they influenced the way in which the nation was perceived and the way the politics of national belonging were practiced.

What is at stake here, then, is a revision of common assumptions concerning the history of nationalism. My argument is intended as a contribution to a "spatial turn" in the historiography of nationalism. For the most part, the dynamics of nationalism have been located within the nation-states at issue: as long traditions and continuities of a national "essence," as "imagined communities," as reactions to the disruptive effects of modernization, as "invented traditions," or as new departures by social groups that aimed at a different kind of modernity. My examples have suggested, however, that the particular form that nationalism and the representation of the nation took around 1900 need to be read in the context of interactions and entanglements on a global scale. The shifts and changes in the discourse of nationalism thus appear not only as effects of internal trajectories, as the familiar picture would suggest, but just as much as part of the larger process we retrospectively call globalization.

This not only refers to the obvious fact that the nation-state concept, in many countries, was the result of cultural transfers. This is well recognized in many (if not all) theories of nationalism. Benedict Anderson and others have stressed the degree to which the nation was a product of relationships.[52] In particular in the colonial world the nation-state was thus an import that superseded traditional forms of belonging and loyalty. It remained, to use Partha Chatterjee's phrase, a "derivative discourse."[53] It is thus widely recognized that the institution of the nation-state has traveled. However, the specific meanings and dynamics of nationalism are generally seen as emanating from local conditions. The spread of the "nation form" (Etienne Balibar), in other words, may be the product of systemic conditions of world order, while the particular ideological contents of nationalism are assumed to derive from cultural traditions and to draw on legacies entirely from within.[54] What I have argued, instead, is that the way the nation was defined, understood, and practiced—the particular contents of nationalism—owed more to the global context in which it was constituted than has hitherto been recognized.[55]

Notes

* An extended version of this chapter was published as "Globalization Effects: Mobility and Nation in Imperial Germany, 1880–1914," *Journal of Global History* 3 (2008): 43–66.

1. A. Bebel, *Für und wider die Commune. Disputation zwischen den Herren Bebel und Sparig in der "Tonhalle" zu Leipzig* (Leipzig, 1876).
2. L.J. Rupp, "The Making of International Women's Organizations," in *The Mechanics of Internationalism*, eds. M.H. Geyer and J. Paulmann (Oxford, 2001), 205–34, 233.
3. S. Berger, *The Search for Normality: National Identity and Historical Consciousness in Germany Since 1800* (New York, 1997).
4. For an overview of research on German nationalism, see D. Langewiesche, "Nation, Nationalismus, Nationalstaat. Forschungsstand und Forschungsperspektiven," *Neue Politische Literatur* 40 (1995), 190–236.
5. G. Eley, *Reshaping the German Right: Radical Nationalism and Political Change after Bismarck* (New Haven, 1980); R. Chickering, *We Men Who Feel Most German: A Cultural Study of the Pan-German League, 1886–1914* (Boston, 1984).
6. C. Geulen, *Wahlverwandte. Rassendiskurse und Nationalismus im späten 19. Jahrhundert* (Hamburg, 2004), 30. See also P. Weindling, *Health, Race, and Politics in Germany between National Unification and Nazism 1870–1945* (Oxford, 1989).
7. D. Blackbourn and G. Eley, *The Peculiarities of German History: Bourgeois Society and Politics in Nineteenth-Century Germany* (Oxford, 1984).
8. For the latest statement on the issue, see the synthesis by P. Walkenhorst, *Nation-Volk-Rasse: Radikaler Nationalismus im Deutschen Kaiserreich 1890–1914* (Göttingen, 2007).
9. A. Honold and K.R. Scherpe, eds., *Mit Deutschland um die Welt. Eine Kulturgeschichte des Fremden in der Kolonialzeit* (Stuttgart, 2004); B. Kundrus, ed., *Phantasiereiche. Zur Kulturgeschichte des deutschen Kolonialismus* (Frankfurt, 2003).

10. S. Conrad and J. Osterhammel, eds., *Das Kaiserreich transnational. Deutschland in der Welt 1871–1914* (Göttingen, 2004); C. Torp, *Die Herausforderung der Globalisierung. Wirtschaft und Politik in Deutschland, 1860–1914* (Göttingen, 2005).
11. D. Hoerder, *Cultures in Contact: World Migrations in the Second Millennium* (Durham, 2002); A. McKeown, "Global Migration, 1846–1940," *Journal of World History* 15 (2004), 155–90.
12. K.J. Bade, *Europa in Bewegung. Migration vom späten 18. Jahrhundert bis zur Gegenwart* (Munich, 2000); D. Hoerder and J. Nagel, eds., *People in Transit: German Migrations in Comparative Perspective, 1820–1930* (Cambridge, 1995).
13. U. Herbert, *Geschichte der Ausländerpolitik in Deutschland. Saisonarbeiter, Zwangsarbeiter, Gastarbeiter, Flüchtlinge* (Munich, 2001).
14. See K.J. Bade, ed., *Deutsche im Ausland – Fremde in Deutschland. Migration in Geschichte und Gegenwart* (Munich, 1992); K. O'Donnell, R. Bridenthal and N. Reagin, eds., *The Heimat Abroad: The Boundaries of Germanness* (Ann Arbor, 2005).
15. Earlier traditions of nationalism, of course, were likewise bound up with global contexts. See C.A. Bayly, *The Birth of the Modern World 1780–1914: Global Connections and Comparisons* (Oxford, 2004), 112–14, 199–245.
16. B.D. Naranch, "Inventing the Auslandsdeutsche: Emigration, Colonial Fantasy, and German National Identity 1848–71," in *Germany's Colonial Pasts*, eds. E. Ames, M. Klotz and L. Wildenthal (Lincoln, 2005), 21–40.
17. See D.J. Walther, *Creating Germans Abroad: Cultural Policies and National Identity in Namibia* (Athens, 2006).
18. On German migration to Brazil, see G. Brunn, *Deutschland und Brasilien 1889–1914* (Cologne, 1971).
19. K. Leonhardt, "Die deutschen Kolonien im Süden von Chile," *Das Auswandererproblem* 5 (1912), 7–53.
20. G.A. Stolze, *Gedanken eines Hinterwäldlers Brasiliens über sociale Verhältnisse, besonders in Bezug auf die deutsche Auswanderung nach Brasilien* (Leer, 1895), 5.
21. W. Breitenbach, *Aus Süd-Brasilien. Erinnerungen und Aufzeichnungen* (Brackwede, 1913), 208.
22. R. Gernhard, *Reise-Bilder aus Brasilien* (Breslau, 1900), 100.
23. K.A. Wettstein, *Mit deutschen Kolonistenjungens durch den brasilianischen Urwald! Selbsterlebtes. Eine Reise nach und durch Südbrasilien und seine deutschvölkischen Kolonien* (Leipzig, 1910), 195.
24. On the life reform movement, see E. Barlösius, *Naturgemäße Lebensführung. Zur Geschichte der Lebensreform um die Jahrhundertwende* (Frankfurt, 1997); G. Eley and J.N. Retallack, eds., *Wilhelmianism and its Legacies: German Modernities, Imperialism, and the Meanings of Reform 1890–1914* (New York, 2003).
25. Quoted from J. Radkau, "Die Verheißungen der Morgenfrühe. Die Lebensreform in der neuen Moderne," in *Die Lebensreform. Entwürfe zur Neugestaltung von Leben und Kunst um 1900*, ed. K. Buchholz (Darmstadt, 2001), 55–60, 59.
26. H. Hesse, *Kindheit und Jugend vor Neunzehnhundert*, vol. 2 (Frankfurt am Main, 1978), 10, 67.
27. Quoted from K.A. Wettstein, *Brasilien und die deutsch-brasilianische Kolonie Blumenau* (Leipzig, 1907), 1.
28. Gernhard, *Reise-Bilder*, 44.
29. See Herbert, *Geschichte der Ausländerpolitik*, 25–27.
30. J. Zimmerer, *Deutsche Herrschaft über Afrikaner. Staatlicher Machtanspruch und Wirklichkeit im kolonialen Namibia* (Münster, 2001).
31. See J. Zimmerer, "Colonialism and the Holocaust: Towards an Archaeology of Genocide," in *Genocide and Settler Society: Frontier Violence and Child Removal in Australia*, ed. D.A. Moses (New York, 2004), 49–76. For a critique, see S. Malinowski and R. Gerwarth, "Der Holocaust als 'kolonialer Genozid?' Europäische Kolonialgewalt und nationalsozialistischer Vernichtungskrieg," *Geschichte und Gesellschaft* 33 (2007), 439–66.
32. P. Grosse, *Kolonialismus, Eugenik und bürgerliche Gesellschaft in Deutschland 1850–1918* (Frankfurt, 2000); B. Kundrus, *Moderne Imperialisten. Das Kaiserreich im Spiegel seiner Kolonien* (Cologne 2003), 219–79.

33. A.L. Stoler, "Rethinking Colonial Categories: European Communities and the Boundaries of Rule," *Comparative Studies in Society and History* 31 (1989), 134–61.
34. See L. Wildenthal, *German Women for Empire, 1884–1945* (Durham, 2001), 121–29.
35. Wildenthal, *German Women*, 86.
36. See D. Gosewinkel, *Einbürgern und Ausschließen. Die Nationalisierung der Staatsangehörigkeit vom Deutschen Bund bis zur Bundesrepublik Deutschland* (Göttingen, 2001), 263–77.
37. J. Wertheimer, *Unwelcome Strangers: East European Jews in Imperial Germany* (New York, 1987).
38. H. Neubach, *Die Ausweisung von Polen und Juden aus Preußen 1885/86* (Wiesbaden, 1967).
39. M.F. Zumbini, *"Die Wurzel des Bösen." Gründerjahre des Antisemitismus: Von der Bismarckzeit zu Hitler* (Frankfurt, 2003), 556.
40. Adolf Hentze, Hannover, to Colonial Office, 1 March 1907, in: Federal Archives Berlin Lichterfelde, R 1001/2090, 109.
41. PSAB, I. HA Rep 87 B, No. 221, Director of the Feldarbeiterzentralstelle to the Secretary of State of the Interior, Berlin, 22 April 1911.
42. PSAB, I. HA Rep 87 B, No. 221, 20 February 1913. See also J. Nichtweiß, *Die ausländischen Saisonarbeiter in der Landwirtschaft der östlichen und mittleren Gebiete des Deutschen Reiches. Ein Beitrag zur Geschichte der preußisch-deutschen Politik von 1890 bis 1914* (Berlin, 1959), 138–43.
43. E. Lee, *At America's Gates: The Exclusion Era 1882–1943* (Chapel Hill, 2003), 9.
44. M. Weber, "Die nationalen Grundlagen der Volkswirtschaft. Vortrag am 12. März 1895 in Frankfurt am Main [Bericht des Frankfurter Journals]," in *Max Weber Gesamtausgabe*, vol. 4.2, W.J. Mommsen and R. Aldenhoff, eds., (Tübingen, 1993), 724–25.
45. Herbert, *Geschichte der Ausländerpolitik*; Nichtweiß, *Saisonarbeiter*.
46. Gosewinkel, *Einbürgern*; Grosse, *Kolonialismus*.
47. See M. Krajewski, *Restlosigkeit. Weltprojekte um 1900* (Frankfurt, 2006).
48. W.D. Smith, *The Ideological Origins of Nazi Imperialism* (New York, 1986), 146–52.
49. W. Lepenies, *The Seduction of Culture in German History* (Princeton, 2006).
50. See J. Fisch, "Zivilisation, Kultur," in O. Brunner et al., eds., *Geschichtliche Grundbegriffe. Historisches Lexikon zur politisch-sozialen Sprache in Deutschland*, vol. 7 (Stuttgart, 1992), 679–774.
51. J. Campbell, *Joy in Work, German Work: The National Debate, 1800–1945* (Princeton, 1989).
52. See B. Anderson, *Imagined Communities* (London, 1983).
53. P. Chatterjee, *Nationalist Thought and the Colonial World: A Derivative Discourse* (Minneapolis, 1993).
54. E. Balibar, "The Nation Form," in *Race, Nation, Class: Ambigious Identities*, eds. E. Balibar and I. Wallerstein (London, 1991), 86–106.
55. I have greatly benefited from the powerful argument in C.L. Hill, *National History and the World of Nations: Writing Japan, France, the United States, 1870–1900* (Durham, 2008).

Chapter 20

Imperial Germany under Globalization

Cornelius Torp

In the nineteenth century the world became much smaller, and the speed with which this happened impressed contemporaries. "Modern transportation," noted the State Secretary of the Interior, Graf Posadowsky, in a speech to parliament when submitting a new German customs tariff in 1901, has brought "countries which are thousands of miles away from us into a geographical market position as if they were in front of the doors of our customs offices." The "globe" has been "pressed together" as if "it were a rubber ball."[1] This compression of time and space was caused by the transportation and communication revolutions in the nineteenth century and the enormous, rapid increase in the worldwide economic integration which accompanied these revolutions. In the last few years, economic historians—and, soon thereafter, other historians too, given the transnational political cross-linking, imperialism and cultural transfers across national borders—have increasingly labeled the decade before 1914 the first wave of globalization, indeed, globalization's Belle Époque.[2]

The extent of worldwide economic integration on the eve of World War I—and the term globalization is used here only in this limited, economic sense—looks quite impressive even from today's perspective. Since the middle of the nineteenth century, world trade had grown so rapidly and continuously that shortly before the globalization backlash brought about by the "Second Thirty Years War" of the twentieth century,[3] the level of world trade was comparable with that of the 1970s and 1980s. This explosion in world trade was accompanied by a radical convergence of the international prices for goods, suggesting the development of an integrated world market. At the same time, new worldwide investment possibilities allowed international capital to become increasingly mobile; the mobility reached in the second half of the "long" nineteenth century was, in fact, in many regards greater than at present. Finally, the level of mass migration and immigration reached in the years between 1850 and 1914 was historically unique, up to the present day. If one looks at the European emigration to the countries of the New World, the transnational, internal European migration, which also numbered in the millions, and the migration flows within the nation-states, which took on completely new dimensions, it appears reasonable to assume that in the late nineteenth century there was a global labor market, a global market for wages.[4]

It is clear that such a fundamental change in the global economic framework had to have an impact upon the societies of the nation-states and their policies. This is true, for example, in regard to mass migration and immigration, to the overturning of traditional ways of life and norms and values affected by global economic developments, as well as to the effects of globalization on citizenship law and the discourse on nationalism.[5] It is perhaps even truer for tariff and trade policy, as here the world economy and the policies of the nation-states came more directly into contact than anywhere else. Globalization and the speed with which it developed had a profound impact upon the individual economies of the nineteenth century, thoroughly breaking down well-known and customary relationships. Absolute and relative prices moved at a breathtaking tempo, new social and political lines of conflict appeared; those hurt by Germany's growing integration into world markets became active and organized. Most countries responded to the new situation by putting up walls of protectionist tariffs. Of the major states, only Great Britain remained true to the principle of free trade—although even here there was a significant protective tariff movement. In contrast, after the late 1870s almost all of continental Europe, even allowing for individual differences, increasingly turned to protectionism. This was true as well for the Latin American countries and for those British colonies granted independence in this period; they also introduced protective tariffs for their industries which were usually much higher than those in Europe. Since the beginning of the nineteenth century, the United States had been a stronghold of protectionism; here, too, since the 1860s the tariffs on industrial products had increased significantly.

German protectionism before World War I—this is my thesis—can be adequately understood only when interpreted as part of the international response to the rapid integration of the world's economies. In order to show how far this interpretation differs from the previous explanations of German foreign trade policy from 1870–1914, I will, first, describe briefly the traditional historical approaches. Second, I will sketch, broadly, the economic and social effects of the German economy being integrated into world markets, before I turn, third, to the most important stages of German tariff and trade policy. To conclude, I will attempt to evaluate German protectionism within the framework of the international context and against the backdrop of possible alternatives.

I

The history of German protectionism before 1914 is not a *tabula rasa*. Although there are comparably few empirical studies, historians quite early recognized the centrality of tariff and trade policy as an important area of political conflict. Accordingly, trade policy plays a key role in the competing interpretations of the German Empire. There is a broad consensus among otherwise diverging interpretations concerning the most important stages of German foreign trade policy and how to interpret these. All agree that the German customs tariff of 1879, along with the increasingly protective tariffs of the 1880s, marks a clear turning point, after a quarter of a century of ever-increasing free trade. Historians agree furthermore that after the short intermezzo of the Caprivi treaties, when the German government was friendly toward trade and reduced the tariffs on agrarian products, with the Bülow tariff of 1902 German tariff and trade policy returned to the protectionism begun under Bismarck. At the same time, historians have asserted that as a result of the break with the principles of Caprivi's trade policies and the higher level of tariffs vis-à-vis the Bismarck period, Germany after the turn of the twentieth century moved into an era of high protectionism.

In contrast, there are clear differences in the competing narratives of the German Empire concerning the explanation of German protectionism and the interpretation of individual events. An especially influential view, which can be traced back to the Berlin historian Eckart Kehr, who died young in 1933, and which was later further developed by especially Alexander Gerschenkron, Hans Rosenberg, and Hans-Ulrich Wehler, sees the durable and long-lasting political alliance of heavy industry and large landowners as the driving force behind German tariff and trade policy.[6] Since the late 1870s, this coalition of "rye and iron" is said not only to have put into practice a protectionist tariff policy centered on defending their class interests and hostile to consumers, but also to have determined to a large degree, as a conservative, anti-socialist "cartel of the patriotic and productive classes," the course of German politics. Ruthlessly, "Junkers and industrial tycoons" pushed through their protectionist interests and implemented a protective tariff policy, shamelessly to their advantage, at the cost of consumers and exporters. At the same time, the unfortunate coalition of heavy industry and large landowners contributed, through their defensive efforts to uphold their position, to leading Germany into the catastrophe of World War I, burdening German history with a heavy mortgage. In this context, some historians have even portrayed the protectionist turnaround of 1879, which was said to be the birthplace of the unholy alliance of "rye and iron" as "one of the most important wrong decisions in German history and thus in the European history of the nineteenth century," with consequences reaching all the way to National Socialism.[7]

This sweeping, far-reaching interpretation has not gone unchallenged. Very quickly other historians pointed out that in the years preceding 1879 it was less the Prussian Junkers and more the agricultural associations in the western part of rural Germany who came out in favor of agricultural tariffs.[8] James C. Hunt has argued that not only those who owned large farms, but also those who owned smaller and medium-sized farms, who in theory were manipulated by the large agrarians, profited from the German grain tariffs. These tariffs, together with a series of de facto protectionist measures, such as laws and measures against animal diseases, effectively shielded the farmers from international competition. In other words, it is a mistake to speak of an agrarian protectionism that gave preference in a lopsided manner to the East Elbian grain producers.[9]

In general, since the end of the 1970s historians have increasingly questioned the "Kehrite" interpretations of the amount of influence wielded by the elite of the German Empire. According to this criticism, the key to understanding the history of the German Empire lies not in a "manipulation from above," but in a self-mobilization "from below"[10]—this has been emphasized above all by a group of British historians. Furthermore, the durability and resilience of the agrarian-industrial coalition has been questioned. The phase of the so-called "politics of rallying together" (*Sammlungspolitik*), when the government at the turn of the twentieth century reinvented the protective tariff alliance of 1878/79, made evident, according to these critics, the structural fragility and disunity of the coalition of agriculture and heavy industry.[11]

Although the competing interpretations of German protectionism differ in many central points, they do have one thing in common. Both those who emphasize the importance of the alliance of Junkers and heavy industrialists and those who criticize this interpretation give too much weight to the social and political power constellations within Germany when they attempt to explain the decisions and the tendencies of the German tariff and trade policy. This is a reflection of the way historians traditionally see history through the lens of the nation-state. This way of seeing things began in Europe in the nineteenth century and moved out from Europe through the world. Even today this perspective informs most traditional political history as well as social history and other alternative approaches to history. The nation-state was and still is considered the self-evident unit of historical analysis. This corresponds to an endogenous understanding of development: the conviction that social and political conditions and processes can best be explained by examining the internal structures and the internal conflicts of the national societies themselves.

In contrast to this, I believe that taking into consideration the first wave of economic globalization before 1914, which transcended the boundaries of the nation-state, greatly improves our understanding of the history of these years. This is neither to argue for economic reductionism nor to suggest that the history of German foreign trade policy must be fully rewritten from the perspective of globalization. Still, what is involved here is more than just a transnational complement to the traditional way of looking at things through the lens of national history. Rather, my argument aims to link together the advancing global economic integration before World War I *causally* with economic, social, and political processes within the German nation-state. In so doing it will become clear that in the nineteenth century much of that which historians have described in regard to

German protectionism as the result of endogenous forces was in truth part of an international reaction to the challenges of globalization. Of course, although globalization was international, its specific repercussions were different in every country and can only be fully understood by taking into consideration factors drawn from national histories.

II

"World trade reaches into the smallest German working-class hut," so summed up shortly before World War I the liberal economist Paul Arndt the effects of integrating Germany into the world economy.[12] And, indeed, the significance of the world markets for Germany was almost omnipresent in everyday life—in consumption, in the workplace, among all social classes. In the last half century before 1914, the German economy was becoming integrated into world markets at an astounding rate. Some dry numbers may suffice here to document this development. Measured in current prices, German exports increased from 2,353 million marks in 1872 to 10,097 million marks in 1913; in other words, they more than quadrupled. As German exports grew even more quickly than world trade, Germany steadily worked its way up the hierarchy of the export countries. The German share of world exports in the five years 1874–78 with 9.5 percent was just a little more than half that of Great Britain; but by the last year before the war it had become almost equal, with 13.1 percent. Indeed, the three great export nations, Great Britain, Germany, and the United States, were now almost equal. Accordingly, foreign trade became increasingly more important for the German economy. As both exports as well as imports grew more quickly than the Gross Domestic Product (GDP), in the last five years before the war the degree of integration of the German economy into world markets reached a level never seen before, with an export quota of 15.8 percent and an import quota of 19.2 percent.[13] This meant on the one hand that the German economy, more than ever, depended on the import of foodstuffs, raw materials, and industrial semi-finished and finished products from abroad. On the other hand, exports became a demand factor of decisive importance for German industry.

Looked at from an economic and long-term perspective, there can be no doubt that the German economy as a whole profited enormously from the international division of labor. Over the middle and short term, however, the effects of being included into world markets had a quite wide-ranging impact upon different economic sectors and sections of the population. On the one side were the winners of globalization. Among these were, of course, those economic branches which lived directly and exclusively from foreign trade such as, for example, much of the shipping industry. Among these were also those branches of industry which, on the one hand, obtained their raw materials and intermediate products from abroad and which, on the other hand, were extremely competitive in world markets, selling a large portion of their products abroad—above all engineering and machine-building, and the chemical and electrical industries. Quite often the demand for exports formed the foundation for an expansion in production, producing substantial economies of scale, leading to a significant reduction in unit costs. For some individual companies or sectors, the world market had a similar or even greater significance than the internal German market. Thus, in 1913 German companies had a world export share of 46 percent in the field of the electrical industry, in international comparison a singularly top position—and they sold more than a quarter of their products abroad; at Siemens it was even 36.2 percent.[14] The situation was even more extreme for the German dye companies, which dominated the industry with approximately 90 percent of the world market; in 1913 the so-called "small I.G.," to which BASF, Bayer and Agfa belonged, achieved 82 percent of their sales outside of Germany.[15] Finally, the group with the largest number of winners from globalization was the consumers. They profited from the expansion in the available goods as well as from the decline in prices of food and other consumers goods as a result of the international competition.

In contrast, those branches where there was strong competition from imports, as, for example, large sections of the German cloth industry, can be counted among the losers of globalization and the beneficiaries of protectionist measures. Furthermore, those sectors, such as German heavy industry and the soda industry, which although quite competitive in world markets, had also formed well-functioning cartels, which enabled an effective differentiation between prices in the world market and in internal markets, also profited from tariffs. The sector of the economy most hurt by globalization and therefore most interested in protectionist measures was German agriculture. In spite of the enormous advances in productivity in German agriculture, in the last decades before World War I and especially in the often criticized East Elbian agriculture,[16] German farmers, as a result of their comparatively high production costs—above all because of the use of artificial fertilizers and high land prices—were unable to keep up with the low-price foreign competition in a free market world. This was true for German cattle farmers, and especially true for grain farmers, who since the 1870s were confronted with an invasion of grain from overseas and with a dramatic decline in prices for their goods.[17]

The importance of the economic interests which either profited or suffered from the ever-advancing integration of the German economy into world markets meant that globalization was one of the most important forces behind the formation of business pressure groups. As in many other countries, in Germany such groups were born largely within the context of and along the lines of disagreement on foreign trade policy controversies. If one follows closely the process of the formation of these associations then one finds that one of the basic assumptions of the endogenous tariff theory is confirmed, namely that those who are interested in protection generally have a greater incentive to organize than those who are likely to profit from free trade. This is because the protective effect of a trade barrier is usually direct and immediate for the individuals who benefit from it, whereas the damage caused by it is indirect and diffuse.[18] The structural head start which protectionist interests enjoyed in regard to their organization can be observed in the early founding (1876) of the first and most important industrial umbrella association, the Central Association of German Industrialists (*Centralverbands Deutscher Industrieller (CVDI)*), which from the very beginning had practically no other goal than "protecting national labor" through a system of protective tariffs. To achieve this goal the CVDI carried out an extremely effective lobbying. However, the pressure association which was by far the most powerful and the most successful in pursuing its goals was the Agrarian League (*Bund der Landwirte (BdL)*). It had been founded in 1893 as a direct reaction to the trade treaties concluded by von Caprivi, which were perceived as being anti-agriculture, and to the worldwide decline in grain prices at the beginning of the 1890s. The organizational strength and the assertiveness of this agrarian pressure group reflects on the one hand the comparatively homogenous and intensely pronounced protectionist interests within German agriculture. On the other hand, the Agrarian League's effectiveness resulted from the leadership's constant efforts to meet any possible diverging of the interests within agriculture with the demand for "the greatest possible degree of uniform protection" for "*all* of the important branches of agriculture."[19]

Those industrial branches interested in unhindered access to markets throughout the world did not have a great deal to put forward to oppose the vehement resistance of the powerful agricultural associations. This was certainly because of the much more heterogeneous interests in the secondary sector in regard to trade policy issues, especially in comparison to agriculture. This picture of organizational weakness for both industry and commerce is not changed by taking into consideration the founding of the decidedly free trade lobbying associations such as the Central Department for Trade Treaties (*Centralstelle für Vorbereitung von Handelsverträgen*) (1897) and the Trade Treaty Association (*Handelsvertragsverein*) (1900). Internally divided, defensive in their orientation, founded too late and without much of an ability to mobilize broad masses, they were unable to exert a decisive influence on the foreign trade policy decision processes.[20]

The in part dramatic shift in income and wages caused by globalization and the potential disputes resulting from this contributed significantly to breaking up German society and politics before World War I along social-economic lines. The first cleavage which opened up under the pressure of increasing integration into world markets was between agriculture and industry. For the alliance between agriculture and heavy industry, which had existed since 1879 without any difficulties through the 1880s, a very serious conflict came up between their organizations over Caprivi's trade policy. The CVDI, which was dominated by heavy industry, had greeted the Russian-German trade treaty of 1894 "with joy," and those members of the *Reichstag* who were close to the CDVI had voted for the trade treaty. Since this treaty had been strongly opposed by the agrarians,[21] the agrarian representatives accused the industrialists of "great ruthlessness,"[22] believing that the existing "pact" between industry and agriculture had been "broken."[23] The policy of an agrarian-industrial coalition, initiated shortly before the turn of the century under the auspices of the Prussian Finance Minister, Johannes von Miquel, was able to patch over this break only for a short time. Even before the Bülow tariff was passed at the end of 1902 the instability of this coalition had become clear. The fragility resulted from the fact that the trade policy interests of the coalition partners were diametrically opposed to each other in key points. It became clear that not only the finished product industries, but also the heavy industry in West Germany, which was worried about its export possibilities, was ultimately unwilling to tolerate the exorbitant increase in tariff protection demanded by the agrarian pressure groups, as this threatened to torpedo the conclusion of new trade treaties.[24]

The second line of tension brought forth by globalization was the conflict of interests between rural producers and urban consumers, which became ever more politically explosive. This became especially clear in the election campaigns for parliament between 1890 and 1903, as tariff and trade policy advanced to a central point of contention in the political debates. Increasingly during this period the government lost its ability to set the agenda and define the topics of the election campaigns to the propaganda machines on the political right and left. On the one side of the political spectrum, the agrarian interest organizations, above all the BdL, set the tone with their demand to seal off Germany from the world market. On the other side, the Social Democrats protested quite effectively against the "hunger tariffs." In so doing they established themselves already within the course of the debates which culminated in the reform of the customs tariffs in 1902[25] as the party of the urban consumer—and not only later, as has often been assumed, in the struggle against the increase in meat prices in the decade before World War I.[26]

III

The first wave of globalization imposed increasingly restrictive conditions on German tariff and trade policy—in part as a direct result of the increasing dependency upon foreign trade, in part indirectly under the pressure of changing internal political conditions on the one hand and, on the other hand, the upward spiral of international protectionist measures. In the half century before World War I, the Prussian-German government increasingly saw its room to maneuver in the realm of foreign trade policy limited. At the beginning of this period, in the 1860s and early 1870s, the integration into world markets and the pressure from economic interests had not played a significant role in determining German trade policy. The significance in this phase of an economic constellation characterized by strong economic growth was not so much that it moved the free trade project forward as that the economic situation made it difficult for the opposition to free trade to develop. Decisive was rather an ideological factor: the victory among the elites in all of Europe, including Prussia, of the idea of free trade as well as the instrumentalization of this idea by the practitioners of Prussian power politics in their struggle for hegemony in Central Europe.[27]

The transition to protective tariffs in 1878/79 cannot be adequately explained without taking into consideration the changing global economic conditions: the world economic crisis which had been ongoing since 1873 as well as the flooding of Europe with grain from overseas, which started a little later. The consequences of this were profound: the organization of those affected and the articulation of their interests, the discrediting of liberal economic ideas, and the change in international trade policy in the direction of protectionism. How the customs tariff of 1879 came into being shows, however, that nothing more was created than the possibility of a protectionist turnaround and thus a new political constellation, whose outcome was fully open. It reveals to what degree Bismarck was the "*Macher*," the architect of the protectionist change of direction, and that it was essentially only because of his permanent interventions that the various factions who supported tariffs, whose paths repeatedly diverged from one another, stayed together until the end. In the key role played by Bismarck one can also see the relatively large scope of action which the executive still had at the time, which made it possible for the Chancellor to pursue far-reaching, autonomous goals in the realm of financial and internal policy, which went far beyond the limited realm of foreign trade policy.[28]

Only a decade and a half later—this is made clear by the discussions of the trade treaties proposed by Caprivi—this degree of political freedom had been reduced to a minimum. This confirms once again the historical interpretation that the 1890s were a decisive period in modern German history.[29] Now, for the first time, German foreign trade policy faced pressure from two different sides at the same time, which in both cases had their origins in globalization, and which increasingly limited the government's room to maneuver.

On the one hand, the integration of the German Empire into world markets had advanced so far that German foreign trade policies had to take note of it. This became clear when the protectionist tide, which had been rising worldwide from the 1870s up to the 1890s, reached a level that threatened to do serious damage to German exports and thus to the complete economic development of Germany. Two important export markets for German goods increasingly closed their borders to German industrial products. In the United States, the McKinley tariff of 1890 marked a new peak in a protectionism which had been worsening since 1861 (Morrill tariff). With Russia, Germany was even heading toward a tariff war, which escalated at the beginning of the 1890s and which caused significant damage to both sides. When at the same time, on top of this, the collapse of the European trade treaty system, which had been founded by Cobden and Chevalier in 1860 and from which Germany had profited as a result of its most-favored nation treaties and the conditions of the French-German peace treaty, became visible on the horizon, German foreign trade policy was under massive pressure to act. If the numerous bilateral treaties were to be allowed to expire without being replaced by new ones—and there were no new initiatives from France, which up till then had been the center of European trade treaties—then Europe was threatened with a "war of all against all" in trade policy.[30] In light of this precarious situation, Caprivi and the civil servants advising him decided to follow a new course in their trade policy. They broke with Bismarck's "autonomous" tariff policy and concluded a series of long-term trade treaties, all of which were based on the principle that Germany should lower its agricultural tariffs and receive concessions in return from its trading partners in regard to industrial tariffs. The high degree to which the German economy was dependent on imports and exports, so the Chancellor when he explained this step to parliament, made it appear "self-evident ... that to continue down the previous path" of sealing off Germany in terms of trade policy "could mean the ruin not only of our industry, of our working class, but also perhaps of even our state."[31]

Exactly this policy of sealing off Germany from world markets, on the other hand, was increasingly demanded by the powerful movement to protect agriculture which had come into being in response to the globalization of the market for agricultural products in a complex interplay of rural self-mobilization and control by the leadership of the agricultural pressure organizations. That the government attempted to help agriculture with economically valuable compensation measures such as lifting the "proof of identity" for grain did not change the fact that the agrarians believed themselves to have been left alone in their "life and death struggle."[32] Furiously attacked, Caprivi, the hated Chancellor, "without an acre or a stalk of grain to his name," was not up to the pressure from the agrarian side. His career came to an end in the whirlwind let loose by the agricultural pressure organizations.

The conflict came to a climax with the controversies over the question of how Germany should respond in terms of its tariff and trade policy to the economic globalization occurring at the turn to the twentieth century. Although the treaties negotiated by Caprivi were scheduled to run out in 1903, already in 1897 the responsible government agencies began working on a new customs tariff to replace the general tariff which had been in place since 1879. The rates of the new tariff—and this was its political significance—were to be the foundation for all future trade treaty negotiations. Soon after the ministries had begun working on the preparations for the Bülow tariffs, as they would later be known in recognition of the man who was chancellor when the tariffs became law, it became clear that the basic social antagonism between those who were the losers in the process of globalization—and who demanded to be protected—and those who supported a trade policy oriented to exporters and consumers, was being fought, too, in the offices of the ministries. At the end of this debate within the executive branch, which was disputed quite harshly, the compromise reached most closely reflected the opinions not of those who supported a high level of protectionism, but rather of those who were in favor of a limited protective tariff. (Given the internal political power constellation, a decidedly free trade policy was never a realistic alternative.) In the final analysis the government supported a trade policy which was less protectionist in its orientation than that favored by the majority in parliament, who were under much more pressure from the protectionist lobbying organizations. If this decision had been made according to the will of the parliamentary majority, then the tariff would have been much higher for agricultural products than had been proposed in the government's original draft—which, to be sure, raised the tariffs on agricultural products considerably, but not to a truly prohibitive level.

When in December 1902 parliament finally passed the tariff reform, five years after work on it had begun, contemporaries looked back on a political debate which was among the most bitter, lengthy, and far-reaching controversies in the whole history of the German Empire.[33] Especially the debate in parliament, which had lasted over a year, brought forth acutely once again the fault lines which existed between the political left and the protectionist majority, within the protectionist majority itself as well as between the protectionist majority and the government. Thus, just the opposite of that which Finance Minister Miquel had projected in 1897 turned out to be the case. Miquel had made a case before the Prussian State Ministry for a "national economic policy" with the argument that it could be achieved through "the cooperation of the large and significant economic groups," that this was "the appropriate means to bring the parties closer together" and to allow the existing "political differences ... to recede into the background."[34] Given the explosiveness inherent in the tariff question, an explosiveness which in the last analysis resulted from the fact that the incomes and the living conditions of various social groups were affected in very different ways by the first globalization, in the end the government just worked to be finished in any way possible with this difficult material, without being caught and squeezed between the various interests. Every long-term government strategy—including, indeed especially, the long-term strategy of an agrarian-industrial coalition—remained increasingly less important than a policy of muddling through. At the same time, every previous freedom of movement to instrumentalize customs and trade policy for other purposes disappeared; even solving pressing financial policy issues receded into the background as a secondary objective.

IV

Taken as a whole, the response of the German customs and trade policy to the challenges presented by globalization before World War I was ambivalent. On the one hand, the customs and trade policy went a long way toward meeting the protectionist demands of those who had organized into powerful organizations and who loudly supported their interests. As a result, the nominal tariff burden, above all on agricultural products, taken as a whole, rose significantly after 1879, and then, after the Caprivi-treaties expired, increased once again with the Bülow tariff. At the same time, the agricultural lobby was able to push through extensive packages of veterinary rules and other measures not related to tariffs which effectively protected it from competition on the world markets. Together, both measures ensured that the German prices for agricultural products remained throughout this period significantly above the prices on the world markets.

An exact quantification of the various consequences of the German agricultural protectionism is very difficult, because there are considerable uncertainties in regard to the sources and methodological problems. Still, there is little doubt that from an economic perspective the effects were clearly negative. All of the measures to support agricultural prices were in essence subventions to preserve and maintain agriculture, directing considerable resources into factors of production which were actually inefficient, which slowed down the structural changes in the economy at great cost, and which did not fully take advantage of the international division of labor. The farmers—and in contrast to what is put forward by a long-lasting myth, not just the farmers to the east of the Elbe, but also the farmers in the rest of Germany—profited from a large-scale redistribution of wealth by the state, and pocketed what was at times a quite lavish economic surplus. The consumers had to pay the cost of the generous system to protect agriculture, for their cost of living went up considerably in comparison to Great Britain, which remained committed to free trade.[35] The tariff on grain alone, part of the so-called Bülow tariffs, placed a burden on the budget of urban working-class families of more than 2 percent, often even more than 3 percent of their family income.[36]

The analysis of the economic and social costs of the German agricultural protectionism is one thing; yet did the decision makers in the German Empire have a realistic political alternative? Especially in regard to the prehistory of the reform of the customs tariffs in 1902 one can doubt whether the Prussian-German government would have been able to decrease significantly the in part existing, in part projected protection of agriculture against the public pressure organized by the agricultural interest associations and the decidedly protectionist majority in parliament, even if it had seriously wanted to do so. Even without the important political position of the Prussian landed nobility—this is shown by the example of the French agricultural protectionism, which was very similar to the German one in its most important characteristics[37]—at a time when approximately 40 percent of the working population was still employed in agriculture, and thus the incomes of a substantial portion of the population were considerably threatened by the integration into the world markets, there was scarcely any other option than to attempt to support those affected and to lessen the pressure of international competition through protectionist measures. Anything else would likely have seriously endangered the social peace and the stability of the political system. Studies on the relationship between trade openness and the extent of social security spending in OECD countries suggest that only after World War II did an efficient and productive social welfare state apparatus enable many industrial countries to compensate possible losers from globalization, without having to swing over to the path of a protectionist policy, with its negative repercussions on world trade.[38]

In a sense, protecting agriculture in order to pacify was the price which had to be paid in German trade policy, taking into account, and that is its other side, that Germany before World War I was one of the leading export nations in the world, to a large degree dependent upon world markets. Historians have willingly conceded this for Caprivi and for the trade treaties concluded while he was chancellor; however, for the period after this they have strongly opposed such an interpretation, following fully the contemporary criticism by Social Democrats and Liberals. There are many good arguments to be made for revising this perspective and emphasizing more strongly than before the continuities in the tariff and trade policy, reaching back from the beginning of the 1890s up till World War I. These continuities reveal a long-term consideration of German export interests and Germany's integration into world markets.

One needs to emphasize that the basic elements of the trade policy inaugurated by Caprivi remained unchanged even after the turn of the century. First, Germany continued to follow a policy of long-term trade treaties, using the Bülow tariff as the basis. As a result, Germany remained up till World War I the center of the European trade treaty system, a position it had taken over from France at the beginning of the 1890s. Second, in spite of powerful public relations efforts by the agrarian lobby, the German government continued to subscribe to the principle of the unlimited most-favored nation, which prevented German exports from being placed at a disadvantage in other countries and which furthermore generalized the reductions in tariffs which the Germans had granted in trade treaties. Third, with the exception of the legally obligatory minimal rates for the four main grain sorts—wheat, rye, oats and barley—which the agricultural pressure organizations were able to push through, the basic decision even in regard to the customs tariff of 1902 was against a double tariff and in favor of a uniform tariff, whose rates could be reduced in trade treaty negotiations, as there was no fixed, specified minimum level. Adhering to these basic principles of the previous trade policies, which guaranteed the stability of the general conditions and which thus made long-term planning possible, met the demands which were raised, in unison and with emphasis, by all the pressure groups from trade and industry, from the Centralverband up to the Trade Treaty Association.

What furthermore speaks against a break in the German foreign trade policy before World War I is that the tariff burden of the German imports, measured as a percentage, which can be considered a fair measure of the actual protectionist *niveau*,[39] hardly changed in the quarter century before 1914 in contrast to the nominal tariff rates. Because of the movement of prices on the world markets, neither the reductions in the tariffs as a result of the Caprivi treaties nor the increase in the rates in the Bülow tariff could be found in a corresponding development of the relative tariff burden. If one compares the five years from 1895 to 1899 with the five years from 1909 to 1913, it is clear that the average tariff burden on those imports liable to customs remained constant at around 19 percent. In other words, the average increase in tariffs as a result of the new tariffs in 1906 merely compensated for price increases in the world's markets. It is interesting that this is even true for foodstuffs, as for these items the new tariffs were increased the most. However, because of parallel developments in world market prices, the actual level of protection remained relatively constant (1895–1899: 23.6 percent, 1909–1913: 23 percent). Indeed, the average tariff burden on all imports into Germany declined slightly in the same period (1895–1899: 10 percent, 1909–1913: 8.6 percent), as the percentage of imports liable to duties declined from 53 to 45.8 percent of the total.[40]

In international comparison, the level of protectionism in the German Empire before World War I was at best in the lower-middle field. If one takes as the measure of protectionism the percentage of the tariff burden on all imports, then Germany was for the years 1909–1913 with an average of 8.6 percent at approximately the same level as Austria-Hungary (7.6 percent) and France (8.7 percent). Only Denmark, Switzerland, the Netherlands, and Great Britain were less protectionist—and even Great Britain had a tariff level of 5.6 percent of the value of its imports. Most of the other states of continental Europe had, in contrast, a significantly higher tariff level than Germany. The German rate was far removed from that of the United States (21.4 percent) and Russia (29.5 percent), which were the true bastions of protectionism.[41]

In conclusion, it should be pointed out that the perspective favored here looks at merely one aspect of the link between the first economic globalization and of the German economy and politics. This essay was most interested in the impact of globalization upon German society and politics and in tracing how Germany responded in terms of its trade policy to changing worldwide economic conditions. By concentrating on this dimension, of course, I did not want to suggest that globalization was an anonymous power which came out of nowhere, or that Germany was its "victim." Germany was an integral part of the global economy in the years before World War I. German firms helped shape in important ways the first wave of globalization. At the same time, German protectionist measures had important repercussions on the trade policies of other nation-states and on the process of globalization itself. The history of this complex interplay of globalization and the politics and economics of nation-states, which can often scarcely be disentangled, has yet to be written.

Notes

1. *Stenographische Berichte über die Verhandlungen des Deutschen Reichstags* (StenBerRT), 1900/1903, 2909 (3 December 1901).
2. See only K.H. O'Rourke and J.G. Williamson, *Globalization and History. The Evolution of a Nineteenth-Century Atlantic Economy* (Cambridge, MA, 1999); id., "When Did Globalisation Begin?," *European Review of Economic History* 6 (2002), 23–50; J. Osterhammel and N.P. Petersson, *Geschichte der Globalisierung. Dimensionen, Prozesse, Epochen* (Munich, 2003); C. Torp, "Weltwirtschaft vor dem Weltkrieg. Die erste Welle ökonomischer Globalisierung vor 1914," *Historische Zeitschrift* 279 (2004), 561–609; C. Conrad, *Globalisierung und Nation im Deutschen Kaiserreich* (Munich, 2006).
3. For the concept of a "Second Thirty-Years War" see H.-U. Wehler, *Deutsche Gesellschaftsgeschichte*, vol. 4 (Munich, 2003), and the contribution by J. Echternkamp in this volume.
4. See J.G. Williamson, "The Evolution of Global Labor Markets since 1830: Background Evidence and Hypotheses," *Explorations in Economic History* 32 (1995), 41–196; id., "Globalization, Labor

Markets and Policy Backlash in the Past," *Journal of Economic Perspectives* 12, no. 4 (1998), 51–72; O'Rourke and Williamson, *Globalization and History*, 119–66.
5. Cf. the contributions to this volume by Sebastian Conrad and Thomas Mergel.
6. See E. Kehr, *Schlachtflottenbau und Parteipolitik 1894–1901* (Berlin, 1930); id., *Der Primat der Innenpolitik*, ed. H.-U. Wehler (Berlin, 1965); A. Gerschenkron, *Bread and Democracy in Germany* (1943), reprint (Ithaca, 1989); H. Rosenberg, *Große Depression und Bismarckzeit. Wirtschaftsablauf, Gesellschaft und Politik in Mitteleuropa* (1967) (Frankfurt, 1976); H.-U. Wehler, *Das Deutsche Kaiserreich 1871–1918* (1973), 6th ed. (Göttingen, 1988). Cf. now C. Torp, "The Alliance of 'Rye and Iron' under the Pressure of Globalization. A Reinterpretation of Germany's Political Economy before 1914," *Central European History* 43 (2010), 401–27.
7. Rosenberg, *Große Depression*, 182.
8. See K.W. Hardach, *Die Bedeutung wirtschaftlicher Faktoren bei der Wiedereinführung der Eisen- und Getreidezölle in Deutschland 1879* (Berlin, 1967).
9. See J.C. Hunt, "Peasants, Grain Tariffs, and Meat Quotas: Imperial German Protectionism Reexamined," *Central European History* 7 (1974), 311–31.
10. Cf. only R.J. Evans, ed., *Society and Politics in Wilhelmine Germany* (London, 1978); G. Eley, *Reshaping the German Right. Radical Nationalism and Political Change after Bismarck* (1980), 2nd ed. (Ann Arbor, 1991); D. Blackbourn, *Class, Religion, and Local Politics in Wilhelmine Germany. The Center Party in Württemberg before 1914* (Wiesbaden, 1980); D. Blackbourn and G. Eley, *The Peculiarities of German History. Bourgeois Society and Politics in Nineteenth-Century Germany* (Oxford, 1984).
11. See G. Eley, "Sammlungspolitik, Social Imperialism and the Navy Law of 1898," *Militärgeschichtliche Mitteilungen* 15 (1974), 29–63.
12. P. Arndt, *Deutschlands Stellung in der Weltwirtschaft*, 2nd ed. (Leipzig, 1913), 12.
13. C. Torp, *Die Herausforderung der Globalisierung. Wirtschaft und Politik in Deutschland 1860–1914* (Göttingen, 2005), 60–62, 66, 372.
14. W. Feldenkirchen, *Siemens, 1918–1945* (Munich, 1995), S. 646 (table 1), 647 (table 2), 662 (table 21).
15. G. Plumpe, *Die I.G. Farbenindustrie AG. Wirtschaft, Technik und Politik 1904–1945* (Berlin, 1990), 50f.
16. See J.L. van Zanden, "The First Green Revolution: The Growth of Production and Productivity in European Agriculture, 1870–1914," *Economic History Review* 44 (1991), 215–39; O. Grant, "'Few better farmers in Europe?' Productivity, Change, and Modernization in East-Elbian Agriculture 1870–1913," *Wilhelminism and Its Legacies. German Modernities, Imperialism, and the Meanings of Reform, 1890–1930*, eds. G. Eley and J. Retallack (New York, 2003), 51–72; id., *Migration and Inequality in Germany 1870–1913* (Oxford, 2005), 215–52.
17. See, e.g., K.H. O'Rourke, "The European Grain Invasion, 1870–1913," *Journal of Economic History* 57 (1997), 775–801; H.-U. Wehler, *Deutsche Gesellschaftsgeschichte*, vol. 3 (Munich, 1995), 685ff.
18. See only B.S. Frey, *Internationale Politische Ökonomie* (Munich, 1985), 22ff.; H. Weck-Hannemann, *Politische Ökonomie des Protektionismus. Eine institutionelle und empirische Analyse* (Frankfurt, 1992), 58ff.
19. *Deutsche Tageszeitung*, 25 December 1900, emphasis in the original.
20. See Torp, *Herausforderung der Globalisierung*, 214–45.
21. H.A. Bueck, *Der Centralverband Deutscher Industrieller, 1876–1901*, vol. 1, (Berlin, 1902), 477.
22. J.v. Mirbach-Sorquitten, StenBerRT 1893/94, 1419 (26 February 1894).
23. W.v. Hammerstein, StenBerRT 1893/94, 1903 (16 March 1894).
24. See Bueck, *Centralverband*, vol. 1, 586–606; CVDI to Bülow, 18 September 1902, Bundesarchiv (BA), R 1501, 118918, Bl. 16.
25. See J. Sperber, *The Kaiser's Voters. Electors and Elections in Imperial Germany* (Cambridge, 1997), 212–40; B. Fairbairn, *Democracy in the Undemocratic State. The German Reichstag Elections of 1898 and 1903* (Toronto, 1997), 45–68, 209–40.

26. Cf. C. Nonn, *Verbraucherprotest und Parteiensystem im wilhelminischen Deutschland* (Düsseldorf, 1996), 23–83, 240–80, 313f.
27. See H. Böhme, *Deutschlands Weg zur Großmacht. Studien zum Verhältnis von Wirtschaft und Staat während der Reichsgründungszeit 1848–1881* (Cologne, 1966), 100–166; H.-W. Hahn, *Geschichte des Deutschen Zollvereins* (Göttingen, 1984), 165–88.
28. See Rosenberg, *Große Depression*; H.-U. Wehler, *Bismarck und der Imperialismus* (1969), 2nd ed. (Frankfurt, 1985), 61–111; Böhme, *Deutschlands Weg*, 341–586; I.N. Lambi, *Free Trade and Protection in Germany 1868–79* (Wiesbaden, 1963), 73–149.
29. See the contribution by Helmut Walser Smith to this volume.
30. Caprivi's speech in the Reichstag. *StenBerRT* 1890/92, 3302 (10 December 1891).
31. Ibid.
32. Count Kanitz. *StenBerRT* 1893/94, 1513 (1 March 1894).
33. See D.M. Bleyberg, "Government and Legislative Process in Wilhelmine Germany: The Reorganization of the Tariff Laws under Reich Chancellor von Bülow 1897–1902" (PhD diss., University of East Anglia, 1979); Torp, *Herausforderung der Globalisierung*, 211–91.
34. Meeting of the Preußisches Staatsministerium, 22 November 1897, Bundesarchiv, R 43, 2028, Bl. 30.
35. See already C.v. Tyszka, *Löhne und Lebenskosten in Westeuropa im 19. Jahrhundert* (Munich, 1914), 259–90.
36. My own calculations, based on W. Gerloff, "Verbrauch und Verbrauchsbelastung kleiner und mittlerer Einkommen in Deutschland um die Wende des 19. Jahrhunderts. Eine konsum- und finanzstatistische Studie," *Jahrbücher für Nationalökonomie und Statistik* 35 (1908), 35.
37. See R. Aldenhoff-Hübinger, *Agrarpolitik und Protektionismus. Deutschland und Frankreich im Vergleich, 1879–1914* (Göttingen, 2002).
38. See D.R. Cameron, "The Expansion of the Public Economy: A Comparative Analysis," *The American Political Science Review* 72 (1978), 1243–61; D. Rodrik, "Why Do More Open Economies Have Bigger Governments?," *The Journal of Political Economy* 106 (1998), 997–1032; E. Rieger and S. Leibfried, *Grundlagen der Globalisierung. Perspektiven des Wohlfahrtsstaates* (Frankfurt, 2001).
39. Economic historians often use the ratio of the duties collected to imports to describe the level of protectionism. However, there are two methodological problems with this: on the one hand, the effect of non-tariff trade barriers is not taken into consideration. On the other hand, the measure is also blind in regard to tariffs which are so high that they are prohibitive and therefore actually are not levied.
40. *Statistisches Handbuch für das Deutsche Reich*, ed. Kaiserlich Statistisches Amt, part 2 (Berlin, 1907), 588; *Statistisches Jahrbuch für das Deutsche Reich* 31 (1910), 314; ibid. 35 (1914), 364, my calculations.
41. P. Bairoch, "European Trade Policy, 1815–1914," *The Cambridge Economic History of Europe*, vol. 8, ed. P. Mathias and S. Pollard (Cambridge, 1989), 76, 139, mistakenly states that the German level was only 7.9 percent. Germany's position in the international ranking of protectionism is confirmed by A. Estevadeordal's calculations which are based on a different methodological approach: "Measuring Protection in the Early Twentieth Century," *European Review of Economic History* 1 (1997), 89–125.

Chapter 21

German Industry and American Big Business, 1900–1914

Volker Berghahn

This contribution deals with aspects of the history of the Wilhelmine empire and its embeddedness in the international system before 1914 that have been overshadowed during the last two decades by more fashionable genres of historical writing, such as the history of daily life and gender, of minorities, popular culture, and identity. By contrast, I am interested here in problems of political economy and of the role of economic actors before World War I. What has motivated me to contribute this essay to a volume that is largely concerned with non-economic questions is the hope that economic history will once again attract more research in the future. However, my approach is not a quantitative one. Rather I start from the existing and certainly indispensable statistical foundations that have been built by others in order to proceed to a more qualitative analysis at the center of which appear economic elites and their interactions with their counterparts in other countries, their perceptions of the world with their judgments, prejudices, and misjudgments.

There is of course a good deal of valuable work on the German business community and the agrarians in their domestic setting.[1] My focus here is on American businessmen and their attitudes toward Germany. I am basing my approach on the consideration that these businessmen will provide a view from the outside both of the German industrial system and of German society and its political system that is missing from the history books, even though this American elite was better informed about the development of Wilhelmine Germany on account of its many visits and in some cases also through family ties. The question posed here is therefore: how did American big business view the German Empire, and do their assessments help us to understand a development that ended in the outbreak of war in 1914?

There are a number of important studies of German-American relations before 1914 that examine various aspects of this relationship, but do so mainly from a political and cultural perspective.[2] Four of these are to be discussed here because they have influenced the lines of argument of this contribution and have also guided me toward sources that are still underused. The work that has to be mentioned first of all in this connection is the two volumes that Alfred Vagts, a refugee from Nazism, published with Macmillan in 1935.[3] Remarkably, the study appeared in German, although its timeframe did not go beyond 1906. Even over seventy years later, it impresses by its extraordinarily broad empirical base that threatens to overwhelm the reader and makes it difficult to see the wood for the trees.

Only in a few places does Vagts say more explicitly what his book is ultimately about. Thus, he arrives after some two thousand pages of his "historical examination of the relations between two states" at the conclusion that "high capitalism," having reached "the stage of the 1890–1906 period," had, during the process of the "rationalistic economization of social relations" stopped short of "a regulation of foreign policy problems and hence of removing the traditional pillars of foreign policy-making and militarism." It had done so "generally respectfully and reluctantly, if not even cowardly" and most "probably in consideration of domestic politics and class." More than that, this "high capitalism" had even permitted the traditional elites "to put its own works in jeopardy, if not even to destroy them."[4]

Referring to theories that were more widely discussed in his time, Vagts added that German and American imperialism before 1914 "did not necessarily—[at least] to a lesser extent than German militarism that was also conditioned by class— ... spring from the overall economic constitution and its structure," but from the "formation, tradition and instincts in both societies that were partially pre-capitalist." After all, those who were guilty of those conflicts represented "minorities, capitalist and personal ones, which had interests in those conflicts"; they represented "segments of the national economy (armaments industry, the capitalist press) and—more frequently and primarily—political and bureaucratic elites, whose noble activities the capitalists in their majority interests were too cowardly to contradict."

We shall have to come back at the end of this essay to Vagts' question of capitalist "cowardice." What has to be noted here is that he stresses the "significance of structural pressures," on the one hand, but is also and ultimately concerned with the "impact of personal criteria that were separate from structures"; these to Vagts were criteria that were the result of "tradition, interest in status quo preservation, adaptation to the present" and that refer the analyst to "the development of the political process within the national framework and international rivalry."[5] However interesting and rich in detail Vagts' two volumes are, in the context of this contribution they suffer from two weaknesses. To begin with, there is the problem that the timeframe up to 1906 is too short. Secondly, the economic elites of Germany and the United States make no more than an indirect appearance. The bulk of his empirical material stems from ministerial files, newspaper clippings, and the papers of assorted diplomats and politicians.

When many new archival sources had become available a generation later, it was Ragnild Fiebig-von Hase who earned much praise for her work on German-American relations before 1914.[6] Although her main study, as if in competition with Vagts, comprises some eleven hundred pages, she, unlike the latter, chose a clearly delineated focus, i.e., Latin America as an area of international and especially German-American conflict. However, she, too, like many other authors, approached her subject after a brief outline of the larger economic picture predominantly from the perspective of diplomatic history, and ends her analysis with the Venezuelan crisis of 1902–3. Two years later, she published an article on "German-American economic relations, 1890–1914, in the era of protectionism and international integration" that was cast more broadly.[7] Here she put forward not only useful statistical material for the entire period, but also discussed the structural differences between the two industrial systems.

The third study to be mentioned here is by Ute Mehnert and bears a title that, at first glance, does not seem relevant to our topic: "Germany, America and the 'Yellow Peril.' The Career of a Political Catchword in Great Power Politics, 1905–1917."[8] Its significance nevertheless lies in the fact that she moves the story beyond Vagts and Fiebig-von Hase to a global level, and expands the traditional trans-Atlantic perspective by a trans-Pacific one. Accordingly, Mehnert makes East Asia and the catchword about the "Yellow Peril" that gained currency in the West the "starting-point of an analysis in diplomatic history." Her main interest is in the "question of the origins of a global international system of states that provided an expanded sphere of action to the foreign policies of the European great powers and the U.S."

This means that she turns, on the one hand, against Paul Kennedy[9] who, while highlighting "the growing importance of the U.S. in the world economy and its increasing political engagement in areas beyond the Western Hemisphere," places that country "at the periphery of a Eurocentric international system" because the Americans decided to abstain from formal alliances.[10] The United States by contrast remains politically central to Mehnert. Moreover, she criticizes Reiner Pommerin with respect to Germany's policy toward the United States after 1905/6. He had argued that the German emperor and his advisors had been aiming to reduce conflict potentials and had concentrated on Europe instead of continuing to pursue the German *Weltpolitik* of the turn of the century.[11] This is why Pommerin believes that Berlin missed the significance of two new players on the international stage in the years before 1914, i.e., the United States and Japan.

This interpretation, according to Mehnert, moved "German-American relations to an isolated plain and reduced expansionist clashes of interest to sham conflicts that were primarily due to misunderstandings and political miscalculations."[12] However, the presence of the "'Japanese Danger' as a constant factor in German and American policy-making" points, she argued, in "another direction." In fact, "the integration of the catchword into the foreign-policy conceptions and decision-making processes of both powers" makes clear that the United States and Germany "continually oriented their political calculations toward a global international system." This, Mehnert concluded, means that both powers had a "clear consciousness of the interaction between the power constellations in the Atlantic and the Pacific space."

The fourth and final author with whose help the approach to this essay is to be delineated is Magnus Brechtgen.[13] Although he is primarily interested "in personality networks and international politics," he presents very helpful economic data at the beginning of his voluminous study. This, together with the materials collected by Fiebig-von Hase in her above-mentioned article and the statistics that Cornelius Torp examines at the beginning of his recent book, offers a very good quantitative foundation for dealing with the more qualitative aspects of the German-American economic relationship before 1914.

However, the main significance of Brechtgen's work lies in the ways in which, while accepting the Atlantic-Pacific framework of Mehnert, he uses the available economic data to determine if the global system of international relations nevertheless had a center of gravity around which his own empirical research might be organized. As he demonstrates by reference to how the great powers of the time projected their economic power abroad, the developments of the decade before World War I clearly pointed to the existence of a triangle composed of Britain, Germany, and the United States. In comparison to this triad, the capacities of France, Russia, and other European states to project their economic and political might abroad were considerably weaker. This analysis enables Brechtgen to break away from the Eurocentric position that had informed Kennedy's work and to expand it to the Atlantic region. No less importantly, he succeeds in showing on the basis of the statistics he presents that the United States became the strongest player in the British-German-American triangle.

However, at the center of his subsequent analysis appears a political rather than an economic question. Starting from the probably correct assumption (that Vagts had also articulated), i.e., that Germany's economic elites did not play a decisive role in the decision-making processes in Berlin during the July Crisis of 1914, his book inevitably moves into the political history of the prewar decades. Accordingly, the rest of his study is devoted to a most careful examination of British-German-American relations from the vantage point of the major political actors. Thus, the two American ambassadors to Berlin, Cecil Spring Rice and Harvey White, are very frequently cited. Their political networks, activities, and perceptions are discussed in considerable detail. Brechtgen can demonstrate convincingly that the United States, as the strongest and rising great power, was intensively courted by both Berlin and London, and that American foreign policy well before World War I had increasingly turned in a direction that was pro-British, on the one hand, and anti-German, on the other.

Brechtgen's volume is therefore most valuable as a political history of British-German-American relations "in modern perspective."[14] But as far as I can see, there is still no study that deals with the Atlantic triangle from the perspective of the three business elites. Such a study can of course not be provided in this essay. All we can hope to do is to make a start that draws on a limited number of primary sources. This explains why the subsequent analysis is primarily based on two influential newspapers, the *Wall Street Journal* (WSJ) and the *New York Times* (NYT).

The question therefore is what is to be found in these papers in the way of information as well as judgments relating to Britain and Germany. What were the major economic themes that they took up and what changes did these themes undergo in the years up to World War I? This approach does of course contain many methodological problems so that my conclusions are merely preliminary, all the more so because limitations of space do not make it possible to quote American businessmen and their attitudes towards Europe more extensively or to reprint longer passages from the two newspapers. All I can do is to present in a nutshell the major topics in the hope that the basic lines of the pre-1914 development can be brought out. In defense of this methodology it is perhaps also important to realize that a lot of information can be gleaned from these two newspapers. How far it diverges from what is to be found in company archives or the private papers of businessmen is of course a task that will have to be taken up by future research that looks at individual economic actors and firms that operated in the Atlantic triangle.

Let me begin with two more general observations that emerge from the two papers. Firstly, the amount of reporting shows very clearly how intensive transatlantic exchanges had become before 1914. There was first of all the information that reached New York by telegraph. However, the extent of the exchange of people is no less astonishing. Throughout the nineteenth century most travelers had been emigrants from Europe, anxious to settle in the United States. However, by 1900 this stream had begun to dwindle quite dramatically, not least from Central Europe.[15] Now it was wealthy Europeans who booked a cabin on one of the fast steamers of the great British, German, and American shipping lines.

On the route from West to East it was with increasing frequency American passengers who had come to even greater wealth and who with their wives or even their children wanted to tour Europe. Among these travelers was a growing number of businessmen who traveled on their own. They wanted to gain a firsthand impression of Europe, to gauge opportunities from cooperations and investments, and to inform themselves about the national business climates and cultures. It would be interesting to know more precisely how strong this traffic was to other parts of the globe. But it seems safe to assume that it did not reach the volume of the travel across the Atlantic and that it did not reach the same dimensions as at the end of the twentieth century, which is why the concept of globalization should also be used with some caution for the pre-1914 period. Still the exchange of people was enormous and very lucrative for the shipping companies, to which must be added the exchange of raw materials and finished industrial goods, so impressively reflected in the statistics collated by Torp and Brechtgen.

Secondly, scrutiny of the two American newspapers confirms what can be gleaned from Brechtgen's tables: the British-German-American triangle was indeed the center of gravity. France appeared less frequently, and Russia as well as Austria-

Hungary even more rarely. Over the years it is also possible to see not merely in the statistics but also in the newspaper commentaries how Britain was slowly losing ground in the competition with the United States and Germany. From the American perspective, that is at the core of this article, Germany appeared ever more brightly on the radar screen of the business community as an economic power but also as a political one.

Let me deal with the positive sides of this American preoccupation with the German Empire first. At the turn of the century, it is fair to say that there continued to exist considerable tensions that had resulted from the tariff increases that both countries had introduced in previous years.[16] Relations were also badly affected by the Venezuelan crisis. But after 1900 business contacts and trade took place in an atmosphere that was in principle amicable. There were, it is true, the attempts of the Krupp trust to break into the American steel market that aroused suspicion.[17] Conversely, the *Hamburg-Amerika-Linie* tried to protect itself against "Americanization," as it was literally put in 1902.[18] In subsequent years, however, the respective chambers of commerce tried hard to improve relations. At the time of the First Moroccan Crisis, the *Wall Street Journal* stated explicitly that the United States did not harbor any hostile feelings against the German empire.[19]

When American businessmen therefore traveled to Europe, they regularly also explored opportunities for cooperations, participations, and even direct investments. But rather than foreign direct investment (FDI), it was still the opening of agencies and sales offices that was at the top of the list. Only a few American companies decided to establish production facilities in Europe, just as conversely it was only a few German enterprises that began to manufacture in the United States.[20] Up to 1914, it was particularly International Harvester that saw opportunities in the market for agricultural machinery and therefore built a factory in Neuss on the Rhine, north of Cologne. Merganthaler Linotype had similarly good experiences with its printing machines, sold in both Germany and Britain through agencies. Otis Elevators and Woolworth's department stores entered the European market. On the other hand, the Kayser glove-making company ran into trouble from its Saxon competitors, and later Standard Oil became the target of much controversy in Germany. Meanwhile various banks and the electrical and chemical industries, among which the latter went from strength to strength in the decades before 1914, worked closely with their American counterparts.[21]

While more specific impressions of the many business travelers were transmitted to a narrower circle of colleagues within their companies, they felt quite free to offer their general impressions of Europe, and of Britain and Germany in particular, when they stepped off the boat in New York.[22] Waiting on the pier, they would find a bevy of journalists who were keen to obtain a statement from them. Finally, there were speeches by businessmen before clubs and associations that were reprinted in the papers as well as interviews. They all give a good first impression of what the travelers had seen and noted.

There has been a good deal of research on American businesses' organizational and cultural imports to Europe before 1914 and on those European businessmen who came to the United States to inform themselves about new production and management methods. They are perhaps the best proof that the United States had meanwhile emerged as a major industrial power. These visitors would view factories in Pennsylvania, Ohio, or Michigan, and would also engage with the ideas of Frederick Taylor and the Scientific Management movement or with those of Henry Ford concerning mass production and mass consumption.

These contacts time and again raised the question of how far Taylorism and Fordism might be imported into Europe.[23] However, this was also a time when the Americans tried to learn from the Europeans, and especially from German industry. Both newspapers repeatedly carried reports and commentaries on the German system of education and on the training of apprentices that American business should study seriously. In 1907 there was a discussion of the advantages of the German system of banking as compared to the American one.[24]

Overall it is difficult to overlook the new self-confidence that the Americans displayed after the turn of the century, if not before. They saw themselves as the first industrial power of the future.[25] Later such views were put forward somewhat less forcefully. The business community was still convinced that the United States had the edge, especially in electrical engineering. However, a comparison between the performance of AEG (*Allgemeine Electricitäts-Gesellschaft*) and General Electrics reveals that the two companies were in a neck-and-neck competition. Germany's rise is also reflected in the growing consumption of copper, partly imported from the United Stataes. Soon the question was raised if it was German big business that was America's real competitor, rather than the British, and that it might one day even overtake America.[26]

These developments gave rise not only to the issues of learning from others but also of critical comparison, in the course of which one tended to stress the differences between the two industrial systems. These debates are particularly interesting in the context of this article because there were structural factors in Germany that the Americans increasingly registered as negatives not to be emulated across the Atlantic. Prominent among these negatives was the organization of the German market, on which there appeared an increasing number of comments.[27] As is well known, the Sherman Act of 1890 had cemented the principle of market competition in the United States. It outlawed the conclusion of cartels (i.e., horizontal agreements between independent firms over prices, production quotas, etc.) and syndicates (i.e., joint sales organizations) as well as attempts by single companies to achieve a monopoly position in the market. This meant that the American concentration movement of the late nineteenth century was pushed in the direction of oligopolistic competition that by and large also left enough room for smaller enterprises. The main purpose of the Sherman Act, some later modifications notwithstanding, was to protect the consumer against the powerful producers.

The German Empire went in the opposite direction with the formation of cartels that tended to protect the producers against competition.[28] In 1897 the Reich Court rendered an opinion that declared horizontal agreements to be legally binding contracts. This made it possible for cartels to sue companies that tried to leave a cartel and to adopt, quite legally, discriminatory practices against non-members. It is true that some American companies also favored the formation of cartels, and the Webb-Pomerene Act later permitted the participation of American firms in international cartels. Still, it is significant that the impulse for the formation of such international combinations tended to come from the European end, and from the Germans in particular, and that they were often directed against the United States. What is important in the pre-1914 context is that the two industrial systems took divergent paths as far as the question of the organization of the market was concerned—a question that is central to any capitalist system. Above all, this divergence was noted by the American side. The two countries were not only competitors on the world market but also developed a different conception of the meaning of capitalist competition.[29]

After this, it was but a small step for the Americans to take a more general view that the Germans inclined towards a collectivism that was sharply delineated from the American creed of individualism.[30] Although American businessmen continued to talk about good relations with the Germans despite their commercial rivalry, the peculiarities of the German "mentality" became a new focus of discussion.[31] And while hitherto economic assessments had remained quite separate from political ones, they increasingly began to overlap in the last years before World War I. Here the increasing mistrust of American diplomats observing the German monarchy may have impacted on American business attitudes, just as conversely commercial tensions were registered by politicians and bureaucrats.[32] By 1913, concerns about the growing indebtedness of Germany and the early indications of an impending recession were added to a sense that relations were deteriorating.

The political developments after 1905 no doubt contributed to this feeling. The United States had contributed to finding a solution to the First Moroccan Crisis in the course of which Washington inevitably began to ask itself what might have motivated the kaiser to unleash it and, more broadly, what the larger ambitions of German *Weltpolitik* could be.[33] If the monarch appeared to be the "Trade Lord of Europe"[34] and as a man of peace to some American business travelers, they were clearly deceiving themselves. To some extent their illusions may have been due to the soft line that Berlin pursued toward Washington after the Venezuelan debacle. Nor should the impact of German cultural propaganda be underestimated.[35] Perhaps it was also a latent admiration that many American entrepreneurs who traveled to Europe felt for the social prestige that the aristocracy continued to enjoy. Although Wilhelm II seems to have made it his business to charm American visitors, there was a growing suspicion that he was a hypocrite and that his actual policies were really disturbing the international peace. The expansion of the German Navy was primarily directed against Britain, but American businessmen recognized the dangers of the Anglo-German naval arms race that soon expanded into an arms competition on land against France and Russia. The main explanation they had for Germany's increasingly aggressive foreign policy was that it was inherent in the structures of the Prusso-German constitutional system and the powerful role it gave to the military.[36]

A number of scholars have investigated how Wilhelmine *Weltpolitik* affected Washington's diplomacy and how the Americans were moved more and more to support the British side, a development that London had worked hard to foster.[37] Even if Berlin, alarmed by this shift, pursued an increasingly conciliatory course towards the United States, the "cold war" against Britain continued, although it had become clear that Wilhelm II and his naval minister Alfred von Tirpitz were losing their arms race against the Royal Navy. These were developments that filled the American business community with apprehension. They feared that rising international tensions and the emergence of immobile alliance blocs might explode into a European war that would cost billions of dollars and badly damage, if not destroy, the international trading system.[38]

It was at this point that what might be called an Anglo-Saxon liberal vision of international order came to the fore, that had first been adopted by Britain in the early nineteenth century, that Herbert Spencer had discussed in his books in the latter years, and that the British businessman Norman Angell had revived in 1911 in his bestseller *The Grand Illusion*. Therein he made a powerful argument that arms competitions and wars among great powers were completely unproductive and indeed (self-)destructive and that in the era of industrialism and world trade they represented atavisms from a bygone pre-capitalist age of militarism.[39]

In line with this paradigm, it was the *Wall Street Journal* that once more referred to the contrast between political systems and civilian societies that devoted themselves to commerce (even if it was not exactly peaceful), and those that were organized militaristically toward war, ironically this time just a few days before Wilhelm II signed the mobilization order that triggered World War I: "The whole world is engaged in business as never before. Industrial Germany in thirty years has far outrun military Germany. ... Throughout the civilized world villages have become mill centers; towns have become cities; empires have succeeded states, and the Empire in the modern world is commercial and not martial."[40] Accordingly militarism and war were seen not only by the *Wall Street Journal* but also by the American business community more generally as a great misfortune,[41] and this is what World War I then in fact turned out to be, to an extent that even the key decision-makers in Berlin (and Vienna) had not imagined. There were a few gloomy predictions about how this war would change the world, but even they were hardly pessimistic enough.

However, the kaiser and his advisers did not share such Angellian views of the world which is why they had rejected all proposals to reduce armaments that had also been circulating in the American business community before 1914.[42] More than that, under the Reich constitution, Wilhelm II had the legal authority and power to assert the martial principle against the commercial one. In light of the aggression of the Central Powers, the United States was now fully pulled into the camp of those who had become the victims of German aggression, even if it took until 1917 for Washington formally to join the alliance that ultimately defeated Germany.

However, most businessmen on the American east coast had long before 1914 come to hold the view that had now turned out to be no more than a pious hope, that "no civilized nation in the world today can raise armies for aggression."[43] Of course, this did not mean that they did not also adhere to the idea that states can and must "readily raise armies and war treasuries for defense." As we now know, this was also the belief with which the majority of Germans marched off to the front, after the kaiser and his advisers had convinced them that they had been attacked and were now called upon to defend the Fatherland. Although many German businessmen, among them Albert Ballin, the Hamburg shipping magnate, shared the view that a European war would be a catastrophe, they, too, accepted the kaiser's declaration of war as justified. But they did so not because they were too "cowardly," as Alfred Vagts had argued in the 1930s, but because they were excluded from the decisions to unleash this war and allowed themselves to be led by the nose by the monarchical government in Berlin.

It has not been possible in this short article to do full justice to the topic that I mapped out in the introduction. Instead I have tried to present the basic outlines of how American businessmen and two influential newspapers viewed the German industrial system and the Hohenzollern monarchy. The next step would be to test the issues that have been presented here against other sources, in the same way Brechtgen did in his study with respect to the political-diplomatic developments within the British-German-American triangle. It is to be hoped that such investigations will yield new insights into the relationship between economics and politics, and into the dynamics of the pre-1914 international system.

Notes

1. See, e.g., H. Kaelble, *Industrielle Interessenpolitik in der Wilhelminischen Gesellschaft* (Berlin, 1967); H.-J. Puhle, *Agrarische Interessenpolitik und preussischer Konservatismus im Wilhelminischen Reich* (Hannover, 1967).
2. See, e.g., H.W. Gatzke, *Germany and the United States. "A Special Relationship"* (Cambridge, MA, 1980); A. Sedlmaier, *Deutschlandbilder und Deutschlandpolitik* (Wiesbaden, 2003).
3. A. Vagts, *Deutschland und die Vereinigten Staaten in der Weltpolitik*, 2 vols. (New York, 1935).
4. Vagts, Vol. II, 2017, also for the following.
5. Thus the conclusion of Magnus Brechtgen, *Scharnierzeit 1985–1907* (Mainz, 2006), 21.
6. R. Fiebig-von Hase, *Lateinamerika als Konfliktherd der deutsch-amerikanischen Beziehungen, 1890–1903*, 2 vols. (Göttingen, 1986).
7. Idem, "Die deutsch-amerikanischen Wirtschaftsbeziehungen, 1890–1914, im Zeichen von Protektionismus und internationaler Integration," *Amerikastudien* 33 (1988), 329–57.
8. U. Mehnert, *Deutschland, Amerika und die "Gelbe Gefahr." Zur Karriere eines Schlagworts in der grossen Politik, 1903–1917* (Stuttgart, 1995).
9. P. M. Kennedy, *The Rise of the Anglo-German Antagonism* (London, 1980).
10. Mehnert, *Deutschland*, 15.
11. R. Pommerin, *Deutschland und Amerika. Die USA in der Politik der Reichsleitung, 1890–1917* (Cologne, 1986).
12. Mehnert, *Deutschland*, 16.
13. Brechtgen, *Scharnierzeit*.

14. A. Hillgruber, "Politische Geschichte in moderner Sicht," *Historische Zeitschrift* 216 (1973), 329–52. Brechtgen's book was influenced by Klaus Hildebrand's work on foreign policy issues.
15. See, e.g., K.J. Bade, *Population, Labor, and Migration in 19th and 20th Century Germany* (Oxford, 1987).
16. On the conflicts over tariffs, see, e.g., C. Torp, *Die Herausforderung der Globalisierung. Wirtschaft und Politik in Deutschland, 1860–1914* (Göttingen, 2005). On the Venezuelan crisis see, apart from the studies by Fiebig-von Hase, H.H. Herwig, *Germany's Vision of Empire in Venezuela, 1871–1914* (Princeton, 1986); N. Mitchell, *The Danger of Dreams. German and American Imperialism in Latin America* (Chapel Hill, NC, 1997); *New York Times* (NYT), 3 March 1900; NYT, 21 May 1901; NYT, 21 December 1901; NYT, 17 August 1902; NYT, 13 December 1902; NYT, 21 December 1902.
17. See, e.g., NYT, 10 August 1903; *Wall Street Journal* (WSJ), 30 July 1903; NYT, 30 August 1903 ("The Krupp Invasion").
18. NYT, 12 November 1901; WSJ, 12 January 1904 (with the heading: "American Invasion"); NYT, 27 December 1900; NYT, 22 April 1901; NYT, 24 May 1901; NYT, 22 October 1901 (with the heading "American Danger"); NYT, 17 February 1902.
19. WSJ, 17 January 1906.
20. Among those German firms that dared to make direct investments was, e.g., the chocolate manufacturer Stollwerck.
21. On International Harvester: WSJ, 1 September 1909; WSJ, 8 January 1910; WSJ, 10 March 1910; WSJ, 1 September 1910; WSJ, 26 September 1910 (with statistics to highlight successes). On Merganthaler: WSJ, 22 July 1910. On Otis: 3 August 1912. On Woolworth: WSJ, 29 August 1913. On Kayser: WSJ, 24 August 1912; NYT, 17 August 1912; NYT, 18 August 1912. On Standard Oil: WSJ, 15 March 1911; WSJ, 5 August 1912; WSJ, 8 May 1914; NTY, 3 May 1902; NYT, 23 February 1910; NYT, 15 October 1912. On banks: C. Kobrak, *Cooperation, Conflict, Men, and Markets: Deutsche Bank and the United States, 1870 to the Present* (New York, 2007); WSJ, 20 January 1914; NYT, 4 November 1905; NYT, 10 October 1906. On Coal: WSJ, 15 December 1908. On the chemical industry: W. Abelshauser, ed., *German Industry and Global Enterprise* (New York, 2004); WSJ, 22 July 1905. On the electrical engineering industry: WSJ, 20 May 1904.
22. See, e.g., M. Nolan, *Visions of Modernity* (New York, 1994); WSJ, 23 March 1903; NYT, 4 January 1903; NYT, 20 January 1907; NYT, 11 September 1910.
23. See, e.g., S. Haber, *Efficiency and Uplift* (Chicago, 1964); H. Braverman, *Labor and Monopoly Capital*, 1974; R. Kanigel, *Our Best Way. Frederick Taylor and the Enigma of Efficiency* (New York, 1997); NYT, 6 July 1902; NTY, 8 September 1907.
24. On training: NYT, 7 August 1904; WSJ, 12 October 1905; WSJ, 15 April 1905; WSJ, 20 May 1905; WSJ, 2 June 1905; NYT, 10 August 1913. On banking: WSJ, 28 December 1907; NYT, 1 February 1908; WSJ, 9 October 1909 (relating to the Reichsbank). On city administration: WSJ, 8 February 1908; NYT, 18 August 1913.
25. See, e.g., NYT, 7 January 1901; NYT, 21 May 1901; NYT, 17 April 1902; NYT, 20 May 1903; WSJ, 26 March 1904.
26. On electrical engineering: WSJ, 27 January 1912; WSJ, 12 March 1912. On copper consumption: WSJ, 21 February 1911; WSJ, 16 August 1911. On Germany's rise: WSJ, 5 November 1907; WSJ, 13 September 1909; WSJ, 15 September 1909; 3 December 1909.
27. On the American Antitrust tradition see, e.g., R.B. Heflebower, "Monopoly and Competition in the United States of America," E.H. Chamberlin, ed., *Monopoly and Competition and their Regulation* (London, 1954), 110–49; R.F. Himmelberg, ed., *The Rise of Big Business and the Beginning of Antitrust and Railroad Regulation, 1870–1900*, Vol. I (New York, 1994); WSJ, 4 March 1905. During the initial years there was still a good deal of resistance on the part of American industry against these laws. See, e.g., WSJ, 5 October 1910; WSJ, 14 November 1911; NYT, 17 November 1911.
28. See, e.g., V. Hentschel, *Wirtschaft und Wirtschaftspolitik im wilhelminischen Deutschland* (Stuttgart, 1978); H. Pohl, ed., *Kartelle und Kartellgesetzgebung in Praxis und Rechtsprechung vom 19.*

Jahrhundert bis zur Gegenwart (Stuttgart, 1985); T.P. Kovaleff, ed., *The Antitrust Impulse*, Vol. I (Armonk, NY, 1994); WSJ, 9 October 1903; WSJ, 12 January 1904; WSJ, 15 April 1905; WSJ, 30 May 1906; WSJ, 4 April 1908; NYT, 15 August 1912; NYT, 18 August 1912. On the German side there were a few industrialists who preferred the American system, but they were unable to assert themselves against the majority who favored cartels and syndicates. WSJ, 6 January 1906.

29. For a synthesis see V.R. Berghahn, *The Americanization of West German Industry, 1945–1973* (New York, 1986), 2–39; WSJ, 4 February 1911.
30. WSJ, 23 September 1911.
31. WSJ, 21 January 1911; WSJ, 19 July 1911.
32. On the growing mistrust see Brechtgen, *Scharnierzeit*, 273–354; WSJ, 1 September 1906; WSJ, 25 February 1907 (voicing the suspicion that Germany was trying to outmaneuver the Americans); NYT, 12 December 1909; NYT, 26 November 1910 (with a warning from no lesser person than Alfred Mahan, the naval strategist, about the "Teutonic menace").
33. WSJ, 14 April 1906, with a warning that Germany was aiming for supremacy. NYT, 30 August 1906, with a similar message.
34. NYT, 11 May 1906; WSJ, 22 July 1911. Andrew Carnegie allowed himself to be charmed by Wilhelm II: NYT, 8 June 1913.
35. See Pommerin, *Deutschland*. See also WSJ, 25 February 1907; WSJ, 15 October 1912; 15 March 1913.
36. WSJ, 22 April 1913, dividing the country into an "old" and a "new" Germany.
37. See, e.g., R.R. Doerries, *Imperial Challenge. Ambassador Count Bernsdorff and German-American Relations, 1908–1917* (Chapel Hill, NC, 1989).
38. WSJ, 20 May 1905; WSJ, 12 March 1913; WSJ, 13 March 1913. In October 1913, Paul Warburg, the banker, was no longer prepared to offer a favorable prognosis for Germany: WSJ, 30 October 1913. See also, NYT, 27 January 1912; NYT, 1 December 1912.
39. Norman Angell, *The Great Illusion* (London, 1911); NYT, 13 March 1911.
40. WSJ, 28 July 1914.
41. WSJ, 12 November 1912; WSJ, 13 November 1913.
42. NYT, 9 March 1913.
43. WSJ, 28 August 1914.

Select Bibliography

Abelshauser, W. (ed.). 2004. *German Industry and Global Enterprise*, New York.
Aengenvoort, A. 1999. *Migration – Siedlungsbildung – Akkulturation. Die Auswanderung Nordwestdeutscher nach Ohio, 1830–1914*, Stuttgart.
Albistur, M. and D. Armogathe. 1977. *Histoire du féminisme français*, 2 vols, Paris.
Aldenhoff-Hübinger, R. 2002. *Agrarpolitik und Protektionismus. Deutschland und Frankreich im Vergleich, 1879–1914*, Göttingen.
Altgeld, W. 1992. *Katholizismus, Protestantismus und Judentum. Über religiös begründete Gegensätze und nationalreligiöse Ideen in der Geschichte des deutschen Nationalismus*, Mainz.
Anderson, B. 1991, *Imagined Communities: Reflections on the Origins and Spread of Nationalism*, 2nd edn., London.
Anderson, M.L. 2000. *Practicing Democracy. Elections and Political Culture in Imperial Germany*, Princeton.
Angell, N. 1911. *The Great Illusion*, London.
Applegate, C. 2005. *Bach in Berlin, Nation and Culture in Mendelssohn's Revival of the St. Matthew Passion*, Ithaca.
——— and P. Porter (eds.). 2002. *Music and German National Identity*, Chicago.
Aron, J.-C. (ed.). 2008. *Entre violence et conciliation: la resolution des conflits socio-politiques en Europe au 19e siècle*, Rennes.
Augustine, D.L. 1994. *Patricians and Parvenus. Wealth and High Society in Wilhelmine Germany*, Oxford.
Bade, K.J. 1987. *Population, Labor, and Migration in 19th and 20th-Century Germany*, Oxford.
——— (ed.). 1992. *Deutsche im Ausland – Fremde in Deutschland. Migration in Geschichte und Gegenwart*, Munich.
——— 1998. *Europa in Bewegung. Migration vom späten 18. Jahrhundert bis zur Gegenwart*, Munich.
——— 2005. *Land oder Arbeit? Transnationale und interne Migration im deutschen Nordosten vor dem Ersten Weltkrieg*. Retrieved 29 July 2009, from Institute for Migration Research and Intercultural Studies at Osnabrück University: http://www.imis.uni-osnabrueck.de/BadeHabil.pdf.
——— et al. (eds.). 2007. *Enzyklopädie Migration in Europa. Vom 17. Jahrhundert bis zur Gegenwart*, Paderborn.

Bader-Zaar, B. 2008. *Das Frauenwahlrecht: Vergleichende Aspekte seiner Geschichte in Großbritannien, den Vereinigten Staaten von Amerika, Österreich, Deutschland und Belgien, 1860–1920*, Vienna.

Bairoch, P. 1989. "European Trade Policy, 1815–1914," in P. Mathias and S. Pollard (eds.), *The Cambridge Economic History of Europe*, vol. 8, Cambridge, 1–160.

Bard, C. 1995. *Les Filles de Marianne. Histoire des Féminismes, 1914–1940*, Paris.

—— (ed.). 1999. *Un siècle d'antiféminisme*, Paris.

Barth, B. 2003. *Dolchstosslegenden und politische Desintegration*, Düsseldorf.

Bauer, E.E. 1992. *Wie Beethoven auf den Sockel kam. Die Entstehung eines musikalischen Mythos*, Stuttgart.

Baycroft, T. and M. Hewitson (eds.). 2006. *What is a Nation? Europe 1789–1914*, Oxford.

Becker, W. 2000. *Das Bismarck-Reich – ein Obrigkeitsstaat? Die Entwicklung des Parlamentarismus und der Parteien 1871–1890*, Friedrichsruh.

Bereson, R. 2002. *The Operatic State. Cultural Policy and the Opera House*, London.

Berger, S., M. Donovan and K. Passmore (eds.). 1999. *Writing National Histories: Western Europe since 1800*, London.

—— and C. Lorenz (eds.). 2008. *The Contested Nation: Ethnicity, Class, Religion and Gender in National Histories*, Basingstoke.

Berghahn, V.R. 1971. *Der Tirpitz-Plan. Genesis und Verfall einer innenpolitischen Krisenstrategie unter Wilhelm II.*, Düsseldorf.

—— 1986. *The Americanization of West German Industry, 1945–1973*, New York.

—— 1994. *Imperial Germany, 1871–1914. Economy, Society, Culture, and Politics*, Providence.

Biard, N. (ed.). 2009. *Combattre, tolérer ou justifier? Ecrivains et journalists face à la violence d'Etat (XVI-XXXe siècle)*, Mont Aignan.

Blackbourn, D. 1980. *Class, Religion, and Local Politics in Wilhelmine Germany. The Center Party in Württemberg before 1914*, Wiesbaden.

—— 1987. *Populists and Patricians. Essays in Modern German History*, London.

——, and G. Eley. 1984. *The Peculiarities of German History*, Oxford.

Blanning, T. 2008. *The Triumph of Music. Composers, Musicians and their Audiences, 1700 to the Present*, London.

Blaschke, O. 2000. "Das 19. Jahrhundert: Ein Zweites Konfessionelles Zeitalter?," *Geschichte und Gesellschaft* 26, 38–75.

—— (ed.). 2002. *Konfessionen im Konflikt. Deutschland zwischen 1800 und 1970: ein zweites konfessionelles Zeitalter*, Göttingen.

—— 2009. *Offenders or Victims? German Jews and the Causes of Modern Catholic Antisemitism*, Nebrasca.

Bock, G. 2000. *Frauen in der europäischen Geschichte. Vom Mittelalter bis zur Gegenwart*, Munich.

Boemeke, M., R. Chickering and S. Foerster (eds.). 1999. *Anticipating Total War: The German and American Experiences, 1871–1914*, Cambridge.

Boll, F. 1992. *Arbeitskämpfe und Gewerkschaften in Deutschland, England und Frankreich. Ihre Entwicklung vom 19. zum 20. Jahrhundert*, Bonn.

Bond, B. 2002. *The Unquiet Western Front: Britain's Role in Literature and History*, Cambridge.

Bösch, F. 2009. *Öffentliche Geheimnisse. Skandale, Politik und die Medien in Deutschland und Großbritannien 1880–1914*, Munich.

Bouchey, V. 2009. *Les anarchistes contre la république 1880–1914: contribution à l'histoire des réseaux sous la troisième république*, Rennes.

Brechtgen, M. 2006. *Scharnierzeit, 1885–1907*, Mainz.
Bretting, A. and H. Bickelmann. 1991. *Auswanderungsagenturen und Auswanderungsvereine im 19. und 20. Jahrhundert*, Stuttgart.
Breuilly, J. 1993. *Nationalism and the State*, 2nd edn., Manchester.
——— 2005. "Modernisation as Social Evolution: The German Case, c.1800–1880," *Transactions of the Royal Historical Society* 15, 117–47.
——— 2007. *Nationalism, Power and Modernity in Nineteenth-Century Germany*, London.
Caine, B. 1997. *English Feminism, 1780–1980*, Oxford.
Cannadine, D. 1980. *Lords and Landlords. The Aristocracy and the Towns 1774–1967*, Leicester.
Chamberlin, E.H. (ed.). 1954. *Monopoly and Competition and Their Regulations*, London.
Chickering, R. 1984. *We Men Who Feel Most German: A Cultural Study of the Pan-German League, 1886–1914*, Boston.
——— 2000. "Militärgeschichte als Totalgeschichte im Zeitalter des totalen Krieges," in T. Kühne and B. Zieman (eds.). *Was ist Militärgeschichte?* Paderborn, 301–12.
——— 2007. *The Great War and Urban Society in Germany: Freiburg 1914–1918*, Cambridge.
——— and S. Förster (eds.). 2000. *Great War and Total War: Combat and Mobilization on the Western Front, 1914–1918*, Cambridge.
——— and ——— (eds.). 2003. *The Shadows of Total War. Europe, East Asia, and the United States, 1919–1939*, Cambridge.
——— u. a. (eds.). 2005. *A World at Total War. Global Conflict and the Politics of Destruction, 1937–1945*, Cambridge.
Clausewitz, C. von. 1976. *On War*, M. Howard and P. Paret (eds. and trans.), Princeton.
Conrad, S. 2008. *Deutsche Kolonialgeschichte*, Munich.
——— 2010. *Globalisation and Nation in Imperial Germany*, Cambridge.
——— and J. Osterhammel (eds.). 2004. *Das Kaiserreich transnational. Deutschland in der Welt 1871–1914*, Göttingen.
Conze, E. and M. Wienfort. 2004. *Adel und Moderne. Deutschland im europäischen Vergleich im 19. und 20. Jahrhundert*, Cologne.
Conze, W. and J. Kocka. 1985. "Einleitung," in idem (eds.), *Bildungsbürgertum im 19. Jahrhundert*, vol. 1, Stuttgart, 9–26.
Conzen, K. 1976. *Immigrant Milwaukee 1836–1860. Accommodation and Community in a Frontier City*, Cambridge.
Coogan, J.W. 1981. *The End of Neutrality: The United States, Britain and Maritime Rights 1899–1915*, Ithaca.
Cooper, C. 2005. *Colonialism in Question. Theory, Knowledge, History*, Berkeley.
Dahlhaus, C. 1980. *Die Musik des 19. Jahrhunderts*, Wiesbaden.
Dahrendorf, R. 1967. *Society and Democracy in Germany*, New York.
Del Fabbro, R. 1996. *Transalpini. Italienische Arbeitswanderung nach Süddeutschland im Kaiserreich 1870–1918*, Osnabrück.
Demarcation and Exchange, "National" Music in 19th Century Europe, *Journal of Modern European History* 5 (2007), eds. S.O. Müller and L. Raphael.
Dietrich, T. 2004. *Konfession im Dorf. Westeuropäische Erfahrungen im 19. Jahrhundert*, Cologne.
Doerries, R.R. 1989. *Imperial Challenge. Ambassador Count Bernsdorff and German-American Relations, 1908–1917*, Chapel Hill.
Dowe, D. et al. (eds.). 1999. *Parteien im Wandel. Vom Kaiserreich zur Weimarer Republik*, Munich.

Dreyer, M. 1987. *Föderalismus als ordungspolitisches und normatives Prinzip. Das föderative Denken der Deutschen im 19. Jahrhundert*, Frankfurt a.M.
Dunker, A. (ed.). 2005. *(Post-) Kolonialismus und deutsche Literatur: Impulse der angloamerikanischen Literatur- und Kulturtheorie*, Bielefeld.
Echternkamp, J. (ed.). 2005. *Die deutsche Kriegsgesellschaft 1939 bis 1945. Zweiter Halbband: Ausbeutung, Deutungen, Ausgrenzung*, Munich, transl. 2010. (*Germany and the Second World War vol. XIX/1–2*).
—— (ed.). 2008. *German Wartime Society 1939–1945: Politicization, Disintegration, and the Struggle for Survival*, Oxford.
—— and S. Martens (eds.). 2007. *Der Zweite Weltkrieg in Europa. Erfahrung und Erinnerung*, Paderborn.
—— and S.O. Müller (eds.). 2002. *Die Politik der Nation: Deutscher Nationalismus in Krieg und Krisen 1760–1960*, Munich.
Eibl, K. 1995. *Die Entstehung der Poesie*, Frankfurt.
Eley, G. 1974. "Sammlungspolitik, Social Imperialism and the Navy Law of 1898," *Militärgeschichtliche Mitteilungen* 15, 29–63.
—— 1980. *Reshaping the German Right: Radical Nationalism and Political Change after Bismarck*, New Haven.
—— 1986. *From Unification to Nazism: Reinterpreting the German Past*, Boston.
—— (ed.). 1996. *Society, Culture, and the State in Germany, 1870–1930*, Ann Arbor.
—— and J.N. Retallack (eds.). 2003. *Wilhelmianism and its Legacies: German Modernities, Imperialism, and the Meanings of Reform 1890–1914*, New York.
Epkenhans, M. 1991. *Die wilhelminische Flottenrüstung 1908–1914: Weltmachtstreben, industrieller Fortschritt, soziale Integration*, Munich.
Evans, R.J. (ed.). 1978. *Society and Politics in Wilhelmine Germany*, London.
—— 2009. *Cosmopolitan Islanders. British Historians and the European Continent*, Cambridge.
Fairbairn, B. 1997. *Democracy in the Undemocratic State. The German Reichstag Elections of 1898 and 1903*, Toronto.
Fandel, T. 1997. *Konfession und Nationalsozialismus. Evangelische und katholische Pfarrer in der Pfalz 1930–1939*, Paderborn.
Fiebig-von Hase, R. 1986. *Lateinamerika als Konfliktherd der deutsch-amerikanischen Beziehungen, 1890–1903*, 2 vols., Göttingen.
Fischer, F. 1972. *War of Illusion. German Policies from 1911 to 1914*, New York.
—— 1979. *Bündnis der Eliten. Zur Kontinuität der Machtstrukturen in Deutschland 1871–1945*, Düsseldorf.
Fitzpatrick, M. 2008. *Liberal Imperialism in Germany: Expansionism and Nationalism, 1848–1884*, New York.
Förster, S. and J. Nagler (eds.). 1997. *On the Road to Total War. The American Civil War and the German Wars of Unification, 1861–1871*, Cambridge.
Frie, E. 2004. *Das Deutsche Kaiserreich*, Darmstadt.
Friedrichsmeyer, S. et al. (eds.). 1998. *The Imperialist Imagination: German Colonialism and Its Legacy*, Ann Arbor.
Fritzsche, P. 1996. *Reading Berlin 1900*, Cambridge, MA.
Funck, M. 2010. *Feudales Kriegertum und militärische Professionalität. Der Adel im preußisch-deutschen Offizierkorps 1860–1935*, Berlin.
Funk, A. 1986. *Polizei und Rechtsstaat. Die Entwicklung des staatlichen Gewaltmonopols in Preußen 1848–1914*, Frankfurt a.M.

Fussell, P. 1975. *The Great War and Modern Memory*, New York.
Gall, L. (ed.). 1993. *Stadt und Bürgertum im Übergang von der traditionalen zur modernen Gesellschaft*, Munich.
Gatti, A. 1964. *Caporetto*, ed. Alberto Monticone, Bologna.
Gatzke, H. 1980. *Germany and the United States. "A Special Relationship,"* Cambridge, MA.
Gellner, E. 2006. *Nations and Nationalism*, 2nd edn., Oxford.
Gerschenkron, A. 1943. *Bread and Democracy in Germany*, reprint Ithaca, 1989.
——— 1968. *Continuity in History and other Essays*, Cambridge.
Geulen, C. 2004. *Wahlverwandte. Rassendiskurse und Nationalismus im späten 19. Jahrhundert*, Hamburg.
Geyer, M. 1980. *Aufrüstung oder Sicherheit*, Wiesbaden.
——— 2006. "Rückzug und Zerstörung 1917," in G. Hirschfeld, G. Krumeich and I. Renz (eds.), *Die Deutschen an der Somme 1914–1918*, Essen, 163–201.
Gienow-Hecht, J.C.E. 2009. *Sound Diplomacy. Music and Emotions in Transatlantic Relations, 1850–1920*, Chicago.
Giesen, B. 1998. *Intellectuals and the Nation: Collective Identity in a German Axial Age*, Cambridge.
Gilman, N. 2003. *Mandarins of the Future. Modernization Theory in Cold War America*, Baltimore.
Gosewinkel, D. 2001. *Einbürgern und Ausschließen. Die Nationalisierung der Staatsangehörigkeit vom Deutschen Bund bis zur Bundesrepublik Deutschland*, Göttingen.
Grant, O. 2005. *Migration and Inequality in Germany 1870–1913*, Oxford.
Green, A. 2001. *Fatherlands: State-Building and Nationhood in Nineteenth-Century Germany*, Cambridge.
Grießmer, A. 2000. *Massenverbände und Massenparteien im wilhelminischen Reich. Zum Wandel der Wahlkultur 1903–1912*, Düsseldorf.
Grimm, D. 2009. *Souveränität. Herkunft und Zukunft eines Schlüsselbegriffs*, Berlin.
Gross, G. 2002. "Das Dogma der Beweglichkeit," in B. Thoss and H.-E. Volkmann (eds.) *Erster Weltkrieg Zweiter Weltkrieg*, Paderborn, 143–66.
Groß, G.P. 1989. *Die Seekriegführung der kaiserlichen Marine im Jahre 1918*, Frankfurt.
Gross, M.B. 2004. *The War against Catholics. Liberalism and the Anti-Catholic Imagination in Nineteenth-Century Germany*, Ann Arbor.
Grosser Generalstab. 1902. *Kriegsbrauch im Landkriege*, Berlin.
Gründer, H. 2000. *Geschichte der deutschen Kolonien*, Paderborn.
Günther, G. 1979. "Life as Poly-Contexturality," in idem, *Beiträge zur Grundlegung einer operationsfähigen Dialektik*, vol. 2, Hamburg, 283–306.
Haber, S. 1964. *Efficiency and Uplift*, Chicago.
Hankel, G. 2003. *Die Leipziger Prozesse. Deutsche Kriegsverbrechen und ihre strafrechtliche Verfolgung nach dem Ersten Weltkrieg*, Hamburg.
Hardach, K.W. 1967. *Die Bedeutung wirtschaftlicher Faktoren bei der Wiedereinführung der Eisen- und Getreidezölle in Deutschland 1879*, Berlin.
Harrison, B. 1978. *Separate Spheres. The Opposition to Women's Suffrage in Britain*, London.
Hartmann, M. 2002. *Der Mythos von den Leistungseliten. Spitzenkarrieren und soziale Herkunft in Wirtschaft, Politik, Justiz und Wissenschaft*, Frankfurt.
Hatton, T.J. and J.G. Williamson. 1998. *The Age of Mass Migration. Causes and Economic Impact*, Oxford.
Haupt, H.-G. and D. Langewiesche (eds.). 2004. *Nation und Religion in Europa. Mehrkonfessionelle Gesellschaften im 19. und 20. Jahrhundert*, Frankfurt.

Hause, S.C. and A.R. Kenney. 1984. *Women's Suffrage and Social Politics in the French Third Republic*, Princeton.
Healy, M. 2004. *Vienna and the Fall of the Habsburg Empire: Total War and Everyday Life in World War I*, Cambridge.
Hentschel, V. 1978. *Wirtschaft und Wirtschaftspolitik im wilhelminischen Deutschland. Organisierter Kapitalismus und Interventionsstaat?* Stuttgart.
Herbert, U. 2001. *Geschichte der Ausländerpolitik in Deutschland*, Munich.
Herwig, H.H. 1986. *Germany's Vision of Empire in Venezuela, 1871–1914*, Princeton.
Hettling, M. 1999. *Politische Bürgerlichkeit*, Göttingen.
——— and S.-L. Hoffmann (eds.). 2000. *Der bürgerliche Wertehimmel*, Göttingen.
Hildebrand, K. 1995. *Das vergangene Reich. Deutsche Außenpolitik von Bismarck bis Hitler, 1871–1945*, Stuttgart.
Hill, C.L. 2008. *National History and the World of Nations. Writing Japan, France, the United States, 1870–1900*, Durham.
Himmelberg, R.F. (ed.). 1994. *The Rise of Big Business and the Beginning of Antitrust and Railroad Regulation, 1870–1900*, vol. 1, New York.
Hirschfeld, G. et al. (eds.). 2003. *Enzyklopädie Erster Weltkrieg*, Paderborn.
Hobsbawm, E. 1994. *Age of Extremes. The Short Twentieth Century, 1914–1991*, London.
Hobson, R. 2002. *Imperialism at Sea: Naval Strategic Thought, the Ideology of Sea Power and the Tirpitz Plan, 1875–1914*, Boston.
Hoerder, D. and J. Nagel (eds.). 1995. *People in Transit. German Migrations in Comparative Perspective, 1820–1930*, Cambridge.
Hoffmann-Nowotny, H.-J. 1970. *Migration. Ein Beitrag zu einer soziologischen Erklärung*, Stuttgart.
Hohls, R. and K.H. Jarausch (eds.). 2000. *Versäumte Fragen. Deutsche Historiker im Schatten des Nationalsozialismus*, Munich.
Hölscher, L. (ed.). 2007. *Baupläne der sichtbaren Kirche. Sprachliche Konzepte religiöser Vergemeinschaftung in Europa*, Göttingen.
Holton, S.S. 1986. *Feminism and Democracy: Women's Suffrage and Reform Politics in Britain, 1900–1918*, Cambridge.
Honold, A. and K.R. Scherpe (eds.). 2004. *Mit Deutschland um die Welt: Eine Kulturgeschichte des Fremden in der Kolonialzeit*, Stuttgart.
——— and O. Simons (eds.). 2002. *Kolonialismus als Kultur: Literatur, Medien, Wissenschaft in der deutschen Gründerzeit des Fremden*, Tübingen.
Horne, J. and A. Kramer. 2001. *German Atrocities 1914: A History of Denial*, New Haven.
Hughes, M. 2002. *The English Musical Renaissance and the Press 1850–1914: Watchmen of Music*, Aldershot.
Hull, I.V. 2003. "Military Culture and the Production of 'Final Solutions' in the Colonies: The Example of Wilhelminian Germany," in R. Gellately and B. Kiernan (eds.), *The Specter of Genocide*, Cambridge, 141–62.
——— 2003. "Military Culture, Wilhelm II, and the End of the Monarchy in World War I," in A. Mombauer and W. Deist (eds.), *The Kaiser*, Cambridge, 235–58.
——— 2005. *Absolute Destruction: Military Culture and the Practices of War in Imperial Germany*, Ithaca.
Hunt, J.C. 1974. "Peasants, Grain Tariffs, and Meat Quotas: Imperial German Protectionism Reexamined," *Central European History* 7, 311–31.
Jackson jr., J.H. 1997. *Migration and Urbanization in the Ruhr Valley, 1821–1914*, Atlantic Highlands.

Jarausch, K.H. 1973. *The Enigmatic Chancellor*, New Haven, CT.
——— and M. Geyer. 2003. *Shattered Past. Reconstructing German Histories*, Princeton.
Jefferies, M. 2008. *Contesting the German Empire, 1871–1918*, Oxford.
Jeismann, M. 1992. *Das Vaterland der Feinde. Studien zum nationalen Feindbegriff und Selbstverständnis in Deutschland und Frankreich 1792–1918*, Stuttgart.
Jessen, R. 1991. *Polizei im Industrierevier. Modernisierung und Herrschaftspraxis im westfälischen Ruhrgebiet 1848–1914*, Göttingen.
Jones, L.E. and J. Retallack (eds.). 1992. *Elections, Mass Politics, and Social Change in Modern Germany*, Cambridge.
Just, M. 1988. *Ost- und südosteuropäische Amerikawanderung 1881–1914. Transitprobleme in Deutschland und Aufnahme in den Vereinigten Staaten*, Wiesbaden.
Kaelble, H. 1967. *Industrielle Interessenpolitik in der Wilhelminischen Gesellschaft*, Berlin.
Kaiser, W. and C. Clark (eds.), 2003. *Culture Wars. Secular-Catholic Conflict in Nineteenth-Century Europe*, Cambridge.
Kanigel, R. 1997. *Our Best Way. Frederick Taylor and the Engima of Efficiency*, New York.
Karl, R.E. 2002. *Staging the World: Chinese Nationalism at the Turn of the Twentieth Century*, Durham.
Keegan, J. 1994. *A History of Warfare*, London.
Kehr, E. 1930. *Schlachtflottenbau und Parteipolitik 1894–1901*, Berlin.
——— 1965. *Der Primat der Innenpolitik*, ed. H.-U. Wehler, Berlin.
Kennan, G.F. 1979. *The Decline of Bismarck's European Order. Franco-Russian Relations, 1875–1890*, Princeton.
Kennedy, Paul M. 1980. *The Rise of the Anglo-German Antagonism*, London.
Kern, S. 2003. *The Culture of Time and Space 1880–1918*, Cambridge, MA.
King, J. 2002. *Budweisers into Czechs and Germans: A Local History of Bohemian Politics, 1848–1948*, New Jersey.
Klejman, L. and F. Rochefort. 1989. *L'égalité en marche: le féminisme sous la Troisième Republique*, Paris.
Kleßmann, C. 1978. *Polnische Bergarbeiter im Ruhrgebiet 1870–1945. Soziale Integration und nationale Subkultur einer Minderheit in der deutschen Industriegesellschaft*, Göttingen.
Knox, M. 2000. *Hitler's Italian Allies*, Cambridge.
——— 2007. *To the Threshold of Power, 1922/33: Origins and Dynamics of the Fascist and National Socialist Dictatorships*, Cambridge.
Kobrak, C. 2007. *Cooperation, Conflict, Men, and Markets: Deutsche Bank and the United States, 1870 to the Present*, New York.
Kocka, J. 1985. *Facing Total War: German Society, 1914–1918*, Cambridge.
——— (ed.) 1987. *Bürger und Bürgerlichkeit im 19. Jahrhundert*, Göttingen.
——— (ed.). 1989. *Bürgertum im 19. Jahrhundert*, 3 vols., Munich.
——— 1989. "Einleitung," in idem (ed.), *Bildungsbürgertum im 19. Jahrhundert*, vol. 4, Stuttgart, 9–20.
——— 2000. "Bürgertum und Sonderweg," in P. Lundgreen (ed.), *Sozial- und Kulturgeschichte des Bürgertums*, Göttingen, 93–110.
——— and J.A. Mitchell (eds.). 1993. *Bourgeois Society in 19th Century Europe*, Oxford.
Kohlrausch, M. 2005. *Der Monarch im Skandal. Die Logik der Massenmedien und die Transformation der wilhelminischen Monarchie*, Berlin.
Köllmann, W. 1974. *Bevölkerung in der Industriellen Revolution*, Göttingen.

Koselleck, R. 1991. "Drei bürgerliche Welten? Zur vergleichenden Semantik der bürgerlichen Gesellschaft in Deutschland, England und Frankreich," in H.-J. Puhle (ed.), *Bürger in der Gesellschaft der Neuzeit*, Göttingen, 14–58.
Kovaleff T.P. (ed.). 1994. *The Antitrust Impulse*, vol. 1, Armonk, NY.
Kühne, T. 1994. *Dreiklassenwahlrecht und Wahlkultur in Preussen 1867–1914. Landtagswahlen zwischen korporativer Tradition und politischem Massenmarkt*, Düsseldorf.
Kundrus, B. 2003. *Moderne Imperialisten. Das Kaiserreich im Spiegel seiner Kolonien*, Cologne.
—— (ed.). 2003. *Phantasiereiche: Zur Kulturgeschichte des deutschen Kolonialismus*, Frankfurt am Main.
—— (regional ed.). 2008. "Section: Germany." In P. Poddar, R.S. Patke, and L. Jensen (main eds.), *A Historical Companion to Postcolonial Literatures – Continental Europe and its Empires*, Edinburgh, 198–251.
Laak, D. van. 2005. *Über alles in der Welt: Deutscher Imperialismus im 19. und 20. Jahrhundert*, Munich.
Lambi, I.N. 1963. *Free Trade and Protection in Germany 1868–79*, Wiesbaden.
—— 1984. *The Navy and German Power Politics, 1862–1914*, Boston.
Langewiesche, D. 1989. "'Volksbildung' und 'Leserlenkung' in Deutschland von der wilhelminischen Ära bis zur nationalsozialistischen Diktatur, *IASL* 14, 108–25.
—— 1995. "Nation, Nationalismus, Nationalstaat. Forschungsstand und Forschungsperspektiven," *Neue Politische Literatur* 40, 190–236.
—— 2002. *Politikstile im Kaiserreich. Zum Wandel von Politik und Öffentlichkeit im Zeitalter des "politischen Massenmarktes,"* Friedrichsruh.
Large, D. and W. Weber (eds.). 1984. *Wagnerism in European Culture and Politics*, Ithaca.
Lässig, S., K.H. Pohl and J. Retallack (eds.). 1998. *Modernisierung und Region im wilhelminischen Deutschland. Wahlen, Wahlrecht und Politische Kultur*, 2nd edn., Bielefeld.
Leed, E. 1979. *No Man's Land: Combat and Identity in World War I*, Cambridge.
Leerssen, J. 2006. *National Thought in Europe: a Cultural History*, Amsterdam.
Levinger, M.B. 2000. *Enlightened Nationalism: The Transformation of Prussian Political Culture, 1806–1848*, Oxford.
Lindenberger, T. 1995. *Straßenpolitik. Zur Sozialgeschichte der öffentlichen Ordnung in Berlin 1900–1914*, Bonn.
Lourens, P. and J. Lucassen. 1999. *Arbeitswanderung und berufliche Spezialisierung. Die lippischen Ziegler im 18. und 19. Jahrhundert*, Osnabrück.
Ludendorff, E. 1920. *Urkunden des Obersten Heeresleitung über ihre Tätigkeit 1916/18*, Berlin.
Luhmann, N. 1982. *The Differentiation of Society*, New York.
—— 1997. *Die Gesellschaft der Gesellschaft*, 2 vols., Frankfurt.
—— 1998. *Observations on Modernity*, Stanford.
—— 2007. *The Reality of the Mass Media*, Cambridge.
Lundgreen, P. (ed.). 2000. *Sozial- und Kulturgeschichte des Bürgertums*, Göttingen.
Lupfer, T.T. 1981. *The Dynamics of Doctrine*, Leavenworth Papers, No. 4.
Malinowski, S. 2003. *Vom König zum Führer. Sozialer Niedergang und politische Radikalisierung im deutschen Adel zwischen Kaiserreich und NS-Staat*, Berlin.
Mann, M. 2005. *The Dark Side of Democracy. Explaining Ethnic Cleansing*, Cambridge.
Maugue, A. 1987. *L'identité masculine en crise au tournant du siècle, 1871–1914*, Paris.
Mazon, P. and R. Steingrover (eds.). 2005. *Not So Plain as Black and White: Afro-German Culture and History, 1890–2000*, Rochester.
Mehnert, U. 1995. *Deutschland, Amerika und die "Gelbe Gefahr." Zur Karriere eines Schlagworts in der grossem Politik, 1903–1917*, Stuttgart.

Merriman, J. 2009. *Dynamite Club: l'invention du terrorisme à Paris*, Paris.
Meyer, S.C. 2003. *Carl Maria von Weber and the Search for a German Opera*, Bloomington.
Michalka, W. (ed.). 1994. *Der Erste Weltkrieg: Wirkung, Wahrnehmung, Analyse*, Munich.
Ministero della Guerra. 1932. *Le istruzioni tattiche del Capo di Stato Maggiore dell'Esercito degli anni 1914–1915–1916*, Rome.
Mitchell, M. 1997. *The Danger of Dreams. German and American Imperialism in Latin America*, Chapel Hill, NC.
Mondini, M. 2006. *La politica delle armi. Il ruolo dell'esercito nell'avvento del fascismo*, Rome.
Müller, S.O. 2002. *Die Nation als Waffe und Vorstellung: Nationalismus in Deutschland und Großbritannien im Ersten Weltkrieg*, Göttingen.
——— 2007. *Deutsche Soldaten und ihre Feinde. Nationalismus an Front und Heimatfront im Zweiten Weltkrieg*, Frankfurt a.M.
——— and J. Toelle (eds.). 2002. *Bühnen der Politik. Die Oper in europäischen Gesellschaften im 19. und 20. Jahrhundert*, Vienna.
Müller-Dreier, A. 1998. *Konfession und Politik, Gesellschaft und Kultur des Kaiserreichs. Der Evangelische Bund 1886–1914*, Gütersloh.
Naumann, F. 1905. *Demokratie und Kaisertum*, Berlin.
Nelson, R.L. (ed.). 2009. *Germans, Poland, and Colonial Expansion to the East: 1850 through the Present*, Houndmills.
Nipperdey, T. 1990/1992. *Deutsche Geschichte 1866–1918*, 2 vols., Munich.
Nolan, M. 1994. *Visions of Modernity*, New York.
Nolan, M.E. 2005. *The Inverted Mirror: Mythologizing the Enemy in France and Germany, 1898–1914*, New York.
Nonn, C. 1996. *Verbraucherprotest und Parteiensystem im wilhelminischen Deutschland*, Düsseldorf.
O'Donnell, K., R. Bridenthal and N. Reagin (eds.). 2005. *The Heimat Abroad. The Boundaries of Germanness*, Ann Arbor.
O'Rourke, K.H. and J.G. Williamson. 1999. *Globalization and History. The Evolution of a Nineteenth-Century Atlantic Economy*, Cambridge, MA.
Offen, K. 2000. *European Feminisms 1700–1950. A Political History*, Stanford, CA.
Offer, A. 1989. *The First World War: An Agrarian Interpretation*, Oxford.
Olivier, B. 2007. *Théorie de la Fédération*, Paris.
Osterhammel, J. 2009. *Die Verwandlung der Welt: Eine Geschichte des 19. Jahrhunderts*, Munich.
Owzar, A. 2006. *"Reden ist Silber, Schweigen ist Gold." Konfliktmanagement im Alltag des wilhelminischen Obrigkeitsstaates*, Konstanz.
Ozkirimli, U. 2010. *Theories of Nationalism*, 2nd edn., London.
Paletschek, S. and B. Pietrow-Ennker (eds.). 2004. *Women's Emancipation Movements in the 19th Century: A European Perspective*, Stanford, CA.
Passmore, K. (ed.). 2003. *Women, Gender and Fascism in Europe, 1919–45*, Manchester.
Paulmann, J. 2000. *Pomp und Politik. Monarchenbegegnungen in Europa zwischen Ancien Régime und Erstem Weltkrieg*, Paderborn.
Pauly, W. 1993. *Der Methodenwandel im deutschen Spätkonstitutionalismus*, Tübingen.
Payne, S.G. 1995. *A History of Fascism. 1914–1945*, Madison.
Perkins, B. 1968. *The Great Rapprochement. England and the United States, 1895–1914*, New York.
Perkins, D. 1960. *A History of the Monroe Doctrine*, London.

Perraudin, M. and J. Zimmerer (eds.). 2009. *German Colonialism and National Identity*, London.
Peters-Schildgen, S. 1997. *"Schmelztiegel" Ruhrgebiet. Die Geschichte der Zuwanderung am Beispiel Hernes bis 1945*, Essen.
Peukert, D.J.K. 1986. *Grenzen der Sozialdisziplinierung. Aufstieg und Krise der deutschen Jugendfürsorge, 1878–1932*, Cologne.
—— 1987. *Die Weimarer Republik*. Frankfurt.
—— 1989. *Max Webers Diagnose der Moderne*. Göttingen.
Pino, E. 2001. "La regolamentazione tattica del Regio Esercito Italiano e la sua evoluzione nell'ultimo anno del conflitto," in G. Berti and P. Del Negro (eds.), *Al qua di là del Piave*, Milan, 275–308.
Planert, U. 1998. *Antifeminismus im Kaiserreich. Diskurs, soziale Formation und politische Mentalität*, Göttingen.
—— (ed.). 2000. *Nation, Politik und Geschlecht. Frauenbewegungen und Nationalismus in der Moderne*, Frankfurt.
Plunkett, J. 2003. *Queen Victoria. First Media Monarch*, Oxford.
Pluviano, M., and I. Guerrini. 2004. *Le fucilazioni sommarie nella prima guerra mondiale*, Udine.
Pohl, H. (ed.). 1985. *Kartelle und Kartellgesetzgebung in Praxis und Rechtsprechung vom 19. Jahrhundert bis zur Gegenwart*, Stuttgart.
Pommerin, R. 1986. *Deutschland und Amerika. Die USA in der Politik der Reichsleitung, 1890–1917*, Cologne.
Puhle, H.-J. 1967. *Agrarische Interessenpolitik und preussischer Konservatismus im Wilhelminischen Reich*, Hannover.
Pyta, W. 2007. *Herrschaft zwischen Hohenzollern und Hitler*, Munich.
Reif, H. 1979. *Westfälischer Adel 1770–1860. Vom Herrschaftsstand zur regionalen Elite*, Göttingen.
Rendall, J. (ed.). 1987. *Equal or Different: Women's Politics 1800–1914*, Oxford.
Retallack, J. 2006. *The German Right, 1860–1920. Political Limits of the Authoritarian Imagination*, Toronto.
—— (ed.). 2008. *Imperial Germany 1871–1918. The Short Oxford History of Germany*, Oxford.
Ritter, G.A. (ed.). 1997. *Wahlen und Wahlkämpfe in Deutschland. Von den Anfängen im 19. Jahrhundert bis zur Bundesrepublik*, Düsseldorf.
—— (ed.) 2006. *Friedrich Meinecke. Akademischer Lehrer und emigrierte Schüler. Briefe und Aufzeichnungen 1910–1977*, Munich.
Rohe, K. 1992. *Wahlen und Wählertraditionen in Deutschland. Kulturelle Grundlagen deutscher Parteien und Parteiensysteme im 19. und 20. Jahrhundert*, Frankfurt a.M.
Roller, K. 1994. *Frauenmigration und Ausländerpolitik im Deutschen Kaiserreich. polnische Arbeitsmigrantinnen in Preußen*, 2. Aufl. Berlin.
Rosenberg, H. 1967. *Große Depression und Bismarckzeit. Wirtschaftsablauf, Gesellschaft und Politik in Mitteleuropa*, Berlin.
—— 1969. *Probleme der deutschen Sozialgeschichte*, Frankfurt a.M.
—— 1978. *Machteliten und Wirtschaftskonjunkturen. Studien zur neueren deutschen Sozial- und Wirtschaftsgeschichte*, Göttingen.
Rupp, L.J. 1997. *Worlds of Women: The Making of an International Women's Movement*, Princeton.
Samson, J. (ed.). 2002. *The Cambridge History of Nineteenth-Century Music*, Cambridge.

Schaser, A. 2006. *Frauenbewegung in Deutschland, 1848–1933*, Darmstadt.
Schieber, C.E. 1923. *The Transformation of American Sentiment toward Germany, 1870–1914*, Boston.
Schimank, U. and U. Volkmann. 1999. *Gesellschaftliche Differenzierung*, Bielefeld.
Schöning, J. (ed.). 1997. *Triviale Tropen: Exotische Reise- und Abenteuerfilme aus Deutschland 1919–1933*, Munich.
Schröder, J. 2003. *Die U-Boote des Kaisers: Die Geschichte des deutschen U-Boot-Krieges gegen Großbritannien im Ersten Weltkrieg*, Bonn.
Schulz, A. 2005. *Lebenswelt und Kultur des Bürgertums im 19. und 20. Jahrhundert*, Munich.
Scott, J.W. 1996. *Only Paradoxes to Offer. French Feminists and the Rights of Men*, Cambridge.
Sedlmaier, A. 2003. *Deutschlandbilder und Deutschlandpolitik. Studien zur Wilson-Administration (1913–1921)*, Stuttgart.
Smith, H.W. 2008. *The Continuities of German History. Nation, Religion, and Race across the Long Nineteenth Century*, New York.
Smith, L.V., S. Audoin-Rouzeau and A. Becker. 2003. *France in the Great War*, Cambridge.
Smith, W.D. 1986. *The Ideological Origins of Nazi Imperialism*, New York.
Speirs, R. and J. Breuilly (eds.). 2005. *Germany's Two Unifications: Anticipations, Experiences, Responses*, Basingstoke.
Speitkamp, W. 2005. *Deutsche Kolonialgeschichte*, Stuttgart.
Sperber, J. 1997. *The Kaiser's Voters. Electors and Elections in Imperial Germany*, Cambridge.
Steinbach, P. 1990. *Die Zähmung des politischen Massenmarktes. Wahlen und Wahlkämpfe im Bismarckreich*, 3 vols., Passau.
Steinert, O. (2003). *"Berlin – Polnischer Bahnhof!" Die Berliner Polen; eine Untersuchung zum Verhältnis von nationaler Selbstbehauptung und sozialem Integrationsbedürfnis einer fremdsprachigen Minderheit in der Hauptstadt des Deutschen Kaiserreichs (1871–1918)*, Hamburg.
Steinmetz, G. 2007. *The Devil's Handwriting: Precoloniality and the German Colonial State in Qingdao, Samoa, and Southwest Africa*, Chicago.
Stolleis, M. 1992. *Geschichte des öffentlichen Rechts in Deutschland*, vol. 2, Munich.
Swidler, A. 1986. "Culture in Action: Symbols and Strategies," *American Sociological Review* 51, 273–86.
Tenbruck, F.H. 1989. "Bürgerliche Kultur," in idem, *Die kulturellen Grundlagen der Gesellschaft*, Opladen, 251–72.
Tenfelde, K. 1994. "Stadt und Bürgertum im 20. Jahrhundert," in idem and H.-U. Wehler (eds.). *Wege zur Geschichte des Bürgertums*, Göttingen, 317–53.
Thoß, B. and H.-E. Volkmann (eds.). 2002. *Erster Weltkrieg – Zweiter Weltkrieg: ein Vergleich. Krieg, Kriegserlebnis, Kriegserfahrung in Deutschland*, Paderborn.
Tilly, C. u.a. 1975. *The Rebellious Century, 1830–1930*, Cambridge.
Torp, C. 1998. *Max Weber und die preußischen Junker*, Tübingen.
——— 2005. *Die Herausforderung der Globalisierung. Wirtschaft und Politik in Deutschland 1860–1914*, Göttingen.
——— 2010. "The 'Coalition of "Rye and Iron"' under the Pressure of Globalization: A Reinterpretation of Germany's Political Economy before 1914," *Central European History* 43, 401–427.
Tyrell, H. 1998. "Zur Diversität der Differenzierungstheorie. Soziologiehistorische Anmerkungen," *Soziale Systeme* 4, 119–49.
Ullmann, H.-P. 1995. *Das Deutsche Kaiserreich, 1871–1918*, Frankfurt.
Urbach, K. (ed.) 2007. *European Aristocracies and the Radical Right 1918–1939*, Oxford.

Vardi, G. 2009. "The Enigma of German Operational Theory: The Evolution of Military Thought in Germany, 1919–1938," PhD diss., The London School of Economics and Political Science.

Vick, B. 2002. *Defining Germany: the 1848 Frankfurt Parliamentarians and the National Question*, New Haven.

Wahl, A. 1980. *Confession et Comportement dans les campagnes d'Alsace et de Bade 1871–1939. Catholiques, Protestants et Juifs*, 2 vol., Strasbourg.

Walkenhorst, P. 2007. *Nation – Volk – Rasse: Radikaler Nationalismus im Deutschen Kaiserreich 1890–1914*, Göttingen.

Walker, N. (ed.). 2003. *Sovereignty in Transition*, Oxford.

Walther, D.J. 2006. *Creating Germans Abroad: Cultural Policies and National Identity in Namibia*, Athens.

Webb, S.B. 1977. "Tariff Protection for the Iron Industry, Cotton Textiles and Agriculture in Germany, 1879–1914," *Jahrbücher für Nationalökonomie und Statistik* 192, 336–357.

——— 1982. "Agricultural Protection in Wilhelminian Germany: Forging an Empire with Pork and Rye," *Journal of Economic History* 42, 309–326.

Wehler, H.-U. 1969. *Bismarck und der Imperialismus*, 2nd edn, Frankfurt 1985.

——— 1973. *Das deutsche Kaiserreich 1871–1918*, 6th edn 1988, Göttingen.

——— 1975. *Modernisierungstheorie und Geschichte*, Göttingen.

——— 1987–2008. *Deutsche Gesellschaftsgeschichte*, 5 vols, München.

——— 2000. *Nationalismus. Geschichte – Formen – Folgen*, München.

Weichlein, S. 2004. *Nation und Region. Integrationsprozesse im Bismarck-Reich*, Düsseldorf.

Weitowitz, R. 1978. *Deutsche Politik und Handelspolitik unter Reichskanzler Leo von Caprivi 1890–1894*, Düsseldorf.

Wennemann, A. 1997. *Arbeit im Norden. Italiener im Rheinland und Westfalen des späten 19. und frühen 20. Jahrhunderts*. Osnabrück.

Wertheimer, J. 1987. *Unwelcome Strangers. East European Jews in Imperial Germany*, New York.

Wildenthal, L. 2001. *German Women for Empire, 1884–1945*, Durham.

Winter, J. and A. Prost. 2005. *The Great War in History. Debates and Controversies 1914 to the Present*, Cambridge.

——— and J.-L. Robert (eds). 1999–2007. *Capital Cities at War: Paris, London, Berlin, 1914–1919*, 2 vols., Cambridge.

Zantop, S. 1997. *Colonial Fantasies: Conquest, Family, and Nation in Precolonial Germany, 1770–1870*, Durham.

Ziemann, B. 2007. "The Theory of Functional Differentiation and the History of Modern Society. Reflections on the Reception of Systems Theory in Recent Historiography," *Soziale Systeme* 13, 220–229.

——— 2007. *War Experiences in Rural Germany, 1914–1923*, Oxford.

——— and T. Mergel. 2007. "Introduction," in B. Ziemann and T. Mergel (eds). *European Political History 1870–1913*, Aldershot.

Notes on Contributors

Volker Berghahn, Seth Low Professor of History at Columbia University. Current research interests: transatlantic relations in the twentieth century. Select publications: *America and the Intellectual Cold Wars in Europe*, Princeton: Princeton University Press, 2001; *Industriegesellschaft und Kulturtransfer. Die deutsch-amerikanischen Beziehungen im 20. Jahrhundert*, Göttingen, 2010.

Olaf Blaschke, Lecturer in Modern History at the University of Trier. Current research interests: religion in modern history, history of books and publishing. Select publications: *Offenders or Victims? German Jews and the Causes of Modern Catholic Antisemitism* ("Studies in Antisemitism," published for the Vidal Sassoon International Center for the Study of Antisemitism, Jerusalem), Lincoln, NE and London, 2009; *Verleger machen Geschichte. Historiker und Buchhandel seit 1945 im deutsch-britischen Vergleich*, Göttingen, 2010.

Dirk Bönker, teaches military history at Duke University, North Carolina. Current research interests: history of the military, warfare, and militarization in Germany and the United States in the late-nineteenth and twentieth centuries. Select publications: *Militarism in Global Age: Naval elites in Germany and the United States before World War I*, Ithaca, forthcoming 2012.

John Breuilly, Professor of Nationalism and Ethnicity at the London School of Economics and Political Science. Select publications: *Nationalism, Power and Modernity in Nineteenth-Century Germany*. German Historical Institute, London, 2007; edited volume (together with Ronald Speirs): *Germany's Two Unifications: Anticipations, Experiences, Responses*, New York, 2005; *Austria, Prussia, and the Making of Germany 1806–1871*, 2nd edition, London, 2011.

Roger Chickering, Professor (emer.) of History at the Center for German and European Studies, Georgetown University, Washington. Current research interests: political history of German agriculture. Select publications: *The Great War and Urban Life: Freiburg, 1914–1918*, Cambridge, 2007; edited Volume (together with Stig Förster): *War in an Age of Revolution, 1775–1815*, Cambridge, 2010.

Sebastian Conrad, Professor for Modern History at the Freie Universität, Berlin. Select publications: *Deutsche Kolonialgeschichte*, Munich, 2008; *Globalisierung und Nation im Deutschen Kaiserreich*, Munich, 2006; *Globalisation and the Nation in Imperial Germany*, Cambridge, 2010.

Jörg Echternkamp, Senior Fellow at the Militärgeschichtliches Forschungsamt, Potsdam, Co-Editor of the journal *Militärgeschichtliche Zeitschrift*, and Visiting Lecturer at Martin-Luther-University of Halle-Wittenberg. Current research interests: European military history, 19th–21st centuries. His major publications include *Nach dem Krieg*, Zürich, 2003; *Kriegsschauplatz Deutschland 1945*, Paderborn, 2006; edited volume: *German War Time Society 1939–1945*, 2 vol., Oxford, 2008–2012; edited volume (together with Wolfgang Schmidt and Thomas Vogel): *Perspektiven der Militärgeschichte*, München, 2010; *Die wichtigsten Fragen: Der Zweite Weltkrieg*, München, 2010; edited volume (together with Stefan Martens): *Experience and Memory. The Second World War in Europe*, Oxford/New York, 2010.

Dieter Grimm, Professor (emer.) of Law at the Humboldt-University, Berlin and at Yale Law School, New Haven, CT. Current research interests: constitutionalism beyond the national state.

Heinz-Gerhard Haupt, Professor of Social History at the University Bielefeld, currently furloughed at the European University Institute, Florence. Current research interests: social history and political history of modern Europe; methodology of comparative history. Select publications: edited volume (together with Jürgen Kocka): *Comparative and Transnational History, Central European Approaches and New Perspectives*, New York, 2009; edited volume (together with Dieter Langewiesche): *Nación y religión en Europa. Sociedades multiconfesionales en los siglos XIX y XX*, Zaragoza, 2010; edited volume (together with Wilhelm Heitmeyer): *Control of Violence. Historical and International Perspectives on Violence in Modern Societies*, New York, 2010.

Manfred Hettling, Professor for Modern History at the Martin-Luther-University, Halle-Wittenberg. Current research interests: the middle class in analogy, political death cult in Germany, social history of circles of marriage. Select publications: edited volumes: (together with Jörg Echternkamp), *Bedingt erinnerungsbereit? Soldatengedenken in der Bundesrepublik*, Göttingen, 2008; (together with Gesine Foljanty-Jost) *Formenwandel der Bürgergesellschaft – Japan und Deutschland im Vergleich*, Halle, 2009.

MacGregor Knox, Stevenson Professor of International History (emer.) at the London School of Economics and Political Science. Select publications: *Mussolini Unleashed, 1939–1941*, Cambridge, 1986; *Common Destiny: Dictatorship, Foreign Policy, and War in Fascist Italy and Nazi Germany*, Cambridge, 2000; *Hitler's Italian*

Allies: Royal Armed Forces, Fascist Regime, and the War of 1940–1943, Cambridge, 2009; *To the Threshold of Power 1922/33: Origins and Dynamics of the Fascist and National Socialist Dictatorship*, vol. 1, Cambridge 2007.

Alan Kramer, Professor of European History at Trinity College, Dublin. Current research interests: international history of concentration camps; the First World War, esp. Italian prisoners of war, and economic warfare and blockades. Select publications: edited volume (together with John Horne) *German Atrocities 1914. A History of Denial*, London, 2001; *Dynamic of Destruction. Culture and Mass Killing in the First World War*, Oxford, 2007.

Birthe Kundrus, Professor for Social and Economic History at the University of Hamburg. Current research interests: the history of National Socialism, colonial/postcolonial studies. Select publications: edited volumes: *A Historical Companion to Postcolonial Literatures – Continental Europe and its Empires*, Edinburgh, 2008 (as regional editor, main editors: Prem Poddar, Rajeev S. Patke, and Lars Jensen); (together with Beate Meyer) *Die Deportation der Juden aus Deutschland. Pläne. Praxis. Reaktionen. 1938–1945*, Göttingen, 2004.

Stephan Malinowski, Teaching and Research Fellow at the University College, Dublin. Current research interests: the history of colonization. Select publications: *Vom König zum Führer. Sozialer Niedergang und politische Radikalisierung im deutschen Adel zwischen Kaiserreich und NS-Staat*, Berlin, 2003; Edited volume (together with Corinna Unger) "Modernizing Missions: Approaches to 'Developing' the Non-Western World after 1945," *Journal for Modern European History* 8 (2010).

Thomas Mergel, Professor of Twentieth-Century European History at Humboldt University, Berlin. Select publications: *Großbritannien seit 1945*, Göttingen, 2005; *Propaganda nach Hitler. Eine Kulturgeschichte des Wahlkampfs in der Bundesrepublik 1949–1990*, Göttingen, 2010.

Sven Oliver Müller, Research Group Leader of the Max Planck Research Group "Felt Communities? Emotions in European Music Performances" at the Max Planck Institute for Human Development, Berlin. Current research interests: the emotional reception of Richard Wagner; European cultural history in the nineteenth century; history of nationalism. Select publications: *Deutsche Soldaten und ihre Feinde: Nationalismus an Front und Heimatfront im Zweiten Weltkrieg*, Frankfurt, 2007; "Analysing Musical Culture in Nineteenth-Century Europe: Towards a Musical Turn?" *European Review of History* 17 (2010), 835–859.

Ute Planert, Professor of Modern History/History Didactics at the Bergische Universität, Wuppertal. Current research interests: the era of Napoleon in global perspective, transition from pre-modern to modern societies, eugenics in international comparison. Select publications: *Der Mythos vom Befreiungskrieg.*

Frankreichs Kriege und der deutsche Süden. Alltag, Wahrnehmung, Deutung, 1792–1841, Paderborn, 2007; *Krieg und Umbruch in Mitteleuropa um 1800. Erfahrungsgeschichte(n) auf dem Weg in eine neue Zeit*, Paderborn, 2008; *Antifeminismus im Kaiserreich*, Göttingen, 1998.

James Retallack, Professor of History and German Studies at the University of Toronto. Current research interests: German regional history; nationalism; antisemitism; electoral politics; historiography. Select publications: *The German Right, 1860–1920: Political Limits of the Authoritarian Imagination*, Toronto/ Buffalo/ London, 2006; *Imperial Germany 1871–1918. The Short Oxford History of Germany*, Oxford and New York, 2008.

Cornelius Torp, Lecturer at the Martin Luther University of Halle-Wittenberg, Department of History, and currently Research Fellow at the Freiburg Institute for Advanced Studies. Select publications: *Die Herausforderung der Globalisierung. Wirtschaft und Politik in Deutschland 1860–1914*, Göttingen, 2005; edited volume (together with Michael G. Müller): "Transnational Spaces in History," *European Review of History* 16 (2009), No. 5.

Helmut Walser Smith, Martha Rivers Ingram Professor of History and Director of the Max Kade Center of European and German Studies at Vanderbilt University. Current research interests: cultural history of the German nation, 1500–2000. Select publications: *The Continuities of German History: Nation, Religion, and Race across the Long Nineteenth Century*, New York, 2008; edited volume: *The Oxford Handbook of Modern German History*, Oxford, 2011.

Benjamin Ziemann, Professor of Modern German History and Co-Director of the Centre for Peace History at the University of Sheffield. Current research interests: peace movements in the cold war; scientification of the social in the twentieth century. Most recent book publications: *War Experiences in Rural Germany, 1914–1923*, Oxford/New York, 2007; *Katholische Kirche und Sozialwissenschaften 1945–1975*, Göttingen 2007; *Sozialgeschichte der Religion. Von der Reformation bis zur Gegenwart*, Frankfurt/New York, 2009; edited volume (together with Bernd Ulrich): *German Soldiers in the Great War. Letters and Eyewitness Accounts*, Barnsley, 2010; edited volume (together with Miriam Dobson): *Reading Primary Sources: The Interpretation of Texts from Nineteenth- and Twentieth-Century History*, London, 2008.

Subject Index

19th century (long), 23, 132–33, 194–95, 297
20th century (short), 189–90, 194–95, 202

A

Action française, 120
Africa 215–16, 253–255, 258–59, 274, 284–89, 293
agriculture, agrarians, 22, 27, 32, 75, 91–92, 147, 162, 268, 273–77, 285, 290, 299–300, 302–04, 306–09, 313
Alsace, Alsace-Lorraine, 269
antifeminism, antifeminist movement, 107–20
aristocracy, 38, 91, 174, 176–78, 320
arts, 27, 39, 42–44, 46, 74, 175–76, 179–184
Asia, 258, 315
audiences, 180–81, 201
Austria-Hungary, 220–21, 269, 276, 310
authority, authoritarianism, 2, 9, 11, 28, 30, 32–33, 37, 40, 42, 45, 48, 52, 54–56, 61, 72, 83–93, 98–99, 101, 103–04, 227–28, 234–35, 267–68, 277, 321

B

BDF (Bund Deutscher Frauenvereine) [Federal Association of Women's Organizations], 111, 116
Belgium 12, 125, 129–30, 198, 227–28, 234, 239, 242–44
Berlin, 30, 39–40, 43, 71, 85, 90, 100, 112, 116, 144, 146–47, 168, 174–82, 271, 276, 283
Bolshevism, 192, 242, 245, 247
bourgeois women's movement, 110–11
bourgeoisie, middle-class, 3–4, 11, 24–26, 41–42, 57, 69, 71, 86–87, 91, 93, 116, 120, 131–34, 138, 142–52, 157–69, 175, 178–79, 181, 192, 253, 255, 262, 285–86, 291
Brazil, 270, 278, 285–86
Bülow tariff, 299, 304, 306–09
Bund der Landwirte [Agrarian League], 91, 303

C

catholicism, Catholics, 46, 48, 70, 76, 90–92, 117–18, 120, 125–39, 177, 240, 244, 273, 277–78
CDI (Centralverband Deutscher Industrieller) ([Central Association of German Industrialists]), 303
China, 253, 256, 275, 287
citizenship, 14, 29, 48, 278, 283, 288–91, 298
colonialism, 13, 25, 253–62, 287
Confederation, German, 52–60, 63, 91
Conservatism, Conservatives, Conservative Party, Tories, Unionist Party, 25, 32, 37, 39, 44, 58, 92, 110, 113, 115, 118, 120, 149, 151, 299
constitution, 24, 48, 51–52, 55–58, 60, 62–63, 69, 76, 83, 91–92, 99, 103, 114, 176, 321
cultural history, 8–9, 26, 130, 148, 151, 161, 163, 166–67, 204–07, 210

D

democracy, democratization, 3, 23–26, 28, 32,52, 46, 48, 69, 74, 76, 83–84, 87–88, 90–91, 100, 141, 144–45, 147, 165, 167, 234, 256
Deutsche Arbeit, 292
Deutscher Fußballbund [German Football League], 41

E

education, 6, 71, 98, 108–10, 118, 144, 146, 159, 161, 198, 293, 319
elections, 84, 87–88, 91–93, 109, 111–12, 167–68, 173, 304
Empire, Holy Roman, 54–55
eugenics, 6–7, 30–31
expressionism, 43

F

Fascism, 25–29, 37, 119, 121, 149, 166, 221–22, 243
    Vaterlandspartei [Fatherland Party], 111, 117, 247
Federal state, 51–63, 86–87
Fischer controversy, 1, 14
France, 4, 11–13, 23, 29, 54–55, 69, 71, 75, 97–105, 107–09, 111–13, 117–20, 126, 129–30, 132, 146, 175, 179–83, 190, 198, 205, 208, 215, 219, 227–28, 232–34, 239–43, 246, 258–59, 261, 269, 273, 282, 292, 305, 309–10, 316–17, 320
Franco-Prussian War, 241
functional differentiation, 38–40, 42, 44–45, 47–48, 138

G

gender, gender history, 8, 10, 12, 22, 84, 107, 112, 116–17, 120, 128, 131, 138, 178, 183, 197, 210, 221, 285, 313
German colonies, 253–61, 285–88, 291, 293
German Revolution 1918, 45, 83, 117, 150, 166–67, 247
Germanness, 276, 284, 286, 288–89, 291, 293
globalization, 7–8, 10, 13–24, 162, 269, 281–83, 290, 292–294, 297–98, 300–08, 310, 317
Great Britain/ British Empire, 12, 69, 71–75, 103, 107–10, 113, 115–17, 119–20, 179–81, 197, 203, 217, 219, 228–33, 258–59, 261, 290, 292, 298, 301, 308, 310, 316–18, 320–21
Great Depression, 27, 167

H

Historiale de la Grand Guerre (Peronne), 205
Historikerstreit, 29

historiography, 1–2, 4, 6–11, 14, 21–24, 28, 40, 47, 69, 84, 86, 97, 128, 132–34, 146, 151, 189, 193, 195, 198, 202, 204–06, 210, 254, 282, 293
Historische Sozialwissenschaft [historical social science], 1–2, 4, 8, 158, 206
Holocaust, 6, 25, 29–31, 33, 287

I

imperialism, 193, 254–55, 257–58, 282, 287–88, 297, 314
Impressionism, 43
Independent Social Democratic Party [Unabhängige Sozialdemokratische Partei Deutschlands], 41
industrialism, industrialists, 291, 300, 303, 321
internationalization, 116, 281–82
interwar period, 37, 67, 119, 193–94, 198
Italy, 71, 74, 76, 130, 146, 180, 213, 220–221, 269, 274, 283

J

Japan, 315
Jews, 29–32, 92, 115, 120, 144, 146, 197, 239–40, 242–45, 247–48, 262, 276–77, 282–83, 288–90
Junkers, 86, 143–47, 151, 299–300

K

Kulturkampf, 46, 84, 125–35, 138

L

Labour Party (Britain), 110, 113–14
law, military/maritime, 232, 234
left liberals, 86
Liberalism, Liberals, 3–4, 10, 48, 86, 109–10, 120, 126, 132, 135, 138, 141, 144, 147, 149, 192, 309

M

mass media, 11, 13, 39–42, 116
mass politics, 11, 73, 77, 83–84, 90–92, 285
master narrative, 2, 4–5, 8, 28, 196, 227
methodology, 1, 5, 8–9, 44, 58–59, 62, 99, 157, 161–62, 167, 191, 193, 195–97, 201–02, 204–07, 209, 211, 242, 257, 317
middle-classes (bourgeoisie) *see* bourgeoisie

Index

migration, 13, 71, 247, 255, 259–61, 267–79, 283–91, 297–98

military, militarism, military history, military culture, 2, 7, 9–10, 12, 22, 24, 27, 32–33, 37, 40, 42, 69, 71–72, 76, 86–87, 98–99, 101, 104, 115–16, 118, 145, 147–49, 189–98, 204–05, 207–08, 210, 213–23, 227–35, 241–46, 255–56, 269, 314, 321

minorities, ethnic, 70, 73, 313–14

mobility, 204, 221, 267, 269–71, 278, 281, 283–84, 286–87, 289–92, 297

modernity, 'the modern,' modernization, 1–3, 5–10, 23–31, 33, 37–48, 67–69, 72–77, 83–86, 88–93, 107–08, 115–16, 120, 131, 133, 141–51, 158–65, 180, 227, 261, 284–85, 293, 321

monarchism, monarchy, 42, 45, 52–53, 55–56, 75, 87, 97–98, 104, 150, 166, 176–77, 214, 218–19, 320, 322

music, 12, 173–84, 261

N

nation, nationalism, 5, 7–8, 10, 12, 13–14, 21–23, 25–26, 28–33, 37, 41, 52–53, 55–59, 63, 67–77, 84–87, 91–92, 98–100, 102, 108–09, 115, 117–18, 120, 132–34, 173–84, 192, 194, 214–16, 218–19, 221–22, 228, 230, 240, 255–56, 268, 273, 276–79, 281–94, 298, 300, 307, 310

National Liberal Party, 107

National Socialism, 2–4, 6–7, 27, 37, 127, 132, 142, 148, 150, 166–68, 192, 195, 197, 222–23, 254, 257, 261–62, 293, 299

Nationaler Frauendienst [National Women's Service], 111

navy, 228–35, 320–21

NSDAP, 27–28, 117, 152

P

parliament, parliamentarism, parliamentarization, 3, 37, 48, 76, 84, 86–92, 97, 103, 110–15, 119, 128, 167, 259, 297, 304, 306–08

Parti republican radical et radical-socialiste, 118–19

particularism, 53, 62, 88

Poles, Poland,193, 197, 223, 239,241–45, 247, 256, 262, 272–73, 275–76, 282, 288–90, 292

political culture, 2, 13, 24, 28, 68, 71, 83–85, 88, 91–92, 97, 118, 131, 168, 176, 247, 278

Political mass market, 83, 85, 88–89, 93

political mobilization, 90

polycontexturality, 46–48

postmodernism, 46, 72–73, 208

press, 39–40, 46, 86, 88, 104, 115, 128, 131, 150, 174–176, 178, 181, 186, 214

pronatalism, 118

protectionism, 143, 298–310, 315

protestantism, Protestants, 27, 44, 46, 76, 126–27, 129–34, 138, 277, 285

Prussia, 4, 9, 11, 25, 56–57, 60, 69, 75–76, 84, 86–87, 101, 110–11, 125, 135, 141–43, 145–47, 150–52, 176, 178, 214, 216, 219–20, 246, 256, 273, 275–76, 287–90, 299, 304, 308

R

race, racism, 6, 22, 120, 195, 198, 239–40, 245–46, 262, 276, 287

racial hygiene, 30, 115

reformism, 88–89, 148, 286

regionalism, regional politics, 88, 112, 210, 268–69, 273–74, 277

Reichstag, 28, 30, 70, 89–93, 288, 303

religion, 11, 21, 25, 27, 29, 33, 39, 43–47, 67, 88, 118, 120, 125–29, 131–39, 209, 277

Revolution 1848, 21, 56, 75, 110, 283

Revolution 1918, 83, 150, 166–67

Revolution, Russian (Bolshevik), 202

Rheinbund, 68

Russia, 29, 232–33, 276, 283, 287, 289–90, 305, 310, 316–17, 320

S

Sammlungspolitik [politics of rallying together], 300

Social Darwinism, 193, 246, 261

Social Democratic Party, Social Democratism, Social Democrats, 41, 48, 90, 92, 103, 110–11, 113, 149, 177–78, 181, 256, 275, 278, 281, 304, 309

social history, 3, 8–9, 11, 38, 44, 68, 70, 72, 76–77, 107, 141–42, 157–58, 161, 163, 167, 169, 204–07, 300
Socialism, Socialists, 26, 41, 70, 86, 92, 100–03, 107, 118–19, 126, 129, 132, 221, 256, 299
sociology, 2, 10, 23, 25, 30, 38–39, 44–47, 86, 213, 2155, 267
Sonderweg, 2–8, 10, 12, 23–26, 29, 31–33, 37, 71, 83, 86–87, 107, 138/, 158–59, 165–67, 176, 227, 239, 282
sovereignty, 10, 51–63, 173, 181, 214, 258
sports, 40–42, 46
submarine warfare, 12, 228–31, 234–35
suffrage, 87, 92, 107–20

T

trans-national history, 8, 13, 168
tariffs, 297–310, 318
taste, 179
Third Reich, 21, 23, 25–26, 28, 31–32, 145, 246
Third Republic (France), 97–98, 100–1, 104, 113, 118–20, 146
Thirty Years' War, 191
Total War, 12, 148, 190–92, 195–97, 206–208, 218, 222, 242
trade and commerce, trade policy, 14, 229, 298–300, 302–10
Trade Unions, 100, 113, 118, 278, 291

U

ultramontanism, ultramontanists, 126
unitarism, 62
United States of America, 22, 55, 60, 102, 109, 114, 201, 219, 230–33, 235, 255, 258, 268, 270, 272–74, 277–78, 283–85, 290–92, 298, 301, 305, 310, 314–21
urbanism, urbanization, 5, 45, 70, 162, 204, 271–73

V

vanishing point, 28–31, 37, 46
Versailles treaty, 190, 195, 197, 222, 243, 253
violence, 7, 10–12, 22–24, 28–29, 33, 71, 97–104, 191–94, 196–97, 202, 207–08, 214–15, 229, 234, 240–48, 256, 258, 272
Völkisch Movement, 88, 115, 148–49,
Volksgemeinschaft [people's community], 48, 164

W

warfare, 12, 22, 108, 148, 190, 192, 194, 198, 207–08, 210, 214–16, 218, 227–35, 239–41, 243–44, 246–48
Wars of Unification, 69
Weimar Republic, 2–3, 27–28, 30–32, 47, 62–63, 83–84, 111, 117, 128, 167, 192, 247, 261, 273
working classes, 9, 41, 99–102, 118, 132, 149, 157, 161, 178, 275, 277–78, 291, 301, 306, 308
world economy/ world trade, 281, 232, 297–98, 301, 308, 315, 321
World War I, 1, 7–8, 10, 12–13, 22, 24–26, 32, 43–44, 48, 83, 85, 107, 109–120, 126, 130, 134, 138, 149, 167, 178, 182, 189–98, 201–06,210–11,213, 227–28, 231, 233–235, 241–44, 246, 248, 253, 257, 268–71,273–74, 276, 278, 282, 287, 297–304, 307–10, 313, 316–317, 320–21
World War II, 2, 7, 12, 62, 136, 142, 151, 189, 198, 201, 203, 206–07, 235, 239, 241, 243, 246–47, 257, 268, 278, 308

Z

Zollverein, 75–76

Index of Persons

A

Adenauer, Konrad, 128, 135
Albrecht, Eduard, 55
Alexander II, 102
Allen, William Sheridan, 91
Anderson, Benedict, 294
Anderson, Margret, 83–84, 89, 91, 227
Angell, Norman, 321
Applegate, Celia, 86
Arndt, Paul, 301
Asquith, Herbert Henry, 114

B

Bach, Johann Sebastian, 180
Bade, Klaus, 267–68, 283
Balibar, Etienne, 294
Ballin, Albert, 322
Bassermann, Ernst, 107
Bauer, Hermann, 231
Bauer, Max, 218
Baumann, Zygmunt, 6
Bebel, August, 90, 107, 281–82
Becker, Winfried, 87–88
Beethoven, Ludwig van, 180–81
Bell, Gertrude, 114
Berghahn, Volker, 8, 23, 84
Bethmann-Hollweg, Theobald von, 217
Bevin, Ernst, 130
Beyschlag, Willibald, 126
Bismarck, Otto Fürst von, 7, 21, 32, 57, 72, 84, 87, 90–92, 128, 174, 215, 253, 299, 305
Blackbourn, David, 4, 24–26, 84, 86, 91, 144, 160, 206, 256–57
Blaskowitz, Johannes, 245
Blum, Léon, 119
Bodin, Jean, 54–55, 59
Böhler, Jochen, 247

Boll, Friedhelm, 100
Bond, Brian, 203
Borcherdt, Rudolf, 148
Brecht, Bertolt, 260
Brechtgen, Magnus, 316–17, 322
Brentano, Lujo, 141
Brepohl, Wilhelm, 273
Briand, Aristide, 119
Brodevini, Luigi, 274
Bruendel, Steffen, 247
Buisson, Ferdinand, 132
Burns, Ken, 201
Busch, Ernst, 244
Busch, Wilhelm, 129

C

Cadorna, Luigi, 220
Calhoun, John, 55, 59
Caprivi, Georg Leo Graf von, 258, 299, 303, 305–07, 309
Carnot, Sidi, 102
Catherine II, 32
Ceva, Lucio, 216
Chatterjee, Partha, 287, 294
Chickering, Roger, 149, 196
Claß, Heinrich, 150
Cohen, Stanley, 103
Conrad, Sebastian, 255
Conze, Eckert, 152
Conze, Werner, 23
Conzen, Kathleen, 270
Cooper, Frederick, 261
Corinth, Lovis, 43
Cramer, Kevin, 227

D

D'Annuncio, Gabriele, 221
Dahn, Felix, 129

Darre, Richard Walther, 148
Darwin, Charles, 6
De Gaulle, Charles, 190, 193
Dernburg, Bernhard, 259, 289
Dickenson, Edward Ross, 28, 88
Dilthey, Wilhelm, 45
Dirlewanger, Oskar, 193

E

Edward VII, 177
Ehrhard, Albert, 125
Eibl, Karl, 162–63, 165
Eisenstadt, Shmuel N., 5
Eley, Geoff, 4, 24–26, 31–32, 91, 110
Elgar, Edward, 180
Elias, Norbert, 28
Engels, Friedrich, 90
Erlander, Tage, 130
Evans, Richard, 4

F

Fabbro, René del, 274
Fabri, Friedrich, 285
Fairbairn, Brett, 83–84, 89
Falkenhayn, Erich von, 216–17, 244
Falter, Jürgen, 27
Ferguson, Niall, 21
Fiebig- von Hase, Ragnild, 315–16
Fischer, Fritz, 1, 14, 23, 151, 193
Ford, Henry, 319
Förster, Stig, 196, 198
Foucault, Michel, 6, 28
Freytag, Gustav, 91–92, 288
Fussell, Paul, 203–04

G

Gagern, Heinrich von, 56
Gall, Lothar, 159
Gauly, Thomas, 128
Gay, Peter, 22
Geertz, Clifford, 142
Gellner, Ernest, 67
George, Stefan, 148
Gerber, Carl Friedrich, 59
Gernhard, Robert, 286
Gerschenkron, Alexander, 23, 32–33, 299
Geyer, Michael, 85, 218, 228
Gierke, Otto von, 85
Ginzburg, Carlo, 209
Giolitti, Giovanni, 216

Goebbels, Joseph, 244
Goethe, Johann Wolfgang von, 68, 156
Goldberg, Hans-Peter, 92
Goltz, Colmar von der, 243
Görlitz, Walter, 143
Gosewinkel, Dieter, 262
Graf, Friedrich Wilhelm, 133
Gramsci, Antonio, 26–27
Green, Abigail, 86
Greiner, Bernd, 196
Grießmer, Axel, 92
Groener, Wilhelm, 217, 219, 222
Gross, Michael, 84, 136
Günther, Gotthard, 46

H

Habermas, Jürgen, 28
Haeckel, Ernst, 164
Halder, Franz, 241, 243–44
Hamilton, Alexander, 57
Handlin, Oscar, 270
Harden, Maximilian, 150
Harrison, Mark, 203
Hartmann, Michael, 148
Healey, Maureen, 210
Healy, Róisín, 84
Hentze, Adolf, 289
Herbert, Ulrich, 31
Hesse, Hermann, 286
Hewitson, Mark, 87
Heydrich, Reinhard, 243
Hildebrand, Klaus, 3
Hillgruber, Andreas, 3
Himmler, Heinrich, 245
Hindenburg, Paul von, 27, 150, 217–18
Hintze, Otto, 235
Hirschfeld, Gerhard, 192, 204
Hitler, Adolf, 27, 30–32, 127, 129, 223, 242–43, 245
Hobsbawm, Eric, 7, 99, 191
Hohenlohe-Schillingsfürst, Chlodwig, 126
Holborn, Hajo, 21–22, 25
Horne, John, 227
Hull, Isabel, 227, 231
Hunt, James C., 299

J

Jackson, James Jr., 272
Jarausch, Konrad, 85
Jeismann, Michael, 282,

Index

Jellinek, Georg, 61
Johannsen, Anja, 101
Jünger, Ernst, 149

K

Kästner, Erich, 260
Kedourie, Elie, 67–68, 72
Keegan, John, 204
Kehr, Eckart, 3, 299
Keiter, Heinrich, 128, 131
Kennan, George, 189, 202
Kennedy, Paul, 315–16
Kocka, Jürgen, 23, 133, 158, 168, 206
Kohlrausch, Martin, 150
Kohn, Hans, 22
Köllmann, Wolfgang, 271
Koselleck, Reinhart, 167
Kramer, Alan, 227
Kreuzer, Marcus, 88
Kühne, Thomas, 84, 87–88

L

Laband, Paul, 59–61
Langewiesche, Dieter, 87, 166, 282
Leed, Eric, 204
Lees, Andrew, 88
Lenin, Wladimir Iljitsch, 22
Lepsius, Rainer M., 162
Lerner, Daniel, 147
Levsen, Sonja, 262
Liebermann, Max, 43
Liebert, Eduard von, 286
Lindenberger, Thomas, 100
Lorenz, Chris, 88
Lossberg, Fritz von, 217
Ludendorff, Erich, 217–220, 241, 244
Luhmann, Niklas, 46
Luxemburg, Rosa, 235

M

Mann, Thomas, 260
Mannheim, Karl, 87
Marc, Franz, 43
Markham, Violet, 114
Marx, Karl, 1, 277
Maurenbrecher, Romeo, 55
Mehnert, Ute, 315–16
Meinecke, Friedrich, 21–23, 68, 150
Mergel, Thomas, 84
Mill, John Stewart, 113

Miquel, Johannes v., 304, 307
Mommsen, Hans, 164
Mommsen, Wolfgang J., 161
Moore, Barrington, 23
Mosse, George, 22
Most, Johann, 103
Müller, Eugen, 241
Münster, Georg Herbert Graf zu, 102
Musil, Robert, 148
Mussolini, Benito, 221

N

Naranch, Bradley, 284
Naumann, Friedrich, 91, 144, 150
Nietzsche, Friedrich, 164
Nipperdey, Thomas, 3, 9, 43, 87, 162, 166
Nolte, Paul, 7, 23

O

Oldenburg-Januschau, Elard von, 150
Osterhammel, Jürgen, 255
Ottley, Charles, 234

P

Parsons, Talcott, 41
Perrot, Michelle, 100
Peukert, Detlev K., 6, 26–29, 31
Pius IX, 129
Plessner, Hellmuth, 23, 164
Ploetz, Alfred, 30, 32
Pohl, Hugo von, 231
Pomp, Rainer, 150
Pound, Ezra, 22
Preuß, Hugo, 85, 141, 146
Prost, Antoine, 205–06, 209, 211
Pufendorf, Samuel von, 54–55

R

Radbruch, Gustav, 86
Ratzel, Friedrich, 292
Ravachol, 101–02
Redern, Friedrich Wilhelm, 176
Reimann, Aribert, 194
Rellstab, Ludwig, 175
Rémond, René, 133
Repp, Kevin, 88
Retallack, James, 25
Rice, Cecil Spring, 316
Ritter, Gerhard, 21, 23, 257
Robert, Jean-Louis, 204
Rosanvallon, Pierre, 98, 118

Rosenberg, Hans, 21–23, 25, 91, 142–45, 147, 149, 151, 299
Rosenhaft, Eve, 92
Rosenstock-Huessey, Eugen, 23
Ross, Ronald, 84
Rossino, Alexander, 244
Rüdin, Ernst, 30
Rupp, Leila, 281

S

Saint-Saëns, Camille, 181–82
Schiller, Friedrich, 68, 146
Schmoller, Gustav, 44, 141
Schnabel, Franz, 132–33
Schönberger, Christoph, 87
Schorske, Carl, 91
Schreiber, Gerhard, 198
Schumpeter, Josef, 162
Schwabach, Paul von, 146
Seeckt, Hans von, 243
Seydel, Max, 58–62
Simmel, Georg, 45
Skowronnek, Richard, 246
Slevogt, Max, 43
Smetana, Betrich, 180
Smith, Helmut Walser, 91, 133
Sombart, Nicolaus, 144, 162
Spenkuch, Hartwin, 86
Stalin, Josef, 22
Stein, Bernhard, 129
Stern, Fritz, 22
Stirk, Peter, 87
Stockfeld, Ola, 184
Stoler, Ann, 288
Stolleis, Michael, 55, 62
Ströbel, Heinrich, 41
Stülpnagel, Joachim von, 219, 222
Suval, Stanley, 83, 89

T

Taylor, Frederick, 319
Tenbruck, Friedrich, 162, 165
Ther, Philipp, 256
Thoma, Richard, 63
Thompson, Alastair, 92
Thompson, Kenneth, 104
Thoß, Bruno, 192

Tilly, Charles, 100, 159–60
Tilly, Richard, 100
Tirpitz, Alfred von, 231, 321
Tocqueville, Alexis de, 56–57
Torp, Cornelius, 316–17
Treitschke, Heinrich von, 57–58, 60
Triepel, Heinrich, 62
Troeltsch, Ernst, 23, 44
Turner, Frederick Jackson, 286

V

Vagts, Alfred, 314–16, 322
Virchow, Rudolf, 128
Viviani, René, 112, 119
Voigt, Wilhelm, 40

W

Wagner, Patrick, 150
Wagner, Richard, 180–81
Wagner, Siegfried, 182
Waitz, Georg, 56–57, 59–60
Ward, Humphry, 114
Watson, Janet, 210
Weber, Carl Maria von, 180
Weber, Max, 2, 6, 43–44, 47, 142–47, 151, 160, 162, 164, 166, 180, 290
Wehler, Hans-Ulrich, 3, 9, 23–24, 32, 37, 39, 51, 70–71, 87, 91, 98, 107, 162, 166, 191, 202, 206, 255, 268, 299
White, Harvey, 316
Wildenthal, Lora, 288
Wilhelm II, 101, 144, 174, 176–77, 253, 256, 320–21
Wilhelmi, Bruno, 286
Wilson, Woodrow, 235,
Winkler, Heinrich August, 23
Winter, Jay, 204–06, 209, 210–11

Y

Younger, Kenneth, 130

Z

Zimmer, Oliver, 134
Zimmerer, Jürgen, 287
Zorn, Philipp, 60
Zumbini, Massimo Ferrari, 289
Zwahr, Hartmut, 159